Understanding Peacekeeping

Understanding Peacekeeping

Second edition

ALEX J. BELLAMY AND PAUL D. WILLIAMS
WITH STUART GRIFFIN

polity

First published in 2010 by Polity Press

Reprinted 2010, 2011, 2012

Polity Press
65 Bridge Street
Cambridge CB2 1UR, UK

Polity Press
350 Main Street
Malden, MA 02148, USA

ISBN-13: 978-0-7456-4185-0 (hardback)
ISBN-13: 978-0-7456-4186-7 (paperback)

A catalogue record for this book is available from the British Library.

Typeset in 9.5 on 13 pt Swift Light
by Toppan Best-set Premedia Limited
Printed and bound in Great Britain by MPG Books Limited, Bodmin, Cornwall

The publisher has used its best endeavours to ensure that the URLs for external websites
referred to in this book are correct and active at the time of going to press. However, the
publisher has no responsibility for the websites and can make no guarantee that a site
will remain live or that the content is or will remain appropriate.

Every effort has been made to trace all copyright holders, but if any have been
inadvertently overlooked the publisher will be pleased to include any necessary credits in
any subsequent reprint or edition.

For further information on Polity, visit our website: www.politybooks.com

Contents

Figures

Maps

Boxes

Tables

Abbreviations

AFP	Australian Federal Police
AMIS	African Union Mission in the Sudan
AMISOM	AU Mission in Somalia
APC	armoured personnel carrier
ASEAN	Association of Southeast Asian Nations
ASF	African Standby Force
ASPI	Australian Strategic Policy Institute
AU	African Union
AusAID	Australian Government Overseas Aid Program
BINUB	United Nations Integrated Office in Burundi
CACI	Consolidated Analysis Centers Inc.
CAR	Central African Republic
CEMAC	Economic Community of Central African States
CIAT	International Committee for the Support of the Transition (DRC)
CIS	Commonwealth of Independent States
CIVPOL	Civilian Police
CNN	Cable News Network
CPA	Comprehensive Peace Agreement (Sudan)
CPP	Cambodian People's Party (PRK)
DDR	disarmament, demobilization, reintegration
DFID	Department for International Development
DFS	UN Department of Field Support
DOMREP	Mission of the Representative of the Secretary-General in the Dominican Republic
DPA	UN Department for Political Affairs; Darfur Peace Agreement (2006)
DPKO	UN Department of Peacekeeping Operations
DRC	Democratic Republic of Congo
DSL	Defence Systems Limited
EC	European Community
ECOMICI	ECOWAS Mission in Côte d'Ivoire
ECOMOG	Military Observer Group of the Economic Community of West African States

ECOSOC	United Nations Economic and Social Council
ECOWAS	Economic Community of West African States
EISAS	Executive Committee on Peace and Security Information and Strategic Analysis Secretariat
EO	Executive Outcomes
EU	European Union
EUFOR RD	European Union Reserve Deployment
EUPM	European Union Policing Mission
FDLR	Forces Démocratiques de Libération du Rwanda
FNI	Nationalist and Integrationist Front (DRC)
FNLA	Frente Nacional de Libertação de Angola
FOMUC	CEMAC Mission in the CAR
FPUs	formed police units
FYROM	Former Yugoslav Republic of Macedonia
G-8	Group of Eight States: US, Canada, Britain, France, Germany, Italy, Japan, Russian Federation
GPOI	Global Peace Operations Initiative (G-8)
GPSP	Global Peace and Security Partnership
GWOT	Global War on Terror (US-led)
IASC	Inter-Agency Standing Committee
IBL	Institutionalization before liberalization strategy
ICC	International Criminal Court
ICRC	International Committee of the Red Cross
ICSC	International Commission for Supervision and Control
ICTR	International Criminal Tribunal for Rwanda
ICTY	International Criminal Tribunal for the former Yugoslavia
IDG	International Deployment Group (Australian Federal Police)
IDPs	Internally Displaced Persons
IEMF	Interim Emergency Multinational Force (DRC)
IFM	Isatabu Freedom Movement (Solomon Islands)
IFOR	Implementation Force (NATO-led)
IMF	International Monetary Fund
IMTF	Integrated Mission Task Force
INTERFET	International Force in East Timor
IPMT	International Peace Monitoring Team (Solomon Islands)
IPOA	International Peace Operations Association
IPTF	International Police Task Force
IRC	International Rescue Committee
ISAF	International Security Assistance Force (Afghanistan)
ISDS	International Security and Defence Systems Ltd
ISF	International Stabilization Force (Timor-Leste)
JEM	Justice and Equality Movement (Sudan)
JNA	Yugoslav People's Army
KFOR	Kosovo Force

KLA	Kosovo Liberation Army
KPC	Kosovo Protection Corps
KPS	Kosovo Police Service
LAS	League of Arab States
LDK	Democratic League of Kosovo
LRA	Lord's Resistance Army (Uganda)
LTTE	Liberation Tigers of Tamil Eelam (Sri Lanka)
MAES	AU Electoral and Security Assistance Mission (Comoros)
MEF	Malaita Eagle Force (Solomon Islands)
MFO	multinational force observers
milobs	military observers
MINUCI	United Nations Mission in Côte d'Ivoire
MINUGUA	United Nations Verification Mission in Guatemala
MINURCA	United Nations Mission in the Central African Republic
MINURCAT	United Nations Mission in the Central African Republic and Chad
MINURSO	United Nations Mission for the Referendum in Western Sahara
MINUSAL	Mission of the United Nations in El Salvador
MINUSTAH	United Nations Stabilization Mission in Haiti
MIPONUH	United Nations Civilian Police Mission in Haiti
MISAB	Inter-African Mission to Monitor the Implementation of the Bangui Agreements
MONUA	United Nations Observer Mission in Angola
MONUC	United Nations Organization Mission in the Democratic Republic of Congo
MPLA	Movimento Popular da Libertação de Angola
MPRI	Military Professional Resources Incorporated
MSF	Médecins Sans Frontières
NAM	Non-Aligned Movement
NATO	North Atlantic Treaty Organization
NCC	National Consultative Council (East Timor)
NGO	Non-Governmental Organization
NLA	National Liberation Army (Macedonia)
NPFL	National Patriotic Front of Liberia
OAS	Organization of American States
OAU	Organization of African Unity
OCHA	UN Office for the Coordination of Humanitarian Affairs
ODI	Overseas Development Institute (UK)
OHR	Office of the High Representative (Bosnia)
OLMEE	OAU's Liaison Mission in Ethiopia/Eritrea
ONUB	United Nations Operation in Burundi
ONUC	United Nations Operation in the Congo
ONUCA	United Nations Observer Group in Central America

ONUMOZ	United Nations Operation in Mozambique
ONUSAL	United Nations Observer Mission in El Salvador
OSCE	Organization for Security and Cooperation in Europe
P-5	Permanent Members of the UN Security Council (Britain, China, France, Russian Federation, US)
PAE	Pacific Architects and Engineers
PBC	United Nations Peacebuilding Commission
PBF	United Nations Peacebuilding Fund
PBSO	United Nations Peacebuilding Support Office
PDK	Party of Democratic Kampuchea (Khmer Rouge)
PIF	Pacific Islands Forum
PLO	Palestine Liberation Organization
PMR	Pridnestrovskaia Moldavskaia Respublica
PRK	People's Republic of Kampuchea
PRTs	Provincial Reconstruction Teams (Afghanistan)
PSC	private security company
R2P	responsibility to protect
RAMSI	Regional Assistance Mission to the Solomon Islands
RDHQ	Rapidly Deployable Headquarters
RECAMP	Reforcement des capacitiés africanes de maintien de la paix
RENAMO	Resistencia Nacional Mocambicana
ROE	rules of engagement
ROTC	Reserve Officer Training Corps
RPF	Rwandan Patriotic Front
RRF	rapid reaction force
RSIP	Royal Solomon Islands Police
RUF	Revolutionary United Front of Sierra Leone
SADC	Southern African Development Community
SAIC	Science Applications International Corporation
SEA	Sexual Exploitation and Abuse
SFOR	Stabilization Force (NATO-led) in Bosnia
SHIRBRIG	Standby High Readiness Brigade
SLM/A	Sudan Liberation Movement/Army
SMC	Strategic Military Cell
SNC	Supreme National Council (Cambodia)
SPLM/A	Sudan People's Liberation Movement/Army
SRSG	United Nations Special Representative of the Secretary-General
SWAPO	South West African People's Organization
SWAPOL	South West African Police
TCCs	troop-contributing countries
TRW	TRW Automotive (part of the Northrop Grumman Group)
TSZ	Temporary Security Zone (Ethiopia–Eritrea)
UN	United Nations

UNAMA	United Nations Assistance Mission in Afghanistan
UNAMIC	United Nations Advance Mission in Cambodia
UNAMID	AU/UN Hybrid Operation in Darfur (Sudan)
UNAMIR	United Nations Assistance Mission in Rwanda
UNAMSIL	United Nations Mission in Sierra Leone
UNAVEM I	United Nations Angola Verification Mission I
UNAVEM II	United Nations Angola Verification Mission II
UNAVEM III	United Nations Angola Verification Mission III
UNDOF	United Nations Disengagement Observer Force
UNDP	United Nations Development Programme
UNEF I	United Nations Emergency Force I
UNEF II	United Nations Emergency Force II
UNEPS	United Nations Emergency Peace Service
UNFICYP	United Nations Peacekeeping Force in Cyprus
UNGOMAP	United Nations Good Offices Mission in Afghanistan and Pakistan
UNHCR	Office of the United Nations High Commissioner for Refugees
UNICEF	United Nations International Children's Emergency Fund
UNIFIL	United Nations Interim Force in Lebanon
UNIIMOG	United Nations Iran-Iraq Military Observer Group
UNIKOM	United Nations Iraq-Kuwait Military Observation Mission
UNIOSIL	United Nations Integrated Office in Sierra Leone
UNIPOM	United Nations India-Pakistan Observer Mission
UNITA	União Nacional para a Independência Total de Angola
UNITAF	Unified Task Force (Somalia)
UNITAR	United Nations Institute for Training and Research
UNMEE	United Nations Mission in Ethiopia and Eritrea
UNMIBH	United Nations Mission in Bosnia and Hercegovina
UNMIH	United Nations Mission in Haiti
UNMIK	United Nations Mission in Kosovo
UNMIL	United Nations Mission in Liberia
UNMIS	United Nations Mission in Sudan
UNMISET	United Nations Mission in Support of East Timor
UNMIT	United Nations Mission in Timor-Leste
UNMOGIP	United Nations Military Observer Group in India and Pakistan
UNMOT	United Nations Mission of Observers in Tajikistan
UNOCI	United Nations Mission in Côte d'Ivoire
UNOGIL	United Nations Observation Group in Lebanon
UNOMIG	United Nations Observer Mission in Georgia
UNOMIL	United Nations Observer Mission in Liberia
UNOMSIL	United Nations Observer Mission in Sierra Leone
UNOMUR	United Nations Observer Mission in Uganda/Rwanda
UNOSOM I	United Nations Operation in Somalia I
UNOSOM II	United Nations Operation in Somalia II

UNPA	United Nations Protected Area (Croatia)
UNPOL	United Nations Police
UNPREDEP	United Nations Preventive Deployment Force (Macedonia)
UNPROFOR	United Nations Protection Force (former Yugoslavia)
UNSAS	UN Standby Arrangements System
UNSCOB	United Nations Special Committee on the Balkans
UNSMIH	United Nations Support Mission for Haiti
UNTAC	United Nations Transitional Authority in Cambodia
UNTAES	United Nations Transitional Administration for Eastern Slavonia, Baranja, Western Sirmium
UNTAET	United Nations Transition Authority in East Timor
UNTAG	United Nations Transitional Assistance Group (Namibia)
UNTEA	United Nations Temporary Executive Authority
UNTMIH	United Nations Transition Mission in Haiti
UNTOP	United Nations Tajikistan Office of Peacebuilding
UNTSO	United Nations Truce Supervision Organization
UNYOM	United Nations Yemen Observation Mission
WFP	World Food Programme
WHO	World Health Organization

Acknowledgements

In writing the second edition of this book we have received assistance from a variety of sources. We would like to thank the Australian Research Council, the Economic and Social Research Council (UK) and the University of Queensland for their financial assistance with various parts of this project. Intellectually, the book has benefited from comments, conversations, advice and additional material from several people, especially Doug Brooks, Don Daniel, William Durch, Victoria Holt, Jacques Paul Klein, Daniela Kroslak, Edward Luck, Sarah Martin, Michael Pugh, Natalia Rayol, Thomas Weiss and Nicholas Wheeler. Paul would also like to acknowledge the insights of the participants in the Partnership for Effective Peacekeeping in Washington, DC. In addition, Stuart Griffin played an important part in helping to draft the first edition of this volume and he has our thanks. At Polity, we are grateful for the advice and help we received from Emma Hutchinson, Rachel Donnelly and Louise Knight. Louise in particular helped develop the idea for a second edition and has guided it to fruition with her usual expertise. Polity's anonymous reviewers also provided incisive comments which helped improve the manuscript in several ways. Finally, Sara Davies and Ariela Blätter have our love and thanks, once again, for putting up with us during the whole process.

The authors and publisher would like to thank the following for permission to use copyright material: Figure i.i, © 2009. Reprinted with permission from UCDP (Uppsala Conflict Data Program); table 1.1, figures 2.1, 2.2, 2.3, 9.2, box 2.3 © 2009. Reprinted with permission from UN Publications Board; boxes 7.2, 7.3 © 1956. Reprinted with permission from UN Publications Board; table 2.2 © 2006 by Routledge. Reprinted with permission from Taylor & Francis Books UK; tables 2.5, 15.4, box 15.2 © 2006 by Henry L. Stimson Center. Reprinted with permission from the Henry L. Stimson Center; figures 8.1 (adapted), 8.2 (adapted) © Crown Copyright 1995 and 1999/MOD. Reproduced with the permission of the Controller of Her Majesty's Stationery Office; figure 9.1 © 2001 by Simon Chesterman. Reprinted with permission from Oxford University Press; figure 12.1 © 2009. Reprinted with permission from GlobalSecurity.org; table 13.3 © 2006, The Brown Journal of World Affairs. Reprinted by permission of the publisher; figure 14.1 (adapted), table 14.1 (adapted) © 2005 by Deborah D. Avant. Reprinted by permission of the author and Cambridge University Press; table 15.1, box 17.2 © 2002. Reprinted with permission from the UN Publications Board; table 15.2 © 2006 by Koninklije BRILL NV. Reprinted by permission of the publisher.

Every effort has been made to trace the copyright holders, but if any have been inadvertently overlooked, the publishers will be pleased to make the necessary arrangements at the first opportunity.

Guide to Companion Website

This book is supported by a companion website, at www.politybooks.com/up2, which contains a range of additional materials relating to *Understanding Peacekeeping*. These include links to other websites with relevant information about peace operations and a definitive list of UN peace operations, as well as a guide to non-UN peace operations since 1945. It also offers additional case studies related to the typology of operations discussed in part III of the book:

- chapter 7: UNTSO in the Middle East (1948–present);
- chapter 8: UNOMSIL/UNAMSIL in Sierra Leone (1998–2005);
- chapter 9: ONUC in the Congo (1960–4);
- chapter 9: Operation Desert Storm in the Gulf (1990–1)
- chapter 9: Operation Allied Force in Kosovo/Serbia (1999)
- chapter 9: Haiti (1990–present);
- chapter 10: ONUSAL in El Salvador (1991–5);
- chapter 11: The transitional administration in Bosnia (1996–present);
- chapter 12: INTERFET in East Timor (1999–2000);
- chapter 12: KFOR in Kosovo (1999–2008).

The online case studies are organized in precisely the same way as those covered in the book and are meant to provide supplementary material for those who are interested. We will endeavour to ensure that this website is kept up to date.

Introduction

The answer to the question of whether peacekeeping works is a clear and resounding yes.

Fortna (2008b: 173)

According to data gathered by the Uppsala Conflict Data Program (UCDP), since the early 1990s the number and intensity of armed conflicts involving the world's governments has reduced by as much as 40 per cent (see figure I.1). Some analysts have argued that a significant part of the credit for this should be given to peace operations (Human Security Centre 2005; Mack 2007). The number of battle deaths per armed conflict is also falling, but this does not necessarily mean there are fewer overall war deaths, since most fatalities occur because of excess non-violent mortality – i.e. from disease and malnutrition. The same period has also witnessed a growing proportion of armed conflicts ending through negotiated settlements rather than the military victory of one of the conflict parties (Licklider 1995; Harbom et al. 2006). Although there is no evidence that the presence of peace operations can successfully facilitate peace agreements (Greig and Diehl 2005), such operations *do* significantly reduce the likelihood of wars reigniting after such agreements have been concluded (Fortna 2003, 2004, 2008b). Specifically, where peacekeepers are deployed, the likelihood of war reigniting falls by 75 to 85 per cent compared to those cases where no peacekeepers are deployed (Fortna 2008b: 171). In the post-Cold War era, traditional peacekeeping operations deployed with the consent of the belligerents reduced the likelihood of war reigniting by as much as 86 per cent. For large and complex multidimensional operations – often deployed in regions with unstable consent and lingering violence – the figure remained above 50 per cent (Fortna 2004: 283). These figures are all the more important if we consider that the single most important factor in determining a country's risk of descending into war is whether it has endured armed conflict in the previous five years (Collier et al. 2003). By dramatically reducing the risk that armed conflicts will reignite, peace operations make a vital contribution to reducing the frequency and lethality of war in our world.

But the contribution of peace operations to world politics does not end there. When peace operations have been tasked with preventing or ending

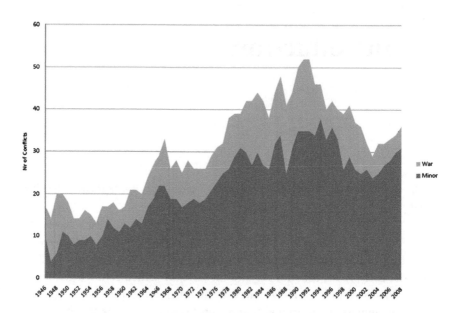

Source: UCDP, at www.pcr.uu.se/research/UCDP/graphs/charts_and_graphs.htm.

Figure I.1 *State-based armed conflicts by intensity and year, 1946–2008*

genocide and mass killing by directly challenging the perpetrators, they have significantly increased the probability that the slaughter can be slowed or stopped (Krain 2005). Moreover, the greater number of actors that come together to challenge the perpetrators of mass slaughter, the more pronounced these positive effects can be (Krain 2005: 383). Recent statistical analyses also support Samantha Power's claim that, 'for all the talk of the futility of foreign involvement' in cases of genocide and mass killing, the evidence categorically points to the fact that even small steps by concerned outsiders save lives' (Power 2002a: 73; 2002b). Big steps, properly coordinated and executed, can save lots of lives. In only a third of cases where it was practised has outside intervention either had no effect in terms of saving lives or made matters worse (Seybolt 2007: 270). In these cases, there is a correlation between the size, composition and legitimacy of an operation and its ability to save lives. Not surprisingly, well-equipped operations despatched with the support of international society are much more likely to save lives than contentious, ill-equipped and ill-conceived operations.

Peace operations can also make a positive contribution to building stable, democratic peace in the medium and long term. This is important because, while they can stop the violence, enforcement operations cannot sow the seeds of long-term peace. On the other hand, consent-based operations cannot stop the violence but are quite effective in helping belligerents build long-term, democratic peace when they choose to put down their arms (Doyle and

Sambanis 2000: 795). Properly conceived, therefore, if enforcement operations can lay the foundations for a subsequent consensual operation, peace operations can make a significant contribution to building long-term stable peace.

None of this is meant to obscure the myriad problems, crises and moments of shame that are clearly part of the history of peace operations. In the 1990s, the world's governments and (most of) their peacekeepers infamously stood aside as Rwanda, Bosnia and large swathes of Africa burned. Botched peace operations made matters worse in Somalia, while some individual peacekeepers physically abused their prisoners – including children. Corrupt and criminal peacekeepers have also endangered and abused the very people they were sent to protect (Razack 2004). In West Africa, the Democratic Republic of Congo (DRC), Somalia and elsewhere, peacekeepers have raped and sexually exploited women and girls and traded arms with warlords (see chapter 16). Ineffectual peacekeepers and peacemakers have failed to resolve protracted disputes in the Middle East, Cyprus and Western Sahara and to make their agreements stick in places such as Bosnia, Haiti and Darfur.

When it comes to understanding peacekeeping, therefore, the stakes are very high indeed. Done well, peace operations can protect civilians from harm, facilitate the implementation of peace agreements and significantly improve the chances of long-term peace. But there is considerable room for improvement. Failures, abuses and crimes hurt people, undermine the legitimacy of peace operations and reduce the likelihood of stable peace. As the number of operations continues to grow, and as they become more complex in terms of both the actors who conduct and authorize them and the tasks they perform, it is imperative that students, analysts and practitioners alike have a sophisticated understanding of peacekeeping – its key concepts and theories, its contested histories, its different variants and its future challenges. That is the purpose of this book.

Understanding peacekeeping

Although the term 'peacekeeping' was invented in the 1950s, the international management of political violence has a far longer history. As international society's most sustained attempt to work in an organized and usually multilateral fashion to reduce and manage armed conflict, understanding the theory and practice of peacekeeping sheds important light upon trends and developments in global politics more generally. In particular, it provides important insights into the codes of conduct that states have collectively devised to cope with life in an international society of states (Bull 1977), the relationship between the great powers and the maintenance of international peace and security, and the creation and diffusion of shared norms about the appropriateness of warfare itself and legitimate conduct within wars. Yet, at the same time, to gain a sophisticated understanding of peacekeeping we must remain sensitive to how it fits in with the ebb and flow of global political currents.

When we do this it becomes apparent that there is not a complete consensus about the role that peace operations should play in global politics, though there are arguably more points of agreement today than at any time previously (see chapter 5). In general terms, a struggle persists between those who see the role of peace operations in global politics in mainly 'Westphalian' terms and those who see it in more ambitious, 'post-Westphalian' terms. In the former view the primary function of peace operations is to *assist* the peaceful settlement of disputes *between* states. From this perspective, the conduct, ideological persuasion and political organization of states, as well as the relationship between state and society, should not concern peacekeepers, so long as states subscribe to the Westphalian norms of sovereign autonomy and non-interference in the domestic affairs of other states. In its most extreme form, this perspective suggests that human suffering within states, no matter how grotesque, should not concern peacekeepers unless it directly threatens international order and the maintenance of peace and security between states.

In contrast, the post-Westphalian conception of peace operations suggests that, in the long run, peaceful relations between states require liberal democratic regimes and societies within states. This is based on the assumption that domestic peace and the way a state conducts its foreign relations is inextricably linked to the nature of its political system and society. From this perspective, threats to international peace and security are not limited to acts of aggression between states but may also result from violent conflict and illiberal governance within them. Moreover, proponents of this view generally argue that states have a responsibility to protect their own populations from genocide, war crimes, crimes against humanity and ethnic cleansing, and that when they manifestly fail to do so international society acquires a duty to protect vulnerable populations (see Evans 2008; Bellamy 2009; chapters 5 and 15). Consequently, the role of post-Westphalian peace operations is not limited to maintaining order *between* states but instead takes on the much more ambitious task of promoting and sometimes enforcing peace, security, and political, institutional, social and economic reconstruction *within* states. This is to be achieved by creating liberal democratic polities and societies within states that have experienced violent conflict. In principle, there is no intrinsic reason why advocates of limiting sovereignty in cases of genocide, crimes against humanity, ethnic cleansing or state collapse must be committed to building liberal economies, societies and polities within states. But in practice, with the notable exception of proponents of the 'light footprint' approach adopted by NATO and others in Afghanistan (see chapters 10 and 11), post-Westphalian peace operations have generally been committed to implanting the seeds of liberal democratic statehood (see Paris 2004).

In many respects, this ongoing struggle between Westphalian and post-Westphalian conceptions of peace operations reflects a tension in the UN Charter over whether the security of states or the security of human beings should be prioritized (see chapter 1). In addition, the struggle reflects different concerns about the legitimacy of peace operations and the scope of multilateral authority vis-à-vis sovereign authority more generally. It also reveals different ideas about how best to promote international peace and security. The main supporters of the Westphalian conception of peace operations have traditionally been post-colonial states in Asia and Africa, the USSR/Russia and China (e.g. UN 2000). In contrast, at least after the Cold War, the most vocal supporters of the post-Westphalian conception of peace operations have traditionally been Western states and humanitarian NGOs such as Human Rights Watch and the International Crisis Group.

Although this struggle has not been conclusively resolved, it has tilted heavily in favour of the post-Westphalian conception. One particularly important symbolic moment came in late 2005, when over 150 UN member states acknowledged their responsibility to protect their citizens from genocide and mass atrocities and promised to take steps to prevent such crimes (see chapter 5). More recently still, in early 2008, the UN adopted a set of 'principles and guidelines' for peace operations that included the protection of civilians as a key function (see chapter 15). All this suggests that there is growing support for some of the basic principles of the post-Westphalian view of peace operations. However, it is important to note that many states (especially in Asia) remain deeply sceptical about post-Westphalian peace operations and that some of its ostensible champions have been prepared to modify their position by adopting a 'light footprint' approach to building peace. Significantly, these debates have been shaped by the ongoing processes of globalization.

The changing political environment

The term 'globalization' can obscure as much as it reveals. However, as an umbrella term used to encompass a variety of complex and interrelated processes it has become difficult to avoid. The way that we understand it is discussed in more detail in chapter 1, but it is worth noting at the outset three particularly important ways in which contemporary globalization is impacting on peace operations. First, it has facilitated a distinctive form of violent conflict commonly known as 'new wars' that reflect the ongoing erosion of the state's monopoly on legitimate organized violence (Kaldor 1997, 1999). Typically, 'new wars' take place within states or are transnational in character and often involve multiple belligerents of different types, significantly adding to the complexity of the problems confronting peacekeepers. Second, the spread of global communications has contributed to a growing awareness of political strife and humanitarian crises around the world, fuelling calls from Western and non-Western civil society groups for international society to assume greater responsibility for the protection of vulnerable populations. This, in turn, has contributed to an increasing demand for peacekeepers (see chapters 4 and 5). Third, contemporary globalization has forced the UN, regional arrangements and individual states to pay greater attention to an increasingly diverse array of non-state actors, many of whom, such as humanitarian NGOs, the International Financial Institutions (IFIs), and warlords and their supporters, play important roles in either maintaining or disrupting international peace and security.

The combination of these developments highlights the three issues that lie at the heart of this book:

1 the ongoing struggle between proponents of the more limited Westphalian conception of peace operations and the more ambitious agenda of those who understand them in post-Westphalian terms;
2 the challenge of meeting the increasing demand for more peacekeepers to undertake increasingly complex operations – including closing the gap between theory and practice and improving understanding of the practical challenges that confront peace operations;
3 understanding the effects of the growing number and variety of non-state actors upon contemporary violent conflicts and the efforts of peacekeepers to resolve them.

All peace operations reflect a desire on the part of those states that authorize them and those that participate in them to limit the scourge of war. As a result, debates about what peace operations are for, and what strategies peacekeepers should use, revolve around different conceptions of the causes and nature of violent conflict, disputes about the relative value of sovereignty and human protection, differences over the foundations of stable peace, and contending political priorities. Peace operations have therefore always been ad hoc responses to particular problems, despite recent attempts to develop common doctrine and strengthen the UN's institutional capacity to conduct and manage them (see chapters 2 and 5). This is why these operations continue to defy simple categorization based on the tasks peacekeepers fulfil in different historical periods (see chapters 3–5), and also why an approach that focuses on the role that peacekeeping plays within global politics more broadly is needed. This book addresses that very problem.

Structure of the book

In order to explore these issues, this book is divided into four parts. There is also a companion website (www.politybooks.com/up2) which contains additional case studies, maps, links and information about UN and non-UN peace operations. Part I of this book, 'Concepts and Issues', provides an overview of the main theoretical debates and technical issues relevant to contemporary peace operations. Chapter 1 investigates different ways of understanding peace operations and their relationship to broader processes and trends within global politics. As the number, range and complexity of peace operations has grown, so too has the number of theories and concepts used by analysts and practitioners alike to explain and understand them. This chapter considers different ways of defining peace operations and contending theories about them before analysing how globalization and ideas about 'sovereignty as responsibility' have impacted upon them. Chapter 2 then develops this approach by identifying different types of peacekeepers (individual states and coalitions, and international organizations, especially regional arrangements and the UN) and how peace operations are put together. After analysing some of the most significant types of non-UN peace operations, the chapter summarizes the UN's peace operations machinery in more detail.

Part II, 'Historical Development', provides a narrative overview of how the theory and practice of peace operations has developed from the 1800s to the present day. Chapter 3 examines some of the historical antecedents of UN peace operations, such as the conference and congress systems of the nineteenth century, as well as the activities of the League of Nations. It then goes on to highlight the main theoretical and practical developments in UN peace operations during the Cold War. The story of how peace operations continued to develop after the end of the Cold War is the subject of chapter 4. This begins by charting how the end of superpower confrontation saw UN member states place an increasing number of demands upon peacekeepers without a requisite rethinking of the nature, role and scale of peace operations. This gap between the tasks given to peacekeepers and the means supplied to them resulted in a number of high-profile failures (in Angola, Somalia, Rwanda and Bosnia) and a global decline in peace operations during the late 1990s. Chapter 5 takes up the story from the turn of the twenty-first century and explores the lessons that were learned from the failures of the 1990s and the gradual rebirth of peace operations in the new millennium. Since 2003 there has been a steady expansion of peace operations, bringing with it new challenges and problems – not least how to find enough troops to satisfy the world's increasing demand for peacekeepers.

As part II demonstrates, UN peace operations have not evolved in a straightforward or linear manner with a 'clean' division between Cold War and post-Cold War operations. In reality, the picture is far messier: the UN and other actors have undertaken different types of operations at different times and in different parts of the world. Part III, 'Types of Peace Operations', sets out a conceptual framework supported by practical case studies that highlight the distinctive characteristics of seven different types of peace operations. These are based on what each type is supposed to achieve. In other words, the primary distinction between the seven types of peace operations lies in the *intended ends* they hope to achieve rather than the *means* that are employed to achieve them. The seven different types of peace operations are as follows.

- *Preventive deployments* Usually conducted with the consent of the host state, preventive operations deploy peacekeepers in order to prevent either violent conflict from emerging in the first place or a specific threat to a civilian population from materializing.
- *Traditional peacekeeping* These operations are intended to support peacemaking between states by creating the political space necessary for the belligerent states to negotiate a political settlement. Traditional peacekeeping takes place in the space between a ceasefire agreement and the conclusion of a political settlement. Traditional peacekeepers do not propose or enforce particular political solutions; rather, they work with the consent of the belligerents and try to build confidence in order to facilitate political dialogue.
- *Wider peacekeeping* These operations are intended to fulfil the aims of traditional peacekeeping as well as certain additional tasks (such as the delivery of humanitarian relief) in a context of ongoing conflict. They developed as an ad hoc response to the breakdown of ceasefires or political agreements that enabled the original deployment of a traditional or assisting transition operation, combined with a belief on the part of peacekeepers that they should continue to have some sort of role (often humanitarian) in the conflict area.
- *Peace enforcement* These operations aim to impose the will of the UN Security Council upon the parties to a particular conflict. Peace enforcement operations are the closest manifestation of the collective security role originally envisaged for the UN by the authors of its Charter, though they depart from that vision in important respects.
- *Assisting transitions* These multidimensional operations involve the deployment of military, police and/or civilian personnel to assist the parties to a conflict in the implementation of a political settlement or the transition from a peace heavily supported by international agencies to one that is self-sustaining. They tend to take place after *both* a ceasefire *and* a political settlement have been reached. External actors play mediatory or peacemaking roles that pave the way for a political settlement, but peacekeepers are not deployed until the settlement has been concluded. The mandate of transitional operations usually revolves around the implementation of the peace settlement.
- *Transitional administrations* These are also multidimensional operations deployed after a peace agreement of some sort, but they are distinguished by their assumption of sovereign authority over a particular territory. In addition to keeping the peace, protecting civilians, enforcing peace agreements, and the other activities associated with large and complex operations, transitional administrations have the authority to make and enforce the law, exercise control over all aspects of a territory's economy, preside over a territory's borders, regulate the media, manage property law, run schools, hospitals, the sanitation system, the electricity grid, the

roads and other forms of transportation, and administer the judicial system.

- *Peace support operations* These are designed to help establish post-Westphalian peace. That is, they aim to establish liberal democratic political systems and societies within states. They combine robust military forces capable of limited peace enforcement tasks, should a ceasefire break down, with a strong civilian component that often includes civil administration, humanitarian agencies and police and justice officers. Peace support operations attempt the impartial enforcement of a political settlement, the substance of which may have been dictated by the interveners and supports the establishment of liberal democracy.

These types of operations have not developed in any consistent chronological order. Nor are they mutually exclusive. A single operation may well move back and forth between these various aims or may involve more than one of these roles simultaneously (see James 1990). We have made extensive use of case studies in part III to illustrate the complexities encountered by individual missions.

Having considered the theoretical debates surrounding peace operations, their historical evolution, and the different types of operations in practice, part IV, 'Contemporary Challenges', assesses the major issues facing peacekeepers for the foreseeable future. The challenges considered in this part of the book might be categorized into two broad types. The first revolves around the problem of satisfying the increasing global demand for peacekeepers. This has been compounded by competing requirements for troops emanating from the 'Global War on Terror' and ongoing large-scale military commitments in Iraq and Afghanistan. Chapters 13 and 14 examine two alternative sources of peacekeepers to augment the UN's efforts – regionalization (the use of regional arrangements) and privatization (the use of private contractors). The challenge in relation to regional arrangements is for the UN to find an appropriate relationship with those organizations that are in the business of conducting peace operations. This is especially important in circumstances where enforcement activities are likely to occur. The challenge in relation to private contractors is to work out what roles they can and should legitimately play in contemporary peace operations and how best to ensure that they remain both efficient and accountable.

The second set of challenges for contemporary peace operations revolves around the expansion of their scope and gradual professionalization. In particular, chapters 15–17 focus on three of the most prominent areas that have seen a rapid expansion in terms of their profile but where much more work is needed to overcome some of the formidable obstacles: the protection of civilians, consideration of gender issues, and policing. While the last decade has witnessed the protection of civilians and policing become core functions of many UN peace operations, there is no consensus on how and by whom these tasks should be carried out. In addition, the UN's public image has been badly damaged by a series of scandals involving the sexual exploitation and abuse of local populations and where critics have accused peacekeepers of spreading HIV/AIDS. Tackling these problems and promoting what the UN calls effective 'gender mainstreaming' is thus an important aspect of future peace operations.

We conclude by reflecting on the likely future trajectory of peace operations. Five years on from the first edition of *Understanding Peacekeeping*, it remains our conviction that peace operations play a vitally important role in managing armed conflict, supporting stable peace and – increasingly – protecting endangered populations. However, to borrow a phrase from the former UN Secretary-General Kofi Annan, peace operations stand at a 'fork in the road'. Through past experience and theoretically informed analysis, we have a better understanding today of what it takes to build stable peace and the roles peacekeepers can play in the process. Although this has created renewed global demand for peace operations, peacekeepers have often been sent on difficult missions without the necessary resources and political support. We hope this book can help people understand why they should be given both.

PART I

Concepts and Issues

CHAPTER ONE

Peace Operations in Global Politics

The fullest perspective on peacekeeping...is one which places it firmly in the context of international politics.

James (1990: 13-14)

This chapter investigates different ways of understanding peace operations and their relationship to broader processes and trends within global politics. As the number and range of peace operations has grown, so too has the number of theories and concepts used to understand them. Meanwhile, processes of globalization are transforming global politics from an activity primarily involving states to one characterized by transnational relations between different types of politically significant actors which are connected by potentially global communications. Both the theory and practice of peace operations have been indelibly shaped by this changing global context. Initially, peacekeeping was concerned chiefly with creating the conditions for the peaceful settlement of disputes *between* states. This approach to peacekeeping is most closely associated with a Westphalian approach and 'traditional peacekeeping' (see chapter 7). On the other hand, new post-Westphalian conceptions of liberal peace insist that, because liberal democratic states are peaceful in their relations with one another, peace operations need to be in the business of fostering and maintaining a world order based on liberal democracy. Buttressing these claims are shifting conceptions of sovereignty. Whereas the Westphalian order rested on a notion of sovereignty that granted states protection from interference by outsiders, the post-Westphalian account is based on the notion of 'sovereignty as responsibility' – the idea that sovereigns enjoy the right to non-interference only insofar as they protect the fundamental rights of their citizens. Today, this post-Westphalian account is in the ascendancy but continues to be resisted by those who believe that it risks undermining sovereignty and, in turn, international peace and security itself. Many of today's debates about the nature and direction of peace operations can be traced back to these two very different conceptions of world order and the different roles afforded to peace operations by each of them.

In order to analyse the roles peace operations play in global politics, this chapter proceeds in three parts. The first considers different ways of defining peace operations. The second explores different theories of peace operations, showing how theory shapes the questions we ask, the way we approach peace operations and, ultimately, the answers we get. The final section sets out some of the basic principles of the Westphalian conception of international society and the role of peace operations within it before evaluating how globalization, 'new wars' and ideas about 'sovereignty as responsibility' have introduced a post-Westphalian challenge.

1.1 Defining peace operations

We need to begin by defining what we mean by peace operations. Definitions are important because without them we cannot narrow down a field of study or argue meaningfully about it. Definitions are also important because they all have consequences that lead the analyst in some direction while closing down others. Ultimately, however, definitions are just tools that are useful only insofar as they help us to understand better the issue in question.

On the face of it, there is little agreement between analysts, governments and international organizations about what peace operations are and the differences between terms such as 'peacekeeping', 'peacemaking' and 'peacebuilding'. Indeed, governments and international organizations have been prone to label many different kinds of military activity as 'peacekeeping', sometimes in an attempt to legitimize their activities (see James 1969: 9; Finnemore 2003). For example, when US forces invaded Grenada in 1983 to overthrow a communist-leaning military junta, US President Ronald Reagan labelled his forces the 'Caribbean Peace Keeping Force' (Diehl 1994: 4). In a similar vein, the Russian government described its counter-insurgency wars in Chechnya as peacekeeping and, more recently, US coalition forces in Iraq have on occasion been labelled peacekeepers (MacQueen 2006: 1).

The situation is not helped by the fact that the terms 'peacekeeping' and 'peace operation' are not found in the UN Charter. Of course, most definitions are not as obviously self-serving as Ronald Reagan's, but all of them are informed by their author's interests, experiences and values. We also need to bear in mind that, when we are dealing with a political activity such as peacekeeping, two actors looking at the same phenomenon might genuinely come up with two quite different ways of defining and conceptualizing their experience (Williams 2010). So politically charged is the question of defining peace operations that the UN has still not clearly stipulated what it means by the term. Member states remain divided as to the proper scope of UN interventionism and the relative merits of concepts such as neutrality, impartiality and the use of minimum force. As such, rather than define 'peace operations', the UN's *Handbook on Multidimensional Peacekeeping Operations* simply lists the military and civilian tasks that peacekeepers are commonly required to fulfil (see table 1.1).

The UN repeated this approach in 2007 when it came to developing what was initially referred to as 'capstone doctrine' to guide the conduct of its peace operations. Rather than specify precisely what peace operations were,

TABLE 1.1 The peacekeepers' tasks

Military	Civilian
Assist in implementing peace agreement	Help former belligerents implement complex peace agreements
Monitor a ceasefire or cessation of hostilities	Support delivery of humanitarian assistance
Provide a secure environment	Assist in the disarmament, demobilization and reintegration of ex-combatants
Prevent the outbreak or spillover of conflict	Supervise elections
Lead states or territories through a transition to stable government based on democratic principles	Build rule of law capacity
Administer a territory for a transitional period	Promote respect for human rights
	Assist economic recovery
	Set up transitional administration as a territory moves to independence

Source: (DPKO 2003: 2–3).

the DPKO simply identified 'peacekeeping' as one of five 'peace and security activities':

- *Conflict prevention* including structural and diplomatic measures to prevent disputes from developing into violent conflict;
- *Peacemaking* the use of diplomatic measures to bring hostile parties to a negotiated agreement;
- *Peacekeeping* the use of military, police and civilian personnel to lay the foundations of sustainable peace;
- *Peace enforcement* the use of military and other measures to enforce the will of the UN Security Council;
- *Peacebuilding* 'a range of measures aimed at reducing the risk of lapsing or relapsing into conflict' (DPKO 2007: 10–11)

Although the categorization of tasks and situating of peace operations in a broader spectrum of measures designed to prevent and limit the incidence and lethality of armed conflict is useful in itself, it does not get us very close to a definition. For instance, we might ask which of these tasks are *necessary* for a mission to be considered a peace operation. This same problem arises in relation to various academic definitions of peace operations which focus on their functions (see James 1990: 1–8; Durch 1996a: 8). Diehl, Druckman and Wall (1998: 38–40), for instance, put forward twelve different types of peacekeeping operations ranging from 'traditional peacekeeping' to 'sanctions enforcement', while Demurenko and Nikitin (1997) identify seven types. Such taxonomies tend to be quite self-referential. Although they shed light on how missions are put together and tasked, they tell us little about the changing role of peace operations or the underlying rationale of the activities described. Moreover, they tend to be quite inflexible. For example, Paul Diehl and his collaborators have pointed out that other typologies forget that operations might involve the performance of multiple tasks simultaneously or alternate between different types (Diehl et al. 1998: 38).

In the absence of a UN definition, many people look to the earliest proponents of peace operations or the earliest historical examples for a guide to defining peacekeeping. Three such definitions are set out in box 1.1. The first two definitions are too narrow. Goulding's definition would exclude peace operations by non-UN actors such as regional organizations (see chapters 2 and 13), while Diehl's would exclude all those international missions not composed of lightly armed troops. Among these would be at least one of the UN's earliest peace operations, ONUC in the Congo (1960–4; see chapter 3). By contrast, the third definition – proposed in an International Peace Academy (now Institute) handbook for peacekeepers – is in one way too broad in that it captures almost any attempt at third-party mediation and in another way too narrow by insisting upon the deployment of *multinational* troops, police and civilians, thus ruling out missions conducted by a single state. What is more, all three definitions assume that peacekeeping is defined by the performance of particular tasks. The tasks they identify were indeed performed in many of the earliest UN missions, but some early missions went well beyond them. The aforementioned mission to Congo (ONUC) was engaged in state-building,

Box 1.1 Definitions of peacekeeping

Field operations established by the United Nations, with the consent of the parties concerned, to help control and resolve conflicts between them, under United Nations command and control, at the expense collectively of the member states, and with military and other personnel and equipment provided voluntarily by them, acting impartially between the parties and using force to the minimum extent necessary. (Goulding 1993: 455)

Peacekeeping is...the imposition of neutral and lightly armed interposition forces following a cessation of armed hostilities, and with the permission of the state on whose territory those forces are deployed, in order to discourage a renewal of military conflict and promote an environment under which the underlying dispute can be resolved. (Diehl 1994: 13)

The prevention, containment, moderation, and termination of hostilities between or within states, through the medium of a peaceful third party intervention organised and directed internally, using multinational forces of soldiers, police and civilians to restore and maintain peace. (International Peace Academy 1984)

peace enforcement and human rights promotion, and the UN mission to Cyprus (UNFICYP) also had a human rights component (Månsson 2005).

This is also why it makes little sense to categorize peace operations chronologically. It is common, for instance, to distinguish two or three 'generations' of peacekeeping or peacemaking (Goulding 1993; Mackinlay and Chopra 1992). But defining peace operations this way obscures more than it illuminates, because there have always been different types of peace operation and their development cannot be easily broken down into chronological eras (see parts II and III).

Boutros-Ghali's *An Agenda for Peace* (1992) marked something of a watershed for the way peacekeeping was defined and conceptualized. The Secretary-General argued that peacekeeping was one of four tools that the UN could use to prevent and resolve conflict around the world, the other three being 'preventive diplomacy' (diplomatic action to prevent conflicts becoming violent), 'peacemaking' (activities designed to bring hostile parties together by peaceful means) and 'peacebuilding' (activities to build peace after a conflict in order to avoid its recurrence). Within this schema, Boutros-Ghali defined peacekeeping as:

> the deployment of a United Nations presence in the field, hitherto with the consent of all the parties concerned, normally involving United Nations military and/or police personnel and frequently civilians as well. Peacekeeping is an activity that expands the possibilities for both the prevention of conflict and the making of peace. (1992: § 20)

The significance of Boutros-Ghali's definition lay not in its wording – like those considered earlier, it assumed that peacekeeping necessarily involved the UN – but in its broader conceptualization, namely the idea that peacekeeping was one of several ways in which third parties might contribute to preventing, resolving or managing violent conflict and the rebuilding of communities thereafter.

Most subsequent definitions of peace operations have tended to put forth a broad general definition of a class of activity (labelled either peacekeeping or peace operations) with several distinct subsets, leaving out the actual composition (heavily armed, lightly armed, etc.) of the force. This is important because a mission's composition does not determine its nature. A lightly armed mission to impose the UN's will on recalcitrant belligerents is still an enforcement operation – albeit a chronically weak one. Likewise, a ceasefire monitoring mission equipped with tanks and fighter jets is still a ceasefire monitoring mission. Given the increasing prevalence of peace operations conducted by non-UN organizations (a far from novel endeavour), most contemporary definitions also reject the idea that only the UN can conduct peace operations. Thus, William Durch (2006a: xvii) defined peace operations as 'internationally authorized, multilateral, civil-military efforts to promote and protect…transitions from war to peace'. According to New York University's Center on International Cooperation (CIC), military deployments by non-UN actors can be considered peace operations if they are 'conducted by regional organizations or ad hoc coalitions of states with the stated intention to (a) serve as an instrument to facilitate the implementation of peace agreements already in place, (b) support a peace process, or (c) assist conflict prevention and/or peacebuilding efforts' (CIC 2006: 152).

Our definition is similar in kind to these. For the purposes of this book: *peace operations involve the expeditionary use of uniformed personnel (police and/or military) with or without UN authorization, with a mandate or programme to:*

(1) *assist in the prevention of armed conflict by supporting a peace process;*
(2) *serve as an instrument to observe or assist in the implementation of ceasefires or peace agreements; or*
(3) *enforce ceasefires, peace agreements or the will of the UN Security Council in order to build stable peace.* (See Williams 2010)

Peace operations are therefore one general type of activity that can be used to prevent, limit and manage violent conflict as well as rebuild in its aftermath. Other parts of the international toolkit include conflict prevention, peacemaking and peacebuilding, which involve the use of civilian agencies and NGOs in the reconstruction of polities, economies and societies. While each of these terms is contested, we will refer to them in the same manner as the UN (as set out above). In part III of the book we discuss seven types of peace operations, differentiated by their primary purpose: preventive deployments, traditional peacekeeping, wider peacekeeping, peace enforcement, assisting transitions, transitional administrations and peace support operations. The next section of this chapter turns to different ways of thinking theoretically about peace operations.

1.2 Theorizing peace operations

Until very recently, there were few self-conscious attempts to think theoretically about peace operations. One exception was Indar Jit Rikhye, who argued that peacekeeping provided a mechanism for resolving international conflicts without superpower involvement and involved the mobilization of international society to create the necessary conditions (Rikhye 1984: 234; cf. Rikhye et al. 1974: 8–18). But this theory tells only part of the story about the role of peace operations in the Cold War – that related to 'traditional peacekeeping' (see chapter 7; James 1994a). Another exception was the various attempts to conceptualize and test peacekeeping as a form of third party-mediation. A. B. Fetherston (1995) argued that there was a gap between the practice of peacekeeping (which was primarily about mediation in her view) and its theory. She sought to fill that gap by proposing a theory of peacekeeping predicated on theories of conflict resolution. In a similar vein, William Zartman (1985) tested the effectiveness of different types of third-party intervention, finding that it was likely to be effective only when the parties to the conflict had reached a 'mutually hurting stalemate', and Fen Osler Hampson (1996) found that one of the principal determinants of success was the level of commitment on the part of the third parties themselves (see Paris 2000: 29).

To be sure, plenty of work on peace operations has had theoretical content. Indeed, the majority of the literature involves detailed studies of individual operations, often organized around a common framework of analysis to facilitate comparison (e.g. Durch 1996b, 2006b; Berdal and Economides 2007). Others have used more or less theory to explain why certain countries have adopted particular policies towards peace operations and why those policies have changed over time (e.g. Briscoe 2004; Stamnes 2007). A final subset of theoretically engaged studies has focused on the lessons that ought to be learned from past peace operations in order to improve future chances of success (e.g. Doyle and Sambanis 2000, 2006; Howard 2008; Fortna 2008b). These have even included the development of theoretical accounts of the *unintended* consequences of peace operations (Aoi, de Coning and Thakur 2007). These types of studies have helped shed light on the general causes of success for peace operations, the contextual factors that make success more likely and the relative effectiveness of regional organizations (Bellamy and Williams 2005b; Diehl and Cho 2006). Others have focused almost exclusively on the failure of peace operations, leading one to believe – wrongly, in our view (see the Introduction) – that the world would be a better place without them (e.g. Jett 1999; Fleitz 2002; Polman 2003).

Given that peace operations are such practical activities, students might ask why we need to think theoretically about them at all. Indeed, some analysts have made precisely this argument. Somewhat paradoxically, Ryan (2000: 43) noted a need to produce 'a stronger conceptual framework for peacekeeping' while cautioning against 'too much theorizing', and Bures (2007) argued that 'macrotheory' was likely to obscure as much as it illuminated. A more important point was made by Roland Paris (2000: 44) when he argued that the study of peace operations had suffered from a 'cult of policy relevance'. This created a situation where 'students of peace operations...neglected broader macrotheoretical questions about the nature and significance of these operations for our understanding of international politics. This omission has stunted the intellectual development of the field and isolated the study of peace operations from other branches of international relations.'

We should, therefore, ask what gets missed from the study of peace operations if we neglect theory. The short answer is an awful lot; from the gendered effects of some peacekeeping practices (Whitworth 2004) to the ideational foundations of peace operations (Barnett and Finnemore 2004) and the wider regional consequences of international interventions (Pugh and Cooper 2004). All investigations of social phenomena are guided by some theory or other, whether we recognize it or not. Theories help us to make sense of complex and seemingly random social interactions. They tell us what to look for, what types of actors are important, and what counts as valid or valuable knowledge about particular phenomena. Theories inform the methods we use and the causal connections we draw, our values and our politics (see Booth 2007: 182–208). It is precisely because theory, broadly understood, is so important in guiding the questions we ask and the answers we reach that the UN has been unable to define peace operations. The protagonists to that debate know only too well that the way we define things shapes the way we conceptualize them and, in turn, our interests and our behaviour. It is therefore dishonest to claim to be working without theory when one studies political phenomena, including peace operations, for we cannot know what those phenomena are without theories. Although there is no single theoretical or methodological framework that can pose or answer the myriad questions associated with peace operations (see Druckman and Stern 1999), it is incumbent on analysts to be self-consciously theoretical and ask basic questions about what we are looking at and why, and what is excluded when we look at something in a particular way.

In this regard, it is a welcome development that the early twenty-first century has seen a steady growth in theorizing about peace operations. This has provided a range of answers to questions about what we should study and how we should study it. In the remainder of this section we will briefly evaluate several different ways of addressing these questions, first by considering the different levels and units of analysis we can employ in studying peace operations and then by assessing some of the most important newly emerging theories.

The question of what to study depends on *ontology*. Put simply, ontology refers to theoretical assumptions about the structures, actors and causal relations that constitute reality (Booth 2007: 184). In relation to peace operations, this raises questions about who the primary actors are, whose perspectives should be taken into account, and how we understand the relationship between social structures such as capitalism or 'world culture' and human behaviour. Two of the most pressing dilemmas of ontology relate to units of analysis and levels of analysis: the former relates to the type of actor whose behaviour we want to explain (individuals, ethnic groups, insurgencies, states, international organizations, etc.) and the latter to the level at which we want to study that unit (international society, regions, individual governments, particular government departments, etc.) (see Wight 2006: 102–8). Taking a lead from Kenneth Waltz, the pioneer of neorealist theory in International Relations, most analysts tend to separate units and levels of analysis into three: the international system, the state and the individual (Waltz 1959). In relation to peace operations, however, studies sometimes tacitly adopt a different approach, following the military's distinction between three levels of war: *strategic* (the policy-making/strategic level), *operational* (the direction of the mission) and *tactical* (the direction of individual mission components on the ground). As noted earlier, most studies of peace operations are conducted at the 'state' or the operational level, yet barely any acknowledge that they are operating at only one of several potential levels of analysis. Consequently, they overlook considerations such as the global forces that influence the direction and impact of an operation and – at the other end of the spectrum – the perceptions of marginalized individuals and groups within the theatre of operations itself. A first step, therefore, is to recognize that peace operations can – and should – be studied from a multiplicity of levels. The problem is that the three levels identified by neorealists and military thinkers are not enough. Instead, we suggest that peace operations can be studied from *at least* five different levels (see figure 1.1).

Both the general phenomenon of peace operations and individual missions can be studied at each of these five levels, and a comprehensive theory of peace operations would need to account for each (and other potential levels) as well as the relationships between them. It should instantly be clear that by opening peace operations up to ontological scrutiny we have immediately widened the range of analysis beyond the operational level. This helps to highlight the types of things that are missed when we focus on only one level and suggests the need for new theories and methods to assist us in understanding peace operations at the other levels.

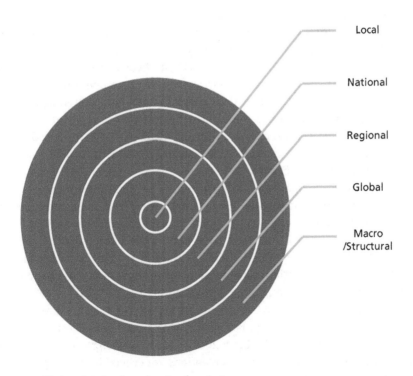

Figure 1.1 *Levels and units of analysis*

Macro- or *structural*-level theories of the sort envisioned by Roland Paris try to explain the deep structural factors that shape the way peace operations are understood and practised. These include factors such as 'global culture', the world economy and the forces of patriarchy that produce gender discrimination (see below).

Global-level theories are interested in decision-making in global organizations such as the UN. These focus on the role played by legitimacy, norms and power politics in shaping political decisions or the way in which organizations develop their own 'pathologies' that influence the way they see the world, interact with others and behave.

Regional-level analysis can help explain how states in given regions reach shared understandings about the role of peace operations which may be different from those of other regions. They have also helped identify how patterns of conflict can spread across borders and how a peace operation in one country might 'displace' conflict into neighbouring states. Pugh and Cooper (2004), for example, show how the traditional focus on single missions obscures the way in which conflicts – and therefore missions – are interlinked, a point demonstrated by a regional perspective on three recent West African conflicts (Sierra Leone, Liberia and Côte d'Ivoire).

As we noted earlier, studies of peacekeeping have typically operated at the *national* level by focusing on either individual missions or the policies of individual countries. Such studies have become increasingly sophisticated in recent years. Often, country- or mission-level studies are comparative in nature, with studies organized around a common framework of analysis to permit cross-comparison (e.g. Durch 1993b, 1996b, 2006b). Others, such as Katharina Coleman (2007), use constructivist theories from International Relations to shed light on particular aspects of peace operations through comparative analysis. Coleman does this to understand better why states prefer to conduct peace operations under the auspices of regional organizations, finding that peacekeepers are concerned about the legitimacy of their operations and that legitimation can be acquired by working through regional organizations (also see chapter 2).

Given that peace operations aim to build sustainable peace in war-torn societies, it is surprising that until very recently the *local* level has been almost entirely excluded from the way they were assessed and understood. That this level is now included is owing in large part to the influence of feminism. Studies at this level have highlighted the ways in which masculinized and militarized peace operations have actually made some segments of the local population more insecure, through the commission of sexual exploitation and abuse (see chapter 16). What is more, anthropological studies have helped shed light on what local populations actually think about the presence of foreign peacekeepers (e.g. Pouligny 2006) – an astonishing earlier omission when one considers that positive perceptions are crucial if peace operations are to accomplish their goals. This approach has generated calls for local actors to be better included in decision-making about the peace processes that will affect their lives in profound ways (Chopra and Hohe 2004a, 2004b). Another approach to understanding peace operations at the local level is to investigate the psychology of the peacekeepers themselves and uncover 'the thoughts, feelings, and behaviours of individuals who attempted to establish peace' in order to understand the factors that shape the effectiveness and well-being of individual peacekeepers (Britt and Adler 2003: 4).

No single level is necessarily better or more accurate than the others, and a comprehensive theory of peace operations would have to take account of each level and the relations between them. The important point to recognize is that, whether self-consciously or not, analysts *choose* the level and unit of analysis; they are neither natural nor predetermined. Neither do they stand in isolation from the other levels. In the chapters that follow, our analysis will draw insights and perspectives from each of the levels. Before that, however, we will briefly survey four of the main theories relevant to peace operations – liberal peace theory, global cultural theory, cosmopolitanism and critical theory – in order to shed light on the question of how we should study them.

Liberal peace theory

Without doubt this is the most influential theory in relation to peace operations. Indeed, in their attempt to construct zones of stable peace (Boulding 1978), both the theory and practice of peace operations are informed by an often unspoken commitment to the liberal peace (see Paris 1997, 2002, 2004). At the interstate level, liberal peace is based on the observation that democratic states do not wage war on other states they regard as being democratic. This is not to argue that democracies do not wage war at all or that they are less warlike in their relations with non-democracies; only that democracies tend not to fight each other. In addition, liberal democracies are said to be the least likely states to descend into civil war or anarchy.

Exponents of this theory generally present two reasons to explain why that might be. First, through their legislatures and judiciaries, democratic systems impose powerful institutional constraints on decision-makers, inhibiting their opportunities for waging war rashly (Owen 1994: 90). These inhibitions are further strengthened by the plethora of international institutions (such as the UN) to which liberal democratic states are tied. Democracy prevents civil war primarily because it guarantees basic human rights and offers non-violent avenues for the resolution of political disputes. The second explanation of liberal peace is normative and holds that democratic states do not fight each other because they recognize one another's inherent legitimacy (ibid.) and have shared interests in the protection of international trade which are ill-served by war (Hegre 2000). Within states, the legitimacy associated with democracy makes it very difficult to mobilize arms against the prevailing order, reducing the likelihood of civil wars.

In arguing that peace operations are informed by liberal peace theory, we mean – by and large – that peace operations have tried to create stable peace by promoting and defending the principles that underpin liberal peace. This is most apparent in those peace operations that seek to build peace *within* states – which are increasingly becoming the norm (see section 1.3). These operations try to build stable peace by enabling the creation of democratic societies and liberal free market economies. They are often supported in this endeavour by Western NGOs (Richmond 2003: 1). There is also, however, a broad consensus that fostering liberal peace can contribute to reducing violent conflict *between* states. As box 1.2 shows, these beliefs are shared by powerful people and organizations, including two successive secretaries-general of the UN, the UNDP and a president of the United States. To be fair, there does indeed seem to be a link (though not a straightforward one; see Jarstad and Sisk 2008) between liberalism, democracy and peace, and, as we noted in the Introduction, the reduction in the frequency and lethality of war has gone hand in hand with both increased international activism and the spread of formal democracy.

Box 1.2 Advocates of liberal peace

There is an obvious connection between democratic practices – such as the rule of law and transparency in decision-making – and the achievement of true peace and security in any new and stable political order. These elements of good governance need to be promoted at all levels of international and national political communities. (Former UN Secretary-General Boutros Boutros-Ghali: 1992: § 59)

Democracies don't attack each other…ultimately the best strategy to insure our security and to build a durable peace is to support the advance of democracy elsewhere. (US President Bill Clinton, in the 'State of the Union Address', New York Times, 26 January 1994)

Sound national and local legislatures and judiciaries are critical for creating and maintaining enabling environments for eradicating poverty. Legislatures mandate differing interests and debate and establish policies, laws and resources priorities that directly affect people-centred development. Electoral bodies and processes ensure independent and transparent elections for legislatures. Judiciaries uphold the rule of law, bringing security and predictability to social, political and economic relations. (UNDP policy document 1997: 14)

The right to choose how they are ruled, and who rules them, must be the birthright of all people, and its universal achievement must be a central objective of an Organization [the UN] devoted to the cause of larger freedom…The United Nations does more than any other single organization to promote and strengthen democratic institutions and practices around the world. (Former UN Secretary-General Kofi Annan 2005a: §§ 148 and 151)

Although liberal peace is the dominant theory that underpins contemporary peace operations, its application remains controversial. China and many states in the global South, for example, argue that peace operations should be limited to assisting states and other actors to resolve their differences and should not be used to impose a particular ideology (Morphet 2000). From this perspective, stable peace can only be built on the maintenance of peace between states (Owen 2000), and this requires respect for the sanctity of national sovereignty (discussed in the following section). Because of these concerns, overt support from the UN for a broad liberal agenda in its peace operations has been limited to one of three situations. First, there are occasions when the parties to a conflict themselves invite the UN or other organizations to help install democratic government, as in the cases of Cambodia, Namibia and, more recently, Sierra Leone and Burundi. Second, the UN Security Council has sometimes defended democratically elected governments ousted by coups d'état (e.g. Haiti and Sierra Leone), though it has not done so consistently (e.g. Pakistan, Congo-Brazzaville and Mauritania). In the case of Haiti in the early 1990s, the Council resolved that the illegal removal of a democratically elected government constituted a threat to regional peace and security (Byers and Chesterman 2000: 287). In 1997 it likewise found that the overthrow of the elected government of Sierra Leone was a threat to peace, demanded that it be restored, and welcomed an ECOWAS intervention that did just that (Roth 1999: 405–6). Finally, the UN and other actors have sometimes attempted to create liberal peace in places where the state has failed to exert effective authority, such as Bosnia after 1995 and Kosovo and Timor-Leste after 1999 (see chapter 11).

There are other problems with the logic of liberal peace besides these political problems. Roland Paris (2004) found that the rapid democratization and marketization of post-war societies could have destabilizing effects and undermine the chances of long-term stable peace. Others deny liberal peace's basic empirical assumption by pointing to wars between or within democracies or arguing that the dataset remains too small to draw statistically relevant conclusions (e.g. Mearsheimer 1994). Echoing realist sentiments expressed by E. H. Carr ([1939] 1995) in the late 1930s, a third group of critics argue that the values underpinning liberal peace are not universal or causally connected to peace but reflect the ideological preferences of the world's most powerful actors (Barkawi and Laffey 1999).

Global culture and peace operations

Drawing on world polity theory (see Finnemore 1996), Roland Paris (2003) argues that the international normative environment – a 'global culture' comprised of formal and informal social rules that guide international life – shapes the design of peace operations in fundamental ways (see box 1.3). Global culture helps determine the sorts of activities that are considered

Box 1.3 The global cultural determinants of peace operations

Peacekeeping agencies and their member states are predisposed to develop and implement strategies that conform with the norms of global culture, and they are disinclined to pursue strategies that deviate from these norms. In short, the design and conduct of peacekeeping missions reflect not only the interests of the key parties and the perceived lessons of previous operations, but also the prevailing norms of global culture, which legitimize certain kinds of peacekeeping policies and delegitimize others....[G]lobal culture constrains...peacekeeping by limiting the range of strategies that peacekeepers can realistically pursue. Peacekeeping agencies seem willing to rule out normatively unacceptable strategies a priori without even considering the potential effectiveness of these strategies as techniques for fostering peace, which is the stated goal of peacekeeping; and concerns about international propriety appear, at least on some occasions, to take precedence over considerations of operational effectiveness. (Paris 2003: 442–3 and 451)

appropriate for peace operations and rules out others, irrespective of whether or not they actually aid progression towards peace. Thus, despite its relatively good post-1945 track record, international trusteeship has been 'disqualified' as a policy tool because of its putatively neocolonial overtones. At the same time, the dominance of liberal peace theories – which hold that democratic states with market economies are less prone to conflict than those having other systems of governance – has pushed peace operations towards the early adoption of competitive elections and economic liberalization despite evidence of their destabilizing potential (see Paris 2004). From this perspective, the triumph of liberalism and its domination of global culture can tell us more about the shape of contemporary peace operations than lessons learned from past operations. To improve the effectiveness of peace operations we need first to understand the ideas that shape them.

Cosmopolitanism

An emerging cosmopolitan approach insists that the maintenance of truly stable international peace and security requires a particular way of understanding, organizing and conducting peace operations. Drawing from cosmopolitan political theory, cosmopolitan conceptions of global governance which emphasize inclusivity and accountability (e.g. Held 1995; Caney 2005) and principles of conflict resolution (Miall et al. 2005), Tom Woodhouse and Oliver Ramsbotham have called for the development of cosmopolitan peace operations (see also Curran and Woodhouse 2007). They argue that cosmopolitan peace operations should be conducted by a standing UN Emergency Peace Service (UNEPS) comprising specially trained military and civilian personnel. UNEPS would be capable of protecting civilians from harm and implementing the full range of the UN's human security agenda (Woodhouse and Ramsbotham 2005: 153).

This is a contemporary variant of the proposal for a UN standing army that dates back to the organization's origins (see Roberts 2008). Between 1945 and 1948, there was a broad consensus that the UN should have its own army capable of deterring and reversing aggression. Provisions were made in the UN Charter for a Military Staff Committee to control and manage the army, and the US went so far as to assign military capabilities – including an Aircraft Carrier Battle Group and some 40,000 soldiers – to the endeavour (Lorenz 1999). The plan was scuppered by Soviet fears that a UN army would be an American stooge, but it has been resuscitated at various times through history (see chapter 6).

Some years before Woodhouse and Ramsbotham's proposal, Mary Kaldor called for peace operations to be redesigned as instruments of 'cosmopolitan law enforcement' (1999: 124–31; 2006). According to Kaldor, since 'the key to resolving new wars is the construction of legitimate political authority', the solution lay in the 'enforcement of cosmopolitan norms, i.e. enforcement of international humanitarian and human rights law' that would enable the protection of civilians and capture of war criminals (2006: x, 132). In her schema, cosmopolitan peace operations involve the creation of a new type of professional combining soldiering with policing skills. Such operations would recognize that it is unreasonable for peacekeepers to expect the unqualified consent of all belligerents – one of the basic tenets of traditional peacekeeping (see chapter 7) – and seek to secure the consent and support of the victims instead (ibid.: 135). This, Kaldor recognized, would require peace operations to use force against those that threatened civilians and would therefore involve risking the lives of peacekeepers. These ideas have been criticized for their simplistic portrayal of contemporary conflicts as involving only innocent civilians and their tormentors (Hirst 2001: 86), but some of Kaldor's proposals – such as the need for a new conception of impartiality and the centrality of civilian protection – correspond closely with some of the ideas set out by the UN's Brahimi Report in 2000 (see chapter 5). Moreover, cosmopolitan calls for a UNEPS-type entity has gained some support in recent years and was endorsed in principle by Sir Brian Urquhart and Satish Nambiar, two leading figures in UN peacekeeping (Johansen 2006). However, persuading governments of the merits of UNEPS remains an uphill battle.

Critical theory

Drawing on the work of Robert Cox (1996), the social theorists of the Frankfurt School (especially Horkheimer 1972) and writers working under the label of critical security studies (e.g. Booth 2007; Wyn Jones 1999), several analysts have applied critical theory to the study of peace operations (see Bellamy and Williams 2005a). Critical theory starts from the presumption that theory is never politically neutral. Instead, it 'is always *for* someone and *for* some purpose. All theories have a perspective' (Cox 1981: 128). The *purpose* of critical theory is human emancipation, understood as the freeing of people 'from those oppressions that stop them carrying out what they would freely choose to do, compatible with the freedom of others' (Booth 2007: 112). As such, approaches to peace operations informed by critical theory typically examine two big and important questions:

1　What theories, values, ideologies, interests and identities shape the way we understand peace operations, and whose theories, values, ideologies, interests and identities are best served through the current practices of peace operations?
2　What theories and practices of peace operations are most likely to advance human emancipation and how might such advances be achieved?

In addressing the first question, some critical theorists have argued that peace operations maintain (and are informed by) a particular understanding of international peace and security that is ostensibly compatible with the capitalist global political economy (Pugh 2003: 40). Global capitalism creates peripheral regions of the global economy where the state and economic development collapse into anarchy and competition between warlords, who use violence to serve their economic interests. As new economic networks based on substate violence arise, so whole regions cease to be normal members of the Westphalian society of states (see below). Because its wealth depends on international trade, the global centre has an interest in preventing areas descending into the sort of anarchy that inhibits trade and the exploitation of raw materials. In most cases, the global centre is unwilling to sacrifice men and materiel to bring peace to peripheral regions of the world and uses a range of proxies instead – including the UN, regional organizations and humanitarian agencies – in order to maintain peace. Sometimes, however, the centre is prepared to act and despatches its own soldiers as peacekeepers. According to this theory, peace operations aim to establish and protect a neoliberal economic order (Pugh 2004: 41; Duffield 2001) or impose the 'normalcy' of democracy on chaotic parts of international society (Zanotti 2006). Similar perspectives are held by those who do not self-consciously identify with critical theory. For instance, Roland Paris (2002: 638; 2004) argued that post-Cold War peacebuilding missions try to 'transplant the values and institutions of the liberal democratic core into the affairs of peripheral host states'. Likewise, Christopher Clapham (1998) maintained that peacemaking has typically, and contentiously, focused on the creation of liberal constitutions.

In order to understand how peace operations might contribute to human emancipation, critical theorists seek to give voice to 'the poor, the disadvantaged, the voiceless, the unrepresented, the powerless' (Said 1994: 84). They share with feminists and anthropologists the view that it is important to seek out and illuminate the perspectives, concerns and experiences of those whose voices are often unheard – marginalized groups, ordinary citizens, women and children. Turning our attention to these groups helps shed light both on the things that make people insecure (local violence, domestic violence, rape, poverty, inadequate healthcare, etc.) and on under-explored avenues for human emancipation. Such avenues might include understanding the coping strategies that victims and potential victims take to protect themselves, the local mobilization of women's groups to address chronic problems, and taking the opinions and contributions of marginalized groups – especially women – into account in the construction of peace processes and agreements (e.g. Stamnes 2004). Indeed, even the UN Security Council has begun to pay attention to this agenda, and in October 2000 passed Resolution 1325, recognizing the importance of female participation in all peace and security initiatives, requiring UN personnel to receive gender training, setting out the need to protect women and girls and their human rights during and after armed conflict, and calling for gender mainstreaming throughout the UN system (discussed further in chapter 16).

The four theoretical approaches discussed above provide different ways of understanding peace operations. They do not exhaust the potential options or cover every aspect of the five levels of analysis described earlier. Nor do they dictate what methods ought to be used. But they do remind us that our decisions about what to study and how to study it will profoundly affect both the results analysts come up with and the policy agendas that flow from them. It is important, therefore, to understand which theoretical tradition and which level or unit of analysis we adopt and reflect upon what is excluded by that choice. Exclusion is an inevitable consequence of studying a phenomenon as complex and multifaceted as peace operations, but it is important that we acknowledge what is missing from our own studies and value insights gathered from alternative perspectives and levels.

1.3 Peace operations and contemporary world politics

Having explored different ways of defining and theorizing peace operations, this final section outlines the changing nature of international order and the place of peace operations within it. Our basic claim here is that peace operations were initially conceived as a tool for maintaining order between states in an international society based on rules arising from state sovereignty, especially non-aggression and non-interference in the domestic affairs of other states. We label this context the 'Westphalian' society of states. Within this society, the principal role of peace operations was the facilitation of peaceful settlements *between* states. As globalization has gathered pace, so the relationships between states and societies have deepened, casting doubt on the political significance of state boundaries and giving rise to new ideas about sovereignty. According to these new ideas, states enjoy full sovereign rights only if they fulfil certain responsibilities towards their citizens, such

as protecting them from genocide and mass atrocities. Within this conception of international society, which we label 'post-Westphalian', the role of
peace operations is to assist states in fulfilling these responsibilities and,
where necessary, to assume those responsibilities when the host state proves
itself unable or unwilling to do so. Although this conception has come into
ascendancy and informs the majority of contemporary UN peace operations,
it remains highly controversial. It is resisted by some states of the global
South, who continue to defend the Westphalian order. In what remains of
this chapter, we will unpack this story a little more. We first evaluate the
Westphalian conception, then briefly look at globalization before focusing on
the post-Westphalian conception.

The Westphalian order

The Westphalian order takes its name from the Westphalian settlements
concluded at the end of Europe's Thirty Years' War (1618–48), which took
place between the 'Union' of Protestant German princes and free cities and
the 'League' of their Catholic counterparts (Jackson 2000: 162–7). Politically,
the treaties recognized the territorial sovereignty of the approximately 300
states and statelets within Europe. They also symbolized the sovereign state's
success in prevailing over other forms of political organization (see Tilly 1992)
and its acquisition of five key monopolies:

1 the right to monopolize control of the instruments of violence;
2 the sole right to collect taxes;
3 the prerogative of ordering the political allegiances of citizens and of
   enlisting their support in war;
4 the right to adjudicate in disputes between citizens;
5 the exclusive right of representation in international society. (Linklater
   1998: 28)

The treaties also reaffirmed the Peace of Augsburg (1555) at which the principle of *cujus regio ejus religio* was formulated, whereby each ruler declared
which brand of Christianity (Protestantism or Catholicism) would hold exclusive rights within their territories and other rulers agreed to respect the
sovereign's right to determine his country's religion (Jackson 2000: 163).

The state's success in Europe brought with it the development of three
fundamental norms (Jackson 2000: 166–7). The first norm held that the king
was emperor in his own realm. Thus, sovereigns were not subject to any
higher political authority. The second was that outsiders had no right to
intervene in a foreign jurisdiction on the grounds of religion, and the third
affirmed the European balance of power as a means of preventing one state
from making a successful bid for hegemony that would, in effect, re-establish
empire on the continent. According to Jackson (ibid.: 182), these three norms
created an international order that permitted different cultures and nations

to live according to their own preferences while respecting the rights of others to do likewise and avoiding the danger of assimilation.

Although we use the label 'Westphalian' to describe this order, these norms evolved incrementally and took nearly three hundred years to develop fully. We should also not make the mistake of thinking that this system was anything like universal. Despite the ascendancy of sovereign states, most of Europe was actually governed by empire (Russian, Austrian and Ottoman) until 1918 and the norms of international society applied only to European – and a small handful of non-European – states. A quite different set of rules applied in the colonized world (see Keene 2002). Finally, the norms and practices that characterized European diplomacy in this Westphalian order were Christian and Latin (Stern 1999: 65–9). The defining characteristics of this expanded body of rules are summarized in box 1.4.

After the Second World War the Westphalian order expanded to cover the entire globe, as former colonies sought to take their place as sovereign states (see Bull and Watson 1984; Jackson 2001). Between 1947 and 1967, the society of states expanded from about fifty to over 160 (Jackson 2001: 46) and today numbers 192. In some places the transition to sovereign statehood was relatively peaceful, but in others – such as Indochina, Algeria and Congo – decolonization was a bloody, protracted and hard-fought affair. If a global Westphalian order was to survive, it was thought necessary to close some of the loopholes evident in its pre-1945 order. In particular, how could one protect a sovereign's right to rule if there was no barrier to strong states simply overpowering weak states to impose their will upon them? With decolonization and the expansion of the Westphalian order, therefore, came calls to protect the sanctity of state sovereignty through law.

Box 1.4 The Westphalian conception of international law

1 The world consists of, and is divided into, sovereign territorial states which recognize no superior authority.
2 The processes of law-making, the settlement of disputes, and law enforcement are largely in the hands of individual states.
3 International law is oriented to the establishment of minimal rules of coexistence; the creation of enduring relationships among states and people is an aim, but only to the extent that it allows state objectives to be met.
4 Responsibility for cross-border wrongful acts is a 'private matter' concerning only those affected.
5 All states are regarded as equal before the law: legal rules do not take account of asymmetries of power.
6 Differences among states are often settled by force; the principle of effective power holds sway. Virtually no legal fetters exist to curb the resort to force; international legal standards afford minimal protection.
7 The minimization of impediments to state freedom is the 'collective priority'.

Source: Held et al. 1999: 37–8

These concerns were aired by a number of small states during the drafting of the UN Charter in 1945. Australia, Bolivia, Brazil and Norway all argued that it should proscribe the use of force completely and without legal loopholes (Chesterman 2001: 49). This, combined with a concern to prevent potential future Hitlers, produced Article 2(4) of the UN Charter, prohibiting the use of force (see chapter 2). Latin American states also argued that the UN should contain rules protecting their sovereign right to determine their own form of government. Article 2(7) thus insisted that the new organization would not interfere in the domestic affairs of its members (see chapter 2). In the subsequent years, the message from the post-colonial world was loud and clear. In 1960, the UN General Assembly issued its Declaration on the Granting of Independence to Colonial Countries and Peoples. Adopted by a majority of eighty-nine votes to none, with nine abstentions, the declaration proclaimed that 'all peoples have the right to self-determination; by virtue of that right they freely determine their political status and freely pursue their economic, social and cultural development' (in Shaw 2003: 227).

For the leaders of many post-colonial states, there was a direct relationship between a people's right freely to determine its political status and the non-interference rule. After all, they argued, there could be no right of national self-determination if powerful states felt entitled to interfere in the affairs of the weak. The General Assembly's 1970 Declaration on Principles of International Law Concerning Friendly Relations stated categorically that:

> No state or group of states has the right to intervene, directly or indirectly, for any reason whatever, in the internal or external affairs of any other state. Consequently, armed intervention and all other forms of interference or attempted threats against the personality of the state, or against its political, economic and cultural elements, are in violation of international law.

Many academics support this argument and maintain that, because national communities are so different, and because difference is a good worth preserving, international order can be achieved only by rigid adherence to Westphalian principles (Jackson 2000: 291; 2005: 73, 100). They argue that it is a short road from relaxing the Westphalian order's non-interference rule to relegitimizing colonialism. International commitment to the Westphalian order remains widespread and steadfast. It is a position endorsed by a majority of states in the General Assembly, by many international lawyers and by some groups of politicians and activists in the West.

It was in the context of a pre-eminent Westphalian order that peace operations originated and developed (see part 2). Westphalian-style peace operations are concerned primarily with the peaceful resolution of disputes between states but might also assist states in the suppression of separatist movements or in the building of state capacity. Upholding and protecting Westphalian values, however, such operations acted only with the consent of the sovereign states involved and sought merely to create the conditions necessary to facilitate the resolution of conflicts by state parties. But since the end of the Cold War the Westphalian order – and its attendant conception of peace operations – has come under challenge from processes of globalization and changing ideas about the meaning of sovereignty.

Contemporary globalization and 'new wars'

It is often argued that recent transformations in peace operations are the result, by and large, of the end of the Cold War. Another important but often overlooked fact is the role of globalization in this transformation. Globalization can be understood as an uneven set of processes that affect all areas of human activity, not just the economy. Chief among the list of motors driving globalization are technological developments, especially in the field of communications, economic growth and integration, and the expansion of the Western influence. Much of the literature on globalization assumes that, as it accelerates and intensifies, so the 'limits to national politics' are increasingly exposed (Held et al. 1999: 1). Consequently, state power is often depicted as retreating in the face of globalization and the revival of non-state sources of power and authority (e.g. Ohmae 1995; Strange 1996). In practice, however, instead of becoming politically redundant, states exist in a mutually constitutive relationship with globalization (Clark 1997). States thus both constitute a principal driver of globalization and are being radically transformed by it. This is hardly surprising if we take seriously insights from historical sociology that states and transnational forces (such as capitalism and religion) have often interacted with each other in this way (Mann 1986, 1993; Tilly 1992). But globalization has not affected the world evenly. Whereas the policies of the most powerful states – especially the US and the G-8 and more recently the G-20 – have actively facilitated the acceleration of economic globalization, weaker states have generally been forced to react to processes initiated elsewhere. As a result, the nature and impact of globalization differs from region to region (Hay 2000). An instructive guide to globalization is provided by the five characteristics identified by Held et al. (1999: 8).

1 Globalization can best be understood as a process or set of processes rather than a singular condition.
2 The spatial reach and density of global and transnational interconnectedness have created complex webs and networks of relations between communities, states, international institutions, non-governmental organizations and transnational corporations which make up the global order.
3 Few areas of social life escape the reach of globalization.
4 By cutting across political frontiers globalization is associated with both the de-territorialization and re-territorialization of socio-economic and political space.

Box 1.5 The actors in global politics

- Nearly 200 governments, including 192 members of the United Nations
- 77,200 transnational companies, such as Shell, Barclays Bank, Vodafone, Microsoft, Coca-Cola and Ford (these parent companies have just over 773,000 foreign affiliates)
- 10,000 single-state NGOs, such as Freedom House (US) and Population Concern (UK), which engage in significant international activities
- 246 intergovernmental organizations, such as the UN, NATO, the African Union, the European Union and the International Coffee Association
- 7,300 international NGOs, such as Amnesty International, the Baptist World Alliance and the International Red Cross, plus a similar number of less well-established international caucuses and networks of NGOs

Source: adapted and modified from Willetts 2008: 332.

5   Power relations are deeply inscribed in the very processes of globalization. In particular, globalization concerns the expanding scale of the networks through which power is organized and exercised.

The processes of contemporary globalization have clearly affected the way in which peace operations are conceptualized and conducted (see Jakobsen 2002), but the exact nature of those effects is contested. David Held et al. (1999: 1–2) have identified four key questions that lie at the root of the many controversies and debates about globalization: What is globalization and how should it be conceptualized?, Does contemporary globalization represent a novel condition?, Is globalization associated with the demise, the resurgence or the transformation of state power? and Does contemporary globalization impose new limits to politics? If so, how can globalization be 'civilized' and democratized? These questions have, in turn, stimulated five main sources of contention in the globalization debate: conceptualization, causation, periodization, the trajectories and the political impacts of globalization (ibid.: 10–14).

Although some analysts argue that globalization is a recent phenomenon, this is not a view we share. Instead, we understand globalization as being a set of processes with a long history, some of which pre-date modernity (see Barkawi 2006). It is for this reason that several analysts have attempted to periodize its development into historical phases in order to gain a more sophisticated appreciation of the novel features of globalization in the contemporary era.

A variety of analysts have suggested that, particularly since 1945, the processes of globalization have given rise to a distinctive form of armed conflict commonly labelled 'new wars' (see Kaldor 1999, 2006; Newman 2004; Münkler 2005). According to Mary Kaldor, in these 'new wars' the traditional

---

Box 1.6 The main elements of the 'new wars' thesis

- New wars are intrastate rather than interstate wars.
- New wars take place in the context of state failure and social transformation driven by globalization and liberal economic forces.
- In new wars, ethnic and religious differences are more important than political ideology.
- In new wars, civilian casualties and forced displacement are dramatically increasing. This is primarily because civilians are being deliberately targeted.
- In new wars, the breakdown of state authority blurs the distinction between public and private combatants.

Source: Newman 2004.

---

distinctions between war (violence between states or organized political groups for political reasons), organized crime (violence by private associations, usually for private gain) and large-scale violations of human rights (violence by states or private groups against individuals, mainly civilians) are blurred. 'New wars' are distinguished from old, interstate wars primarily by their distinct goals, methods and systems of finance, born out of the erosion of the relevant state's monopoly of legitimate organized violence. This led one analyst to describe them as 'state disintegrating' wars (Münkler 2005: 8; see also box 1.6).

The goals of combatants can be understood in the context of a struggle fought between cosmopolitan and exclusivist identities, the latter seeking to control a given population by ethnically cleansing all those of a different identity or who espouse a cosmopolitan political opinion. The 'new wars' are fought through a novel 'mode of warfare' that draws on both guerrilla techniques and counter-insurgency, though the main target for attack is usually the civilian population and not other militia groups or government forces. This mode of warfare is distinctive because decisive confrontations are typically avoided and territory is controlled through political manipulation and fear rather than winning 'hearts and minds'. 'New wars' are financed by a globalized war economy that is decentralized and increasingly transnational, and in which the fighting units are often self-funding through plunder and the black market (see also Keen 2001; Duffield 2001). This means that some people can benefit from continued warfare. As David Keen has observed, for some belligerents, 'Winning may not be desirable: the point of war may be precisely the legitimacy which it confers on actions that in peacetime would be punishable as crimes' (1998: 11–12). Finally, to make matters worse, 'new wars' often generate crises such as famine or occur alongside natural disasters, creating 'complex emergencies' (Keen 2008).

Understood in this manner, peacekeepers operating in such environments must try and address the challenges raised by their particular strain of identity politics, their mode of warfare, and their globalized systems of finance.

Kaldor argued that the resolution of 'new wars' requires 'cosmopolitan law enforcement' wherein peacekeepers are mandated to enforce human rights law and reconstitute legitimate political communities (1999: 10–11). This goes well beyond the image of international assistance or peacekeeping envisaged by advocates of a Westphalian order and implies the emergence of a post-Westphalian conception of international order based on the idea of 'sovereignty as responsibility' (see chapter 2).

The post-Westphalian approach

Post-Westphalian conceptions of world order have been around for a long time but came to the fore after the end of the Cold War. Echoes of this approach can be heard in the Preamble of the UN Charter, which in many other ways is a document prescribing Westphalian rules for the world. In the Preamble, member states promised to 'reaffirm faith in fundamental human rights, in the dignity and worth of the human person' – an ambition that goes well beyond the maintenance of stable peace between states through rules of mutual coexistence. In the post-Cold War era, leading proponents of the post-Westphalian conception of world order included the former British prime minister Tony Blair and Francis Deng, the UN's Special Representative on Internal Displacement and then Special Representative on the Prevention of Genocide. The key tenets of the Westphalian and post-Westphalian approaches are set out in table 1.2 below.

During NATO's 1999 intervention in Kosovo/Serbia, Blair travelled to the US to shore up American support for the war, and gave a now famous

TABLE 1.2 Westphalian and post-Westphalian approaches

	Westphalian	Post-Westphalian
Sovereign responsibility	Limited to relations with other states	Relations with other states *and* for treatment of citizens
Non-interference	Absolute (more or less) right of sovereigns	Dependent on fulfilment of responsibilities to citizens
Peace operations (inter-state)	Most frequent. Consensual activity designed to facilitate peaceful settlement of disputes between states	Less frequent. Usually designed to facilitate peaceful settlement of disputes between states
Peace operations (intra-state)	Less frequent. Limited engagement to assist states deployed only at request of host state	Most frequent. Extensive engagement to facilitate or sometimes impose liberal democratic polities and economies
Key advocates	China, India, Cuba, NAM	Western Europe, UN Secretary-General

Box 1.7 Tony Blair's 'doctrine of the international community'

We live in a world where isolationism has ceased to have a reason to exist. By necessity we have to co-operate with each other across nations. Many of our domestic problems are caused on the other side of the world...We are all internationalists now, whether we like it or not. We cannot refuse to participate in global markets if we want to prosper. We cannot ignore new political ideas in other countries if we want to innovate. We cannot turn our backs on conflicts and the violation of human rights within other countries if we want still to be secure...

The most pressing foreign policy problem we face is to identify the circumstances in which we should get actively involved in other people's conflicts. Non-interference has long been considered an important principle of international order. And it is not one we would want to jettison too readily...But the principle of non-interference must be qualified in important respects. Acts of genocide can never be a purely internal matter. (Blair 1999)

speech in Chicago in which he set out a new, post-Westphalian, 'doctrine of the international community' (see box 1.7). He argued that sovereignty should be reconceptualized because globalization was changing the world in ways that made the traditional Westphalian approach anachronistic. According to Blair, global interconnectedness created a responsibility for international society to deal with egregious human suffering wherever it occurred because, as US President John F. Kennedy had argued in the 1960s, in an interdependent world, 'freedom is indivisible and when one man is enslaved who is free?'. Individual sovereigns were responsible to international society for the welfare of their own citizens because, in an era of globalization, domestic problems spread across borders causing international mayhem (Blair 1999).

The idea that sovereignty ought to entail certain responsibilities had been put forth a few years earlier by Francis Deng and his colleagues. Deng, a well-respected former Sudanese diplomat, was appointed Special Representative on Internally Displaced People (IDPs) by Boutros-Ghali in 1993. As wars became less a matter between states and more a struggle between competing state and non-state actors, so the proportion of civilians killed and displaced increased. When Deng was appointed, there were some 25 million IDPs globally (Weiss 2007: 90). If these civilians crossed an international border they would be entitled to claim refugee status, providing that their host was either a signatory to the 1951 Refugee Convention or accepting the help of the UNHCR (see Davies 2007). As IDPs, however, they were afforded no special protection and remained vulnerable to the whims or failings of their home state. Deng recognized that this made them particularly vulnerable and noted that they suffered significantly higher mortality rates than the general population (2004: 18–20).

To argue his way around the use of sovereignty to deny international assistance for IDPs, Deng postulated an alternative, post-Westphalian, account.

Instead of being a barrier against international involvement, sovereignty was described as a state's responsibility to protect its neediest citizens. Where a state was unable to fulfil its responsibilities, it should invite and welcome international assistance to 'complement national efforts' (Deng 2004: 20). The best way for a vulnerable or failing state to protect its sovereignty, Deng argued, was by inviting international assistance. The corollary of sovereignty in this view, therefore, is accountability. The host state is made accountable to its citizens, and international society acquires a responsibility to assist that state or, in extreme cases, to act to fulfil its responsibilities to its citizens even without the state's consent. As Deng et al. (1996: 1) put it:

> Sovereignty carries with it certain responsibilities for which governments must be held accountable. And they are accountable not only to their national constituencies but ultimately to the international community. In other words, by effectively discharging its responsibilities for good governance, a state can legitimately claim protection for its national sovereignty.

This post-Westphalian understanding of international society holds that states receive their sovereign rights only if they fulfil their responsibilities to their citizens, chief among them the protection of civilians from arbitrary killing. This implies a very different role for peace operations to that envisaged by a Westphalian conception of international society. According to the post-Westphalian perspective, peace operations need to be in the business of protecting human rights where host states prove unwilling or unable to do so, and of helping to build states capable of fulfilling their responsibilities in the long term. It is not hard to see how this post-Westphalian conception of sovereignty is closely related to the liberal peace theory described earlier. If the aim of peace operations is to help build states and societies capable of fulfilling their responsibilities, and if we believe that liberal and democratic societies are most effective in this regard, then it stands to reason that peace operations need to be in the business of aiding the spread of liberal democracy. According to at least two analysts, building peace out of 'new wars' requires the transformation of governing systems along liberal lines by external interveners (Ottaway and Lacina 2003: 75). As the remainder of the book sets out in more detail, this conception of peace operations is currently in the ascendancy and is closely associated with the expansion of the roles and responsibilities granted to peacekeepers.

Despite this, however, MacQueen (2006: 11) argues that peace operations remain 'largely Westphalian' because they are concerned principally with regulating a state-based international system. Our view is that an increasing number of peace operations are concerned primarily with the internal nature and composition of states themselves rather than with relations *between* states. However, MacQueen is partly right, because liberal peace theory tells us that democratization and liberalization within states is a necessary precursor to peace between them.

Although ascendant and increasingly evident in the work of the UN and other international organizations, the post-Westphalian conception remains controversial and is opposed by defenders of the Westphalian order, most of whom are found in the global South. The Chinese government, for instance, has argued that Deng's account of sovereignty is merely a thinly veiled attempt to legitimize great power interference in the domestic affairs of sovereigns, while Cuba detected an attempt 'to forcibly impose certain ideological conceptions of human rights on a number of countries, chiefly, though not exclusively, in the Third World' (in Deng et al. 1996: 12). This debate, between advocates of Westphalian sovereignty and proponents of the new post-Westphalian approach, underpins many contemporary arguments about the function and purpose of peace operations, including strengthening the UN's capacity to deploy peacekeepers, funding issues, the protection of civilians, the use of force, the relationship between troop contributors and the Security Council, the role of regional organizations and coalitions of the willing, the relationship between peace operations and human rights, the monitoring of elections, the most appropriate path to economic reconstruction, the meaning of and necessity for host state consent, and the indicators of success and failure.

As we mentioned earlier, the post-Westphalian conception has become more popular since the end of the Cold War. In their design, most contemporary peace operations go well beyond the parameters set out by the Westphalian conception and interfere in many aspects of domestic political life. As a result, peace operations tend to be larger and more complex than in the past (Durch and Berkman 2006: 12). What is more, in 2005, the UN General Assembly formally endorsed the idea that states have a responsibility to protect their citizens from genocide and mass killing and that, when they failed to do so, this responsibility transferred to the UN (see Evans 2008; Bellamy 2009). It is important, however, to bear in mind that the Westphalian account continues to hold sway among many post-colonial states, which fear that the new approach erodes their right to determine their own path and opens the door to great power interference in their domestic affairs. A useful way of conceptualizing the debate is to follow former UN Secretary-General Kofi Annan's caricature of it as a struggle between two conceptions of sovereignty, each of which protects certain values worth preserving (see box 1.8).

1.4 Conclusion

It is important to recognize the concepts and theories that inform the way we understand peace operations and their relationship with world politics more generally. Without this understanding, we are likely to overlook the way in which our unspoken theories and assumptions determine what we think is important and the way that the theory and practice of peace operations is informed by certain political commitments. Although often insight-

Box 1.8 Kofi Annan: two conceptions of sovereignty

In reality, this 'old orthodoxy' [traditional sovereignty] was never absolute. The Charter, after all, was issued in the name of the 'the peoples', not the governments, of the United Nations. Its aim is not only to preserve international peace – vitally important though that is – but also 'to reaffirm faith in fundamental human rights, in the dignity and worth of the human person'. The Charter protects the sovereignty of peoples. It was never meant as a license for governments to trample on human rights and human dignity. Sovereignty implies responsibility, not just power... Can we really afford to let each state be the judge of its own right, or duty, to intervene in another state's internal conflict? If we do, will we not be forced to legitimise Hitler's championship of the Sudeten Germans, or Soviet intervention in Afghanistan? (Annan 1998a)

To those for whom the greatest threat to the future of international order is the use of force in the absence of a Security Council mandate, one might ask... in the context of Rwanda: If, in those dark days and hours leading up to the genocide, a coalition of States had been prepared to act in defence of the Tutsi population but did not receive prompt Council authorization, should such a coalition have stood aside and allowed the horror to unfold?

To those for whom the Kosovo action heralded a new era when States and groups of States can take military action outside the established mechanisms for enforcing international law, one might ask: Is there not a danger of such interventions undermining the imperfect, yet resilient, security system created after the Second World War, and of setting dangerous precedents for future interventions without a clear criterion to decide who might invoke these precedents, and in what circumstances? (Annan 1999d)

ful, discussions of peace operations that are not open about their own theoretical and political preferences exclude potentially valuable insights and perspectives. This leads to partial explanations that overlook a potentially rich and diverse range of alternative perspectives, which, in turn, inhibits rather than enlightens our understanding of peace operations. It is important to scrutinize our theoretical assumptions, to understand which level or unit of analysis we are operating at, and to remain curious about the perspectives, interests and values that are being left out. Until very recently, one of the most obscured perspectives in this field of study was that of the *subjects* of peace operations – the very people that the peacekeepers are ostensibly helping.

Today's world is shaped by contemporary globalization, which has facilitated important challenges to the Westphalian order. Events that happen in one part of the world invariably impact on others – be that through flows of refugees and migrants, trade (both legal and illicit) or communication. Such connectivity has given rise to the argument that international society as a whole has a 'responsibility to protect' individuals from grave breaches of their human rights in situations where their own state is either unwilling or unable to do so. This has prompted a radical rethinking of the meaning of sovereignty to include responsibility and has prompted protracted and ongoing debate about the proper role of peace operations in world politics. Many states and other actors continue to argue that the principles of Westphalian international society ought to be privileged and should temper the commitment to liberal peace that informs most contemporary peace operations. Stable peace, they argue, can only be achieved by creating spaces and institutions for states to resolve their differences peacefully on the basis of consent and mutual respect for the principle of non-interference. What goes on inside states should not concern peace operations unless their hosts invite them.

In contrast, the post-Westphalian view holds that states have responsibilities to their citizens, instability in one state is likely to destabilize others, and individual states are accountable to international society. International society, in turn, has a responsibility to assist and – if needs be – force states to fulfil their responsibilities. Because liberal democratic polities tend to be better at protecting their citizens from genocide and mass killing, as well as settling their disputes with other democracies without resorting to war, peace operations should be in the business of rebuilding war-shattered societies along liberal democratic lines. Only in this way can stable peace be assured, because the Westphalian conception does nothing to tackle the underlying causes of war, such as injustice, human rights abuse and poverty. Although the post-Westphalian conception is certainly in the ascendancy, it remains controversial, with the result that the place of peace operations in world politics and its future trajectory remains contested, inconsistent, unpredictable and uncertain.

Having set out some of the basic parameters for the study of peace operations, chapter 2 explores who the peacekeepers are, which institutions and ideas guide what they do, and how they are in the process of changing in the contemporary world.

CHAPTER TWO

Who are the Peacekeepers?

Peacekeeping is often closely associated with the UN (e.g. Durch 1994a). Many analysts credit a Canadian diplomat, Lester Pearson, with the invention of peacekeeping because of his efforts to establish what is often considered the UN's first such operation, the UN Emergency Force (1956–67). This was deployed to Egypt shortly after that country had been invaded by the UK, France and Israel in what became known as the Suez Crisis (see chapter 7). But the UN is not the only actor that conducts or authorizes peace operations. Consequently, in this book we use the term 'peacekeepers' as an umbrella label to refer to those individuals and groups who perform the different tasks discussed in part III. In general terms, peacekeepers usually operate under the banner of particular states or international organizations. States sometimes conduct operations alone but more commonly they act as part of a coalition, alongside other willing states. Although not all international organizations conduct peace operations, it is the UN and certain regional arrangements that have most commonly engaged in such activities.

Sometimes, the UN Security Council explicitly authorizes other actors to carry out peace operations on its behalf to maintain what the UN Charter refers to as 'international peace and security'. This delegation or subcontracting of responsibilities by the UN is discussed in more detail in chapters 13 and 14 with reference to regional arrangements and private contractors. However, operations are not always authorized by the UN even though they may support the organization's objectives or those of a particular UN mission. Thinking about peace operations in these terms enables us to develop a typology based on the type of actors that conduct them (i.e. individual states, coalitions of the willing, or formal regional arrangements and other international organizations) and their relationship to the UN (i.e. whether they are UN 'blue helmet' operations, UN-authorized operations or non-UN operations). Table 2.1 sets out this typology with some examples.

This chapter provides an overview of these different types of peacekeepers. In doing so it shows that, although it has become the primary peacekeeping actor and source of international legitimacy, peace operations should not be thought of as being synonymous with the UN. Specifically, the first and second sections discuss the roles played by pivotal states and regional arrangements respectively. In the third section we focus on the single most important peace-

TABLE 2.1 Peace operations: a typology with examples

Actor	UN operations	UN-authorized operations	Non-UN operations
UN blue helmets	UNEF, UNFICYP, UNOSOM II, UNMIL, MONUC	n/a*	n/a
Other inter-national organizations	n/a	NATO (KFOR) in Kosovo (1999–) ECOWAS in Côte d'Ivoire (2003–4) EU in Bosnia (2004–)	ECOWAS in Liberia (1990–7)† NATO in Kosovo (1999)†† SADC in Lesotho (1998)
Coalition of the willing	n/a	UNITAF in Somalia (1992–3)†† INTERFET in East Timor (1999) ISAF in Afghanistan (2002–)	RAMSI in Solomon Islands (2003–)†
Individual government	n/a	No examples	UK in Sierra Leone (2000)† South Africa in Burundi (2001–3)†

Notes: †Missions subsequently welcomed by the UN Security Council in either a resolution or a presidential statement.
††Missions conducted without host government consent.
*'n/a' refers to the fact that these categories do not apply, whereas 'no examples' mean that these categories are theoretically possible but as yet untried.

keeping organization, the UN, and summarize how it assembles and manages its operations. The final section sketches the discernible trends in what can be labelled 'partnership peacekeeping' – that is, where different types of actors engage in various forms of cooperation to achieve their objectives.

2.1 Unilateral action, pivotal states and coalitions of the willing

Peace operations are sometimes initiated and led by individual states, acting either unilaterally or as *pivotal states* in tandem with others in coalitions of the willing. Pivotal states initiate, lead and provide a significant material contribution to a peace operation, which may or may not be authorized by the UN or be conducted under the auspices of a regional arrangement. Often, the material contribution made by other members of the coalition or organization is insubstantial, leading one analyst to argue convincingly that pivotal states try to form coalitions in order to enhance the legitimacy of these operations rather than to share the material burdens (Coleman 2007).

Individual states might wish to influence the future direction of a conflict or mitigate its impact on regional and/or human security for one or more of four principal reasons. First, *regional hegemons* occasionally lead peace operations in order to press their own claims to territory, economic benefits or access to natural resources, or to support the socio-political ambitions of allies. Often, such hegemons also have a vested interest in maintaining regional order and the prevailing regional status quo. Russian peacekeeping and mediation through the CIS in Abkhazia/Georgia and Nigerian peacekeeping through ECOWAS in West Africa provide good examples of regional hegemons acting as pivotal states initiating and leading peace operations to maintain regional order. This type of peacekeeping may be a thinly veiled attempt to secure the hegemon's perceived interests, which may or may not produce positive humanitarian outcomes. Although the impartiality and legitimacy of such operations can be challenged, experiences in West Africa and Russia's 'near abroad' suggest that the effects are not always entirely negative. First, regional hegemons have an interest in maintaining order in their neighbourhood. Second, they are by definition more militarily capable than their neighbours and therefore may make the most effective peacekeepers. Finally, regional hegemons may have a good understanding of the dynamics of the conflict they are trying to manage, though they are also more likely to have an economic and political interest in the outcome of the conflict.

Unilateral actors and pivotal states may be *former colonial powers* that continue to have close economic, political and social ties with their former colonies. For example, French troops garrisoned in Côte d'Ivoire acted as peacekeepers after the outbreak of civil war there in 2002. Similarly, France acted as a pivotal state when it sponsored MISAB in the Central African Republic (1997–8) (MacQueen 2002: 96–104; Berman and Sams 2000: 222–8). Britain's Operation Palliser in Sierra Leone in 2000, in support of President Kabbah's government and the beleaguered UN operation UNAMSIL, resulted from a mixture of motives, but a sense of attachment resulting from the former colonial relationship was certainly one of them (Williams 2001). Another set of former imperial relations is provided by Russia and what it refers to as its 'near abroad'. Here Russia has exploited the ambiguities around the term 'peace operations' to cover its hegemonic ambitions in its local region. In Moldova in 1992, for example, some 12,000 troops from the Russian 14th Army were deployed to the breakaway republic of Transdnestr as part of a so-called disengagement force. In reality, the troops acted to buttress the Transdnestrian secession (McNeill 1997: 99). The US's historic connection with Liberia also partly explains why the George W. Bush administration was prepared to provide off-shore support to the deployment of UNMIL in 2003. Former colonial powers may be motivated by the desire to support elected or friendly governments, help maintain regional order, protect perceived economic and political interests, support humanitarian concerns, or protect significant communities of nationals from the metropole.

Third, *concerned neighbours* might conduct unilateral operations or act as a pivotal state when internal conflict, economic collapse and/or massive human rights abuse occur in their own 'backyard' (see James 1990). They may be prompted to act by concerns that the effects of conflict may spill across the border as well as regard for the welfare of neighbouring populations. For instance, the Italian-led operation in Albania in 1997 was prompted by the desire to stem the flow of Albanian refugees into Italy, a perceived need to restore regional order, and humanitarian concerns (Bellamy 2002a: 64). Similarly, Australia acted as a pivotal state in creating the INTERFET mission to East Timor in 1999, primarily because of domestic pressure to do something to protect an endangered population near Australia's borders (Chalk 2001: 42; Dee 2001: 9).

Finally, *great powers* might act unilaterally or as pivotal states in initiating and leading peace operations. As Hedley Bull put it, great powers may play a role in promoting international order by 'exploiting their preponderance in such a way as to impart a degree of central direction to the affairs of international society as a whole' (1977: 200). Because great powers often have a vested interest in preserving the international status quo, they may act unilaterally or in concert to preserve it, which was particularly the case in nineteenth-century attempts to manage international order (see chapter 3), and also during the Cold War, when the superpowers recognized 'spheres of influence, interest and responsibility' (ibid.: 212). For instance, in 1982, Israel's refusal to allow the UN to supervise the withdrawal of PLO forces from Beirut persuaded the Americans to seek alternative options, and it was the US that acted as a pivotal state in the creation of the multinational force deployed to Lebanon (Diehl 1994: 58–60; McDermott and Skjelsbaek 1991). In this case, the US was prompted to act to maintain stability in a distant region out of concerns for global order and the threat of violent escalation that was carried by the Middle East conflict, as well as to secure its own interests in the region.

There are therefore four primary reasons why individual states might conduct unilateral operations or act as pivotal states, though the reasons are not limited to these four broad types. Such operations may, or may not, be conducted under the auspices of an international organization. Indeed, there is an important distinction to be made between *unilateral action*, which is quite rare, and cases where *pivotal states*, motivated by one of the four concerns described above, assemble a coalition of the willing. Acting as a pivotal state within a coalition of the willing may provide the operation with additional resources, but the principal concern is usually international legitimacy, which is especially important when an operation is undertaken outside the auspices of the UN. Consequently, while states may sometimes choose to act alone or to lead others in coalitions, it is more common for peace operations to be organized and coordinated by international organizations. While the UN has been the most significant organization in this regard, it is by no means the only one.

2.2 International organizations: regional arrangements

Although we deal with the subject of regional peacekeeping in greater detail in chapter 13, it is useful to raise briefly some of the central issues here. Regional arrangements recognized by the UN may conduct peace operations under Chapter VIII of the UN Charter. This encourages them to engage in activities designed to achieve the peaceful resolution of conflicts within their region, as long as they keep the Security Council informed about their initiatives. In practice, however, some regional arrangements, including ECOWAS, SADC and NATO, have conducted peace enforcement operations without explicit authorization from the UN Security Council.

International organizations are significant actors in initiating peace operations, and it has been suggested that they have considerable functional and normative advantages over unilateral action (Abbott and Snidal 1998). First, it is claimed that they can often operate with greater legitimacy than individual states (Claude 1966; Coleman 2007) and that they have permanent bureaucratic structures that can be used both to create and manage field operations and to offer a forum for galvanizing support and coordinating action in responses to crises. These organizations are also said to possess a normative capacity to influence state behaviour and the standards, rules and conceptual parameters of peace operations (see Barnett and Finnemore 2004: ch. 5).

In relation to peacekeeping, international organizations can play at least four positive roles.

1 They help to set the rules for the peacekeepers themselves. Contributing states should work within the organization's agreed rules and to the mandate it provides.
2 They may provide greater accountability than unilateral actions or coalitions of the willing organized by pivotal states and often possess internal procedures for auditing operations.
3 In cases where the state that hosts the conflict is also a member of the organization in question, there may be a greater inclination to accept its involvement than that of a strong regional hegemon or coalition.
4 International organizations may have collective institutional memories based on past experiences that can influence the development of peacekeeping norms.

However, international organizations also confront several shortcomings that may undermine their normative and functional potential. First, the cost of accountability may be cumbersome decision-making processes and bureaucratic structures that are ill-suited to conducting complex operations (Esman 1995: 43–7). Furthermore, peacekeeping under the auspices of an international organization does not necessarily confer legitimacy on an operation. International legitimacy also depends upon the organization, the historical context and the nature of the intervention itself (Kieh 1998; Wheeler 2001). Finally, organizations vary not only in terms of their membership, purpose, bureaucratic structure and legitimating function, but also in terms of their capabilities, role and moral standing (Alagappa 1998: 20–1).

At this stage it is sufficient to note that regional arrangements have played a significant and growing role in the conduct of peace operations, especially in Europe and Africa. However, the participation of regional bodies in peace operations raises important issues of legitimacy and impartiality as well as the nature of their relationship with the UN. While we discuss the so-called regionalization of peace operations in chapter 13, the next section of this chapter focuses on the single most important international organization in the realm of peace operations: the UN.

2.3 The United Nations

This section provides an overview of the legal and bureaucratic frameworks within which UN peace operations are conducted, as well as the main issues involved in assembling and financing them. The historical evolution of UN peace operations and the doctrine underpinning them is discussed in part II of the book (chapters 3–5).

The legal framework for UN peace operations

Although peace operations are undertaken by many different actors, the history and development of international peacekeeping is now intimately related to the activities of the UN. The primary aims of the UN are set out at the beginning of its Charter. Article 1(1), for instance, states that one of the organization's central purposes is 'to maintain international peace and security, and to that end: to take effective collective measures for the prevention and removal of threats to the peace.' This rationale is usually cited as the legal basis for peacekeeping. However, the Charter contains a fundamental ambiguity between the priority it affords to state sovereignty and human rights. On the one hand, the Preamble and Article 1(3) state that one of the purposes of the UN is to encourage respect for human rights. But this is tempered by Articles 2(4) and 2(7), which reaffirm the principle of sovereign inviolability (see box 2.1). Article 2(7) has been widely interpreted as precluding UN involvement in the internal affairs of its members. That said, the notion of domestic jurisdiction has a relative quality that depends on the full range of international obligations undertaken by a particular state. Domestic jurisdiction can therefore legally prohibit UN activity only if a state has not signed up to particular treaties. Thus, for example, the UN is legally able to take a position on the domestic governance of any state that has pledged to promote the Universal Declaration of Human Rights (Conforti 2000: 134–6). Article 2(7) does not prohibit the Security Council from taking action against

> ## Box 2.1 Sovereignty and human rights in the UN Charter
>
> We the peoples of the United Nations determined...to reaffirm faith in fundamental human rights, in the dignity and worth of the human person, in the equal rights of men and women and of nations large and small. (Preamble)
>
> [One of the purposes of the UN is] [t]o achieve international co-operation in solving international problems of an economic, social, cultural or humanitarian character, and in promoting and encouraging respect for human rights and for fundamental freedoms for all. (Article 1(3))
>
> All Members shall refrain in their international relations from the threat or use of force against the territorial integrity or political independence of any state, or in any other manner inconsistent with the Purposes of the United Nations. (Article 2(4))
>
> Nothing contained in the Charter shall authorise the United Nations to intervene in matters which are essentially within the domestic jurisdiction of any state or shall require the Members to submit such matters to settlement under the present Charter; but this principle shall not prejudice the application of enforcement measures under Chapter VII. (Article 2(7))

states whose domestic politics it believes pose a threat to international peace and security.

It was widely understood that during the Cold War the UN should focus on interstate conflicts. If the consent of the belligerents was not present, or if the conflict was internal (as in Congo, 1960–4), there tended to be considerable opposition to any UN military activities. For instance, both the Soviet and French governments opposed the UN's enforcement activities in Congo and refused to contribute to the peacekeeping budget (see chapter 3). By contrast, after the Cold War, the UN's greater involvement in intrastate conflict increased the salience of the tension between sovereignty and human rights and further blurred the distinction between domestic and international issues (Woodhouse and Ramsbotham 1998). As discussed in chapter 1, however, efforts to reconceptualize the relationship between sovereignty and human rights may help to overcome this apparent tension.

The specific measures available to the UN to maintain international peace and security are set out in Chapters VI, VII and VIII of the Charter. Chapter VI deals with pacific measures that can be taken with the consent of the belligerents, Chapter VII deals with enforcement measures, while, as noted above, Chapter VIII sets out the UN's relationship with regional arrangements. According to Article 33(1), the pacific measures available to the UN include negotiation, inquiry, mediation, conciliation, arbitration, judicial settlement and resort to regional agencies or arrangements. Until the turn of the twenty-first century, traditional peacekeeping operations were usually authorized under Chapter VI (see chapter 7). Chapter VII arrangements were originally designed to facilitate collective security activities but are now also used to authorize the use of force by peacekeepers to pursue a variety of tasks (see chapter 9). Articles 41 and 42 provide for forceful non-military and military responses respectively. The authorization of such enforcement measures requires the Security Council to identify a 'threat to international peace and security'. Since the enlargement of the Security Council in 1965 from eleven to fifteen members, enforcement measures have required 'an affirmative vote of nine members including the concurring votes of the permanent members', as set out in Article 27(3).

The Charter's authors envisaged that threats to international peace and security would consist primarily of aggression by one state against another. Over time, however, the Security Council has identified an increasing number of issues as constituting such threats. During the Cold War, for instance, a rebellion in South Rhodesia (1965) and South Africa's nuclear weapons programme (1977) were pinpointed (Chesterman 2001: 130). It was the post-Cold War era, however, that witnessed a dramatic expansion in the Council's understanding of threats. Arguably the landmark resolution in this regard was number 688: passed in the immediate aftermath of the Gulf War (1991), this perceived the flow of Kurdish refugees beyond Iraq's borders as a threat to the peace. Since then, the Council has identified a range of different threats, including state collapse (e.g. Resolution 794), the overthrow of a democratically elected government (e.g. Resolution 841), HIV/AIDS (e.g. Resolution 1308), international terrorism (e.g. Resolution 1373) and nuclear proliferation (e.g. Resolution 1540), as well as humanitarian suffering (e.g. Resolution 770), massive human rights abuse (e.g. Resolution 1199) and the massacre of civilians (e.g. Resolution 1674) within a state.

In light of the close relationship between peacekeeping and the UN, it is important to note that the Charter neither explicitly mentions the concept, nor contains provisions for peacekeeping operations. Peacekeeping was not envisaged as part of the organization's role, which was often thought to lie primarily in establishing a system of collective security (Roberts 1996). This had three important effects on the development of peace operations. First, in practice, UN peace operations have developed as ad hoc responses to particular crises. Second, the key concepts of traditional peacekeeping (consent, impartiality, minimum use of force) were developed through practice. As a result, their meaning is contested and often interpreted differently in contemporaneous missions. Third, member states have reinterpreted the Charter's provisions over time. This helps explain why the definition of what constitutes a threat to international peace and security has changed over time and why there are so many different ways of defining peace operations themselves (see chapter 1).

Matters relating to international peace and security may be brought to the attention of the Security Council by three institutions: the Secretary-General, the General Assembly and individual members of the Security Council.

The Secretary-General   Under Article 99, 'The Secretary-General may bring to the attention of the Security Council any matter which in his opinion may threaten the maintenance of international peace and security.' Because it would make little political sense for any Secretary-General to invoke Article 99 without the support of the permanent members of the Security Council, its formal use has been limited to three occasions: over decolonization in the Congo (1960), in response to the Iranian hostage crisis (1979) and in relation to the armed conflict in Lebanon (1989). As part of his remit, the Secretary-General has also appointed a variety of Special Representatives on such matters as internally displaced persons and the prevention of genocide and mass atrocities. Once the Council has become seized of a particular matter and a peace operation has been deployed, the Secretary-General continues to advise the Council by providing periodic reports about the missions.

The General Assembly   The General Assembly has always been able to play a role in relation to matters of international peace and security by applying pressure on the Council to undertake peacekeeping operations. Indeed, the UN's first peace operation, UNSCOB in Greece (1947–51), was authorized by the Assembly rather than the Security Council. In addition, under the Assembly's 'Uniting for Peace Resolution' passed in 1950, it is empowered to recommend collective measures whenever the Security Council is unable to reach a decision (see box 2.2). This resolution was originally passed to counter Soviet threats to veto further Security Council resolutions with regard to the ongoing war in Korea (see chapter 9). To pass such a resolution there must be a two-thirds majority of the Assembly in favour. Although the 'uniting for peace' option has been used to facilitate UN action (on ten occasions), including to establish UNEF I during the Suez Crisis (1956) and ONUC in Congo (1960), it remained controversial because it brought the primacy of the Security Council into question. Indeed, as Edward Luck observed, not only has this procedure

Box 2.2 'Uniting for peace' in the UN General Assembly

If the Security Council, because of the lack of unanimity of the permanent members, fails to exercise its primary responsibility for the maintenance of international peace and security in any case where there appears to be a threat to the peace, breach of the peace, or act of aggression, the General Assembly shall consider the matter immediately with a view to making appropriate recommendations to Members for collective measures, including in the case of a breach of the peace or acts of aggression the use of armed force when necessary, to maintain or restore international peace and security. If not in session at the time the General Assembly may meet in emergency special session within twenty four hours of the request therefor. Such emergency special session may be called if requested by the Security Council on the vote of any seven members, or by a majority of the Members of the United Nations. (General Assembly Resolution 377 (V, A1), 3 November 1950)

fallen out of favour in recent times – it was last used to take action against Israel in 1997 – but its primary function was always 'to make a political point rather than to authorize the kinds of specific actions that the Charter clearly intended to be left to the Council' (Luck 2006: 70). The General Assembly, through its Fifth Committee, also plays important roles in relation to the financing of peacekeeping operations (see box 2.5).

The Security Council   The Security Council's powers are set out in Chapters V–VIII and XII of the Charter, where it is given primary responsibility for the maintenance of peace and security. Its resolutions are binding on all member states, who are in turn required to assist in their fulfilment should the Council instruct them to do so. The Security Council consists of fifteen member states (expanded in 1965 from the original eleven). There are five permanent members (China, France, the Russian Federation, the UK and the US), and ten members are elected by the General Assembly on a two-year rotational basis. Resolutions (except on procedural matters, where the veto is not applicable) require nine affirmative votes and the concurrence of the permanent members. Although the tendency of the P-5 members to use their veto has decreased since the end of the Cold War, the practice is not unknown and has on occasion been used to terminate a peace operation. This happened when China vetoed the extension of UNPREDEP's mandate in Macedonia in 1999 and when the US vetoed the extension of UNMIBH's mandate in Bosnia in 2002. In addition, it is important to note that a veto does not have to be cast to influence the shape of the Council's activities. As the permanent representative of Jamaica put it, 'the mere presence of the threat of the veto or its possible use more often than not determined the way the Council conduct[ed] its business' (cited in Hulton 2004: 239).

In the post-Cold War era, the Council has taken a more proactive approach to addressing issues of international peace and security and engaging in dialogue with other relevant actors, both within and outside the UN system (see Hulton 2004). One example has been the increased use of fact-finding missions to parts of the world under discussion within the Council. These can help increase public awareness about the issue in question and better inform Council members of the facts on the ground (this is particularly important for the non-permanent members, who may lack other sources of reliable information about the issue in question). In addition, since the late 1990s the Council has engaged in substantive and regular dialogue with NGOs about issues of peace and security. This important development started in 1992 under the so-called Arria formula, when the Venezuelan permanent representative to the UN, Diego Arria, invited fellow members of the Council to meet away from the Council's chambers with independent experts on the Balkans. Since then, the relationship between the Council and various NGOs has been strengthened, largely on account of the efforts of the NGO Working Group on the Security Council founded in 1995.

The bureaucratic framework for UN peace operations

Before the creation of the Department of Peacekeeping Operations (DPKO) in February 1992, UN peace operations were assembled and managed on what was effectively an ad hoc basis. For example, UNEF I in the Sinai (1956–67) was neither authorized nor created by the Security Council. Instead, the then Secretary-General, Dag Hammarskjöld, took it upon himself to offer his 'good offices' to end the dispute, and the General Assembly authorized UNEF I under Resolution 1000 on 5 November 1956. The office of the Secretary-General assumed responsibility for organizing the operation, raising the force itself by lobbying potential troop contributors, borrowing the commanding officer from UNTSO, creating its mandate and developing the rules of engagement (Baehr and Gordenker 1994: 78). The other Cold War operations were assembled in a similar way. Regardless of whether the Secretary-General, General Assembly or Security Council was responsible for creating a particular mission, they were all set up, structured and deployed from scratch.

In 1961, Hammarskjöld created the Office for Special Political Affairs, run by two Under-Secretaries-General. This gave the UN a limited planning and implementation infrastructure for peacekeeping that proved adequate for dealing with the small numbers of operations undertaken during the Cold War. However, this system was clearly deficient when it came to planning and running larger numbers of complex operations. Its shortcomings were quickly exposed by the rapid expansion of peacekeeping operations between 1988 and 1992 (see chapter 4). The UN's new operations in Angola, Namibia and Cambodia, which included peacekeeping and peacebuilding functions, were too complex to be organized by the twenty or so full-time staff in the Office for Special Political Affairs. In addition, the separation of peacekeeping and related functions across several departments and bureaus (such as the Field Operations Division and the Department of Administration and Management) meant that more than twenty Under-Secretaries-General reported directly to the Secretary-General, often without coordinating their activities with each other (Durch 1994c: 62). For example, the various civilian and military components of UNTAC in Cambodia conducted separate and uncoordinated mission surveys and developed distinct mission plans before they were deployed.

In 1992 the UN Secretariat was restructured and the DPKO was created to alleviate some of these problems. The UN began to develop a greater institutional capacity for peacekeeping by providing the DPKO with an Office of Planning and Support for mission planning and logistics, a Field Missions Procurement Section, a permanently staffed Situation Room, and a Lessons Learned Unit. The creation of the Lessons Learned Unit in 1995 gave the UN for the first time an institutional memory in relation to peacekeeping and an institutional capacity to begin addressing broader conceptual issues.

Nevertheless, institutional planning, implementation and learning pro-blems continued. For instance, the reformed UN peacekeeping structure con-tinued to spread responsibility widely and disassociated planning issues (the DPKO and the Department of Administration and Management) from peace-making and peacebuilding diplomacy (the Department of Political Affairs and Executive Office of the Secretary-General) (Akashi 1998).

A practical manifestation of these problems occurred in 2000, when the Department of Political Affairs (DPA) and the DPKO came into conflict over the control of UNTAET in East Timor. Previously, UN operations in East Timor had been managed by the DPA. Although UNTAET would have significant civil functions, it was also mandated to provide a safe environment, which brought many of its activities within the remit of the DPKO. After a protracted inter-necine struggle the DPKO assumed responsibility for the operation, a decision that some argued led to an overly militarized operation and slowed down UNTAET's long-term peacebuilding functions (Thakur 2001).

In order to address some of these bureaucratic problems, the *Report of the Panel on United Nations Peace Operations* (UN 2000), nicknamed the Brahimi Report after its chairman, Lakhdar Brahimi (see chapter 5), recommended that the UN Secretariat should be given significantly more capabilities to reduce the huge gap between the ends peace operations were being asked to achieve and the means the organization's members provided to achieve them. In particular, it recommended significantly more resources should be devoted to headquarters support of UN peace operations and the creation of new agencies to enhance the Secretariat's ability to engage in information-gathering and strategic analysis. Although the DPKO was expanded consider-ably in light of the panel's recommendations (to just over 500 staff in 2006), many of its proposals related to information-gathering and strategic analysis were rejected by the UN's member states. One change that did subsequently occur was the merging in 2001 of the DPKO's Lessons Learned and Policy Planning Units to form the Peacekeeping Best Practices Unit. The Best Practices Unit is part of the Office of the Under-Secretary-General for Peacekeeping Operations and is formally intended to 'coordinate the development of guide-lines and recommendations for the better planning, conduct, management and support of peacekeeping operations'.

One of the goals of the Brahimi reform agenda was to equip the DPKO with sufficient capacity to launch one new multidimensional operation per year. However, during the early years of the twenty-first century UN peacekeeping experienced a major surge in demand (see chapter 5). In practice, the DPKO had to cope with the start-up or expansion of about three field missions per year. By mid-2007, this meant that the ratio of DPKO staff to field personnel was an unbearable 1:149 (Barcena 2007: 4).

In light of the surge in demand for UN peacekeeping, in 2007 the new Secretary-General, Ban Ki-moon, proposed a more radical restructuring to cope with the expansion and complexities of peace operations. These reforms saw the restructuring of the DPKO; the creation of a separate Department of Field Support (DFS), headed by an Under-Secretary-General and with a remit to administer and manage field personnel, finances and information/communications technology; increases in working-level resources in both departments and in other parts of the UN Secretariat; and new capacities and integrated structures (supposedly to match the growing complexity of mandated activities). The DFS was intended to provide an institutional home for officials whose sole focus would be to find the logistical support and solve all the supply chain issues necessary to make peace operations function efficiently. Although some member states were initially very reluctant to approve the splitting of the DPKO and the creation of the DFS, the new Secretary-General made it a central part of his agenda. Officially, the Under-Secretary-General for the DFS has no political mandate, but a remit to provide the logistics that will enable the UN to achieve its objectives on the ground. Nevertheless, it soon became clear that the department's role would also entail providing something of a reality check to the UN Security Council's political decisions by informing the Council of what was actually possible given logistical constraints.

The approved package of reforms included 287 new posts, although the Secretary-General had originally proposed 400 extra posts. Procurement operations were kept under the Department of Management, rather than becoming part of the restructured DPKO. Some member states expressed concern that the creation of two departments would fracture the unity of command and effort so central to the success of any peace operation. Part of the anxiety stemmed from the fact that these reforms reversed the merger of the political and logistical components of peacekeeping that had taken place in 1993–4 precisely to achieve more coordinated and coherent planning. Another key concern was how the relationship between the two Under Secretaries-General would work in practice. The theory was that the head of the DFS would report to and take direction from the head of the DPKO. But, as Michael Pugh has cautioned, this may turn out to be 'a recipe for confusion and dis-integration' (2008: 416). The current organization of the DPKO and DFS are shown in figures 2.1 and 2.2 respectively.

Another important aspect of these reforms was the creation of a separate office overseeing the 'Rule of Law and Security Institutions' in recognition of the increasing importance of policing and the rule of law to peace operations (see chapter 17). Originally, the small policing component of a UN peace operation was managed by the military division. As such, UN police were often referred to as 'CIVPOL' (civilian police) to distinguish them from their military colleagues. As peace operations became more complex, however, so the role of policing expanded, creating, in turn, a growing understanding of the wider tasks associated with establishing the rule of law. Such tasks include managing and overseeing the judiciary and running and reforming national prisons. In this context, it made little sense to house policing in the military

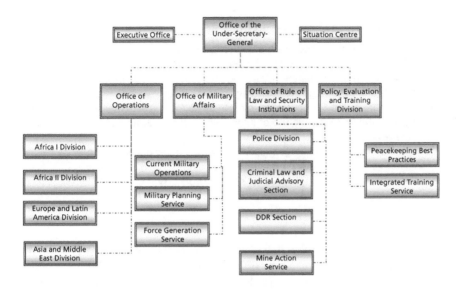

Source: www.un.org/Depts/dpko/DPKOchart.pdf.

Figure 2.1 *The UN Department of Peacekeeping Operations*

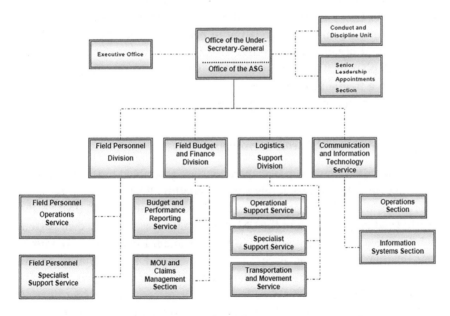

Source: www.un.org/Depts/dpko/DFSchart.pdf.

Figure 2.2 *The UN Department of Field Support*

> **Box 2.3 Peace operations, 2010**
>
> Goal 1: Recruit, prepare and retain high quality personnel.
> Goal 2: Set out doctrine and establish standards for peacekeeping operations.
> Goal 3: Establish effective partnerships, integrated missions and predictable frameworks of cooperation with regional organizations.
> Goal 4: Secure essential resources to improve operational capacity (especially in rapid response and policing), the use of information technology, and public information strategies.
> Goal 5: Establish integrated organizational structures at headquarters and in the field.
>
> *Source*: www.un.org/Depts/dpko/dpko/po2010.pdf.

office and these other related activities with civilian officers. As part of the reform process, therefore, a new office was created, bringing both UN policing (now relabelled UNPOL) and the wider rule of law activities under one institutional roof.

Looking to the future, in November 2005 the Under-Secretary-General for Peacekeeping Operations, Jean-Marie Guéhenno, had circulated an inter-office memorandum to all DPKO headquarters and mission staff outlining his priorities for the next five years. Entitled 'Peace Operations 2010', the memorandum contained five goals, relating to personnel, doctrine, partnerships, resources and organization (see box 2.3). This remains the strategic framework and plan of action to achieve the DPKO's mission: 'to protect and strengthen a fragile peace through the effective planning, conduct, support and transition out of UN peace operations'.

Assembling UN peace operations

Box 2.4 describes how UN peace operations are assembled in theory. In practice, however, the process rarely works smoothly. First, the more complex operations involve many other UN agencies, such as the UNHCR, UNICEF, the World Food Programme and the UNDP. Each agency is led by its own personnel, is tasked separately, and has different standard operating procedures. The relationship between each agency, the Special Representative of the Secretary-General who has overall responsibility for a UN operation, the Resident or Humanitarian Coordinator who is responsible for coordinating and managing the organization's relief and development programmes, and the military force commander is often ambiguous. This can create practical problems with regards to the command and control of an operation and the interpretation of its mandate (e.g. Bagshaw and Paul 2004).

There are further problems associated with actually assembling a military component for any mission. First, it was common practice to choose the force commander only after the force had been assembled (usually from one of the

Box 2.4 Assembling a United Nations peace operation

The UN has no army. Each peace operation must be designed to meet the requirements of each new situation; and every time the Security Council calls for the creation of a new operation, its components must be assembled 'from scratch'. Today, most UN peace operations are authorized by the fifteen-member Security Council. The Council also determines its mandate. Authorizing a new operation requires at least nine votes in favour and is subject to a veto by the negative vote of any of the Council's five permanent members (China, France, the Russian Federation, the UK, and the US). Security Council votes are also required to change the mandate or strength of an existing mission.

Once a mission is authorized, the Secretary-General chooses the Force Commander and asks Member States to contribute troops, civilian police or other personnel. Supplies, equipment, transportation, communication, and logistical support must also be secured from Member States or from private contractors. The type and amounts of such resources are determined on the basis of detailed mission assessment plans conducted by UN personnel, usually after visiting the proposed theatre of operations. Civilian support staff include personnel assigned from within the UN system, loaned by Member States and individuals recruited internationally or locally to fill specific jobs.

The Secretary-General makes recommendations on how the operation is to be launched and carried out, and reports on its progress; the Department of Peacekeeping Operations (DPKO) is responsible for day-to-day executive direction, management and logistical support for UN peace operations worldwide. This includes supporting a number of political missions such as the UN Assistance Mission in Afghanistan, the UN Officer in Timor-Leste, and the UN Integrated Office in Sierra Leone.

Most missions are headed by a Special Representative of the Secretary-General. Senior military officers, staff officers and military observers serving on UN peace operations are directly employed by the UN, usually on secondment from their national armed forces. Peacekeeping troops – the Blue Helmets – participate in UN peace operations under terms negotiated between their Governments and the UN. They remain under the overall authority of those Governments while serving under UN operational command. Police officers are also contributed by the UN's Member States and serve on the same basis as military observers, i.e. as 'experts on mission' paid for by the UN.

The lead-time required to deploy a mission varies, and depends primarily upon the will of Member States to contribute troops to a particular operation. The timely availability of financial resources and strategic lift capacity also affect the time necessary for deployment. In 1973, for example, elements of the second UN Emergency Force (UNEF II) were deployed in the Middle East within 24 hours. However, for some missions with highly complex mandates or difficult logistics, or where peacekeepers face significant risks, it may take months to assemble and deploy the necessary elements.

Source: Adapted from www.un.org/Depts/dpko/dpko/faq/.

major troop-contributing countries). Only then would the force commander be brought to UN headquarters to meet his deputies (from other contingents) and relevant UN personnel. Often this occurred after the majority of mission planning had already been conducted. Second, it was quite common for little or no formal training to be given to the mission's staff officers before command

and control of the operation shifted to them. In recent years the UN has made significant progress in its efforts to provide peacekeepers with relevant training, notably through attempts to develop a capstone doctrine, but, as discussed more extensively in part IV, there remains considerable room for improvement. Third, although the UN nominally commands peacekeeping missions unless a country is specifically tasked to lead the operation, in practice each contingent has considerable leeway to act at the discretion of its highest ranking national officer and remains under the authority of its home government. During peace operations national contingents regularly communicate directly with their home state, adhere to their own rules of engagement and choose whether or not they will obey the force commander. Finally, each component of the force may vary considerably in terms of its peacekeeping experience, the resources available to it and the languages spoken by its troops, as well as their basic military competence.

The lack of strong institutional command and control capabilities has also adversely affected UN peacekeeping. For instance, UN peace operations in Angola, Bosnia, Cambodia, Congo, Rwanda, Sierra Leone and Somalia were all challenged by the unilateral actions of individual contingents. However, because participation in peacekeeping is voluntary, both the professional quality of the personnel and their primary motivations vary (Blum 2000; Durch 1994c: 62–3).

Since the early days of UN peace operations, over 130 member states have contributed military and police personnel. In total, nearly 1 million personnel have served under the UN flag. During the Cold War, a norm developed that peacekeeping operations should not be conducted by either the superpowers or former colonial powers. This helped pave the way for a variety of small states and middle powers to establish reputations as willing and able peacekeepers, including, among others, Canada, the Scandinavian states, Ireland and India. Through their peacekeeping activities, these troop-contributing countries (TCCs) gained useful experience for their personnel as well as international prestige and moral weight at the UN and beyond. In addition, their commitment gave the UN regular access to forces with peacekeeping experience. With the end of the Cold War, however, a different pattern of TCCs began to emerge. Not only did the great powers begin to get more involved in peace operations but, starting with the UNTAC operation in Cambodia, the norm restricting the participation of former colonial powers also began to erode. By 1993, for instance, the four largest TCCs to UN operations were France, the UK, Canada and the Netherlands (Luck 2006: 38). In addition, a much larger number of countries began to contribute personnel to peace operations (see Findlay 1996).

Shifts in the nature of UN TCCs have continued into the twenty-first century. In particular, it has become apparent that states from the developing world have been providing an increasingly large proportion of the UN's peacekeepers. Table 2.2 shows the ten states that consistently provided the

TABLE 2.2 Top ten contributors of troops and police personnel to UN operations, based on monthly averages over a three-year period (2003–2005)

Rank	Country	Total	Monthly	2005	2004	2003
1	Pakistan	264,236	7,340	114,235	94,344	55,657
2	Bangladesh	233,393	6,483	103,007	87,344	43,042
3	India	146,539	4,071	75,708	36,902	33,929
4	Nigeria	111,886	3,108	36,068	41,485	34,333
5	Ghana	98,577	2,738	36,799	36,350	25,428
6	Nepal	84,537	2,348	41,551	28,501	14,485
7	Jordan	79,648	2,212	36,180	24,507	18,961
8	Uruguay	76,476	2,124	29,644	25,743	21,089
9	Ethiopia	72,439	2,012	41,041	30,315	1,083
10	Kenya	62,244	1,729	17,914	22,834	21,496

Source: Luck 2006: 39.

most troops and police personnel during the surge in UN peace operations that occurred between 2003 and 2005. The ten are made up of four states in Asia, four states in Africa, and one each from the Middle East and South America. Over the same time period, however, Western states have significantly reduced the numbers of troops they contribute to UN peace operations. As table 2.3 demonstrates, this is the case for both the Western great powers (France, UK, US) and Western middle powers.

According to DPKO figures, as of 31 December 2007, the UN was deploying 84,309 military and police personnel provided by 119 TCCs. The main suppliers continued to be Pakistan, Bangladesh and India, each contributing over 9,000 personnel, followed by Nepal, Jordan and Ghana, with about 3,500 each, and then Nigeria, Uruguay and Italy, with about 2,500 each. The permanent five members of the Security Council were ranked 11th (France, 1,944), 13th (China, 1,824), 38th (UK, 362), 42nd (US, 316, of which only eight were troops), and 43rd (Russia, 293). In addition, some of the UN's previously stalwart contributors had virtually stopped contributing troops to its peacekeeping operations, confining their input instead to police and/or military observers. For example, Canada provided only fifteen troops, Norway eleven, Australia nine, Sweden three and New Zealand just one.

Although the West's contribution to contemporary UN peace operations is relatively small, this does not mean it has abandoned all forms of peacekeeping. Instead, it has placed more of its personnel in so-called hybrid missions (involving the UN but where the Western troop contribution sits outside UN command and control structures – see table 2.4 and section 2.4) and contributions outside the UN system altogether (including unauthorized peace

TABLE 2.3 Western troop contributions to UN peace operations, 2001–2006

	2001*	2002*	2003*	2004*	2005*	2006*
Total UN peacekeepers	47,151	44,260	36,948	60,745	67,468	74,841
West (broad)**	11,231	10,113	7,530	6,147	5,948	6,242
West (broad) % of total UN	23.8%	22.85%	20.3%	10.2%	8.8%	8.34%
West (major powers)***	3,137	2,881	2,004	2,078	1,315	1,925
West (major powers) % of total UN	6.65%	6.5%	5.4%	3.4%	1.9%	2.57%
P3****	2,103	1,832	1,371	1,556	1,333	1,501
P3 % of total UN	4.45%	4.1%	3.7%	2.5%	1.97%	2%

Notes: * DPKO figures (based on August each year), which include all troop, police and civilian contributions.
** Australia, Portugal, Poland, the US, the UK, New Zealand, Ireland, France, Slovakia, Austria, Germany, Finland, Canada, Italy, Spain, Hungary, Turkey, Sweden, Bulgaria, Romania, Denmark, Norway, the Netherlands, the Czech Republic, Switzerland, Japan, Belgium, Slovenia, Greece, Croatia, Bosnia, Lithuania, Iceland, Estonia, Albania, Serbia and Montenegro.
*** The US, the UK, France, Germany, Italy, Spain, Japan.
**** The US, the UK, France.

Source: Bellamy and Williams 2009: 45.

TABLE 2.4 P-3 troops deployed to non-UN financed peace operations, 2000–2006

	2000	2001	2002	2003	2004	2005	2006
France	8,467	8,180	5,989	8,885†	7,280†	7,460†	8,573†
UK	7,654	6,015	3,450*	3,265	2,815	4,900	6,990
US	16,858	15,225	6,510#	5,580	2,966	2,995	14,573

Notes: UK and US figures 2003–6 exclude troops deployed in Iraq (and Kuwait) and those engaged in Operation Enduring Freedom in Afghanistan (and Pakistan).
† Includes 3,800 troops stationed in Côte d'Ivoire outside of UNOCI.
* Excludes 11,000 troops officially engaged in peace support operations in Iraq.
# Excludes troops deployed in operations Enduring Freedom and Iraqi Freedom.

Source: Bellamy and Williams 2009: 47.

operations conducted with or without the consent of the host state, and financial and technical support for peace operations conducted by non-Western regional organizations such as the African Union and ECOWAS).

Financing UN peace operations

Paying for the UN's peace operations has always been a source of political debate and sometimes of controversy. As a result of the financial crisis generated by the UN's mission in Congo (1960–4) a separate peacekeeping budget was established, although some operations were subsequently funded by voluntary contributions. Financing UN peacekeeping is based on the scale of assessments for the UN's regular budget, first informally adopted in 1973. The P-5, however, pay an additional charge towards UN peacekeeping of about 22 per cent on top of their regular UN assessments. The process of financing UN peace operations is summarized in box 2.5.

Since 2000, and following US-led pressure, a series of reforms were enacted that altered the distribution of payments within the UN's peacekeeping budget. This resulted in a change from the old system (based on four categories of states: P-5, developed, developing and least developed) to a new system (based on ten categories of states, labelled A through J) for raising peacekeeping assessments that differed from the general UN dues (see table 2.5). Under the new system, the P-5 states were relieved of approximately 2 per cent of UN peacekeeping costs (Durch et al. 2003: 122–8).

The United States saw the greatest reduction, however, with its share of the UN peacekeeping budget reduced from 30 to 31 per cent to about 26.5 per cent. At the 2004 rate, this saved the American taxpayer some $164 million a year (Durch and Berkman 2006: 37). The world's poorest countries also benefited from these reforms. The forty-nine Group J (least developed) states received a 90 per cent discount on their peacekeeping dues, leaving them

Box 2.5 Financing United Nations peace operations

All UN Member States contribute to the cost of the organization's peace operations. How much each state pays is based on a special scale of assessments applicable to peacekeeping devised by the General Assembly. This scale takes into account the relative economic wealth of Member States but also requires the Permanent Members of the Security Council to pay a larger share because of their special responsibility for maintaining international peace and security. The scale is now reassessed periodically to determine the most appropriate levels of assessment for three-year cycles e.g. 2004–6 and 2007–9. The current scale has ten levels ranging from A (the highest) through J (the lowest). As of 1 January 2007, the top ten providers of assessed contributions to UN peace operations were: the US (26%), Japan (17%), Germany (9%), the UK (8%), France (7%), Italy (5%), China (3%), Canada (3%), Spain (3%) and the Republic of Korea (2%). In addition, many states also make voluntary contributions on a non-reimbursable basis in the form of transportation, supplies, personnel and financial contributions above and beyond their assessed share of peacekeeping costs.

Between 1948 and mid-2008 the UN is estimated to have spent $54 billion on peacekeeping operations. By way of comparison, during 2006 governments worldwide spent over $1,150 billion on military activities (SIPRI 2007a). Since the 1960s, UN peacekeeping has faced a persistent financial crisis with many states paying their assessments late or only partially. As of 31 December 2008, the amount of peacekeeping arrears stood at approximately $2.88 billion. The annual amount of peacekeeping arrears is shown in figure 2.3.

Source: Compiled by authors and adapted from
www.un.org/Depts/dpko/dpko/contributors/financing.html.

with a bill of around $6,700 per year. The eighty-one members of Group I (the next category up) received an 80 per cent discount and on average paid $488,000 each. Without the discounts, Group J states would be liable for $67,000 and Group I for $2.4 million apiece (ibid.). It is important to recognize, however, that some of these Group I and J states spend the highest amount on their national defence per dollar spent on UN peacekeepers. For every dollar given to UN peacekeeping by Group J states, some $12,000 goes on national defence. For Group I states that figure is around $7,000. By contrast, P-5 states spend on average $642 on national defence per dollar of spending on peace operations and other developed states (mainly European) spend just $178 (ibid.: 39). Thus, while the West is often criticized for not spending enough on UN peace operations, Western states do typically spend much more on UN operations relative to overall defence spending than the least developed states, suggesting that the latter could contribute more financially if they restrained domestic defence spending.

The controversy surrounding peacekeeping finance has intensified as the budget has risen. Before 1988 the UN routinely spent around $300 million a year on peacekeeping, a figure that more than doubled the following year and rose to $3.6 billion in 1993. By 2005, expenditure on peace operations had reached more than $4.5 billion (see figure 2.3). The DPKO's estimated cost of

TABLE 2.5 Old and new UN peacekeeping scales of assessment

As of January 1999					As of January 2005				
Old groups	Payment relative to regular scale	Group criteria	Number of members	Percentage funded by each group	New groups	Payment relative to regular scale	Group criteria (per capita income)	Number of members	Percentage funded by each group
A	121.1%	P-5	5	46.89	A	122.5%	P-5	5	45.25
B	100%	Developed	26	51.09	B	100%	Developed	32	50.13
					C	92.5%	n/a	5	0.82
					D	80%	<$10,188	1	1.51
					E	60%	<$9,189	3	0.01
C	20%	Developing	60	2.01	F	40%	<$8,150	2	0.29
					G	30%	<$7,131	4	0.34
					H	30%	<$6,112	9	0.28
					I	20%	<$5,094	81	1.38
D	10%	Least Developed	97	0.02	J	10%	Least Developed	49	0.01

Source: Durch and Berkman 2006: 37.

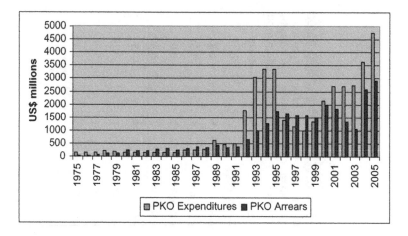

Source: www.globalpolicy.org/finance/tables/pko/expendarrears.htm.

Figure 2.3 *UN peacekeeping expenditure vs. arrears by all member states, 1975–2005*

UN peace operations between July 2008 and June 2009 is approximately $7.1 billion. Part of the problem is that many rich states have refused to pay their peacekeeping assessments on time, causing a persistent financial crisis staved off only by the practice of volunteer states loaning money and equipment to the UN. By the end of 2008, the level of outstanding contributions to peacekeeping was just under $3 billion, but this figure fluctuates constantly.

Another source of controversy has involved the motives driving TCCs. It has been suggested that some of the world's poorest states have sought to use troop contributions to peacekeeping as a source of revenue (Berman and Sams 2000; Blum 2000: 59–61). Because the UN has traditionally reimbursed contributing governments at a flat rate for the troop units they supplied, states supplying expensive military equipment could receive as little as one-quarter of their costs, while states sending ill-equipped forces could receive as much as 3.5 times their expenditure (Durch 1994b: 50). Such disparities have sometimes caused considerable friction between contributing states. Five of the top contributors to UN peace operations (India, Pakistan, Bangladesh, Ethiopia and Jordan) are countries with very high ratios of defence spending relative to UN peacekeeping dues (Durch and Berkman 2006: 39), suggesting that they are capable of contributing troops that are worth significantly more than the UN dues. The existence of ill-equipped contingents in the field also had an adverse effect on the UN's procurement system. The DPKO encouraged contingents to bring the necessary equipment with them when they deployed, but the desire to enhance legitimacy and impartiality by achieving a wide geographic spread of peacekeepers, coupled with the need for larger numbers of troops, meant that a significant proportion of the equipment and logistical support was supplied by a slow and costly commercial procurement process – hence the criticism that peacekeeping was undermined by a payment system that allowed operations to become profit-making exercises for those states least prepared to undertake them.

A powerful counter-argument, however, is that, because they are often responsible for creating peace operations, it is only right and proper that the P-5 states pay the lion's share of the bill. Moreover, if the powerful and wealthy states were seriously concerned about the poor quality of equipment and training used on peace operations, they could have displayed a greater willingness to share their equipment and provide more effective training. This has led a variety of analysts and UN officials to call for better troop standby arrangements, including the idea of having several multinational brigade-sized forces and support services on call, and reviving the idea of creating UN standing forces (see Langille 2000; Roberts 2008; and chapter 6). Finally, the reimbursement system allows several leading troop contributors (Ghana, Nigeria, Kenya, Uruguay and South Africa) to contribute brigade-sized forces despite having below-average spending ratios. That is, reimbursements allow them to contribute to the UN even though they spend less on national defence relative to peacekeeping dues than their peers.

2.4 Partnership peacekeeping

Particularly since the end of the Cold War, the different types of peacekeepers (states, coalitions and international organizations) have engaged in a variety of cooperative activities. Norrie MacQueen (2006) has referred to this as 'partnership peacekeeping'. While there is no simple and completely accurate way to classify the various relationships that have developed between the different types of peacekeepers because they have been *sui generis*, it is possible to sketch four broad types.

First, there have been cases where actors adopted a sequential division of labour whereby one actor initially conducted an operation and then passed the peacekeeping baton to another actor. Examples include cases where one international organization has handed responsibility to another, and also cases where a multinational coalition has passed responsibility to an international organization. Examples in the former category are ECOWAS forces handing over to the UN in Sierra Leone (1999–2000) and Liberia (2003); NATO's decision to turn its operations in Bosnia (2004) and Macedonia (2003) over to the European Union; and the African Union handing over the responsibility for peacekeeping in Burundi (2004) to the UN. Examples in the latter category include the Multinational Force in Haiti preparing the environment for the UN mission MINUSTAH to take over in 2004; and NATO's decision in 2003 to take command of the International Security Assistance Force in Afghanistan from the coalition of states that had previously run it.

A second form of partnership peacekeeping has involved cooperation between two types of actors deployed concurrently within the same conflict zone. This has most commonly taken the form of linked peacekeeping–observer operations, where the UN and another operation provide a combination of peacekeeping and observer capacities in separate but coordinated commands (Jones and Cherif 2004). Examples of this type of partnership are UNOMIL and ECOMOG in Liberia (1993–7); UNOMSIL and ECOMOG in Sierra Leone (1998–2000); and UNOMIG and the CIS operation in Abkhazia/Georgia (1993–present). On other occasions, personnel from multiple institutions have worked within the same conflict zone but carried out different functions while maintaining separate command structures. In the DRC, for example, the UN's peacekeepers in MONUC received various forms of support from EU peacekeepers, including rapid reaction forces such as Operation Artemis (2003) and EUFOR RD (2006), and security sector reform missions such as EUPOL Kinshasa (2005–7) and EUSEC RD Congo (2005–present).

A third type of partnership peacekeeping has occurred where what Bruce Jones has called 'integrated operations' have been established, wherein multiple institutions pool their capabilities under a single operation command (Jones and Cherif 2004). To date, examples of this type of cooperation have been confined largely to the Balkans, particularly the missions in Bosnia and Kosovo, where a variety of institutions – including the UN, NATO, the EU and the OSCE – took responsibility for different dimensions of the mandate.

The final type of partnership peacekeeping has involved the construction of a hybrid operation where two institutions joined together to establish working procedures. To date, the African Union–UN Hybrid operation in Darfur (UNAMID) remains the only example of this type. Rodolphe Adada of the Republic of Congo, appointed Joint AU–UN Special Representative designate for UNAMID, was tasked to report to both the UN Secretary-General and the AU Commission chairperson. In turn, Adada was to receive directives from both the AU's Peace and Security Commissioner and the UN Under-Secretary-General for Peacekeeping Operations. The day-to-day functioning of the force was to be in accordance with the concept of operations jointly agreed by the AU and the UN. From the beginning of 2008, however, the command and control structures for the mission were officially provided by the UN. Given the complexities involved, it is unlikely that many missions will opt to follow this model.

In general terms, while these forms of partnership peacekeeping may offer the opportunity to create pragmatic and flexible responses to difficult circumstances and provide a way of pooling resources, they also suffer from a variety of problems, not least those related to coordination and chain of command issues, as well as problems related to funding – both the potential for different salary levels and the sustainability of finance from poorer institutions.

2.5 Conclusion

Three central conclusions emerge from our investigation of who the peace-keepers are. First, with their functional and normative advantages, international organizations are the most significant and legitimate peacekeepers, with the UN predominant among them. International organizations can construct norms that shape state behaviour and act as legitimizing bodies – conferring the stamp of international legitimacy on state practice. The UN in particular has played a central role in the creation of new norms in international society (Claude 1966; Weiss and Daws 2007). However, the ad hoc nature of UN peacekeeping made the organization and its members slow to recognize the implications of the expansion of its post-Cold War operations and the transition from a Westphalian towards a post-Westphalian international society. As Adam Roberts (1993: 4) noted in the early 1990s, the UN's preoccupation with making its existing peacekeeping infrastructure more efficient detracted from the even more critical task of re-examining the premises underpinning the concepts and practices themselves. Second, the increasing demand for peacekeepers encouraged an expansion of both unilateral and multilateral peacekeeping activity outside the auspices of the UN. Third, the different types of peacekeepers have begun to develop various partnerships to tackle the significant challenges confronting them.

PART II

Historical Development

CHAPTER THREE

The Early Peacekeepers

Peace operations are not unique to the twentieth century. Indeed their origins lie in attempts by the great powers in the nineteenth and early twentieth centuries to manage conflicts, protect imperilled Christians and impose their collective will on other powers (Chesterman 2001; Finnemore 2003). Important threads of continuity and parallels exist between these older activities and what we now call peace operations. The idea that great powers have special responsibilities for maintaining peace and security can be traced back to antiquity. The Roman Empire, for instance, established the idea that law enforcement should cross political boundaries (Buzan and Little 2000: 200) and that all peoples were governed by a universal law, the *ius gentium*. In the modern era powerful states have frequently justified intervention in the affairs of others on the grounds of protecting fundamental human rights, the natural order or the wider peace. Sometimes this has been for the greater good, as with the belated British stand against the international slave trade. More often, however, such claims were merely a pretext for self-interest, as with the 'standard of civilization' idea that was employed to legitimize colonialism. For instance, in 1884, Jules Ferry told the French parliament that 'the superior races have a right vis-à-vis the inferior races...they have a right to civilize them' (in Conklin 1997: 13). Likewise, John Stuart Mill, one of the foremost liberal thinkers of the nineteenth century, argued that despotism was necessary to educate natives about the importance of obeying government, the first step to civilization (Mill 1991: 34–40).

International organization and collective action in pursuit of peace and security began in earnest during the nineteenth century. It was in the growth of European cooperation in the post-Napoleonic period that the first steps were taken towards collective action to preserve peace between states. Importantly, this period also saw the great powers award themselves special legal responsibilities for the maintenance of international peace and security and requisite rights to intervene in the affairs of others. Interestingly, these claims to special rights and responsibilities were supported by weaker members of international society – a form of 'legalized hierarchy' that is today evident in the structure of the UN Security Council, which bestows unique rights and responsibilities upon its permanent members (Simpson 2004; see chapter 2). Most attempts by Europe's great powers to maintain order were driven either by selfish motives or, in the case of several interventions in the Middle East, solidarity with Christian communities outside Europe. In the aftermath of the First World War, these early efforts prompted bolder attempts to institutionalize international cooperation in the twentieth century – first through the League of Nations and then via the UN.

This chapter examines the rise of international organization and some of the antecedents of today's peace operations. It starts by analysing attempts to keep the peace and uphold common interests during the nineteenth century, then discusses the work of the UN's predecessor, the League of Nations. It concludes with an overview of UN peacekeeping during the Cold War.

3.1 Nineteenth-century peace operations

In 1815, France and the victorious powers in the Napoleonic Wars (Austria, Britain, Prussia and Russia) gathered at the Congress of Vienna and agreed to create the so-called Concert of Europe (see Ikenberry 2001: 80–116; Clark 2005: 85–108; and box 3.1). This system attempted to manage potential great power conflicts and prevent one power dominating the others. For our purposes, it is important to identify four related yet distinct forms of European cooperation enabled by the Concert of Europe:

Box 3.1 Reflections on nineteenth-century multilateralism

The conference system did not inaugurate a rule of law or produce an impartial agency politically superior to national states and capable of upholding the moral standards of a larger community. It was a system of de facto great power hegemony, and the fact that its arrangements frequently resulted in collective or international decisions did not mean that those decisions were necessarily wise or just.... When all is said and done, the political conference system contributed more to awareness of the problems of international collaboration than to their solution and more to opening up the possibilities of multilateral diplomacy than to realizing them. But it produced the prototype of a major organ of modern international organisation – the executive council of the great powers. (Claude 1963: 28)

The political order that emerged from the Vienna settlement combined elements of the old European logic of balance with new legal-institutional arrangements meant to manage and restrain power. Its most important departure from previous peace agreements was that it sought to cope with problems of menacing states and strategic rivalry by tying states together through treaties and a jointly managed security consultation process. It foreshadowed but fell short of the 1919 and 1945 settlements, which tackled a wide range of security, political, and functional problem areas, established semi-permanent multilateral institutions, and created more invasive agreements that extended further into the domestic polities of the participating states. (Ikenberry 2001:114)

1 a collective agreement to cooperate in protecting the international status quo through a system of preventive diplomacy and peacemaking;
2 an agreement by a smaller group of the great powers (the Holy Alliance) to protect the domestic status quo by intervening in support of monarchs under threat from nationalist revolutionaries;
3 a series of collective ad hoc interventions aimed at protecting human rights, usually those of Christian communities in the Balkans (Greece) and Middle East but also slaves;
4 loose agreements setting out colonial responsibilities and the collective use of force to protect shared colonial interests.

Each of these forms of collective action evolved through the course of the nineteenth century and produced their own types of 'peace operation' (see table 3.1). Interestingly, the concert system itself served to deter potentially destabilizing intervention (such as a proposed 1822 Russian intervention in the Balkans) more than it acted as a catalyst for collective peace operations (Booth and Wheeler 2008: 110). However, the Vienna settlement failed to deal with the question of how the great powers should deal with a fragmenting

TABLE 3.1 Early peace operations

International status quo	Domestic status quo	Humanitarian	Colonial
1848–9: Swedish peace force for Schleswig-Holstein	1821: Austrian intervention in Naples	1817: UK begins naval operations against slave traders; 1837: Anglo-French naval operations against slave traders	1820s: Multinational operations against Barbary pirates
	1848: Russian intervention in Hungary (in support of Austrian government)	1827: Multinational intervention to protect Greek Christians from Turkish–Egyptian forces	1878: British occupation of Cyprus (while still an Ottoman territory)
		1860–1: French occupation of Syria	1878: Austro-Hungarian occupation of Bosnia (while still an Ottoman territory)
		1898: US intervention in Cuba	1898: International mission to Crete
			1900: International response to the Boxer Rebellion
			1913: International force in Albania

and increasingly brutal Ottoman Empire (Holsti 1991: 155; Mitzen 2005: 412). As a result, most nineteenth-century operations concerned themselves with the Ottoman Empire, and a large number of those had an ostensible humanitarian dimension.

Conflict management in Europe

The Concert of Europe was created to protect the interests of Europe's great powers. In this system, preserving the peace was synonymous with securing the interests of the great powers, which in practice meant maintaining a balance of power to prevent future French revanchism (Kissinger 1994: 86, 91). This experiment in international organization was brought to a halt, however, by the revolutions of 1830 and 1848, which reduced the level of great power consensus and thus the likelihood of collective action by the concert powers (see Hobsbawm 1962: 104). Despite the breakdown of the congress system and the proliferation of wars in Europe (Crimean War, Italian wars of unification, Austro-Prussian War and Franco-Prussian War), the great powers continued to cooperate occasionally to defend the status quo and prevent more widespread war. This was usually done through diplomacy – as in the Balkans crisis of 1822 – but occasionally it involved military action, as in 1848 when, at the behest of the great powers, Sweden intervened between Prussia and Denmark over the contested territory of Schleswig-Holstein (Schmidl 2000: 7; MacQueen 2006: 24).

Defending the domestic status quo

In 1821, Austria, Prussia and Russia effectively defected from the Vienna settlements and established the so-called Holy Alliance, empowering themselves to intervene against states 'which have undergone change of Government due to revolution' (Clark 2005: 94). Britain rejected the idea that revolutions granted a *prima facie* right of intervention and the conservative powers' argument that the internal constitution of states presented a threat to international peace and security, arguing that it was Napoleonic expansionism, not French republicanism, that had caused the wars of the past decades (Simpson 2004: 202). In 1822, the Holy Alliance sent expeditionary forces to help the monarchs suppress revolutions in Naples and Spain, drawing sharp criticism from Britain and the United States. When Spain's South American dominions revolted in 1823 and the allies considered intervention, Britain's foreign secretary, Canning, insisted that his government should reject any right for external powers to dictate the terms of a state's internal constitution, while the United States responded with the 'Monroe doctrine', opposing European interference in the Americas (Chesterman 2001: 23).

Defence of Christians and human rights

A number of collective military interventions in the nineteenth century were putatively concerned with the protection of Christian civilians from attack. In its attempts to address the problem of conflict in the Balkans, the Congress of Berlin (1878) provides evidence of emerging agreement about the new ethical principles which ought to govern international society. These were first espoused in the American Declaration of Independence (1776) and the French Declaration of the Rights of Man (1789). As the Ottoman Empire had gradually imploded in the early nineteenth century, Turkish repression of Christians became increasingly frequent and vicious. In the 1820s, the Ottomans responded brutally to a series of Christian uprisings in Greece and Serbia. Great power interest was prompted by both the perceived strategic importance of the region and concerns about the treatment of Christians, particularly Greeks (Medlicott 1956: 22–7). Britain initially turned a blind eye to Greek suffering for fear of encouraging Russian intervention in the Balkans, but by 1827 this position became untenable in the face of public outcry about Turkish atrocities. Britain and France joined Russia in signing the London Treaty (6 July 1827), which explained the grounds for intervention as being to prevent 'all the disorders of anarchy', end the endemic piracy in the region and put a 'stop to the effusion of blood' and 'evils of every kind' (in Westlake 1910: 319 n.3). The allied forces destroyed the Turkish and Egyptian navies, laying the seeds for Greek independence. Similar dynamics were at play in 1860 when France intervened in Ottoman Syria to protect Maronite Christians, thousands of whom had been slaughtered by Druze and Muslims on Mount Lebanon and in Damascus (see Brownlie 1963: 340; Chesterman 2001: 32). Another case occurred in 1898, when the US intervened in Cuba after Spanish policies that resulted in the deaths of around 100,000 Cuban civilians (see Bass 2008: 317–28).

Colonial policing

A majority of nineteenth-century interventions were related to colonial concerns. These included the British occupation of Cyprus (1878 onwards), the Austrian trusteeship in Bosnia (Malcolm 1994: 133–51), and the collective action undertaken in 1900 by the eight major powers most intimately engaged in China (Austria, France, Germany, Britain, Italy, Japan, Russia and the United States) to rescue their diplomatic missions during the Boxer Rebellion. In line with our argument that international society during this period was guided by two sets of rules – one for (mainly European) sovereign states and one for the colonial world – most of these missions were ultimately concerned with managing and protecting the colonial status quo. Towards the end of the century, the great powers even began to accept a limited degree of collective oversight of their colonial possessions. For example, although the 1885

Treaty of Berlin was concerned almost entirely with free trade, it also committed colonial rulers to 'watch over the preservation of the native tribes, and to care for the improvement of the conditions of their moral and material well-being' (Article 5) (Keith 1919: 58–63). This sowed the seeds for the trusteeship system and future UN transitional administrations (see chapter 11).

International organization continued to develop at the turn of the century. In 1899 and 1907, state representatives from around the world gathered at The Hague at two great conferences assembled with the grand intention of abolishing war. Although they failed in that endeavour, these conferences secured important agreements that limited recourse to war and the means that states could use in wartime, such as banning the use of poison gas. In particular, the second conference created a system of voluntary arbitration of disputes between systems and elicited a pledge from states that they would not wage war without providing prior warning, in the form of either a declaration or an ultimatum, detailing the grounds for war (Lauterpacht 1933: 27–8). Unfortunately, these pledges were put to the test in 1914, when alliance politics and balance of power logic transformed a regional problem in Austria-Hungary's newest territory, Bosnia, into the 'war to end all wars'.

3.2 The League of Nations

The 'war to end all wars', or First World War, was the first fully industrialized war and engulfed all the world's major powers. It left approximately 20 million people dead and contributed directly to the conditions of generalized poverty and social dislocation in which a further 20 million died of Spanish influenza immediately after the end of the war. Such devastating losses at the heart of the 'civilized world' stimulated mass movements for social change. It also had a powerful impact on politicians, publics and academics alike. Four main conclusions were drawn about the causes of the war and the activities needed to prevent any repetition: that war was now expensive and senseless, and should no longer be considered an ordinary instrument of state policy; that this particular war resulted from state leaders getting caught up in processes no one could control; that the causes of war lay in misunderstandings between leaders and in the lack of democratic accountability within the states involved; and that the underlying tensions which provided the rationale for conflict could be removed by the spread of statehood, democracy and – we would add – international organization (Hollis and Smith 1991: 18).

These reflections contributed to a resurgence in international organization and the creation of the League of Nations in 1919. Based in Geneva, Switzerland, the League was characterized by a broad membership which extended far beyond Europe's great powers; by the time of its demise, sixty-three states had been members at one time or another (Walters 1969: 64–5). The League represented a far more ambitious attempt to manage interna-

Box 3.2 Key articles of the Covenant of the League of Nations

Article 11.1: Any war or threat of war, whether immediately affecting any of the Members of the League or not, is hereby declared a matter of concern to the whole League, and the League shall take any action that may be deemed wise and effectual to safeguard the peace of nations.

Article 15.1: If there should arise between Members of the League any dispute likely to lead to a rupture, which is not submitted to arbitration or judicial settlement in accordance with Article 13, the Members of the League agree that they will submit the matter to the Council.

Article 16.1: Should any member of the League resort to war in disregard of its covenants under Articles 12, 13 or 15, it shall ipso facto be deemed to have committed an act of war against all other Members of the League, which hereby undertake immediately to subject it to the severance of all trade or financial relations, the prohibition of all intercourse between their nationals and the nationals of the Covenant-breaking State, and the prevention of all financial, commercial or personal intercourse between nationals of the Covenant-breaking State and the nationals of any other State, whether a member of the League or not.

Article 16.2: It shall be the duty of the Council in such cases to recommend...what effective military, naval or airforce the Members of the League shall severally contribute to the armed forces to be used to protect the covenants of the League.

Box 3.3 Selections from Woodrow Wilson's fourteen points (January 1918)

I.   Open covenants of peace, openly arrived at, after which there shall be no private international understandings of any kind, but diplomacy shall proceed always frankly and in the public view.
IV. Adequate guarantees given and taken that national armaments will be reduced to the lowest point consistent with domestic safety.
V.   A free, open-minded, and absolutely impartial adjustment of all colonial claims, based upon a strict observance of the principle that in determining all such questions of sovereignty the interests of the populations concerned must have equal weight with the equitable claims of the government whose title is to be determined.
XIV. A general association of nations must be formed under specific covenants for the purpose of affording mutual guarantees of political independence and territorial integrity to great and small states alike.

tional society than the Concert of Europe. In principle at least, it was founded not on the narrow self-interest of the great powers but on common ideas and values – principally the idea of collective security and the values expressed in US President Woodrow Wilson's 'fourteen points' (see box 3.3). One aspect of the concert system that was preserved, however, was the idea that the great powers should play an executive role in international organization (see the quotation from Inis Claude in box 3.1). This role was enshrined in the form of the League's Council, of which the great powers would be permanent members (see Simpson 2004: 157–8).

Although the great powers wielded considerable influence within the League, the organization institutionalized the basic rights of other sovereign states to participate in managing international society. Its central body was the Council, which was tasked with taking key decisions and establishing collective responses to international crises and conflicts. All member states were represented in the Assembly, which had mainly consultative and declaratory functions. The new organization also had a Secretariat that was responsible for its day-to-day running, though it was small in size. The League's primary function was the provision of collective security. Collective security refers to the idea that all members of international society have a responsibility to contribute to collective action to prevent and repel aggressors (see box 3.4).

According to Kupchan and Kupchan (1991), ideal collective security organizations exhibit three characteristics: certainty, utility and inclusivity. However, the League missed the mark in all of these areas in both its Covenant and its practice. Certainty was undermined by the fact that the Covenant required decisions to be made on the basis of unanimity. In the case of Japan's invasion of Manchuria in 1931, for example, the Council hesitated to apply sanctions that Wilson had envisaged as being 'immediate and automatic'. The

Box 3.4 The idea of collective security

The term 'collective security' normally refers to a system, regional or global, in which each participating state accepts that the security of one is the concern of all, and agrees to join in a collective response to aggression. In this sense it is distinct from, and more ambitious than, systems of alliance security, in which groups of states ally with each other, principally against possible external threats. (Roberts 1996: 310)

Collective security involves a recognition by states that 1) they must renounce the use of military force to alter the status-quo and agree instead to settle...their disputes peacefully; 2) they must broaden their conception of the national interest to take account of the interests of the international community as a whole; and 3) they must overcome the fear which dominates world politics and learn to trust one another. (Baylis 2001: 264)

The aim of any collective security system is to preserve, and ensure the observance of, certain community defined values. The determination of what are these community values in the case of the United Nations – what constitutes a threat to, or breach of, international peace and security – and what is the appropriate measure to maintain and restore peace has been left to the Security Council under Chapter VII of the Charter. (Sarooshi 2000: 285)

subsequent failure to apply sanctions in 1935 against Italy after it attacked Abyssinia – itself a member of the League – was another case in point. These episodes led many states to view the League as little more than a reinstitutionalization of the Concert of Europe rather than the collective security system that Wilson had envisioned (Armstrong 1982: 35).

The League also had problems in relation to 'utility'– i.e. the ability to mobilize all forms of diplomatic, moral, economic and military coercion available to its members. Once again the need for unanimity stymied Wilson's aspirations, and powerful states (including the UK and the US) suggested that members could decide individually how to respond to aggressors. The final characteristic of 'inclusivity' meant that collective security systems should encompass all members of international society. Here again the League suffered from two central problems: not only was 'membership' impossible for large (colonized) sections of the planet, but the League failed to persuade the great powers to work within it (while Germany and Japan joined late and left early, the United States was completely absent, and after joining late the Soviet Union was subsequently expelled).

From the outset, therefore, the League was based on a very imperfect concept of collective security whereby responses to aggression would be selective, the means of response would vary, and important members of international society were absent. Nevertheless, these problems did not entirely preclude the League's playing a role in maintaining international peace and security. In 1920 it took responsibility for two controversial aspects of the post-war peace agreements. First, it supervised the international administration of Germany's industrial heartland, the Saar basin. After the war, the Saar coal mines were placed under French control as part of the reparations package, but the British and US governments rejected French claims that they should annex the territory completely (Walters 1969: 89). As a compromise, while the Saar was included within a French customs union, it was to remain under international administration for a period of fifteen years, after which time a plebiscite would decide the region's long-term future. The League appointed a five-man commission to supervise the administration of the territory and effectively exercised full governmental control for over a decade. As the plebiscite approached, however, international concern increased that the vote would provoke an outburst of political violence. Adolf Hitler's Nazi Party had come to power in Germany in 1933 and was inciting German nationalism in the Saar (James 1990: 76). In response, the League exercised its authority to station armed forces on the territory and deployed an international force of 3,300 troops, comprising British and Italian soldiers supported by small contingents of Swedish and Dutch troops. The international force was guided by two key principles that would later come to inform early UN peace operations: the operation required the host's consent and the use of force was permitted for self-defence alone (James 1990: 77). These early peacekeepers maintained law and order in the run-up to the plebiscite and allowed the League to oversee a free and fair process that saw the Saarlanders vote overwhelmingly for reunification with Germany.

The second case involved the future of the port of Danzig. Danzig's population was overwhelmingly German, but the post-war redrawing of the European map left it physically separated from Germany and claimed by the new Polish state. While its future was debated within the League's Assembly and Council, two battalions of Allied troops occupied the territory under the authority of a British administrator (James 1990: 26). After the withdrawal of the temporary Allied administration in November 1920, the port and its surrounding territory was made a 'free city' and placed under the League's protection. The League's High Commissioner for Danzig was integral to the development of its democratic constitution and to the arbitration of disputes between it and Poland. This was intended to be a permanent solution to the problem. However, by the mid-1930s Danzig presented the League with further difficulties when the city's government became dominated by Nazis. This soured its relationship with both the League and Poland.

In addition, between 1920 and 1922 the League supervised a variety of post-war plebiscites held in Schleswig, Allenstein and Marienwerder, the Klagenfurt basin, Upper Silesia and Sopron (James 1990: 27–32). This was done through League missions comprising civilians, police and soldiers from disinterested states – operations labelled 'plebiscite peacekeeping' by Norrie MacQueen (2006: 28–9). Most of these missions were handled by commissions supported by international military forces, numbering between 450 and 3,000 troops. But in the case of the hotly disputed territory of Upper Silesia (Germany and Poland), 15,500 British, French and Italian troops were deployed alongside a plebiscite commission that also took temporary control of the region's police forces. In addition the League engaged in international mediation, including in the Åland Islands dispute (1920), the Albanian issue (1921–3) and the Greco-Bulgarian conflict (1925).

Although some of these activities went smoothly, there were also signs of fundamental weaknesses, particularly in cases where disputants did not consent to arbitration or intervention, such as the dispute between Poland and Lithuania over Vilna (1920–2) (James 1990: 33–5). Similarly, when Manchuria (1931) and Abyssinia (1935) were invaded the League was unable to live up to the aspirations of collective security (Bartlett 1992: 153–8, 179–83). By the end of the 1930s, therefore, the League had become an international irrelevance. As a result, the organization became less concerned with providing collective security and more intent on preserving the status quo and the Anglo-French position within it. Unsurprisingly, the League ultimately suffered a similar fate to the Concert of Europe.

The League's failure is often seen as a crucial factor in the descent into the Second World War. E. H. Carr (1995), for instance, saw it as sounding the death knell of idealism, while the organization was vilified by subsequent generations of political realists. However, the League was an incomplete project that was neither genuinely inclusive nor allowed to pursue collective security in the way that its architects had originally intended. Despite, or arguably because of, these failings it began to carve out a particular role for itself in mediation, the supervision of plebiscites and the organization of transitional arrangements. Similar activities became important aspects of the UN's 'traditional peacekeeping' and 'assisting transition' type operations (see chapters 7 and 10).

3.3 The United Nations and peace operations during the Cold War

The UN was conceived as the successor to the failed League of Nations by the Western allies during the Second World War. The catastrophic loss of life and physical devastation caused by the war, coupled with the invention of the atomic bomb, convinced international leaders that international organization was more necessary than ever. Taking up the idea that great powers should play a legalized executive role in world politics, the main wartime allies (Britain, France, the Soviet Union and the United States) saw themselves as the 'four policemen' and initially conceived the UN as the vehicle through which they would police world affairs. The 'police', plus China, were given special rights (permanent membership of the Security Council and veto powers; see chapter 2) but also bore, in the words of US Secretary of State John Stettinius, 'the principal responsibility for action' (in Goodrich and Carroll 1947: 415). For all its problems, this combination of special rights and responsibilities, and the guarantee that the UN could never act against the interests of the great powers (of 1945), ensured their continued participation in the new organization and helped it survive the global chill of the Cold War (see Thakur 2006: 33).

The vision of a UN led by the world's policemen was severely circumscribed during the Cold War, and current assessments of the UN Security Council see it more as an instrument of crisis management than an institution concerned with policing international law (Lowe et al. 2008). In addition to the Cold War politics that stymied the potential for consensus among the superpowers, the UN faced some profound tensions as to its proper role in the world, tensions which arose from different ideas about the lessons of the Second World War. These tensions are similar in kind to those between the two visions of sovereignty described in chapter 1 and are also evident in the Charter itself. The horrors of the Second World War produced a somewhat contradictory response from international society, largely because three concerns pulled world leaders in different directions.

First, the experience of war created a strong impetus for outlawing it as an instrument of state policy. Second, the monstrosities perpetrated by Nazism, fascism, Japanese nationalism and Stalinism, combined with the immense contribution to the war effort made by colonized peoples in India, Indochina,

Africa and elsewhere, strengthened the belief that peoples had a right to govern themselves. This helped discredit the idea of empire and bolster calls for decolonization. But it also presented the problem of how to protect the subsequent new states from interference by the world's great powers. In addition to the ban on force, the key protection afforded to the new states was the principle of non-interference. Finally, the Holocaust and other horrors persuaded international society to place aspirations for basic human rights at the heart of the new order. The tension this created within the UN Charter set in train the core dilemma that we explored in chapter 1: how should states behave in cases where the principles underlying good neighbourliness (mutual respect for sovereignty, non-interference, etc.) collide with those relating to the protection of human rights? Or, put another way, how should the UN behave if the pursuit of peace and security requires that it interferes in the domestic affairs of its members?

Because chapter 2 set out the mechanics of putting together UN peace operations and part III of this book provides an overview of peace operations in practice, this section briefly outlines the origins and development of UN peace operations during the Cold War.

The early impact of the Cold War on the UN's work can be illustrated by its failed attempts to create a standing army and its response to North Korea's invasion of its southern neighbour. The first victim of the Cold War was the proposal for the UN to have its own standing army to enforce the decisions of the Security Council. The Charter's drafters had originally conceived the idea that, in order to avoid the uncertainty that had characterized the League's collective security system, the UN's member states would provide the organization with a standing military force. This 'UN army' would be politically directed by the Security Council and commanded by a UN Military Staff

TABLE 3.2 The UN: lessons learned?

Problem with the League	Remedy in the UN
'Empty chairs' – absence of US, USSR, Germany, Japan	Permanent Security Council members with veto powers; non-permanent members elected by General Assembly
Lack of credible enforcement power and international authority	Chapter VII empowers Security Council to use all means; Article 43 creates a military staff as prelude to international armed force
Lack of universality – League became more about collective defence (of Britain and France) than collective security	General Assembly is all-inclusive – all states can be members; General Assembly oversees the work of the UN, including the Security Council
Inactivity and delay	Creation of a larger, permanent Secretariat with technical expertise

Committee. These provisions were written into the UN Charter (e.g. Articles 42 and 43), and negotiations began in 1945 to establish the force. It may be surprising nowadays, but one of the leading advocates of the UN army in 1945 was the United States. The US government went so far as to indicate which forces it would set aside for the new UN force – around 40,000 soldiers, sailors and airmen, including an aircraft carrier battle group (see Lorenz 1999). This American activism raised concerns in Moscow that the UN army would be a front for the Western allies, and the Soviet Union pulled out of the negotiations. The idea of building a UN army died in 1948, although there have been repeated efforts to resurrect it (see box 6.4, pp. 168–9).

The US-led intervention in Korea in 1950 ostensibly suggested that, unlike the League, the UN had the capacity to play a leading role in collective security (see chapter 9). However, the peculiar circumstances in which the intervention was authorized meant that it turned out to be the exception rather than the rule for UN operations during the Cold War. The intervention was facilitated by the Soviet Union's absence from the Security Council, which left it unable to use its veto power. Its absence was in protest at the Council's refusal to recognize the Communists as the rightful government of China. When the Soviets returned to the Council, they ensured that the United States could not continue to use the UN to legitimize its intervention in Korea (see Luck 2006: 49–50). The Korean War was the only explicit example of peace enforcement action against a sovereign state during the Cold War (there are also very few post-Cold War cases; see chapters 4 and 5).

At the same time, however, the UN was beginning to develop alternative ways of contributing to international peace and security. In 1947 the General Assembly reacted to a complaint from the Greek government that its Yugoslav neighbour was actively assisting communist rebels engaged in a civil war against the government by despatching an observation mission (UNSCOB) to report on cross-border movements (see chapter 7). The following year, the Security Council also began to be engaged in two of the world's most pressing crises, the Palestinian conflict and the struggle over Kashmir. This prompted Edward Luck (2006: 32) to describe 1948 as a 'pivotal' year for the Council. The UN despatched a mediator, Count Folke Bernadotte – a Swedish aristocrat who had played a central role in freeing Jews at the end of the Second World War – to the Middle East to facilitate an agreement between the Jews and Palestinians, but he was assassinated by what the Security Council labelled 'a criminal group of terrorists' (Resolution 57, 1948). Bernadotte was replaced by Ralph Bunche. After months of careful and skilful diplomacy, in early 1949 Bunche secured a ceasefire agreement that would be overseen by a UN Truce Supervision Organization (UNTSO) (Pelcovits 1993: 9–17). Bunche was awarded the first Nobel Peace Prize for his efforts (Luck 2006: 32; see Urquhart 1993: 139–200).

UNTSO is often cited as the organization's first peacekeeping operation (Goulding 1993: 452) and it is certainly its longest-lasting. While it has maintained a presence in the Middle East through all the years of turmoil, it has rarely been able to fulfil its mandate on account of variable levels of cooperation from the belligerents and its own limited capabilities. UNTSO was initially established to support a Truce Commission for Palestine, established by the Security Council to oversee a ceasefire (Higgins 1969: 16). The initial figure of around 572 observers deployed to monitor the ceasefire was reduced after the conclusion of an armistice agreement in 1949, which produced a more stable ceasefire (Ghali 1994a: 94). Since then, its size has fluctuated between thirty and a few hundred personnel. With its role limited to monitoring ceasefire agreements, UNTSO has proven unable to prevent the periodic escalation of hostilities in the region, but it has played a valuable role as a source of independent information and training ground for peacekeepers.

On 21 April 1948, the Council issued Resolution 47, which called for India and Pakistan to cease their hostilities in Kashmir and – in an echo of 'plebiscite peacekeeping' – permit a plebiscite to determine the wishes of the Kashmiris. The Council also authorized the creation of a mission (UNMOGIP) to observe the ceasefire and write periodic reports (Luck 2006: 32–3). In the space of a few months that year, and in the wake of the collapse of negotiations about a UN army, the Security Council had begun to carve out a role for itself in the promotion of international peace and security and to lay the foundations of peace operations.

These ad hoc missions began to be conceptualized into a coherent role for the UN through the idea of 'preventive diplomacy'. Most of the credit for this idea went to Secretary-General Dag Hammarskjöld, though at least one analyst argued that the UN's first Secretary-General, Trygve Lie (1946–52), had laid the groundwork (Elabray 1987: 170). This provided the UN with a new collective security role, with peace operations at its heart (Urquhart 1994: 175–85). Hammarskjöld first set out the concept of preventive diplomacy in his annual report to the General Assembly on 31 August 1960. This document described it as the 'main field of useful activity of the UN in its efforts to prevent conflicts or to solve conflicts'. By 'preventive diplomacy', the Secretary-General meant something more specific than simply the use of diplomacy for peacemaking between warring parties. Instead, he saw the UN's primary role as intervening in order to prevent the escalation of local conflicts into regional or global wars involving the superpowers (see chapter 6). This was spelt out most clearly in reference to the UN's mission in Congo (ONUC). Such peace operations were justified, he argued, 'by the wish of the international community to avoid [an] important area being split by bloc conflicts. It is a policy rendered possible by the fact that both blocs have an interest in avoiding such an extension of the area of conflict because of the threatening consequences, were the localization of the conflict to fail' (in Zacher 1970: 67–8). A few years earlier, Hammarskjöld had instructed his envoy to Lebanon that the operation was a 'classic case of preventive diplomacy' which aimed to 'keep the Cold War out of the Middle East' (Urquhart 1994: 265; Schechter 2005).

The terms of reference for what was widely regarded as the UN's first self-styled peace operation, UNEF I – deployed to the Sinai to help defuse the Suez Crisis of 1956 – contributed to the establishment of the core principles of consent, impartiality and minimum use of force (see chapter 7). However, the force did not set a formal precedent because it was widely perceived as responding to the extraordinary problems confronting the post-Suez Middle East. What is more, the relevant actors in that case had very different ideas about the proper purpose of the peace operation. The British and French saw it primarily as a tool that permitted their extrication from Suez while protecting their interests. The United States, in contrast, considered it a way of facilitating British and French withdrawal and securing the support of post-colonial leaders, while the Soviet Union and most of the world's new post-colonial states viewed it – and UN peace operations in general – as a vehicle for advancing decolonization. As a result, UNEF I's terms of reference reflected a political compromise more than an ideal framework for peace operations. In short, the terms of reference represented the most that Canadian diplomat Lester B. Pearson and Hammarskjöld calculated they could get away with without breaking the fragile consensus over UNEF I. The UN went on to conduct several more similar operations before the end of the Cold War (see table 3.3). But it also undertook limited peace enforcement action in the Congo (ONUC) and embarked on missions in the Congo and Dutch West New Guinea (West Irian) that had roles similar to those of 'assisting transitions' (see chapter 10) or 'wider peacekeeping' (see chapter 8) type operations.

Table 3.3 provides details of all the UN's peace operations between 1945 and 1987, when the Cold War era began to end. Perhaps the most striking thing to note is just how few missions the UN conducted during this period – fourteen in total. Another striking feature is that all of the missions, including the UN's war in Korea, were intimately connected with decolonization. UN peace operations during the Cold War were therefore a tool for managing one of the most significant structural shifts in world politics – the globalization of the sovereign state. Closer attention still reveals that almost half of all the UN operations deployed in this period were in the Middle East. This supports the view that peace operations were an important part of the UN's 'preventive diplomacy' role, seeking to prevent local conflicts escalating into a global imbroglio. In the Middle East case, both superpowers recognized the potential for escalation, but neither was prepared to wage war in order to defend their claims and allies in the region. This created an opening for consensus in the Security Council and helps explain the strong regional bias in the deployment of peace operations towards the Middle East. It is worth noting that, by contrast, the same period saw only one UN operation (ONUC) deployed to sub-Saharan Africa, and this too came in relation to a crisis that divided the superpowers. In the Congo case, the United States was keen to prevent the rise of socialism by supporting decolonization while

TABLE 3.3 UN peace operations (authorized, 1945–1987)

Mission	Dates	Purpose
UN Special Commission on the Balkans (UNSCOB)	1947–51	Investigate foreign interference in Greek civil war
UN Truce Supervision Organization (UNTSO)	1948–present	Monitor adherence to terms of General Armistice Agreement in Middle East
UN Military Observer Group in India and Pakistan (UNMOGIP)	1949–present	Monitor Indo-Pakistan ceasefire in Kashmir
UN Force in Korea	1950–3	Peace enforcement in defence of South Korea
UN Emergency Force I (UNEF I)	1956–67	Buffer between Israel and Egypt in the Sinai
UN Observation Group in Lebanon (UNOGIL)	1958	Monitor arms and troop movements in Lebanon
UN Operation in the Congo (ONUC)	1960–4	Restore order and assist Congolese government
UN Temporary Executive Authority (UNTEA)	1962–3	Administer West New Guinea before transfer to Indonesian sovereignty
UN Yemen Observation Mission (UNYOM)	1963–4	Monitor arms and troop movements into Yemen from Saudi Arabia
UN Force in Cyprus (UNFICYP)	1964–present	Maintain order before 1974 Turkish invasion; monitor buffer zone afterwards
UN India–Pakistan Observer Mission (UNIPOM)	1965–6	Monitor ceasefire after 1965 Indo-Pakistan War
Mission of the Representative of the Secretary-General in the Dominican Republic (DOMREP)	1965–6	Observe and report on breaches of the ceasefire in the Dominican Republic
UN Emergency Force II (UNEF II)	1974–9	Act as a buffer between Israel and Egypt in the Sinai
UN Disengagement Observer Force (UNDOF)	1974–present	Monitor the separation of Israeli and Syrian forces on the Golan Heights
UN Interim Force in Lebanon (UNIFIL)	1978–present	Buffer between Israel and Lebanon

opposing – and assisting in the assassination of – the left-leaning Congolese nationalist leader, Patrice Lumumba.

The UN's operation in the Congo (ONUC, 1960–4) was a larger, more complex, costly and multifaceted operation than anything the organization had attempted previously. Although largely successful in terms of accomplishing its mandate, it proved highly controversial, divided the Security Council and helped create a financial crisis for UN peace operations. At its height, almost 20,000 troops were deployed alongside a significant civilian component, and the mission was mandated to fulfil a number of different roles (Abi-Saab 1978; James 1994c). ONUC was mandated to maintain law and order during the Congo's turbulent decolonization after Belgian rule. However, the rapid disintegration of the security situation forced it away from Hammarskjöld's vision of preventive diplomacy (based on the same principles as UNEF I) and towards peace enforcement to help defend the Congo's territorial integrity (Dayal 1976).

The political fallout from ONUC had a profoundly negative effect on UN peace operations. The Soviet Union and France in particular complained that it had exceeded its original mandate and that, having authorized the mission, the Security Council had little control over its direction. In particular, the Soviets condemned the American role in the ousting and assassination of Lumumba and the installation of Mobutu – an American ally, head of the army and, it would later transpire, a corrupt tyrant – as president. They argued that, in supporting Mobutu, ONUC was acting as a proxy for the US, not as an agent of the Security Council. In addition, they complained about the operation's spiralling costs. In protest at both the direction and the cost of the mission, the Soviet Union and France withheld their peacekeeping dues. This caused an immediate funding crisis for UN operations which has never been fully overcome (see chapter 2). Moreover, these two permanent members (the Soviet Union in particular) adopted a much more sceptical approach to UN operations, seeing in them the danger of politicization that had warned the Soviets off the UN army in the 1940s. At French and Soviet insistence several reforms were made to the way that UN peace operations were constituted and managed. Most significantly, operations would be mandated for only six months at a time. This gave the Security Council the opportunity to review individual operations and permanent members the chance to veto the continuation of operations. Although adding to the complexity of managing peace operations, this was a positive development which ensured that UN operations were doing the bidding of the organization as a whole, prevented future politicization, and gave the Security Council a permanent role in overseeing the missions it authorized. Second, the financial crisis sparked by ONUC led to the removal of peace operations expenses from the general UN budget and the creation of a separate peacekeeping budget.

After ONUC, UN peace operations took something of a battering and entered two decades of relative decline. When the 1967 war in the Middle East forced the collapse of UNEF I, the UN and its then Secretary-General, U Thant, were pilloried in the American and British press for failing to prevent the conflict by acceding to Egypt's request to withdraw (Thakur 2006: 328). This was rather unfair, given UNEF's mandate and the Security Council's inability to reach a consensus on how to proceed, but it contributed to a general attitude of pessimism about the potential for peace operations to make a positive contribution to international peace and security (Urquhart 2007: 24). In the twenty-three years that followed ONUC, the UN took on only five new missions, four of which were continuations of previous UN engagements in the Middle East and Kashmir, and the fifth, UNFICYP in Cyprus, was aided by a unique set of circumstances that saw Britain, which had assumed responsibility for security on the island, keen to divest itself of those responsibilities and spread the burden.

Things got particularly bad in the 1970s and early 1980s. A worsening of Cold War tensions reduced the level of consensus in the Security Council. Combined with the enduring financial crisis, this encouraged further retreat from peace operations, with only one new mission (UNIFIL in Lebanon) despatched between 1974 and 1987. This was also a particularly divisive era in the wider UN membership, with the General Assembly increasingly used to push the agenda of the post-colonial world, much of which had organized itself into the Non-Aligned Movement.

In 1971, the Security Council appointed Kurt Waldheim as Secretary-General, undeterred by the fact that he had failed in his bid to be elected president of Austria and that he had served as an officer in the German army during the Second World War. To rub salt into the wound, the Soviet Union vetoed the alternative candidate, the American Max Jakobsen, on the grounds that the Arab world would never accept a Jewish Secretary-General. The General Assembly followed this up by declaring 'Zionism is racism' and calling for a 'New International Economic Order', moves which helped further alienate the United States and other Western governments. To make matters worse still, it later transpired that Waldheim had lied about his military career and had, in fact, been an SS officer and willing volunteer for the Nazis. By 1980, the UN had almost become an irrelevance in the West (Traub 2006: 19–21; Urquhart 2007: 25–6). There was therefore little support for expanding the scope of its peace operations. And, as it turned out, UNIFIL revealed many of the problems that had prompted states to move away from using UN peace operations as a tool of preventive diplomacy. Financial shortfalls and the lack of consent from belligerents persuaded many member states that peace operations could function effectively only if all the conditions set at the time of UNEF I were in place (see chapter 7). It is not surprising that there was a general retreat from peace operations, given the deep divisions that wracked the world along these two axes (USA vs. USSR; West vs. Non-Aligned Movement).

3.4 Non-UN peace operations during the Cold War

It is important, briefly, to recognize that, although many commentators defined peace operations as being synonymous with the UN, the world body was not the only actor engaged in this type of activity during the Cold War.

Indeed, one count suggests that between 1945 and 1987 there were over fifty peace operations conducted by non-UN actors, which are listed on this book's companion website. Undoubtedly, the main problem raised by these missions was that they brought into doubt which actors had the authority to mandate peace operations (Wilcox 1965). This issue arose over Palestine in 1948 (in relation to the Arab League), Hungary in 1956 (in relation to the Warsaw Pact) and the Dominican Republic in 1965 (in relation to the OAS). The upshot of these debates was that the precise nature of the relationship between the Security Council and regional organizations remained heavily contested into the post-Cold War era (see chapter 13). Interestingly, not until the end of the Cold War did non-UN actors seek, and receive, Security Council authorization or approval for their actions.

Table 3.4 provides some important examples of non-UN peace operations during the Cold War. Most were observation missions by third parties involved in brokering peace deals at the request of the belligerents. These include the International Commission for Supervision and Control (ICSC), which involved India, Poland and Canada (representatives of the NAM, communist bloc and Western bloc respectively) in the supervision of a variety of agreements relating to the wars in Indochina between 1954 and 1975 (see Thakur 1984); the deployment of Nigerian peacekeepers to Chad in 1979 to monitor a ceasefire between Chad and Libya; the Commonwealth force deployed in 1979–80 to assist in Rhodesia's transition into Zimbabwe; and the deployment between 1987 and 1990 of some 53,000 Indian troops to Sri Lanka to monitor a peace accord between the Sri Lankan government and LTTE ('Tamil Tigers'). The Indian deployment remains one of the largest peace operations undertaken by either the UN or other actors, surpassed only by the enforcement operations against Korea (1950s) and Iraq (1991) (see Rupesinghe 1989).

Amid the ad hoc deployment of peace operations by third parties, there were also discernible signs of the development of regionalism in relation to peace operations, especially in the Americas and Africa. Neither of these regions, it might be remembered, hosted many UN operations. Indeed, throughout the Cold War, only one UN mission (ONUC) was deployed in Africa and only one tiny mission (DOMREP) was deployed in the Americas. Although its involvement in the Dominican Republic in 1965 was controversial, the OAS developed a track record in deploying regional peace operations and monitors. Its role in this area began as early as 1948 with the despatch of Mexican military observers to monitor a peace accord between Costa Rica and Nicaragua. In the 1950s and 1960s, in addition to the Dominican Republic mission, the OAS oversaw peace agreements between Honduras and Nicaragua (1957), monitored the situation in Panama (1959, 1964), placed a naval quarantine on Cuba (1962), monitored the situation between Venezuela and Cuba (1963–4), and monitored a border dispute between Honduras and El Salvador (1969).

TABLE 3.4 Examples of non-UN peace operations (1948–1987)

Mission	Date	Agent	Purpose
International Mission for Supervision and Control – North and South Vietnam	1954–73	India, Canada, Poland	Monitor implementation of 1954 Geneva Accord
Joint Truce Force – Cyprus	1963–4	UK	Oversee ceasefire agreement between Greek and Turkish communities
Inter-American Peace Force – Dominican Republic	1965	OAS	Oversee ceasefire and elections
Inter-African Force – Zaire	1978–9	OAU	Support regime and oversee withdrawal of foreign forces
Commonwealth Monitoring Force – Rhodesia/Zimbabwe	1979–80	Commonwealth/ UK	Police agreement between government of Southern Rhodesia and the Patriotic Front
OAU Peacekeeping Force I and II – Chad	1980; 1981–2	OAU	Monitor peace between Chad and Libya and implementation of Libyan withdrawal
Multinational Force and Observers – Israel/Egypt	1981–2	US-led coalition of the willing	Oversee Israeli withdrawal from the Sinai
Multinational Force I and II – Israel/Syria/ Lebanon	1982–6	US-led coalition of willing	Interpositionary force at request of Lebanese government
Indian Peacekeeping Forces – Sri Lanka	1987–90	India	Monitor Sri Lankan peace accord

The development of regional peace operations in Africa was more chaotic, involving a wider range of actors and a number of different organizations, including the British-led Commonwealth. Nonetheless, the OAU was actively involved from the start, mainly providing a legitimizing framework for third-party engagement rather than interceding itself. In 1963, Mali and Ethiopia despatched military observers to monitor the Bamako Communiqué, negotiated under the auspices of the OAU between Algeria and Morocco. A year later, Sudan interceded in a conflict between Ethiopia and Somalia under its auspices. In 1974, the OAU created a mediation commission of inquiry to negotiate and monitor an agreement between Mali and Burkina Faso. It was also involved in the despatch of several relatively large peace operations. In 1978–9 it deployed an 'Inter-African Force' of 2,645 troops to assist the government in Zaire and oversee the withdrawal of Belgian and French forces, and in 1981–2 it deployed 2,600 troops to oversee the Lagos Accord in Chad.

Although some of these operations, most notably the LAS activities in the Middle East, were obviously self-serving (see Collelo 1989), others made an important contribution to international peace and security and filled voids where, for one reason or another, the UN was inactive. However, they remained largely outside the UN framework and thus developed in a piecemeal fashion. One of the principal changes in peace operations after the Cold War was the growing recognition of the contribution made by regional arrangements and their increasing incorporation into the UN framework, either through the joint operations or through the authorization or formal recognition of the Security Council (see chapter 13).

3.5 Conclusion

The early history of peace operations is intimately connected to three ideas that have developed along with the society of states. The first is the idea that the great powers have a special responsibility to maintain international peace and security. From the Roman Empire to the Concert of Europe and the UN Security Council, this idea is based on the notion that the great powers have a vested interest in preserving the international order in which they occupy a privileged position. The Concert of Europe, League of Nations and UN are each predicated on what Gerry Simpson (2004) has labelled 'legalized hierarchy'. This is where international society as a whole – including its smaller members – confers upon the great powers special rights and responsibilities and enshrines them in law. Since 1945 this has been done via the UN Charter.

International organization depends on each of the world's most powerful states having a vested interest in preserving the status quo or managing orderly reform. The Concert of Europe and the League of Nations failed at least partly because many powerful states had little intention of supporting collective goals, because they believed the prevailing international order to be fundamentally unjust. The UN's architects attempted to address this problem by creating permanent members of the Security Council with veto powers. While critics have suggested that the veto arbitrarily privileges the five states that were victorious in the Second World War and prevented the UN from operating effectively during the Cold War, the system has important merits. As Roberts and Kingsbury point out, the veto system is superior to the League's decision-making procedures in several ways: it helped to get and keep the great powers within the UN framework; it may have saved the UN both from damaging conflicts with the great powers and from entangling itself in impossible and divisive operations; it has encouraged the habit of consultation between the permanent five states; and it reduces the risk of major discrepancies between power politics and the law of the UN Charter (2000: 41).

The second principal idea tied to the evolution of peace operations was collective security. Specifically, peace operations were established on the idea that wars between and within states were the concern of international society as a whole and could be ameliorated by collective action. The League of Nations and the UN both developed peace operations because they were unable to pursue the form of collective security envisaged by the authors of the Covenant and Charter especially. Moreover, with the decline in the number of interstate wars and the relative increase of intrastate conflicts after 1945, the traditional model of collective security became less and less appropriate for addressing challenges to international peace and security.

Third, the history of international organization and the evolution of early peace operations were both influenced by the growing significance accorded to humanitarian concerns by international society. Nineteenth-century inter-ventions in Greece, Syria and Cuba were inspired by a combination of national self-interest and concerns about the mistreatment of Christian populations. Similarly, much of the League's work in this area (such as plebiscite supervi-sion) displayed a concern for the promotion of liberal democracy, even if that sometimes worked against the short-term interests of the great powers. Finally, it is often overlooked that some of the UN's earliest operations (e.g. ONUC and UNFICYP) were tasked with protecting and promoting human rights (see Månsson 2005). As the next two chapters demonstrate, this was to become a central challenge facing peacekeepers during the 1990s and beyond.

CHAPTER FOUR

Peace Operations during the 1990s

As the Cold War came to an end between 1988 and 1993, peace operations underwent a triple transformation. First, there was a *quantitative transformation*. During this period, the UN conducted more peace operations than it had undertaken in its previous forty years combined. Moreover, traditional peace-keeping contributors were augmented by a flood of new countries, including great powers such as the US, France and the UK, prepared to deploy their troops as UN peacekeepers (see Findlay 1996). Second, there was a *normative transformation* catalysed by a growing belief among some member states that the remit for peace operations should be broadened to take in the promotion of a post-Westphalian conception of stable peace. Finally – and as a result of the normative transformation – there was a *qualitative transformation*. The UN was asked to carry out complex missions reminiscent of ONUC in the 1960s but on a far more regular basis. In places such as Cambodia, Bosnia and Somalia, the UN launched operations that were qualitatively different from earlier missions, marrying peacekeeping with the delivery of humanitarian aid, state-building programmes, local peacemaking and elements of peace enforcement. These missions were also much larger and more expensive than anything the UN had attempted before, with the important exception of ONUC.

By 1995, however, the catastrophes in Angola, Somalia, Bosnia and Rwanda had prompted many states to re-evaluate the value of peace operations and the nature of their contribution to them. It also prompted some senior UN officials to question whether the organization should go 'back to basics' and focus only on conducting operations with the consent of the host parties (Tharoor 1995). The number of UN peacekeepers deployed around the world fell dramatically as member states expressed a preference for working through regional organizations and alliances, such as ECOWAS and NATO, and the Security Council became reluctant to create new missions. This ushered in a period of hesitant introspection at the UN, during which the organization produced reports detailing its failings in Rwanda and Bosnia. These reports identified serious problems with the way in which the UN mandated, orga-nized and conducted its peace operations and exposed gaps between the tasks peacekeepers were expected to fulfil in the post-Cold War era and the concep-tual and material resources made available to them. At the UN's Millennium Summit in 2000, Kofi Annan called for a special panel of experts – led by the former Algerian foreign minister Lakhdar Brahimi – to consider the future direction of UN peace operations.

The post-Cold War era was therefore a seminal time for the development of peace operations. This chapter explores this period in four sections. The first two sections examine the causes and the nature of the triple transformation of peace operations, while the third focuses briefly on some of the high-profile missions in the first half of the 1990s, charts the failure of operations in Somalia, Angola, Bosnia and Rwanda, and describes the subsequent decline of UN peace operations as a popular tool for managing violent conflict. The final part of the chapter looks at what lessons were learned from these failures, concentrating on the UN's internal reports on the 1994 Rwandan genócide and 1995 massacre in the Bosnian 'safe area' of Srebrenica.

4.1 The transformation of peace operations

This section examines different explanations for the transformation of peace operations between 1988 and 1993. Put simply, there was no single overarching cause of the transformation but rather a mixture of factors that increased global demand for peace operations and the willingness of international society to supply the missions and troops requested.

On the demand side, it was commonly argued that the ending of the Cold War created a 'new world disorder' in which ethnic rivalries and 'roguish' behaviour previously held in check by the superpowers exploded into civil war (e.g. Kaplan 1994). This, in turn, created heightened demand for the deployment of peacekeepers in these newly 'volatile regions'. The main problem with this account is that, although the number of armed conflicts peaked in the immediate aftermath of the Cold War in 1992, after this high-point the number of conflicts declined significantly (see figure I.1, p. 2). In the medium term, therefore, the end of the Cold War seems to have significantly reduced rather than increased the number of armed conflicts around the world.

An alternative explanation emphasized that many of the conflicts that erupted during this period were of a particular type – what some analysts described as 'new wars' (see chapter 1). In this account the transformation of peace operations represented a principled response to this new barbarism. The central problem with this view is that the 'new barbarism' associated with the end of the Cold War was not new at all. Protracted Cold War conflicts in Afghanistan, Cambodia, Angola and Central America bore all the hallmarks of barbarism associated with these 'new wars' – deliberate attacks on civilians, warlordism and illegal economic activities (see Slim 2008).

A better place to start is by asking where the requests for peace operations came from. All bar one of the missions created between 1988 and 1993 (UNIIMOG) were 'brokered requests for UN assistance' (Durch 1993a: 17). In other words, they were formally requested by peace agreements or ceasefires brokered by third parties and endorsed by the parties to the conflict. In most cases, the UN played the role of broker, but there were a number of exceptions: UNTAG was the product of a US-led mediation effort through a Contact Group of Western governments and UNAVEM II the product of an initiative spearheaded by Portugal, the Soviet Union and the US (ibid.: 17, 20–2). Of these, the majority (thirteen of the twenty missions authorized between 1988 and 1993) of peace processes addressed conflicts that preceded 1988 and all of those had some connection to Cold War politics. In other words, this period witnessed the conclusion of many civil wars that had been provoked and sustained by the Cold War's ideological struggle. As the superpowers withdrew patronage with the lessening of Cold War hostilities, so it became harder for local clients to maintain their war fighting effort. This created powerful incentives for belligerents to begin the search for a negotiated settlement, and the deployment of peace operations was widely understood to be an important part of that process. The view that peace operations were critical to peace processes and implementing ceasefires was encouraged by the relative success of the smaller operations launched in 1988 and 1989 (see below). Gradually, peace operations became the tool of choice for conflict management applied to new conflicts as well as old.

A rise in demand alone, however, cannot explain the transformation of peace operations. What explains the greater willingness of governments to contribute to and fund more complex peace operations, especially in strategically unimportant parts of the world? Of course, the answer is different for every troop-contributing country, but there are at least three general factors that played a role. First, the disintegration of the Soviet bloc created a much more permissive Security Council, and for the first time powerful states began to envisage its playing a greater role in policing and peace enforcement. Between 1990 and 2002, only twelve draft resolutions were vetoed – by far the lowest rate of vetoing since the establishment of the UN. Nine of these vetoes were cast by the US, six of which were in response to draft resolutions that were critical of Israel. In comparison, between 1945 and 1990, 238 vetoes were cast, an average of forty-three per decade. Cooperation between East and West played a major role in resolving the Central American wars and conflicts in Afghanistan, Namibia, Angola and Mozambique. Moreover, from the late 1980s, China began to adopt a more positive stance on peace operations, increasingly accepting that the UN Security Council had a legitimate role to play in the resolution of conflict and the amelioration of human suffering (Fravel 1996).

Second, three facets of contemporary globalization – the acceleration of democratization, the spread of human rights and the so-called CNN effect (see Robinson 2002) – led more governments to see peace operations as 'politically desirable' (Jakobsen 2002: 274). Globalization was accompanied by the spread of mass communication technology, which permitted the almost instantaneous reporting of humanitarian catastrophes. Combined with the putative triumph of liberalism over communism and the apparent success of peace operations in 1988–9 and the first Gulf War (1990–1), this created expectations among publics in the West and elsewhere that their governments would become engaged in resolving violent conflicts and humanitarian crises overseas. As the former UN Secretary-General Pérez de Cuéllar suggested in 1991, 'we are clearly witnessing what is probably an irresistible shift in public attitudes towards the belief that the defense of the oppressed in the name of morality should prevail over frontiers and legal documents' (in Scheffer 1992: 4). There is plenty of evidence to suggest that participation in peace operations began to look attractive to governments. For example, the UK and France used their contribution to peace operations as justification for their seats on the Security Council (Rifkind 1993: 4; Treacher 2003: 65). The French foreign minister Roland Dumas even suggested that France would place 1,000 troops under permanent UN command. Similarly, states from the former Eastern bloc which aspired to membership of the EC/EU and NATO participated in peace operations to bolster their claim. States seeking to become permanent members of the Security Council (Brazil, South Africa, India, Germany, Indonesia and Nigeria) also committed troops to peace operations partly to support their case (Findlay 1996: 8). Some middle powers such as Canada, Australia and New Zealand saw themselves as 'good international citizens' (Linklater 1992; Evans 1993) and participated in peace operations to help spread the now universal values of democracy and human rights. Rising demand also created more opportunities for some of the world's poorest states to take part in peace operations. This helped them enhance their international reputations and secure small amounts of foreign currency via the system of reimbursements from the UN (Scobell 1994: 190; Berman and Sams 2000: 253). Moreover, the triumph of liberalism encouraged many in the West to believe that peace operations could be used to stop governments mistreating their people, resolve civil wars and spread democracy (Stedman 2001: 3). These three facets of globalization therefore brought the great (Western) powers, internationalist-minded middle powers, and a range of other states together in articulating a new role for peace operations and the UN.

Finally, with the Cold War coming to a close and with no new major new strategic challenges on the horizon, governments had more military capacity to commit to peace operations, and some militaries themselves had an interest in taking on new roles in order to justify their budgets and guard against excessive cuts as part of the 'peace dividend' (see Freedman 1998: 34–5; Jakobsen 2002: 273). This hard material reality created the capacity for military forces to be redirected away from national security towards the pursuit of internationalist goals through peace operations.

There were thus several reasons for the transformation of peace operations, involving both increased demand and the greater willingness and capacity of governments to supply peacekeepers. They are summarized in table 4.1.

TABLE 4.1 Explaining the triple transformation

Demand	Supply
1 End to civil wars brokered by third parties	1 More cooperative Security Council
2 Request for peace operations to monitor and implement peace accords and ceasefires	2 Globalization: media, democratization, human rights create government interest
3 Recognition that peace operations can play an effective role (after 1988–9)	3 Peace dividend: end of Cold War frees military capacity

4.2 The nature of the transformation

It is important to begin by recognizing the gradual nature of the *quantitative* transformation of peace operations. Although rapid by historical standards, the transformation occurred over a number of years and in a relatively ad hoc fashion whereby early successes translated into heightened demand for more – and more complex – UN peace operations. What is more, the *normative* and *qualitative* transformations came after the initial *quantitative* expansion of peace operations. Between 1988 and 1993, the UN created twenty new peace operations (table 4.2). Although the sheer number of new missions represented a transformation in its own right, it did not represent a straightforward, chronological transition between different generations of peacekeeping (Tharoor 1996; cf. Goulding 1993; James 1994b). Instead, the period experienced first a re-engagement and then a gradual expansion of peace operations conducted along similar lines to those during the Cold War and only then the emergence of a whole new type of operation in Somalia and Bosnia. Significantly, even these two missions started life as relatively traditional types of operation but developed gradually – and according to requirements – into something wholly different to what had come before (see chapters 8 and 9).

The first nine of these new operations, mandated between 1988 and 1991, represented more of a re-engagement with Cold War style peacekeeping than a radical transformation. The first five, all authorized during 1988 and 1989, involved monitoring the withdrawal of foreign forces (UNGOMAP, UNAVEM I), monitoring a ceasefire (UNIIMOG), and supervising and overseeing a peace agreement (UNTAG, ONUCA). And, with the exception of UNAVEM I in Angola, which was superseded by UNAVEM II, all five missions were concluded by 1991. These operations were therefore very similar in type to those of the past, but they showed signs of improvisation and change. For example, the missions in Namibia and Central America contained large civilian components. ONUCA also broke new ground by monitoring elections (early signs of the normative transformation) and disarming and demobilizing former rebels (Weiss et al. 1994: 61).

TABLE 4.2 Peace operations established 1988–1993

Mission	Location (dates)	Description
UNGOMAP	Afghanistan and Pakistan (1988–90)	Monitor Soviet withdrawal from Afghanistan
UNIIMOG	Iran–Iraq (1988–91)	Monitor ceasefire
UNAVEM I	Angola (1988–91)	Monitor Cuban withdrawal
UNTAG	Namibia (1989–90)	Supervise transition in Namibia
ONUCA	Honduras, Nicaragua and Guatemala (1989–91)	Monitor compliance with peace agreement
UNAVEM II	Angola (1991–5)	Monitor ceasefire and supervise elections
UNIKOM	Iraq–Kuwait (1991–2003)	Monitor buffer zone
MINURSO	Western Sahara (1991–present)	Organize referendum on independence from Morocco
ONUSAL	El Salvador (1991–5)	Monitor ceasefire, elections, demobilization and human rights
UNAMIC	Cambodia (1991–2)	Plan subsequent UN mission
UNTAC	Cambodia (1992–3)	Monitor ceasefire, organize elections, supervise government, demobilization, refugee return
ONUMOZ	Mozambique (1992–4)	Help implement peace agreement
UNOSOM I	Somalia (1992–3)	Monitor ceasefire, assist humanitarian relief
UNPROFOR	Croatia, Bosnia-Hercegovina and Macedonia (1992–9)	Monitor and secure ceasefires, support humanitarian relief, protect 'safe areas' (1993–5), protect UN personnel
UNOSOM II	Somalia (1993–5)	Establish a secure environment for humanitarian assistance
UNMIH	Haiti (1993–6)	Help implement peace agreement
UNOMIL	Liberia (1993–7)	Support ECOWAS and government implement peace agreement
UNOMUR	Rwanda and Uganda (1993–4)	Monitor Rwanda–Uganda border
UNAMIR	Rwanda (1993–6)	Help implement peace agreement
UNOMIG	Georgia (1993–present)	Verify ceasefire agreement

All five of these missions were also broadly successful. Deploying a force of fifty military observers, drawn from traditional contributors to UN peace operations (Scandinavia, Ireland, Fiji – but also Poland), UNGOMAP successfully verified the withdrawal of Soviet forces from Afghanistan and faced few obstacles, though commentators agree that success was due more to Soviet intentions to fulfil the Geneva Accords more than anything UNGOMAP did (see Birgisson 1993). Although UN Secretary-General Kurt Waldheim had begun attempts to broker peace between Iran and Iraq in 1980, it was not until 1988 – after the two sides had fought themselves to a standstill – that a peace deal was signed. As part of the deal, the UN was invited to deploy an observation mission along the border. With the consent of the belligerents (and more cooperation from Iraq than from Iran), UNIIMOG's 400 observers established and monitored ceasefire lines and conducted confidence-building activities. These activities contributed to cementing what was originally a fragile peace between Iraq and Iran (see Urquhart and Sick 1987). The UN's first attempt to build peace in Angola, UNAVEM I, was a modest contribution to a wider Angolan-led peace effort. Its role was limited to verifying the withdrawal of Cuban fighters from Angola. Though 'not particularly significant' (Fortna 1993a: 385) for Angola itself, assurances of Cuban withdrawal helped mediators build trust in Namibia and sowed the seeds for a more active UN role, embodied in UNAVEM II. This operation had a wider mandate to monitor a ceasefire, with an option for assisting in the organization of national elections (Fortna 1993b).

If UNGOMAP and UNIIMOG helped reaffirm the utility of relatively small UN observation missions in managing the resolution of conflicts between states, the success of the missions in Namibia (UNTAG) and Central America (ONUCA) suggested that, when conducted with the consent of belligerents, UN peace operations could also play an important role in managing the resolution of civil wars. UNTAG stood out as the UN's largest and most ambitious mission since ONUC in the 1960s. Despite several hiccups – including a miscommunicated disarmament process that nearly derailed the whole operation (see Goulding 2002: 139–75) – the operation in Namibia succeeded in overseeing the withdrawal of South Africa and Namibia's transition to independent statehood (see chapter 10). One commentator labelled it 'the first major success' for contemporary UN peace operations (Howard 2008: 52). To this day, Namibia remains one of Africa's most stable states.

The ONUCA mission in Central America had two primary goals – to stop the cross-border supply of arms and fighters into Nicaragua and to build confidence between the government of Nicaragua and the Contra rebels. As with earlier missions, such as UNSCOB, ONUCA proved incapable of detecting and interdicting weapons movement, but it did contribute to creating an environment that made such movements more difficult and therefore less frequent. In 1990, ONUCA's mandate was expanded to include disarming the rebels and overseeing elections. Although some rebels persisted, by the time the mandate expired they numbered fewer than 1,000 and were eventually brought into a negotiated peace process by the Nicaraguan government (Smith and Durch 1993).

Paying attention to these missions suggests that the end of the Cold War did not inspire a sudden and dramatic about-turn in international perceptions of the role of peace operations in world politics. In fact the UN took on more missions that were similar in type to the majority of missions conducted during the Cold War. As they delivered on their initial aims, some of these missions (e.g. ONUCA, UNAVEM) took on new tasks that involved a deeper engagement with internal conflict. In the case of Namibia, a large and complex operation succeeded in accomplishing its mandate within a relatively short timeframe (see chapter 10). This seemed to suggest that UN peace operations were capable of building peace and transforming war-torn societies in a wider range of circumstances than had hitherto (since ONUC) been thought possible.

Partly as a result of these early successes, at the beginning of the 1990s UN peace operations became international society's conflict management tool of choice, and a new raft of large and complex operations were deployed. Most important among these missions were those in Cambodia, Somalia and Bosnia – all of which are discussed in greater detail in part III of this book. The first of these new types of mission, UNTAC, was deployed to manage the transition from war to peace in Cambodia (see Evans 1993: 107–8; chapter 10). The second, UNOSOM I, was first used to monitor a ceasefire in Somalia and assist in the delivery of humanitarian assistance, and the third, UNPROFOR, was initially sent to Croatia and Bosnia to supervise a ceasefire there. In both Somalia and Bosnia, conditions on the ground changed rapidly, and the missions were expanded and given new tasks without necessarily being granted the requisite material resources or doctrinal guidance. Meanwhile, the UN continued to deploy smaller traditional-style missions in Haiti (UNMIH), Liberia (UNOMIL), Rwanda/Uganda (UNOMUR) and Georgia (UNOMIG).

Another important element of this quantitative transformation of peace operations was a growth in the number of states prepared to contribute to UN operations, including many Western states. Before 1992, the US, France and the UK (with the exception of UNFICYP in Cyprus) had not contributed many troops to UN peace operations. Nor, as we noted in chapter 3, was it customary for the great powers to deploy troops, since they were widely seen as being unable to act impartially because of their global interests. However, all three states became actively involved in the peace missions in Cambodia, Bosnia, Somalia and Latin America. This accompanied a general broadening of participation in peace operations, with forty-one states taking part for the first time between 1988 and 1993 (Findlay 1996: 3). Another twenty-one states became involved in non-UN peace operations during this time, most as part of either the US-led multinational force in Haiti (1994) or OSCE and CIS missions in the former Soviet Union (ibid.: 6).

The expansion of peace operations and their seeming effectiveness in helping states and societies to make the transition from war to stable peace encouraged a gradual shift in the *normative* expectations about what peacekeepers ought to do and a *qualitative* change in the tasks they were given. The ending of the Cold War lent credence to the post-Westphalian idea that the spread of liberal democracy constituted the best path to global stable peace (e.g. Fukuyama 1989; Held 1998: 11). Indeed, in 1996 Boutros-Ghali recognized an 'emerging consensus' on the value of liberal democracy (1996: § 15). With increasing frequency, peace operations were given the task of overseeing elections as part of their mandate, helping to support a rapid move towards democracy that saw the proportion of states holding elections increase from 46 to 60 per cent (Paris 2003: 446).

This changing normative environment was given an institutional voice by Boutros-Ghali in 1992. In his first two months of office, the new Secretary-General established the Department for Peacekeeping Operations (DPKO) and appointed Kofi Annan as its head (Goulding 2002: 31). He followed this up in June 1992 with the release of his important report *An Agenda for Peace*. On 31 January 1992, the Security Council had met for the first time at the level of heads of state and instructed the Secretary-General to prepare 'analysis and recommendations' on strengthening the UN for preventive diplomacy, peace-making and peacekeeping. Importantly, the resulting report reflected the commonly held view at the time that, while peace operations had to be adapted to meet the new demand for more complex operations (see box 4.1), the basic concepts and principles of peacekeeping remained sound. The Secretary-General confidently noted that peace operations had 'brought a degree of stability to areas of tension around the world' and that 'the established principles and practices of peace-keeping have responded flexibly to new demands of recent times, and the basic conditions of success remain unchanged' (Boutros-Ghali 1992: §§ 46 and 50). The increasing tendency for operations to be fielded to help implement political settlements presented a range of new challenges for the UN, particularly in relation to providing adequate resources for these new missions. Thus, Boutros-Ghali called for the creation of stand-by arrangements whereby member states would exchange notes with the UN identifying the kind and number of personnel they were prepared to contribute to UN operations (ibid.: § 51); the recruitment of more

---

Box 4.1 *An Agenda for Peace* **on the nature of peacekeeping**

§ 50: The nature of peace-keeping operations has evolved rapidly in recent years. The established principles and practices of peace-keeping have responded flexibly to new demands of recent years, and the basic conditions for success remain unchanged: a clear and practicable mandate; the continuing support of the Security Council; the readiness of the member states contribute the military and civilian personnel, including specialists, required; effective United Nations command at Headquarters and in the field; and adequate financial and logistic support. As the international climate has changed and peace-keeping operations are increasingly fielded to help implement settlements that have been negotiated by peace-makers, a new array of demands and problems has emerged regarding logistics, equipment, personnel and finance, all of which could be corrected if Member States so wished and were ready to make the necessary resources available.

> ### Box 4.2 *An Agenda for Peace* and the new world order
>
> We were all expectant. It was thrilling and we saw possibilities of doing...what the organization was expected to do [in 1945]. So we were all excited. (Kofi Annan, reflecting on the early 1990s, in Barnett 2002: 28)
>
> Now we can see a new world coming into view. A world in which there is the very real prospect of a new world order. In the words of Winston Churchill, a 'world order' in which 'the principles of justice and fair play...protect the weak against the strong'. A world where the United Nations, freed from cold war stalemate, is poised to fulfil the historic vision of its founders. A world in which freedom and respect for human rights find a home among all nations. (President George H.W. Bush 1991)

civilian personnel, especially police; the need for additional training; the creation of a pre-positioned stock of supplies to permit rapid deployment and avoid equipment shortfalls; and the provision of free-of-cost heavy lift capability (ibid.: § 53–4). Recognizing that, in the complex operating environment created by the end of the Cold War, UN operations might have to go beyond peacekeeping and become involved in peace enforcement, Boutros-Ghali called for the creation of 'peace enforcement units' – a variation on the UNEPS proposal (see chapter 1). These units would be kept entirely separate from peacekeeping units. Drawn from member states and comprising troops who volunteer for UN peace enforcement roles, the units would be specially trained, placed on call for use in operations by the Security Council and more heavily armed than peacekeepers (ibid.: § 44).

Although it was an optimistic document, *An Agenda for Peace* issued a thinly veiled warning to member states that it was imperative that they back up their new mandates for larger and more complex peace operations with the requisite resources. In relation to financing, the Secretary-General noted that a 'chasm has developed between the tasks entrusted to this Organization and the financial means provided to it' (1992: § 60). Similarly, the report's conclusion noted that 'the endeavours of the United Nations will require the fullest engagement of all its Members, large and small, if the present renewed opportunity is to be seized' (ibid.: § 80).

The idea that UN peace operations could play a significant and constructive role was warmly received by political leaders and UN officials (see box 4.2). Although some of Boutros-Ghali's proposals – such as the idea of a tax on arms sales and international travel to support UN military operations – were greeted with scepticism (see Meisler 1995: 180; Cockayne and Malone 2007: 80), the US administration initially indicated its intention to help implement some of them. Colin Powell, chairman of the Joint Chiefs of Staff, described peacekeepers as 'warriors of freedom', and President George H. W. Bush offered to allow the UN to train peacekeepers at Fort Dix in New Jersey (Traub 2006: 36).

The *normative* transformation and increased participation of Western great powers in peace operations helped shape ideas about the sorts of activities that peacekeepers should undertake. As we noted earlier, additional tasks were grafted onto ongoing peace operations in an ad hoc fashion without much in the way of strategic thinking about their overall function or doctrinal thinking about what was required to accomplish these goals. In 1993, the UK's House of Commons Foreign Affairs Select Committee issued a report on the expansion of UN peace operations, in which it identified the emergence of eight specific tasks for peacekeepers based on the experience in Angola, Namibia, Central America, Mozambique and elsewhere (see box 4.3). For all its merits, *An Agenda for Peace* barely touched on the activities identified by the British.

In summary, the transformation of peace operations at the end of the Cold War was gradual and ad hoc. It began with a re-engagement with small-scale traditional monitoring missions. When these proved effective tools for managing the transition for war to peace, the Security Council began adding new tasks and expanding the remit given to peace operations. Although this was recognized in *An Agenda for Peace*, the Secretary-General did not spell out ways of reforming the UN to meet the challenge of managing these more complex operations in a better way. However, Boutros-Ghali did sound a warning: that giving the UN more tasks without the material or doctrinal resources needed to fulfil them was a recipe for disaster. Just how prescient that prediction was would be made clear before the end of 1994.

Box 4.3 Peacekeeping tasks (1993)

Military: monitoring ceasefires, cantonment and demobilization of troops, location and destruction of weapons, de-mining, reform and retraining of armed forces, protecting borders, investigating claims of the presence of foreign forces, providing security for elections and helping to rebuild infrastructure

Police: visiting police stations, monitoring police activities, investigating alleged human rights violations by national police forces, training new police forces, enforcing arrests of suspected criminals and protecting the electoral process

Human rights: monitoring human rights, conducting human rights education programmes and investigating human rights violations

Information: explaining the peace settlement, reasons for UN deployment, and opportunities for the future of the country

Elections: observation and verification, through supervision and control of nationally conducted elections, conduct of elections by UN itself

Rehabilitation: short-term and long-term development projects

Repatriation: return and resettlement of refugees

Administration: supervising or controlling the administration of states, control foreign affairs, national defence, public security, finance and information

(Paraphrased from House of Commons 1993: § 35)

4.3 Failures and retreat

The world's new-found faith in the UN's ability to resolve violent conflict and alleviate humanitarian distress by using peace operations was short-lived. Faced with the fact that the traditional approach to peace operations (see chapters 3 and 7) and the resources made available by member states were insufficient to accomplish the increasingly ambitious mandates being handed down by the Security Council in environments where peace and ceasefire agreements were often precarious, those responsible for managing peace operations were repeatedly confronted with an awful dilemma: whether to soldier on, making do with the limited resources, authority and political support offered by international society, or advocate withdrawal. This is precisely how Boutros-Ghali (1994: § 45) described the dilemma facing UNPROFOR in 1993: 'the choice in Croatia is between continuing a mission that is clearly unable to fulfil its original mandate in full or withdrawing and risking a renewed war that would probably result in appeals for UNPROFOR to return to restore peace. Given such a choice, soldiering on in hope seems preferable to withdrawing in abdication.'

Although the UN received much of the blame for what happened in Angola, Somalia, Bosnia and Rwanda – some of it rightly – it is important to note the crucial roles played by its member states. It was member states, not the UN secretariat, that crafted mandates and determined resources, and the mandates for these four operations were not crafted before warnings had been aired in the Council (see Roberts, Anna 2003). What is more, the bungled operation in Mogadishu in October 1993 that marked the beginning of the demise of UNOSOM II was conducted by US soldiers (not UN peacekeepers); the DPKO had warned the Security Council that without adequate resources the so-called safe areas in Bosnia would be vulnerable to attack; and the decision to stand aside during Rwanda's genocide in 1994 was taken against the advice of the UN's force commander on the ground. These missions are discussed in more detail in chapters 8 and 9, but it is worth providing a brief outline here to provide some context for understanding the retreat from UN peace operations in the second half of the 1990s.

The first signs that the UN's record of relative success was about to come to an end came in Angola in 1992. Following UNAVEM I's success in overseeing the withdrawal of Cuban forces, in May 1991 the Security Council established UNAVEM II to oversee the demobilization of ex-combatants and monitor national elections. To accomplish this task, the mission was afforded 350 military observers and 400 civilian election observers (see Anstee 1996; Howard 2008: 37). Earlier missions of this size, such as UNGOMAP, UNAVEM I, UNIIMOG and ONUCA, had succeeded primarily because the belligerents were themselves deeply committed to the peace process. This was not the case in Angola, and UNAVEM II lacked the capacity to operate without high levels of cooperation. Although it succeeded in creating an efficient monitoring and verification system (Fortna 1993b: 402), UNITA rebels and the Angolan govern-ment used the lull in fighting to regroup and rearm rather than disarm and demobilize. When UNITA's leader, Jonas Savimbi, lost national elections in September 1992 by a clear margin, he declared them fraudulent. Fighting broke out the following month, most likely initiated by the government (Lodico 1996: 121). Having failed to disarm the belligerents prior to the elec-tion and unable to influence events afterwards, UNAVEM II was forced to stand aside as the fighting claimed the lives of up to 300,000 people. In what was the most intense fighting of the decades-long civil war, Boutros-Ghali

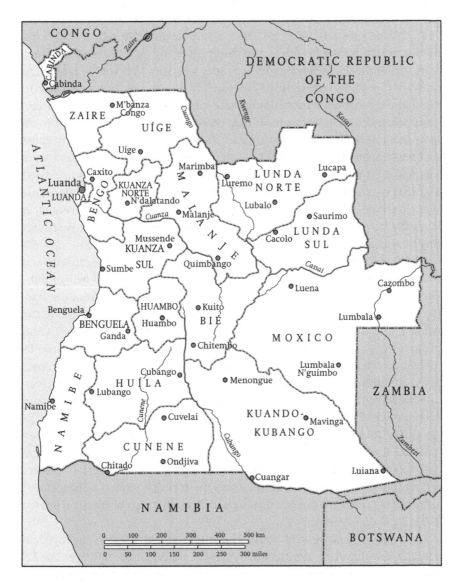

Map 4.1 *Angola*

(1993: 5) reported in September 1993 that a thousand people were being killed each day. Diplomats from the US, Portugal and Russia attempted to broker new agreements, while UNAVEM II soldiered on amid the violence. In early 1995, the parties reached a new ceasefire agreement, and UNAVEM II was replaced with a much larger mission – UNAVEM III.

UNAVEM III was given a broad and ambitious mandate, including monitoring the ceasefire and verifying the withdrawal of combatants, cantoning, disarming and demobilizing combatants, collecting UNITA arms, verifying the movement of government troops, establishing a new national army, clearing mines, coordinating humanitarian activity and overseeing the presidential election. To accomplish this it was provided with 7,000 troops and around 750 civilians (Howard 2008: 39). Once again Savimbi refused to cooperate, first by not cantoning his forces and then by holding back his specialist force from cantonment and refusing to surrender weapons. UNAVEM III lacked the military capability to disarm UNITA forcibly and the civilian capability to assist the government in building state capacity in UNITA-held territory. Thus, when UNAVEM III was wound up on schedule in 1997, it had not come close to completing its mandated tasks. There were, it should be said, some successes. Around 70,000 UNITA soldiers were disarmed and 11,000 were integrated into the national army, humanitarian coordination was improved and shaky coalition government was established (ibid.: 39–40). In the same year, however, UNITA demonstrated its military capacity by intervening in Zaire/DRC in support of Mobutu Sese Seko (Jett 1999: 167) and a year later Angola was plunged back into civil war.

UNAVEM II was the first of the UN's 1990s missions to lack the capacity and mandate to hold a peace together in the face of resistance from belligerents. The mission was unprepared to prevent post-election violence from descending into all-out civil war. The loss of life was probably higher than that of the whole Bosnian war, and its successor UNAVEM III failed to disarm UNITA and prevent the war reigniting in 1998. The failure of UNAVEM II comprised elements typical of later disasters in Somalia, Bosnia and Rwanda: peacekeepers given ambitious tasks without the mandate, resources or political will necessary to fulfil them and sent into an environment where the consent and cooperation of belligerents was shaky at best. Given all this, it is perhaps surprising that the outbreak of violence in 1992–3 did not produce an international outcry and that Angola is not typically listed as one of the UN's 'great peacekeeping failures' of the 1990s. This was because UNAVEM II did not attract international media attention and the Security Council's engagement with Angola during this period was characterized by ambivalence (Howard 2008: 37; Lodico 1996: 123).

The same cannot be said about the international mission deployed to Somalia less than two months after Angola's descent into violence. The US experience in Somalia marked the beginning of the world's (temporary) disengagement with peace operations and was the direct catalyst of the Security

Council's catastrophic 1993 decision to deploy only a small and cheap mission to Rwanda. In January 1991, the so-called United Somali Congress – a loose coalition of warlords led by Mohammed Farah Aidid and Ali Mahdi – drove the government of Siad Barre out of Mogadishu. Soon afterwards, the former allies turned on each other and Somalia descended into anarchy. Attacks on the civilian population and destruction of food sources compounded droughts and caused a massive famine that killed up to 350,000 people in 1992 (Wheeler 2000: 174; Weiss 1999: 78). Although international society had belatedly responded to the crisis by despatching large amounts of emergency aid, without armed protection a significant proportion of it was looted by warlords and thus failed to reach the intended recipients among Somalia's civilian population. In response, the US deployed over 30,000 soldiers in December 1992 to help secure the delivery of aid and assist UN peacekeepers (see chapter 9).

Relations between the US, the UN and various Somali warlords were strained, especially when the peacekeeping mandate was enlarged to include the disarmament of armed militia in addition to securing the delivery of humanitarian relief. On 5 June 1993, militia loyal to Mohammed Aidid killed more than twenty Pakistani peacekeepers who were inspecting a weapons dump as part of the disarmament process (see chapter 9). In the face of such a serious challenge to the credibility of UN peace operations around the world, within days the Security Council issued Resolution 837, which authorized the use of force ('all necessary measures') against those responsible for the attack. The US component of the mission thus became preoccupied with bringing Aidid to justice. Throughout the summer of 1993 the US conducted numerous combat operations against his supporters, killing hundreds of belligerents and Somali civilians. Matters came to a head on 3 October, when US Rangers and Special Forces raided what they thought was a gathering of tribal elders sympathetic to Aidid at the Olympic Hotel. Over 500 Somalis and eighteen Americans were killed in the ensuing battle. Shortly afterwards, President Clinton announced that all American troops would be withdrawn within six months (see Hirsch and Oakley 1995; Lyons and Samatar 1995; Clarke and Herbst 1997).

The White House also subsequently adopted a much tougher line on peace operations, announced by President Clinton at the 1993 General Assembly (see box 4.4). As the then US ambassador to the UN, Madeleine Albright, put it at the time: 'we are coming to the day when countries in need will call the global 911 and get a busy signal' (*The Times*, 13 May 1993). The administration also set out strict guidelines, limiting the potential for future US participation in peacekeeping under Presidential Decision Directive 25 (May 1994). This identified failings in the UN itself as the main reason for the US failure in Somalia and outlined seventeen conditions that would have to be met before the US would take part in a UN operation (Weiss 1997: 223). Since then the US has placed its troops under UN command only as part of the

Box 4.4 US retreat from United Nations peace operations

In recent weeks, in the Security Council, our nation has begun asking harder questions about proposals for new peacekeeping missions: is there a real threat to international peace? Does the proposed mission have clear objectives? Can an end point be identified for those who will be asked to participate? How much will the mission cost?... The United Nations simply cannot become engaged in every one of the world's conflicts. If the American people are to say yes to UN peacekeeping, the United Nations must know when to say no. (President Clinton to the UN General Assembly, 27 September 1993, in Parsons 1995: 252)

preventive mission in Macedonia (UNPREDEP; see chapter 6). As it turned out, the country in need of the global 911 that got no response would be Rwanda.

This US-led retreat from peace operations had a massive impact on the UN's response to the 1994 genocide in Rwanda, not least through the US insistence that any UN mission deployed to Rwanda be small and cheap and its repeated argument in favour of terminating the hapless UNAMIR force once the genocide was under way. In what can only be described as a 'grave accident of timing' (Melvern 2000: 79), the question of what sort of peace operation was required to oversee the implementation of the recently concluded Arusha Accords for Rwanda came up in the Security Council only a week after the eighteen Americans were killed in Mogadishu. Not surprisingly, the US was disinclined to despatch any new mission to Africa, but it was persuaded by European and African governments to consent to a peace operation on the condition that the force be given a narrow monitoring role and costs be kept as low as possible (see Melvern 1997: 335).

The US was not alone in its scepticism towards peace operations. Following the murder of ten of its peacekeepers by extremist militias at the start of the 1994 Rwandan genocide, Belgium reversed its earlier strong support for UNAMIR and decided to withdraw the remainder of its contingent on the grounds that there was no peace to keep and consequently little point placing its soldiers in harm's way. Echoing US sentiment after the death of its troops in Somalia, the Belgian government argued that continued participation in the UN mission was 'pointless within the terms of the present mandate' and exposed its soldiers to 'unacceptable risks' (in Wheeler 2000: 219). The Bangladeshi contingent quickly followed suit. In response, Major-General Roméo Dallaire recommended the reinforcement of his mission in order to avert a humanitarian catastrophe. The Security Council, however, decided instead formally to reduce the UN's presence in Rwanda. Downgraded to a skeleton staff and volunteers, UNAMIR was unable to prevent the genocide, protect the civilian population or punish the perpetrators. In one hundred days, approximately 1 million Tutsi and Hutu moderates were slaughtered – a rate of killing higher than that of the Nazi Holocaust.

Things did not go well in Bosnia either. In Srebrenica alone, between 6 and 16 July 1995, Bosnian Serb forces seized the 'safe area' proclaimed by the Security Council. They expelled the 23,000 Bosnian Muslim women and elderly people and massacred over 7,600 Muslim men and boys – almost all of them were civilians and thousands were first captured and then lined up, shot, and dumped in mass graves. The 'safe areas' policy, devised as a stop-gap by the Security Council amid the unfolding turmoil in Angola, Somalia and Rwanda, was under-resourced and lacked direction (see chapter 8). The Dutch peacekeepers charged with protecting Srebrenica, for example, did not have a mandate to protect the 'safe area' and the civilians sheltering within it, only to defend themselves. Moreover, even if they had enjoyed a more robust mandate, the peacekeepers did not have the numbers, the equipment or the support needed to protect Srebrenica and its people from the Bosnian Serb Army (see Honig and Both 1996). The UN's failure to protect Srebrenica and prevent Europe's worst massacre since the Second World War stimulated a dramatic rethink of Western policy towards Bosnia. The result was a shift to peace enforcement led by a NATO air campaign (Operation Deliberate Force) against the Bosnian Serbs and a more open strategy of providing military support to the Muslim and Croat armies on the ground. In place of the UN, Western states chose to employ force through NATO. Britain and France deployed a NATO rapid reaction force, NATO conducted air strikes, Americans (not the UN) led the Dayton negotiations that brought peace to Bosnia, and the force deployed to keep the peace after the Dayton Accords in 1995 was the NATO-led IFOR.

The political will of member states to mandate and contribute to UN peace operations is related to the operational effectiveness of the organization itself (Berdal 1993: 5). It is not surprising, therefore, that the repeated failure of peace operations between 1992 and 1995 encouraged member states to curb their earlier enthusiasm and limit their commitment. The disasters in Angola, Somalia, Rwanda and Bosnia partly caused (in the case of Somalia) and were partly caused by (in the case of Rwanda) a retreat from peace operations as dramatic as the triple transformation that began between 1988 and 1993. The change in sentiment at the UN can be seen in the words of the Secretary-General in 1994 and 1995 (box 4.5).

One of the obvious consequences of this retreat was the reduction in the number of UN peacekeepers around the world – from over 70,000 in 1993 to fewer than 20,000 in 1996. UN member states, particularly those in the West, were reluctant either to support renewed engagement with the world's trouble spots (Somalia, Afghanistan, Zaire/Congo, Burundi) or to place their troops under UN command and provide the global institution with the resources it needed. Thus, the 20,000 UN peacekeepers were augmented by a further 40,000 working under the command of regional arrangements such as NATO, ECOWAS and the OSCE (see McCoubrey and Morris 2000). Within this context of retreat, the Security Council displayed a growing reluctance

> **Box 4.5 Boutros-Ghali on the failure of UN peace operations**
>
> The international community appears paralysed in reacting…even to the revised mandate established by the Security Council. We must all recognise that in this respect, we have failed in our response to the agony of Rwanda and have thus acquiesced in the continuing loss of human lives. Our readiness and capacity for action has been demonstrated to be inadequate at best, and deplorable at worst, owing to the lack of collective political will. (31 May 1994, in Wheeler 2000: 230)
>
> Peace-keeping in such contexts is far more complex and more expensive than when its tasks were mainly to monitor cease-fires and control buffer zones with the consent of the States involved in the conflict. Peace-keeping today can involve constant danger…It must also be recognized that the vast increase in field deployment has to be supported by an overburdened Headquarters staff that resource constraints have held at levels appropriate to an earlier, far less demanding, time. Meanwhile, there is continuing damage to the credibility of the Security Council and of the Organization as a whole when the Council adopts decisions that cannot be carried out because the necessary troops are not forthcoming. (Boutros-Ghali 1995a: §§ 15, 17, 98)
>
> The limits of peace-keeping in on-going hostilities starkly highlighted by the distressing course of events in the former Yugoslavia have become clearer, as the Organization has come to realize that a mix of peace-keeping and enforcement is not the answer to a lack of consent and cooperation by the parties to the conflict. The United Nations can only be as effective as its Member States may allow it to be. The option of withdrawal raises the question of whether the international community can simply leave the afflicted population to its fate. (Boutros-Ghali 1995b: § 600)
>
> Should there be a mismatch between the international force's mandate and its resources, there would be a risk of failure, of international casualties, and of undermined credibility for those who had put the force into the field. (Boutros-Ghali 1995c)

to authorize new missions, with the largest UN mission deployed in the second half of the 1990s being UNAVEM III in Angola. Between 1995 and early 1999, the Security Council created only three new (and small) missions in regions where the UN was not already active (UNSMIH/UNTMIH, UNOMSIL and MINUGUA). The largest of these was the UNSMIH mission in Haiti, which comprised 1,500 civilian and military personnel, though this was soon reduced to 250 when it handed over to UNTMIH in August 1997. UNOMSIL in Sierra Leone and MINUGUA in Guatemala were both limited to approximately 200 personnel.

In February 1995, before the Srebrenica disaster, Boutros-Ghali had published a supplement to his *An Agenda for Peace* in which he outlined a far less ambitious future for peace operations than that enunciated less than three years earlier. In it he argued that the experience of the previous three years had damaged the credibility of the Security Council and the UN as a whole, because the Council had adopted decisions that could not be carried out since the necessary troops were not forthcoming (see box 4.6). In addition, a lack of funds imposed 'severe constraints' on the UN's ability to deploy the troops that had been offered (Boutros-Ghali 1995a: §§ 98–9).

It appears as if a lack of political will on the part of the P-5 states in particular, combined with the UN's institutional inability to cope with the transformation of peace operations, contributed to a series of high-profile failures. By conservative estimates, around 1.5 million civilians were killed while peacekeepers were present in Angola, Somalia, Rwanda and Bosnia. The failures, the deliberate killing of peacekeepers and the comparatively high financial costs of these missions prompted many states to temper their earlier enthusiasm both for the UN as the primary global agent for international peace and security and for peace operations themselves. On the one hand, states reluctant to place their troops under UN command began to make greater use of regional arrangements or to act unilaterally. On the other hand, for most of the latter half of the 1990s, states were reluctant to authorize, fund or participate in peace operations, despite the continuation of violence in many parts of the world. The final part of this chapter asks what lessons were learned from these experiences.

4.4 Lessons learned?

In November and December 1999, the UN issued landmark reports accepting responsibility and detailing the many failings that had led UN peacekeepers to stand aside amid genocide in Srebrenica and Rwanda respectively. This section provides a brief background and overview of the main findings of these two reports, which helped set the scene for new thinking about the role and proper composition of peace operations evident in many twenty-first-century missions. However, we should begin by focusing on two earlier reports that were not so damning in their criticism of the UN.

The first of the UN's 'lessons learned' reports was produced in February 1994 but not publicly released. The Commission of Inquiry created by the Security Council to investigate the armed attacks on UNOSOM II personnel in Somalia made two important observations and issued a damning recommendation that could be read as an endorsement of the retreat of peace operations. It argued that the mission failed principally because its different military components had no means of communicating with each other directly. A complex and slow process of decision-making was required for one contingent to request assistance from another (Commission of Inquiry 1994: 40). Second, the Commission noted that there was very little coordination at UN headquarters. The US component of UNOSOM II distanced itself from UN elements, creating a situation where information was not shared and common operating procedures and rules of engagement were not established. Importantly, the Commission concluded by insisting that:

> The United Nations should refrain from undertaking further peace enforcement actions within the internal conflicts of states. If the United Nations decides nevertheless to undertake enforcement operations, the mandate should be limited to specific objectives and the use of force would be applied as the ultimate means after all peaceful remedies have been exhausted. (Ibid.: 42)

Most of these recommendations have been heeded. From the mid-1990s to around 2005, the UN tended to refrain from using enforcement measures in civil conflicts, leaving that to NATO, ECOWAS and other regional bodies. It has been inclined to limit the size of its missions both functionally and temporally. As chapter 5 demonstrates, however, from around 2005, UN peace operations have gradually grown in size and begun to use force in order to protect themselves and civilians under their care as well as to coerce 'spoilers'.

The UN was slow to acknowledge its role in facilitating the Rwandan genocide. In 1996, the newly created Lessons Learned Unit of the DPKO issued an internal report which attempted to exonerate the UN while blaming member states. 'UNAMIR', it found, 'seemed always to be one step behind the realities of the situation in Rwanda.' This was a product of operational problems such as the mission's critical lack of transportation (of twenty-two armoured personnel carriers requested, UNAMIR received only eight – all seconded from other missions, and only five of which were roadworthy) and a breakdown of communication between peacekeepers on the ground, troop-contributing countries and UN headquarters in New York. The last encouraged 'a fundamental misunderstanding of the nature of the conflict [which] contributed to false political assumptions and military assessments' (DPKO 1996: § 3). According to the report, UNAMIR's failure to prevent or halt the genocide, however, was also the fault of member states because, 'at the height of the crisis, the unilateral decision of some Governments to withdraw their national contingents left the remnants of UNAMIR even more vulnerable and unable to provide protection to civilians at risk' (ibid.: § 2). Despite this, the report found, UNAMIR persevered and played a constructive role in Rwanda:

> The United Nations and its family of agencies, although after some delay, did exert considerable efforts to assist the Rwandese people, particularly in the rehabilitation of the country's justice system and to alleviate the very harsh conditions of many of the roughly 60,000 detainees in the prisons. UNAMIR itself was instrumental in restoring the telecommunications capabilities of the country, doing road and bridge repairs and rehabilitating basic infrastructure. (Ibid.: § 3).

Although many of the report's forty-three recommendations identified key areas in need of improvement (see table 4.3), they stopped short of assigning institutional responsibility or fault on the part of the UN's agencies, officers and personnel. Moreover, although it identified key problems (e.g. the gap between mandate and means; late/non-deployment of troops), some of its recommendations were contradictory, and it omitted some important pieces

TABLE 4.3 Key DPKO recommendations from *Comprehensive Report* on UNAMIR (1996)

Recommendation	Description
1 Mandates should reflect realities on the ground and be matched with the means to implement them.	UNAMIR's mandate and means were based on a misunderstanding of the conflict and a false assumption that parties supported Arusha Accords.
3 Peacekeepers require intelligence.	UNAMIR and UN headquarters lacked capacity to collect intelligence.
6 Requests for troops should focus on capabilities not numbers.	UNAMIR lacked logistical and communications capabilities.
7 Troops must deploy in a timely fashion.	Authorized expansion of UNAMIR in May 1994 not translated into enhanced capacity on account of late deployment and unwillingness of non-Africans to contribute.
8 Contingents must be fully equipped.	Some African peacekeepers lacked basic equipment.
9 Unilateral troop withdrawals should be discouraged.	Belgian withdrawal announced without consultation; undermined whole mission.
32 An effective political and humanitarian early warning system is needed.	Human Rights Commission reports of deteriorating situation were not circulated across UN system.
34 Missions should have a joint civil–military operations centre (CMOC).	Little coordination of political, military and humanitarian agencies.
36 Protection of civilians is an important humanitarian contribution.	UN should have had a human rights office in Rwanda working with UN police (CIVPOL).
37 Peacekeepers should strive to maintain impartiality in appearance and perception.	Negotiations with Rwandan government and RPF impaired UNAMIR impartiality.

of information. Thus, in response to its recommendation concerning the protection of civilians, the report called merely for the creation of a (civilian) human rights component within UNAMIR with access to the peace operation's logistics. The UN's troops and police officers would have thus been 'made aware of the human rights dimension of the situation in Rwanda' (DPKO 1996: § 16). Kofi Annan himself has argued that it was not lack of knowledge about the human rights situation in Rwanda but the lack of political will on the part of member states to act upon that knowledge that was crucial (in Meisler 2007: 103). In similar vein, it is difficult to see how Recommendation 36 on the protection of civilians does not contradict Recommendation 37, which insists that peace operations remain impartial, in both appearance and fact. Without reconceptualizing impartiality, it is hard to perceive how peacekeepers could stay faithful to the principles of traditional peacekeeping (see chapter 7) while protecting civilians in a hostile environment.

Moreover, the DPKO's report failed to include some important pieces of information. One piece of now well-known information missing from this report is that, shortly before the genocide, one of Major-General Dallaire's cables advised UN headquarters that he had received intelligence about preparations for genocidal killing. In the cable he asked for permission to seize arms caches belonging to militia groups. The cable was passed to the deputy head of the DPKO, Iqbal Riza, who responded on behalf of Annan. Riza replied to the Secretary-General's Special Representative (SRSG) in Rwanda (not Dallaire) that the peacekeepers should not act until given clear instructions from headquarters. The SRSG, Jacques-Roger Booh-Booh, replied that he had high-level political verification of Dallaire's intelligence and that UNAMIR planned to act on it in the next day or two. Riza's response was that UNAMIR did not have a mandate to seize weapons caches or protect civilians and must therefore refrain from doing so. UN headquarters would pass on the intelligence to the US, France, Belgium and the Rwandan government. Riza infamously ended his cable by declaring that 'the overriding consideration is the need to avoid entering into a course of action that might lead to the use of force and unanticipated repercussions' (in Traub 2006: 52). Although the cables were all copied to the Secretary-General, the DPKO did not specifically bring the matter to Boutros-Ghali's attention, nor did they ask the Secretary-General to alert the Security Council. The overarching concern in the wake of Somalia was to guard against overextension in a context where the US was actively arguing against UN peace operations. As Annan explained, 'you can't look at Rwanda without thinking of what happened in Somalia; in fact, they were happening almost simultaneously' (ibid.: 53).

This tendency to try to shield the UN from criticism over Rwanda persisted after the report. In 1998, Kofi Annan was widely criticized for mincing his words on a trip to Rwanda to issue a belated apology. In response to questions at a press conference in Nairobi, he characterized criticism of the DPKO's role (which he led at the time of the genocide) as 'an old story which is being rehashed', telling reporters, 'I have no regrets' (in Traub 2006: 114). While member states must obviously shoulder the blame for providing inadequate support to UNAMIR and then ordering its withdrawal in the face of genocide, the DPKO's report and Annan's public statements failed to address equally troubling questions about the UN's performance. For example, the *Report of the Independent Inquiry* in 1999 argued that, even given its limited size, UNAMIR should have been able to do more to prevent the genocide and protect civilians (Independent Inquiry 1999: 28).

Partly in response to mounting public criticism of the UN's refusal to examine its mistakes in Rwanda properly, and partly in response to internal advice that a more critical examination was a prerequisite for regenerating UN peace operations, in 1999 Annan established an Independent Commission comprising the former Swedish prime minister Ingvar Carlsson, the former South Korean foreign minister Han Sung-Joo, and a retired Nigerian general, Rufus Kupolati, to investigate all aspects of the UN's performance in Rwanda. When Annan received a draft copy of the report, his first inclination was to order its revision, believing that it was too critical of the UN. However, on the advice of senior advisers such as Mark Malloch Brown and the new head of the DPKO, Jean-Marie Guéhenno (2002: 72), who argued that only by reconciling fully with the past could the UN move forward and begin to rebuild credibility and support for peace operations among member states, Annan agreed to leave the text as written by the Inquiry.

The *Report of the Independent Inquiry* opened with a damning but general criticism, insisting that the Rwandan genocide resulted from the failure of the whole UN system (see box 4.6). The 'overriding failure', it argued, was the lack of resources and lack of will to take on the commitment that would have been necessary to prevent the genocide and protect its victims. The lack of resources and will was manifested in UNAMIR not being adequately 'planned, dimensioned, deployed or instructed' in a way that would have 'provided for a proactive and assertive role' in the face of the deteriorating situation in Rwanda (1999: 2). The mission was smaller than recommended by the DPKO, slow to deploy owing to the reluctance of states to contribute troops and debilitated by administrative difficulties. When troops did arrive, they were generally inadequately trained and equipped (ibid.).

All this meant that, when the genocide erupted, UNAMIR was not functioning properly and was mired in problems associated with dysfunctional command and control and a lack of military capacity. 'A force numbering 2,500' (UNAMIR's strength at the time of the genocide), the Inquiry concluded, should have been able to stop or at least limit massacres of the kind which began in Rwanda' at the start of the genocide (1999: 2). That UNAMIR failed to do this was the result of 'fundamental capacity' problems. Among the report's many criticisms and recommendations were ten points critical to improving future UN peace operations.

Box 4.6 Rwanda: failure by the whole UN

The failure by the United Nations to prevent, and subsequently to stop the genocide in Rwanda was a failure by the United Nations as a whole. The fundamental failure was the lack of resources and political commitment devoted to developments in Rwanda and to the United Nations presence there. There was a persistent lack of political will by Member States to act, or to act with enough assertiveness. This lack of political will affected the response by the Secretariat and decision-making by the Security Council, but was also evident in the recurrent difficulties to get the necessary troops for the United Nations Assistance Mission for Rwanda (UNAMIR). Finally, although UNAMIR suffered from a chronic lack of resources and political priority, it must also be said that serious mistakes were made with those resources which were at the disposal of the United Nations. (Independent Inquiry 1999: 1)

1 *Inadequacy of the mandate*   The scope of UNAMIR's mandate was unsuited to the situation in Rwanda and lacked contingencies and fall-back positions. This was a product of a lack of will on the part of member states but also the UN's failure to inform the Security Council accurately about the situation in Rwanda before the genocide.

2 *Implementation of the mandate*   UNAMIR's mandate was implemented cautiously, focusing on preserving the appearance of neutrality under a traditional peacekeeping mandate that was unsuited to the context. UNAMIR should have done more to alert headquarters and the Security Council to the inadequacy of this approach.

3 *Confusion over the rules of engagement*   UNAMIR never received a response to requests for guidance about the rules of engagement, resulting in a critical lack of clarity regarding which rules were in force.

4 *Failure to respond to the genocide*   At the beginning of the genocide, UNAMIR failed to take steps – such as establishing roadblocks and protecting VIPs – to respond to the early massacres. It said that it would protect politicians and failed to do so; civilians who fled to UN compounds in search of protection were sometimes abandoned to their fate. This failure stemmed from poor intelligence and information and the inability of UNAMIR's commander to exert practical command over his troops.

5 *Inadequate resources and logistics*   UNAMIR had only five roadworthy armoured personnel carriers, one helicopter and insufficient medical supplies for its personnel. Troops in Kigali reported that they had one to two days' worth of drinking water, up to two days' worth of food rations and two to three days' worth of fuel reserves.

6 *Inappropriate focus on ceasefire*   Once the genocide had begun, UNAMIR and UN headquarters were focused more on negotiating a ceasefire than they were on protecting civilians. From the Secretary-General down, UN officials held meetings with those associated with the *genocidaires* in which they focused on securing a ceasefire rather than conveying outrage at the genocide.

7 *Lack of analytical capability*   UNAMIR lacked sufficient focus or the institutional capacity systematically to gather and analyse information in order to build an accurate picture of the situation or provide early warning.

8 *Failure to protect*   UNAMIR failed to protect political leaders, civilians and national staff even where promises to protect had been made or where people had gathered seeking the UN's protection. 'Tragically', the report found, 'the trust placed in UNAMIR by civilians left them in a situation of greater risk when the UN troops withdrew than they would have been anyway' (ibid.: 43).

9 *Flow of information*   The flow of information was sporadic, resulting in critical information either being lost or not getting into the hands of appropriate decision-makers. Several members of the Security Council complained that they were not made aware of Dallaire's now famous cable.

10 *Organizational problems* Poor personal relations and unclear lines of communication and authority within UNAMIR and between the Secretary-General, UN staff and the Security Council hindered the transfer of information.

The report concluded, therefore, that the UN's failure in Rwanda was created largely by a critical disjuncture – endemic in many UN operations at the time and explored further in chapter 8 – between the tasks given to the peacekeepers and their conceptual and material tools. For largely political reasons (because the US would not support a large complex operation so soon after Somalia), UNAMIR was conceived in traditional terms, even though its operational context meant that the basic assumptions necessary for traditional peacekeeping were not in place (see chapter 7). These conclusions echoed those of the UN's report on the Srebrenica massacre, issued a month earlier.

Unlike the Rwanda report, the UN's report on Srebrenica was written by the UN Secretariat and issued in the name of the Secretary-General. What made this report different, however, was that, on the advice of those such as Malloch Brown and Guéhenno, who believed that the UN needed to be full and frank in its analysis of past mistakes, the report was not revised by political officers and senior officials. Usually, UN reports are redrafted and the wording finessed as they make their way through the system. When it came to the Srebrenica report, Malloch Brown argued that the integrity and wording of the original report should be preserved, and Annan agreed (Traub 2006).

The report argued that the collapse of Srebrenica was particularly shocking because the town had been designated a 'safe area' by the UN and thousands of civilians had fled there seeking protection. However, the Dutch peacekeepers were denied the resources, support and mandate necessary to protect Srebrenica. In relation to resources, it was garrisoned by approximately 200 Dutch peacekeepers with limited mobility and armed only with light weapons. The peacekeepers were not regularly resupplied and confronted critical shortages of fuel, ammunition and other basic supplies. They faced approximately 2,500 Bosnian Serb soldiers equipped with heavy artillery. In relation to support, on at least three occasions the Dutch commander in Srebrenica requested aerial support – a request denied by UNPROFOR's leadership (with the backing of UN headquarters) for mainly political reasons. In relation to the mandate, Dutch peacekeepers were not expressly authorized to use force to protect civilians in the safe area, and the commander was issued a directive to place force protection ahead of all other considerations (Annan 1999e: §§ 471–4). Annan conceded that 'we were, with hindsight, wrong to declare repeatedly and publicly that we did not want to use air power against the Serbs' (ibid.: § 483).

The report found that, as in Rwanda, these operational problems were rooted in deeper political problems in the Security Council. Once again, the

> ## Box 4.7 Humanitarian aid as a response to ethnic cleansing
>
> Nor was the provision of humanitarian aid a sufficient response to 'ethnic cleansing' and to an attempted genocide. The provision of food and shelter to people who have neither is wholly admirable, and we must all recognise the extraordinary work done by UNHCR and its partners in circumstances of extreme adversity, but the provision of humanitarian assistance could never have been a solution to the problem in that country. The problem, which cried out for a political/military solution, was that a State Member of the United Nations [Bosnia-Hercegovina], left largely defenceless as a result of an arms embargo imposed upon it by the United Nations, was being dismembered by forces committed to its destruction. This was not a problem with a humanitarian solution. (Annan 1999e: § 491)

Security Council was focused on trying to keep the peace when there was no peace to keep (Annan 1999e: § 488) and delivering humanitarian aid in the false belief that this would help remedy the situation (see box 4.7). Moreover, decisions about the nature and direction of UNPROFOR were taken on the basis of false assumptions about Serbian war aims (ibid.: §§ 496–7). As a result, peacekeepers were put into situations where they might be required to use force but without the political support or resources to do so effectively and pursue the strategy through to its conclusion (see Goulding 1996: 15–17).

The report identified a series of lessons for the future, three of which are particularly important here. First, it stated that, when they are deployed without the general consensus of the Security Council and as a substitute for such consensus, peace operations are likely to fail. Peace operations and war fighting are distinct roles, the report argued, and the former must only be deployed with clear mandates and clear support from the UN membership, backed up by the commitment of adequate resources. It is worth quoting the report at length on this point:

> Peacekeepers must never again be told that they must use their peacekeeping tools – lightly armed soldiers in scattered positions – to impose the ill-defined wishes of the international community on one or another of the belligerents by military means. If the necessary resources are not provided – and the necessary political, military and moral judgments are not made – then the job simply cannot be done. (Annan 1999e: § 498)

Second, the report argued that, while safe zones could play a useful role in protecting civilians, it was important to clarify the precise nature of the zone. 'Protected zones', 'safe areas' or 'safe havens' should fall into one of two types. The first are properly demilitarized zones created under the authority of international humanitarian law and enjoy the consent of the belligerents. Safe areas that are not demilitarized or do not enjoy the consent of the belligerents should be 'fully defended by a credible military deterrent' (ibid.: § 499). The two concepts are absolutely distinct and should not be confused, the report argued. Yet this is precisely what happened in Bosnia, where 'safe areas were established by the Security Council without the consent of the parties and without the provision of any credible military deterrent' (ibid.). This problem was foreseen by several members of the Security Council and UN officials, but their warnings went unheeded.

The third and 'cardinal' lesson from Srebrenica was that a strategy of genocide and ethnic cleansing could only be met 'decisively with all necessary means, and with the political will to carry the policy through to its logical conclusion' (Annan 1999e: § 502). Ultimately, only the appropriate threat and use of force is likely to deter attacks and protect the civilian population, and UNPROFOR, like UNAMIR before it, was ill-equipped to fulfil this role.

The double denunciation of UN peace operations in Rwanda and Srebrenica prompted many in the UN Secretariat and several governments to begin thinking about peace operations in new ways. It stood to reason that, if peace-keepers were to be in the business of protecting civilians from genocide and mass atrocities, enforcing ceasefires in the face of wilful defiance and supporting peace agreements even when the commitment of the parties themselves is in doubt, new thinking would be needed about how missions were mandated, staffed and equipped. This led to an emerging view that peace operations should be more complex, multidimensional, forceful and well-equipped, a view which came to be increasingly widely accepted at the beginning of the twenty-first century (Malone and Wermester 2001; Wilkinson 2000).

4.5 Conclusion

Between 1988 and 1993 a triple transformation of UN peace operations began, comprising quantitative, normative and qualitative changes to their role and scope. During this period the UN gradually took on more, and more complicated, operations than in its previous forty years combined. Factors associated with the end of the Cold War, the putative triumph of liberalism, and the acceleration of globalization encouraged governments and the UN to believe that peace operations could help transform war-torn societies by protecting human rights, fostering democracy and enforcing peace. These attitudes were encouraged by important early successes in Central America, Namibia and Cambodia. However, the gradual expansion of peace operations without a requisite growth in the UN's institutional capacity, member states' willingness to provide troops and financial support, and the development of doctrinal thinking left the organization overstretched. In Angola, Somalia, Rwanda and Bosnia, peace operations were despatched without appropriate mandates, information, political support, troops, resources and guidance, and these shortcomings were swiftly and brutally exposed. In Angola, peacekeepers deployed to monitor a ceasefire and elections were utterly ill-prepared and ill-equipped to prevent and mitigate a sharp descent into the worst violence of that country's decades-old civil war. In Somalia, well-intentioned but misguided policies led to peacekeepers being targeted by militias. In Rwanda and Srebrenica, member states and the UN Secretariat lacked the institutional capacity and political will to support their words with appropriate action.

These very public failures damaged the reputation of the UN and prompted a retreat from peace operations as dramatic as their earlier transformation had been. States preferred to use regional mechanisms rather than the UN, and the Security Council became deeply reluctant to endorse anything other than small observation-style missions. UN peace operations thus confronted a 'fork in the road' (Diehl 2000). They faced a choice between going 'back to basics' or reconceptualizing the basics themselves (Tharoor 1996). This was accompanied by a period of introspection at the UN in which important lessons were identified in a series of reports. Building on the momentum generated by these reports, Annan appointed a high-level international panel chaired by the respected former Algerian foreign minister Lakhdar Brahimi to make recommendations for reforming UN peace operations (Malone and Thakur 2001: 11). This sowed the seeds for a reconceptualization of peace operations, which in turn laid the foundations for their resurgence in the twenty-first century.

CHAPTER FIVE

Peace Operations in the Twenty-First Century

As noted in chapter 4, the end of the 1990s was characterized by a period of introspection where states became much more cautious about using peace operations as a tool of conflict management. This began to change in 1999 with high-profile operations in Kosovo and East Timor. During the same year, the Security Council authorized new missions to Sierra Leone and the DRC. This renewed demand for peace operations helped prompt the UN Secretary-General to commission a major report into the conduct and management of peace operations, and a panel of experts under the chairmanship of Lakhdar Brahimi made a series of recommendations which laid the groundwork for a new approach to UN peace operations. This chapter examines the new approach and its impact on contemporary peace operations. We begin by examining the increased demand for peacekeeping at the turn of the twenty-first century, highlighting the hostage crisis in Sierra Leone in May 2000 as a crucial turning point. The second section focuses on the Brahimi Report and its implementation, while the third and final sections explore some of the political issues that have influenced contemporary peacekeeping, the process of UN reform, and experiences in peace operations since 2001.

5.1 Peacekeeping reborn? 1999–2002

In March and September 1999, two military operations began which gave renewed impetus to peace operations by creating fresh demands for peace-keepers and partially restoring faith in their ability to make a positive contribution to international peace and security and the protection of endangered populations. On 24 March, NATO launched Operation Allied Force to prevent a humanitarian catastrophe in Kosovo caused by Serbian ethnic cleansing there. Spearheaded by the KLA, a year earlier the province's politically repressed Albanian population had risen up against the Serbian government. The Serbs retaliated with a wave of killing and ethnic cleansing that claimed the lives of up to 5,000 people. After several aborted attempts to secure a peaceful resolution, NATO intervened with force (see companion website). The intervention, which was not authorized by the Security Council because Russia threatened to veto any such resolution, proved very controversial. A few months later, in September 1999, Australia led a coalition of states into

East Timor to put an end to violence by pro-Indonesian militia in the wake of a UN-supervised referendum on independence. Deployed with the consent of the Indonesian government, INTERFET dramatically improved the security situation, though most of the militia had retreated to Indonesia before the mission's deployment (Annan 2000a; Smith and Dee 2003; and companion website).

These operations created a demand for two new UN peace operations – UNTAET in East Timor and UNMIK in Kosovo – as well as a large NATO-led operation in the Balkans (KFOR). In the same year, the UN Security Council also authorized the deployment of peacekeeping operations to the DRC and Sierra Leone. Within twelve months, therefore, the number of UN peacekeepers around the world more than doubled. The number of peacekeepers deployed under the auspices of non-UN actors also began to grow significantly. There were at least five reasons for this resurgence in peacekeeping.

First, the mid-1990s saw an increased interest in humanitarianism and, perhaps more importantly, the merging of the international development and security agendas (Duffield 2001, 2007). This merger has been dubbed the 'security first' philosophy or the 'new aid paradigm' (Duffield 1997). Its proponents included international institutions such as the UNDP, IMF and World Bank and state-based agencies such as Britain's DFID, USAID and Australia's AUSAID. Towards the end of the 1990s, these institutions began to argue that

TABLE 5.1 Peacekeeping reborn? UN-authorized operations started in 1999

Mission	Location	Lead actor	Mandate	Size (max. deployed)
INTERFET	East Timor	Australia	Deter and disarm militias; provide security	11,000
UNTAET	East Timor	UN	Transitional authority	10,700
MONUC	DRC	UN	Monitor implementation of ceasefire agreement; facilitate humanitarian assistance; protect civilians under imminent threat of physical violence	3,700
UNAMSIL	Sierra Leone	UN	Assist in implementation of the Lomé Agreement; DDR; facilitate humanitarian assistance; protect civilians under imminent threat of physical violence	17,500
UNMIK	Kosovo	UN	Transitional authority	1,000 (civilians)
KFOR	Kosovo	NATO	Verify Yugoslav withdrawal; maintain security; disarm KLA	50,000

'a prerequisite for social development and human rights protection is the security and stability that comes through an effective, impartial and humane introduction of law and order, alongside the extension of sound governance to the military sector itself' (Cooper and Pugh 2002: 14). Following the lessons learned from Bosnia, Somalia and Rwanda, there was widespread recognition that long-term development programmes and humanitarian assistance depended on a relatively secure environment. Without that security, aid would be pilfered and development programmes scuppered by corruption and violence. Thus, throughout the Western aid community there emerged a belief that effective peacekeepers were a vital component of broader humanitarian and developmental programmes.

Second, Western governments became concerned with humanitarian problems in their own neighbourhoods. The interventions and follow-on peace operations in Kosovo and East Timor, for instance, were justified primarily by humanitarian concerns. Attempting to justify NATO's use of force against Yugoslavia, British Prime Minister Tony Blair articulated a vision of a 'new international community', similar in parts to George H. W. Bush's 'New World Order' (see chapter 4). Blair argued that in a globalizing world 'the principle of non-interference must be qualified in important respects', including in instances of large-scale and systematic human rights abuse, ethnic cleansing and genocide (see box 1.7, p. 37). Similarly, prior to the INTERFET operation a US State Department official had noted the existence of a 'massacre quotient' that, when surpassed, would trigger serious international involvement, while observers in Canberra argued that, once the Indonesian-backed militia had started its reign of terror, 'no Australian government could have survived if it stood by and did nothing' (Chalk 2001: 42).

Third, in the case of Kosovo and East Timor (and later Sierra Leone), Western states undertook operations without placing their own troops under the UN's general command structure. In this sense they acted as *pivotal states* working outside, but in support of, the UN (see chapter 2). In particular, NATO (in Kosovo) and Australia (in East Timor) took responsibility for the creation, organization, command and large parts of the funding of the operations. In Kosovo, NATO argued that its unified command structure allowed it to overcome many of the problems associated with the UN: it could take decisions quickly, insist upon basic levels of inter-operability, thus ensuring consistency and proper coordination, and could ensure that the mission was properly staffed and equipped. All these things were thought to be very difficult to achieve within the UN command structure. Australia fulfilled an almost identical role in East Timor. Both operations were conducted in the neighbourhood of the pivotal states/organizations and were motivated by a blend of humanitarianism and perceived national interests. In Kosovo, NATO was concerned that inaction would permit a repeat of the Bosnian bloodbath, generate massive refugee flows and prompt geopolitical instability. Similarly, Australia was confronted with a situation in which continued appeasement of Indonesia became untenable, not least because the US had pressurized its government to permit East Timorese independence and the presence of an international force, and because Canberra's commercial interests (particularly the exploitation of mineral and oil resources in the Timor gap) demanded some form of conflict resolution (Chalk 2001: 4). By devolving responsibility and control over operations to the troop-contributing countries, the Security Council allowed states to participate without placing their soldiers under UN command. This was a particularly important consideration for the US, which was happy to participate in NATO-led operations in the Balkans but was deeply sceptical about UN-led missions (MacKinnon 2000: 38–61).

Fourth, the rebirth of peace operations in Africa was assisted by the activities of states such as Nigeria and South Africa, and the development of regional capacities through Western-sponsored training initiatives such as the US African Crisis Response Initiative (and later the Africa Contingency Operations Training Assistance), Britain's African Peacekeeping Training Support Programme, and France's Reinforcement of African Peacekeeping Capacities programme (RECAMP). From late 2004, these initiatives were largely folded into the G-8 broader Global Peace Operations Initiative (GPOI), which aimed to train 75,000 new peacekeepers worldwide but with a focus on Africa by 2010.

A large part of the rebirth of UN peacekeeping in Africa was a belated response to regional peacekeeping efforts. In both Liberia and Sierra Leone, the UN was slow to support Nigerian-led operations conducted under the auspices of ECOWAS. In Liberia, the UN force (UNOMIL, 1993–7) eventually worked with ECOMOG troops, while in Sierra Leone a significant UN presence did not materialize until early 2000, after Nigeria had decided to withdraw its forces. In South Africa's case, its desire to play a positive international role after apartheid met with mixed results, with the bungled SADC operation in Lesotho in 1998 (Coleman 2007: 160–93) being only partially offset by South African peacekeepers' constructive engagement in Burundi's civil war. South Africa was initially unwilling to commit its peacekeepers to the DRC after the ongoing war there caused a major rift between SADC leaders (Zimbabwe, Angola and Namibia had deployed troops to the DRC in support of embattled President Laurent Kabila initially without SADC's formal approval; see ibid.: 116–59).

Finally, renewed confidence in peace operations was partly induced by attempts to learn from the mistakes of the 1990s and develop new doctrines, institutions and procedures. This saw the emergence of the new concept of 'peace support operations' (see chapter 12). At its fiftieth anniversary summit in 1999, NATO unveiled a new strategic concept that included the traditional alliance goals of collective defence but also developed a new set of missions under the rubric of 'crisis response'. Similarly, the EU announced plans to create a 60,000 strong multinational rapid reaction force capable of fulfilling a range of humanitarian and peacekeeping tasks. In addition, as we noted in chapter 4, the UN embarked on a more systematic process of lesson learning, culminating in the release of the Brahimi Report in 2000 (see section 5.2).

These five factors coalesced at the end of the 1990s to bring about a rebirth of peace operations. As with the transformation of peace operations at the end of the Cold War, the rebirth was slow, incremental and hesitant. This was reflected in the fact that between 1999 and 2002 the UN also terminated six missions (see table 5.2). Moreover, in the years following 1999, only three new missions were created: a traditional peacekeeping operation along the Ethiopia–Eritrea border (UNMEE), a NATO-led security assistance force in Afghanistan (ISAF) and a scaled-down assistance mission for East Timor (UNMISET).

At the end of July 2000, the Security Council authorized a force of just over 4,000 soldiers and civilians to monitor a cessation of hostilities between Ethiopia and Eritrea. Conceived as a traditional peacekeeping operation, UNMEE was mandated to monitor the 'Temporary Security Zone' between the two states' armed forces and to observe and verify their withdrawal. The mission's civilian component was limited to assisting humanitarian agencies with a de-mining programme. Importantly, Security Council Resolution 1320 (15 September 2000) stated that, should the cessation of hostilities agreement collapse, UNMEE would be terminated (see chapter 7).

On 20 December 2001, the Council authorized the deployment of the ISAF in Afghanistan (see chapter 12). Resolution 1386 authorized Britain to lead a force of approximately 4,800 peacekeepers to provide security in the Kabul area after the US-led Operation Enduring Freedom had toppled the Taliban regime. Although ISAF was given a broad mandate, it was initially limited to

TABLE 5.2 UN missions terminated between 1999 and 2002

Mission	Location (dates)	Description	Size
MONUA	Angola (June 1997–Feb 1999)	Peacebuilding, confidence-building, democratization	3,500
UNPREDEP	Macedonia (March 1995–Feb 1999)	Preventive mission	1,100
UNOMSIL*	Sierra Leone (July 1998–Oct 1999)	Monitor security situation, disarmament and demobilization	200
MIPONUH	Haiti (Dec 1997–March 2000)	Assist government with police reform	500
UNMOT	Tajikistan (Dec 1994–May 2000)	Monitor ceasefire	100
UNTAET**	East Timor (Oct 1999–May 2002)	Transitional administration	11,000

Notes: *Replaced by UNAMSIL.
**Replaced by UNMISET.

operating in Kabul and its environs. Over time, the mission was brought under NATO command and expanded its area of operations, and by 2007 had been increased in strength to over 40,000 troops. ISAF also began to participate in enforcement action against remnants of the Taliban and its al-Qa'ida supporters (see ICG 2008a).

The third new mission was actually a scaling-down of the UNTAET operation in East Timor, following the province's transition to full independence in May 2002. Specifically, Security Council Resolution 1410 (17 May 2002) authorized a new mission, UNMISET, which cut the number of UN personnel in East Timor by half, to 5,000. East Timor's transition to independence came earlier than had originally been planned on account of political pressure stemming from accusations that the UN had adopted a quasi-imperial approach to governing by not consulting sufficiently with local actors (Chopra 2000a, 2002). UNMISET's three primary goals were to provide assistance to core administrative structures critical to the viability and political stability of the new state; to ensure interim law enforcement and public security and to assist in the development of a new law enforcement agency, the East Timor Police Service; and to contribute to the maintenance of the external and internal security of East Timor. Rather than building and running the structures of a state, as UNTAET had done, UNMISET's primary role was to assist and supervise the new indigenous authorities. Some analysts (Caplan 2005) worried that the UN's involvement with East Timor had been scaled back too quickly – concerns borne out in 2006, when the country descended into anarchy and was rescued only by renewed foreign intervention (see section 5.3).

Although the new missions in Kosovo and East Timor were configured to take account of the lessons learned from Rwanda and Srebrenica, in both Sierra Leone and the DRC the operations suffered from the familiar problems associated with unclear mandates and a gulf between ends and means. Matters came to a head in Sierra Leone in the first half of 2000, when a deterioration of the security situation exposed weaknesses in the UNAMSIL mission and badly undermined the credibility of UN peace operations once again (see box 5.1 and companion website). UNAMSIL was saved from ignominious failure only by a British military operation launched in May 2000 and subsequent rapid restructuring by the DPKO thereafter.

As with the UN's missions to Somalia, Rwanda, Angola and Bosnia, the mandate for UNAMSIL was prefaced on the false assumption that the principal parties to the conflict in Sierra Leone were committed to the Lomé Peace Accords. In reality, the Revolutionary United Front of Sierra Leone (RUF) was determined to prevent the UN deploying to the diamond-rich areas in which it operated and was deeply concerned about potential reprisals from self-defence groups, known as *kamajors*. On paper, UNAMSIL was one of the UN's larger missions: its initial authorized strength of 6,000 was increased in early 2000 to 11,000 and later to 17,500. However, the mission was not configured

Box 5.1 Sierra Leone: a crucial test for twenty-first-century peace operations

Sierra Leone may be a small country, but this is an enormous challenge for the United Nations. It is in effect no less of a test of the United Nations commitment to conflict resolution in Africa than what we are contemplating for the Democratic Republic of the Congo. It is a test not just of our willingness to intervene...but of the United Nations' actual ability to deliver effective peacekeeping of lasting impact and value. (Sir Jeremy Greenstock, British Ambassador to the UN), S/PV.4099, 7 Feb. 2000, pp. 3–4)

Intended to be 11,000-strong, the force there is the largest UN peacekeeping army in the world. Yet it is pathetically failing. It has become hostage...to the armed gangs of rebel forces who are destabilising the regime it should be defending...If this massive UN presence is incapable of sustaining peace, against a disorderly and largely untrained rabble, one must ask what future there can ever be for the entire principle of humanitarian peacekeeping intervention by the UN. (Hugo Young, in *The Guardian* (UK), 18 May 2000)

to operate in potentially hostile territory. It was painfully slow to deploy, underfunded, poorly organized and commanded, and lacked critically important equipment and properly trained troops. Even UNAMSIL's Indian commander, Vijay Jetley, observed that some contingents 'did not come up to the mark and were an embarrassment both to the countries and to the UNAMSIL' (in Adebajo and Keen 2007: 260). Despite this assessment, Jetley decided to deploy his forces throughout the country and proceed with disarmament and demobilization (Hirsch 2001: 60–1).

When UNAMSIL tried forcibly to disarm RUF fighters in diamond-rich Kono province, the RUF reacted by attacking UNAMSIL, killing four Kenyan peacekeepers and seizing 500 others within a week, including an entire Zambian battalion (Adebajo and Keen 2007: 262). The newly emboldened RUF forces then began to advance on Sierra Leone's capital, Freetown. At that point, Britain sent approximately 1,300 troops to evacuate British and Commonwealth citizens from Freetown in a mission that eventually widened to include supporting UNAMSIL and the government of Sierra Leone. The DPKO also acted swiftly to recalibrate its mission by consolidating its forces around Freetown and the Lungi peninsula (see Hirsch 2001, 2004; Williams 2001). Disaster was narrowly averted in Sierra Leone, but the May 2000 hostage crisis and the factors that contributed to it exposed the fact that much more needed to be done to act on the lessons learned in the 1990s.

For similar reasons, the UN's new mission in the DRC (MONUC) also hung in the balance as the Brahimi panel set about its deliberations. MONUC was initially mandated to oversee the implementation of the Lusaka Peace Agreement (1999), signed by the governments of Angola, the DRC, Namibia, Rwanda, Uganda and Zimbabwe, and later by two rebel groups. It was also tasked with facilitating humanitarian assistance and protecting international staff and the civilian population wherever possible (Roessler and Prendergast 2006: 230). The ceasefire was broken almost as soon as the agreement was signed, and the governments of Rwanda, Uganda and Zimbabwe – all of whom had soldiers deployed inside the DRC – indicated that they would not be withdrawing immediately. To accomplish this large, complex but very vague mandate in a country the size of Western Europe, MONUC was granted an authorized strength of just 5,500 troops. In addition, its deployment was to be conducted in phases that were dependent on the consent and good behaviour of the conflicting parties. Because the latter persisted in fighting, it was not surprising that troop contributors were deeply reluctant to provide soldiers to implement a mandate that was so clearly unachievable within the parameters set by the Security Council. As a result, MONUC peacekeepers did not begin arriving in the DRC in significant numbers until early 2001.

The principal reason for this huge gulf between mandate and means lay in the mission's origins. The basic problem was that 'the war in the Congo was too gruesome and devastating for the West to ignore, but too difficult and too low a priority to address seriously' (Roessler and Prendergast 2006: 253). With the situation deteriorating into what became known as 'Africa's world war', calls grew for the UN to 'do something' to stop it (see Prunier 2009). African leaders in the Security Council had called for the deployment of a large force of 15,000 to 20,000 troops and France called for 10,000 troops, arguing that only an international deployment would bring an end to the fighting. However, in the midst of the crises in Kosovo, Sierra Leone and East Timor, the US and to a lesser extent the UK were reluctant to authorize another large mission. Following precisely the same line of decision-making that had caused the UN to deploy a small and weak force to Rwanda in 1993, the US administration authorized a UN mission to the DRC but insisted that it be limited to 5,000 troops and that it should avoid trying forcibly to disarm non-state actors (Roessler and Prendergast 2006: 250–1). As in Sierra Leone, by 2004–5 MONUC was confronting multiple crises, presenting the Security Council with the option of withdrawing or strengthening the mission (see section 5.3).

In summary, a combination of factors coalesced to bring about a rebirth of peace operations in the early years of the twenty-first century. In particular, there was a palpable surge in the force of humanitarian arguments which made it more difficult for governments simply to ignore widespread suffering. The pragmatic use of pivotal states and regional organizations also opened opportunities for Western states to contribute to peace operations without placing their forces under UN command. However, the crises in Sierra Leone and the DRC highlighted that two major problems had not yet been addressed. First, both missions were deployed on the incorrect assumption that all local actors were genuinely committed to the peace agreements they had signed. Second, the means given to these operations were not sufficient to achieve their stated objectives. It was in this context that the UN

Secretary-General was asked to conduct a thoroughgoing review of the organization's approach to peace operations.

5.2 The Brahimi Report

In March 2000, the UN Secretary-General set up the Panel on United Nations Peace Operations in response to a combination of factors, including the organization's institutional failings, the General Assembly's decision to end the practice of providing 'gratis military staff' to the DPKO, the renewed demand for peace operations, and the near collapse of the UN's mission in Sierra Leone (UNAMSIL) (Durch et al. 2003: 2–3). The panel was chaired by the former Algerian foreign minister Lakhdar Brahimi and comprised a mixture of former diplomats and soldiers. The research and writing was directed by William Durch, senior associate at the Henry L. Stimson Center in Washington, DC, and a leading analyst of peace operations. The panel was given the task of identifying the principal weaknesses in UN peace operations and making practical recommendations to overcome those weaknesses. The Secretary-General promised to do what he could to implement the panel's recommendations (ibid.: 5).

The report was officially launched at the UN's Millennium Summit in September 2000. As instructed, it focused upon how the UN Secretariat's staff working on peace operations might better manage planning, mission support, decision-making and personnel in the field to produce more effective results. But it also contained important insights into how peace operations themselves might be conducted in the future (Gray 2001: 288; and box 5.2).

In order to promote better management of peace operations the report made dozens of recommendations, which for the purposes of summarizing can be divided into four broad areas.

1 *Improving decision-making at UN headquarters* As noted in chapter 4, the UN's reports on the failures in Rwanda and Srebrenica identified major problems with the way that key strategic decisions about peace operations were made. For example, the UN's failure to stop the genocide in Rwanda was caused in part by a breakdown in communications between the peacekeepers in the field and decision-makers in New York, which resulted in members of the Security Council – including its president at that time, New Zealand – not being properly informed about the impending threat of genocide. As New Zealand's permanent representative to the UN at the time later reflected, 'the Rwanda experience proves that the United Nations must drastically improve the quality of the background information received by members of the Security Council about situations that come before them…even in 1993, the situation in Rwanda was more complex and dangerous than was ever indicated to the members of the Council' (Keating 2004: 500–1).

In order to address this problem, the Brahimi Report made several recommendations aimed at improving the flow and quality of information

Box 5.2 The Brahimi Report and the future of peace operations

The United Nations was founded, in the words of its Charter, in order 'to save succeeding generations from the scourge of war'. Meeting this challenge is the most important function of this Organization, and to a very significant degree it is the yardstick with which the Organization is judged by the peoples it exists to serve. Over the last decade, the United Nations has repeatedly failed to meet the challenge, and it can do better today. Without renewed commitment on the part of Member States, significant institutional change and increased financial support, the United Nations will not be capable of executing the critical peacekeeping and peace-building tasks that the Member States assign to it in coming months and years. There are many tasks which United Nations peacekeeping forces should not be asked to undertake and many places they should not go. But when the United Nations does send its forces to uphold the peace, they must be prepared to confront the lingering forces of war and violence, with the ability and determination to defeat them...The Panel concurs that consent of the local parties, impartiality and use of force only in self-defence should remain the bedrock principles of peacekeeping. Experience shows, however, that in the context of intra-state/transnational conflicts, consent may be manipulated in many ways. Impartiality for United Nations operations must therefore mean adherence to the principles of the Charter: where one party to a peace agreement clearly and incontrovertibly is violating its terms, continued equal treatment of all parties by the United Nations can in the best case result in ineffectiveness and in the worst may amount to complicity with evil. No failure did more to damage the standing and credibility of United Nations peacekeeping in the 1990s than its reluctance to distinguish victim from aggressor. (UN 2000: § 1, 9)

transmitted from the field to UN headquarters. It called for more consultation between the Security Council, which mandates operations, and the TCCs that provide the personnel, and for the creation of a standing committee to facilitate this relationship. It also insisted that the Secretariat should be better able to provide timely and accurate advice to the UN's decision-makers and requested the establishment of an Information and Strategic Analysis Secretariat (EISAS) capable of collating and disseminating this information. Moreover, the panel insisted that the way that peace operations were planned and managed should be reorganized to improve professionalism and coordination. Personnel should be recruited exclusively on the basis of expertise rather than on the basis of national quotas. The DPKO's capacity to provide effective and timely guidance would be improved by the creation of a 'Best Practices Unit' responsible for discovering and disseminating 'lessons learned', collating the best new research on peacekeeping, and conducting systematic analysis of relevant issues. Finally, the panel noted that advance planning was not well coordinated and called for the setting up of Integrated Mission Task Forces (IMTFs) comprising officials from the DPKO, DPA, OCHA and the UN's humanitarian and development agencies. IMTFs would coordinate and lead advance planning for peace operations, contributing to their overall effectiveness.

2 *Mandating and resources*   Problems connected with unclear mandates and the gulf between an operation's mandate and the resources given to it were recurring themes in the 1990s that were highlighted in the inquiries into the massacres in Rwanda and Srebrenica. All too often, the Security Council expanded an operation's mandate once it had deployed without ensuring that the mission was given the resources it needed to fulfil the new mandate. The gulf between ends and means that developed as a result was the principal cause of the failures in Srebrenica, Rwanda and Angola.

In order to address this problem, the Brahimi Report made four important recommendations designed to ensure that missions would not be deployed with unrealistic mandates or without the means to implement them properly. First, the DPKO should give realistic advice to the Security Council about the situation on the ground and the potential for a peace operation to work effectively. UN officials should be prepared to spell out precisely what the UN could and could not realistically hope to achieve and to recommend against the deployment of peacekeepers if they did not believe that the conditions for likely success are satisfied (UN 2000: § 64). Second, the Security Council should ensure that mandates are clearly worded and realizable. Third, the Security Council should not authorize an operation until it is confident that it has the means to accomplish its goals. Consequently, Security Council resolutions detailing a mission's mandate and the resources required to fulfil it should be left in draft form until the DPKO advises that member states have promised to provide the necessary resources in a timely fashion. Finally, the report recommended that the way peace operations were financed should be reformed so that financial arrangements are in place before a mission is deployed. In order to meet demands for rapid deployment (see below), it called for the Secretary-General to be granted the authority to utilize up to $50 million from the Peacekeeping Reserve Fund to secure key capabilities and services in advance of a mission being authorized by the Security Council.

3 *Rapid and effective deployment*   Once operations are mandated, the UN should be able to deploy its peacekeepers rapidly and effectively. One of the key problems that dogged UNPROFOR from the outset was that, by the time it deployed, the ceasefire it was supposed to monitor (between Croatia and Serb militia) had broken down and the conflict in Croatia had been surpassed by the explosion of war in Bosnia-Hercegovina. In 1994, twenty-seven states had designated themselves 'Friends of Rapid Deployment' and aimed to provide the DPKO with a rapidly deployable headquarters (RDHQ) through the provision of gratis staff. The RDHQ concept, adopted and developed by Canada, promised to provide the UN with the capacity to plan and manage the deployment of new operations rapidly. However, as we noted earlier, some General Assembly members opposed the provision of gratis staff to the DPKO on the grounds that most of these staff were Westerners and this practice disrupted the national balance in UN staffing

(Langille 2000: 228). Although this proposal failed to win political support, it provided the catalyst for a number of subsequent studies on rapid deployment. For example, in 1995 a Canadian report called for the creation of an effective rapid reaction capability that would require an early warning mechanism, an effective decision-making process, reliable transportation and infrastructure, logistical support, sufficient finances, and well-trained and equipped personnel (Miall et al. 2005: 156). In the same year, Sir Brian Urquhart (1995), one of the pioneers of peacekeeping, added his own thoughts on the idea of a rapid deployment capability. However, Secretary-General-elect Kofi Annan (1996) rejected calls for the UN to develop such capabilities. Conscious of the need to secure consensus among member states, he warned that such a capability would create legal and financial difficulties, was unlikely to deliver the necessary rapid deployment capabilities and – even if it were possible – would take too long to develop.

Working within these parameters, the Brahimi Report made four recommendations aimed at improving the UN's capacity to deploy peacekeepers rapidly and effectively. First, the UN should have the ability to generate forces rapidly by using forces under the Standby Arrangements System (UNSAS), whereby member states are invited to nominate with varying degrees of specificity forces that they are prepared to assign to UN duties in order to quicken the composition of missions (see chapter 2). Ideally, the panel concluded, a traditional mission should be deployable within thirty days and larger, more complex, missions within ninety days. Second, the UN should have the capacity to deploy the forward elements of a peace operation within a few days of a mandate being handed down by the Security Council. Third, to accomplish these goals the Secretariat should be given the capacity to take decisions and make plans rapidly. It would be assisted in this by the creation of EISAS and IMTFs. Finally, the panel concluded that the rapid and effective deployment of the forward elements of a mission required that the UN have its own deployable logistics and communications capabilities.

4 *Effectiveness of deployed forces*   On the question of how to improve the effectiveness of deployed peace operations, the Brahimi Report identified three core requirements. First, in order to avoid repeating the mistakes made in Rwanda, Bosnia, Angola, Somalia and elsewhere, the military component of a peace operation should be robust enough to defend itself effectively, 'confront the lingering forces of war and violence' and protect civilians under its care. 'Peacekeepers who witness violence against civilians should be presumed to be authorised to stop it' within their means (UN 2000: § 62). The report made it clear, however, that this presumed mandate needed to be balanced against the need to match mandate and means, and that the Security Council and Secretariat should avoid writing 'blank cheques' by proffering wide protection mandates without fully examining what would be required to fulfil them. Second, the recommendation was made that UN peacekeepers be required to have basic skills and comply with 'best practices' common to

all UN missions. Finally, this demand would be supported by a renewed emphasis on training for peacekeepers and senior civilian personnel.

The UN membership – including all five of the Security Council's permanent members – welcomed the report (Gray 2001: 268). Nevertheless, the Secretariat experienced considerable difficulty persuading member states to implement its main recommendations (see table 5.3). In particular, several states – many of them key contributors to UN peace operations such as in India – expressed doubts about the legitimacy of 'robustness', arguing that Brahimi's vision constituted an unwelcome departure from the traditional tenets of peacekeeping (ibid.). Some states argued that the scope of peace operations should not be enlarged in the way envisaged by the panel and that 'basic principles' such as consent, impartiality and the minimum use of force only in self-defence should be preserved (UN General Assembly 2002: 2; see section 5.3). They even feared that the switch of language from 'peacekeeping' to 'peace operations' could legitimize forcible humanitarian intervention (ibid.: 3). A Special Committee, created by the General Assembly to follow up on the report, therefore adopted a more cautious and traditional position on peacekeeping than that taken by the Brahimi panel (Gray 2001: 270).

Shortly after the report was published, the Secretary-General outlined the steps necessary to implement its recommendations. In particular, Annan agreed that improving coordination between the Security Council and TCCs was crucial. The Secretariat, he noted, could also 'improve the way it assesses force requirements and devises concepts of operations. It could enhance the quality of military guidance provided in the field. It could promulgate standard operating procedures for a whole host of activities' (Annan 2000b: 9). These goals would be met by establishing IMTFs that would coordinate the efforts of the UN's different agencies and enhance the organization's rapid deployment capabilities. The Secretary-General also called for states to participate more fully in the UNSAS (ibid.: 15–17). Annan requested 'additional resources for the Secretariat', without which the reforms would have little hope of producing results on the ground. However, in a revealing admission, he acknowledged that his 'request does not represent our complete needs, but it is a realistic indication of the areas that need to be strengthened on a priority basis' (ibid.: 22). The following year, the Secretary-General identified five strategic goals for implementing the panel's recommendations and improving UN peace operations (see box 5.3).

Although it was meant to be holistic in its approach to peace operations, in practice the political aspects of the Brahimi Report's recommendations have been sidelined, and UN officials themselves admit that there has been least progress on the decision-making and strategic issues (Harland 2003: 2). For example, some permanent members reportedly worried that, should the Security Council leave mandates in draft form as recommended, political support for a mission could dry up while waiting for the Secretary-General to verify troop commitments. In place of the draft resolutions, the Council

TABLE 5.3 Implementing the Brahimi Report: a scorecard

Issue area	Progress	No progress
Decision-making	– Improved informal consultations between Council and TCCs – Heightened informal consultation between P-5 – 'Planning mandates' issued (MONUC) – IMTFs established for Afghanistan, Liberia and Sudan	– No standing liaison committee for TCCs – Security Council rejects idea of leaving resolutions in draft form until resources provided – DPKO Best Practices Unit created and subsequently expanded and renamed 'Best Practices Section' – IMTFs become briefing venues rather than joint planning venues
Mandate and resources	– DPKO has improved advice on threats and limits to what peacekeepers can achieve – Mandates are clearer, more specific and carefully demarcated – Pre-approval of advance discretionary funds for the Secretary-General denied but process quickened for case-by-case approval (MINUCI, UNMIL)	– Missions authorized without necessary resources being available (e.g. UNAMID)
Rapid deployment	– UN Logistics Depot created at Brindisi, Italy – UN can deploy small number of transport assets and communications at short notice – Small missions deployed in less than one week (e.g. Iraq, Côte d'Ivoire)	– Average duration to full deployment remains around eighteen months – Critical delays in Sudan, Darfur, eastern DRC
Effective deployment	– Missions typically given robust mandates – Peacekeepers taking proactive role in preventing spoilers and protecting civilians (e.g. Haiti, DRC) – Best practice guidelines developed – 'Capstone doctrine' developed – UN Staff College strengthened and training for SRSGs formalized – UNITAR programme on peace operations expanded into a comprehensive programme	– Significant capacity problems remain – UN unable to insist on compliance with best practices – Training of non-UN personnel remains entirely voluntary – Complaints of abuse by UN peacekeepers

Source: based on Annan 2000b, 2000c, 2001c, 2001d; Durch et al. 2003)

Box 5.3 Implementing the Brahimi Report: five strategic goals

1 Enhancing the rapid deployment capability for peacekeeping operations
2 Strengthening the relationship with member states and legislative bodies
3 Reforming the DPKO's management culture
4 Reforming the DPKO's relationship with field missions
5 Strengthening relationships with other parts of the UN system

Source: paraphrased from Annan 2001d: § 7.

...it must be remembered that the success or failure of peacekeeping operations derives above all from the will of the parties to the conflict, of the Security Council, and of other Member States to use this invaluable instrument wisely and well. Regardless of the excellence of any system or machinery, a peacekeeping operation cannot succeed if there is no peace to keep, if it lacks an appropriate mandate, or if it is not given the necessary material and political support in a timely fashion. (Annan 2001d: § 83)

offered 'planning mandates' that would allow the Secretariat to approach potential contributors before a final mandate was handed down (Durch et al. 2003: 19). This approach was trialled in relation to MONUC (UN Security Council Resolution 1327, 2000) but has not been widely used since. Nor has there been significant progress towards institutionalizing cooperation between TCCs, the DPKO and the Security Council, despite Annan having identified this as a priority. In 2001 the Security Council resolved to institutionalize cooperation (in Resolution 1353), but little tangible progress was made thanks to differences over the precise role of TCCs. While a group of thirty-six troop contributors sought a formal subsidiary body as recommended by Brahimi, four of the five permanent members of the Security Council opposed this move, fearing that it had the potential to devolve the Council's authority and hinder its work (see Gray 2001: 283). The problems connected with an absence of consultation were made plain in 2003, when 750 Uruguayan military observers and soldiers not configured for a hostile environment were deployed into the town of Bunia in eastern DRC to replace around 9,000 battle-hardened Ugandan soldiers who were withdrawing at the request of the Security Council. Despite clear warnings pointing to the likely deterioration of the security situation after Uganda's withdrawal, the Uruguayans were deployed with no UN background briefings, no special training, and no guidance about how to interpret and implement their mandate in this context (Ross 2003; see also chapter 15).

In the main, both the report and its implementation focused on the institutional capacity of the UN Secretariat and the bureaucratic organization of individual missions. Issues such as political will, funding and the responsibility of the Security Council have been further marginalized during the subsequent implementation process. This occurred in spite of the importance that the panel attached to these political dimensions (see box 5.3) but was as much a consequence of bureaucratic disputes between the DPKO and DPA over the nature and proper place of 'political' issues as it was a product of pressure from member states (Berdal 2001: 50–1). Of course, a report such as this cannot by itself generate political will, but it could have reiterated its importance in the strongest possible terms. The preoccupation with technical issues looks even more out of place when we remember that the UN reports on Rwanda and Srebrenica clearly demonstrated that *political factors* rather than bureaucratic/institutional factors were primarily responsible for the respective failures. This, of course, is no great revelation. Recall that in 1992 Boutros-Ghali warned that one of the most serious problems facing the UN was the danger of its member states assigning it more and more onerous tasks without giving it the requisite resources to fulfil them (Boutros-Ghali 1992: §§ 4, 7). This issue remains central to the contemporary agenda but, apart from proposing that resolutions be left in draft form until the requisite resources were available and strengthening standby arrangements, the Brahimi Report did not make much headway (though cf. Malone and Thakur 2001).

As table 5.3 attests, even the report's technical recommendations did not necessarily command support when it came to implementation. For a start, the proposal for improved strategic planning and analysis for peace operations was rejected largely because of long-standing opposition to the idea that the UN should have its own information/intelligence-gathering capabilities (see Chesterman 2006). The UN is also still having difficulty obtaining sufficient pledges of reserve contingents of troops. Moreover, even when pledges have been forthcoming, member states have sometimes reneged on them. To give one example, before 2007 the entire UN force in the DRC was covered by just one reserve battalion. This problem is indicative of the fact that member states often make declarations of intent but are less likely to commit money and troops.

Other technical recommendations simply did not work as intended. For example, the IMTF model was widely supported and put into practice in relation to missions in Afghanistan (2001–2), Liberia (2003) and Sudan (2004). But the task forces attracted a high number of participants (over fifty), making it difficult for them to do more than simply offer updates and briefings (Durch et al. 2003: 48). In the end, the DPKO convened its own smaller ad hoc working group for Liberia to perform many of the same tasks envisaged for the IMTFs.

In addition to these difficulties, the report was criticized on a number of grounds. Most significant, given the pressing need to find additional troop capacity to close the gulf between means and ends, was the panel's failure to address non-UN peacekeepers. This was important given that in 2002, for instance, there were approximately 39,000 UN peacekeepers but around 50,000 non-UN peacekeepers deployed around the world (Durch 2003: 4; see Diehl 2008: 66–7) While this oversight is understandable given the report's remit, it is less clear why the panel failed to explore more fully the UN's relationship with regional organizations and other peacekeeping actors, despite its increasing reliance on those actors and the emergence of 'hybrid' operations (see chapters 13 and 14).

In addition, some commentators criticized the report for not going into detail about command and control and the financial aspects of peace operations (Cardenas 2000: 72–3; White 2001: 137–8). Critics have also chided it for ignoring conflict prevention and not devoting enough attention to civil-military relations or the relationship between the UN and local actors in conflict zones. In particular, it was taken to task for not suggesting that UN peace operations should hire more local staff, thereby cultivating the skills and leadership of local citizens (Bell and Tousignant 2001: 44). That said, the question of which locals to hire is clearly a complicated issue. Finally, the report was criticized for being 'largely silent on gender issues' and its apparent inability to draw upon work already undertaken on these issues within the UN system (Whitworth 2004: 127; see chapter 16).

These criticisms notwithstanding, the Brahimi Report marked a significant step forward for UN peace operations, not least by redefining the core tasks of peacekeeping, refocusing basic principles, and setting out a relatively comprehensive programme of UN reform. Although some significant gaps remained, it helped set the agenda for twenty-first-century peacekeeping and laid the foundations for the UN to respond to heightening demands for its peacekeepers. The following section focuses on this more recent expansion of peace operations and shows how the groundwork laid by the Brahimi Report helped change the way the UN conducts peace operations.

5.3 Peace operations after Brahimi

The final section of this chapter examines the progress of peace operations after the Brahimi Report. It begins by reviewing some of the key political issues, focusing on questions about the relationship between peacekeepers and the International Criminal Court and the impact of the US-led 'Global War on Terror' – especially the 2003 invasion and subsequent occupation of Iraq. The second part considers the question of UN reform and one of the main post-Brahimi changes in the way the UN thinks about peace operations – the development of 'capstone doctrine.' Finally, we briefly discuss the practical experience of peace operations themselves and identify some key signs of progress, but also some major challenges and potential dangers.

Politics

The twenty-first century has been a relatively tumultuous time for UN peace operations, especially in terms of the UN's relationship with George W. Bush's administration and the impact of the latter's approach to the International Criminal Court (ICC) and the Global War on Terror (GWOT).

It is well known that one of the keys to making the UN work effectively is maintaining a good relationship with its principal donor – the US. However, the establishment of the ICC on 1 July 2002 placed a considerable strain on the relationship. Although it was heralded by many states and international lawyers as the most progressive development in international law since the establishment of the UN itself, US opposition to the ICC has caused significant problems for peacekeepers. The Bush administration opposed the Court because it feared that US military forces operating overseas would be vulnerable to what it described as 'politicized prosecutions'. Not only did the Bush administration 'unsign' the treaty establishing the ICC, it threatened to veto the renewal of every UN peacekeeping operation until it achieved a blanket amnesty for US and other peacekeeping personnel. Since most UN peacekeeping operations have their mandate renewed by the Security Council every six or twelve months, it was not long before a mission renewal came before the Council – that of UNMIBH in Bosnia-Hercegovina. The US duly vetoed the extension of UNMIBH, even though the operation enjoyed the consent of the Bosnian government and the support of the other permanent members of the Security Council and involved only forty-five Americans (in July 2002 the US had fewer than 750 personnel deployed worldwide with the UN, all but two of whom were civilian rather than military personnel). Ironically, the US did not consider withdrawing its troops from the NATO-led operations in Bosnia and Kosovo, despite the fact that the peacekeepers there came under the jurisdiction of the ICTY. Neither did it withdraw its forces from the territories of states such as Britain, Germany and Japan, all of which had ratified the ICC Statute. Fortunately, by 2002, UNMIBH comprised mainly a police-training programme that was due to hand over to the EU later that year. A compromise was finally reached whereby the US permitted the mission to stay in place in return for a swifter transition to EU control. After some very strained negotiations, an agreement was reached whereby peacekeeping personnel were granted immunity from prosecution by the ICC for a renewable period of one year.

A second issue that affected relations between the US and UN, and impacted in other ways on peace operations more generally, was the GWOT and especially the 2003 invasion of Iraq. There are at least two different ways of thinking about the impact that the GWOT and the Iraq War have had on peace operations. The first can be described as 'optimistic', because it sees peace operations being more likely on account of the perceived convergence between Western national security interests and humanitarian concerns that occurred after the terrorist attacks of 9/11 (Wheeler and Bellamy 2005: 572). The second perspective is that the 'sun has set' on the nascent humanitarianism evident in the 1990s, primarily because the GWOT in general and the West's operations in Afghanistan and Iraq in particular will make them less likely to contribute large numbers of troops to UN operations (Weiss 2004a: 135). In addition, the abuse of humanitarian justifications for the invasion of

Iraq has severely undermined the credibility of the US and the UK in particular to act as champions of more robust civilian protection operations in the future (Evans 2004). As the director of Human Rights Watch put it, one of the most troubling consequences of the attempts to justify the Iraq War in humanitarian terms was that 'it will be more difficult next time for us to call on military action when we need it to save potentially hundreds of thousands of lives' (Roth 2004: 2–3).

The impact of the GWOT and Iraq War on peace operations is therefore hotly contested. Nevertheless, we think at least three trends are clearly apparent. First, the commitment of large numbers of Western troops to Afghanistan and Iraq make the TCCs less likely to contribute to UN and other non-UN peace operations. Second, the moral credibility of states that participated in the invasion of Iraq was diminished, making it more difficult for these traditional leaders to play a major role in shaping the world's response to crises in Darfur, Somalia, the DRC and elsewhere. Finally, the overriding of sovereignty in the case of Iraq has made many states in the global South more wary of international activism without the consent of the host government. As we discuss below, the deferral to host-state consent has made it difficult to craft an effective response to the conflicts in Darfur, Chad and the Central African Republic (CAR). In short, therefore, as demand for peace operations increases, not only has the West become less willing and able to contribute its personnel but the global consensus on international activism has weakened (see chapter 2).

UN reform

Reforming the UN was a centrepiece of Kofi Annan's bid to become Secretary-General and a central demand of the US. The George W. Bush administration encouraged an anti-UN political atmosphere in Washington, which only intensified with Annan's criticism of the invasion of Iraq and the UN's 'oil-for-food' scandal. In 2004 Henry Hyde introduced legislation into Congress aimed at halving America's dues to the UN, which would have caused a financial crisis for the organization overnight. The Bill passed Congress, suggesting that there was some sympathy for it at the White House, and it was widely thought that the Senate would only kill it off (as it subsequently did) if the US was satisfied with the progress of UN reform (Traub 2006: 362).

In September 2003, Annan commissioned a High-Level Panel to examine challenges to international peace and security and the contribution that the UN could make to address those challenges more effectively. In its December 2004 report, the panel set out a range of recommendations relating to the function of the Security Council, the capacity of the Secretariat and the creation of new institutions (UNSG High-Level Panel 2004). Among the recommendations was a call for the UN to create a standing police capacity to improve its ability to deploy police officers at short notice – a clear response to the emergence of police-led operations (see chapter 17). In place of Brahimi's call for mandates to be left in draft form, the panel suggested a system of indicative voting whereby Council members could call for states to declare and justify their positions publicly prior to an actual vote (ibid.: § 257). Annan accepted almost all the High-Level Panel's recommendations in his own blueprint for UN reform, which was taken to a summit of world leaders in 2005 (Annan 2005a). Many of these proposals were adopted at the summit, though in considerably weakened form (see table 5.4 for those most relevant to peacekeeping). For example, the standing police capacity was limited to twenty-five people, hardly enough to make an impact on the UN's seventeen peace operations.

Thus, while progress was made at the 2005 World Summit, it was limited progress at best, and the limitations placed on the Peacebuilding Commission and standing police capacity threatened seriously to constrain their ability to make a positive contribution to peace operations. Even less progress was made on issues such as management reform, with the Secretary-General seeking the authority to make appointments on the basis of merit alone but the UN membership reserving for itself the right to confirm appointments – ensuring that the appointment of senior UN staff will continue to be made for political as much as merit-based reasons.

As we noted in chapter 2, the DPKO itself has undergone a period of reform and restructuring. At the same time, progress has been made on the development of doctrine to guide UN peace operations in the field. There was no UN doctrine (in the normal military sense of the term) owing largely to political

TABLE 5.4 UN reform and the 2005 World Summit: relevant outcomes

Area	2005 outcome	Implementation
Peacebuilding	– Agreement to create a Peacebuilding Commission to spearhead UN's efforts in this area	– Commission supported by a new Peacebuilding Support Office and Peacebuilding Fund – Confused authority: Commission sits under Security Council, General Assembly and ECOSOC – PBSO given limited resources (around twenty staff) – Donations to the Peacebuilding Fund are voluntary and slow to arrive
Standing police capacity	– Agreement to create a standing police capacity	– Capacity limited to twenty-five – No new financial or personnel resources provided
Responsibility to protect	– Endorsement of responsibility to protect principle	– Secretary-General creates a special adviser position to develop plans for translating the principle from words into deeds

sensitivities about the UN prescribing behaviour to member states and a lack of strategic capacity in the DPKO. As we noted earlier, the Brahimi Report's call for the DPKO to be given a capacity for strategic planning and analysis was rejected principally on account of concerns about the potential for such a capacity to challenge the decision-making authority of member states. However, there are signs that states are beginning gradually to lessen their hostility to UN doctrine, and the UN has developed a series of 'guidelines'.

Some progress was also made in terms of thinking about the meaning of key concepts such as 'impartiality' and translating lessons learned into better practice. For example, the 2003 *Handbook on United Nations Multidimensional Peacekeeping Operations* insisted that 'impartiality...does not mean inaction or overlooking violations'. It instructed peacekeepers to 'actively pursue the implementation of their mandate', even if that meant going against the wishes of one or more of the parties to the conflict (DPKO 2003: 56–7).

The *Handbook* was followed up in December 2005, when Kofi Annan (2005d) called for the development of an inventory of terms and peacekeeping doctrine to address various issues, including the protection of vulnerable populations. Shortly afterwards, in March 2006, member states signalled their willingness to address the question of developing UN doctrine, with the General Assembly's Special Committee on Peacekeeping calling upon the Secretariat to prepare a glossary of terminology for 'further development of a peacekeeping doctrine, guiding principles and concepts' (UN General Assembly 2006: § 7).

The development of what was initially labelled 'capstone doctrine' for UN peace operations was led by the DPKO's renamed Best Practices Section. Drafts of the 'doctrine' were written by DPKO staff and presented to member states and experts through a series of regional roundtables. During the consultation process, it became evident that many member states remained reluctant to embrace the very idea of 'capstone doctrine', let alone a systematic rethinking of the way that peace operations were conceptualized and conducted in line with the recommendations of the Brahimi Report. These differences are apparent when comparing early drafts of the doctrine with the final product in two important domains: the status of doctrine and principles of peacekeeping.

Status of doctrine   The most important difference between the early drafts and the finished product was the underlying purpose of the document itself. Whereas the initial intent was to provide guidance and common principles for UN peacekeepers, the final version appeared more an exercise in summarizing the current state of play, much like the 2003 *Handbook*. The third draft of the doctrine (29 June 2007) contained the phrase 'capstone doctrine' in its title and stated that it 'constitutes the highest-level in the doctrine and guidance framework for UN peacekeeping'. The draft continued: 'it is in effect the strategic guidance' for the wider body of material on the conduct of peace operations (DPKO 2007: § 4). Reflecting member states' concerns about UN doctrine, the final draft dropped the phrase 'capstone doctrine' from its title, removed all references to 'doctrine', insisted that the document was 'internal' to DPKO and deleted the intention to provide 'strategic guidance' (DPKO 2008a: § 4). Whereas the original draft purported to offer 'a multi-dimensional doctrine to embrace the complex operations of today' (2007: § 6), the final version simply 'reflect[ed]' the multi-dimensional nature of contemporary operations (2008a: § 6).

Principles of peacekeeping　The draft doctrine argued that the traditional principles of consent, impartiality and non-use of force except in self-defence should be revised and augmented. In their place, the draft proposed six new principles.

1　*Consent*: Peacekeepers should be deployed with the consent of the parties to the conflict.
2　*Impartiality*: 'UN peacekeepers should be impartial in their dealings with the parties to conflict, but not neutral in the execution of their mandate' (DPKO 2007: § 66).
3　*Restraint in the use of force*: Although force must be used in a restrained fashion, it may be employed in circumstances other than self-defence. Peacekeepers may use force to protect themselves, their mandate and groups identified by the mandate (e.g. civilians, humanitarian workers) (§ 69).
4　*Credibility*: To operate effectively in volatile environments, peace operations must be credible. Credibility requires rapid deployment, proper resourcing, ability to deter spoilers and the ability to manage expectations (§§ 73–5).
5　*Legitimacy*: Operations must be seen as legitimate. Legitimacy is conferred through the legal mandate, the firm and fair exercise of the mandate, circumspect use of force, discipline of the peacekeepers, and respect shown to the local population (§§ 76–7).
6　*Promotion of national and local ownership*: Peacekeepers should promote national and local ownership of the peace process (§ 79).

These proposed changes to the basic principles of peacekeeping met with stiff resistance from states reluctant to augment the traditional principles and unwilling to expand the remit of UN activism. In the final draft, credibility, legitimacy and local ownership were downgraded from 'principles' to 'success factors' (DPKO 2008a: §§ 76ff.). Likewise, the proposed expansion of the role of force was revised to read 'non-use of force except in self-defence and defence of the mandate' (§§ 70ff.). Whereas the Brahimi Report had advised that peacekeepers be 'presumed' to have a mandate to protect civilians (with force if necessary) and the draft had permitted force to protect peacekeepers, the mandate and others, the final draft insisted that force could be used only in self-defence and defence of the mandate, when authorized by the Security Council (§ 70). Where neither the Brahimi Report nor the early drafts of the capstone doctrine required that peacekeepers be explicitly authorized to use force to protect civilians, the final version of the 'principles and guidelines' made the use of force in such circumstances contingent on Security Council authorization.

Important changes were therefore made to the proposed capstone doctrine in order to make it less authoritative as a guide to UN peacekeepers and less progressive in the way that it conceptualized the principles of peacekeeping. Nonetheless, the formulation of 'principles and guidelines' itself marks an important step towards clarifying the nature and purpose of UN peace operations as well as best practice. Moreover, the strengthening of the Best Practice Section in the DPKO (see chapter 2) means that this process is likely to be ongoing.

Missions

The years following the release of the Brahimi Report saw a steady increase in the number and size of UN peace operations. By 2008 there were seventeen ongoing operations and over 80,000 troops, police and civilian personnel deployed under the auspices of the UN (see figure 5.1 and table 5.5). In addition, there were also sizeable non-UN deployments (see table 5.6).

There are several important points to draw from these tables. First, post-Brahimi peace operations cover the broad spectrum of types, from

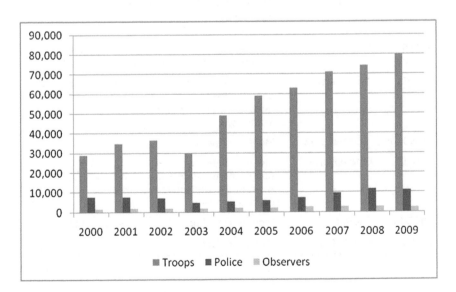

Figure 5.1 *UN peacekeepers in the twenty-first century (figures based on 30 June of each year)*

TABLE 5.5 UN peace operations, 30 June 2008

Name	Location	Mandate	Size (deployed)
MINURSO	Western Sahara	– Supervise referendum	223
MINUSTAH	Haiti	– Support the government in maintaining order – Help build government capacity	8,836
MINURCAT	Chad/CAR	– Humanitarian assistance – Facilitate return of IDPs by protecting civilians	270
MONUC	DRC	– Maintain peace and security – Protect civilians – Assist in reconstruction	18,271
UNAMID	Darfur	– Protect civilian population – Monitor ceasefire – Implement Darfur Peace Agreement	9,000 (of authorized 26,000)
UNDOF	Middle East	– Observe disengagement of forces	1,043
UNFICYP	Cyprus	– Monitor ceasefire	915
UNIFIL	Lebanon	– Verify withdrawal of forces – Monitor ceasefire	13,264
UNMEE	Ethiopia–Eritrea	– Monitor ceasefire – Patrol demilitarized zone	1,686
UNMIK	Kosovo	– Contribute to building state institutions – Oversee establishment of Kosovo Police Service	2,069 (mainly police)
UNMIL	Liberia	– Oversee implementation of peace agreement – Contribute to peace and security	15,318
UNMIS	Sudan	– Oversee implementation of comprehensive peace agreement	10,066
UNMIT	Timor-Leste	– Assist government in maintaining peace and security – Establish effective government institutions	1,668
UNMOGIP	India/Pakistan	– Monitor ceasefire	44
UNOCI	Côte d'Ivoire	– Monitor ceasefire – Contribute to peace and security – Assist in the implementation of a peace agreement	9,196
UNOMIG	Georgia	– Monitor ceasefire	147
UNTSO	Middle East	– Monitor ceasefire	151

TABLE 5.6 Non-UN peace operations, 30 June 2008

Name	Actor	Place	Mandate	Size
AMISOM	AU	Somalia	Support transitional government of Somalia; maintain order	2,200
MAES	AU	Comoros	Defeat insurgents; support government; collect arms; support electoral process	1,500
FOMUC	CEMAC	CAR	Monitor ceasefire	378
Joint Control Commission Peacekeeping Force	Russia-Moldova-PMR	Moldova (Transdnestr)	Monitor ceasefire	1,174
CIS Peacekeeping Forces in Georgia	CIS	Georgia (Abkhazia)	Monitor ceasefire	1,600
South Ossetia Joint Force	Russia-Georgia-S. Ossetia	Georgia (South Ossetia)	Monitor ceasefire	1,500
EUFOR Althea	EU	Bosnia-Hercegovina	Establish Bosnian Police Service	2,504 (police)
EUFOR Chad/CAR	EU	Chad/CAR	Monitor ceasefire; deter violence; oversee implementation of peace agreement	3,000
KFOR	NATO	Kosovo	Maintain peace and security; establish security forces in Kosovo	15,109
ISAF	NATO	Afghanistan	Maintain peace and security; support government of Afghanistan	41,118
MFO	Coalition	Egypt (Sinai)	Observe ceasefire	1,691 (milobs)
Operation Licorne	France	Côte d'Ivoire	Contribute to maintenance of peace and security; support UNOCI	2,400
RAMSI	Australia / Pacific Islands Forum	Solomon Islands	Maintain law and order; disarm rebels; support government rebuilding	750
ISF	Australia and New Zealand	Timor-Leste	Support government in maintaining law and order	1,020

traditional monitoring (see chapter 7) to complex peace support operations with robust mandates (see chapter 12). It is too simplistic, therefore, to argue that the traditional precepts of peace operations have been replaced by new doctrines, because traditional and monitoring-style operations account for half of all UN operations and around a third of all non-UN operations. Moreover, not all traditional operations are small in size. UNIFIL, deployed to Lebanon as part of a peace deal that brought the 2006 conflict between Israel and Hezbollah to an end, is a relatively large operation with a basically traditional mandate. Second, the growth in non-UN operations has not come at the expense of UN operations (see Heldt 2008). As often as not, UN and non-UN actors operate alongside one another, as in the Balkans, Afghanistan, Côte d'Ivoire and Timor-Leste. Indeed, measured in terms of personnel, the number of UN peacekeepers has grown considerably in the twenty-first century (see figure 5.1), while, with the exception of NATO's mission in Afghanistan, the overall number of troops deployed on non-UN missions has remained relatively static (CIC 2008: 3). Third, the Brahimi Report's call for missions to have the capability to protect themselves, their mandates and – where possible – imperilled civilians was reflected both in this partnership between UN and non-UN actors and in the increased average size of UN peace operations. With the notable exceptions of the four missions deployed in Sudan, Chad and the CAR, in 2008 none of the missions listed in tables 5.5 and 5.6 were confronted with a gulf between means and ends as dramatic as that experienced by UNAMSIL in 2000 or UNAMIR in 1994. Fourth, the composition of these operations demonstrates an increased willingness to fit forces to missions. Contemporary missions include military-led operations as well as traditional peacekeeping led by military observers and a new breed of 'rule of law' operations led by police officers (see chapter 17). Finally, in 2008 the overall record of the UN's ongoing operations was relatively strong, despite a number of serious challenges caused primarily by stalling peace processes, a reluctance to contribute forces to the UNAMID operation in Sudan, and a general neglect of the spiralling crisis in Somalia (ibid.). This reluctance to engage in Sudan stood in stark contrast to the rapidity with which contributors moved to deploy 10,000 troops to Lebanon in the space of just four months in 2006.

There are multiple reasons for this growth in the size and number of peace operations, not least a steady increase in demand. Increased demand, however, was not a simple product of higher levels of armed conflict, because this has actually reduced during this period (Human Security Centre 2008). Instead, perceptions of success in places such as the Balkans, Timor-Leste, Burundi and West Africa helped elevate the status of peace operations as a valued tool of conflict management once again. In Sierra Leone and Burundi, for example, UN peacekeepers accomplished their mandates in 2005 and 2006 respectively and handed over to political missions, which came under the auspices of the new UN Peacebuilding Commission.

The fact that peace operations have once again become conflict management tools of choice was most clearly demonstrated after the war between Israel and Hezbollah in July–August 2006. Before that conflict, analysts had questioned the continuing utility of UNIFIL, which had originally been established in 1978 to assist in the provision of security in south Lebanon following Israel's invasion during the Lebanese civil war (CIC 2006). During the 2006 conflict, however, both the parties and the mediators recognized the need for a strengthened deployment of peacekeepers to ensure the demilitarization of southern Lebanon. Although UNIFIL was not authorized to disarm Hezbollah or secure the Lebanese border, it was given a mandate to ensure that southern Lebanon not be used as a staging post for attacks on Israel. Just as importantly, UNIFIL was also provided with the means to accomplish its mandate, with European states (especially France, Italy, Spain and Germany) contributing around 5,500 troops to a mission operating in a relatively small geographic area.

This level of European participation in a UN operation, which had not been seen since the end of UNPROFOR and UNTAES in the Balkans, was facilitated by a unique command structure centred around a strategic military cell (SMC) based at UN headquarters. The SMC, created at the insistence of France and Italy, provides a conduit between the mission commander and the DPKO and ensures that the troop contributors (principally the Europeans) have more control over the mission's operational direction (CIC 2007: 86). The key point here is that the strengthening of a floundering UN peace operation in southern Lebanon was widely seen as a fundamental part of the conflict resolution process. The remainder of this section briefly explores this expansion of peace operations.

As we noted earlier, a key test for UN peace operations in the twenty-first century came in the DRC. We discuss that case in relation to the protection of civilians in chapter 15. Here, however, we are most interested in how the Security Council responded to the crises of 2003–4, when various militia groups in the DRC broke ceasefire agreements and began to wage war on each other and the civilian population in a context where the UN peacekeepers lacked the means and mandate to deter violations, enforce compliance and protect civilians. Most notably, in 2003 militias overran the town of Bunia and posed a very real threat of genocide that was averted only by the timely intervention of the French-led IEMF. The following year, rebels loyal to General Laurent Nkunda overran the town of Bukavu in South Kivu, despite the presence of MONUC peacekeepers, seriously undermining the mission's credibility (CIC 2008: 43).

Unlike in Somalia and Rwanda, when the Security Council responded to challenges such as this by downsizing and withdrawing – effectively leaving the civilian population to its fate – the Council strengthened MONUC. From June to September 2003, France led a coalition of the willing into the town of Bunia in eastern DRC to stem the tide of attacks on civilians.

The relative – though limited – success of that operation provided a catalyst for the staged strengthening of MONUC's mandate and the means placed at its disposal. Between 2005 and 2007, the much-strengthened mission worked alongside government forces to coerce and sometimes forcibly disarm recalcitrant militia and, with the support of an EU Reserve Deployment (EUFOR RD), oversaw national elections. The EU mission helped ensure that post-election violence in Kinshasa, responsible for the death of thirty-two people, did not escalate into more generalized violence or undermine the political process in the DRC (see chapter 6). Throughout the period, sporadic fighting, especially in Ituri province and North and South Kivu, caused widespread civilian displacement, and MONUC peacekeepers often come under attack, sustaining heavy casualties. In all, twenty-two peacekeepers were killed in violent attacks in 2005 and 2006 (CIC 2008: 229).

Similar patterns have also been evident in Côte d'Ivoire and Timor-Leste, which both confronted (and survived) major crises. In 2002, elements of Côte d'Ivoire's military ('Forces Nouvelle') rebelled and launched a failed coup attempt against President Laurent Gbagbo. Fearing a repeat of the bloodshed seen in Côte d'Ivoire's West African neighbours and spurred by France in particular, which had a long-standing relationship with the government and military bases in the country, the Security Council authorized the deployment of a UN mission to operate alongside the French Operation Licorne and to take over from a hastily assembled West African force, ECOMICI. The UN force, UNOCI, was deployed in 2004 to monitor a ceasefire between the two sides in the civil war, maintain a demilitarized 'zone of confidence' between the parties and help implement a peace agreement (Linas–Marcoussis Accords). In late 2004, government forces attacked French peacekeepers, prompting a retaliatory air strike against the Côte d'Ivoire air force and the swift imposition of an arms embargo by the Security Council. As the peace process stalled towards the end of 2005, tensions boiled over and pro-Gbagbo demonstrators began attacking UN personnel, forcing the UN to withdraw from several towns (DPKO 2004b). In the face of this resistance, in 2006 the Security Council increased UNOCI's mandated size by 1,100 and redeployed peacekeepers and UN personnel to the troubled districts. With the support of Nigeria and the African Union, a new peace agreement was concluded at the end of 2007 (the Ougadougou Accords) and the 'zone of confidence' was replaced by a UN policed 'green line', indicating significant (though hesitant) progress towards national unification (CIC 2008: 106–7).

Following Timor-Leste's successful transition to independence in 2002, UNTAET handed over to a smaller support mission (UNMISET) tasked with providing interim law enforcement, assisting in the creation of rule of law institutions, and enabling capacity-building across the government administration. In 2005, amid superficial signs of progress and an absence of violence, the UN's engagement with Timor-Leste was further downsized. This turned out to be premature, as one year later the government dismissed a large portion of the armed forces, sparking an armed rebellion. Timor-Leste's new institutions proved too fragile to maintain law and order, and by May 2006 the state had all but collapsed amid widespread disorder and large-scale population displacement. At the request of the government, Australia and New Zealand deployed peacekeepers to help restore order, and the Security Council – tacitly recognizing that it had authorized a premature withdrawal – established a new mission (UNMIT) with greater capacity to impose law and order and build Timorese capacity. The two missions were augmented at the government's request by a deployment of Portuguese police. This rapid international engagement, spearheaded by Australia, prevented the state's collapse and descent into more generalized violence, though serious tensions remained – made evident by the attempted assassination in 2008 of Timor-Leste's president (Jose Ramos Horta) and prime minister (Xanana Gusmao) (CIC 2008: 84–5).

In Côte d'Ivoire and Timor-Leste, peacekeepers confronted serious challenges that could have undermined the mission. But in both these cases the Security Council, pivotal states, the UN Secretariat and the peacekeepers themselves responded with renewed resolve. The result was a gradual restoration of order. Although serious underlying problems remain in both countries, discernible progress was made. This was in stark contrast to international society's failure to stem the commission of large-scale crimes against humanity in Darfur and other conflicts involving the government of Sudan.

The most serious threat to this new, more robust and confident approach to peace operations comes from the various conflicts – and missions – involving Sudan. The government of Sudan and its proxies are involved in wars or fragile peace processes in the south, east and west of the country, as well as in Chad and the CAR. These conflicts have witnessed the deployment of a UN mission (UNMIS), an AU/UN hybrid mission (UNAMID), two small forces in Chad/CAR (EUFOR Chad/CAR and MINURCAT) and an even smaller CEMAC mission in the CAR. All of these missions are critically vulnerable.

UNMIS was deployed to oversee implementation of the Comprehensive Peace Agreement (CPA) between the government of Sudan and the Sudan People's Liberation Movement/Army (SPLM/A). This included provisions for a government of national unity until the future of the south was decided in a referendum on full independence scheduled for 2011. Although relatively large compared to other UN missions, it is important to bear in mind that UNMIS covers a huge area of underdeveloped territory, lacks crucial capabilities and operates in what is sometimes a hostile environment. What is more, the security situation was complicated by the presence of the Lord's Resistance Army (LRA), a brutal Ugandan rebel organization composed mainly of abducted child soldiers, which maintained bases in southern Sudan until a combination of pressure from the SPLA and UNMIS forced it to relocate much of its operation to the DRC – creating new problems for the peacekeepers in

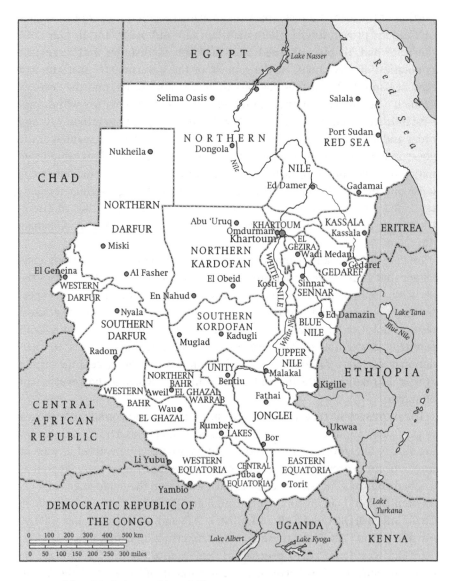

Map 5.1 *Sudan and its neighbours*

MONUC. These problems were compounded by the lack of political progress towards national integration, primarily because the National Congress Party regime in Sudan did not fulfil its commitment to share oil revenues and because integration of the armed forces has not progressed. The widely expected resumption of hostilities started in earnest in mid-2008 around the contested town of Abyei. Meanwhile, UNMIS lacked the capacity to push the process forward or deter significant violations of the CPA. These problems have also been compounded by the disaster in Darfur, which we discuss in chapter 8.

The situation in Sudan has been further compounded by instability in Chad and the CAR. In Chad, a combination of cross-border raids by *janjawiid* militias and an influx of nearly 300,000 refugees from Darfur, along with ongoing fighting between the government and at least three domestic rebel groups, caused over 350,000 people to flee their homes. In 2007 the government of Chad rejected calls for a UN mission to be deployed to Chad and the CAR, consenting only to the deployment of unarmed military observers and police. However, the government's long-standing relationship with France made it amenable to a small EU force deployed mainly in the east of the country (near the border with Sudan/Darfur), with a mandate to protect civilians, especially refugees and IDPs, and facilitate the delivery of humanitarian relief. The small mission of some 3,700 troops known as EUFOR Chad/CAR ran into difficulties even before it deployed, when rebels apparently backed by the government of Sudan attacked Chad's capital, N'Djamena, in early 2008. The violence succeeded in delaying the EU's deployment and reinforcing European reluctance to contribute to it. The EU's efforts are supported by a small UN force known as MINURCAT.

International society's commitment to support peacekeepers in the CAR has been even weaker than in Chad. The small CEMAC mission and the government of the CAR have proven utterly incapable of stemming the tide of violence in the country's north, which effectively descended into anarchy in 2007, causing around 200,000 people to flee their homes – in addition to the approximately 3,000 refugees from Darfur. Although the CAR government supported proposals for a large UN mission to be deployed there and to Chad, these proposals were scuppered by Chad's opposition (CIC 2008: 100).

The gap between international society's rhetorical commitment to peace and security and the protection of civilians, on the one hand, and its lack of political will to provide the necessary troops and resources, on the other, has not only produced a failure to stem the tide of violence in the interconnected conflicts in Sudan, Chad and the CAR. It has also left a string of highly vulnerable, relatively weak and under-resourced peace operations made more problematic by their complex mandates and the inter-institutional relationships between the UN, AU, EU, CEMAC and the relevant governments – not to mention more than ten major rebel groups.

5.4 Conclusion

Significant strides have been made towards making peace operations more effective in the field. There has also been significant – if somewhat limited – progress on reforming the way that peace operations are managed. However, although there has been a general improvement in the performance of peace operations, several missions continued to hang in the balance (especially MONUC), some faced major challenges (UNMIL, UNOCI, MINUSTAH) and others contained some of the ingredients of the worst failures of the 1990s (most notably UNAMID). Moreover, with the increasing size, frequency and complexity of missions, contemporary peacekeeping faces a host of challenges, including delivering on civilian protection, honing the relationship between the UN and non-UN actors, mainstreaming gender, and operationalizing police contingents and police-led missions. These and other contemporary challenges are addressed in detail in part IV of the book. But first, part III provides an overview of the many different types of operations, their assumptions and their limitations.

Types of Peace Operations

CHAPTER SIX

Preventive Deployments

Peace operations tend to be deployed either after or during an armed conflict. The UN Charter, however, gives the organization the task of ridding the world of the scourge of war – that is, *preventing* deadly conflict rather than solely *managing* it or *reconstructing* societies ravaged by war (Hampson and Malone 2002: 77). As UN Secretary-General Boutros-Ghali noted in the mid-1990s, '[i]t is evidently better to prevent conflicts through early warning, quiet diplomacy and, in some cases, preventive deployment than to have to undertake major politico-military efforts to resolve them after they have broken out' (1995a: § 26). However, because peacekeeping developed as a series of ad hoc responses to particular conflicts, the importance of preventing deadly conflict in the first place and developing the appropriate techniques to do this has tended to be overlooked by the UN and other organizations that engage in peace operations. A central challenge for these actors is thus to try and prevent armed conflicts before they erupt.

The aim of this chapter is to examine attempts to do this through the use of preventive deployments. Although the term 'preventive deployments' could encompass a wide range of actors engaged in a very wide range of activities, here we focus on the employment of uniformed personnel (soldiers, military observers and police). Consequently, our discussion does not include the activities of various conflict prevention and peacemaking exercises such as the use of civilian peacemakers, fact-finding missions and other forms of confidence-building measures. Given the shortage of practical examples of this sort of preventive deployment, this is a 'type' of peace operation which currently exists more in theory than in practice. A significant portion of this chapter is therefore devoted to exploring the political reasons why there have not been more preventive deployments. We begin, however, with a brief overview of conflict prevention more broadly in order to illustrate where preventive deployments fit in. We then discuss two concrete cases of preventive deployments, in Macedonia and the Democratic Republic of Congo (DRC), before outlining some of the central problems raised by this type of operation.

6.1 Preventing violent conflict and preventive deployments

In recent years, debates about how best to prevent violent conflict have often revolved around the distinction between structural and operational prevention popularized by the Carnegie Commission on Preventing Deadly Conflict (1997). According to the Carnegie Commission, structural prevention involves strategies to address the root causes of deadly conflict to ensure that crises do not arise in the first place. It encompasses a wide range of activities, including 'putting in place international legal systems, dispute resolution mechanisms, and cooperative arrangements; meeting people's basic economic, social, cultural, and humanitarian needs; and rebuilding societies that have been shattered by war or other major crises' (Carnegie Commission 1997: xxviii). Operational prevention, on the other hand, revolves around measures applicable in the face of an immediate crisis. 'Operational prevention', the Commission noted, 'relies on early engagement to help create conditions in which responsible leaders can resolve the problems giving rise to the crisis' (ibid.: xix). The preventive deployment of armed forces analysed in this chapter falls within the operational category. However, it should be pointed out that the dividing line between operational and structural activities is not always clear and absolute. If, for example, international society established a significant, standing rapid reaction force designed to conduct operational responses in the face of particular crises, the very existence of such a force might also go some way towards having a structural impact by helping to deter the outbreak of future hostilities in some parts of the world.

One useful way of thinking about the relationship between structural and operational prevention is Ken Menkhaus's idea of a conflict prevention chain. Using the chain analogy, Menkhaus suggests that successful policies are

---

Box 6.1 Ken Menkhaus's conflict prevention chain

Link 1: The analytical capacity to predict and understand conflicts: do we know what to look for?

Link 2: The structural capacity to predict and alert: do we have a functional early warning system or systems in place?

Link 3: The operational capacity to prevent: do we have a toolbox of preventative methods?

Link 4: A strategic framework to guide coherent preventative action.

Link 5: The structural capacity to respond: do we have organizations designed, prepared and funded to execute preventative action?

Link 6: The political will to prevent: do significant actors have the commitment to undertake and support preventative action?

Source: Menkhaus (2004).

unlikely to occur if there are any weak links; all of these areas need attention. The links in Menkhaus's chain are described in box 6.1. Understood in this manner, preventive deployments can play especially important roles in Links 3 and 5 of the chain. In order for them to do so, however, we need to understand what tasks are suitable for preventive deployments to undertake (Link 3) and invest relevant organizations with a capacity to deploy troops rapidly to a theatre of operations.

At least three sets of arguments have been used to make the case for an increased use of preventive deployments. The first set is financial – the argument being that it is far cheaper in financial terms to prevent armed conflicts from breaking out than trying to manage them after they have erupted (e.g. UN 2000: § 29). A Carnegie Commission study, for instance, estimated that international society spent about $200 billion on the seven major peace operations of the 1990s, in Bosnia and Hercegovina, Somalia, Rwanda, Haiti, Iraq, Cambodia and El Salvador, exclusive of Kosovo and East Timor. 'The study calculated the cost differentials between these conflict management activities and potential preventive action, and concluded that a preventive approach would have saved the international community almost $130 billion' (Annan 2001a: § 2).

A second set of arguments is institutional. In sum, preventive deployments should be undertaken because a variety of international organizations now exist that are mandated to prevent armed conflict. Chief among these organizations is the UN. As Kofi Annan argued, 'For the United Nations there is no higher goal, no deeper commitment and no greater ambition than preventing armed conflict' (1998b: § 2). Annan was to reiterate this point in a variety of documents throughout his period as UN Secretary-General. Indeed, in his final blueprint for reform of the UN system he stated that 'No task is more fundamental to the United Nations than the prevention and resolution of deadly conflict' (Annan 2005a: § 106). Other organizations, such as the EU, AU and ECOWAS, also have remits that include conflict prevention activities.

A third set of arguments has highlighted the moral imperative to prevent armed conflicts. Here the argument is that civilized actors have a moral responsibility to stop the outbreak of armed conflict, particularly those that might place vulnerable peoples at great risk of death and atrocity (e.g. IISS 2001). This means that preventive deployments should take place whenever civilians are under imminent threat of massacre and not only when they are cheaper than managing or containing conflict or conducted by actors that have official mandates to engage in such activities.

Since the end of the Cold War, senior UN officials have emphasized the need for the organization to become more effective at crisis prevention. The central catalyst in this regard was Boutros-Ghali's report *An Agenda for Peace* (1992). This identified preventive deployments as one instrument that might be used as part of a broader notion of preventive diplomacy. As the Secretary-General argued,

> The time has come to plan for circumstances warranting preventive deployment, which could take place in a variety of instances and ways. For example, in conditions of national crisis there could be preventive deployment at the request of the Government or all parties concerned, or with their consent; in inter-State disputes such deployment could take place when two countries feel that a United Nations presence on both sides of their border can discourage hostilities; furthermore, preventive deployment could take place when a country feels threatened and requests the deployment of an appropriate United Nations presence along its side of the border alone. In each situation, the mandate and composition of the United Nations presence would need to be carefully devised and be clear to all. (1992: § 28; see also §§ 29–32)

An emphasis on preventive efforts was also reaffirmed during Kofi Annan's term as UN Secretary-General. In relation to peace operations specifically, the Brahimi Report recommended that the constituent elements of the UN system should focus on prevention and early engagement 'wherever possible' (UN 2000: § 6c).

Annan's major contribution, however, was his report *Prevention of Armed Conflict* (2001a; see also Annan 1998b). This argued that the UN system needed to move from a culture of reaction to a 'culture of prevention' and set out ten principles to guide the UN's future work in this area (these principles are set out in box 6.2). Rather than creating an office or agency with specific responsibilities for prevention, Annan argued that every arm of the UN should be involved and should mainstream prevention into their work. With regard to preventive deployments, Annan noted that,

> While all peacekeeping operations could be said to have a preventive function in that they are intended to avert the outbreak or recurrence of conflict, their preventive role has been particularly clear where they have been deployed before the beginning of an armed internal or international conflict. This has taken place three times over the past decade, with the United Nations Preventive Deployment Force (UNPREDEP) in the former Yugoslav Republic of Macedonia, the United Nations Mission in the Central African Republic (MINURCA) and a succession of operations in Haiti. (2001a: § 81)

For Annan, these cases provided clear evidence that 'there are circumstances in which preventive deployment of a peacekeeping operation can save lives and promote stability' (ibid.: § 82). He also observed that, in these types of operations, civilian police would have a particularly important function (ibid.: § 84).

Since 1998, concerns about the importance of conflict prevention have also appeared in a series of UN Security Council resolutions. Arguably Resolution 1366 (30 August 2001) was particularly important in acknowledging the principles and commitments set out in Annan's earlier report. Among other things, this resolution expressed the Council's 'determination to pursue the objective of prevention of armed conflict as an integral part of its primary responsibility for the maintenance of international peace and security' (§ 1) and 'its willingness to consider preventive deployment upon the recommendation of the Secretary-General and with the consent of the

Box 6.2 Towards a culture of prevention at the UN

The following ten principles should guide the future approach of the UN to conflict prevention:

1 Conflict prevention is one of the primary obligations of the UN and must be pursued in conformity with the purposes and principles of the Charter.
2 Conflict prevention must have national ownership. The primary responsibility for conflict prevention rests with national Governments, with civil society playing an important role.
3 Conflict prevention is an activity best undertaken under Chapter VI of the Charter.
4 Preventive action should be initiated at the earliest possible stage of a conflict cycle in order to be most effective.
5 The primary focus of preventive action should be in addressing the deep-rooted socio-economic, cultural, environmental, institutional, political and other structural causes that often underlie the immediate symptoms of conflicts.
6 Conflict prevention and sustainable and equitable development are mutually rein-forcing activities. An investment in national and international efforts for conflict prevention must be seen as a simultaneous investment in sustainable development, since the latter can best take place in an environment of sustainable peace.
7 An effective preventive strategy requires a comprehensive approach that encom-passes both short-term and long-term political, diplomatic, humanitarian, human rights, developmental, institutional and other measures taken by the international community, in cooperation with national and regional actors.
8 There is a clear need for introducing a conflict prevention element into the UN system's multifaceted development programmes and activities so that they con-tribute to the prevention of conflict by design and not by default.
9 A successful preventive strategy depends upon the cooperation of many UN actors. However, the UN is not the only actor in prevention and may often not be the actor best suited to take the lead. Therefore, other actors also have very important roles to play in this field.
10 Effective preventive action by the UN requires sustained political will on the part of Member States. First and foremost, this includes a readiness by the membership as a whole to provide the UN with the necessary political support and resources for undertaking effective preventive action in specific situations.

Source: summarized from Annan (2001a: § 169).

Member States concerned' (§ 12). Resolution 1625 (14 September 2005) was similarly important for its focus on Africa, the site of a disproportionate number of the world's armed conflicts.

Under the powers vested in it by the UN Charter, the Security Council may authorize the deployment of armed forces for a variety of purposes, including the prevention of some unwanted development. As discussed above, the UN has argued that most preventive activity is best undertaken with reference to Chapter VI of the UN Charter, which covers the pacific settlement of disputes. Nevertheless, if the Security Council identifies a particular threat to interna-tional peace and security, it may deploy forces preventatively with reference to Chapter VII of the Charter. If the preventive deployment of forces is not authorized to engage in enforcement activities, then Chapter VIII of the Charter is also relevant, because it encourages recognized regional arrangements to undertake such deployments where they might help defuse a conflict. This is usually done with reference to the organization's own region. But, as the case of the EU's deployments to the DRC makes clear, the Security Council may authorize a regional organization to engage in activities outside its own borders.

All preventive deployments beg the fundamental question of what exactly it is that they are trying to prevent. At an abstract level there are two common answers to this question. First, preventive deployments may be designed to ward off the outbreak of armed conflict by enhancing the ability of parties to settle their disputes without resorting to force. This could be done through peacekeepers adopting interpositionary or deterrent roles, monitoring a specific area, or building confidence between the parties. A second answer suggests that such deployments are intended to prevent the escalation of an already existing dispute and therefore stop the recurrence or intensification of hostilities. These two understandings situate preventive deployments in different stages of the conflict cycle. While the first view would see prevention occurring only before the outbreak of armed conflicts, the second perspective could see such deployments despatched at any stage of the conflict cycle.

If preventive deployments are understood to encompass only the first approach (i.e. they are intended to prevent the initial outbreak of armed conflict), then there have been relatively few examples of such operations conducted by the UN or other international organizations. One of these is UNPREDEP in Macedonia, which is discussed later in this chapter. If, on the other hand, preventive deployments are understood more broadly to encompass action aimed at arresting the escalation of already existing conflicts then the number of practical examples increases significantly. Indeed, as Annan noted above, in one sense all peace operations are intended to limit the escalation of armed conflict. In both cases, however, preventive deployments require the ability to react rapidly to unfolding events in the theatre concerned. In the UN's case, the rapid deployment of armed forces would have been made considerably easier if Articles 43 and 45 of the Charter had been implemented as its architects had intended (see box 6.3). These Articles, together with the rest of Chapter VII, envisaged that the UN's member states would place elements of their armed forces at the Security Council's disposal for enforcement operations. In practice, these provisions have never been implemented. As a consequence, in the few cases in which the UN has undertaken a preventive deployment operation, it has been forced to hunt for suitable personnel on an ad hoc basis. This was the case in both the examples discussed below: the UN mission in Macedonia and the EU's force in the DRC.

Box 6.3 Articles 43 and 45 in Chapter VII of the UN Charter

Article 43

1 All Members of the United Nations, in order to contribute to the maintenance of international peace and security, undertake to make available to the Security Council, on its call and in accordance with a special agreement or agreements, armed forces, assistance, and facilities, including rights of passage, necessary for the purpose of maintaining international peace and security.

2 Such agreement or agreements shall govern the numbers and types of forces, their degree of readiness and general location, and the nature of the facilities and assistance to be provided.

3 The agreement or agreements shall be negotiated as soon as possible on the initiative of the Security Council. They shall be concluded between the Security Council and Members or between the Security Council and groups of Members and shall be subject to ratification by the signatory states in accordance with their respective constitutional processes.

Article 45

In order to enable the United Nations to take urgent military measures, Members shall hold immediately available national air-force contingents for combined international enforcement action. The strength and degree of readiness of these contingents and plans for their combined action shall be determined within the limits laid down in the special agreement or agreements referred to in Article 43, by the Security Council with the assistance of the Military Staff Committee.

6.2 Preventive deployment in practice

Preventing war in Macedonia: UNPREDEP and beyond

The UN preventive deployment in Macedonia, UNPREDEP, is one of the few examples available to analysts. Initially established as a small tripwire force to deter Serbian forces crossing Macedonia's northern border, it grew out of an already existing operation, UNPROFOR, which had been deployed to manage the ongoing conflicts in Croatia and Bosnia (see chapter 8). Indeed, from December 1992 to March 1994 the mission in Macedonia was known as UNPROFOR-Macedonia Command and then as FRYOM Command. However, it did not take the UN personnel long to realize that the threat of external invasion was not the only source of potential armed conflict within Macedonia. As a result, the UN's representatives began to call for a broadening of their mandate to include domestic sources of tension (see Williams, A. 2000). In retrospect this proved to be an astute move, for within two years of UNPREDEP's withdrawal in 1999 a low-intensity civil war broke out in Macedonia.

Although the wider context for the UNPREDEP mission was the dissolution of Yugoslavia, the operation's immediate origins lie in a request made in November 1992 by Macedonia's president, Kiro Gligorov, for UN peacekeepers to deploy to his country. Even though Macedonia was not a member of the

Map 6.1 *Macedonia*

UN at the time of Gligorov's request, the Security Council agreed to the despatch of a military presence. Gligorov's central concern was that fighting in Kosovo would spill over into Macedonia and encourage Albanians there to enter into the conflict. Either of these scenarios could have provided a pretext for Serbian forces to enter Macedonia. As a result, Gligorov wanted the UN to help monitor his country's northern and western borders and the ethnic groups in the area.

As it turned out, the peacekeepers were initially given three primary tasks: to establish a presence on the Macedonian side of the new international borders; to monitor and report developments that could threaten the stability of Macedonia; and to deter violence (Security Council Resolution 795, 11 December 1992). Over the next few years the force developed three pillars of activity, related to its military functions, its political functions (notably through the use of its good offices), and what became known as the human dimension (essentially a variety of developmental and peace-building activities conducted by its personnel, often outside of the mission's formal mandate).

As far as the military pillar was concerned, by mid-1993 the UN force comprised approximately 700 peacekeepers from Scandinavia (*c*.400) and the US (*c*.300). Uniquely, for UN operations after the withdrawal of UNOSOM II from Somalia (see chapter 4), US soldiers were placed under UN command. Given the size of the force, its utility was primarily political rather than military. The message was simple: 'hands off Macedonia' (Williams, A. 2000: 42). This made the presence of several hundred US troops particularly important as a signal of Washington's seriousness about protecting Macedonia.

The political pillar did not take shape as quickly, however. This was largely owing to the reluctance of Macedonian authorities to grant the UN force a role in its domestic politics. As a result, it was not until April 1994, when the Security Council broadened the operation's mandate to include the use of its good offices to monitor domestic political issues, that the mission was given its own Special Representative of the Secretary-General. Among its new tasks were confidence-building between the Slav Macedonian and Albanian communities, providing assistance to humanitarian organizations, and giving support to state and non-state actors engaged in improving the country's infrastructure (Stamnes 2004; Stefanova 1997: 113). And it was not until the passing of Security Council Resolution 983 on 31 March 1995 that the mission's name was changed from UNPROFOR FYROM Command to UNPREDEP. Much later, in 1998, UNPREDEP's mandate was expanded once again (under Security Council Resolution 1160) to monitor and report on illicit arms flows and other prohibited activities.

Overall, it is fair to conclude that the UNPREDEP mission played an important role in facilitating Macedonia's relatively peaceful transition from communism to sovereign independence and democracy. According to Stefanova, there was 'a direct causal relationship...between the presence of UNPREDEP and the other preventive initiatives...and the sustained relative stability in the region' (1997: 101). Moreover, as Susan Woodward has observed, in light of the initial challenges to Macedonian sovereignty made by Bulgaria, Greece and some Albanian nationalists within the country, the UN operation also provided 'the psychological reassurance of de facto international recognition that was vital to keeping the politics of [Macedonia's] constitutional questions peaceful' (2008: 423).

In 1998, Prime Minister Tupurkovski tried to improve Macedonia's dire economic situation by negotiating a mutual recognition and trade agreement with Taiwan which, he thought, would bring large amounts of much needed foreign investment. However, not only did Taiwan fail to deliver the trade and aid it had promised, but on 28 February 1999 the Chinese exacted retribution by vetoing the proposed extension of UNPREDEP's mandate. Although the Macedonian government called for the peacekeepers to stay, the Chinese Ambassador in the Security Council argued that the preventive mission was wasting the UN's scarce resources on a country that was not enduring conflict.

Within weeks of China's decision, NATO intervened in Kosovo in an attempt to end the murder and ethnic cleansing of Albanians by Serbian security forces. The Kosovo war had two major effects on Macedonia. First, the Kosovo Liberation Army (KLA) used Macedonian territory as a training base, hiding place and smuggling route, which led to the creation of armed Albanian networks within the country. Second, Serbian ethnic cleansing in Kosovo caused a major influx of Kosovar Albanian refugees into Macedonia. The UNHCR estimated that Macedonia housed 225,000 refugees (equivalent to one-tenth of its entire population).

These two factors, combined with a worsening economy (even before 1991, Macedonia was Yugoslavia's poorest republic), the government's failure to address the grievances of Albanian representatives in parliament, and the absence of peacekeepers, produced an outburst of violence in 2001. Between January and August, the National Liberation Army (NLA), which demanded greater rights for Macedonia's Albanian minority, and the Slav-dominated Macedonian armed forces engaged in a series of skirmishes, which included the shelling of Tetovo by the NLA and artillery responses by the Macedonian army. By mid-2002 the conflict had killed about sixty police and soldiers and generated 13,000 IDPs.

Efforts to prevent an escalation of the violence got off to an inauspicious start. With the UN deadlocked on the issue, the EU took the lead, despatching Javier Solana and Chris Patten to Skopje to help persuade the different parliamentary parties (which included Albanian parties) to work together to find a solution. However, the EU was reluctant to back diplomacy with substantive proposals, and so the buck passed to the OSCE. An OSCE negotiator, Robert Frowick, established contact with the NLA and negotiated a ceasefire agreement with them, which was reciprocated by the Macedonian government. The OSCE then proposed a two-stage plan to prevent further violence. Stage one involved confidence-building measures such as NLA disarmament. Stage two involved an OSCE-sponsored peace process that would produce a comprehensive settlement. The government, however, rejected the plan because it believed that it made too many concessions to the NLA and because it recognized that it had widespread international sympathy for its campaign against the rebels. Unsurprisingly, the collapse of the OSCE initiative prompted the collapse of the ceasefire and an escalation of violence (Bellamy 2002b).

In response to the renewed violence, the EU and the US launched a new initiative. Although the EU–US proposals echoed those of the OSCE, they had greater resonance in Skopje because they were supported by the US government and backed by the possibility of a NATO peacekeeping deployment. Moreover, the EU offered over $30 million of development aid in return for action by the government to address the 'legitimate grievances' of the Albanian population. After extensive negotiations, in August 2001 the two sides agreed to a comprehensive peace plan known as the Ohrid Agreement.

Under the plan, a NATO peacekeeping force of 4,000 was deployed to Macedonia in order to disarm the NLA. For its part, the Macedonian government agreed to address many of the Albanians' grievances by amending the constitution. Although the NATO force was deployed for only thirty days, the UN authorized the continuance of a 'small' NATO-run security force. In March 2003 this was replaced by a smaller EU force of approximately 400 troops known as Operation Concordia. This in turn was replaced in December that year by an even smaller EU police mission, Operation Proxima, which completed its activities in December 2005.

Among other things, the Macedonian case demonstrates that successful preventive deployments depend on three primary factors. First, it is important that domestic and international actors have *early warning* of potential violence. Second, it is important that both domestic parties and international agents have the *political will* to invest material and ideational resources in conflict prevention. This was facilitated by international society's significant prior engagement with conflicts in other parts of the Balkans. Finally, this case shows the importance of having a web of international institutions so that, in situations where one is unable to prevent conflict (as was the case with the UN after the Chinese veto), others are able to take on this role.

The European Union force in the Democratic Republic of Congo (2006)

On 27 April 2006, the EU adopted a Joint Action (2006/319/CFSP) stating that it would deploy a military operation to the DRC during the election process in support of the existing UN peacekeeping operation, MONUC. The Joint Action was adopted following a request from the UN Security Council and with the consent of the host-state authorities. In Resolution 1671, adopted on 25 April, the Security Council had authorized the deployment of an EU force to the DRC 'for a period ending four months after the date of the first round of the presidential and parliamentary elections'. These elections were seen as a crucial step in the DRC's ongoing transition to peace after a variety of ceasefires and agreements were concluded in 2002. EUFOR RD Congo was therefore designed to ensure that the elections did not spark the recurrence of significant violence which might undermine the peace process. In particular, 'Eufor RD Congo was intended first and foremost as a deterrent force in order to prevent and, where necessary, contain acts of armed violence in the capital [Kinshasa]' (Gutiérrez 2006: 5).

In the same way that UNPREDEP had grown out of the UN's earlier engagement with the wars of Yugoslav succession, so EUFOR RD Congo was seen as a 'a logical extension of the Union's involvement in the DRC' (Gutiérrez 2006: 5). Specifically, at the time of EUFOR's deployment, the EU already had two small peace operations engaged in the DRC, both of which were designed to

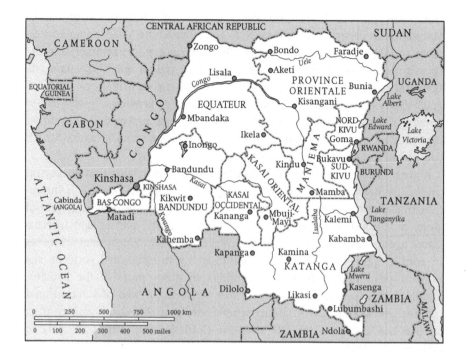

Map 6.2 *The Democratic Republic of the Congo*

help facilitate the democratic transition: EUPOL Kinshasa (a police training force of some forty-five police and civilian personnel) and EUSEC RD Congo (a mission of approximately thirty military and civilian personnel helping to reform the DRC's security sector). Furthermore, between June and September 2003 the DRC had been the site of one of the EU's earliest military missions, the French-led Operation Artemis, which had deployed some 1,200 troops to the eastern town of Bunia to help MONUC peacekeepers protect endangered civilians there. In this sense, the EU had already invested a significant amount of diplomatic capital in assisting the DRC's transition to peace and was not prepared to see it collapse in the final stages.

In military terms, EUFOR RD Congo involved twenty-one EU member states and candidate countries and approximately 3,000 troops. This made it the Union's second largest military operation after Operation Althea in Bosnia and Hercegovina. EUFOR's military command was shared between Germany, the lead nation, and France. Between them, these two states provided more than two-thirds of the force. While its operation headquarters was in Potsdam, Germany, the force itself was composed of three pillars: an advance element was deployed to Kinshasa; an on-call force was stationed in Libreville, Gabon (over 500 miles from Kinshasa); and a strategic reserve was retained in Europe (in France and Germany). Approximately 2,300 troops were deployed to the DRC and Gabon. This pillar structure was adopted in order to provide a realistic deterrent force but also to avoid an unnecessarily heavy military presence in Kinshasa (Solana 2007: 2). Compared to many UN peacekeeping operations, the EUFOR was very well supported. Not only did it have air support from French Mirage jets stationed in Gabon, it incorporated several companies of special forces troops, a Spanish rapid reaction force of some 130 soldiers, and sophisticated intelligence-gathering capabilities, including four B-Hunter drones. Towards the end of the mission, in November 2006, over 1,400 troops were deployed in Kinshasa.

The size and structure of the EU force reflected its preventive nature. As one analyst put it, bearing in mind that the DRC's incumbent president, Joseph Kabila, maintained a presidential guard estimated at about 10,000 soldiers and that several rebel factions were capable of mobilizing similar numbers of combatants, 'even if deployed to its full capacity [EUFOR] could not deal with a large-scale resumption of internal hostilities in the DRC' (Gutiérrez 2006: 21). Nevertheless, EUFOR did prove capable of dealing with small-scale outbreaks of violence. Between 20 and 22 August, for instance, EUFOR units, in conjunction with MONUC peacekeepers, engaged in the protection and evacuation of the visiting diplomats from the International Committee for the Support of the Transition (CIAT), who were trapped at the headquarters of the vice-president and candidate Jean-Pierre Bemba when it came under attack from members of Kabila's presidential guard.

Alongside its military components, EUFOR also initiated an information campaign, complete with its own newspaper called *La Paillote*. This provided Kinshasa's citizens with information about the force and was designed to offset any negative propaganda it might experience from hostile parties and/or unsympathetic locals. *La Paillote* proved particularly useful as a communication outlet for EUFOR in November 2006, when some local residents began attacking its vehicles with stones. EUFOR responded by publishing an appeal informing locals of the dangers that such attacks posed to the victims and to the peace process and explained that EUFOR personnel might be obliged to act in self-defence if its vehicles continued to be blocked or attacked (Gutiérrez 2006: 23).

On 30 November, EUFOR concluded its operations in light of what international society viewed as a reasonably successful set of elections. As the EU's High Representative for Foreign Policy put it, 'We can state that the mission has been a success, both in the way it has been conducted and in its contribution to the overall positive conclusion of the transition in DRC' (Solana 2007: 3). Of course, large political questions remain about whether the expensive international effort to hold the elections essentially endorsed the regime of the incumbent autocrat, Joseph Kabila, but in operational terms EUFOR carried out its mandate efficiently and prevented large-scale renewal of hostilities in and around Kinshasa.

6.3 The politics of preventive deployment

It is clear from the two case studies that preventive deployments can make an important contribution to the forestalling of conflict and escalations of violence. They also illustrate several important points about preventive deployments. First, both of these operations grew out of earlier international engagements with the region in question. It is highly unlikely that UNPREDEP would have emerged if not for the earlier deployment of UNPROFOR. The same is true of the EU's sustained engagement with conflict management in the DRC dating back to 2003. Second, because these missions operated with different understandings of prevention, they took place at very different stages of the conflict cycle. While UNPREDEP was designed to prevent a crisis from erupting, the EU force in the DRC was intended to prevent a recurrence of large-scale violence around a particularly tense period of an ongoing transition from war to stable peace. Third, both of these operations depended on contributions from pivotal states willing to invest money and personnel (Scandinavian countries and the United States in the case of Macedonia, and Germany and France in the DRC). This last point is particularly important, given that the UN has not developed a standing set of armed forces as envisaged by the architects of the UN Charter. As box 6.4 indicates, this has not been because of a lack of relevant proposals (also see chapter 1 on UNEPS). Rather, despite the widespread consensus that international organizations should take prevention more seriously, the reason that there are relatively few examples of preventive deployments is because they raise a whole host of difficult political challenges and dilemmas. These challenges are the subject of the final section of this chapter.

Box 6.4 Proposals for UN standing forces: a very short history

Although Winston Churchill had proposed the creation of an international air force in 1946, little serious discussion was dedicated to the issue of UN standing forces until UN Secretary-General Trygve Lie proposed various types of standing international forces. Between 1948 and 1952 Lie's suggestions included a small UN Guard Force, which could be placed by the Secretary-General at the disposal of the Security Council; a UN Legion, to be composed of over 50,000 volunteers for military service under the UN; and a UN Volunteer Reserve. No significant action was taken on any of these.

In 1957 the Carnegie Endowment for International Peace proposed the creation of a 'UN peace force' to consist of individual volunteers formed into a Standing Force of between 200,000 and 600,000 persons, plus a Peace Force Reserve of between 600,000 and 1.2 million. As it turned out, this proved to be the most ambitious of all proposals on the topic. Needless to say it made little practical headway.

The idea was not seriously debated again until 1992, when UN Secretary-General Boutros Boutros-Ghali made several proposals for standing forces in his report *An Agenda for Peace*. These revolved around the peace enforcement units and standby

Continued

Box 6.4 *Continued*

arrangements laid out in Article 43. Debate was rejoined in 1993, when a former UN Under-Secretary-General for Special Political Affairs, Brian Urquhart, proposed the idea of a standing UN Volunteer Military Force comprised of professionals recruited on an individual basis to create 'a five-thousand-strong light infantry force'.

Following the Rwandan genocide of 1994 a process began whereby existing UN standby arrangements for peacekeeping forces were formalized into what became known as the UN Standby Arrangements System (UNSAS). By April 2005, eighty-three states had made conditional commitments to UNSAS. It is important to note, however, that these standby arrangements were not synonymous with a standing force.

In his *Supplement to An Agenda for Peace*, published in 1995, Boutros-Ghali suggested that in light of events in Rwanda and Bosnia in particular, a rapid reaction force was needed to undertake a range of tasks going well beyond traditional peacekeeping. 'Such a force', Boutros-Ghali argued, 'would be the Security Council's strategic reserve for deployment when there was an emergency need for peace-keeping troops. It might comprise battalion-sized units from a number of countries. . . . They would be stationed in their home countries but maintained at a high state of readiness.' The proposal gained no traction within the Security Council.

Despite the rejection of Boutros-Ghali's proposal, the same year witnessed the creation of a rapid reaction force consisting of troops from France, the Netherlands and the UK within the context of the UNPROFOR mission in Bosnia. In August–September 1995 it was deployed close to Bosnia's besieged capital city of Sarajevo and engaged Serbian forces. Along with NATO's Operation Deliberate Force, its actions helped end the siege. Also in 1995, the Netherlands issued a 'non-paper' calling for a UN Rapid Deployment Brigade. Specifically, it explored 'the possibilities for creating a permanent, rapidly deployable brigade at the service of the Security Council . . . [with] an immediately deployable strength of between 2,000 and 5,000 men [recruited on an individual basis]'. The Dutch envisaged the brigade conducting a wide variety of tasks, including preventive deployment on the territory of a party that felt threatened. In the same year the Canadian government also circulated a study on 'Improving the UN's Rapid Reaction Capability'. This led to a detailed report being presented to the UN in September 1995 which called for major improvements to be made to UNSAS.

Perhaps the most significant of all the proposals of 1995 was the Danish-led working group to develop a multinational rapid deployment brigade. This ultimately led to the establishment of the Multinational Standby High Readiness Brigade for UN Operations (SHIRBRIG) in December 1996. By late 2000 this had grown to some 5,000 personnel and become the basis for several Chapter VI deployments, including the UN peacekeeping operation in Ethiopia and Eritrea (UNMEE). By 2007, SHIRBRIG had sixteen states as members plus seven observers.

More recently, in 2004, the UN Secretary-General's High-Level Panel on Threats, Challenges and Change recommended that 'States with advanced military capacities should establish standby high-readiness, self-sufficient battalions at up to brigade level that can reinforce United Nations missions, and should place them at the disposal of the United Nations.' Since then, however, as Adam Roberts has observed, although the 'idea of a UN standing force was not dead . . . it was in suspended animation'. This was largely because of 'an underlying reluctance on the part of all states to see a major transfer to the UN of their power to use military force'.

Source: paraphrased from Roberts (2008).

The first major difficulty lies in knowing what exactly it is that preventive deployments are supposed to prevent. In sum, what are the warning signs that should trigger international debates about the pros and cons of preventive deployment in a particular context? While international relations scholarship has been relatively good at identifying the underlying causes of armed conflict – that is, those factors that make societies more or less likely to descend into open war – it has been much less successful at identifying what activities will trigger violence in any given context, and when. In this sense, it is difficult to pinpoint when and/or why countries perceived as falling into the 'at risk of armed conflict' category will erupt into violence, and why some of these states have avoided doing so for significant periods of time (see Goldstone 2008). This problem is complicated by the fact that, in any potentially tense political situation, it is rather difficult to gain an accurate picture of what is happening on the ground. Here, the conundrum facing would-be peacekeepers is discerning which voices (local and foreign) to listen to, and hence which warnings of impending crisis to take seriously and which to ignore.

The second major difficulty facing preventive deployments relates to the concept of sovereignty and the crucial role identified for host governments in the UN's approach to prevention. As discussed above, except in very rare cases where such deployments may be used for enforcement purposes, prevention is best undertaken with the consent of the host-state authorities. The problem this raises is that, 'if the Government concerned refuses to admit that it has a problem that could lead to violent conflict and rejects offers for assistance, there is very little outside actors, including the United Nations, can do' (Annan 2001a: § 163). Changing attitudes about the limits of sovereignty and what it means for states to ask for external assistance was a key part of developing what Annan referred to as a 'culture of prevention'.

A third set of challenges revolves around the fact that, if preventive deployments are conducted at all, they are almost certain to be undertaken by large bureaucracies, whether in the form of states or of international organizations. Such bureaucracies present a range of challenges. Arguably the most important in relation to preventive operations are the struggle to secure funds and resources and the problem of showing positive and measurable results. In relation to funding, the central problem 'is the gap between verbal postures and financial and political support for prevention' (UN 2000: § 33). The central challenge is how to persuade cash-strapped organizations that are often required to deal simultaneously with a variety of ongoing crises why they should devote some of their limited resources to a situation which, at present, is not in dire need of external assistance. Since 1990, for instance, the UN has constantly had to manage at least a dozen ongoing peace operations, each of which could always use more resources. In such a context, ring-fencing funds to spend on the prevention of hypothetical future crises will require overcoming a variety of bureaucratic hurdles.

The other major bureaucratic requirement is showing that the organization's resources have been used efficiently and effectively. Here, preventive deployments run up against the problem of proving effective results. As Gareth Evans (2006a), president of the conflict prevention NGO International Crisis Group, has put it, '[p]art of the problem is that it [conflict prevention] doesn't generate immediately visible returns:…you succeed most…when nothing happens, and nobody notices.' Similarly, the Brahimi Report noted how 'preventive action is, by definition, a low-profile activity; when successful, it may even go unnoticed altogether' (UN 2000: § 10). In the case of Macedonia, for example, one might wish to conclude that, because the country remained peaceful while UN peacekeepers were deployed there and civil war erupted soon after they left, it was UNPREDEP's activities that caused the peace. However, the fact that civil war erupted shortly after UNPREDEP's departure does not automatically prove either (a) that it was the activities of UN peacekeepers that kept Macedonia peaceful from 1992 to 1999 or (b) that it was their absence that explains why war broke out in 2001. UNPREDEP's activities may well have been coincidental to peace rather than the direct cause of it. In sum, securing funding and proving positive results are difficult things for preventive deployments to do. Large bureaucracies are therefore less likely to be undertaking them than other types of peace operations.

A fourth set of challenges identified earlier in Menkhaus's conflict prevention chain is the current lack of institutional capacity available for preventive deployments within the UN and other international organizations engaged in conducting peace operations. As discussed in box 6.4, although a variety of standby arrangements exist within the UN system, its member states have consistently avoided furnishing the organization with standing forces. Indeed, member states have also objected to the creation of a small civilian office in the DPA that would provide early warning and help coordinate the UN's prevention activities. Typically, many states worry that these activities amount to intelligence-gathering and hence represent a grave challenge to state sovereignty. Elsewhere, however, some international organizations have started the process of assembling rapid reaction capabilities. As part of its Helsinki Headline Goal (1999) for crisis management, for instance, the EU declared its intention to develop a rapid reaction force comprising up to 60,000 troops that would be deployable worldwide and sustainable for a period of up to one year. This was officially declared operational in late 2001. Since late 2003 the Union has also been developing the concept of smaller battle groups of approximately 1,500 soldiers capable of conducting small-scale and short-term crisis management operations beyond its borders. These are similar in conception to the type of operation carried out by EUFOR RD Congo. The NATO alliance has also developed a significant expeditionary set of capabilities. Of most relevance here is the NATO Response Force. Declared fully operational in late 2006, this force of up to 25,000 troops is intended to conduct the entire spectrum of military operations anywhere in the world and be self-sustaining for a period of thirty days. Beyond the Euro-Atlantic region, since 2003 the African Union has been working to establish an African Standby Force (ASF). It is hoped that, by 2010, the ASF will comprise five regional brigades (of about 4,500 personnel each) that will be available to conduct a range of crisis management operations throughout the continent and perhaps beyond (see Cilliers 2008). While the existence of such forces does not overcome the political issues involved in deciding when and where to deploy them, and to what ends, they do make it easier for the organizations concerned to engage in preventive deployments early in the conflict cycle.

The final set of challenges relate to the issue of political will. Fundamentally, there are relatively few examples of preventive operations because states and international organizations have not seen fit to deploy them. Although political leaders across the globe are likely to respond to different incentives, few preventive deployments are likely to occur unless persuasive arguments are made for them; efficient and effective institutional structures are established that can conduct them; and, at least in the world's democratic states, citizens actively encourage their governments to undertake them and hold their leaders accountable when they fail to respond to foreseeable crises.

6.4 Conclusion

Most peace operations can be understood as reactions to political crises rather than attempts to prevent them erupting in the first place. Despite the relatively positive evidence from operations in Macedonia and the DRC that preventive deployments can be efficient, cost effective and contribute positively to peacebuilding, the UN and other international organizations have conducted relatively few such operations. Particularly since the end of the Cold War, successive UN Secretaries-General and a variety of senior UN officials have made a strong case for the organization to make greater use of preventive deployments. Not only is the UN Charter sufficiently flexible to permit their use in a wide variety of settings, but the relatively small levels of force required in such operations is likely to be well within the scope of the UN's current management structures to command. Although it is highly unlikely that the UN's member states would grant the organization standing forces in the foreseeable future, several other international organizations have started to develop their own rapid reaction capabilities and structures. As these develop, they will make it harder for these organizations to ignore the onset of crises. Until then, however, the majority of peace operations will continue to be deployed after conflict has already broken out. The rest of part III of this book is devoted to analysing the different types of these operations.

CHAPTER SEVEN

Traditional Peacekeeping

Traditional peacekeeping is the conceptual point of departure for all the other types of peace operations. It is often associated with chronological typologies of peace operations, but this is inaccurate (see chapter 1). Chapters 3 to 5 have demonstrated that traditional peacekeeping was neither the sole form of peace operations undertaken during the Cold War nor exclusive to that era. Traditional peacekeeping today comprises both ongoing operations that began during the Cold War and newer ones. This highlights the enduring perception of its utility and also its continued ability to influence the conduct of other types of mission.

The first section of this chapter examines traditional peacekeeping's core assumptions and the historical factors that influenced its development. The second section then considers how it has been applied in practice by looking at UNEF I in the Middle East, the UN's ongoing operation in Cyprus (UNFICYP) and the recently terminated mission in Ethiopia and Eritrea (UNMEE). The final section reflects upon some of the limitations of traditional peacekeeping and raises questions about the value of using it as the conceptual basis for all the other types of operations.

7.1 What is traditional peacekeeping?

Although there is no consensus on what activities constitute traditional peacekeeping, its underlying principles and implied objectives are reasonably clear (Diehl 1994: 13; Durch 1994a: 1–3; Goulding 1993: 452). Traditional conceptions of peacekeeping are premised on the so-called holy trinity of consent, impartiality and the minimum use of force (see figure 7.1).

Traditional peacekeeping is intended to assist in the creation and maintenance of conditions conducive to long-term conflict resolution by the parties themselves, often in conjunction with international mediation (see box 7.1). In practice, this means non-coercive, consent-based activities, usually to support a peace process or interim ceasefire, to help prevent the resumption or escalation of violence, and/or to establish a stable peace. Traditional peacekeeping is therefore what Alan James described as 'an activity of a secondary kind' (1990: 1). It is neither a creative force in wider conflict resolution processes nor a coercive instrument in defence of such processes. As activities of

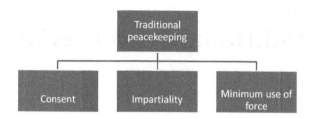

Figure 7.1 *The 'holy trinity' of traditional peacekeeping*

a secondary kind, the creation and success of traditional peacekeeping missions depend upon the consent and positive contribution of the disputants.

Traditional peacekeeping usually takes place in the period between a ceasefire and a political settlement and is designed to cultivate the degree of confidence between belligerents necessary to establish a process of political dialogue. As such, it is based on three assumptions: the primary belligerents are states; the combatant units are hierarchically organized, Clausewitzian militaries; and the protagonists wish to end the conflict and search for a political resolution.

Traditional peacekeeping activities typically range from simple observation and fact-finding to monitoring compliance with the conditions of ceasefires and physical interposition between the belligerents. Peacekeepers monitor

---

Box 7.1 Some popular definitions of traditional peacekeeping

[Operations] involving military personnel, but without enforcement powers…to help maintain or restore international peace and security in areas of conflict. These operations are voluntary and are based on consent and co-operation…they achieve their objectives not by force of arms, thus contrasting them with the 'enforcement action' of the United Nations under Article 42. (UN 1990: 4)

Field operations established by the United Nations with the consent of the parties concerned, to help control and resolve conflicts between them, under United Nations command and control, at the expense collectively of the member states, and with military and other personnel and equipment provided voluntarily by them, acting impartially between the parties and using force to the minimum extent necessary. (Goulding 1993: 455)

Peacekeeping operations are generally undertaken under Chapter VI of the UN Charter with the consent of all the major parties to a conflict, to monitor and facilitate the implementation of a peace agreement. (HMSO 1999: 1.1)

…the imposition of neutral and lightly armed interposition forces following a cessation of armed hostilities, and with the permission of the state on whose territory these forces are deployed, in order to discourage a renewal of military conflict and promote an environment under which the underlying dispute can be resolved. (Diehl 1994: 13)

borders, help establish and patrol buffer zones separating opposing forces, verify the various aspects of demilitarization (including weapons decommissioning and troop withdrawals), and attempt to create a political space that will facilitate a political resolution of the conflict. They do not devise political solutions themselves or enforce agreements between the competing parties.

The conceptual roots of this approach to peacekeeping lie in the Cold War and the UN's attempt to develop a role for itself in the pursuit of international peace and security. Although the architects of the UN Charter envisaged a powerful institution capable of enforcing collective security, the rapid deterioration of relations between its two most influential members, the US and the USSR, meant that many of the instruments that were originally envisaged (including a standing army and a strong Military Staff Committee) failed either to materialize or to take on their assigned role (Lorenz 1999). Superpower rivalry soured working relations and created a lack of consensus in the Security Council. This meant that the organization was unable to fulfil the collective security function that was initially envisaged for it. The 1950 'Uniting for Peace' General Assembly resolution created an alternative way of thinking about the role of the UN in international conflicts, though this was a very different form of collective action than that initially envisaged by the Charter's authors (see chapters 2 and 3).

Within this context the UN adopted alternative techniques to fulfil its role in 'preventive diplomacy' sketched out by Secretary-General Hammarskjöld (see chapter 3), initially through observer missions but later in the form of traditional peacekeeping. Observer missions attempt to monitor a situation with the consent of the concerned parties and report their findings to the UN (Hillen 1998: 33–57). They are usually deployed following a ceasefire agreement in order to provide an impartial international presence to monitor compliance. They can also be deployed within a country to investigate allegations of criminal activity, humanitarian problems or external interference in domestic politics. This was the case with the first UN observer mission, sent to the Balkans in 1947 after Greece requested a UN presence on its territory to monitor the activities of its northern communist neighbours (Albania, Bulgaria and Yugoslavia). Along with early UN efforts on the Indian subcontinent and in the Middle East, UNSCOB was in many respects the forerunner to traditional peacekeeping.

The fragile peace between the communist and non-communist fighters in the wartime Greek resistance movement fractured soon after liberation and Greece descended rapidly into civil war (O'Ballance 1966). As the war spread north, the communists began to receive material support from the surrounding communist states, particularly Tito's Yugoslavia. Greece complained to the UN about this external interference and the organization responded by sending a Commission of Investigation early in 1947. The resulting UNSCOB (1947–51) consisted of two-man teams working in six areas along Greece's northern border. These teams reported back to the mission's small headquarters in Salonika, which in turn sent its findings directly to the General Assembly. Like the later traditional peacekeeping operations that its experiences informed, UNSCOB was meant to be impartial, its activities were entirely consent-based and it had no enforcement capabilities. Also, like its more complex successors, it suffered from variable levels of consent and cooperation from the parties to the dispute and considerable external constraints upon, and interference in, its work (Birgisson 1994a: 81–2).

The Cold War tensions apparent in the Greek civil war and throughout the Balkans more generally were indicative of the environment within which the UN was expected to work. Throughout the conflict the Security Council was deadlocked by Soviet vetoes and its rejection of UNSCOB's findings (Higgins 1981; Bailey and Daws 1998). Nevertheless, the fact that the organization played a limited role in the conflict provided the first example of its adaptation to the political constraints imposed by the Cold War.

During its first decade, the UN undertook two further missions under similar circumstances, in the Middle East (UNTSO, 1948–present) and on the Indian subcontinent (UNMOGIP, 1949–present). Both missions were premised on the same principles as UNSCOB and both were organized and deployed on a similarly ad hoc basis (UNTSO is discussed in more detail on the companion website). Thus, while in retrospect these early observer missions can be viewed as the progenitors of traditional peacekeeping, their significance as a distinct form of engagement was not acknowledged at the time.

While UNSCOB, UNMOGIP and, especially, UNTSO contributed significantly to the formulation of the key concepts of UN peacekeeping, and also highlighted some of its primary limitations, they were not directly responsible for the formalization of a traditional conception of peacekeeping. It was the UN Emergency Force (UNEF I), deployed to the Sinai in 1956, that provided the impetus for the codification of the organization's approach to peacekeeping for the next forty-five years. This mission helped produce a set of concepts that remain influential today. There were four main reasons for this:

- the deepening Cold War made it more difficult for the UN to pursue the collective security role envisaged for it in the Charter;
- the Suez Crisis prompted the organization to consider alternative techniques for promoting international peace and security and gave it a first opportunity to demonstrate that it had an important role to play in international conflicts;
- the greater complexity of UNEF I demanded conceptual clarification of the core tenets underpinning it;
- two highly influential figures, UN Secretary-General Dag Hammarskjöld and the Canadian diplomat Lester B. Pearson, attempted to define a clear role for the UN in international conflict resolution.

More than any other individuals, Hammarskjöld and Pearson created a role for the UN in international peace and security at a time when heightened superpower rivalry threatened to exclude the organization from such issues entirely. Hammarskjöld, in consultation with Pearson and other influential advisers (such as Hans Engen of Norway and Frederick Boland of Ireland), developed the concept of preventive diplomacy (first formally expressed in the UN *Annual Report* of 1960). As we noted in chapter 3, Hammarskjöld conceived preventive diplomacy in a different fashion to the concept of the same name that was later described by Boutros Boutros-Ghali in *An Agenda for Peace* (1992: 11). Hammarskjöld understood it as preventing direct superpower confrontation rather than the violent conflict *per se* (UN 1960). By projecting an image of the UN as the neutral third party attempting to prevent conflict escalation, Hammarskjöld set important boundaries for the organization's activities within a climate of superpower rivalry. The UN thus acquired a significant, albeit limited, role in the maintenance of international peace and security. Within this, peacekeeping became the primary ingredient of Hammarskjöld's conception of preventive diplomacy.

Before the Suez Crisis, the UN's peacekeeping experience had been limited to the observer missions mentioned above. The organization could thus not afford to squander the opportunity to play a prominent role in resolving the crisis presented by the superpowers' mutual determination to avoid serious escalation. The creation of UNEF I was thus crucial, first as a practical demonstration of the UN's worth in such circumstances and subsequently to the development of the key concepts of traditional peacekeeping. The organizing principles that underpinned UNEF I (see box 7.2) became the guiding principles of traditional peacekeeping. They reflected the UN's limited past experience, the Cold War environment and the limited amount of time it had to put a viable operation together.

The details were hammered out in a few frantic days at the beginning of November 1956. Allowed considerable freedom of action by the Canadian government, Pearson played a leading role in the process by first broaching

---

Box 7.2 Hammarskjöld's principles for the conduct of UNEF I

1 UNEF was dependent upon the consent of the parties for both its deployment and future operations.
2 It would not constitute an enforcement action.
3 Its military functions would be strictly limited.
4 It should not in any way seek to influence the politico-military power balance between the parties.
5 It would be temporary in duration.

Source: Second Report of the Secretary-General on the Feasibility of a UN Emergency Force, 6 November 1956 (A/3302).

the idea of a UN force (informally with Hammarskjöld and then formally to the first Emergency Special Session of the General Assembly on 2 November). Hammarskjöld was initially sceptical about the viability of a UN force and spent many hours in discussion with Pearson exploring all the options (Urquhart 1994: 178–9). At Pearson's behest, the General Assembly then formally invited the Secretary-General to submit a report within forty-eight hours on the feasibility of establishing 'a United Nations Force large enough to keep these borders at peace while a political settlement is being worked out' (General Assembly Resolution 998). These discussions between Hammarskjöld and his advisers concerning the potential nature of UN engagement were informed as much by political considerations about what the Security Council would permit the organization to do as by technical thoughts about what the aims and activities of peacekeepers should be (Urquhart 1994: 175–83). With France and Britain directly involved in the crisis and the two superpowers looking to avoid entanglement but nevertheless retaining strong interests in the region, Hammarskjöld believed that the UN needed to be pragmatic rather than idealistic in its approach. This perception contributed to the influential idea that peacekeeping was (and should be) an ad hoc response to particular problems rather than being guided by a rigid blueprint for international action.

Hammarskjöld remained sensitive to the Cold War context and tailored his response accordingly. His subsequent report led to the establishment of UNEF I on 5 November 1956 under General Assembly Resolution 1000, while his second, and final, report written overnight on 5–6 November and presented to the General Assembly the following day 'laid the foundations for an entirely new kind of international activity and set out principles and ideas that were to become the basis for future UN peacekeeping operations' (Urquhart 1994: 180). At its heart lay the 'holy trinity' of consent, impartiality and the minimum use of force.

UNEF I's subsequent claim to be a largely successful operation seemed to confirm Hammarskjöld's position, particularly his decision to keep faith with the lessons of previous observer missions as the basis for the more complicated operations envisaged by his embryonic concept of preventive diplomacy. It also filled him with confidence about the UN's potential in this area. In 1959, for instance, he argued that

> the UN simply must respond to those demands which may be put to it. If we feel that those demands go beyond the present capacity…that in itself is not a reason why I, for my part, would say no, because I do not know the exact capacity of this machine. It did take the very steep hill of Suez; it may take even steeper hills. (UN 1959)

In this sense, UNEF I had a profound impact on the Secretary-General and, by extension, perceptions about the potential for UN peacekeeping more generally. Its core principles were enshrined in the concept of traditional peacekeeping and, largely unquestioned, continued to inform UN operations until the end of the Cold War, when the changed international environment exposed its flaws (see chapter 4).

Those limitations (discussed below) were ever present and reflected the circumstances of the birth of the concept of traditional peacekeeping. The Westphalian character of traditional peacekeeping set the parameters for its techniques and defined its limits. Most obviously, reliance on the 'holy trinity' left no room for more forceful action when notional consent failed to translate into compliance with the UN's demands. This is an inevitable problem for a form of peacekeeping based on the Westphalian premise that its central aim is to create space for others to resolve conflict, not to do so itself. This means that, for traditional peacekeepers, 'the importance of the military factor in the equation of success is considerably less than the political factor' (Mackinlay 1989: 199). Traditional peacekeeping is founded on the assumption that the belligerents have the political will to resolve the conflict, an assumption that is often not supported in practice.

7.2 Traditional peacekeeping in practice

There are numerous examples of traditional peacekeeping operations in both the Cold War and post-Cold War periods (Hillen 1998: 13–30). This section concentrates upon three of the most significant. UNEF I is discussed because it represents the first major military peacekeeping operation which formally laid down the principles upon which traditional peacekeeping would be based. UNFICYP provides a particularly useful and ongoing illustration of the strengths and weaknesses of traditional peacekeeping, while UNMEE represents a more recent example of the challenges posed to traditional operations when the conflict parties withdraw their consent.

UNEF I in Egypt (1956–1967)

UNEF I came in response to the Suez Crisis, which threatened to trigger a wider escalation and possibly superpower confrontation. It provided the first serious test case for the UN to demonstrate that it could play the role of what Hammarskjöld later dubbed a 'preventive diplomat' (UN 1960). The background to the crisis was complex, but the immediate cause was the nationalization of the Suez Canal by President Nasser of Egypt in July 1956 (Rikhye 1978; James 1990: 210–23). Nasser had been frustrated by the British and American decisions to cancel their financial assistance for the building of the Aswan Dam, which had prompted the World Bank to cancel its loan to Egypt. This left Nasser with a potentially bankrupt project, which he decided to bankroll by seizing control of the French-owned Suez Canal. For their part, the Western allies were suspicious of Nasser's nationalism and interpreted his refusal to enter into the Western alliance, his dealings with the Eastern bloc, and his aggressive stance towards Israel as confirmation of his pro-Soviet leanings. Nasser's nationalization of the canal thus provided a convenient justification for Israel, France and Britain (the other major shareholder in the Suez Canal Company) to intervene militarily. Diplomatic activity through the UN during August and September masked military preparations for a combined attack, the details of which were secretly agreed in France on 23 October. The plan was for Israeli forces to launch an attack across Sinai, after which Britain and France would demand that both Israeli and Egyptian forces retreat 10 miles from the canal or face the consequences. An Anglo-French expeditionary force would then be despatched under the pretext of 'protecting' international access to the canal. The plan went ahead six days later when Israel launched its invasion. Britain and France issued their ultimatum the following day before bombing Egyptian military targets on 31 October.

The diplomatic façade did not have the desired effect, not least because the Anglo-French ultimatum was issued *before* the Israelis had advanced to within 10 miles of the canal and the military action appeared to be too well prepared and coordinated to be coincidental. The evident collusion was confirmed within a week when British and French airborne forces landed near the canal's northern entrance, at Port Said and Port Fouad respectively. International condemnation of the attacks was immediate and widespread. The Anglo-French intervention also alienated the United States. President Eisenhower's administration believed that it could not be seen to endorse such behaviour, especially since it risked allowing the Soviet Union to extend its influence in the region. At the UN, the US publicly distanced itself from its allies.

UN calls for a ceasefire were ignored, but a rare instance of superpower consensus allowed the deadlock in the Security Council (engineered by Britain and France) to be by-passed by the General Assembly under the 'Uniting for Peace' mechanism (see chapter 2). The US secretary-of-state, John Foster Dulles, sponsored a resolution calling for an immediate ceasefire (General Assembly Resolution 997). This was followed by Lester Pearson's initiative, which ultimately led to the establishment of UNEF I on 5 November. UNEF I's mandate was considerably more ambitious than anything the UN had undertaken to date and is set out in box 7.3.

Under intense diplomatic and economic pressure, Britain, France and Israel reluctantly acquiesced to a ceasefire on 6 November on the condition that the UN force deploy rapidly. Egyptian cooperation was secured on the condition that the UN entered into a 'good faith' agreement with regards to guaranteeing its national sovereignty (Urquhart 1994: 181–91). The result was that UNEF I's mandate was far more complex than that of any of the UN's previous operations and involved a stronger, though still non-coercive, military component.

As the UN's first armed military force, UNEF I represented a significant development in the organization's approach to peacekeeping. The need for rapid deployment required the UN to mobilize its resources considerably

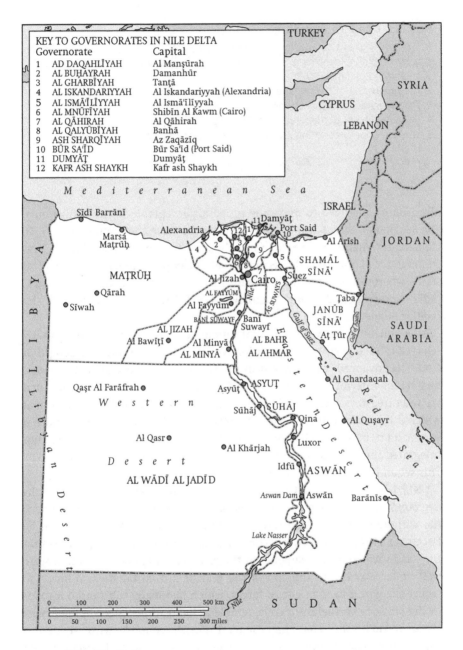

KEY TO GOVERNORATES IN NILE DELTA

Governorate	Capital
1 AD DAQAHLĪYAH	Al Manṣūrah
2 AL BUḤAYRAH	Damanhūr
3 AL GHARBĪYAH	Tanṭā
4 AL ISKANDARIYYAH	Al Iskandariyyah (Alexandria)
5 AL ISMĀ'ĪLĪYYAH	Al Ismā'īlīyyah
6 AL MNŪFĪYAH	Shibīn Al Kawm (Cairo)
7 AL QĀHIRAH	Al Qāhirah
8 AL QALYŪBĪYAH	Banhā
9 ASH SHARQĪYAH	Az Zaqāzīq
10 BŪR SAʿĪD	Būr Saʿīd (Port Said)
11 DUMYĀṬ	Dumyāṭ
12 KAFR ASH SHAYKH	Kafr ash Shaykh

Map 7.1 *Egypt*

faster than had previously been the case. This, coupled with the deadlock in the Security Council, invested the office of the Secretary-General with the authority to implement the decision to intervene. Hammarskjöld assumed full responsibility for mandating and organizing UNEF I, developing it in consultation with a small group of advisers. These consultations were given

Box 7.3 UNEF I's mandate

1 The securing and supervision of a ceasefire by the formation of a buffer zone between British, French and Israeli forces and their Egyptian counterparts (in accordance with Resolution 997)
2 The supervision of the withdrawal of foreign forces from Egyptian territory
3 The supervision of canal clearing operations
4 The patrolling of border areas and deterring of incursions
5 Securing adherence to the provisions of the Egypt–Israel Armistice provisions

Source: UN General Assembly Resolution 1000, 5 November 1956.

direction by the need to make the proposals acceptable to the belligerents. The Secretary-General also took advice from the force commander of UNTSO, Lieutenant-General Burns, whom he subsequently appointed as UNEF I's first commander. Hammarskjöld decided to select troop contingents from neutral states wherever possible, in this case including Brazil, Canada, Denmark, India, Norway, Sweden and Yugoslavia. UNEF I was financed through the regular budget of the UN.

After consultations with potential candidates, ten countries were initially selected to take part in the operation, which had an authorized strength of 6,000. Its advanced units arrived in the region on 15 November. They were met by an interim headquarters staff, seconded from UNTSO, which had arrived three days earlier, and the operation quickly reached full strength, at which it remained until 1965 (Ghali 1994b: 117). UNEF I had a decentralized command structure. Each contingent was led by its own officers and was not integrated into a truly multinational force (Baehr and Gordenker 1994: 79). This set an important precedent for traditional peacekeeping.

UNEF I achieved the first four elements of its mandate within six months (see box 7.3). It rapidly placed itself between the opposing forces, monitored the withdrawal of the Anglo-French contingents (which was completed by December 1956) and effectively controlled the northern Suez Canal area that they had vacated. It also supervised the canal clearing operations that were well under way before the end of the year. It proved far more difficult to secure the withdrawal of Israeli forces, which had made substantial inroads in the Sinai. Nevertheless, a considerable amount of personal diplomacy by Hammarskjöld and Lieutenant-General Burns, coupled with vociferous support from Eisenhower, finally persuaded Israel to pull back. Over the next few years UNEF I set up seventy-two permanent observation posts along the ceasefire lines and the international frontier, and continued to patrol the front line (which extended for nearly 500 km) until the operation ended in 1967. Finally, although UNEF I had neither the capacity nor the mandate physically to stop border incursions by either side, its presence provided an important deterrent, and instances of cross-border raiding reduced considerably during its deployment (Ghali 1994b: 123).

Despite its achievements, UNEF I also displayed considerable weaknesses that warned of future problems. First, it was powerless to prevent the parties breaking the terms of the ceasefire. Second, its reliance on consent meant that it was never able to patrol the Israeli side of the border, nor could it refuse Egypt's request that it leave Egyptian territory before the outbreak of the 1967 war. Finally, because it was meant to create a space to allow the belligerents to reach a political settlement, it could do very little itself to build stable peace in the region. It was caught in the paradoxical position of being a temporary force that could not leave because it was incapable of creating the conditions that would enable it to do so. Instead, the resumption of war between Egypt and Israel forced it to withdraw after eleven years. Of course, these were not faults with UNEF I *per se* because it was not designed to address the underlying issues of the Arab–Israeli conflict or to enforce a particular political resolution. However, its limitations meant that the UN was unable to contribute significantly to building a stable peace despite its long-term presence in the region. This tension was also apparent in UNFICYP.

UNFICYP in Cyprus (1964–present)

UNFICYP was created in 1964 to help manage the escalating violence between the Greek and Turkish communities in Cyprus. The immediate catalyst for violence was the promulgation of a constitution that was designed to protect the rights of both ethnic groups after the island achieved independence from British rule in 1960. However, its elaborate provisions exacerbated animosities and failed to quell the Greek Cypriot desire to be incorporated within Greece. Violence erupted in late 1963 when Archbishop Makarios, the president of Cyprus, proposed amendments to the constitution that would effectively end the special protected status of Turkish Cypriots (Birgisson 1994b: 220–1). Britain, which still had forces stationed on the island, suggested a combined British, Greek and Turkish peacekeeping force under British control (James 1990: 224–5). The Cypriot government agreed with the proviso that the force was authorized by the UN.

The initial peacekeeping force was unable to prevent further violence and was supplanted by a formal UN force, UNFICYP, created on 4 March 1964 by Security Council Resolution 186. UNFICYP was mandated to 'use its best efforts to prevent a recurrence of the fighting and, as necessary, to contribute to the maintenance and restoration of law and order and a return to normal conditions' (Resolution 186). It was not authorized to use coercive force or undertake activities that would affect the political balance in Cyprus. Instead, it was to act as an interposition force, though this time between communities scattered across the island rather than between armed forces separated by clearly demarcated buffer zones. After a considerable struggle to persuade other states to join Britain and provide troops, UNFICYP became fully operational on 27 March 1964 with a complement of 6,200 troops

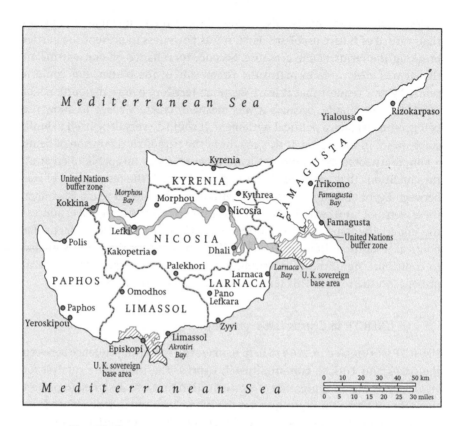

Map 7.2 *Cyprus*

drawn principally from seven contributing states (Austria, Canada, Denmark, Finland, Ireland, Sweden and Britain). The force was commanded by Lieutenant-General Gyani from India. In addition to concerns about the safety of the force in a volatile environment, the UN's financial crisis (generated in large measure by its operation in the Congo; see chapters 2 and 9) made potential contributors more reticent because UNFICYP was to be funded by voluntary contributions, the first time that a mission had been financed in this way. The willingness of Britain and the US to shoulder much of the burden assuaged fears of onerous financial obligations, but the financial concerns of potential troop contributors appeared prescient once UN peacekeeping was formally removed from the regular budget when UNEF II was established in October 1973.

UNFICYP was intended to be deployed for only three months but is still in place today. Between 1964 and 1974 it succeeded in fulfilling its functions but, like UNEF I, lacked the mandate and wherewithal to address the underlying causes of the conflict itself. Thus, when Turkey invaded northern Cyprus in 1974, UNFICYP found itself in a similar situation to that faced by

UNEF I on the eve of the Six Day War in 1967. Unlike UNEF I, however, UNFICYP was able to stay in place during the Turkish invasion and actually engaged in combat to defend itself and endangered civilians around Nicosia. Its activities brought it respect from the civilian population and, eventually, the combatants themselves (Birgisson 1994b: 234). It remained in place after the cessation of hostilities with a modified mandate of monitoring the buffer zone between Turkish-held northern Cyprus and Greek-dominated southern Cyprus, as well as providing humanitarian assistance to over 200,000 displaced persons (James 1990: 229). The island has been partitioned ever since and UNFICYP has remained in place to patrol the 180 mile-long ceasefire line.

Hammarskjöld's successor, U Thant, attempted to reinvigorate the peace process by attaching a dedicated UN mediator to UNFICYP. However, lack of progress towards a final settlement in Cyprus raised fundamental questions about the efficacy of traditional peacekeeping more generally (Sambanis 1999), even before the new missions of the 1990s significantly altered the terms of the debate (James 1989). One issue that became particularly apparent in Cyprus is that the presence of peacekeepers can create a stable status quo – a relatively comfortable stalemate – that encourages belligerents to become disinterested in conflict resolution processes because they are not immediately threatened by violent conflict. In Cyprus, as elsewhere, traditional peacekeeping without effective conflict resolution has tended to preserve the status quo.

Similar challenges remain today, particularly after the failure of the parties to implement the so-called Annan Plan, a revised version of which was submitted to the parties by the UN Secretary-General in March 2004 following six weeks of concerted negotiations and consultations. Annan hoped that in simultaneous referenda the two sides of the island would vote for a united Cyprus to accede to the EU on 1 May 2004. Despite support from the Turkish Cypriots, the plan was overwhelmingly rejected by Greek Cypriots, and hence Cyprus joined the EU as a divided island. In light of these developments, in October 2004 the UN Security Council reduced UNFICYP's military component to 860 on the grounds that the situation there had become 'increasingly benign'. Little political progress was made until 8 July 2006, when the Greek Cypriot leader and the Turkish Cypriot leader signed a set of principles and decisions recognizing that the status quo was unacceptable and that a comprehensive settlement was both desirable and possible. Although a resolution has not been achieved, both parties continue publicly to support the principles contained in the July 2006 statement. As Annan noted in 2007, however, the apparent lack of a viable political process, the relatively benign atmosphere on the island, and the annual cost of approximately $50 million has led an increasing number of actors within international society to question the value added of UNFICYP.

UNMEE in Ethiopia and Eritrea (2000–2008)

The most recent example of a traditional peacekeeping operation was deployed on the cusp of the twenty-first century. This serves as an important reminder that traditional peacekeeping has not become defunct *per se*. Rather it is a tool of conflict management that is best suited to address a phenomenon that has become increasingly rare in world politics: interstate war. However, the fact that UNMEE was terminated in July 2008 highlights the problems of attempting to keep the peace when the belligerent parties withdraw their consent.

After earlier disputes about trade and currency as well as minor border clashes, on 6 May 1998 Eritrean troops launched an attack which took over the Ethiopian-administered settlement of Badme. This prompted a serious escalation in the conflict, as the two sides mobilized between them some 800,000 troops. Various attempts at mediation by the United States, the OAU and the UN proved unsuccessful. In May 2000, therefore, UN Security Council Resolution 1298 imposed an arms embargo on both parties. It was not until 18 June 2000, however, that the two sides signed the Agreement on Cessation of Hostilities. By this time the conflict had cost between 70,000 and 100,000 lives and displaced more than 1.2 million people (Adebajo 2004: 581). It was also evident that Ethiopia had gained the upper hand militarily.

The cessation agreement included provision for a small observer operation. The UN Mission in Ethiopia and Eritrea (UNMEE) was duly authorized on 31 July by UN Security Council Resolution 1312 with an initial strength of up to 100 military observers (plus support staff). Its mandate was to liaise with the conflicting parties, verify the cessation of hostilities, and assist in planning for a future peacekeeping operation.

On 15 September, and following the UN Secretary-General's report to the Security Council of 9 August, Resolution 1320 authorized the deployment of a peacekeeping operation of up to 4,300 troops. A significant proportion of these troops, notably units from the Netherlands, Canada and Denmark, were deployed relatively rapidly as the first operation of the Standby High Readiness Brigade (SHIRBRIG). Over the years, these Western states gradually reduced their presence in UNMEE, leaving India, Jordan and Kenya as the largest contributors. UNMEE's mandate now included monitoring the ceasefire as well as the redeployment of the armed forces of both sides, in line with the temporary security zone (TSZ) envisaged in the cessation agreement. The Security Council stated that the mandate would end following the conclusion of the delimitation and demarcation process for the Ethiopian–Eritrean border. Defining the exact position of the TSZ proved to be UNMEE's first major political challenge. Indeed, it was not until June 2001 that its location was established – and even then this was in principle rather than in practice. Not only did the conflict parties differ on where they thought the boundaries of the TSZ should lie, both sides proceeded to break the rules: while Ethiopia refused to withdraw its troops from certain areas that UNMEE believed to be within the TSZ, notably around Irob, Eritrea denied UNMEE freedom of movement outside of the TSZ and persisted in deploying more than 6,000 militia and 3,000 police within the zone, which greatly exceeded the permissible number stipulated in the terms of the agreement (Martin 2004: 138–43). By December 2000, UNMEE was joined by officials from the OAU's Liaison Mission in Ethiopia/Eritrea (OLMEE).

In the meantime, talks between the Ethiopian and Eritrean governments had continued, resulting in the signing of a comprehensive peace agreement – the Algiers Agreement – on 12 December 2000. Under this agreement, the parties decided, among other things, to 'terminate hostilities between themselves' and 'refrain from the threat or use of force against the other' (Article 1.1); 'release and repatriate' all prisoners of war (Article 2.3); establish 'a neutral Boundary Commission...to delimit and demarcate' the disputed border between the two countries (Article 4); and establish 'a neutral Claims Commission' to address 'the negative socio-economic impact of the crisis on the civilian population' (Article 5).

The Boundary Commission announced its decision on the delimitation of the border on 13 April 2002. Under the Algiers Agreement this was supposed to be 'final and binding' on the parties (Article 4.15). Immediately following this announcement, Security Council Resolution 1430 expanded UNMEE's mandate to include de-mining and other assistance in support of the Boundary Commission's demarcation activities. Initially, Ethiopia and Eritrea both accepted this 'April Decision'. In practice, however, Ethiopia, in particular, prevented its implementation by refusing to allow UNMEE and Boundary Commission staff to cross from Eritrea into Ethiopia. They also questioned the Commission's neutrality and refused to work with UNMEE's force commander, General Cammaert.

Part of the problem was that the Commission's April Decision did not specify the final disposition of the settlement of Badme, which had been at the centre of the dispute. In March 2003, in a set of 'Observations' clarifying its ruling, the Boundary Commission awarded control of Badme to Eritrea. Technically, this upheld Eritrea's position that it went to war in 1998 to defend its territory. The Ethiopian government rejected this ruling as 'totally illegal, unjust, and irresponsible' (Lyons 2006: 8). The Commission responded by condemning Ethiopia's actions as 'an attempt to reopen the substance of the April Decision...and to undermine not only the April Decision but also the peace process as a whole' (cited in Adebajo 2004: 584). The UN Security Council also passed several resolutions (1430, 1466, 1507, 1531) in which it called for Ethiopia's full cooperation with respect to the Boundary Commission. It was not until November 2004 that the Ethiopian government accepted the Commission's ruling in principle, but called for a 'peace-building dialogue' (Lyons 2006: 8).

Believing that the process of legal arbitration had upheld its claims, Eritrea became increasingly frustrated with the UN Security Council's inability to enforce Ethiopia's compliance with the Boundary Commission's ruling. Over time, it therefore began to place greater restrictions upon UNMEE, declaring in late 2007 that the UN force was in effect maintaining Ethiopia's 'occupation' of Eritrean territory (UN Secretary-General 2008a: 5). These restrictions included banning UN helicopter flights in Eritrean airspace, banning UNMEE from conducting night patrols, restricting its supply of diesel fuel (which was cut off entirely from 1 December 2007), hindering the movement of UNMEE personnel, and refusing to accept nationals of certain states, among them the United States, Canada and European countries, as UNMEE personnel (ibid. 2008a: 2–4). UNMEE reported that such activities would compel it to relocate from Eritrea 'and effectively halt its operations' (ibid.: 3). This duly occurred in February and March 2008, when most UNMEE contingents were relocated from Eritrea. (The mission's military personnel on the Ethiopian side continued to carry out their mandated tasks.)

In essence, the problem was that Ethiopia and Eritrea expressed conflicting views on the Boundary Commission's ruling. On 30 November 2007, the Boundary Commission had dissolved itself on the grounds that at that point it considered that it had fulfilled the mandate given to it (UN Secretary-General 2008a: 15). The sticking point was that the Commission did not physically demarcate the border between Ethiopia and Eritrea, not least because the area was heavily mined and it faced significant obstruction from Ethiopia. Instead, it demarcated the boundary with reference to coordinates on a map but without ensuring that these coordinates were represented physically by pillars on the ground. Eritrea accepted what it called the Commission's 'virtual demarcation' as an incomplete but 'important step forward towards the demarcation on the ground' (cited ibid.: 16–23). Later, Eritrea's president argued that 'Whether pillars are placed along the border or not is in fact immaterial for all legal and practical purposes' (cited in UN Secretary-General 2008b: 10). Ethiopia, on the other hand, argued that the Commission's demarcation coordinates were 'invalid because they are not the product of a demarcation process recognized by international law' (cited in UN Secretary-General 2008a: 16–23).

The resulting impasse reflected some of the central challenges facing traditional peacekeeping operations. First, without the cooperation of the conflicting parties, the peacekeepers were unable to fulfil the terms of their mandate. Second, by effectively freezing the conflict and stopping the death toll from rising, UNMEE helped create the conditions whereby there was little pressure on either the parties or the Security Council to push for a political resolution to the dispute. After the April Decision, the Security Council did little to push Ethiopia either to accept the Boundary Commission's ruling or to tackle the underlying causes of the conflict until Eritrea's restrictions on UNMEE placed it back under the international spotlight (Lyons 2006: 19).

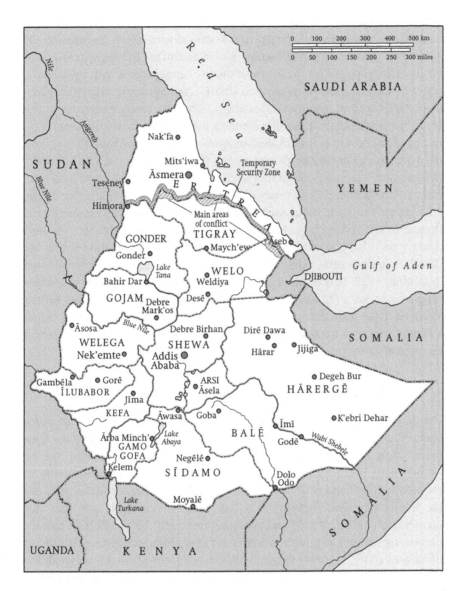

Map 7.3 *UNMEE in Ethiopia and Eritrea*

Third, if they fail to implement legitimate rulings, the presence of UN peace-keepers can come to be resented by one side. In this case, Eritrea came to view UNMEE's presence as helping to maintain Ethiopia's occupation of its territory rather than as facilitating an arbitration process. From UNMEE's perspective, because it had neither the mandate nor the resources to impose an outcome upon the belligerents, it was unable to implement the Boundary Commission's ruling and hence became part of a status quo that all parties regarded as unsatisfactory.

As a consequence of these problems, several members of the Security Council, including the US, began to advocate closing down the mission. By April 2008 the situation had become so contested that the Secretary-General outlined four options for the future of the UN's engagement with the dispute: (1) if Eritrea reconsidered its position UNMEE could proceed with its mission; (2) UNMEE could be terminated, leaving no UN peacekeeping presence in the area; (3) a small observer mission could be deployed in the border area; or (4) liaison offices could be established in Asmara and Addis Ababa to maintain UN readiness to assist the parties in the implementation of the Boundary Commission's decision should they agree to proceed with the physical demarcation of the border (UN Secretary-General 2008b: 11). Shortly afterwards, the governments of both states made it clear to the UN Secretary-General that they would not accept any of the options. This prompted Belgium – the lead country on this issue at the time – to circulate a draft resolution proposing UNMEE's termination. On 30 July, the Council unanimously adopted Resolution 1827. This terminated UNMEE with effect from 31 July and made no provision for a follow-on mission. As one analysis put it, this left Eritrea 'clinging to the legitimacy of its position – backed by international law' while Ethiopia clung 'to the leverage it has by virtue of the de facto situation on the ground' (Security Council Report 2008a: 3).

7.3 Problems

The 'holy trinity' is still widely viewed as a crucial starting point for peace operations, although its limitations have been exposed in many of the UN's more complex operations, raising questions about its wider utility. Nevertheless, it is important to recognize that, in terms of their ability to reduce the likelihood of a war reigniting, traditional peacekeeping missions are highly effective, reducing this risk by as much as 95 per cent (see Introduction). While traditional peacekeeping might be an effective tool for preventing war, it has proven less effective at enabling conflict resolution. As illustrated above, there are two principal sets of problems that limit its ability to facilitate conflict resolution. The first refers to its inability to accomplish its own goals. The second relates to its inability to accomplish wider tasks or actively promote conflict resolution.

In many cases traditional peacekeeping operations have not culminated in the former belligerents concluding a lasting peace settlement as envisaged by the theory of this type of operation. Traditional peacekeeping was intended to help provide an environment conducive to conflict resolution by the parties to the dispute. It is based on a Westphalian conception of the liberal peace that looks to create space for states to resolve their conflicts peacefully. However, far from encouraging long-term conflict resolution, traditional peacekeeping operations have been accused of entrenching conflicts and solidifying partitions (Ratner 1996: 10; MacGinty and Robinson 2001: 30). On the one hand, traditional peacekeeping may help prevent further bloodshed in circumstances where a dispute appears intractable and may facilitate confidence-building measures between belligerents. On the other hand, however, it can remove or at least reduce the imperative to pursue a political settlement. Although traditional peacekeeping aims to create a context in which former belligerents feel confident enough to negotiate a political settlement, such operations were not always explicitly linked to peacemaking efforts and certainly never had control over their outcome.

Moreover, traditional peacekeeping's dependence on the consent of the belligerents creates problems even within the narrow remit of the Westphalian conception of peacekeeping. Reliance on the belligerents' goodwill means that traditional operations are unable to achieve their goals if the combatants do not cooperate. In the case of UNTSO, for instance, persistent violations of the 1949 General Armistice Agreements by all the parties meant that the UN was unable to accomplish its goals. Similarly, as noted above, UNEF I was forced to withdraw from the Middle East in 1967 after continued animosity between Israel and Egypt saw their relationship deteriorate into war. In UNMEE's case, its movement and supplies were restricted, some of its personnel were expelled, and, ultimately, the operation was forced to withdraw completely. Finally, the enforced change to UNFICYP's mandate after the Turkish invasion of 1974 is testimony to the inability of traditional peacekeeping to accomplish goals independently of the wishes of the belligerents.

The second set of problems emerges once peacekeepers are given duties beyond simply monitoring ceasefires and are deployed in environments reminiscent of Kaldor's 'new wars' (1997, 1999). The principle of consent was based on the assumption that the belligerents were states with hierarchical Clausewitzian armies. Consent at the governmental level therefore meant that consent and cooperation could be relied upon lower down the chain of command. This is often not the case in 'new wars'. Not only is consent variable in terms of the appropriate authority changing its mind, it is also multilayered inasmuch as there is no guarantee that all the combatants will consent to peacekeeping even if their political leaders do.

From this post-Westphalian perspective, the principles of impartiality and minimum use of force may also be problematic. Adherence to these principles has tended to exacerbate the problems peacekeepers face when consent is not forthcoming or is variable. UNEF I and II, UNFICYP, UNMEE and other traditional peacekeeping operations were all powerless to prevent open breaches of the agreements they were meant to oversee. Furthermore, their limited military capabilities have sometimes undermined their ability to defend themselves and achieve their objectives.

Nevertheless, the impact of traditional peacekeeping upon other types of peace operations has been profound. The powerful legacy of the 'holy trinity' frequently restricted imaginative thinking when peacekeepers were deployed in 'new wars'. Crucially, the successful acquisition and management of consent depends on a number of variables that have often been overlooked because of the insistence that consent be thought of in absolute terms. While it may (sometimes) have been appropriate for operations to monitor buffers between states, experience has shown that it is not an adequate guide for action in other circumstances. Similarly, although the tendency to treat impartiality as synonymous with neutrality may not have been problematic in traditional peacekeeping, experiences in the 1990s suggested that peacekeepers in wider peacekeeping or peace support operations that maintain 'neutrality' could not accomplish their mandate.

The aims of traditional peacekeeping are thus premised on particular assumptions about their environments that have rarely been borne out in practice. Even during the Cold War, operations in Cyprus (UNFICYP) and Congo (ONUC) did not justify these assumptions. After the Cold War, the conflicts and more complex operations in Somalia, Bosnia, Rwanda, Sierra Leone and elsewhere challenged the efficacy of the 'holy trinity', leaving peacekeepers physically and conceptually unable to deal with a 'new' environment that was actually not new at all. Many of the problems associated with 'wider peacekeeping' (see chapter 8) can be attributed to the application of traditional peacekeeping principles in pursuit of very different objectives and in very different environments to those that shaped their development.

CHAPTER EIGHT

Wider Peacekeeping

Despite the relative success of several assisting transition operations in the first half of the 1990s (discussed in chapter 10), the growth of UN peacekeeping at that time is often associated with the failures of high-profile missions in Bosnia, Rwanda, Somalia and Angola (see chapter 4). For some, a 'crisis of expectations' was caused by the disjuncture between the demands placed on peacekeepers and the means given to them to accomplish their goals (Thakur and Thayer 1995). Peacekeepers took on wider tasks, including both traditional and 'transitional' duties, often within hostile environments, and yet were still expected to adhere to the 'holy trinity' of traditional peacekeeping. While some writers suggest that wider peacekeeping became extinct after the Rwandan and Bosnian bloodbaths, many peace operations have continued to exhibit some of its chief characteristics.

After identifying the central characteristics of wider peacekeeping, this chapter discusses how they shaped international responses to conflict in Bosnia and Rwanda and demonstrates how they can also be detected in more recent missions, such as the African Union's mission in the Darfur region of Sudan, AMIS (2004–7). (An additional case study of the UN operations in Sierra Leone is provided on the companion website.) Finally, the chapter examines some of the weaknesses of wider peacekeeping as a response to the changing conflict environment facing peacekeepers. These weaknesses suggest that, in certain circumstances, 'peace enforcement' and 'peace support operations' may be necessary to accomplish the expanded mandates, though often there is not the political will to authorize or contribute to these types of operations.

8.1 What is wider peacekeeping?

Wider peacekeeping has many different labels. According to the British military doctrine which bears the same name, it refers to 'operations carried out with the consent of the belligerent parties in support of efforts to achieve or maintain peace in order to promote security and sustain life in areas of potential or actual conflict' (HMSO 1995: 2.1). The 'wider' qualification of wider peacekeeping refers to 'the wider aspects of peacekeeping operations carried out with the consent of the belligerent parties but in an environment that may be volatile' (ibid.). Wider peacekeeping is also sometimes referred to as 'second generation peacekeeping' (e.g. Mackinlay and Chopra 1992; Mackinlay 1996). The 'second generation' was distinct from the first generation because such operations tended to take place within states rather than between them and in an environment where the interposition of blue helmets between organized belligerents was either not possible or ineffective. Another term for wider peacekeeping is 'Chapter 6 ½' peacekeeping – used to highlight the problem that wider peacekeeping falls somewhere between the pacific and consensual provisions of Chapter VI of the UN Charter and the enforcement measures envisaged by Chapter VII (Bailey and Daws 1995). The ambiguous 'Chapter 6 ½' nature of such operations is often claimed to lie at the heart of the failures in Bosnia, Rwanda and Sierra Leone (O'Shea 2002: 147). Other labels for wider peacekeeping include 'peacekeeping by proxy' (Charters 2000) and 'strategic peacekeeping' (Olonisakin 2000), both of which emphasize the gap between the demands placed on peacekeepers and the means made available to them.

All these terms refer to similar practices, although each stresses different aspects. Some focus on the new tasks given to peacekeepers while others pay more attention to the changing conflict environment. However, six key characteristics of wider peacekeeping can be identified.

First, despite the existence of formal ceasefires, these operations occur within a context of ongoing violence. Whereas both traditional peacekeeping and assisting transition operations take place after the belligerents have signed a ceasefire agreement, wider peacekeeping takes place either in the complete absence of such an agreement or in situations where agreements are fragile and prone to collapse. In Bosnia, for instance, UNPROFOR negotiated literally hundreds of ceasefires, most of which were broken within twenty-four hours. Similarly, UN missions in both Rwanda and Sierra Leone were plagued by collapsing peace agreements and violence.

Second, wider peacekeeping operations tend to take place during what Mary Kaldor (1999) has labelled 'new wars' rather than in traditional interstate conflicts. Thus, although the armed conflicts in Bosnia, Rwanda, Sierra Leone and Sudan, for instance, witnessed significant external involvement, they were not simply interstate wars in the Westphalian sense.

Third, soldiers engaged in wider peacekeeping are given tasks beyond those of traditional peacekeeping, including the separation of forces, disarming the belligerents, organizing and supervising elections, delivering humanitarian aid, protecting civilians and UN personnel, guaranteeing freedom of movement, host-state capacity-building, monitoring ceasefires, and enforcing no-fly zones (Berdal 1993; Doyle et al. 1997). Although peacekeepers involved in managing transitions in Namibia, El Salvador, Cambodia and Mozambique also took on many of these roles, the context of enduring violent conflict dramatically altered their nature and salience in wider peacekeeping operations.

Fourth, wider peacekeeping operations witnessed the exponential growth of the civilian 'humanitarian community' with whom peacekeepers were often supposed to coordinate their activities. Compared with traditional peacekeepers such as those in the UNEF missions, for example, wider peace-keepers in Bosnia, Rwanda, Sierra Leone and Sudan were confronted with literally hundreds of different governmental and non-governmental organiza-tions, each trying to accomplish different goals. For example, over 200 NGOs were active in Rwanda at the height of the conflict, and in the space of just seven months in Yugoslavia, between February and September 1993, the number of NGOs increased from sixty-five to 127 (Ramsbotham and Woodhouse 1999: 176). More recently, by 2005 there were some 12,000 humanitarian aid workers operating in Darfur (UN 2007b). This created problems of coherence and coordination and contributed to the new tasks given to peacekeepers (see Weiss 1995; Slim 1997).

Fifth, wider peacekeeping missions have frequently changing mandates. Between 1991 and the end of 1995, the Security Council passed eighty-three resolutions on the Croatian and Bosnian wars alone (see table 8.1). Many of these resolutions changed UNPROFOR's mandate, composition, equipment or financing. Even resolutions that did not directly refer to UNPROFOR – such as Resolution 713 – affected its operating environment. The UN's mandate in Bosnia changed rapidly, from a humanitarian remit, to one empowered to use force to assist the delivery of humanitarian supplies, to one charged with deterring violence within 'safe areas' and, finally, to one supporting a NATO-led peace enforcement mission.

Finally, wider peacekeeping operations suffer from a significant gulf between means and ends. Although it entails the adoption of more tasks by peacekeepers, the latter are not provided with the necessary means to accom-plish those tasks. This situation is often reflected in a financial shortfall. For UN-financed operations, this problem is exacerbated by the fact that the organization's peacekeeping budget lacks capital reserves and is unable to borrow significant amounts to cover arrears (McDermott 1994). This caused practical difficulties in Rwanda, for example, when UNAMIR's commander, General Dallaire, was unable to communicate with all his units because he did not have enough radios (Melvern 2000; see box 8.1).

Wider peacekeeping thus exists where Westphalian and post-Westphalian conceptions of peacekeeping collide. On the one hand, some of the wider tasks peacekeepers are asked to carry out on an ad hoc basis point towards a post-Westphalian conception. The delivery of humanitarian aid, the super-vision of displaced people, support for multi-party elections, and the guar-anteeing of freedom of movement all point towards a post-Westphalian understanding of the role of peacekeeping because they are concerned with what goes on within the state in question. However, although wider peace-keeping takes place within 'new wars', its guiding principles draw heavily on the traditional 'holy trinity' of consent, impartiality and minimum force.

After its unhappy experience in Bosnia, the British military tried to resolve the problem of responding to 'new wars' by using traditional peacekeeping techniques. As a result, the formal doctrine of wider peacekeeping is Janus-faced. On the one hand, the doctrine writers defined it in terms of the changing conflict environment and the new tasks given to peacekeepers. From this perspective, it takes place in an environment characterized by numerous parties to the conflict, undisciplined belligerents, ineffective ceasefire(s), the absence of law and order, gross violations of human rights, a risk of armed opposition to UN forces, the active involvement of large numbers of NGOs, the collapse of civil infrastructure, large numbers of displaced persons, and an undefined area of operations (HMSO 1995: 1.7). Consequently, wider peacekeepers must perform more tasks than traditional peacekeepers. British doctrine identified five typical tasks in particular: conflict prevention, demobilization of belligerents, military assistance to civilian agencies, humanitarian relief, and the guarantee and denial of movement. While many of these 'new' tasks had been key features of earlier missions, particularly earlier peace enforcement and managing transition operations, their location within 'new war' environments presented peacekeepers with a distinct set of challenges.

Although British doctrine recognized that the peacekeeping environment had changed, it largely retained the conceptual tools of traditional peacekeeping, claiming that 'wider peacekeeping tasks post Cold War do not reflect a novel development but rather a *changing emphasis* in terms of scale, participation and involvement' (HMSO 1995: 2.4). There was no substantive difference, it reasoned, between traditional peacekeeping and wider peacekeeping. The task at hand was not, therefore, to rethink the role of peacekeeping in global politics. Rather, it was to adapt Westphalian tools to the new environment.

Wider peacekeeping doctrine thus retained traditional peacekeeping's 'holy trinity', including the notion that the preservation of consent was a prerequisite for a successful mission. As figure 8.1 shows, wider peacekeeping doctrine viewed the issue of consent as marking a fundamental distinction between wider peacekeeping and peace enforcement. A wider peacekeeping mission that inadvertently crossed the 'Mogadishu line' (Rose 1998) into peace enforcement would always fail to achieve its goals. A mission could not, it was argued, move from wider peacekeeping to peace enforcement and back again. Consent could be maintained only by adhering to the other two aspects of the 'holy trinity'. First, wider peacekeepers must remain impartial, defined here as being synonymous with neutrality rather than as treating belligerents equally in relation to their adherence to the mandate (as set out in the Brahimi Report or the concept of peace support operations; see chapter 12). As a result, 'all dealings by UN troops, whether operational, administrative or social, should be conducted without favour to any particular party or *any single point of view*' (HMSO 1995: 4.3; emphasis added). Second, the use of force

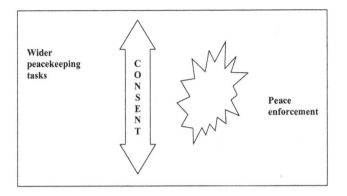

Source: adapted from HMSO (1995: 2.6).

Figure 8.1 *The central role of consent in wider peacekeeping doctrine*

by peacekeepers was identified as the main threat to consent. Field commanders were therefore advised to keep the use of force to a minimum (ibid.: 4.6).

Wider peacekeeping can therefore be understood as an attempt to apply
the principles of traditional peacekeeping – based on ideas about managing
Westphalian interstate conflict – in a post-Westphalian environment. It is
important to remember that, although it claimed to be prescriptive, the
British doctrine was in fact descriptive, trying to make sense of the British
experience in Bosnia. It is unsurprising, therefore, that wider peacekeeping
should make use of established canons, because it is an ad hoc response to a
changing conflict environment and the addition of new tasks.

8.2 Wider peacekeeping in practice

UNPROFOR in Bosnia (1992–1995)

UNPROFOR provides an exemplary illustration of wider peacekeeping. Indeed,
the British military doctrine outlined above has been criticized for drawing
too heavily on the British experience in Bosnia (Connaughton 1995). Between
1992 and 1995 peacekeepers in Bosnia confronted all six characteristics of
wider peacekeeping (outlined above) and tried to resolve the dilemmas they
posed in an ad hoc fashion. The result, according to most commentators, was
a 'miserable and conspicuous disaster' that 'reflected the flawed logic of
bravado that underscored the conception and function of "second-genera-
tion" peace operations' (Adibe 1998: 107). A more judicious assessment found
that UNPROFOR was 'agonised by tough-sounding resolutions [see table 8.1]
followed-up with inadequate human, material, and financial resources'
(Biermann and Vadset 1998: 21).

UNPROFOR's experience can be divided into three phases. The first phase,
from June 1992 to April 1993, saw UN peacekeepers given two primary tasks

TABLE 8.1 UNPROFOR'S changing mandate

Security Council Resolution	Date	Purpose
713	25 Sept 1991	Arms embargo against former Yugoslavia
743	21 Feb 1992	Establishes UNPROFOR to monitor a ceasefire in the UNPAs in Croatia
757	30 May 1992	Imposes sanctions on Serbia and Montenegro
758	8 June 1992	Increases UNPROFOR mandate to include Bosnia and the safe delivery of humanitarian supplies
764	13 July 1992	Empowers UNPROFOR to secure Sarajevo airport and its environs
770	13 Aug 1992	Demands access to all refugee and prisoner of war camps
776	14 Sept 1992	Enlarges UNPROFOR mandate to include the protection of convoys
781	9 Oct 1992	Creates a no-fly zone over Bosnia
787	16 Oct 1992	Deployment of observers to Bosnia's borders to enforce compliance with sanctions
816	31 March 1993	Gives members the right to enforce the no-fly zone
819	16 April 1993	Designates Srebrenica a 'safe area' which should be 'free from armed attack'
824	6 May 1993	Designates Sarajevo, Tuzla, Zepa, Gorazde and Bihac as 'safe areas' and authorizes the strengthening of UNPROFOR by 50 military observers
827	25 May 1993	Creates the International Criminal Tribunal for Yugoslavia (ICTY)
836	4 June 1993	Gives UNPROFOR the task of 'deterring' attacks on the safe areas including the use of air strikes
913	22 April 1993	Gives UNPROFOR responsibility for collecting and storing belligerents' heavy weapons around Gorazde
998	16 June 1995	Welcomes the creation and deployment of the NATO rapid reaction force
1035	21 Dec 1995	Authorizes the deployment of IFOR

(though even this was done incrementally). Created in February 1992, UNPROFOR was initially mandated to monitor a ceasefire agreement between Croatia and Serbia. This agreement signalled a temporary end to six months of violence between the new Croatian state and Croatian Serb militias fighting alongside the Yugoslav People's Army (JNA) that had virtually destroyed Vukovar and Dubrovnik. Together, the rebel Serbs and the JNA had seized

Map 8.1 *Bosnia and Hercegovina*

around one-third of Croatia's territory. Having agreed a ceasefire, the Croats and Serbs accepted the creation of UN Protected Areas (UNPAs) in the Serb-held regions. The UNPAs were to be free from armed attack by the Croats but were also to be demilitarized by the Serbs. UNPROFOR was to supervise compliance with the ceasefire agreement (a traditional peacekeeping task). The opposing sides had agreed a ceasefire, and peacekeepers were interposed between them while political leaders sought a lasting political settlement.

At the outset UNPROFOR consisted of 13,000 troops, civilian personnel and a largely ineffective civilian police element (Gow and Smith 1992). Strangely, given that UNPROFOR's mission was originally confined to Croatia, the UN decided that its headquarters should be in Sarajevo, Bosnia. Its deployment took many months owing to disagreements about who would pay for the mission, what its rules of engagement would be, and who would command it (Gow 1997), and it did not become fully operational until June 1992. By that time, the decision to locate the UN's headquarters in Sarajevo looked most apposite. Although the situation in Croatia remained relatively calm the violence had spread to Bosnia, with the Bosnian Serbs backed by the JNA seizing great tracts of land in eastern Bosnia and forcing hundreds of thousands of Muslim and Croatian Bosnians from their homes (Burg and Shoup 1999).

By the summer of 1992, the UN was confronting a humanitarian catastrophe in Bosnia. The Bosnian Serb strategy of ethnic cleansing had created 500,000 refugees at the time of UNPROFOR's creation and three times that number by the time it was deployed. The death toll had also begun to increase alarmingly towards 50,000 (by the end of the war that figure reached 250,000). The Security Council reacted by enlarging UNPROFOR's mandate. In June 1992 it was officially extended into Bosnia and given the additional task of supporting the delivery of humanitarian aid. Peacekeepers were given little or no guidance about how precisely they were supposed to do this, and their primary mission remained the supervision of a ceasefire that did not exist. 'How can we keep the peace when there is no peace to keep?' was a question asked by many soldiers given just that task (see Stewart 1993). Along with the European Community Monitoring Mission, UNPROFOR's ceasefire supervision role became an irrelevance, limited to providing reports (albeit important) of the shifting frontlines, civilian casualties and flows of displaced persons.

The additional task, then, was to facilitate the delivery of humanitarian aid by international organizations such as the World Food Programme and NGOs such as Oxfam. This presented a number of problems, especially as regards the mandate and the use of force. All the belligerents (but the Bosnian Serbs in particular) attempted to control the flow of aid around the country. Roadblocks often obstructed aid convoys, and international lorries carrying aid became prime targets for looting and destruction. However, UNPROFOR lacked both the means and the mandate to enforce the delivery of aid. The problem was that the mandate stipulated that UNPROFOR could use force only in self-defence. Even if a commander decided to interpret self-defence in broad terms – as several contingents tended to do – the UN lacked the resources to follow such a policy through. Both UNPROFOR and the aid agencies therefore depended on the consent of warlords to carry out their tasks, and by negotiating and dealing with them the peacekeepers inadvertently enhanced the warlords' legitimacy. By paying 'taxes' in goods and cash to secure the transit of aid they also enriched the warlords and helped fund the war (Schierup 1999). UNPROFOR was confronted with a Faustian dilemma: bargain with the warlords and deliver *some* aid or refuse to bargain and deliver much less aid. Most UNPROFOR commanders chose the first option.

As disquiet began to grow in the Western media and among peacekeepers about the UN's failure to halt the bloodshed, questions were raised about the possibility of extending UNPROFOR's mandate to include the use of force. In October 1992 the Security Council declared a 'no-fly zone' over Bosnia and gave member states authority to enforce it. NATO took up this authorization. However, the no-fly zone did little to affect the situation on the ground, which continued to worsen. Although humanitarian aid sustained thousands of people through the harsh Bosnian winter, the peacekeepers had little noticeable impact on the fighting.

Spring 1993 saw UNPROFOR enter a new phase. In the face of continuing violence, the Security Council created 'safe areas' in Srebrenica, Sarajevo, Gorazde, Zepa, Tuzla and Bihac. The safe areas were all major towns or cities held by the Bosnian government but besieged by Bosnian Serb forces, who systematically targeted civilians with shells and sniper fire. The Security Council demanded that civilians be 'free from armed attack' and authorized UNPROFOR to deter such attacks. But problems stemmed from the belief that there was a rigid distinction between wider peacekeeping and peace enforcement. In his report to the Security Council, Boutros-Ghali advised that, for the safe areas policy to work, UNPROFOR would need to be reinforced by 34,000 additional troops. However, the Security Council opted for a 'light option' and authorized only 7,600 additional troops (UN 1994: 2). As a result, the Secretary-General noted, 'the effective implementation of the safe-area concept depends on the degree of consent by the parties on the ground' (ibid.: 3). In other words, the success of the safe areas policy depended upon the Bosnian Serbs.

UNPROFOR was not authorized to use force to ensure that humanitarian supplies were delivered. Besieged towns such as Srebrenica were therefore dependent for supplies on Bosnian Serb goodwill. But goodwill was in short supply, and malnutrition and disease set in. A by-product of creating so-called safe areas was that most of Bosnia became a hostile region in which UN peacekeepers had very little power. Moreover, when, in summer 1995, the Bosnian Serbs decided to overrun the safe areas, UNPROFOR had neither the capability nor the mandate to prevent them from doing so. In July 1995 the Bosnian Serbs seized the safe area of Srebrenica from a small contingent of Dutch peacekeepers, massacring more than 7,500 civilians as they did so (Honig and Both 1996). The Dutch commander in Srebrenica, General Herrimans, requested air strikes to repel the Serbs – as he was entitled to do under Resolution 836 (4 June 1993), which permitted UNPROFOR to 'deter attacks against the safe areas'. But UNPROFOR's commander, General Joulwan, and the Special Representative to the Secretary-General, Yasushi Akashi, feared that substantial air strikes would take UNPROFOR across the 'Mogadishu line' and so blocked the demand. The Bosnian Serbs seized the safe area and massacred its male inhabitants virtually unimpeded by the UN.

The fall of Srebrenica, the subsequent fall of Zepa and the near collapse of Gorazde and Bihac prompted the Security Council to rethink its strategy. The British and French created and deployed a rapid reaction force (RRF) that had more robust rules of engagement. After consistent pressure from the US, on 30 August 1995 NATO launched Operation Deliberate Force. Supported with artillery from the RRF, Deliberate Force was a sustained air campaign against the Bosnian Serbs. This was the end of wider peacekeeping in Bosnia and the start of peace enforcement (see chapter 9). Within four months the Bosnian war was over.

UNAMIR in Rwanda (1993–1994)

UNAMIR confronted many of the same problems that plagued the wider peacekeeping mission in Bosnia. It was deployed to keep a peace based on the Arusha Accords of August 1993 but was given neither the means nor the mandate to accomplish its mission. UNAMIR peacekeepers were therefore unable to deter or halt the genocide that began only hours after President Habyarimana's plane was shot down at Kigali airport on 6 April 1994. In 100 days, *Interahamwe* and *Impuzamugambi* militias and their Hutu supporters killed approximately 800,000 Tutsis and up to 50,000 of their Hutu opponents.

Although the difference between 'Hutus' and 'Tutsis' in Rwanda is unclear, most accounts suggest that the Belgian imperialists favoured the minority Tutsis, whom they deemed culturally superior to the Hutus. However, during the transition to independence, which began in 1959, the Hutus seized control of the state in a bloody conflict that led to a mass exodus of Tutsis. This large refugee population proved to be an ideal recruiting ground for armed militia, and the Tutsis staged a number of armed incursions into Rwanda aimed at toppling the government. The government responded with violent repression, such as in 1973 when a Tutsi attempt to seize power was met with severe reprisals. At the same time, however, Juvenal Habyarimana, a Hutu, staged a coup and seized control of the state. The relative stability enjoyed by Rwanda was threatened in 1990 by the emergence of a new Tutsi army, the Rwandan Patriotic Front (RPF), which was based in Uganda. Three years of guerrilla war followed, with the RPF claiming substantial amounts of territory in Rwanda. This was in spite of the fact that the French government had deployed soldiers to help Habyarimana's forces fend off the RPF assault (see Kroslak 2007). In 1993, facing defeat and fearing opposition from more extremist Hutu politicians, and pressurized by international society, Habyarimana concluded a power-sharing agreement with the RPF under the Arusha Accords. UNAMIR was created to observe compliance. The primary problem the mission faced was that some of Habyarimana's Hutu opponents had a more radical agenda and, probably after killing the president, unleashed their planned genocide on the country (see Prunier 1995; Melvern 2006). For the 100 days of genocide, UNAMIR was powerless to stop the slaughter in many areas, although at one stage it did manage to protect up to 30,000 people (Des Forges 1999: 689).

The Arusha Accords had three key facets: a ceasefire agreement, an agreement to create a transitional government that included the RPF, and the deployment of a peacekeeping force to supervise their implementation (Destexhe 1995: 46). Although international society had been instrumental in pressurizing the parties to sign, there was little will to organize an effective peacekeeping force (Jones 2001). Article 54 of the accords called for a neutral international force to provide security for the inhabitants of Rwanda's capital, Kigali, by protecting civilians, supervising arms dumps and disarming militias (Uvin 1998: 97). This clearly implied that a force capable of more than traditional peacekeeping was needed. Unlike UNPROFOR, which was initially envisaged as a traditional interpositionary force, the peace that UNAMIR was meant to keep was dependent on the adoption of wider tasks that required greater capabilities than its peacekeepers possessed.

When the question of creating UNAMIR came before the Security Council, the political will to create and pay for a force capable of accomplishing wider peacekeeping tasks was lacking. Security Council Resolution 872 (5 October 1993) envisaged it as a small operation assisting transition, limiting its task to monitoring the agreement and restricting even that to a 'weapons secure area established by the parties'. A major reason for the Council's reluctance to establish a stronger presence was that the decision on whether to create it and what kind of mission it should be came only two days after the death of eighteen American soldiers in Mogadishu, Somalia (see chapters 4 and 9). It was, as Linda Melvern (2000: 79) put it, 'a grave accident of timing'. However, it was not only American reluctance to countenance another Somalia that dictated that UNAMIR would be conceptualized in traditional terms. Although Boutros-Ghali campaigned for a UN peacekeeping mission, his reports insisted that it should be of the traditional variety.

UNAMIR was thus incapable of facilitating the implementation of the Arusha Accords. For example, according to the UN Secretariat, it did not have a mandate to collect weapons, protect civilians, or assist with the repatriation of refugees as had been stipulated (Adelman and Suhrke 1996: 7; Melvern 2000: 79–80). Instead, the Council authorized a force that was too small to manage Rwanda's transition. The initial assessment of force commander General Roméo Dallaire and the DPKO had been that 8,000 troops were necessary. This assessment had been reduced to 4,500 to deter a Security Council veto, but still the Council authorized the deployment of only 2,548 peacekeepers. In the wake of Somalia and an American Congressional decision to cancel an emergency peacekeeping contingency fund, the US pushed to reduce UNAMIR's budget. At the insistence of the American Ambassador to the UN,

Madeleine Albright, the Security Council instructed the Secretary-General to 'consider ways of reducing the total maximum strength of UNAMIR...[and] to seek economies' (Bennis 2000: 128). The Americans argued that the mission should not cost more than $10 million a month (Melvern 2000: 85). As a result, four months later only half the authorized number of peacekeepers had been deployed, and those that were remained woefully under-equipped.

Some of the negative effects that this had on UNAMIR are described in box 8.1. It was a small and cheap force conceptualized in traditional terms, even though its original rationale, set out in the Arusha Accords, called for a force capable of managing the transition from civil war to peace. At the beginning of 1994 it became clear to Dallaire and others that arms were being imported and distributed throughout the country. It was also clear that UNAMIR had neither the mandate nor the means to prevent that from happening, a point recognized by both Dallaire and the Special Representative to the Secretary-General, Jacques Booh-Booh (Prunier 1995: 206; Dallaire 2003).

The Security Council met to discuss extending UNAMIR's mandate for a further six months on 5 April 1994, shortly before the genocide erupted. On the one hand, the US argued that progress towards democracy was too slow and that the UN should consider withdrawing completely. On the other, Boutros-Ghali reported that progress was being made, though he omitted to tell the Council that Dallaire had complained about the lack of resources at

---

Box 8.1 UNAMIR: small and cheap

UNAMIR was forced to operate without adequate resources. From the very start, the operation found it difficult to obtain even basic supplies such as eating utensils, and at one stage was unable to file situation reports because it ran out of paper. One symbolic story suggested that, after months of begging for them, flashlights arrived but were without batteries. Many of the peacekeeping troops that did appear lacked not only training but also basic items such as boots. Despite this desperate situation, in the initial stages of the genocide UNAMIR's personnel watched a series of cargo planes arrive empty and without provisions into Kigali airport and leave with foreigners aboard. UNAMIR's military component fared little better. The official version was that it consisted of three infantry battalions, one engineer company, a transportation section (with four utility helicopters), one logistics company, one medical platoon, 331 military observers, a force headquarters, a movement control unit and a field hospital. It was to have at its disposal twenty-two armoured personnel carriers (APCs) and eight military helicopters in order that it could respond rapidly to developing events. In practice, however, no military helicopters arrived, while only five of the eight APCs that found their way to Rwanda were serviceable. These were Czech-made BTR-80s (on loan only), which arrived in early March 1994. Unfortunately, they lacked tools, spare parts, mechanics and manuals and had only limited ammunition. In addition, they were worn out from use in the UN mission in Mozambique, and shortly after their arrival they became inoperable.

Sources: Barnett (2002: 92, 100); Melvern (2000: 85).

his disposal and warned about the imminent danger of mass killing (Melvern 2000: 113). The Council agreed to extend but further restrict the mandate, and demanded that UNAMIR should withdraw if the transitional government was not fully operational by the end of the extended period of time. One day later, Habyarimana was dead and the genocide had begun.

The UN now discussed three main options: withdraw UNAMIR because it was a traditional peacekeeping force with no peace to keep; escalate the mission to a peace enforcement operation; or keep a symbolic UNAMIR presence in place – a traditional peacekeeping force inside a bloody wider peacekeeping context. The situation deteriorated when ten Belgian peacekeepers were killed by Hutu militia, prompting Belgium – which had provided the strongest military contingent – to order an immediate withdrawal of its forces (Suhrke 1998). Boutros-Ghali pressurized Dallaire to advocate a complete withdrawal, but he refused, insisting that UNAMIR could still serve a useful purpose no matter how small (Magnarella 2000: 34). After much prevarication, the Security Council decided formally to reduce UNAMIR to 270 observers, although approximately 450 chose to remain (Melvern 2000: 174). The downsized UNAMIR did what it could. It organized prisoner transfers, conducted mediation and tried to support the delivery of humanitarian aid. There were repeated attempts to withdraw the force until, on 17 May, the Security Council authorized a force of 5,500 troops to join the mission. In practice, however, Resolution 918 was a sham: 'no equipped troops were available for Rwanda, and, even if there had been, there was no airlift' capability (ibid.:197). As a result it was not until early July that foreign soldiers arrived in Rwanda. At this stage France led an operation to the southwest of the country to create safe areas and protect displaced people. But by that time most of the killing had stopped (see Prunier 1999). As the genocide progressed, the RPF gradually defeated the Rwandan government's army and the militia forces, eventually driving many of them out of the country.

UNAMIR's inability to prevent or halt the genocide prompted a considerable amount of soul searching at the UN. In presenting the report of an independent inquiry as to what went wrong, Kofi Annan admitted that

> All of us must bitterly regret that we did not do more to prevent it. There was a United Nations force in the country at the time, but it was neither mandated nor equipped for the kind of forceful action which would have been needed to prevent or halt the genocide. On behalf of the United Nations, I acknowledge this failure and express my deep remorse. (Annan 1999f)

As mentioned in chapter 4, the inquiry found that 'the failure by the United Nations to prevent, and subsequently to stop the genocide in Rwanda was a failure by the United Nations system as a whole' (Independent Inquiry 1999: 1). That failure was a product of the lack of resources and a lack of will on the part of international society (ibid.: 22). There was a critical disjuncture, endemic in wider peacekeeping, between the tasks given to peacekeepers and

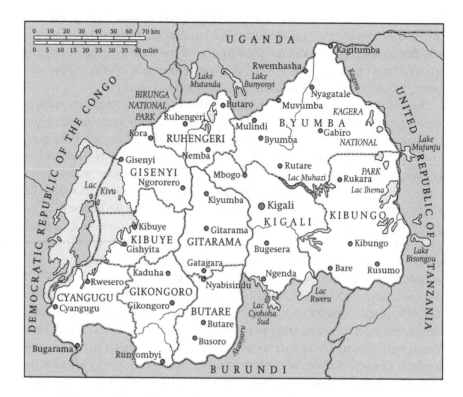

Map 8.2 *Rwanda*

their conceptual and material tools. UNAMIR was conceived in traditional terms, even though its operational context was very different to those of successful assisting transition operations (see chapter 10). The rhetoric of shame that followed the Rwandan experience prompted Western states in particular to think about peacekeeping in new ways. Rather than focusing on consent, they turned their attention to the capabilities needed to fulfil the wider tasks. This led to an emerging view that peacekeepers should be more forceful and better equipped. As we discussed in chapter 5, this view is now most commonly associated with the Brahimi Report. After Rwanda there was a growing tendency to think of peacekeeping in terms of enforcing peace (see chapter 9) and peace support (see chapter 12). Unfortunately, even after the terrible experiences of UN peacekeepers in Bosnia and Rwanda, several peace operations – particularly in Africa – continued to display the characteristics of wider peacekeeping. A good example of this is the African Union's mission in the Darfur region of Sudan.

AMIS in Sudan (2004–2007)

In early 2003 two rebel movements, the Sudan Liberation Movement/Army (SLM/A) and the Justice and Equality Movement (JEM), launched a series of attacks against Sudanese government targets in the western region of Darfur (see map 5.1, p. 150). The government retaliated by conducting a counter-insurgency campaign against the rebels and their supporters wherein its troops were supported by a variety of militia forces popularly referred to as the *janjawiid*. By early 2004 the war in Darfur had left thousands dead and hundreds of thousands displaced from their homes, and pushed millions into the UN's category of 'conflict affected people' (see Flint and de Waal 2005; Prunier 2005). Throughout 2004, Darfur's conflict was characterized by large-scale and systematic war crimes and crimes against humanity perpetrated primarily by the government's forces and the *janjawiid* militias it supported (see International Commission 2005). Because the government of Sudan did not consent to a UN peace operation in Darfur, it was left to the African Union (AU) to muster a response.

The catalyst for the AU's peacekeeping operation in Darfur was the signing on 8 April 2004 of the N'djamena Humanitarian Ceasefire Agreement between the government of Sudan, the SLM/A and the JEM. This helped produce the Addis Ababa agreement on 28 May 2004 which included the formation of a Ceasefire Monitoring Commission. At this point the AU decided to deploy military observers and a small protection force to monitor the agreement. In early June about eighty AU observers were deployed, along with some 300 Nigerian and Rwandan troops. Unfortunately, the ceasefire agreement quickly broke down and the AU observers were left to monitor events in an ongoing war zone.

Spurred on by international calls to 'do something' in response to the civilian suffering evident in Darfur, the AU expanded its peace operation in a series of phases. On 20 October 2004 it authorized an increase in the number of AMIS personnel to 3,320, and in April 2005 this number was expanded to more than 6,000 troops and 1,560 civilian police. The further expansion came after the AU acknowledged that its force was 'extremely stretched to implement its mandate' (AU 2005a: § 3). It also recognized that, in spite of its efforts, 'the number of people displaced and at risk in Darfur has doubled since last year and continues to rise' (AU 2005b: § 103). Elements of the enhanced force were to be deployed with external assistance (the US flew in the Rwandan battalion while France provided airlift for the Senegalese continent). In addition, Canada provided twenty-five transport helicopters and 100 armoured personnel carriers. By this stage the AU was publicly envisaging a force of some 12,000 uniformed personnel being deployed to Darfur by the spring of 2006. As it turned out, its numbers peaked at just under 8,000.

Although it is fair to say that in its areas of deployment AMIS personnel made some significant differences, the operation was plagued by three major problems – mandate issues, incapacity issues, and operating in an environment of ongoing conflict – each of which are depressingly familiar for wider peacekeeping missions and badly hampered its ability to bring stability to Darfur.

Like that of other wider peacekeeping operations, AMIS's mandate underwent a series of changes. The first controversial issue concerned whether or not the Nigerian and Rwandan troops that made up the initial protection force would undertake civilian protection tasks. In late July the AU Assembly stated that the protection force's mandate would include 'the protection, within the capacity of the Force, of the civilian population' (AU 2004a: § 8). In August 2004 Rwanda's president, Paul Kagame, announced that his 'forces will not stand by and watch innocent civilians being hacked to death like the case was here in 1994. If it was established that the civilians are in danger, then our forces would certainly intervene and use force to protect civilians.' Nigeria, on the other hand, agreed with the Sudanese government's position that AU peacekeepers were to use force only in self-defence.

The next problem also revolved around the issue of civilian protection and came with the expansion of AMIS's mandate in October 2004. At this point, the AU Peace and Security Council authorized 'the enhanced AMIS' to undertake a wide range of tasks. Among these were contributing to a secure environment for the delivery of humanitarian relief and the return of refugees and displaced persons to their homes; monitoring and verifying events throughout Darfur; checking that the police were performing their tasks properly; investigating allegations of violations of the ceasefire; and protecting civilians and conducting humanitarian operations.

Not surprisingly, it was the civilian protection element of the mandate that generated the most immediate problems. The AU's communiqué of October 2004 stated that AMIS should 'Protect civilians whom it encounters under imminent threat and in the immediate vicinity, within resources and capability, it being understood that the protection of the civilian population is the responsibility of the Government of Sudan'; and 'Protect both static and mobile humanitarian operations under imminent threat and in the immediate vicinity, within capabilities' (AU 2004b). This phraseology caused considerable confusion among AMIS commanders on the ground, most of whom were unsure of how they were supposed to relate to government forces when they encountered civilians in 'imminent threat'. It was also very unclear as to what type of civilian protection initiatives were within AMIS's 'resources and capability', given its meagre and thinly stretched force levels. In many respects this situation left AMIS in the worst of all worlds inasmuch as local civilians expected its personnel to protect them from the *janjawiid* militias and government soldiers, for they had neither the force levels nor, indeed, a crystal-clear mandate to do so. Eventually, even the chairperson of the AU Commission, Alpha Omar Konare, admitted that 'AMIS' current mandate…is not clearly understood by commanders at all levels' (AU 2006: § 105v).

The third debate about AMIS's mandate came after the signing of the Darfur Peace Agreement (DPA) in May 2006. The agreement's security provisions gave AMIS what Kofi Annan called 'a myriad of new and formidable tasks' (2006: § 29). These included civilian protection and (potentially forcible) disarmament of parties that did not sign the agreement, as well as drawing all the maps of which parties controlled what areas (see Stimson Center 2006). The AU also acknowledged that it was 'acutely aware of the limitations of the capacity of AMIS to fulfil the onerous responsibilities for monitoring and verification under the DPA....To undertake the numerous tasks specified requires additional forces, improved logistics, and a more robust mandate' (*Sudan Tribune* 2006).

As it turned out, the DPA, which initially was signed only by the government of Sudan and one breakaway faction of the SLM/A led by Minni Minawi, quickly collapsed. This left AMIS in an even more precarious position than it had been previously, because its role as overseer of the DPA's security provisions meant that the rebel groups that had not signed up to the agreement accused the AU peacekeepers of siding with the government, which still claimed that the DPA represented a legitimate peace deal and called for AMIS to take action against parties that would not agree to it.

The final set of problems related to the question of how best the UN could help support the beleaguered AU force. On 31 August 2006, the UN Security Council passed Resolution 1706. This authorized the UN's peacekeeping mission in southern Sudan, UNMIS (which had been deployed there in 2005 to assist in the implementation of the Comprehensive Peace Agreement which ended the civil war between the government and rebels in the south of the country), to help AMIS 'support implementation of' the DPA and N'djamena Humanitarian Ceasefire Agreement. To this end it authorized UNMIS to expand by up to 17,300 troops and 3,300 civilian police. Although the resolution stated that deployment should begin no later than 1 October 2006 and that the process of transition to a UN force should be completed 'no later than 31 December 2006', the sticking point was that it 'invited' the consent of the Sudanese government. The government of Sudan, however, refused to accept the resolution and demanded that any peacekeeping operation in Darfur must consist primarily of African troops.

AMIS also faced major problems because of its lack of resources. This left it unable to fulfil numerous aspects of its mandate. First, it lacked sufficient numbers of troops to monitor the whole of Darfur – an area the size of France. To give an indication of how badly under strength AMIS was it is useful to recall that two rules of thumb are commonly used to calculate the necessary force size for civilian-protection operations. The first is based on the assumption that two to ten soldiers are required for every 1,000 inhabitants within the crisis zone. Given Darfur's population of approximately 6 million, on this calculation AMIS should have had between 12,000 and 60,000 personnel. The second method is based on the protection force being at least the size of the largest indigenous armed force. According to the best available estimates, roughly 40,000 to 45,000 government troops were operating in Darfur and the *janjawiid* forces were between 10,000 and 20,000 strong. On this measure AMIS should have comprised a minimum of 10,000 and potentially 45,000 troops. On either of these measures, it was far too small to offer genuine protection to a majority of Darfur's civilians.

The other major problems were that AMIS was under-resourced in the crucial areas of logistics, transport and communications. Partly because of a lack of vehicles such as APCs and helicopters, and partly because of restrictions of movement placed on it by the government, it was not well equipped to enable it to get around Darfur. It also lacked vital equipment, from GPS facilities to night-vision goggles. In addition, by mid-2005 it became apparent that many AMIS personnel were not receiving their salaries.

The final and in many ways the most fundamental problem that AMIS faced was the lack of a workable political settlement to end the war in Darfur. As a consequence its personnel were left trying to engage in wider peacekeeping tasks in the midst of a live war zone. Not only did this leave it literally caught in the crossfire, but it began to be seen as another participant in the war rather than as a facilitator of peace. AMIS personnel started being fired upon in early 2005 and suffered their first casualties in October that year. The largest single massacre of peacekeepers occurred on 29 September 2007 at its Haskanita camp. This left ten peacekeepers dead and several more wounded, bringing the total number of AMIS deaths to nearly thirty. Later that year, in the face of mounting international pressure, the government of Sudan finally agreed to allow a hybrid AU–UN force known as UNAMID to deploy to Darfur. This officially replaced the AMIS mission on 31 December 2007. In practice, however, the remaining AMIS peacekeepers were simply re-hatted and new peacekeepers were slow to arrive.

How did AMIS fare in relation to its long and complicated mandate (see Williams 2006)? First of all, in the areas where it established a presence, both the security and the humanitarian situations did tend to improve. As the Joint Implementation Mechanism concluded in June 2005, AMIS's presence 'provided a very positive influence' (cited in Annan 2005b: 17). In particular, the number of clashes between the belligerent parties diminished, as did the number of attacks on civilians. However, as Kofi Annan noted, by that stage in the war 'the decrease in attacks may also be a function of a reduced number of targets' (ibid.: 11). In terms of the wider elements of the mandate relating to civilian protection, AMIS did not fare so well. Indeed, it is important to recall that responsibility for the direct physical security for the IDP camps lay primarily with the Sudanese police – a police force widely distrusted by the IDPs because many of them turned out to be 're-packaged' *janjawiid* or government soldiers. Furthermore, AMIS was criticized for allowing militias to attack civilians and each other in its presence. The force also suffered the indignity of having local SLM/A commanders impede its deployment to an increasing number of rebel-held areas.

Of course, these problems do not mean that all AMIS personnel performed poorly as individuals. The peacekeepers on the ground should not be blamed for factors beyond their control, including a lack of relevant training, doctrine, materiel (especially communications equipment and vehicles), and intelligence-collection capacity. In short, AMIS personnel had insufficient resources to achieve the mandate.

After several years in the field, AMIS proved unable to facilitate the return of the IDPs and refugees to their homes; nor was it able to repair the damage done to the land, settlements and livestock by the *janjawiid* and government forces. In addition, it was unable to address the underlying governance issues that lay at the heart of Darfur's crisis. In this sense, despite the best efforts of AMIS personnel, stable peace in Darfur remained elusive.

8.3 Problems

Although the major problems with wider peacekeeping were identified in the aftermath of the Rwandan genocide, several peace operations continued to bear its hallmarks. The UN's independent inquiry into its failure in Rwanda gave a useful indication of the central problems associated with wider peacekeeping (also see chapters 4 and 5):

- inadequate mandate. UNAMIR's mandate was based on the ill-founded assumption that the parties would adhere to the Arusha Accords. As the report pointed out, 'the UN mission was predicated on the success of the peace process. There was no fall-back, no contingency planning for the eventuality that the peace process did not succeed' (Independent Inquiry 1999: 23). The same can be said for UNPROFOR, AMIS and other peace operations.
- the mandate could not be implemented. The mandates were worded vaguely, using words such as 'assist'. In all the cases discussed above, where there was a situation of ongoing violence and a breakdown in the peace process, it became unclear as to what or whom it was that peacekeepers should be assisting.
- confusion over the rules of engagement. Because the mandates were unclear, the peacekeeper's rules of engagement were also vague and subject to constant change. As a general rule, each of the missions considered here treated the 'Mogadishu line' of consent (figure 8.1) as absolute, even if that meant that the mission was unable to accomplish its wider goals. This approach raised particularly acute dilemmas with regard to civilian protection issues (see chapter 15).
- inadequate resources and logistics. At least initially, all three missions discussed above lacked the troops, equipment and logistical capability to fulfil their mandates. The 'safe areas' policy in Bosnia resulted in peacekeepers (in Srebrenica in particular) being stranded without supplies for months on end. The same is true of peacekeepers deployed in outlying regions of Darfur, and virtually the entire UNAMIR force.
- the failure of political will. James Gow's (1997) diplomatic history of the Bosnian war was aptly titled *The Triumph of the Lack of Will*. Sitting at the

crossroads of Westphalian and post-Westphalian conceptions of peace operations, wider peacekeeping reflects the idea that peacekeeping in contemporary war zones requires the adoption of 'wider' tasks, but it also reveals a deep reluctance on the part of UN member states to give the organization's peacekeepers the means to fulfil these objectives successfully. In each of the cases analysed here, states were willing to authorize new peacekeeping missions but were unwilling to pay for them to be appropriately resourced.

• wider peacekeeping suffers from organizational problems. Sometimes, rifts appear across different national contingents within the same peace operation, as occurred most publicly in UNAMSIL after a confidential report written by the force commander, General Jetley, was leaked to the international media (see companion website). But it is also a problem in the sense of coordinating across different agencies which often get in each other's way and work at cross-purposes. In Bosnia, for instance, peacekeepers were mandated to protect the delivery of humanitarian aid, but there was no wider assessment of the impact that this was having on either the belligerents or the suffering civilian populace. Not only can the militarization of an aid operation jeopardize years of progress in fields such as confidence-building but, conversely, uncoordinated activities by aid agencies can hamper peacekeeping operations by, for instance, sustaining local warlords and militating against the use of force by the UN or other engaged organizations. Moreover, the UN secretariat, and the DPKO in particular, were unable to manage the vast flow of information generated by these operations. The stories of both Srebrenica and Rwanda are littered with examples of information flows breaking down, of complex decision-making processes producing inertia, and of multiple lines of communication spreading confusion.

As we have seen, wider peacekeeping operations are plagued by the gulf between means and ends. They are an ad hoc response to the challenges raised by 'new wars' but they have remained founded upon Westphalian concepts and habits. In Bosnia, Rwanda, Darfur and other war zones, international society has called upon peacekeepers to undertake a long list of onerous tasks beyond the traditional activities but proved reluctant to give them the means to achieve them. In practice, therefore, states retained what they believed were tried and tested peacekeeping techniques in inappropriate conditions. Thus, consent was placed at the conceptual heart of wider peacekeeping and its maintenance was understood as being the most important aspect of the operation. But, as the case studies in this chapter have highlighted, consent was always precarious, since at least one side usually benefits from the use of force. Moreover, while formal wider peacekeeping doctrine suggested that it was the actions or inactions of peacekeepers that were the primary cause of a loss of consent, in these four cases, compared to the strategic calculations

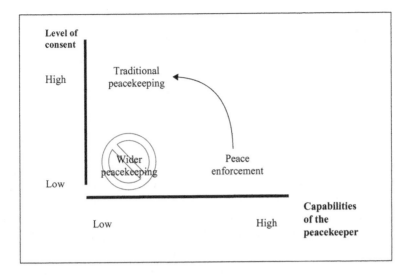

Source: adapted from HMSO (1999).

Figure 8.2 *Consent and capability: the unenviable position of wider peacekeeping*

of the belligerent parties, the actions of the peacekeepers themselves had little influence on the breakdown of consent and the upsurge in violence.

The arrows in figure 8.2 represent the preferred operational direction of a peacekeeping operation. In terms of its practical experiences, wider peacekeeping sits in the bottom left-hand corner, the environment that an operation – even one deployed to a hostile environment – should avoid at all costs. Nevertheless, all the operations discussed here find themselves in this unenviable position, one in which they lacked the consent of the parties and the capability to enforce the mandate. This is caused by the combination of continuing support for the Westphalian conception of peacekeeping coupled with the failure of adherents to the post-Westphalian conception to back their words with actions and money in areas of the world that are peripheral to their geostrategic interests. The next chapter analyses those operations where the need to enforce the will of the UN Security Council was considered more important than achieving the consent of the local parties.

CHAPTER NINE

Peace Enforcement

Peace enforcement is generally considered to be synonymous with activities sanctioned under Chapter VII of the UN Charter. Occasionally, the UN resorted to peace enforcement measures during the Cold War, but it was not until the 1990s and the dramatic increase in the passage of Chapter VII resolutions that the concept became widely utilized. The issue of peace enforcement has raised several important questions about the UN's role in maintaining international peace and security, not least whether the organization is capable of using force to preserve its values and, perhaps more fundamentally, whether it should.

This chapter starts by exploring the distinctive characteristics of the UN's concept of peace enforcement. It then examines peace enforcement in practice by considering both an example of Westphalian enforcement that is closely related to collective security and was orchestrated by the UN Security Council (Korea) and an example of the post-Westphalian variety, conducted in Somalia, which aimed to maintain order and public security. (Several other cases of peace enforcement are discussed on the companion website.) Finally, the chapter outlines some of the main challenges associated with this type of operation.

9.1 What is peace enforcement?

As the UN and other actors became involved in more complex operations, so the neat distinctions between traditional types of peacekeeping and peace enforcement have eroded in practice. In conceptual and legal terms, however, there remain important characteristics that continue to distinguish peace enforcement from other types of operations. In particular, peace enforcement is concerned with activities that fall under Chapter VII of the UN Charter: 'Action with respect to threats to the peace, breaches of the peace, and acts of aggression'. Enacting Chapter VII gives the Security Council the authority (1) to determine when a threat to, or breach of, international peace and security has occurred; (2) to order provisional measures under Article 40; and (3) to order enforcement measures to be taken against a state or entities within a state.

Although this seems relatively clear in theory, in practice it has not always been easy to identify either when the Security Council has invoked Chapter

VII or which sections of a resolution refer to Chapter VII and which do not. As a consequence, it is important to understand how Security Council practice on this issue has developed. As was argued in a recent study by the organization Security Council Report (2008b), among the most relevant questions are: Does the form of a Council decision matter – is an explicit mention of Chapter VII necessary? Is a reference to Chapter VII necessary to authorize member states to use force? Is a reference to Chapter VII necessary to authorize a robust mandate for a UN operation involving the use of military force? Is it the Council resolution or the rules of engagement (ROE) and concept of operations that determine whether a UN operation will be able to use force? And is a reference to Chapter VII necessary to impose sanctions? Some of the study's answers to these questions are summarized in box 9.1.

It is reasonably clear that between 1946 and 1989 the UN invoked Chapter VII on twenty-four occasions (see table 9.1). In comparison, between 1990 and 1999 there were a further 166 Chapter VII resolutions (and the number has continued at a similar rate into the twenty-first century). Enforcement measures usually refer to the imposition of either economic sanctions (under Article 41) or military sanctions (under Article 42). To date, the UN has authorized the use of military force for a wide range of purposes. Among these have been to restore or maintain international peace and security; to enforce sanctions; to defend the personnel of peacekeeping operations; to provide physical protection to civilians in conflict zones; to protect humanitarian activities; and to intervene in so-called internal conflicts.

For many commentators and practitioners alike, the idea of collective security provides the intellectual basis for the UN's conception of peace enforcement (see box 3.4, p. 78). In its classic sense, the concept of collective security referred to 'a system, regional or global, in which each state in the system accepts that the security of one is the concern of all, and agrees to join in a collective response to threats to, and breaches of, the peace' (Lowe et al. 2008: 13). As Boutros-Ghali suggested, in *An Agenda For Peace*,

> [i]t is the essence of the concept of collective security as contained in the Charter that if peaceful means fail, the measures provided in Chapter VII should be used, on the decision of the Security Council, to maintain or restore international peace and security in the face of a 'threat to the peace, breach of the peace, or an act of aggression'. (1992: § 42)

This general rule, however, is qualified by Article 51, which preserves 'the inherent right of states to individual or collective self-defence', at least until the Security Council has taken the appropriate measures. In practice, of course, the UN has functioned in a far more selective manner than envisaged in an ideal system of collective security. This has led some analysts to suggest that the UN was neither set up as a collective security system – the Charter contains no reference to collective security and contains several departures from such a system, not least the veto power of the P-5 (which kept the great

Box 9.1 Security Council action under Chapter VII

The Council has general powers under articles 24 and 25 to adopt binding decisions, and such decisions do not always need to be taken under Chapter VII. Even when the Council does use its Chapter VII powers, it is not essential to have an explicit reference either to the chapter itself or to a particular article thereof. Resolutions adopted under Chapter VII may also (and usually do) include provisions which are non-binding.

Interpretation of Council resolutions is, therefore, a complex art. In order to ascertain the Council's intent and the powers it may be using in a particular resolution, it is necessary to analyse (1) the overall context; (2) the precise terms used in the resolution; and (3) (sometimes) the discussions in the Council – both at the time of adoption and subsequently. Although the express mention of Chapter VII is not essential, the Council seems in recent times to recognize increasingly the significant importance of clarity. The clearer the language adopted, the better the prospects for effectiveness and credibility of Council decisions. This may not be possible on every occasion, but it seems that on balance the Council is conscious of the need to avoid ambiguity.

Chapter VII powers must be used for the establishment of Council-mandated sanctions regimes – although an explicit reference to the chapter or Article 41 is not essential. Similarly, use of Chapter VII powers is required to authorize member states or a UN peacekeeping operation to use force – but again an explicit reference to the chapter is not essential. However, the problems generated by uncertain consent, concern about legal ambiguity, and deployment in increasingly hostile operational environments increasingly led the Council to begin to approve UN operations and to authorize the use of force with explicit reference to Chapter VII. In recent times, therefore, authorizing resolutions have consistently included: (1) a determination in accordance with Article 39; (2) the chapeau 'acting under Chapter VII'; and (3) an operative paragraph containing a 'decision' to authorize member states to use force.

Such was the case with authorizations regarding Iraq (resolutions 678, 1483 and 1511), Somalia (resolutions 794 and 1744), Bosnia (resolutions 770, 787, 816, 820, 836, 908, 1031, 1088, 1174 and 1575), Albania (resolutions 1101 and 1114), Rwanda (Resolution 929), Haiti (resolutions 875, 940 and 1529), the Great Lakes/Democratic Republic of the Congo (resolutions 1080, 1484 and 1671), the CAR (Resolution 1125), Sierra Leone (Resolution 1132), Kosovo (Resolution 1244), Timor-Leste (Resolution 1264), Afghanistan (resolutions 1386 and 1510), Liberia (Resolution 1497), Côte d'Ivoire (resolutions 1464 and 1528) and Chad/CAR (Resolution 1778).

The practical conduct of UN peacekeeping operations – and whether force is actually used or not – is typically influenced more strongly by factors such as the concept of operations and ROE rather than by the language of the mandate itself. In such cases, what happens in practice may be largely dependent upon the political and operational environment in which the mission is expected to discharge its mandate.

Source: paraphrased from Security Council Report (2008b: 1–2, 22, 36–37).

powers safe from Council action against them) and Chapter VIII's reference to regional arrangements (which acknowledged that the UN would be unable to address all threats to international peace and security) – nor operated as such a system in practice (Lowe et al. 2008: 13). Compared to the League of Nations, however, and in terms of the three characteristics of collective secu-

TABLE 9.1 Chapter VII resolutions, 1946–1989

24 resolutions	
Palestine	54 (1948); *62 (1948)
Korea	†82 (1950); †83 (1950); †84 (1950)
Congo	*146 (1960); †161 (1961); †169 (1961)
Southern Rhodesia	†217 (1965); †221 (1966); *232 (1966); 253 (1968); 277 (1970); 288 (1970); 314 (1972); *386 (1976); 388 (1976); 409 (1977)
East Pakistan	†307 (1971)
Cyprus	†353 (1974)
South Africa	418 (1977); †421 (1977)
Falkland Islands (Islas Malvinas)	†502 (1982)
Iran–Iraq	*598 (1987)

Notes: *Resolution refers to a specific article in Chapter VII, but not explicitly to Chapter VII itself.
†Resolution uses wording that contains only an implicit reference to Chapter VII.

Source: Chesterman (2001: 237).

rity systems (certainty, utility and inclusivity) that we discussed in chapter 3, the UN can be understood as an imperfect system of collective security.

One serious problem with the application of Chapter VII measures stems from the fact that, while the Charter's authors envisaged the Security Council possessing its own armed forces, in practice the UN has been forced to try and establish a system of collective security by authorizing other entities to use force on its behalf. Although the Charter created an institutional framework for such a force in Article 43, which established the Military Staff Committee, we have already discussed (in chapter 6) the numerous (failed) attempts to establish standing forces for the UN. This has left a persistent gap between the theoretical provision for UN military enforcement measures and the practical lack of a UN military capability. In *An Agenda for Peace*, Boutros-Ghali (1992) suggested that the Military Staff Committee should be resuscitated in the context of Chapter VII operations rather than traditional peacekeeping operations. To this end, he called for member states to make armed forces available to the UN. Such a step, he argued, would itself be a deterrent to potential aggressors, since it would advertise that the Security Council possessed a means of response (see box 9.2). The Military Staff Committee did not establish an auspicious track record in this regard. By the time of the 1991 Gulf War, it had held no substantive meetings since 1948, had undertaken no preparatory staff work or contingency planning, and had concluded no agreements with member states to make forces available to the Council under Article 43 (Urquhart 2000: 83).

Box 9.2 Peace enforcement units

43) ...The ready availability of armed forces on call could serve, in itself, as a means of deterring breaches of the peace since a potential aggressor would know that the Council had at its disposal a means of response....It is my view that the role of the Military Staff Committee should be seen in the context of Chapter VII, and not that of the planning or conduct of peace-keeping operations.

44) ...I recommend that the Council consider the utilization of peace-enforcement units in clearly defined circumstances and with their terms of reference specified in advance. Such units from Member States would be available on call and would consist of troops that have volunteered for such service. They would have to be more heavily armed than peace-keeping forces and would need to undergo extensive preparatory training within their national forces. Deployment and operation of such forces would be under the authorisation of the Security Council and would, as in the case of peace-keeping forces, be under the command of the Secretary-General. I consider peace-enforcement units to be warranted as a provisional measure under Article 40 of the Charter. (Boutros-Ghali 1992)

Today, the UN still has no 'peace-enforcement units' as envisaged by Boutros-Ghali. The Security Council has therefore been forced to delegate its Chapter VII powers to UN principal organs, UN subsidiary organs, UN member states or regional arrangements (Sarooshi 2000: 4). According to Boutros-Ghali, such delegation was necessary because 'neither the Security Council nor the Secretary-General [had] the capacity to deploy, direct, command and control operations for [enforcement purposes], except perhaps on a very limited scale' (1995a: § 77). When a particular entity is delegated Chapter VII powers by the Security Council it is conferred with the UN's seal of legitimacy to carry out the necessary enforcement measures. In turn, the way in which the delegate exercises those Chapter VII powers will affect the Security Council's future as a source of international legitimacy. The delegation of Chapter VII powers does not involve a complete transfer of power, since a delegation can always be revoked and the Security Council retains its right to exercise those powers (Sarooshi 2000: 7).

On the positive side, the process of delegation provides the UN with an enforcement capacity it would not otherwise have, is more legitimate than the unilateral use of force by states without UN authorization, and can provide a greater degree of operational coherence. On the other hand, the arrangement can have a negative impact on the UN's credibility and stature, and entities authorized to carry out Chapter VII tasks may go beyond their delegated mandate (Boutros-Ghali 1995a: § 80). In the experiences analysed below, the main culprit in this regard was the United States, particularly in the Congo (covertly) and Somalia (overtly). This highlights the historically close relationship between US interests and the Security Council's authorization to use force. This, in turn, raises the uncomfortable point that the main deterrent to would-be aggressors is fear of US military power rather than the UN's security system *per se* (Urquhart 2000: 86).

From the outset, the UN's architects realized that the organization would need to have a mixture of military and non-military means at its disposal. In particular, the Charter envisaged the use of various types of sanctions (Article 41) and military force (Article 42) as the organization's primary coercive instruments. Before 1990 the use of economic sanctions and arms embargoes by the UN was relatively rare, but their use increased markedly during the 1990s. Their main purpose was 'to modify the behaviour of a party that is threatening international peace and security and not to punish or otherwise exact retribution' (Boutros-Ghali 1995a: § 66). Since 1990 the Security Council has imposed economic sanctions on some twenty targets, with mixed but always controversial results (see Cortright et al. 2008). During the early 1990s, a significant part of the controversy stemmed from the widespread recognition that the use of general trade sanctions was a blunt instrument that raised questions about the legitimacy of inflicting suffering on a population as a whole in order to exert an uncertain degree of pressure on political leaders whose primary concern may not be the welfare of their citizens. By far the most contentious case in this regard was Iraq (see Lynch 2008).

Partly in recognition of this problem, since 1994 all new UN sanctions regimes have been targeted. That is, they consist of various packages of financial sanctions, travel bans, arms embargoes and commodity boycotts rather than general trade sanctions (Cortright and Lopez 2000, 2002). Financial sanctions, for instance, were initially imposed only on government assets. Starting with the case of Haiti in 1994, the Council has also targeted the accounts of designated individuals and groups, such as the Haitian military junta, UNITA leaders in Angola and the Taliban regime in Afghanistan. In 2001 the UN imposed sanctions upon Liberia because of its continued material and financial support for the Revolutionary United Front in Sierra Leone (Security Council Resolution 1343). This was the first time that it had imposed sanctions upon one state because of its defiance of sanctions against another (Cortright and Lopez 2002: 17). The following year the UN significantly broadened the scope of sanctions by demanding that member states take action within their own borders to criminalize the financing of terrorist activities (Security Council Resolution 1373). However, while sanctions form an important part of the UN's enforcement armoury, they do not directly require the involvement of peacekeepers. Arguably the closest association between peace operations and sanctions has been in relation to arms embargoes, the results of which have been the subject of considerable debate (see Tierney 2005; SIPRI 2007b). The remainder of this chapter concentrates upon the UN's use of the military instrument.

In *An Agenda for Peace*, Boutros-Ghali (1992: § 43) made clear that the option of taking military action in defence of the Charter's principles 'is essential to the credibility of the United Nations as a guarantor of international security'.

Because the UN lacks its own armed forces, once Article 42 has been invoked it is up to the member states to make armed forces and facilities available to the Security Council so that it may carry out its mandate or delegate its powers to an appropriate entity. In practice, it is possible to distinguish two varieties of the use of military force: Westphalian and post-Westphalian. Westphalian peace enforcement refers to those occasions when the UN has authorized the use of force against a particular state in response to an act (or acts) of interstate aggression. From this perspective, the liberal peace thesis requires enforcement measures to promote liberal practices between states, such as refraining from the use of force (except in self-defence) and respecting diplomatic protocol and the territorial integrity of other states. Such practices evolved out of the European states system of the nineteenth century and were central components of Woodrow Wilson's liberal vision of the post-First World War order (see chapter 3). Examples are the UN's authorization of force against North Korea following its invasion of South Korea in June 1950 and against Iraq following its invasion of Kuwait in August 1990.

Post-Westphalian enforcement, on the other hand, refers to those occasions when the UN has authorized the use of force against a state or non-state entity in response to acts of violence that may have occurred primarily within the borders of a particular state, such as the massacre of civilians or attacks against UN personnel. Examples of this sort of enforcement activity include the UN's use of force in the Congo in the early 1960s, in Somalia in the early 1990s and in eastern DRC in the early twenty-first century, NATO's use of force in Bosnia during Operation Deliberate Force, the multinational force assembled to evict the military junta in Haiti in 1994, and INTERFET in East Timor in 1999.

9.2 Peace enforcement in practice

Westphalian forms of collective peace enforcement have been relatively rare. The case analysed here is the UN's involvement in the Korean War – specifically, its delegation of its enforcement powers to a US-led coalition of member states. The post-Westphalian variety of peace enforcement was relatively rare until the early 1990s, after which the numbers of this type of operation increased substantially. The example offered here is of the international intervention in Somalia during the early 1990s. Additional examples of both types (the Gulf War, ONUC and MINUSTAH) are available on the companion website.

The unified command in Korea (1950–1953)

The Korean War was the first occasion when the UN authorized the use of force by a coalition of states under Chapter VII (see Stueck 2008). The authorization came in response to North Korea's invasion of South Korea on 25

June 1950 across the 38th parallel. The 38th parallel represented the military boundary between the two halves of Korea established in 1945. Within three days the Security Council passed two resolutions, both under Chapter VII. Resolution 82 (25 June 1950) defined North Korea's 'armed attack' as a 'breach of the peace' and called upon the 'authorities of North Korea to withdraw forthwith their armed forces to the 38th parallel'. Resolution 83 (27 June) recommended that UN member states 'furnish' South Korea with 'such assistance…as may be necessary to repel the armed attack and to restore international peace and security in the area'. Just over a week later, on 7 July, the Security Council recommended that 'all Members providing military forces and other assistance pursuant to the aforesaid Security Council resolutions make such forces and other assistance available to a unified command under the United States' (Resolution 84). This resolution also requested that the US designate a commander for the forces. On 8 July, President Truman duly assigned General MacArthur to that role. The Security Council delegated command and control to the US primarily because of the overwhelming contribution it made to the UN force (Sarooshi 2000: 110). This generated significant criticism of the UN, which many states believed was acting as a stooge for the US to carry out its own war aims throughout the conflict.

All forces and other assistance by member states were given on a voluntary basis, and in total fifteen states provided troops for the operation. In the face of such an effective opposition the North Korean forces were soon pushed back beyond the 38th parallel, and by November 1950 the UN forces were nearing Korea's border with China. Not surprisingly, this prompted Chinese intervention, which successfully drove the UN forces back towards the 38th parallel. After causing approximately 4 million deaths and stimulating intense disagreements between and within both sides, the war ground to a halt with the signing of an armistice on 27 July 1953. This established a new truce line close to the 38th parallel.

The Korean case raises two particularly relevant issues for a discussion of UN peace enforcement. The first concerns the decision-making process whereby the UN Security Council authorized the use of force in Korea. The initial resolutions on Korea (resolutions 82 to 84) were only possible because the Soviet Union was boycotting the Council at the time over its decision not to allow a representative from the People's Republic of China to sit in place of the member representing Chiang Kai-shek. Although the Soviet absence undoubtedly made it easier for the US to get its own way in the Council, several non-permanent members, notably Egypt, India and Yugoslavia, were not totally uncritical of Washington's proposals, and all of them either abstained or voted against the first resolutions. When the Soviet Union resumed its seat at the Council on 1 August it was able to wield its veto to preclude any further Security Council resolutions. This prompted the United States to transfer its efforts into the arena of the UN General Assembly. After much politicking, on 3 November 1950 the Soviet veto in the Council

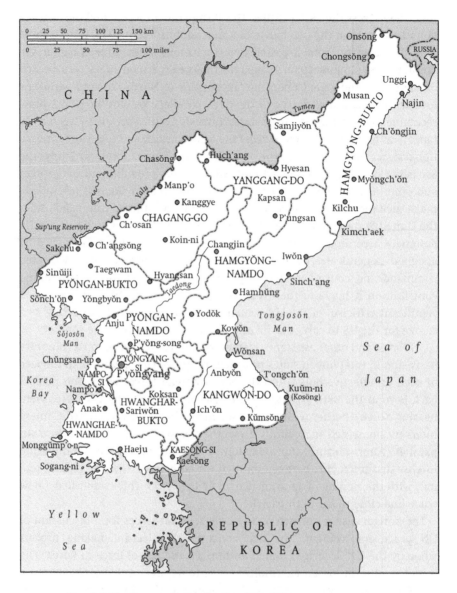

Map 9.1 *The Democratic People's Republic of Korea*

was circumvented when the Western powers successfully transferred debate on the issue of Korea into the General Assembly by invoking what has become known as the 'Uniting for Peace' procedure (see chapter 2). While the Soviets voted against the proposal, they could not veto it because the transfer of an issue from the Council to the Assembly is considered a procedural issue and therefore not subject to the veto. In the resolution the Assembly confirmed the mandate of the US-led forces in Korea, perpetuated the legality of the military action, asked the Collective Measures Committee to consider additional actions to meet the North Korean and Chinese attacks, and kept the UN involved in the diplomatic efforts to end the war (Zaum 2008: 159). This scenario demonstrates how peace enforcement is often inextricably related to the wider context of relations between the great powers and the P-5 states within the Security Council. In this case, the context was one of Cold War rivalry. The episode also 'persuaded Moscow once and for all of the advantages of full participation' within the Security Council (Stueck 2008: 277).

The second issue concerns the outcomes that peace enforcement measures are intended to achieve. The problem that faced the US commanders of the UN force in Korea was discerning what outcomes would constitute the successful completion of their mandate, given the vague nature of the phrase 'restore international peace and security to the area' (Resolution 83). The US commanders had to decide whether their mandate simply required the North Korean forces to be repelled beyond the 38th parallel or whether they should pursue the fleeing North Korean forces beyond the 38th parallel in line with the General Assembly's wishes (under Resolution 376 (V), 7 October 1950) and contribute to the establishment of an independent, democratic and united Korea (see Sarooshi 2000: 115–19).

As it turned out, the UN forces initially advanced north of the 38th parallel but were subsequently themselves repelled by the Chinese and North Korean forces and settled for an armistice based upon a truce line near the 38th parallel. Indeed, MacArthur's decision to pursue the North Korean forces to the Chinese border exceeded his own president's orders. Arguably because of the military balance, the UN force also decided that the establishment of a united and democratic Korea lay beyond the mandate's terms. As the US secretary of state argued at the time, although the US and UN both desired a united and democratic Korea, 'I do not understand it to be a war aim. In other words, that is not sought to be achieved by fighting, but it is sought by peaceful means, just as was being attempted before the aggression' (in Sarooshi 2000: 118). In this case, therefore, the Security Council's inability to define a clear political outcome for its enforcement measures was resolved primarily by the balance of military forces on the ground. This was to happen regularly in future operations as well.

UNOSOM I and II and UNITAF in Somalia (1992–1995)

The UN's involvement in Somalia followed a deadly combination of protracted civil war and famine that killed at least 350,000 Somalis in 1992 alone and left 70 per cent of the population suffering severe malnutrition (Clark 1993: 213–14; see also Clarke and Herbst 1997). By the time Somalia's representative at the UN formally requested assistance in January 1992, the country had no functioning government (see Sahnoun 1994). In response, the Security Council adopted Resolution 733. This called for a ceasefire between the warring factions, imposed an arms embargo, called for the Secretary-General to deploy a fact-finding mission, and requested increased levels of humanitarian assistance. In light of the ongoing violence within Somalia the UN established a peacekeeping force, UNOSOM, under Security Council Resolution 751 (24 April 1992). It was intended, among other things, to protect the humanitarian assistance operations. However, the small force (which eventually numbered approximately 3,500) was unable to operate effectively in the context of ongoing violence and persistent attempts by various militias to steal humanitarian relief supplies or extort concessions from international agencies attempting to deliver aid.

In an effort to create a stable environment in which humanitarian assistance could be effectively disbursed, in December 1992 the UN Security Council passed Resolution 794. This authorized the Secretary-General and any cooperating member states to use 'all necessary means to establish as soon as possible a secure environment for humanitarian relief operations in Somalia'. It also provided the legal basis for Operation Restore Hope, the name given to the US-led Unified Task Force designed to create such an environment. The UNITAF operation comprised some 38,000 troops, approximately 25,000 of whom were American. Confronted by such an overwhelming display of force, the vast majority of Somali warlords and their militias curtailed their activities against the UN and personnel from the various aid agencies. Unfortunately, such cooperation did not endure.

UNITAF's problems began in earnest when its commanders and the Secretary-General differed over the definition of what constituted 'a secure environment' for the delivery of humanitarian assistance. The key disagreement revolved around the issue of disarming the various factions in and around Mogadishu. The Secretary-General argued that, because UNITAF had not disarmed these various militia forces, it had not completed its objectives within the capital city, let alone the rest of Somalia. Washington took a different view, claiming that UNITAF had achieved what it had set out to do. Amid these arguments, UNITAF's mission officially expired on 4 May 1993, at which point many of its troops were absorbed into the successor force, UNOSOM II. Shortly before this, the Secretary-General had recommended that the new mission be given the right to use military force. On 26 March 1993, therefore, the Security Council passed Resolution 814. This duly stated: 'Acting under Chapter VII...UNOSOM II [should] assume responsibility for the consolidation, expansion and maintenance of a secure environment throughout Somalia...and...to organise a prompt, smooth and phased transition from UNITAF to UNOSOM II.' UNOSOM II was given the unenviable objectives of providing 'a secure environment' and ensuring 'the rehabilitation of the political institutions and economy of Somalia'. Unlike UNITAF, UNOSOM II was placed under the command of the Secretary-General's Special Representative to Somalia, a retired American admiral, Jonathan Howe, until his resignation in February 1994.

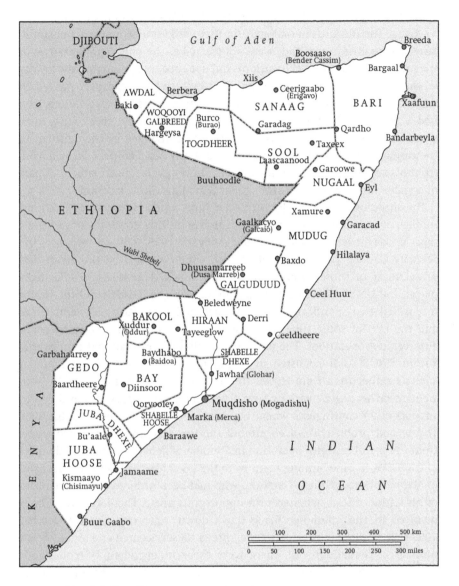

Map 9.2 *Somalia*

Left with the task of disarming the various warring factions, UNOSOM II was inevitably drawn into Somalia's fractious clan politics. This presented the peacekeepers with a series of difficult challenges. In particular, UNOSOM II needed to devise strategies that would persuade the warlords to cooperate with the disarmament process without bestowing unwarranted political legitimacy upon them. The difficulty was that, while the warlords and their supporters were responsible for extorting humanitarian NGOs and looting aid deliveries, they also commanded a not insignificant degree of political support within the local population. For the peacekeepers it was important to engage the warlords in dialogue, for they could not be ignored, but simultaneously to ensure that they were not treated as the only representatives of the local populace. Since the warlords did not appear to command the loyalty of the majority of locals (see Sahnoun 1994), the peacekeepers needed to engage more effectively with other local organizations and associations who had a greater stake in peace, and in all likelihood would speak for greater numbers of people whose voices had been marginalized by the fighting. In the case of General Mohammed Farah Aidid, UN peacekeepers chose to confront his supporters without making a credible case for disarmament as part of a viable broader political strategy for Somalia's reconstruction.

The situation took a deadly turn on 5 June, when twenty-three Pakistani soldiers were killed while trying to disarm militia loyal to Mogadishu's most powerful leader, General Aidid (Melvern 1995: 324). In response, the Security Council passed Resolution 837, which authorized the arrest and prosecution of those responsible for the attack. This decision effectively placed the UN's peacekeepers in a state of war with Aidid's militia. It also intensified two significant problems that had been facing General Howe and the UN for some time. The first is a common feature of many peace enforcement operations. The problem was that several national contingents within UNOSOM II persisted in taking their orders from their national capitals rather than from Howe. The Italian contingent, for example, even went as far as paying various Somali leaders not to attack it and failed to support other contingents when they came under fire (Clapham 2002: 204). The second problem revolved around the fact that there were also forces from UN member states operating in Somalia which were not formally part of UNOSOM II. Chief among them were the US soldiers under the command of Major General William Garrison, who had been ordered to capture Aidid or his senior officials whenever the opportunity arose. These were the troops involved in the infamous 'Black Hawk down' operation on 3–4 October 1993 that resulted in the deaths of eighteen US servicemen and an unknown number of Somalis. In all, there were three independent US commands (Sarooshi 2000: 189–90). Clearly these factors made it very difficult for UNOSOM II to maintain cohesion and achieve its objectives.

The situation calmed somewhat after 9 October, when Aidid's faction declared a unilateral cessation of hostilities against UNOSOM II. Nevertheless, stung by the loss of its soldiers, Washington announced its intention to withdraw its troops from Somalia by 31 March 1994. European governments quickly followed suit, thus effectively ending the military enforcement action in the country (UNOSOM II's ability to carry out military enforcement action was officially terminated with the passing of Security Council Resolution 897 on 4 February 1994). The last UN troops left Somalia in March 1995. For all the bloodshed, they left behind a situation not too dissimilar from the one they had initially encountered in 1992.

9.3 Challenges

The UN has been relatively successful, within its own limited terms of reference, when it has engaged in Westphalian enforcement operations, as in the Korean and Gulf wars. Such cases have, however, been relatively rare compared to situations where the UN has authorized enforcement measures in response to internal wars with significant international dimensions – that is, post-Westphalian enforcement. This latter type of operation is concerned with what transpires within states and enters a qualitatively different terrain from Westphalian enforcement. The important question for the world's peacekeepers is whether post-Westphalian enforcement operations are something that the UN and other actors should be in the business of conducting, and, if so, in what circumstances they should take place (see Tharoor 1995).

As we can see from the historical cases discussed above, peace enforcement operations raise several challenges. First, the often vaguely worded nature of many enforcement mandates has generated questions of interpretation, particularly over the specific conditions that need to be achieved in order to terminate enforcement measures. Such arguments were particularly evident in the operations in Korea and Somalia. In addition, the debates that occurred prior to the US-led invasion of Iraq in March 2003 were at least partially related to the way in which the previous set of enforcement measures, conducted against Iraq since 1990, had been concluded. This case shows that, even in what appear to be relatively clear-cut cases of Westphalian enforcement, establishing criteria for success can be difficult.

In the post-Westphalian environment the challenges are even more pronounced. As a result, analysts have called for greater clarity in the use of enforcement mandates. In relation to the UN, for instance, Trevor Findlay has argued that all UN missions involving armed military personnel should be given Chapter VII mandates; that the Security Council should stop using the euphemism 'all necessary means' and be more precise in its intentions; that a UN Staff College be established to prepare senior officers for leadership roles in UN operations; and that the UN must overcome '[t]he great lacuna in all efforts to improve UN peace operations…doctrine' (2002: 384). Findlay's points are particularly pertinent in relation to civilian protection tasks. As we discuss in more detail in chapter 15, especially since 1999, a variety of peace operations have engaged in low-level enforcement activities in the name of civilian protection but have done so without clear mandates and relevant doctrine.

Second, given the lack of a UN army and the organization's overstretched and under-funded bureaucratic mechanisms, there are a variety of prudential concerns about whether the UN is in any position to conduct large-scale enforcement measures effectively. These include the fact that the UN's member states have been unwilling to pay for effective forces; that when the member states have deployed troops, they have been loath to place them under foreign control; that the UN's members lack a common military doc-trine; that the UN's bureaucratic structures are ill-prepared to oversee the day-to-day management of large-scale military operations; and that the UN's political process means it is often reluctant to distinguish victim from aggres-sor – exhibited most starkly in Bosnia and Rwanda. Aside from the crucial practical questions of command and control involved in enforcement opera-tions, of particular importance here is whether the contributing states can maintain the political will to sustain enforcement measures when faced with rising costs and the increased likelihood of casualties. Although the UN's two Westphalian enforcement operations in Korea and the Gulf achieved the specific terms of their mandates, they generated very large numbers of casual-ties in the process. Post-Westphalian enforcement, on the other hand, has met with mixed results. While on occasion military power has been used with some success to promote humanitarian activities (for example UNITAF in Somalia), other operations (such as UNOSOM II) have experienced severe problems and resulted in the deaths of significant numbers of peacekeepers. Figure 9.1 shows a clear increase in UN peacekeeping fatalities in the early 1960s (at the height of the ONUC operation) and again in the early 1990s, when peacekeepers engaged in enforcement action in Somalia, Bosnia and elsewhere. It also shows that during the twenty-first century, when most operations involved some form of enforcement activity beyond self-defence, the UN has sustained consistently high levels of fatalities.

The third issue revolves around whether the UN should be engaged in war fighting at all. Westphalian enforcement measures are clearly designed to

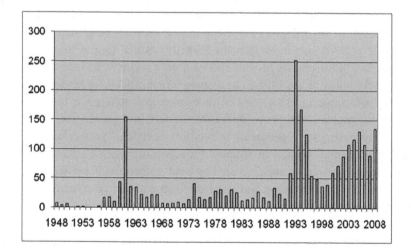

Source: Compiled by the authors from DPKO figures at www.un.org/ Depts/dpko/dpko/factsfigs.shtml.

Figure 9.1 *UN peacekeeping fatalities, 1 January 1948 to 31 December 2008*

protect a pluralist society of states, to guard against imperialism and to reduce the use of force between states. As a result, they have received support from the vast majority of the UN's member states. In contrast, the UN's attempts at post-Westphalian enforcement have been criticized as constituting a form of neo-imperialism because they impose Western preferences about the organization of polities, societies and economies through the use of force if necessary (see Chandler 2000). This problem has often been exacerbated because of the close association between the use of US military power and the UN's enforcement activities. In both the cases analysed here the United States was central to the enforcement measures concerned. This has raised concerns among the UN's members who are wary of Washington's political agenda. It also raises the more general question of whether the UN and other actors can undertake large-scale peace enforcement operations without American participation.

Finally, there is a series of debates about whether enforcement measures might prove counter-productive to the goal of building stable peace in the longer term. According to the Westphalian conception of peace operations, enforcement measures are specifically intended to maintain peace between sovereign states. From this perspective, the occasional use of force to restore international order is a price worth paying to uphold the norm of non-intervention and the general rule of non-use of force in international society. From a post-Westphalian perspective, however, not only does the use of force become necessary far more often but its future benefits in cases of civil war are far less obvious. From this perspective, force may often be required to deal with groups who persistently refuse to commit to peace agreements and continue to use violence to impede peace processes. Stedman (1997) has labelled such groups 'spoilers'. Using force against spoilers raises a number of difficult challenges for the UN and other actors. Not only is there a problem of identifying who the spoilers are in any given theatre of operations, there is also a quandary if the spoiler groups represent a significant proportion of the local population. In particular, using force against popular local groups may make the process of national reconciliation exceedingly difficult and jeopardize the chances for building stable peace.

Peace enforcement thus raises a host of difficult challenges. Indeed, for some, the phrase itself is an oxymoron. It was at least partly in an attempt to provide more coherent answers to these difficult questions and analyse how military power could be used to build stable peace that the UN and other actors developed the concept of 'peace support operations'. We examine these operations in more detail in chapter 12.

CHAPTER TEN

Assisting Transitions

Transition operations involve the deployment of military, police and/or civilian personnel to assist the parties to a conflict in implementing a political settlement or to help in the transition from a peace heavily supported by international agencies to a self-sustaining peace. Whereas traditional peacekeeping typically takes place in the period between a ceasefire and a political settlement, transitional operations tend to take place after *both* a ceasefire *and* a political settlement have been reached. The UN, other organizations and individual states may act as mediators (or peacemakers) to pave the way for a political settlement, but the peacekeepers are not deployed until the settlement has been concluded. The mandate of transitional operations usually revolves around the implementation of the peace settlement.

There are many different subcategories of transitional operations, but the most pronounced difference is between missions that aim to *assist transitions* – the subject of this chapter – and *transitional administrations* – which are analysed in the following chapter. The most important difference between these two types of operation is that the former works in cooperation with the host state and under its authority and the latter assume the full reins of government and sovereign authority. Underpinning this distinction, however, is a political and philosophical difference over the best way to foster stable peace. Assisting transition operations is informed by what has become known as the 'light footprint' approach. This holds that stable peace can be built only by local actors themselves and that international society's role is to support those actors in a non-intrusive fashion (see below). Transitional administrations, on the other hand, rest on the assumption that local actors can build stable peace only once they have the institutional capacity, political culture and economic infrastructure necessary to sustain it. There are also other important differences: historically, transitional administrations have tended to be the product of prior enforcement operations or other forms of international coercion, whereas assisting transition operations tend to be products of peace settlements arrived at by the parties themselves (albeit often with international mediation); transitional administrations tend to be larger than assisting transition operations; transitional administrations are usually backed by robust military forces with a broad mandate to use force, while some assisting transition operations may be authorized under Chapter VI of

TABLE 10.1 Assisting transition operations and transitional administrations compared

	Assisting transition	Transitional administration
Authority	1 Sovereign authority remains with national authorities 2 Authority grounded in local consent	1 Temporary assumption of sovereign authority by UN or other external actor 2 Authority grounded in international mandate (usually UN Security Council)
Philosophy	'Light footprint'	Building institutions necessary for stable peace: • New York consensus • institutionalization before liberalization • republican peace
Purpose	Type 1: Assist national authorities/signatories to peace settlements in implementing peace settlement Type 2: Assist in the transition from peace to self-sustaining stable peace	Govern territory and prepare it for transition to full self-government, independence or reintegration
Source (typical)	Peace settlement agreed by major parties to the conflict	International imposition through armed force, economic coercion, or diplomatic pressure
Geography (typical)	Small, medium and some large territories	Typically limited to small territories
Operating principles	Consent, impartiality, minimum force	Robust rules of engagement in pursuit of decisions by the transitional administration and UN Security Council

the UN Charter and rely primarily on local consent; finally, transitional administrations have been limited almost exclusively to relatively small territories, whereas assisting transition missions have been used in both small and large territories (e.g. El Salvador and Namibia) (Caplan 2005). These differences are summarized in table 10.1.

Assisting the transition from war to stable peace is a difficult and long-term undertaking. Some analysts claim that almost half of all countries emerging from civil war descend back into war within five years (Collier et al. 2003: 7; for a critique of this figure, see Suhrke and Samset 2007). It is therefore surprising that UN operations aimed at assisting such transitions have been relatively successful in accomplishing their mandates. The risk of future war drops by 95 per cent when a peace mission is deployed with the consent of the belligerents (Fortna 2003: 108). Another study has shown that interventions aimed at facilitating a peace agreement are likely to save lives because there is a high correlation between peace agreements and an end to violence (Doyle and Sambanis 2000: 794).

10.1 What are assisting transition operations?

Assisting transition operations aim to assist a process of transition to stable and self-sustaining peace within particular states. They are 'transitional' in three related senses. First, and most obviously, they deal with state transition. They aim to facilitate the successful implementation of a political settlement by playing a role in managing or facilitating the process itself. In principle, this reduces the risks run by combatants engaging in peace processes, as it holds out the promise of impartial international oversight and enhances the likelihood of meeting substantive goals by marshalling international resources in support of the peace process. Second, they are 'transitional' because – in theory at least – they have a clear beginning and end. They begin within the signing of a political settlement that includes a call by the parties to the conflict for international assistance in implementing the settlement and – historically – have concluded with some formal indication that the transition itself has come to an end. This is usually signalled by the formal recognition of a new state (as in the case of Namibia) or the holding of 'free and fair' elections (as in the case of Cambodia). In the past few years, however, it has been recognized that the abrupt end of international assistance in the wake of a single 'free and fair' election may leave only a fragile peace. In a landmark report in 2001, the UN Secretary-General acknowleged that the UN has often withdrawn or significantly downsized peace operations 'only to see the situation remain unstable, or sink into renewed violence (Annan 2001b: 1). Thus, an emerging type of assisting transition operation, now supported by the UN's Peacebuilding Commission (created in 2005), aims to assist countries in the transition from internationally supported peace to self-sustaining stable peace by helping them to build the necessary capacities (see figure 10.1). By 'self-sustaining', we mean a peace that can endure without major international assistance. This occurs when a state and society is able to resolve conflicts without violence.

Within the category of assisting transition operations there are therefore two broad types: those that aim to implement the terms of a peace settlement and those that aim to build a self-sustaining stable peace. Assisting transition operations facilitate the implementation of a peace settlement and then the transition to self-sustaining peace. The latter type of operation, which is relatively new, may follow any type of peace operation. For instance, the UN assistance mission in Sierra Leone (UNIOSIL) followed the successful completion of UNAMSIL, a wider peacekeeping operation (see Olonisakin 2008: 124–30).

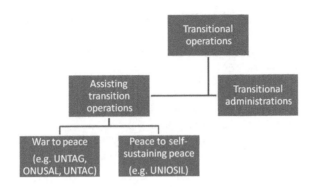

Figure 10.1 *Varieties of transitional operation*

Assisting transition operations are qualitatively distinct from other types of operation (except transitional administrations) because they take place at a different stage in the conflict cycle. Like transitional administrations and peace support operations, however, they have a significant civilian component because they have to address the full range of issues connected with the transformation of states and societies from war to peace. Since these operations are concerned with the implementation of peace accords, they usually have important military functions associated with the disarmament, demobilization and reintegration (DDR) of combatants and the maintenance of public order during the process of demilitarization. These military tasks may involve traditional peacekeeping responsibilities, such as patrolling neutral zones, major routes and cantonment areas, as well as separating combatants and monitoring troop movements and verifying the disarmament of armed groups. However, because they are conducted at the behest of the parties to the conflict, these operations are not technically exercises in enforcement but are predicated on the same 'holy trinity' as traditional peacekeeping (though consent is not static and peacekeepers can take measures to manage and enhance it). The military component exists alongside multiple civilian components responsible for managing various aspects of transition, including civil administration, policing, capacity-building, refugee return and rehabilitation, and the organization and supervision of elections. Sometimes, these missions are primarily or exclusively civilian in character. Thakur and Schnabel (2001: 12) refer to these operations as 'peace reinforcement'. We prefer the label 'assisting transition' because they are *not* mandated to enforce peace, but are concerned with the implementation of agreements freely entered into and overseeing a transition to self-sustaining stable peace (see box 10.1).

As we mentioned earlier, assisting transition operations are prefaced on what has become known as a 'light footprint' approach to building peace. This is most often associated with Lakhdar Brahimi's approach to building peace in Afghanistan after the US-led invasion of 2001 (see Annan 2002a; Traub 2006: 160–4).

> ## Box 10.1 Attributes of assisting transitions operations
> - Durable ceasefire
> - Political settlement agreed by the major parties to the conflict that includes a request for international assistance
> - Multifaceted mandate: concerned with all the major aspects of peaceful transition
> - Multidimensional: military, police and civilian components, although some missions may comprise primarily or exclusively civilians or police
> - Success depends on the consent of the local parties
> - The mission is predicated on the traditional principles of consent, impartiality and minimum use of force.

The light footprint philosophy involves using international agencies to accomplish certain tasks, such as the provision of security in some major cities, capacity-building support for the state bureaucracy, and training and equipping a national army and police service, while permitting indigenous leaders to develop their own preferred type of polity and retain ownership of the overall rebuilding process. In sharp contrast to the transitional administrations in the Balkans and East Timor (see chapter 11), international agencies in Afghanistan did not insist upon the institution of a particular form of government but instead left these decisions to the local representatives who participated in the *loya jirga*. As long as certain basic conditions were satisfied (some form of democracy, an open economy, respect for basic human rights), international agencies were prepared to allow the Afghan government to control and direct the rebuilding effort (Chesterman 2004: 89–92).

There are clearly some advantages to the light footprint philosophy, not least its underlying principle that the purpose of international engagement is to facilitate the development of local initiatives. With local ownership of peace processes come sustainability and the capacity to resolve conflicts peacefully. But this approach also raises a number of problems. First, by placing authority in the hands of local elites, it runs the risk of legitimating spoilers, embedding tyranny and reinforcing the very structures and actors that caused violent conflict in the first place. Moreover, this approach makes the peace process potentially hostage to the demands of political leaders, delaying progress. Second, as the comparative figures for Kosovo and Afghanistan noted above demonstrate, the light footprint can serve as a cover for chronic under-investment and limited engagement. In Afghanistan, this approach to security allowed the resurgence of the Taliban and produced only modest gains in relation to economic growth, education and infrastructure. As a RAND study concluded, 'low input of military and civilian resources yields low output in terms of security, democratic transformation, and economic development' (Dobbins et al. 2003: 7). Many of these same problems were encountered in the UN's assisting transition operations in West New Guinea and Cambodia especially.

10.2 Assisting the transition from war to peace in practice

During the Cold War, the UN conducted thirty-two missions (including peace operations, election monitoring missions and political missions) to assist the process of decolonization, some of which helped lay the foundations for the UN's future role in transitional processes (Ratner 1996: 112–16). The UN's role in the decolonization of the western half of New Guinea was illustrative of the prospects and potential pitfalls of assisting transition operations.

In 1962, bilateral negotiations between Indonesia and the former colonial power, the Netherlands, resulted in an agreement to transfer sovereignty over the territory to Indonesia through a transitional authority under the auspices of the UN. At that time, the eastern half of New Guinea was administered by Australia under the UN's trusteeship system. Launched in October 1962, UNTEA was mandated by the General Assembly's endorsement of the Dutch–Indonesian agreement (Dunbabin 2008: 500). It was to be a mission of short duration, taking responsibility for the territory's administration and security until May 1963, when it was scheduled to be handed over to Indonesia. The deal also made provisions for an 'act of free choice' for West Papuans to decide whether to accept Indonesian rule. This was to be administered by the Indonesians, however, not the UN.

Although UNTEA had no formal mandate from the General Assembly or the Security Council, the terms of the peace treaty gave it a broad remit to administer West New Guinea in preparation for its transfer to Indonesia. Its responsibilities ranged from civil administration to supervision of policing and the provision of military security (Ratner 1996: 109–12). The UN assumed responsibility for running all the territory's major administrative departments. The UN's Iranian head of mission, Djalal Abdoh, referred to as 'the administrator', was given the freedom to determine the size of the security force, and 1,500 Pakistani peacekeepers were deployed to carry out this task (MacQueen 2006: 109). Because there were very few Papuans able to replace Dutch colonial administrators and UNTEA had neither the time nor mandate to build administrative capacity in the territory, most government positions were filled by Indonesian civil servants from the main island of Java. As MacQueen argues, these civil servants 'quickly came to dominate the territory's administration in a way alarmingly reminiscent of a colonial government' (2006: 109).

UNTEA proved successful in overseeing Dutch withdrawal, maintaining order, and handing over administration of West New Guinea to Indonesia. This was largely the result of a combination of Dutch eagerness to complete their withdrawal, global support for Indonesian rule – which was widely seen as a necessary part of decolonization – and a general antipathy towards heavy involvement. However, Indonesia did not follow through on its commitment to respect the wishes of the territory's Papuan inhabitants. Rather than being

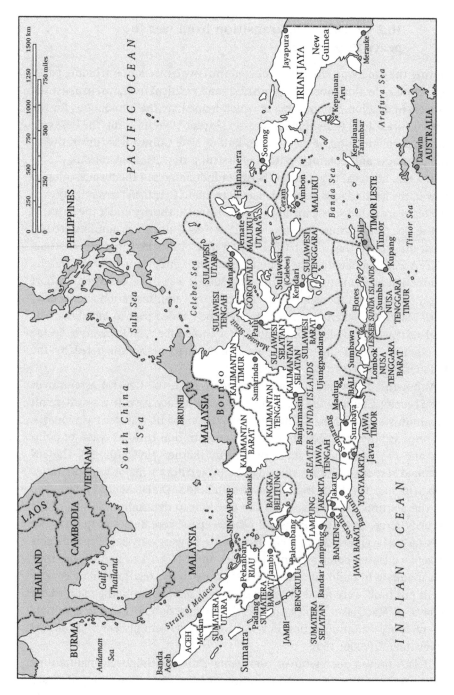

Map 10.1 *Indonesia*

a proper referendum, the 'act of free choice' held six years after UNTEA's withdrawal consisted of a consultation with Indonesian-appointed councils. Unsurprisingly, they overwhelmingly endorsed Indonesian rule. Thereafter Papuan dissent was met with state repression, but this generated little international interest in the matter (MacQueen 2006: 110).

While this experience demonstrated that the UN was capable of taking primary responsibility for the administration of a territory, it also showed the potential pitfalls of simply carrying out the belligerents' wishes. On the one hand, the mission's successes emanated from its limited mandate and short duration and the high levels of consent that flowed from the fact that the UN was merely managing the implementation of an agreement already concluded by the Dutch and Indonesians. This translated into a stable environment conducive to a smooth transition. On the other hand, however, UNTEA's primary role was to manage and legitimize a morally problematic *fait accompli*, wherein West Papuans were not given the opportunity to express their wishes, and Indonesia used political repression to impose its authority on the territory. The UN was therefore placed in the unenviable position of successfully executing its narrow mandate while being unable to build stable peace or reaffirm respect for human rights.

In the remainder of this section we analyse two major assisting transition operations. The first, UNTAG, assisted Namibia's transition from war and South African rule to peace and independence. The other, UNTAC, oversaw the transition from protracted civil war to peace in Cambodia (ONUSAL's efforts in El Salvador are discussed on the companion website).

UNTAG in Namibia (1989–1990)

UN involvement in South West Africa stretched back to 1945 when it took over responsibility for former League of Nations trust territories. The League had devolved responsibility for South West Africa (a former German colony) to South Africa after the First World War. However, South Africa refused to recognize UN authority over the territory after the Second World War and began a push for annexation. After it extended apartheid there in the 1960s, the General Assembly revoked South Africa's right of administration. In 1970 the Security Council followed suit (in Resolution 276). In addition, in 1971 the International Court of Justice declared South Africa's continued occupation of Namibia to be illegal. The South West African People's Organization (SWAPO), formed in 1960, began conducting a guerrilla war against South Africa with the help of Angola's pro-Soviet regime. The UN maintained its interest in South West Africa's fate through a Contact Group or so-called Western five (UK, France, Canada, US, West Germany). In 1978 its settlement plan for an independent Namibia gained the Security Council's approval (in Resolution 435). Under this plan, the Secretary-General created UNTAG.

By the end of the 1980s, SWAPO and the South Africans had fought themselves to a stalemate. The ending of the Cold War, however, contributed to the removal of patronage from both sides and made the prospect of an independent Namibia more palatable to the West. During the Cold War, SWAPO's Angolan links had made the West baulk at Namibian independence and consequently drag its feet on the matter (MacQueen 2006: 188–9). Moreover, under intense domestic and international pressure, South Africa began the process of dismantling apartheid in earnest. All of this created a context conducive to a negotiated settlement based on managing Namibia's transition to independence. On 22 December 1989 the Namibian Accords were signed between Angola, Cuba and South Africa, paving the way for Namibia to begin its UN-assisted transition to independence.

UNTAG's mandate comprised a series of agreements and resolutions rather than a single definitive text. During a decade of negotiations its original mandate thus underwent considerable revision. For instance, agreements were concluded regarding Namibia's future constitution and the nature of its democratic process, which expanded UNTAG's remit considerably. Although it did not administer the territory directly (that was left to South Africa), UNTAG monitored or supervised all the major aspects of the transition process, including the elections, police activities and reform, and the withdrawal or disarmament and demobilization of the parties to the conflict. Some commentators argue that the ambiguities in UNTAG's mandate proved constructive in the sense that generally high levels of consent allowed it to engage in what Stanley and Holiday termed 'constructive mission creep' (1997: 25). In other words, UNTAG was occasionally able to exploit its wide and somewhat ambiguous mandate to undertake activities that it was not specifically tasked to perform. It was able to counteract South Africa's presence, maintain the appearance of impartiality (by and large) and monitor and strengthen security; most importantly, it 'was [able] to build confidence in and legitimise the peace process, the elections, and the result of the transition: the new state of Namibia' (Fortna 1994: 362).

The Secretary-General's Special Representative, Martti Ahtisaari, argued that the only way to ensure free and fair elections as a precursor to the transition to independence was to change Namibia's political culture first. UNTAG therefore focused on relieving racial tensions, curbing police and military violence, ensuring an end to SWAPO violence, and educating the wider society about democracy (Howard 2008: 66). To accomplish this, it attempted to position itself as a 'source of authentic and objective' information and recognized that its legitimacy would depend on its ability to deal with challenges to the transition while maintaining its perceived impartiality. This was no small challenge in a deeply divided country that had experienced decades of colonial oppression and racial discrimination (ibid.).

The period of extended negotiation prior to UNTAG's deployment provided the operation with an unusually long time to prepare. This allowed Ahtisaari time to recruit key staff, organize his team and conduct advance training and planning (Ratner 1996: 118). Most importantly, it gave UNTAG's personnel the opportunity to become better acquainted with the dynamics of the conflict. Ahtisaari and his force commander, Indian Lieutenant-General Dewan Prem Chand, frequently visited Namibia in the years preceding deployment. Thus, by the time UNTAG was deployed, in April 1989, its key personnel were widely conversant with the situation on the ground and were clear about their objectives.

When UNTAG left Namibia one year later, it had completed its mandate in full. It had overseen the withdrawal of South African forces and the disarming of Namibian forces that had fought against SWAPO, had supervised 'free and fair' elections to the new Constituent Assembly, and had facilitated South Africa's handover of state administration to the new Namibian authorities. Nevertheless, it had encountered serious challenges along the way. For example, on its first day of operation, 1 April 1989, the mission was plunged into an immediate crisis when around 500 SWAPO fighters (other estimates put the figure at 1,000 to 2,000) crossed the border from Angola into northern Namibia in violation of the peace agreement (Goulding 2002: 155; Jaster 1990: 35–40). South Africa believed the move was an aggressive attempt to strengthen SWAPO's hand by increasing its number of fighters inside Namibia relative to the number based in Angola. The British prime minister, Margaret Thatcher, interceded and asked the South Africans to keep their forces in barracks unless asked to do otherwise by the UN (Thatcher 1993: 529). With only 300 military observers on the ground, UNTAG was in no position to enforce a ceasefire. Facing the potential collapse of the peace process, the UN authorized the South Africans to use force. South Africa and its allies engaged the SWAPO forces, and SWAPO in turn reinforced its fighters inside Namibia (Goulding 2002: 153). Around 300 SWAPO fighters and thirteen South Africans were killed in the fighting. As SWAPO began to retreat and the fighting died down, Ahtisaari brought the South Africans together with other key states (Angola, Cuba, US, USSR) for crisis talks amid fears that South Africa would walk away from the process and ask the UN to leave. However, a combination of domestic factors (an ailing economy, a determination to rid themselves of expensive military commitments and the dismantling of apartheid) and international pressure (principally from Thatcher) persuaded South Africa to remain committed to the process (ibid.: 154–8; Howard 2008: 64).

To this day it remains unclear whether SWAPO was deliberately violating the peace deal in order to strengthen its position or whether the incident was a product of a tragic misunderstanding about where SWAPO fighters were supposed to be cantoned. Most agreements over the previous decade had involved SWAPO fighters being disarmed in Namibia, but the terms had been changed shortly before UNTAG's deployment and without the direct participation of SWAPO. As a result, there are a number of different ways of apportioning blame. Some commentators squarely reproach SWAPO's leader and the subsequent president of Namibia, Sam Nujoma. Others, including the UN's senior peacekeeping official at the time, suggest that the UN must shoulder some of the responsibility and that it should have delayed disarmament and demobilization until after the UN force was fully deployed (Goulding 2002: 158). Either way, UNTAG was saved by a combination of the parties' determination to implement the peace settlement and rapid diplomatic engagement with the crisis.

A further problem was related to the democratic process itself. South Africa had hoped to exert continuing influence in Namibia through a pro-South African political party, the Democratic Turnhalle Alliance (DTA), but, when it became clear that the DTA was unlikely to prevent an electoral landslide for SWAPO, the South Africans engaged in 'dirty tricks' to deny the former rebels a convincing victory (MacQueen 2006: 190). In the end, both sides – though mainly the DTA – engaged in voter harassment, intimidation and violence. In particular, evidence emerged that members of the notorious South African commando unit Koevoet had been absorbed into the South African-dominated South West African Police (SWAPOL), rather than being disbanded as promised, and were continuing to intimidate the population. In response to these reports, the UN increased the size of its own policing contingent, ultimately providing 1,500 international police officers to monitor SWAPOL's activities. South Africa was placed under considerable international pressure and finally withdrew all ex-Koevoet forces from SWAPOL towards the end of October 1989 (Jaster 1990: 34–42). UNTAG's response to this strategy of intimidation restored international and domestic confidence in its ability to manage the transition and helped ensure a largely free and fair election (Howard 2008: 82).

In addition to these specific crises, UNTAG suffered problems related to its overall size, logistics, procurement and command and control (Alden 1997: 55; Fortna 1994: 366–7). The Secretary-General had originally estimated that the UN would need 25,000 troops for the mission, but the Security Council was never likely to authorize a mission this large (Diehl and Jurado 1993: 62). When the Security Council reduced the nominal strength of 7,500 to a mere 4,650, it appeared to some that the mission was not sufficiently staffed to execute its mandate (Jaster 1990: 35). Aside from the logistical difficulties of supervising elections for a population of 1.4 million people who were widely dispersed across a large (around the size of UK and France combined) and inhospitable terrain (Diehl and Jurado 1993: 63), UNTAG did not have the wherewithal to control territory and guarantee security. Given Namibia's geographic size and the relative smallness of UNTAG's military component, the mission's military mandate was clearly unrealistic (see box 10.2).

As there were 30,000 South African troops in Namibia and a similar number of SWAPO fighters in neighbouring Angola and Zambia, both the South Africans and the UN had concerns about UNTAG's ability to maintain order after South Africa's withdrawal (Fortna 1994: 362). The history of UN

> **Box 10.2 The mandate of UNTAG's military component**
> - Monitor the cessation of hostilities.
> - Restrict opposing forces to their bases.
> - Supervise their disarmament or withdrawal from the country.
> - Monitor the activities of those forces that were to perform civil tasks during the transition.
> - Guard against border infiltrations.
> - Supervise general demilitarization (especially non-SWAPO forces and paramilitary organizations).
> - Assist the UN's civilian agencies in securing the safe return of refugees.
> - Provide a secure environment for elections.

peacekeeping has many examples of small UN forces replacing much larger national or regional contingents and failing in this respect. Two of the most famous cases are UNAMSIL's replacement of ECOMOG in Sierra Leone and MONUC's replacement of Ugandan troops in the Congolese town of Bunia. In both cases, UN peacekeepers confronted an immediate emergency and required external assistance. In the Namibian case the SWAPO incursion challenged the UN's credibility, but, once the immediate emergency was resolved, UNTAG's inability to fulfil the military aspects of its mandate never seriously threatened the mission owing to the parties' deep-seated commitment to the peace process. The South African defence forces completed their phased withdrawal on schedule and – guaranteed a victory at the ballot box – SWAPO did not attempt to use its military arm to fill the void.

The successful supervision of the November 1989 election was undoubtedly UNTAG's single largest achievement. Although overall responsibility for the territory's administration lay with the South African administrator-general, Louis Pienaar, UNTAG had authority to oversee his activities. Approximately 2,000 UN election monitors tried to educate people and build confidence and awareness of the process by publicizing it widely and demonstrating that UNTAG could provide both a stable security environment and effectively monitor the election process itself. Voter turnout was around 97 per cent and, as predicted, the election resulted in an overwhelming victory for SWAPO. Although South Africa later admitted to trying to influence the election by unconstitutional means (Fortna 1994: 370–1), and suspicions remained that it both planned and did much worse (Diehl and Jurado 1993: 65), Ahtisaari was able to declare that a free and fair election had taken place.

According to one analyst, UNTAG's 'operational complexity exceeded earlier cases by many orders of magnitude', as it combined complex civil and military tasks (Ratner 1996: 123). Although this may be overstating the point – ONUC (1960–4), for instance, was just as complex an operation – UNTAG's mandate did take UN peacekeepers well beyond their normal remit. In addition to overseeing security, South African withdrawal and elections, it facilitated the return of some 50,000 Namibian refugees. All this allowed UN Secretary-General Pérez de Cuéllar to claim that UNTAG 'proved the executive ability of the United Nations in successfully managing a complex operation' (1990: 2).

Four factors are commonly identified as the principal reasons for UNTAG's success.

1 *The parties were committed to the peace settlement* Both SWAPO and South Africa were committed to a managed transition to independence. As Goulding (2002: 175) put it, 'the objective of bringing Namibia to independence through an internationally monitored democratic process was opposed by no one except a few right-wing extremists in South Africa and Namibia.' Neither side believed that it could achieve its political objectives by violent means and both preferred to have the process overseen by the UN. The peace settlement's basic principles were also well established and well understood. This basic commitment meant that, although both sides sought to gain advantage (SWAPO through incursions, South Africa through SWAPOL), neither was prepared to risk the overall peace process (also see Howard 2008: 87).

2 *The positive engagement of external actors* Although UNTAG was not 'micromanaged' by UN headquarters and its principal officials were free to interpret the mandate broadly (see below), high-level political support from both global powers (the UK) and regional actors (Angola and Zambia) was available when needed and played a critical role in limiting the damage caused by the incursion crisis and persuading South Africa to cease its attempts to use intimidation to improve the DTA's electoral chances. This positive engagement was produced by 'almost universal international support' for the peace plan (Goulding 2002: 175).

3 *Context-sensitive interpretation of the mandate* Given ambiguities about how particular parts of the mandate were to be interpreted, Ahtisaari and his staff were able to fashion a strategy that suited the environment and to respond flexibly to crises. This involved recognizing that free and fair elections would require a wholesale restructuring of Namibian political culture and expressly permitting South African forces to engage their former enemies militarily during the incursion crisis. Because the plan had been ten years in the making, this was well understood by the parties (Goulding 2002: 175).

4 *Peacekeeping innovation* UNTAG was the first mission to become heavily engaged in police monitoring and training, public information, and disseminating and enforcing electoral codes of conduct. It was also one of the first missions to work through regional and district centres and emphasize the creation of mechanisms for the resolution of disputes (Howard 2008: 87). All of these measures helped consolidate democratic transition and were replicated in other missions.

UNTAC in Cambodia (1991–1993)

UNTAC, deployed between November 1991 and September 1993, was a large and wide-ranging operation that is widely described as a major success by analysts and participants alike (e.g. Akashi 2001: 149–54; Lee Kim and Metrikas 1997: 132–3; Thayer 1998: 162–3). Schear (1997: 175), for example, argued that 'future historians may well look back at UNTAC as the organization's high point in multidimensional peacekeeping.' However, most observers also accept that it was a flawed operation and that Cambodia remained unstable after UNTAC's departure (ibid.: 176; Sanderson 2001: 165–6; Le Billon and Bakker 2000: 82–6). After UNTAC withdrew, there was no follow-up mission or agreement about what role the Khmer Rouge should play in political life. This allowed Cambodia's Vietnamese-installed leader, Hun Sen, to dispute the legitimacy of the 1993 election results and eventually to seize power in a 1997 coup.

Cambodia's tragic history is too complex to explore thoroughly here, but it is important to sketch some key events. After gaining independence from France in 1953, Cambodia (Kampuchea) was a monarchy under Prince Norodom Sihanouk until he was overthrown by a military coup in 1970. Bloody civil war followed between the military government and Pol Pot's

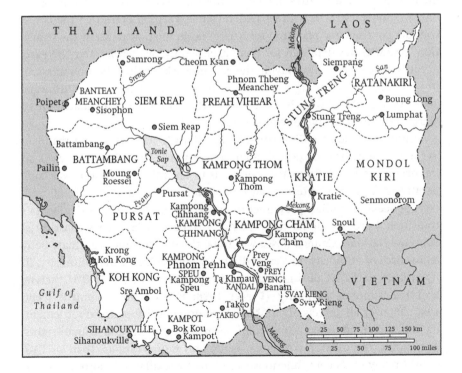

Map 10.2 *Cambodia*

Maoist Khmer Rouge, or Party of Democratic Kampuchea (PDK). The Khmer Rouge seized power in 1975 and unleashed a bloody reign of terror aimed at establishing an agrarian, peasant-based, communist society (see Evans and Rowley 1990). Between 1975 and 1979 the Khmer Rouge committed genocide against its own people and was responsible for the death of around 2 million persons, more than a quarter of Cambodia's entire population (see Le Billon and Bakker 2000: 74; Jackson 1989: 3; Chandler 1997: 43–8). The genocide was stopped by a Vietnamese invasion which installed its own puppet regime, the People's Republic of Kampuchea (PRK), which was later led by Hun Sen – himself a former member of the Khmer Rouge. Although Vietnam secured approximately 85 per cent of Cambodia's territory, a civil war rumbled on between the PRK, backed by Vietnam and the Soviet Union, and the Khmer Rouge and its monarchist allies, backed by China, ASEAN, France, the US and the UK (Thayer 1998: 147). International society punished the PRK and Vietnam for overthrowing the Khmer Rouge with a devastating sanctions regime that left the country destitute (Wheeler 2000: 89–100).

As in El Salvador and Namibia, the end of the Cold War opened a space for conflict resolution as the superpowers removed their patronage from the belligerents. From 1987 onwards, negotiations between the four major protagonists and influential states (especially France and Indonesia) led first to ceasefires and partial agreements and finally to a comprehensive peace settlement. Four related treaties, known as the Paris Peace Accords, were signed on 23 October 1991. As with UNTAG, advance warning permitted the UN to conduct contingency planning for a large-scale mission to assist the transition. UNAMIC was deployed for this purpose only two weeks after the Paris Accords were signed. After laying the groundwork for the follow-on mission, in particular by providing estimates of the number of combatants (Howard 2008: 145), UNAMIC was absorbed into UNTAC, which was mandated on 15 March 1992 in Security Council Resolution 745.

According to Boutros-Ghali (1995b: 3), UNTAC's size, scope and mandate 'set a new standard for peacekeeping operations'. The mission marked an important landmark for peace operations in several ways. First, it was comparatively large: its eighteen-month mandate authorized nearly 22,000 military, police and civilian personnel to engage in every aspect of Cambodia's transitional process. Under the Paris Accords, Cambodia's newly constituted Supreme National Council (SNC) was to be the 'unique and legitimate body and source of authority' in Cambodia but would delegate that authority, in its entirety, to UNTAC during the transition process (Article 6). UNTAC thereby acquired 'supreme authority' (Thayer 1998: 151) or 'direct control' (Peou 1997: 98) over all aspects of Cambodia's comprehensive political settlement, including civil administration, public security, elections and human rights. As a result, the mission was much wider and more complex than UNTAG, even if many of its core functions were broadly similar. It is also important to note that, however wide this authority, it did not represent a transfer of sovereign authority to UNTAC, and thus this mission should not be seen as a transitional administration.

UNTAC soon found that it did not enjoy universal consent and was vulnerable to attack. Boutros-Ghali (1995b: 15), for instance, subsequently acknowledged that its activities were shaped as much by the situation on the ground as by the Paris Accords. By the time the operation deployed, some four months after the peace accords, the security situation had deteriorated and the ceasefire was being broken on a regular basis. More ominous still was the continuing Khmer Rouge intransigence. When UNTAC's Australian force commander, Lieutenant-General John Sanderson, declared the mission's military component ready to oversee the disarmament and demobilization of armed groups, the Khmer Rouge simply refused to cooperate. Instead, it escalated attacks on the other groups, including UNTAC itself. The SRSG, Yasushi Akashi, instructed the Secretary-General that the Khmer Rouge was 'trying to gain what it could not get in the battlefield or in the Paris negotiations, that is, to improve its political and military power to such an extent that the other parties will be placed at a distinctive disadvantage when UNTAC leaves' (Akashi 1995: 206). By late 1992 the Khmer Rouge had effectively withdrawn from the peace process, retreating into its strongholds along the Thai–Cambodian border and returning to full-scale violence.

UNTAC's 15,000-strong military component therefore faced a host of problems within a few months of deployment. As a result of Khmer Rouge intransigence, which the latter justified by claiming (falsely) that the presence of ethnic Vietnamese in Cambodia demonstrated that the Vietnamese army had not fully withdrawn, the mission's mandate was modified to include securing a peaceful environment for the forthcoming elections (Lee Kim and Metrikas 1997: 119). This hinted at a shift to enforcement, something that Sanderson was keen to guard against. Sanderson believed, probably correctly (see Doyle and Suntharalingam 1994: 128), that UNTAC did not have the military capability to defeat the Khmer Rouge and that pursuing this course of action would only worsen matters. UNTAC's unwillingness to confront the Khmer Rouge forcibly drew criticism, stalled the disarmament process, which was never fully completed, and cast doubt upon its military credibility. This encouraged other armed groups to violate the ceasefire (Lee Kim and Metrikas 1997: 119–21). The deteriorating security situation also had an adverse effect upon other aspects of UNTAC's operation.

For instance, the mission's role in civil administration was severely hampered (Schear 1997: 158–61). Although UNTAC had the legal authority to play a leading role in all aspects of governance, in practice the Cambodian government continued to govern around the UN while areas that remained under Khmer Rouge control remained entirely out of its reach (Doyle 1994: 80–4). In addition, UNTAC suffered from a series of logistical problems, including a lack of engineering and de-mining capacity, which further limited its areas of operation; relatively ineffective intelligence; and poor communications, which made interaction within the mission and between the mission and the local population difficult at times (Berdal and Leifer 1996). Despite these problems, the mission succeeded in returning 360,000 refugees to their homes and organizing a free and fair election (Findlay 1995: 52–4).

As the May 1993 elections approached, the security situation remained unstable, with 'a partitioned Cambodia, armed to the teeth, and a violent campaign of civil terror waged among the factions, and against UNTAC' (Doyle and Suntharalingam 1994: 126). The situation became so desperate that Akashi subsequently admitted that UN volunteers would have been withdrawn had the mission suffered a single additional fatality (Akashi 1994: 205). UNTAC itself was frequently targeted, mainly by the Khmer Rouge but also by supporters of the Cambodian People's Party (CPP, formerly the PRK). During the course of the mission, eighty-four UN personnel were killed.

In such circumstances, that the election took place at all was a significant achievement. UNTAC prepared for the election by launching a massive public information campaign, spearheaded by the mission's radio station. In the end, the pro-Sihanouk FUNCINPEC party, which had borne the brunt of the intimidation, won the most seats in the Constituent Assembly (though not enough to govern alone), with 45 per cent of the vote. Given the precarious security situation, the registration of almost all of Cambodia's 5 million eligible voters and a 90 per cent election turnout were major successes, indicating that UNTAC had succeeded in educating the country about democracy and building confidence in its ability to oversee a free and fair election.

Overall, therefore, UNTAC is best understood as a qualified success. On the positive side, it succeeded in verifying the withdrawal of Vietnamese forces and overseeing an election that transferred sovereign authority to a Cambodian government, and assisted in improving humanitarian conditions. The mission also withdrew on schedule in September 1993. On the downside, it left behind a precarious political situation, failed to disarm the armed groups (especially the Khmer Rouge), stimulated economic problems by introducing inflation, and created social problems such as prostitution (Berdal and Leifer 1996: 53; Whitworth 2004: ch. 2). Moreover, there had been little attempt to foster national political reconciliation, and the lack of a follow-on mission left the coalition government that emerged from the 1993 election highly vulnerable. Although FUNCINPEC emerged as the largest party, Hun Sen refused to hand over power on the grounds that Sihanouk had collaborated with the Khmer Rouge. Keen not to delay its departure, UNTAC organized a compromise whereby FUNCIPEC and Hun Sen ruled jointly. In 1997, however, Hun Sen seized complete power in a coup, the results of which were legitimized by a less than free and fair election the following year. These problems notwithstanding, however, Cambodia did not return to large-scale violence, and without its international supporters the Khmer Rouge collapsed. Pol Pot died and his second in command was arrested and tried for crimes against humanity by the Cambodian authorities.

Where UNTAC succeeded it was because of factors similar to those identified in Namibia: a degree of local political support; a benign international environment, especially the removal of foreign patronage; and the work of the mission itself. However, three other points help explain why UNTAC was a more qualified success than UNTAG.

1 *Elite support was relatively shallow*   Although there was a general commitment to the peace process, key actors, in particular Hun Sen's government and the Khmer Rouge, believed that the transition process would undermine their sources of power and authority (Lizee 1993: 38). The problem's source lay in the Paris Accords, which had prioritized rapid consensus over the establishment of clear mechanisms for resolving disputes, reforming the state and promoting national reconciliation (Roberts 2001: 38–9). As a result, government bodies were highly politicized and not easily susceptible to reform. They successfully resisted UNTAC's efforts at reform, made possible by the lack of a clear enforcement mechanism. This, in turn, encouraged other parties to believe that UNTAC was incapable of creating an impartial government system (Doyle 1995: 69; Peou 1997: 201). The resulting shallowness in elite support created a fragile democratic system subject to traditional networks of power and authority and meant that the indigenous military, police and civilian bureaucracy consistently attempted to limit UNTAC's impact. For their part, the Khmer Rouge remained a largely unreconstructed spoiler throughout the process.
2 *UNTAC failed to oversee the maintenance of security*   UNTAC's failure to establish a secure environment undermined the election's credibility, delayed humanitarian, human rights and economic programmes, and permitted the continuing use of intimidation to procure political support (Bull 2008: 107; Peou 1997: 201).
3 *UNTAC was guided by a predetermined timetable*   The fixed timetable for withdrawal and the absence of a follow-on mission meant that the UN did not have the opportunity to protect the modest gains made by UNTAC or transition to a longer-term programme of assistance aimed at supporting self-sustaining stable peace. In Cambodia, the election was widely seen as an end in itself.

10.3 Problems and causes of success

Studying the missions in West New Guinea, Namibia and Cambodia – as well as the mission in El Salvador (see companion website) – it is clear that there are some recurrent problems and causes of success (see table 10.2 for a summary). As a general type, assisting transition operations have been among the UN's most successful. Their success depends on a range of factors, including the political commitment of the parties to the conflict, a relatively stable security situation and international support, as well as the way the missions themselves are composed and act.

TABLE 10.2 Problems and causes of success in assisting transition operations

Problems	Causes of success
Missions wholly dependent on local consent	Political commitment of the parties to the conflict
Military components not capable of fulfilling mandates in the face of determined opposition	Relatively secure environment
Missions focused on short-term order, not long-term justice	Benign international environment and active diplomatic support from external actors
Organizational problems	Activist and creative approach to interpreting mandate
Limited long-term commitment can undermine gains made by the mission	Mission composition reflecting emergent needs (e.g. policing)

Because we have covered the causes of success in some detail in the preceding discussion, here we focus on some of the recurrent problems. First, because these missions are dependent on host-government support, powerful domestic actors may prevent them accomplishing their goals. The South African administration in Namibia, the Salvadoran security forces, and the CPP/PRK in Cambodia all successfully opposed or undermined the UN's work at some point. This reliance on consent – so crucial to mission success – created problems in relation to human rights commitments and the transition to self-sustaining stable peace in the long term.

Second, in all these cases, the missions' military components were insufficiently strong to fulfil their mandate in the face of determined opposition. Because the missions were deployed with the consent of the host government they were not entitled to use force against the government, but in Namibia and Cambodia the UN faced serious security challenges to which it was not able to respond. In all three cases, the UN lacked the material wherewithal properly to verify the disarming and demobilizing of armed groups.

Third, some critics have argued that the peace settlements that underpinned these operations favoured negative peace over justice and long-term stable peace. John Pilger (1994: 401–94), for example, condemned UNTAC for relegitimizing the Khmer Rouge by allowing it a place in the peace process, pointing to the support this genocidal group had received from key members of the Security Council (US, UK, China and France) between 1979 and 1991.

Fourth, to a greater or lesser extent, each operation suffered from organizational problems in relation to logistics, equipment, coordination and command. Whether it was delayed deployment, as in Namibia, or ineffective policing of human rights abusers, as in Cambodia, these problems reduced the UN's impact and could have undermined the whole mission.

Finally, UNTAC, especially, highlighted the limits of international society's commitment to building stable peace in war-torn states. In that case, elections were seen as an end in themselves and there was little provision for follow-up assistance to build on the progress made by UNTAC. This last problem points to the need for a longer-term approach to assisting transitions, one that focuses on the transition from internationally supported peace to self-sustaining peace. Although the establishment of MINUSAL suggests that this concern was recognized in the early 1990s, only since 2001 has the UN begun to consider this issue systematically. This is reflected in its deployment of similar missions in Burundi, Sierra Leone and Tajikistan. Moreover, the UN Peacebuilding Commission, created in December 2005, was intended to help coordinate the delivery of long-term assistance through civilian-led missions that follow on from full-scale peace operations. The following section discusses this second type of assisting transition operations, focusing briefly on the missions in Burundi, Sierra Leone and Tajikistan before turning to the Peacebuilding Commission.

10.4 Assisting the transition from peace to self-sustaining stable peace

UN Secretary-General Kofi Annan recognized the need to develop a capacity to manage better the transition from peace to self-sustained stable peace in his 2001 report on the exit and closure of peace operations. Annan (2001b: 4) noted that 'more than once during the last 10 years the United Nations has withdrawn a peacekeeping operation, or dramatically altered its mandate, only to see the situation remain unstable, or sink into renewed violence.' The 'ultimate purpose' of a peace operation, he argued, was 'the achievement of a sustainable peace'. In the aftermath of civil wars, peace 'becomes sustainable, not when all conflicts are removed from society, but when the natural conflicts of society can be resolved peacefully through the exercise of State sovereignty and, generally, participatory governance.' Annan advocated a mixture of heavy involvement and the 'light footprint' approach. In his words, 'to facilitate such a transition, a mission's mandate should include peace-building and incorporate such elements as institution-building and the promotion of good governance and the rule of law, by assisting the parties to develop legitimate and broad-based institutions' (ibid.: 8 and 10). To achieve sustainable peace, the Secretary-General maintained, it was necessary to consolidate internal and external security; strengthen political institutions and good governance; and promote economic and social rehabilitation and transformation (ibid.: 20). The need to strengthen the UN's capacity to support this process was widely recognized outside the UN (see Ponzio 2007: 7). In 2000, for instance, the Security Council had created UNTOP to assist the process of building peace in Tajikistan, and in 2006 it despatched similar missions to Burundi (BINUB) and Sierra Leone (UNIOSIL). These initiatives were supported by efforts to improve the UN's institutional capacity to assist states in making the transition to self-sustaining stable peace.

Field missions

The relatively small civilian missions in Tajikistan, Burundi and Sierra Leone provide the best examples of UN missions that are designed to assist countries make the transition from (usually fragile) peace to self-sustaining stable peace.

The UN assistance mission in Tajikistan (UNTOP, 2000–7) was somewhat different from the other two, in that BINUB and UNIOSIL were follow-on missions to major UN peace operations. After gaining independence from the Soviet Union in 1991, Tajikistan was plunged into a civil war between the Russian-backed Tajik government and the United Tajik Opposition (UTO), which comprised liberal democrats and Islamists. Between 50,000 and 100,000 people were killed in the fighting (Kolsto 2000: 76). In September 1993 the CIS deployed 25,000 – mainly Russian – peacekeepers, and the two sides agreed a ceasefire twelve months later. The UN deployed a small monitoring mission (UNMOT) to work alongside OSCE monitors deployed at the request of the government, which was withdrawn at the same time as parliamentary elections in February 2000.

In June 2000, the Security Council established UNTOP to assist with the provision of peacebuilding activities in Tajikistan. UNTOP's work focused on facilitating dialogue between political and civil society groups on national reconciliation, the provision of human rights and conflict management training to government officials, and the training of electoral commission staff. Although the mission contributed to efforts to avoid a return to war, little progress towards self-sustaining peace was made. None of Tajikistan's post-2000 elections were deemed free and fair, political opposition and media freedom were repressed by the government, and corruption, poverty and instability remained rife (CIC 2007: 140–1). A combination of evidence that UNTOP was having little impact, belief that Tajikistan was unlikely to relapse into war, and Tajik opposition to the mission prompted the Security Council to terminate it in mid-2007. The key lessons drawn from UNTOP were that, absent wider international engagement and a commitment from the host government, these operations are unlikely to have a major impact.

UNIOSIL was established in August 2005 as a follow-on presence for UNAMSIL (see companion website). It was mandated to support the government of Sierra Leone in consolidating peace and to coordinate the UN's humanitarian and development activities in the country. The work of its forty military observers and police and around 300 civilian staff and volunteers has focused on providing assistance to the national authorities in preparing, organizing and overseeing elections, supporting the work of the Special Court for Sierra Leone, and delivering programmes developed by the Peacebuilding Commission (see below).

In Burundi's case, BINUB became the UN's presence in the country after its larger peacekeeping operation, ONUB, was wound down in late 2006. Comprising twenty military and police observers and around 400 civilian staff and volunteers, BINUB was mandated to assist the government in the consolidation of peace (Security Council Resolution 1719, 25 October 2006). The bulk of its funding came through the UN Peacebuilding Commission. It also attempted to promote national reconciliation through dialogue on issues such as immunity from prosecution for faction leaders. Although some progress was made – for instance the creation of a special tribunal and truth and reconciliation commission – Burundi still faced huge challenges. Most notably, little progress was made on disarming and demobilizing some of the rebels and integrating armed groups into a new national army and police service (CIC 2008: 96–7).

These missions represent an important departure from the past practice of terminating UN engagement at the end of a peace operation. Consolidating peace through protracted engagement in support of the government is widely seen as an essential component of reducing the likelihood of relapsing into war and assisting the transition into self-sustaining peace. However, experiences in Tajikistan and Burundi in particular suggest that this sort of operation is likely to encounter serious problems. Not least, without strong political commitment from the parties it is difficult to see how these small missions can make much of a difference to peace consolidation. This is why a body such as the UN Peacebuilding Commission is potentially so important to the success of missions such UNIOSIL and BINUB.

The UN Peacebuilding Commission

In 2004, Kofi Annan's High-Level Panel on UN Reform (see chapter 5) called for the establishment of a Peacebuilding Commission (PBC) supported by a Peacebuilding Support Office (PBSO) provided by the Secretariat (see box 10.3).

The proposal was broadly welcomed and adopted at the UN's 2005 World Summit – though without its preventive component, which won very little support. The Commission's mandate was to bring together 'all relevant actors to marshal resources and to advise on and propose integrated strategies for post-conflict peacebuilding and recovery' (UN 2005b: 98). The PBC is subsidiary to the General Assembly, the Security Council and ECOSOC and acts as an 'advisory body' for the Assembly and two Councils. It includes an equal number of representatives from the three bodies, and the top five financial contributors and troop contributors to UN peace operations are also granted membership.

The PBC was formally established by concurrent Security Council (Resolution 1645, 20 December 2005) and General Assembly (Resolution 60/180, 30 December 2005) resolutions, which gave the institution three primary purposes:

> ### Box 10.3 The UN Secretary-General's High-Level Panel recommends a Peacebuilding Commission
>
> There is 'no place in the United Nations system explicitly designed to avoid State collapse and the slide to war or to assist countries in their transition from war to peace'. The Commission should be charged with enabling the UN to act in a 'coherent and effective way' on a broad continuum of measures ranging from early warning and preventive action to post-conflict reconstruction. The Commission would:
>
> - identify countries at risk;
> - organize and coordinate assistance;
> - oversee the transition from war to peace and peacekeeping to peacebuilding;
> - fulfil the twin roles of conflict prevention and post-conflict reconstruction;
> - facilitate joint planning across the UN system and beyond;
> - provide high-level political leadership.
>
> *Source*: UNSG High-Level Panel (2004).

1   to bring together all relevant actors to marshal resources, to provide advice, and to propose integrated strategies for post-conflict peacebuilding;
2   to focus attention on the necessary reconstruction and institution-building efforts to ensure post-conflict recovery and sustainable development;
3   to provide recommendations and information to improve coordination of all relevant actors.

The PBC is an 'advisory body' that operates on the basis of consensus among its thirty-one state members. It organizes 'country specific meetings' to assess the needs of individual states that come onto its agenda. Countries may come onto the agenda at the request of the Security Council, ECOSOC or the General Assembly with the consent of the state concerned, and in exceptional circumstances at the request of the concerned state or the Secretary-General (General Assembly Resolution 60/80, 30 December 2005, § 15). Even where consensus between PBC members and UN agencies is possible, the PBC lacks the formal authority to coordinate UN bodies and agencies. As one commentator put it, 'its influence within the UN stems entirely from the quality of its recommendations, the relevance of the information it shares, and its ability to generate extra resources' (Ponzio 2007: 8). Funds for the Commission's fifteen-strong support office (the PBSO) are to be met from existing resources. In addition to salaries and associated personnel costs, the PBSO receives an annual operating budget of $1.2 million sourced from the Department of Political Affairs (Stimson Center 2007: 3).

The third element of the UN's new peacebuilding capacity is the Peacebuilding Fund (PBF). The fund was created as an alternative to increased assessed contributions and is managed by the head of the PBSO and administered by the UNDP. The decision-making process associated with its distribution is quite cumbersome and involves country-level reports, steering committees (comprising UN agencies, bilateral donors, NGOs and the host government), and requests by the PBC and/or the Secretary-General. The PBF is intended to fill an important funding gap between the conclusion of a peace treaty and the commencement of fully fledged peacebuilding measures. Rather than providing substantive funding, its role is envisaged as 'catalytic' – helping to stimulate further funding by other donors (PBSO 2007). Although the Secretary-General had set an initial target of $250 million per year, by October 2008 the UN's member states had deposited only a little over $242 million. At this stage, the largest single donors to the fund were Sweden (*c.*$42 million), the UK (*c.*$36 million) and Norway (*c.*$32 million).

By mid-2007 the fund had begun dispersing a small amount of this income on projects in Sierra Leone and Burundi, the PBC's first two cases. A little over $5 million (of a projected total of $25 million) had been assigned to Sierra Leone for capacity-building in the police service and youth enterprise development. Burundi fared somewhat better, receiving $15.5 million for projects on resolving land disputes, anti-corruption measures, national reconciliation, supporting the role of women in the peace process, creating a national human rights commission, improving the judicial system, the disarmament of small arms, and barracking the national army (PBSO 2007).

It is too early to make definitive judgements about the extent to which the PBC, PBSO and PBF have improved the UN's capacity for assisting the transition to self-sustaining stable peace. The PBC began work in October 2006, focusing on providing support to the UN's civilian-led missions in Sierra Leone and Burundi. The scope of its work was subsequently expanded to a wider range of countries, including Guinea-Bissau, the Central African Republic, Côte d'Ivoire, Liberia and Nepal. Early signs suggest that its political character makes it better suited to acting as a catalyst for attracting government donations for the UN's civilian-led operations (Ponzio 2007: 10). Early indicators also suggest that the PBC is unlikely to play a decisive role in coordinating UN agencies, not least because it lacks both an explicit mandate to do this and the bureaucratic capacity and financial power to be an effective coordinator. Its coordination role is therefore more one of providing a high-level forum for agencies, donors and the states concerned to identify peacebuilding priorities, develop strategic plans, and initiate relatively small but high profile programmes that support missions in the field such as UNIOSIL (International Peace Academy 2006). The danger is that the PBC might simply 'duplicate, confuse and divert scarce resources' already dedicated to particular countries (Ponzio 2007: 10). Indeed, this very concern was raised by the African Development Bank shortly after the Commission started its work (PBC/1/BD1/SR.1, 18 May 2007, § 44).

Even with the narrow confines of its mandate and resources, however, there are ways in which the PBC could make a positive contribution to assisting the transition to self-sustaining stable peace. As a high-level commission it has the potential to become an engine for augmenting donations and resources in support of already existing long-term missions and programmes such as UNIOSIL. From Afghanistan to Angola, long-term efforts to build stable peace by fostering strong institutions and viable economies are woefully under-resourced, and the PBC could play a useful role as a focal point for generating the necessary resources. It could also prove significant in ensuring that states deliver on their pledges of assistance. In Burundi, for example, by early 2006 only 66 per cent of the $1.1 billion pledged by donors in 2000 had been disbursed (Evans 2006b: 5). In addition, the PBC builds an important bridge between the Security Council and the World Bank. All too often, the security and economic wings of the UN have acted at cross-purposes – the latter using economic coercion to instil neoliberal marketization and the retreat of the state and the former seeking to enhance state capacity. Sometimes, as in the cases of Sierra Leone and Rwanda, World Bank policies have contributed to political instability and violence (Williams 2004). By bridging the gap between security and economics, the PBC could mitigate these effects and provide a forum for articulating consolidated peacebuilding strategies.

10.5 Conclusion

Assisting transition operations are among the UN's most successful, primarily because they deploy after the conflict parties have concluded both a ceasefire and a political settlement. There are broadly two types of assisting transition operation: the first assists states and societies from war to peace, usually marked by the formation of a new government after elections or the creation of a new state; the second is a civilian-led mission to assist states and societies establish self-sustaining stable peace. Typically, both types of mission are successful to the extent that the major local parties allow them to be. Although they often involve a high level of intrusiveness in a state's domestic affairs – and a willingness to play an activist role was a key contributor to success in some cases – it is important to remember that assisting transition operations are predicated on a Westphalian conception of peace operations. The UN's role is to *assist* states to achieve goals that they have set for themselves (albeit usually with the help of international mediators) rather than to *impose* political solutions. Consequently, these operations are not suited to environments where violent conflict is ongoing. Indeed, the Westphalian conception insists that peacekeepers should not be deployed where there is no peace to keep.

CHAPTER ELEVEN

Transitional Administrations

Transitional administrations have been described as the 'Rolls Royce of conflict management strategies' (Caplan 2005: 256). They are comprehensive and wide-ranging operations that involve the assumption of sovereign authority over a particular territory by external actors, usually the UN. In addition to keeping the peace, protecting civilians, enforcing peace agreements, and the other activities associated with complex operations, transitional administrations have the authority to make and enforce the law, exercise control over all aspects of a territory's economy, preside over a territory's borders, regulate the media, manage property law, run schools, hospitals, the sanitation system, the electricity grid, the roads and other forms of transportation, and administer the judicial system (ibid.: 3). Although other types of operation may be engaged in similar activities, none of them have sovereign authority, making transitional administrations quite distinctive. As we noted in chapter 10, in 1962–3 UNTEA was authorized to administer the disputed territory of West New Guinea. The UN did not undertake a similar operation until January 1996, with the establishment of the Transitional Administration for Eastern Slavonia (UNTAES). Within the following four years, however, it was authorized to administer even more ambitious projects in Bosnia, Kosovo and East Timor. In association with other organizations such as the EU, the OSCE, ASEAN and the World Bank, the UN engaged in all the activities of government in these four territories. In taking on this sovereign authority and extensive range of tasks, the challenge confronting the UN was nothing less than conceiving and implementing 'a set of norms appropriate to the political tasks of international stewardship' (Caplan 2002: 11). It is important to note at the outset, however, that since 2000 the UN has refrained from creating new transitional administrations, leading at least one prominent analyst to question whether there will be sufficient international political will to take on transitional administrations in any but the most exceptional of circumstances (Caplan 2005: 256).

The rationale behind transitional administration is the idea that establishing zones of stable peace depends not only on the provision of military security through the wider tasks given to peacekeepers but also on the creation of functioning liberal polities, economies and societies, all guided by the rule of law (see Duffield 2001: 11; Mandelbaum 2002: 6). This rationale is itself predicated on three key assumptions. First, in addition to not fighting one another, genuinely democratic societies that are governed by the rule of law do not descend into violent conflict because they contain legitimate structures for non-violent conflict resolution that help ease the societal security dilemma (Roe 2005; Snyder and Jervis 1999). Indeed, the rule of law itself provides a framework for the peaceful resolution of disputes (Stromseth et al. 2006: 78; see chapter 17). Second, liberal peace requires vibrant civic associations and a capitalist market economy. These associations are believed to contribute to the development of key 'democratic attributes' such as tolerance, compromise, and a willingness to settle disputes peacefully. Where these attributes are absent, as in war zones, international society must implant them in the interests of building stable peace. Finally, in territories affected by war, the institutions of liberal democracy are assumed to be fragile and require sustained protection by external agencies, especially in parts of the world where there is no history or culture of liberal democracy. Confronted with malevolent systems of governance in the Balkans and East Timor, the UN and other agencies therefore attempted to cultivate stable peace by nurturing liberal polities, economies and societies.

Although the idea of international trusteeship is not new, this chapter focuses on its contemporary manifestation in the form of transitional administrations. It begins by summarizing some of the different approaches to establishing stable peace in war-torn societies. Building on this discussion, the second part of the chapter analyses the transitional administrations conducted by the UN in Kosovo and East Timor (a case study of the transitional administration in Bosnia is available on the companion website). The final part of the chapter reviews debates about the utility and legitimacy of UN transitional administrations.

11.1 What are transitional administrations?

In the second half of the 1990s, the UN assumed sovereign-like responsibility in four territories: Bosnia, Eastern Slavonia, East Timor and Kosovo. Before this, the exercise of international support to formerly war-torn territories had been limited to the UN's trusteeship system, the provision of assistance to interim governments (ONUSAL), formal partnerships with retreating occupiers (UNTAG), and the exercise of limited control over belligerent parties, including the host government which remained sovereign (UNTAC) (Chopra and Hohe 2004b: 242). The four transitional administrations were distinct, however, in that they temporarily assumed sovereign-like authority over the territory in question. The regulations governing the UN Mission in Kosovo (UNMIK), for instance, granted the Special Representative 'all legislative and executive authority with respect to Kosovo, including the administration of the judiciary' (UNMIK/REG/1001, section 1, 25 July 1999). Likewise, the UN's High Representative in Bosnia was empowered to promulgate laws, appoint

and dismiss government officials, and remove elected representatives irrespective of their seniority if he or she judged them to be violating the Dayton
Peace Accord or jeopardizing its implementation. Several other peace operations, such as MINUSTAH (Haiti), UNMIL (Liberia) and MONUC (DRC), share
many of these characteristics but lack the element of sovereign-like
authority.

In the late 1990s, transitional administrations appeared to be the logical
next step in the UN's attempts to stabilize war-torn societies. From today's
vantage point, however, it is becoming increasingly clear that this model is
likely to be used only in exceptional circumstances. Three of the four administrations were part of the world's response to the dissolution of Yugoslavia
and the fourth, in East Timor, was conducted in a context of near unanimity
in international society about the territory's status and future direction.
What is more, as Richard Caplan (2005) points out, these four cases shared
some striking contextual similarities: all were geographically small territories and in each case the former ruler's claim to authority had either entirely
collapsed or was subject to serious challenge. In addition, all four administrations were in areas thought strategically important by Western states and
the missions were led, endorsed and financially supported by Westerners.
These reasons give some indication as to why these four territories were the
focus of so much effort and attention while other areas equally (or more)
in need of transitional administration – most notably Somalia – have been
overlooked.

There is little consensus about how transitional administrations should go
about their business. Since the end of the Cold War, international attempts
to administer war-torn territories have been guided by the interrelated concepts of peacebuilding (Barnett et al. 2007), nation-building (Fukuyama 2005)
and state-building (Paris and Sisk 2008). To summarize crudely some of the
key distinctions between these concepts, peacebuilding is usually understood
as being activities undertaken (often but not exclusively by foreign personnel)
to encourage stable, self-sustaining peace; state-building is best thought of as
activities undertaken to construct the institutional foundations and infrastructure necessary for the effective governance of a particular territory;
while nation-building refers to the more explicitly normative and ideological
attempts to construct a group of people who adhere to a particular national
identity. These activities raise many fundamental moral and practical questions about the ethics of outsiders governing insiders; the type of states to be
built and what road maps should guide the process; and how to build new
states without adequate resources, especially given that the enterprise is
likely to be managed by actors which have 'attention deficit disorder' when
it comes to such projects (Chesterman 2004: 253).

Even if we take peacebuilding as the guiding philosophy behind transitional administrations, we find a range of different perspectives about its
scope and nature (see box 11.1). These different perspectives partly influence

Box 11.1 Competing definitions of peacebuilding

The practical implementation of social change through socio-economic reconstruction and development. (Galtung 1975: 282)

Peacebuilding should be concerned with changing the belligerent and antagonistic attitudes that foster violent conflict at the grassroots level. (Ryan 1990: 50)

Peacebuilding is action to identify and support structures which will tend to strengthen and solidify peace in order to avoid a relapse into conflict. (Boutros-Ghali 1992: § 21)

Peacebuilding underpins the work of peacemaking and peacekeeping by addressing structural issues and long-term relationships between conflictants...peacebuilding aims to overcome the contradictions which lie at the root of the conflict. (Miall et al. 1999: 22)

Peacebuilding can be defined as a policy of external international help for developing countries designed to support indigenous social, cultural and economic development and self-resilience, by aiding recovery from war and reducing or eliminating recourse to future violence. (Pugh 1995: 328)

'...activities undertaken' on the far side of conflict to reassemble the foundations of peace and provide the tools for building on those foundations something that is more than just the absence of war. Thus, peace-building includes but is not limited to reintegrating former combatants into civilian society, strengthening the rule of law (for example, through training and restructuring of local police, and judicial and penal reform); improving respect for human rights through the monitoring, education and investigation of past and existing abuses; providing technical assistance for democratic development (including electoral assistance and support for free media); and promoting conflict resolution and reconciliation techniques. (UN 2000: § 13)

contending ideas about the most legitimate and effective ways of overseeing the transition from war to peace. In the remainder of this section we examine different ways of understanding peacebuilding, identify four central concerns, and then review the contemporary debate about the most legitimate and effective approaches.

Although each of the definitions in box 11.1 emphasizes different issues, there are certain important aspects on which they agree and which are important for understanding the purpose of the UN's transitional administrations.

First, like assisting transition operations, transitional administrations take place after an armed conflict has officially ended and a political settlement has been reached. However, whereas the former are usually products of agreements freely entered into by the parties, transitional administrations have tended to follow international enforcement actions/operations, and the final settlement may be drafted by external actors rather than by the actual parties to the conflict. The transitional administration in Bosnia was based on the

Dayton Peace Agreement, which was written by American diplomats and preceded by NATO military operations against the Bosnian Serbs (Operation Deliberate Force). The transitional administration in Kosovo was based on a military-technical agreement written by NATO and imposed on Yugoslavia through the use of force and UN Security Council Resolution 1244. Similarly, in East Timor, the nature of the political settlement (independence following a period of internationally managed transition) was dictated and enforced by the Security Council.

Second, actors engaged in transitional administrations are concerned with identifying and tackling the root causes of armed conflict at all levels, from the local to the national (Galtung 1975; Lederach 1995). This recognizes the important point that the causes of conflict are often structural rather than simply the product of immediate political disputes or roguish politicians. It is not enough, therefore, for transitional administrations to create a space for conflict resolution. They must also establish the institutional capacities, legitimate processes and locally owned cultures necessary to ensure the peaceful resolution of disputes in the long term (see Albert 2000: 177–9).

There are many broad schools of thought about the most appropriate way of building stable peace within transitional administrations (see table 11.1). The first may be described as the 'New York orthodoxy'. This suggests that the best way to build peace is by emphasizing processes of economic liberalization and rapid democratization. Economic liberalization involves measures, such as low taxes and tariffs and small government involvement in the economy, that are designed to stimulate economic growth. Rapid democratization involves the holding of early elections. This approach was adopted most obviously by the transitional administration in Bosnia (discussed in the next section).

TABLE 11.1 Contending approaches to transitional administrations

Approach	Key ideas
New York orthodoxy	International agencies should foster rapid economic growth through market economies and the rapid democratization of the political system.
Neocolonial critique	Transitional administrations are new forms of colonialism that rule without the consent of the governed.
Institutionalization before liberalization/state-building	International actors should focus on building the institutions of state before progressing to liberalization and democratization.
Republican peacebuilding	International actors should foster peaceful social dialogue and allow the indigenous population to set their own path.

A second approach emphasizes the need to build robust state institutions before unleashing the forces of marketization and democratization. From this perspective, the chief problem with the way the UN has organized its transitional administrations is that they are not based on a sober assessment of what works best in post-war settings. This view is premised on the belief that the fragility all too evident in many post-conflict operations is caused by problematic neoliberal assumptions about democratization and economic liberalization which actually impede efforts to develop government capacity and foster political reconciliation. As a result, evidence suggests that, while there is some move towards democracy in the short term, this is often followed in subsequent years by backsliding towards autocracy on account of a failure to instil democratic cultures and institutions (Fortna 2008a: 71).

To a greater or lesser extent, each of the UN's transitional administrations was premised on the 'New York orthodoxy' thesis – the idea that neoliberal polities and societies are more stable and peaceful than the alternatives. They attempted to foster liberal peace by moving rapidly to establish democratic government and marketize the economy. According to Roland Paris, however, the rush to hold early elections before national reconciliation, institution-building and the development of civil society can have two 'destabilizing effects' (2004: 235). First, the 'winner takes all' mentality fostered by elections encourages political intimidation, extortion, cheating and conflict – none of which is conducive to peacebuilding. Second, as political parties are typically organized on ethnic lines, elections can entrench social divisions. Where parties are led by ethnically based elites, elections can also lend the veneer of democratic legitimacy to the nationalist or patrimonial politics that helped cause the war in the first place.

Likewise, economic liberalization places a premium on competition (the essence of capitalism), which can exacerbate rivalries. Neoliberalism's insistence on 'small government' can involve the withdrawal of already weak states from the provision of basic services and infrastructure, reducing indigenously driven human development, increasing aid dependency and undermining the state's domestic legitimacy. In addition, attempts to privatize industries without the requisite institutional capacity to regulate complex financial transactions leads to 'crony capitalism', whereby ownership is corruptly transferred, often in return for political favours. Rather than dampening conflict, Paris argues, these policies exacerbate it and fundamentally weaken the host state's capacity to govern. The most vivid example of this was the near collapse of Timor-Leste's government in early 2006. Here a weak state was unable to maintain order in the face of unrest caused by a combination of political intrigue and economic inequality (see below). But there is also evidence of these factors at work in Bosnia and Kosovo, especially in the economic sector.

In response, state-builders such as Paris argue that the task of rebuilding after war should begin with the construction of institutions, infrastructure and human capacity. Specifically, Paris calls for an approach based on 'institutionalization before liberalization' (IBL), whereby the competitive forces of elections and market economies are released only when the state and society have the capacity to manage and regulate competition peacefully and mitigate its worst effects.

Paris's strategy stems from the recognition that during the transition towards market democracy war-torn states are susceptible to five 'pathologies': the problem of 'bad' (non-liberal) groups within civil society; the opportunistic behaviour of 'ethnic entrepreneurs' who garner political support by exploiting inter-communal distrust; the risk that elections may serve as focal points for destructive societal competition; the danger posed by local saboteurs, who may win power democratically but then sabotage the transition to democracy to perpetuate their own rule; and the disruptive and conflict-inducing effects of economic liberalization (2004: 159–68). The IBL strategy is 'designed to anticipate and avert' these pathologies by, among other things, postponing elections until moderate political parties have been established and mechanisms are in place to ensure compliance with election results; designing electoral rules that reward moderation rather than extremism; encouraging non-violent and inter-communal civic associations; regulating incendiary 'hate speech'; promoting economic reforms that moderate rather than exacerbate societal tensions; and developing effective security institutions and a professional, neutral bureaucracy (ibid.: 187–207). Paris envisages his IBL strategy taking at least five years, and probably much longer (see box 11.2).

If anything, this approach would involve an even deeper level of engagement with post-war societies than that already embarked upon by transitional administrations. As Paris notes, peacebuilders have traditionally been reluctant to interfere in local media (except in Kosovo, where a uniform code of conduct was imposed), have tended to steer clear of meddling in the affairs of political parties, and have expressed concerns that delayed elections could create democratic deficits. Nonetheless, the IBL position has been endorsed in many quarters. Simon Chesterman (2004: 12), for instance, argued that his primary concern 'is not that transitional administration is colonial in character' but 'that sometimes it is not colonial enough'. Likewise, Richard Caplan concluded that some transitional administrations precipitately downsized their engagement, leaving significant gaps in state capacity. This analysis proved highly prescient. Writing in 2004–5, Caplan (2005: 218) identified especially serious gaps in the East Timorese government's capacity to maintain law and order – gaps brought about by the UN's sudden withdrawal. Caplan was proved correct in 2006, when the country descended into anarchy and was rescued only by foreign intervention (ICG 2006; see below). But there is also an obvious problem with this perspective, evoked by Chesterman's reference to 'colonialism'.

Box 11.2 Institutionalization before liberalization: six priorities

1 *Delay elections until conditions are ripe*: elections are likely to be an effective way of distributing political authority only when they can be conducted in a free and fair manner, when they are unlikely to produce violence, and when there are good grounds for believing that the twin principles of majority rule and absolute respect for minority and individual rights that are fundamental to democratic politics are deeply embedded and likely to be adhered to.

2 *Design electoral systems that reward moderation*: peacebuilders should create constitutional arrangements that require candidates for high office to seek support from different factions, thus rewarding political figures who promise to work for more than just their own constituency.

3 *Promote good civil society*: peacebuilders should provide logistical and financial support to those associations that cross factional boundaries. At the same time, they should be prepared to 'shut down' those civil society associations that promote hatred and intolerance.

4 *Control hate speech*: although free speech is a bastion of democracy, an entirely free press in the immediate aftermath of war can lead to the proliferation of factional outlets and the dissemination of hate speech. Peacebuilders should deal with this by fostering responsible news outlets and acting to 'shut down' hate speech outlets forcibly when they incite violence and genocide.

5 *Adopt conflict-reducing economic strategies*: economic liberalization should be slowed in order to dampen its negative effects (such as corruption, clientalism, state incapacity, etc.) and should contain measures to guard against conflict-causing economic iniquities. These measures may involve economic redistribution, safety-nets for the most disadvantaged, and the provision of education and public health.

6 The common denominator is the need to rebuild effective state institutions: the aforementioned recommendations are all based on the key priority of building effective state bodies (a constitution, police, armed forces, judiciary, parliament, etc.) with effective infrastructure and open political participation.

Source: Paris (2004: 188–207).

A group of critics maintain that the evident problems associated with transitional administrations efforts are caused principally by the external actors themselves. These writers see the echoes of colonialism as the most fundamental difficulty with attempts to build peace through such administrations. From this perspective, the UN has played a quasi-imperial role, imposing political and economic systems without consulting the people who will be most affected. This creates a democratic deficit, only worsened by Paris's suggestion that elections should be delayed until after outsiders have built the institutions of government.

It was for these reasons that Jarat Chopra (2000a) – a former senior UN official in East Timor – accused the UN of setting up its own unaccountable and non-democratic 'kingdom' in the country. Chopra argued that UNTAET's top-down approach excluded the East Timorese themselves from the process of state-building, resulting in international administrators having only superficial impact on the country's institutions and political culture. It was this superficiality – brought about in part by UNTAET's quasi-imperial outlook and in part by its own capacity problems – that sowed the seeds of subsequent state failure, he argued (Chopra 2002: 995). Rather than promoting sustainable democracy and self-government, the UN and other agencies are said to be fostering undemocratic practices, aid dependency and unsustainable polities by imposing ideologies, processes and institutions without reference to the local inhabitants. David Chandler (2001: 87) has taken this argument a step further by suggesting that the agreements which provide transitional administrations with the broad-ranging powers described earlier lack legality and legitimacy; they are also one-sided inasmuch as, while local parties are bound by them, the international agencies charged with implementing them are not. According to Chandler, the ideology underlying transitional administrations is colonial and racist because it implies that certain groups are mere 'helpless victims of governments and the forces of the world market' and therefore unable to determine their own political affairs (also see Chandler 2000, 2006).

One potential way around this set of criticisms is Michael Barnett's (2006) concept of 'republican peacebuilding'. This starts from the premise that state-building projects confront 'a dual crisis of security and legitimacy' (2006: 92). This is most likely to be overcome, Barnett argues, if insiders and outsiders can agree on procedural rules and principles to underpin the decision-making process. Consequently, state-builders should not automatically set a course for market democracy and figure out how to overcome the challenges in the way. Rather they should focus on earning the respect and trust of the local population by gaining 'societal agreement regarding the proper procedures for deciding and pursuing collectively acceptable goals' (ibid.: 93). For Barnett, republicanism's emphasis on deliberation, constitutionalism and representation makes it the best package of principles currently available to meet this objective (box 11.3).

Building versatile republics would thus seem a better way to achieve stable peace than pushing the liberal vision of market democracy upon local

---

Box 11.3 Michael Barnett on republican peacebuilding

Unlike liberal peacebuilding, which uses shock therapy to push postconflict states toward some predetermined vision of the promised land, republicanism's emphasis on deliberative processes allows space for societal actors to determine for themselves what the good life is and how to achieve it. It is incremental. Unlike liberal peacebuilding, which has the vices of all grand social-engineering experiments, republicanism's emphasis on basic design principles and deliberative processes provides the shell for improvisation and learning informed by experience. Finally, republican peacebuilding offers principles not only for building states after war but also for conducting peacebuilding operations. The concern with arbitrary power extends beyond the postconflict state; it also includes the exercise of power by peacebuilders. (Barnett 2006: 90–1)

societies that may not want to be transformed in this manner. In more practical terms, Barnett argues that, despite its limitations, the 'light footprint' approach in Afghanistan was far more preferable than the coalition provisional authority model adopted in Iraq.

Naturally, Barnett's republicanism invests significant faith in the power of deliberation and constitutionalism to overcome differences of interests among competing factions. But, as the cases of Bosnia and Kosovo attest, lengthy deliberation may not significantly alter group interests (see below). At this point, it is not entirely clear how a republican strategy to provide the security and order within which serious deliberation could take place would differ greatly from the orthodox approach. Similarly, Barnett's approach may underestimate the extent to which global forces are pushing newly (re-) created states to become market democracies. If, for example, a new government wants debt relief or loans from the international financial institutions, or to join the World Trade Organization, it is difficult to see how it can resist for long the pressure to liberalize. While the major actors engaged in state-building are market democracies, it would require them to engage in probably unrealistic levels of other-regarding behaviour to allow the states they help build to develop in ways that are incompatible with their own ideals.

There is also the difficult question of effectiveness posed earlier by Chopra. As Barnett's republican peacebuilding makes clear, reform processes are most effective when they are legitimate and 'owned' by the subjects of reform themselves. If government is to be effective and sustainable, it has to be legitimate. Legitimacy in this context refers to the extent to which the political leadership, state institutions and rule of law enjoy the consent and support of the wider domestic population (Chesterman et al. 2005: 364). There are two key components of this kind of legitimacy. First, legitimacy is fostered by the creation and development of institutions that 'fit' the wider community's preferences. Institutions, laws and other political processes have to be organic to the community rather than imposed by outsiders. In relation to the rule of law, this creates potential difficulties for transitional administrations when local institutions and practices fall short of international human rights standards, for example, or when traditional forms of justice exist alongside the formal system – as in East Timor. In the East Timor case, international agencies attempted to bridge the divide by creating a panel of experts comprised of East Timorese and international legal experts charged with developing a new legal code. The panel developed a code that combined international human rights standards with elements of Indonesian law that had prevailed in East Timor before 1999. The state authorities also permitted the continuation of traditional forms of justice for certain crimes, including the use of village-based forgiveness rituals instead of war crimes trials for some militia members.

In relation to the creation of political institutions, this approach – which has been used in part in Afghanistan and Iraq – follows the path set out by

Barnett and focuses on creating a mechanism by which local elites themselves design the political system. In Afghanistan this was done in a non-democratic fashion through a council of tribal elders – the *loya jirga*. In Iraq, the US-led coalition attempted to democratize the process by holding early elections to determine who would play a role in constitution-writing. As it turned out, the Iraq model left the process open to political factionalism and created an opportunity for radicals and spoilers to shape the structure of government and chronically delay progress.

The other key element is 'ownership'. The ownership principle holds that the local population must be directly connected to peacebuilding and that power-sharing is most likely to succeed when driven by indigenous actors (Sisk 1996: 118). The local population should be engaged in decision-making as far as possible and should be informed and consulted about the direction of the whole process. Where decisions are made by external actors, it is important that those decisions are understood to be in the best interests of the local population and clearly connected to the achievement of the final outcome. Decentralization – something akin to the EU principle of subsidiarity, whereby decisions should be taken as close as possible to those who will be most affected by them – is often considered a good way to encourage local ownership. Of course, as Chesterman, Ignatieff and Thakur (2005: 364) point out, the urge to decentralize has to be balanced against the necessity of building strong, stable and sustainable institutions in the centre and the need to foster national unity. After all, decentralization can open the door to fragmentation, as in Bosnia.

There is clearly no easy answer to the question of how best to design transitional administrations. While there is broad agreement that indigenous capacities must be built and that legitimacy and ownership are key components, there is much less agreement about how international agencies should go about doing this. In some respects there is a payoff between short-term effectiveness and legitimacy and ownership – the more local ownership is granted the more reflective of local politics the peace process is likely to be. This can be both a strength and a curse: a strength because local ownership helps ensure that the new institutions and processes reflect the values and concerns of the host population; a curse because it exposes the transitional administration to manipulation by some of the very actors that caused and profited from conflict in the first place and risks entrenching atavistic forces and legitimizing disruptive actors.

What might be referred to as the orthodox approach after the Cold War has followed a sectoral, sequential and liberal blueprint. In short, state-building mandates have been organized around different sectors of activity with the goal of building market democracies – that is, states with a liberal democratic polity and market-oriented economy. While the exact number of sectors often differs from mission to mission, a common framework is set out in box 11.4.

Box 11.4 Transitional administrations: key sectors

- *Military*: end armed conflict and disarm, demobilize and reintegrate combatants who have no place in the reformed armed forces.
- *Legal*: establish or reconstitute a system of criminal justice based on the rule of law, complete with police, courts and prisons.
- *Governance*: design systems that establish who rules and under what conditions and increase the 'efficiency, effectiveness and responsiveness of government per-formance' (Grindle 1997: 5).
- *Economic*: provide and enable local institutions to sustain essential services and employment and foster economic growth.
- *Social*: reassure minorities, promote human rights and support the education, infor-mation and communication systems.

The process is often considered to be sequential inasmuch as it is assumed that little progress can be made in the other sectors until military security is provided (see Marten 2004). In terms of funds and personnel, it is usually the military sector that accounts for by far the largest proportion. This orthodoxy has been the subject of much discussion, not least because of the inherent tensions of state-building. As Chesterman (2004: 239) argued, transitional administrations are plagued by problems of inconsistency, inadequacy and irrelevance which challenge 'the very idea of creating a legitimate and sus-tainable state through a period of benevolent autocracy: the means are incon-sistent with the ends, they are frequently inadequate for those ends, and in many situations the means are irrelevant to the ends'. In addition, it is very difficult to know when indigenous institutions are capable of functioning unaided (see Jackson 2000: 300–1). Delaying the full transfer of authority risks the appearance of neocolonialism, whereas transferring authority too quickly risks leaving behind structures that are incapable of surviving political crises. The following section addresses these issues in more detail by examining two of the most significant transitional administrations, in Kosovo and East Timor.

11.2 Transitional administrations in practice

Kosovo (1999–present)

Roland Paris (2004: 212) has argued that the transitional administrations in Kosovo and East Timor were more informed by the logic of IBL than their predecessor in Bosnia (analysed on the companion website), evidenced by the more gradual democratization and liberalization process and greater empha-sis on institution-building. For example, whereas national elections were held nine months into the transitional administration in Bosnia, Kosovo had to wait twenty-nine months and East Timor twenty-two months (Caplan 2005: 125). However, institution-building and national reconciliation in Kosovo

Map 11.1 *UNMIK in Kosovo*

have been impeded by uncertainty over its final status and economic reconstruction has taken a decidedly neoliberal form.

The dissolution of Yugoslavia began in Kosovo. Kosovo has historic attach-
ments to Serbia, but around 90 per cent of the province's inhabitants are
Albanian. Under Yugoslavia's 1974 constitution Kosovo enjoyed a degree of
autonomy, which attracted a backlash among Serb nationalists that cata-
pulted Slobodan Milošević to power in Belgrade. In the late 1980s, Kosovan
autonomy was stripped back and political power was vested in the Serb
minority. Albanian schools were closed, Albanian public workers lost their

jobs, and order was maintained by police brutality. This sparked a non-violent resistance movement that created a parallel Kosovo Albanian state. However, the non-violent movement failed to attract international attention, and a combination of factors, including Kosovo's exclusion from the Dayton Peace Accords and the 1997 collapse of Albania itself, which permitted the flow of arms into Kosovo, facilitated an armed rebellion spearheaded by the Kosovo Liberation Army (KLA) in 1998. The Serb authorities responded with a wave of ethnic cleansing that left up to 10,000 Kosovo Albanians dead. In early 1999, NATO intervened and launched a bombing campaign that forced Serbia to withdraw its forces from Kosovo and permit the creation of a transitional administration overseen by the UN and supported by a large NATO-led peace support operation (KFOR) (see Vickers 1998; Judah 2000).

Whereas the transitional administration in Bosnia was mandated with the agreement of the parties, UNMIK was imposed upon Kosovo by the UN Security Council following an enforcement operation conducted by NATO. Security Council Resolution 1244 (1999) set out a broad mandate covering the NATO-led peace support operation (KFOR) and the transitional administration (see box 11.5).

As in Bosnia, the transitional administration was divided into four pillars:

- Pillar I: civil administration (UN);
- Pillar II: humanitarian assistance (UNHCR);
- Pillar III: institution-building (OSCE);
- Pillar IV: economic reconstruction (EU).

Box 11.5 Security Council Resolution 1244 and the transitional administration in Kosovo

The UN shall 'establish an international civil presence in Kosovo in order to provide an interim administration for Kosovo under which the people of Kosovo can enjoy substantial autonomy from the Federal Republic of Yugoslavia, and which will provide transitional administration while establishing and overseeing the development of provisional democratic self-governing institutions to ensure conditions for a peaceful and normal life for all inhabitants of Kosovo'. The transitional administration was tasked with:

- supporting the distribution of humanitarian aid;
- supporting the reconstruction of infrastructure;
- protecting human rights;
- maintaining law and order in association with peacekeepers;
- performing civil administration;
- developing democratic institutions;
- assuring the return of refugees and displaced persons.

It was also granted 'full authority over all aspects of civil administration'.

Source: Søbjerg (2006: 65).

A fifth pillar, security, was provided by the NATO-led (later EU-led) peace support operation (KFOR), which sat outside the transitional administration. With the return of most refugees and displaced persons in 2000, the humanitarian pillar was replaced by a UN-led security and justice pillar focused on instituting the rule of law and security sector reform (Søbjerg 2006: 66; Baskin 2006: 78).

The overall strategy set out in Resolution 1244 identified five phases of operation, beginning with the creation and establishment of the transitional administration itself, the gradual transfer of administration to Kosovars and preparation for elections, the actual holding of elections, the establishment of a new government and provisional administration, and the full transfer of the transitional administration to a new permanent civil administration (Søbjerg 2006: 68). In his mission guidance, the UN Secretary-General elaborated on this mandate and tasked the mission with establishing multi-ethnic government institutions, the application of international instruments on human rights, pluralistic party structures, administrative procedures of democratic governance, and a viable market-based economy (Fox 2008: 94). The mission completed the first three phases by 2001 and was then stalled in the fourth phase by deep disagreements in international society about Kosovo's final status.

The major strategic concern for the transitional administration was that the UN had willingly engaged in creating a transitional administration without a clear political vision of Kosovo's future status (see Chesterman 2002: 47). Serbia and its Russian ally insisted that the province should remain a part of Serbia and should be reintegrated. Kosovo's Albanian majority insisted that it must become an independent state, and many Western governments believed that this was the only realistic way of securing lasting peace in the region. In the administration's initial months the ambiguity this created did not pose too much of a problem, because after the Serbian withdrawal Kosovo lacked even the most basic institutions of governance. UNMIK's primary challenge at this stage was to establish basic institutions that made use of the human resources employed by the 'shadow state' built by the Kosovar Albanians in the 1990s – replete with a taxation system, law enforcement, and education and health services (Clark 2000) – and the institutional resources of the discredited Serbian state in Kosovo.

While the absence of a clear political vision for Kosovo may have assisted the UN's activities initially by creating a degree of exploitable ambiguity, the lack of clarity soon began to jeopardize the mission (IICK 2000: 262). In particular, it constrained efforts to build government institutions and local capacity by limiting the degree of authority that could be transferred to Kosovo's elected representatives (Yannis 2004: 76). The fate of the Kosovo Protection Corps (KPC) provides one good example of how uncertainty about Kosovo's final status complicated the transitional administration's work. Formed largely from KLA personnel, the KPC was seen by many Kosovar

Albanians and some NATO states as a future armed force for an independent Kosovo, which with NATO training and democratic control could become an important bulwark of democracy and stability – as has happened throughout the rest of Central Europe (see Cottey et al. 2002). However, in the administration's first years, NATO was unable to lead such training because only states can have legitimate armed forces, and there was no agreement within international society about whether Kosovo would become a state or not. Thus, the KPC remained lightly armed, poorly funded and lacking a specific role in the peacebuilding process. Not surprisingly, it became a magnet for organized crime and was at times associated with Albanian radicalism.

At the outset, the administration simply rejected Kosovar Albanian demands for independence (see Fox 2008: 86). But as the demand was repeated, and as it became clear to many that independence was the only realistic exit strategy, more international actors began to embrace this option despite ongoing resistance from Serbia and Russia. In 2003, the Security Council adopted a Constitutional Framework that set out a policy referred to as 'standards before status' – the idea that Kosovo's civil administration should reach certain benchmarks in relation to human rights, democratization, bureaucratic efficiency and the rule of law. Unofficially, this approach held that Kosovo had to achieve 'political maturity' before the question of independence or reintegration could be addressed (Chesterman 2001: 6). However, it was unclear how its progress towards these benchmarks would be monitored, who would be authorized to declare the province in compliance, and whether compliance would result in Yugoslavia and Russia dropping their opposition to independence (Søbjerg 2006: 69–70). In December 2003 the UN's framework was distilled into a set of 'Standards for Kosovo', which involved developing a multi-ethnic and democratic polity with European levels of economic development. This was followed by an implementation plan which set out which institutions were responsible for which areas, as well as identifying appropriate timeframes and supporting actors (ibid.). To supporters of independence this constituted a clear pathway to recognition, but opponents continued to resist this interpretation. In 2005 the Security Council issued a statement calling for negotiations on Kosovo's final status, claiming (not altogether convincingly) that the province had made good progress towards achieving the goals set out in the implementation plan (Knudsen 2006: 167, n.26).

Those negotiations stalled in 2006 as both sides refused to compromise, and in 2007 the UN Secretary-General's Special Envoy for Kosovo, Martti Ahtisaari, proposed a pathway to 'conditional independence' which involved a phased transition to full independence based on the achievement of key goals – especially the protection of Kosovo's multi-ethnic character. The process would be overseen by an International Civilian Representative, similar to the High Representative in Bosnia, with powers to annul laws and remove officials (Fox 2008: 95–7). Throughout the negotiations, Serbia continued to oppose independence, while Russia and China in particular prevented the Security Council from reaching a consensus on the matter by insisting that any solution to the Kosovo agreement should be achieved with the consent of both parties (Kosovo and Serbia). When the talks collapsed, the US indicated its willingness unilaterally to recognize Kosovo as an independent state. On 17 February 2008, Kosovo's president, Hashim Thaci, declared independence, and the US and many EU states recognized the new state's sovereignty, despite strong opposition from Serbia and Russia. The unilateral declaration significantly heightened tensions in the region, and the Serbian government pledged to do all it could short of the use of force to undermine Kosovo's independence (see Weller 2008).

Kosovo did not face the same challenges as Bosnia in relation to elections, though the transitional administration has found it difficult to encourage Kosovo's Serb population to participate in the election process, making it difficult to realize the establishment of a multi-ethnic polity. There have also been instances of voter intimidation and violent attacks on journalists, particularly those critical of hardline Albanian nationalists. Nevertheless, the political wing of the KLA was transformed into a legitimate political party and faced competition from the Democratic League of Kosovo (LDK), which had spearheaded the non-violent resistance of the 1990s. Indeed, the LDK won the presidency in the province's first two elections (Baskin 2006: 79). It was evident that UNMIK had learned important lessons from the Bosnian experience with elections. Rather than being seen as measures of success in themselves, elections were viewed as one part of a much wider process. In Kosovo, elections were delayed and important distinctions were made between local, regional and national level elections (ICG 2000). Furthermore, although all parties were obliged to adhere to strict rules about appropriate democratic conduct, the electoral system remained relatively simple, increasing the transparency and legitimacy of the process.

The two most problematic areas in Kosovo have been economic reconstruction and political reconciliation. Several years into the transitional administration, Kosovo's economy remains heavily dependent on remittances and official transfers and a significant portion of the workforce are employed by international organizations and NGOs (Baskin 2006: 84). Unemployment, a key indicator of economic development, remains at over 50 per cent. This economic malaise has helped feed a burgeoning organized crime sector which further undermines the economy, as well as challenging progress on the rule of law and national reconciliation by encouraging corruption and violence (see Pugh 2006: 119–21).

The economic reconstruction programme is managed primarily by the EU's Stability Pact, concluded in June 1999 between the EU and several Balkan states, including Bosnia. Noting the reciprocal relationship between sustainable peace, 'good neighbourly relations' and economic reconstruction, the pact's solution was to create 'vibrant market economies based on sound macro policies' that were 'open to greatly expanded foreign trade and private sector investment' and which included the promotion of privatization (§ 10). More specifically, the pact's largest benefactor, Germany (which has donated around $500 million), identified nine key goals, among them anti-corruption measures and the promotion of free media. Only one of these objectives related to creating a market economy and 'promoting economic prosperity' (German Government 2002). Indeed, it appears to some commentators that the EU's strategy for economic reconstruction rests on the assumption that creating institutions and a culture conducive to free trade will suffice (Gligorov 2000: 2).

This raises several problems for the economic reconstruction element of the transitional administration in Kosovo. First, while freer trade would promote cooperation between the UN administrations in Bosnia and Kosovo and their former adversaries, the Stability Pact does not address the structural weakness of Balkan economies, including, most urgently, 'macro-economic imbalances, feeble capital inflows and an inability to create prerequisites for growth on a sustained basis' (Daianu and Veremis 2001: 9). Second, adhering to neoliberal economic principles may further weaken an already fragile state. Third, rather than stamping out corruption, privatization can contribute to the creation of 'crony capitalism', where industries are sold to political allies and bought with proceeds accrued from war or criminal activities (see Le Billon 2008). Finally, in contrast to its stated objective of promoting economic efficiency and independence, the reconstruction programme has encouraged an unhealthy culture of dependency on foreign aid (Kekic 2001).

The second key problem for UNMIK has been fostering political reconciliation. In the immediate aftermath of NATO's 1999 intervention, thousands of Serbs fled north to Serbia and there were numerous attacks on Serb civilians by Kosovar Albanian radicals associated with the KLA. Since 1999 there have also been sporadic attacks on Serb Orthodox churches. KFOR's inability to prevent these attacks resulted in a de facto ethnic partition of Kosovo, with the majority of Kosovo's Serbs living in Mitrovica or in heavily guarded enclaves. The Serb part of Mitrovica itself was infiltrated by Serb militia leaders and organized criminals. Ethnic tensions have erupted into violence on occasion, most notably in 2004, when rumours that a group of Serbs had caused the deaths of three Kosovar Albanian boys in Mitrovica led to an outburst of rioting and armed fighting that left nineteen civilians dead and UN property destroyed (Søbjerg 2006: 67). Although power-sharing was a critical component of Resolution 1244, the Secretary-General's directive and the implementation plan, in practice the inclusion of Serbs in government institutions has been very limited, and Serb parties were not widely consulted prior to the release of the implementation plan or the Ahtisaari plan (Jarstad 2008: 127).

At the time of writing, it is too early to tell whether the declaration and partial recognition of independence will destabilize Kosovo or whether it will provide the political pathway that the transitional administration has long needed. Uncertainty about Kosovo's final status inhibited efforts to build institutions and revive the economy. It also made political reconciliation difficult because the uncertainty encouraged both parties to hold onto their diametrically opposed positions. Despite sporadic outbursts of violence, on the whole the transitional administration has succeeded in laying the groundwork for a more stable peace, though huge challenges remain. Not least, Kosovo's economic malaise demonstrates some of the problems with the neoliberal, marketization approach, whereby a reliance on private investment has failed to deliver the opportunities necessary for growth which, in turn, has fostered aid dependency.

East Timor (1999–2002)

In contrast to the situation with Kosovo, there was broad international consensus, including both former ruling powers, Indonesia and Portugal, about East Timor's future status. Shortly after Portugal's withdrawal in 1975, Indonesian forces invaded East Timor. Indonesian sovereignty was recognized by very few states (Australia was one of the handful that did) and East Timorese guerrillas (Falintil) launched a violent rebellion. Over the following twenty years, up to a quarter of East Timor's population died as a result of Indonesian repression and government-induced famine. Under immense international pressure, Indonesia finally consented in 1999 to a UN-supervised referendum on independence. The East Timorese voted for independence by a massive majority, but Indonesian-backed militia unleashed a wave of killing, ethnic cleansing and property destruction. With Indonesian consent, INTERFET was deployed to restore order and hand over to a UN transitional administration (UNTAET) that would supervise East Timor's transition to independence (see Smith and Dee 2003; companion website).

Under Security Council Resolution 1272, UNTAET was mandated to administer East Timor until it became independent and effectively constituted the territory's legal sovereign with international legal personality, exceeding the authority granted the transitional administrations in Bosnia and Kosovo (Chopra 2000b: 36; Caplan 2005: 20). UNTAET divided its work into eight 'ministerial-like' portfolios and administered the territory until East Timor achieved full independence in May 2002 (Fox 2008: 103). At this point the country became known as Timor-Leste.

Despite the relatively benign environment, UNTAET still faced significant challenges. While it had the advantage of being able to draw upon the recent experiences in Bosnia and Kosovo, the mission did not have the luxury of subcontracting significant elements of the process to large and capable organizations such as NATO, the EU and the OSCE. Thus, while UNTAET benefited from the clarity of the expected outcome, the UN faced immense challenges in piecing together the necessary capacities and deploying them rapidly

(Caplan 2005: 24). Once it did get up to speed, the mission's relatively short-term timeframe and an approach that focused on achieving specific measurable objectives meant that too little attention was paid to building institutional capacity and the non-material components of a functioning polity, such as communal trust and national reconciliation (Bull 2008: 189). In 2008, for example, President Ramos Horta suggested that state incapacity resulted primarily from a lack of sufficiently qualified bureaucrats capable of administering the state budget effectively and efficiently (Horta 2008).

In addition, the broad consensus over East Timor's final status created unrealistic expectations about how long it would take to build a functioning state and self-sustaining peace. UNTAET was widely criticized for adopting a timeframe, based on UNMIK's experience, that was widely perceived as being too slow and cautious for East Timor. In addition to being denigrated for not handing over authority to the East Timorese quickly enough, UNTAET was also condemned for not adequately consulting the local population about important decisions and regulations. Critics argued that, despite the existence of significant local expertise, the UN dictated the pace of reform, the nature of the country's constitution, and the creation and implementation of laws (Chopra 2000a; see Chesterman 2002). For instance, although the UN established a National Consultative Council (NCC) in East Timor, local leaders expressed considerable frustration both with the limited powers they could

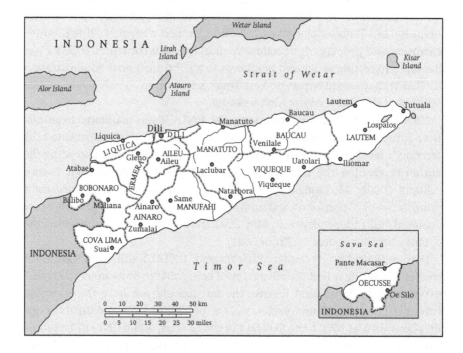

Map 11.2 *Timor-Leste*

exercise themselves and with the unwillingness of international officials to engage in serious consultation (Caplan 2002: 42). In December 2000, East Timorese members of the cabinet threatened to resign over what they saw as UNTAET's failure to share decision-making authority and provide them with adequate resources (Caplan 2005: 116). As Caplan suggests, 'this incident and other expressions of frustration spurred the United Nations to put East Timor independence on a more accelerated path' (ibid.). In response, the NCC was replaced by the National Council, a more powerful and representative body. However, the new council's members were still appointed rather than elected, and ultimate authority for decisions rested with the SRSG, Sergio Vieira de Mello. Three months after the resignation threat, de Mello announced elections to the Constituent Assembly which would pave the way for the creation of a wholly East Timorese cabinet to succeed the transitional cabinet (ibid.: 117).

The transfer of effective authority from the UN to the indigenous administration took place incrementally but with a clear timetable that was linked to the achievement of particular objectives. National elections were not held until August 2001 after a concerted programme of civic education about democracy (Caplan 2005: 123). Although most commentators declared UNTAET's political component a successful example of how international actors can assist processes of transition (Jardine 2000; Maley 2000), others worried that the transition had taken place prematurely and that the new East Timorese state lacked the capacity to resolve disputes and overcome crises (Caplan 2005).

The problems caused by the weakness of the East Timorese state were exacerbated by the weakness of its economy. World Bank and IMF programmes were funded by special voluntary donations to an East Timor Trust Fund, which had limited reconstruction programmes for community-based and micro-enterprise projects. Moreover, the post-independence Falintil government was reluctant to take on additional debts to fund major infrastructure projects because it worried that its debt interest repayments would cripple the fledgling economy in the long term. In the meantime, small-scale reconstruction projects did little to rebuild an economy devastated by nearly thirty years of oppression. Furthermore, some key donor states sometimes appeared more concerned with their own economic interests than with those of the region they were trying to reconstruct. Having led the INTERFET force, Australia strongly encouraged the new East Timor government to grant it revenue from oil and gas in the Timor Straits. Upon independence, Timor-Leste, as Asia's newest and poorest state, was heavily dependent on revenue from these resources.

Concerns that an 'unholy alliance' of East Timorese and leftist activists in the West, who were critical of UNTAET's slowness in transferring authority to indigenous bodies, and Western governments keen to keep their commitments to a minimum had prompted a premature downsizing and withdrawal were proved well-founded in 2006. In February that year about 500 East Timorese soldiers went on strike, demanding better accommodation and complaining that the promotions system was ethnically biased. The government ordered troops back to barracks and, when they refused, sacked them. Sacked soldiers descended on Dili and, with the police unable to maintain order, generalized violence and rioting erupted between rebel and loyal troops and between troops and the police. In the end, thirty-seven people were killed and 150,000 forced from their home before order was restored with the help of rapidly deployed Australian and Portuguese troops and police (ICG 2006). At least 50,000 remained displaced in 2008 (ICG 2008b). The rebel ringleaders were arrested, but later escaped from prison and in 2008 attempted to assassinate President Ramos Horta and Prime Minister Xanana Gusmao.

The near collapse of Timor-Leste in 2006 demonstrated three key points. First, UNTAET had downsized too quickly and had not created a state capable of managing crises and resolving disputes. Second, the transitional administration had not paid enough attention to national reconciliation or invested sufficient energy in helping to create a functioning multi-party democracy. Third, as we noted in chapter 10, it is important to follow up large operations with assistance missions that furnish ongoing support in order to ensure that progress towards stable peace is deeply embedded.

11.3 Conclusion

To what extent has the assumption of sovereign authority by the UN succeeded in laying the foundations for stable peace? Unsurprisingly, many different answers have been offered. What can be said of both missions analysed here is that, at the time of writing, living conditions were significantly better than they were before the missions were deployed. On the downside, however, violence, ethnic tension, economic fragility, and government incapacity remain. Timor-Leste and Kosovo have endured sporadic outbursts of deadly violence. In Kosovo, seventeen people were killed in riots sparked by allegations that Serbs had chased an Albanian boy into a river, where he drowned. Dozens were killed when Timor-Leste descended into anarchy in 2006. Ethnic tensions are evident across all transitional administrations and all are characterized by high unemployment and low economic growth. Of course, some have fared better than others. The transitional operation in Eastern Slavonia (UNTAES) successfully reintegrated the region into Croatia. Moreover, refugee return has been slow but has progressed, the economy has grown, unemployment has fallen and ethnic violence is rare. On the other hand, Timor-Leste's economy has barely grown at all; discontent and economic woes have provoked mutinies, riots and gang violence; and the Timorese police and military forces proved utterly incapable of maintaining order in 2006. Indeed, it is highly likely that the state would have collapsed had it not received rapid international security assistance. Likewise, Bosnia and Kosovo remain fractured societies characterized by economic stagnation. But, despite these problems, there has been no generalized violence, all four territories are now governed by democratic governments, basic human rights are safeguarded, and economies – still poor – are better than they were.

Transitional administrations provoke three important debates. First, there are arguments that relate to the debate between proponents of the Westphalian and post-Westphalian conceptions of peace operations. Transitional administrations are predicated on a post-Westphalian view of the role of peace operations that sees violent conflict primarily as a consequence of 'bad' governance and suggests that the maintenance of international peace and security is strengthened by the proliferation of liberal democratic polities. In support of this position, proponents point to evidence suggesting that conflict is less likely in places with legitimate and effective state institutions and thriving market economies (e.g. Lake 1990). Although these post-Westphalian ideas have been widely accepted and incorporated into the working practices of a range of UN and non-UN operations, as we saw earlier, critics dispute that the UN should be in the business of creating a particular type of state and argue that the liberal democratic model might not be appropriate for communities where traditional modes of governance and economy prevail. They prefer the 'light footprint' approach that guides assisting transition operations (see chapter 10).

The second debate revolves around the question of ownership. We noted earlier that critics argue that transitional administrations are a form of neocolonialism that create democratic deficits (e.g. Chopra 2000a; Chandler 2000, 2006). Comparisons with colonial forms of government are constructed by the exclusion of local actors from decision-making and the imposition of liberal economies. However, transitional administrations have a difficult balancing act to manage. If they delay transitioning to local actors they leave themselves open to the charge of neocolonialism; if they move ahead too quickly with elections (as in Bosnia – see the companion website) or the transfer of political authority (as in East Timor) they risk legitimizing destructive political forces or exposing fragile states to profound dangers without having first helped them build the capacity to manage those dangers.

The third debate revolves around the world's capacity to manage transitional administrations and build effective states out of war-torn societies. There are three important and related issues here. The first concerns the UN's capacity to deliver sufficient technical expertise quickly enough. In Bosnia and Kosovo it was able to subcontract key aspects of the administration to organizations such as the OSCE, the EU and NATO, but that was not possible in East Timor, and the UN struggled to bring together sufficient technical expertise across the whole range of government responsibilities. The second issue pertains to international society's short attention span. Transitional administrations require significant resources over the long term. Although there are too few cases to draw general conclusions, international society's eagerness to downsize the only non-European administration casts doubt on its commitment to building strong and legitimate states. The third issue relates to the unintended consequences of transitional administrations. The influx of thousands of well-paid international professionals can skew local economies, causing inflation, the redirection of scarce local resources towards catering for the internationals, and aid dependency. Combined, these factors can undermine efforts to build local capacity. As we begin to understand these unintended consequences better, so transitional administrations can take action to mitigate their effects, but this typically requires a deeper and longer-term engagement with the host country (see Aoi et al. 2007).

CHAPTER TWELVE

Peace Support Operations

Peace support operations are multifaceted missions that combine a robust military force with a significant civilian component (HMSO 1999). Their aim is to support robustly the transformation of war-torn societies into (usually, but not exclusively, liberal democratic) societies capable of sustaining stable peace. To that end, peace support operations typically involve the deployment of multinational forces, usually (but not exclusively) authorized by the UN Security Council, that have both the means and the mandate to respond effectively to breaches of the peace and other activities associated with 'spoilers' – actors who use violence to undermine peace processes for political, religious or economic reasons (Stedman 1997). The purpose of the military force is not to police buffer zones while the belligerents make peace or to observe and verify peace agreements but rather to provide public security, actively disarm belligerents and help to implement either a peace agreement or the wishes of the UN Security Council.

In practice, because peace support operations are often associated with Western peacekeepers, who are being deployed on UN missions in diminishing numbers, they have typically been used either as a prelude to the creation of a transitional administration intended to establish a functioning (liberal democratic) state (as in East Timor), alongside an ongoing transitional administration (East Timor, Bosnia and Kosovo), or in other operations in which the West is heavily invested (Afghanistan). This involves an extensive expansion of peacekeeping functions to include the maintenance of public order, policing (see chapter 17), capacity-building in the security sector, infrastructure reconstruction, and national reconciliation (see Mackinlay 1998). The development of the concept of peace support operations comprises the merging of ideas developed in assisting transitions, wider peacekeeping and peace enforcement and marks an attempt to overcome the problems of each.

The sources of the peace support operations concept are set out in three important places. The first source is British peacekeeping doctrine (Wilkinson 2000; Woodhouse 1999). According to this doctrine, peace support operations are:

> multi-functional operations involving military forces and diplomatic and humanitarian agencies. They are designed to achieve humanitarian goals or a long-term political settlement and are conducted impartially in support of a UN or OSCE mandate.

These include peacekeeping, peace enforcement, peacemaking, peacebuilding and humanitarian operations. (HMSO 1999: 1.1)

The second source is the *Report of the Panel on United Nations Peace Operations*, the so-called Brahimi Report (see chapter 5). This concluded that 'peace-keepers must be able to carry out their mandate professionally and successfully. This means that United Nations military units must be capable of defending themselves, other mission components, and the mission's mandate' (UN 2000: x). Both documents represent a response to the perceived failings of wider peacekeeping and peace enforcement operations in the 1990s. The third source is the American doctrine on 'support and stability operations' and 'peace operations', although it takes a slightly different approach and uses a different terminology (see Department of the Army 2003; Joint Publication 2007).

This chapter begins by outlining the concept of peace support operations before analysing some of the most important examples, namely, IFOR/SFOR/EUFOR in post-war Bosnia and ISAF in Afghanistan. (The companion website gives additional case studies on KFOR in Kosovo and INTERFET in East Timor.) The final part of the chapter reflects on the problems with peace support operations. These include the danger of constructing a two-tiered system of peacekeeping, the debate about which approach to stable peace (Westphalian or post-Westphalian) peacekeepers should be in the business of pursuing, and practical questions about rapid deployment and the effective coordination of military and civil activities.

12.1 What are peace support operations?

Peace support operations embody a particular approach to three fundamental issues facing peacekeepers: (1) the use of force and its relationship to the principles of consent and impartiality; (2) how to close the gap between mandate and means; and (3) the place of the military component within a broader, civilian-led peace operation. In the rest of this section we focus on these three issues in more detail.

A common conclusion reached by analysts was that the use of force by UNOSOM II in Somalia and UNPROFOR in Bosnia was ineffective because it had not been part of an overall strategic plan (Roberts, A. 1995). Peace enforcement as part of a wider operation is very different to war-fighting in the name of international peace and security. To get around this problem, analysts argued that there was a need to reconceptualize consent as something more malleable than previously acknowledged. This was achieved by rethinking the range of potential military activities within peace operations. Whereas other approaches distinguish sharply between non-coercive and consensual peacekeeping and peace enforcement, the peace support operations concept distinguishes between peace enforcement within a peace operation and war-fighting. This allows the 'Mogadishu line' to be drawn more flexibly, as illustrated in figure 12.1.

In military terms, the peace support operations concept insists that it is possible to use force in a peace operation without losing impartiality. This move is based on the idea that neutrality and impartiality – often conflated in the theory and practice of peace operations – are quite different things. Whereas neutral peacekeepers play no political role whatsoever, refusing to take sides even in the face of breaches of a ceasefire, peace agreement or Security Council resolution, impartial peacekeepers discriminate between belligerents according to their compliance with the terms of the peace operation's mandate and treat like breaches in similar ways (see Donald 2002). In other words, impartiality simply means treating everyone according to the same principles, whereas neutrality means opting not to take a position. Peace support operations rest on the view that it is possible to use force occasionally without undermining a mission's impartiality. Indeed, in the face of serious challenges from spoilers, impartiality might *require* the use of force. In order to retain the appearance of impartiality, though, any use of force must be directed against a specific breach of the mandate or peace agreement, linked to a clearly defined outcome, conducted discriminately and proportionally, and carefully explained to the host population. To achieve this, the military component of a peace operation must be 'robust', as the Brahimi Report insisted. In other words, it must be able to move swiftly

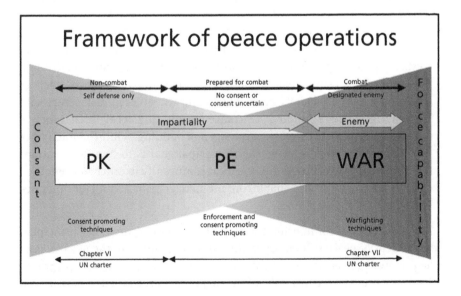

Source: Department of the Army (2003: 4–14).

Figure 12.1 *Consent and impartiality in peace support operations*

where necessary from a traditional peacekeeping posture, based on consent and cooperation, to peace enforcement *and back again*.

Whereas wider peacekeeping conceptualized consent in absolute terms, peace support operations doctrine recognizes that consent is variable, multi-layered and malleable.

- *Variable consent*: the level and nature of consent changes across a mission. Parties which give their consent at the outset may change their minds and vice versa. Parties might also fragment on the question of whether or not to grant consent. Consent may be shallow or deep: shallow consent refers to a situation where actors tolerate a peace operation and do not actively seek either to undermine it or to cooperate proactively; deep consent implies that actors actively cooperate with the peace operation.
- *Multilayered consent*: consent operates at a number of levels. While a faction leader or government may give their consent, it does not always follow that local fighters will do likewise – and vice versa. This is particularly true in cases where the conflict is not between two disciplined armies – as is often the case in 'new wars' – as instructions from political leaders are less likely to be implemented by subordinates.
- *Malleable consent*: peacekeepers can influence the level of consent they enjoy through 'consent management' activities. If we understand consent to be a fluctuating factor, it follows that peacekeepers themselves have an important role to play in promoting and maximizing consent and mitigating the possible loss of consent in cases where the use of force is necessary. Consent management activities aim to strengthen an operation's legitimacy in the eyes of the host population (see Mersiades 2005). Techniques include ensuring that peacekeepers are closely engaged with the local community through activities such as regular foot patrols and establishing 'drop-in centres'; the provision of public information through the radio and print media; conducting 'quick impact projects' such as helping to rebuild schools, places of worship and other infrastructure; and providing capacity-building assistance by training local inhabitants in trades such as electrical work, carpentry and building. While these activities contribute to peacebuilding, their principal goal is to improve relations between the peacekeepers and the local community in order to strengthen and deepen consent and enable consent management in difficult times (see Flint 2001; Lehmann 1999).

In addition to reconfiguring the way we understand these key principles, the concept of peace support operations draws attention to the need to close the perceived gap between mandate and means that plagues many operations. This was a central conclusion of all the major 'lessons learned' reports issued at the turn of the twenty-first century (discussed in chapters 4 and 5). The Brahimi Report recommended that the Security Council change the way it makes decisions but said little about practical strategies for closing the gap between mandate and means in the field. In practice, peacekeepers in peace support operations have developed two, quite different, strategies. The first is carefully to delimit the scope of the mandate, as happened with IFOR and ISAF. An alternative strategy was pursued in Kosovo and East Timor. In these cases, the peacekeepers were given a broad mandate on the understanding that a large and capable force would be deployed, and there was a close link between the 'pivotal actors', which were the primary troop contributors (NATO and Australia), and the construction of the mandate in the Security Council.

The third important innovation of the peace support operations concept is the recognition that the military component is only one element in a broader multi-agency engagement aimed at creating a liberal democratic society. As Kofi Annan put :

> State sovereignty, in its most basic sense, is being redefined by the forces of globalization and international cooperation. The state is now widely understood to be the servant of its people, and not vice versa…[with] renewed consciousness of the right of every individual to control his or her destiny. These parallel developments demand of us a willingness to think anew – about how the United Nations responds to the political, human rights and humanitarian crises affecting so much of the world. (Annan 1999d)

Military tasks in peace operations therefore need to be related to these broader tasks of the mission. SFOR in Bosnia, for instance, played a vital role in providing both security and material assistance, which allowed the civil authorities to run elections (Cousens 2001). Similarly, in East Timor and Kosovo the military took on wider roles beyond the simple provision of physical security. These included maintaining and constructing infrastructure, assisting with institutional capacity-building, and cooperating with others in community projects by providing trucks and manpower. This entails more than simply recognizing that the performance of civilian tasks might help military peacekeepers win and deepen local consent. It also involves recognition of the fact that military peacekeepers play a supporting role to civilian agencies. Ultimately, it is civilian-led activities such as the delivery of humanitarian assistance, institution-building and the establishment of good government, economic reconstruction and national reconciliation that lay the foundations for self-sustaining stable peace. According to the concept of peace support operations, the role of military peacekeepers is to create an environment that is conducive to those activities. This adds an additional layer of complexity because it requires that military commanders consider the effect their actions are likely to have on a wide range of civilian activities, among them those undertaken by humanitarian agencies. For example, peacekeepers that deliver humanitarian relief need to consider whether their actions politicize aid and undermine the appearance of neutrality on which many aid agencies rely for their safety (see Kennedy 2004; Slim 2001a, 2001b). In theory, if not always in practice, the military component of a peace support operation is subordinate to the civilian components.

In summary, peace support operations should be able to close the gulf between means and ends by being robust and proactive in consent management. They are also explicitly concerned with assisting broader political, social and economic transformations (see chapters 10 and 11). As such, the military component is seen as one of several components and not necessarily the most significant, as it was in wider peacekeeping and peace enforcement.

12.2 Peace support in practice

IFOR and SFOR in Bosnia (1995–2004)

IFOR was deployed in the immediate aftermath of the Dayton Peace Agreement concluded at the end of 1995 (see map 8.1, p. 199). The agreement invited IFOR to secure the Inter-Entity Boundary Line between Bosnia's two entities, the Croat–Muslim Federation (formally known as the Federation of Bosnia and Hercegovina) and Republika Srpska; oversee the drawing down of regular military forces and the disbandment of irregular units; supervise the withdrawal of all 'foreign forces', notably forces from Serbia proper and the approximately 2,000 Mujahadeen fighters on the Bosnian government side; and administer a programme of disarmament which included the states of Yugoslavia and Croatia and demanded a 2:1 ratio of arms between the Bosnian government and Republika Srpska. Significantly, IFOR was not specifically mandated to maintain public security, as the parties themselves pledged to maintain a 'safe and secure environment' (Cousens and Harland 2006: 63). Its primary tasks were quite traditional: separate the armed forces, oversee the cantonment of troops and heavy weapons, and stabilize the ceasefire. What made IFOR a peace support operation were its robust composition and rules of engagement, its secondary tasks, among them the protection of civilians and the apprehension of persons indicted for war crimes, and the fact that it sat alongside a civilian-led transitional administration (see ibid.: 69).

The force formed part of a broader UN mission tasked with implementing the Dayton Agreement. As well as issues of military implementation, the international presence under the auspices of the Office of the High Representative (OHR) was mandated to run elections, construct and implement a constitution, develop a system of human rights protection, return refugees to their original homes, and construct and manage public corporations and a judicial system (see chapter 11; Chandler 2000: 44–54). IFOR itself was authorized by the Security Council (Resolution 1031) but commanded by NATO. Initially it consisted of almost 60,000 soldiers, including a large American contingent (approximately 15,000 troops) and an important Russian contingent (around 2,000 troops) that also operated under NATO command (although in practice the Russians exercised considerable autonomy).

Although IFOR had a broad mandate to assist with the implementation of the Dayton Agreement and a robust force with a clear command structure, it imposed limitations on its own role. Specifically, the mission focused almost exclusively on its primary tasks and neglected its secondary tasks, creating what the US general Wesley Clark labelled a 'huge gap in the Bosnia food chain' (in Holbrooke 1998: 252). This agenda was led by the US, which believed that trying to apprehend war criminals, maintain public order, build civilian infrastructure and carry out policing functions would both put peace-keepers' lives at risk and lead to so-called mission creep (Bert 1997: 230; Freedman 1994: 54). In practical terms this meant that, among other things, the OHR was not allowed to use IFOR flights to transport goods and people. Carl Bildt, Bosnia's first High Representative, argued that the US government deliberately obstructed his work, restricted his office's mandate and deprived it of funds (Bildt 1998: 174).

Although IFOR was well equipped and funded, the decision to focus on the primary objectives and neglect the secondary mission created significant problems. First, the various national contingents behaved differently, even those that were part of NATO. At the outset of the operation, the British and French contingents continued to apply the lessons they had learned when they had deployed the rapid reaction force alongside UNPROFOR in 1995 (see chapter 8). This approach combined the use of force in limited and specific ways with more traditional consent-based approaches to peacekeeping (Murray and Gordon 1998). The US contingent, on the other hand, stood out because it either declined to use force at all or, when it did, used a massive amount. In Bildt's words, 'in their mode of operation, there was very little between doing nothing and a massive use of military force'; moreover, 'they were very much concerned with their own security' (1998: 303).

The second major problem was that little progress was made on tackling the nationalists' power base and challenging the sources of violence against civilians. The effects of IFOR's decision not to engage in the maintenance of public order were compounded by the fact that the mission's police compo-nent had neither the mandate nor the capacity (numbering only 350 people) to 'fill the breach' (Cousens and Harland 2006: 91). As a result, only a handful of persons indicted for war crimes were apprehended, and many of them continued to dominate public life (Cousens 2001: 133; Bose 2002). The con-tinuing dominance of the nationalists dissuaded refugees from returning home, and, in perhaps the clearest example of IFOR's failure to address the power of the nationalists and provide public order, the mission failed to prevent the flight of between 60,000 and 100,000 Serbs from Sarajevo at the violent behest of Serb warlords. The Serbs that fled were housed mainly in the former homes of Bosnian Muslims, inhibiting future refugee returns (Cousens 2001: 134; Cousens and Harland 2006: 91). There were even sporadic cases of 'ethnic cleansing' and intimidation. IFOR's lack of positive action at this stage created subsequent problems primarily because the lack of refugee return helped to solidify the boundaries between the Bosnians, Serbs and Croats and the nationalist warlords were able to legitimize themselves through the ballot box. Both these factors became important impediments to the peacebuilding project.

Although the US in particular had insisted that NATO's military presence in Bosnia be restricted to twelve months, by the end of 1996 it was clear that a military withdrawal would in all likelihood undo the fragile peace. Thus, the Security Council replaced IFOR with SFOR, giving it a wider mandate to assist with civilian implementation. Nevertheless the perception remains that IFOR's slow start created problems for SFOR and impacted negatively on the wider mission (McMahon 2002: 22).

Like IFOR, SFOR was initially mandated for a set period (eighteen months) but outlived this timetable primarily because of the widespread beliefs that its tasks had not been completed and that its withdrawal would plunge Bosnia back into civil war. The transition from IFOR to SFOR was accompanied by a significant downsizing of the military force, which was reduced to around 30,000 (and in November 2004 to 7,500) but then augmented with a major expansion of the policing component to include some 1,700 unarmed police monitors. The US contingent was reduced by half and then to a mere 750 by 2001 (ICG 2001: i). SFOR was given a broader civilian role than its predecessor, to encompass a more direct role in the provision of public security, the pursuit and apprehension of persons indicted for war crimes, and the provision of assistance to agencies engaged in the creation of legitimate and democratically controlled indigenous armed forces.

SFOR interpreted its role as involving three key components. First, it aimed to provide support to other implementing agencies and the process of institutional reform. There was little progress towards the creation of a single national army on account of resistance from the country's three military entities (the Bosnian government, Bosnian Croat, Republika Srpska). While the Dayton Agreement gave IFOR/SFOR the authority to supervise the deployment of these armed groups, it did not give them the right to insist on the creation of a national army (Cousens and Harland 2006: 103). In 1997–8 SFOR provided assistance in Bosnia's election process and in 1997 SFOR forces seized a Serbian television station that was undermining the OSCE and UN-led electoral process by transmitting nationalist propaganda (Clark 2001: 102–6). It also began monitoring Republika Srpska's 'special police' units, which were suspected of holding secret arms caches and were widely considered to be de facto nationalist paramilitaries (Cousens and Harland 2006: 103). In addition, SFOR was engaged in efforts to tackle corruption and weaken the power of the nationalists. For example, in March and April 2001, SFOR forces assisted the OHR in its investigation of the Hercegovacka Banka, which was providing illegal funding to Croatian extremists (ICG 2001: 4–5).

Second, SFOR employed a relatively wide definition of public security in interpreting its mandate, to incorporate the provision of security for returning refugees. In 2001 alone, there were over 400 reports of attacks against returning refugees, and SFOR responded by stepping up patrols and supporting civilian-led return efforts (ICG 2001: 6). However, such efforts were not uniform. Russian and Italian peacekeepers, for example, refused to intervene in cases of harassment and violence against returning refugees in Bratunac and Bijeljina. The US responded to this problem by setting up its own military establishment in Bratunac to encourage refugees to return and to provide security to those feeling unprotected by the Russian and Italian contingents (ibid.: 7).

The third key component of SFOR's activities was an increasingly proactive pursuit of people indicted by the ICTY for war crimes, crimes against humanity and genocide. At the outset, IFOR commanders insisted that the NATO-led force did not have the authority to arrest suspects (Vallieres-Roland 2002: 2). However, as it became clear that the relatively open presence of indictees around Bosnia was a destabilizing factor that made it more difficult to remove the nationalist stranglehold over Bosnian politics, NATO insisted that the pursuit of suspects remained a civilian task but that SFOR could act in support of the OHR (Cousens and Harland 2006: 102). Advocates of this policy insisted that long-term peace and stability could only be achieved if war crimes suspects were apprehended. Between 1997 and 2002 SFOR apprehended thirty-nine war crimes suspects, though a series of major operations failed to capture the Bosnian Serb leader Radovan Karadzić and Ratko Mladić (NATO 2002: 127). In 2008, however, Karadzić was arrested by Serbian police in Belgrade.

Although SFOR succeeded in overcoming many of the key problems encountered by IFOR by taking a more proactive role in assisting civilian agencies and providing public security, it was hampered in a number of ways, with the result that, rather than ending with a complete withdrawal, it was obliged to hand over to an EU-force (EUFOR) in December 2004. On the one hand, as noted earlier, different contingents interpreted their civilian roles differently, particularly when it came to issues such as refugee protection and the apprehension of suspected war criminals. On the other hand, IFOR's slow start and lack of strategic vision meant that many problems were left unaddressed, enabling resistance to ideas such as refugee return and the illegitimacy of local paramilitaries to become more deeply embedded in Bosnian society.

In late 2004, a EUFOR force of 6,500 peacekeepers (Operation Althea) took over from SFOR, although NATO retained a headquarters in Sarajevo to continue its work on the creation of a single national army to replace the three entity armies (Cousens and Harland 2006: 111; Kim 2005). EUFOR's principal roles have involved continuing the work of SFOR in contributing to the maintenance of public order, dealing with persons indicted for war crimes, and ensuring compliance with the military aspects of the Dayton Agreement. One area that proved particularly significant was ensuring that the entity armies abide by Dayton's disarmament demands. This involved collating intelligence and inspecting weapons facilities, and in one case entailed EUFOR closing down an underground weapons storage facility in Republika Srpska that it deemed 'not required for civil or military use' (Cousens and Harland 2006: 111).

Despite the fact that the missions in Bosnia enjoyed extraordinary levels of military capability compared to most of the other peace operations studied in this book, progress there has been painfully slow. This was in large part a result of IFOR's decision to focus only on its primary military objectives and not such secondary objectives as the provision of public order and the pursuit of persons indicted for war crimes. Current US thinking about peace support operations holds that there is a short window of opportunity (the 'golden hour') immediately after deployment where rapid progress can be made. There is no doubting that IFOR had the military capacity to effect rapid changes in the areas of disarmament and demobilization, public security and the pursuit of war criminals, but concerns about casualties and potential mission creep pushed the military leadership into a passive posture, leaving these problems to be tackled by SFOR and EUFOR. Moreover, efforts to reform Bosnia's security sector were greatly impaired by the decision not to mandate the phased assimilation of the three entity armies into a single Bosnian army.

Criticism of the peace support operation in Bosnia should be tempered, however, by two considerations. First, IFOR/SFOR and EUFOR successfully implemented the military aspects of the Dayton Accord, prevented a slide back into war, and – by proceeding slowly and incrementally – successfully managed local consent despite engaging in sporadic acts of limited enforcement. Second, in cases where they became involved in actively supporting the High Representative's political goals, NATO and EU peacekeepers attracted criticism for overstepping their mandate and acting in a neocolonial manner (e.g. Knaus and Martin 2003). Such criticisms, when aired by Bosnians themselves, can have a negative impact on consent. Peacekeepers therefore confront a difficult balancing act whereby the requirement for them to support civilian agencies and maintain public order might lead them into conflict with local political actors, and this might, in turn, undermine local consent.

The ISAF in Afghanistan (2001–present)

The ISAF was deployed in late 2001 in the aftermath of the collapse of the Taliban regime as a result of the US-led Operation Enduring Freedom. The idea for such a force was raised in the Bonn Agreement of 5 December 2001, which established the interim Afghan authority led by Hamid Karzai. Its inclusion in the Bonn Agreement was initially resisted by the anti-Taliban 'Northern Alliance', whose forces were in control of Kabul at the end of the war. However, pressure was brought to bear on the alliance and it grudgingly acquiesced (Thier 2006: 541). The ISAF was then authorized by the Security

Council, acting under Chapter VII, in Resolution 1386 of 20 December 2001. It was authorized to assist the interim Afghan authority in the maintenance of security in Kabul and the surrounding area and granted the power to use 'all necessary means' in the execution of its mandate. The British government agreed to take the lead in putting the force together and to command it for a three-month period. After considerably longer than three months, the UK handed over to a Turkish command, which, in turn, handed over to a Dutch–German command in early 2003. Most NATO members were initially reluctant to take on a large and potentially open-ended role in Afghanistan. Thus, although the ISAF was given a robust mandate, its rules of engagement were carefully limited by its commanders. While its troops were entitled to use force to protect themselves and to intervene in active crime situations, they were not to interpose themselves between warring factions or seize and hold territory (ibid.: 543).

In the early stages of the operation, therefore, the most notable feature of ISAF was its limited nature: its area of operations consisted only of the Kabul area, extending at its farthest reach to the Bagram airbase. It also limited its activities. Although Resolution 1386 authorized the force to assist in the maintenance of security in the Kabul area, the British government limited this role to conducting patrols and trying to build local peace and security capacities. Nevertheless, once on the ground the British military did expand

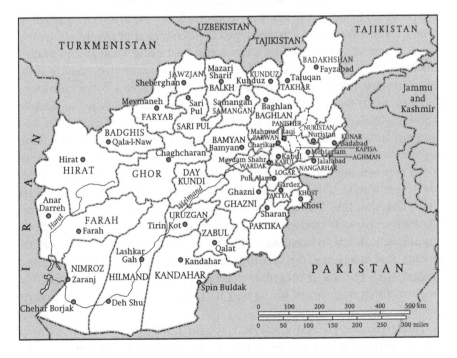

Map 12.1 *Afghanistan*

its role. For example, in response to repeated raids on homes by criminals, British soldiers sealed off the village of Barjay each evening in order to protect the villagers. In addition, the force found itself preventing disruption of the *loya jirga*, the traditional Afghanistan national decision-making process. From the outset, Hamid Karzai, Lakhdar Brahimi, a range of NGOs, and Afghan public opinion called for the expansion and extension of ISAF, but troop contributors were reluctant to heed the calls (Thier 2006: 543). Moreover, the US was adamant that it opposed expansion and would not itself contribute troops, partly because it was worried that the international force could obstruct its ongoing military campaign against the Taliban and their allies, and partly because it did not want to make an open-ended commitment to nation-building in Afghanistan (Hoon 2001; ICG 2002).

In late 2002 the US dropped its opposition to expanding ISAF, and in August 2003 command of the operation was passed to NATO. Two months later the Security Council passed Resolution 1510, which authorized ISAF to operate outside Kabul. This significantly expanded its mandate, asking it to establish a secure environment for peacebuilding in Afghanistan and support the Afghan government. However, despite the widening scope of the mandate, NATO members remained reluctant to commit extra troops. By 2005 the force comprised only 8,200 soldiers – an expansion of only 3,000 despite the massive geographical extension of its mandate.

In order to secure positive effects across the country with such limited resources, ISAF gradually embraced the 'Provincial Reconstruction Teams' (PRTs) model first developed by the Operation Enduring Freedom coalition in 2002–3. The PRTs model was developed by US forces after the initial deployment of specialized civil affairs units. It involved using small groups of civil affairs soldiers (fifty to a hundred), operating from protected bases to fulfil two primary roles: first, through capacity-building and other measures, helping to strengthen the Afghan government and its ability to operate throughout the country; second, removing the root causes of conflict and support for terrorism by assisting in economic reconstruction, the rebuilding of infrastructure, the provision of education, and the fostering of better relations between the Afghan government and local power-brokers (Thier 2006: 497). In late 2003, Germany established a PRT in the Kunduz region, the first to be linked to ISAF. This model was soon extended across Afghanistan, with ISAF's country-wide strategy linked to a network of twenty-five PRTs. These combined military and civilian staff, who assumed responsibility for coordinating and managing the security and reconstruction efforts in a given region. Each PRT was managed by a national contingent, which means that each is different in terms of the way it is structured, its priorities and its activities.

This expansion in ISAF's role was accompanied by an expansion in its size. By early 2008 it numbered 34,000 troops, 14,000 of whom were from the US. This expansion was also necessitated by a marked deterioration of the

Box 12.1 Afghanistan: insurgency resurgent in 2006

- Attacks on Enduring Freedom/ISAF forces increased from 900 in 2005 to 2,500 in 2006.
- Attacks increased to 600 per month by November 2006, from 300 in March of that year and 130 a month in 2005.
- US military statistics showed a total of 4,542 attacks using small arms in 2006, up from 1,558 in 2005.
- Road-side bombings increased from 800 in 2005 to 2,800 in 2006.
- There were 139 suicide bombings in Afghanistan in 2006; just thirty occurred between 2002 and 2005.
- Eighty-three aid workers were killed, fifty-two were kidnapped and nearly 800 were wounded.
- Many attacks have also focused on soft targets, such as schools and government officials.
- Taliban units up to 400 strong engaged security forces in southern Afghanistan.
- Endemic violence in Zabol and Oruzgan rendered the provinces too insecure to permit population surveys.

Source: Scott (2007: 6).

security situation in much of Afghanistan, thanks to the spreading influence of a resurgent Taliban. In 2007 the Taliban had established a presence in 54 per cent of the country and mounted regular attacks on both ISAF and the civilian population (see Senlis 2008: 17–18; box 12.1).

In response, ISAF launched a number of military offensives against Taliban militia operating from bases in Afghanistan's mountainous region and in Pakistan. As a result, both ISAF and civilian casualties had escalated dramatically (see table 12.1), with around 4,000 Afghans killed in 2006 (Scott 2007: 9). Moreover, the deteriorating security situation meant that the emphasis for ISAF in the south and east of the country had to shift away from reconstruction towards war-fighting, with the British contingent reporting that it was engaged in its most fierce and protracted combat since the Second World War (ibid.). This shift to war-fighting and relatively high casualty levels prompted many governments to question their commitment to ISAF. In 2008, Canada, whose forces had suffered high levels of casualties after bearing a significant portion of the fighting, threatened to withdraw its troops unless other NATO members (especially Germany, France, Italy and Spain) increased their contributions and expressed a readiness to deploy their forces to unstable regions. With Germany, Italy and Spain reluctant to do so, a crisis was narrowly averted only by a French commitment to deploy 1,000 extra troops. Another consequence of war-fighting was that civilian casualties caused by ISAF and NATO air forces attracted strong criticism from the Afghan government and undermined efforts to improve the mission's legitimacy and local consent (ibid.: 4).

TABLE 12.1 ISAF fatalities in Afghanistan (as of 10 August 2009)

Country	Casualties
US	779
UK	196
Canada	128
Germany	33
France	28
Spain	25
Denmark	24
The Netherlands	19
Italy	15
Australia, Romania	11 each
Poland	10
Estonia, Norway	4 each
Czech Republic, Latvia	3 each
Estonia, Sweden, Turkey, Portugal	2 each
Czech Republic, Finland, Lithuania, South Korea	1 each
Total	**1305**

Although the security situation in Afghanistan's north was relatively stable, this was mainly a result of the cooperation of the region's armed political leaders. Some analysts worried that this cooperation was based on a fragile calculation of interests on the part of the north's leadership and that support for the Karzai government could evaporate if the leaders received better offers from elsewhere (ICG 2008a). Other indicators also exhibited a marked deterioration. For example, in 2006, 165,000 hectares of land were used for poppy cultivation, a figure that grew to 193,000 hectares in 2007 despite ISAF's best efforts. In Helmand province, a Taliban stronghold, up to 43 per cent of agricultural land was being used for poppy cultivation.

While there can be little doubt that, other than its failure to disarm militia groups fully, ISAF's mission around Kabul was a success, the deterioration of the security situation across Afghanistan in 2006–7 raises important questions about the peace support operation there. Of course, exogenous factors beyond the control of ISAF played a significant part. In 2001 a significant proportion of the Taliban sought shelter from Operation Enduring Freedom in neighbouring Pakistan and used the mountainous border region to regroup in preparation for renewed attacks into Afghanistan. The upsurge in violence in 2006 centred upon those provinces (Helmand and Oruzgan) that are adjacent to the Taliban's heartland. The border with Pakistan is mountainous and therefore all but impossible to control. Despite several incursions, Pakistan remained reluctant to target the Taliban and its supporters on its side of the border, and potential ISAF/NATO raids over the border remain highly controversial. Moreover, the Taliban took advantage of agreements reached between ISAF and local tribal leaders whereby the force withdrew to base and allowed the tribal leaders to provide security. In one of its most daring raids in 2006, the Taliban seized the town of Musa Qala in Helmand province from one such group of tribal leaders, forcing ISAF to launch an enforcement operation to recapture it (Scott 2007: 9). There are, however, several aspects of ISAF itself that have contributed to the mounting problems in Afghanistan. These are: (1) the incremental fashion in which ISAF was expanded; (2) an absence of unity of purpose; (3) a fragmented military mission; and (4) an ineffective approach to reconstruction. We briefly survey each of these factors in turn, but together they represent a failure to integrate the various elements of international engagement in Afghanistan into a coherent whole.

Incremental expansion   Doctrine writers have come to recognize that the first few months of a mission are critically important because there is a narrow window of opportunity in which to make fundamental changes to a country's political system (see Stephenson 2007). The Brahimi Report also recognized this point, pointing out that a mission's credibility and legitimacy was shaped by the manner of its early deployment. Because Western governments wanted to avoid becoming involved in an open-ended commitment to nation- and state-building in this part of the world, they adopted a very limited approach to establishing stable peace in Afghanistan. Thus, in its first year, ISAF was rightly criticized for being under-ambitious (ICG 2002). To undertake a complex and dangerous mission in Afghanistan, a country shattered after twenty-five years of war and a major bombardment by the US Air Force, ISAF was initially given fewer than 5,000 troops and focused exclusively on Kabul. During this early phase, while it may well have improved security in Kabul, ISAF had little, if any, positive effect on security elsewhere in the country, where the Taliban and its allies continued to operate and poppy production began to thrive. This had multiple effects: it gave the Taliban time and space to regroup; tribal elders were forced to make provisions for their own post-Taliban security without the assistance or influence of an international force, entrenching old – and often violent – ways of pursuing security; opportunities for rapidly reconfiguring Afghan politics after the collapse of the Taliban were missed; international actors were unable to make a rapid and positive difference to livelihoods; and the credibility and legitimacy of ISAF outside Kabul was impaired.

No unity of purpose   The second problem that plagued ISAF was a lack of unity of purpose. It operated in Afghanistan alongside the US-led coalition's ongoing Operation Enduring Freedom, a UN civilian assistance mission (UNAMA), an

EU-led policing mission, and a series of bilateral reconstruction programmes. Within ISAF itself, there were important differences of opinion among troop contributors, leading some analysts to argue that many states were contributing in order to satisfy their NATO obligations rather than to make a significant difference in Afghanistan itself (ICG 2008a: 12). In the mission's early phase, for example, the British turned down Canada's offer of troops because they would have fulfilled similar roles to the British and thus risked widening the mission geographically (Hoon 2001). Later on, in the face of a resurgent Taliban in 2007–8, many contributors refused to increase troop numbers or permit the deployment of their troops to unstable regions (ICG 2008a). The German government, which contributed 900 soldiers, insisted that the need for ISAF to retain its impartiality meant that it should be entirely separate from Operation Enduring Freedom and refused to deploy its troops in the country's south and east, where they were most needed to confront the Taliban. In the first year of its deployment, these problems allowed the US to distance itself from ISAF and, indeed, from the whole project of reconstructing Afghanistan (ICG 2002: 12). The different approaches resulted in different priorities. For example, while some states (e.g. the US) emphasized the importance of poppy eradication, others (e.g. the UK) argued that this was not a priority and that ISAF should tackle the causes of poppy cultivation (the influence of warlords and economic deprivation) before embarking on eradication proposals. Another consequence was that regions fell in and out of focus depending on the security situation. Another was that there was no consistency across PRTs. The problem – not just one of coordination – reflected deeper uncertainties and disagreements. As Roland Paris (2007a: 2) argued, 'too often, unrelated problems are misdiagnosed as coordination failures because they manifest themselves, superficially, as disorderliness or ineffectiveness in the field, whereas in fact they reflect deeper frustrations, tensions and uncertainties in the state-building enterprise.'

A fragmented military mission   Without doubt, ISAF lacked the troops needed to succeed in Afghanistan. The most obvious indicator of this was that, while it successfully engaged Taliban forces, it often lacked the wherewithal to hold territory once seized, forcing it to return to the same area to tackle the Taliban at a later date. However, it was also plagued by a deeper problem stemming from its fragmented structure. First of all, ISAF and Operation Enduring Freedom commands were not integrated, with the result that they not only failed to support each other as much as they could have done, they sometimes worked at cross purposes. Moreover, the tasks of the two forces overlapped considerably – Enduring Freedom ran PRTs and conducted peacekeeping; ISAF sometimes engaged in war-fighting. Second, each had different priorities. Enduring Freedom was concerned primarily with combating terrorism and destroying poppy cultivation. Its activities, however, often directly impacted upon ISAF. For example, poppy eradication could have a negative effect on local levels of consent and impoverish farmers. When conducted without a strategy for maintaining economic livelihoods through other means, these operations undermined ISAF's legitimacy. Sometimes, Operation Enduring Freedom targeted Taliban-related poppies but not poppy cultivation associated with allies, thereby impairing ISAF's perceived impartiality (ICG 2008a).

A third element of fragmentation was within ISAF itself. Because different regions and sectors were controlled by different national contingents with their different priorities, it proved very difficult to coordinate across regions and sectors. This had significant and negative consequences. For example, the US took the lead in the military sector, including disarmament, while Germany and then the EU led the policing sector; Germany had promised to retrain the Afghan police but then deployed only forty police trainers (Paris 2007b: 39). The US demanded that the Northern Alliance disarm and integrate themselves into the new national Afghan army, whose composition would reflect Afghanistan's ethnic make-up. The Northern Alliance, however, preferred to remain within an ethnically homogenous group in order to maintain its cohesion and military strength and therefore transferred its leadership and fighters to the national police service. It was able to do this because the police reform sector – run by Germany/the EU, not the US – was much less developed than the military reform sector and lacked a strategy, plan and resources, and the two sectors (military and police) were left uncoordinated (ICG 2008a).

Finally, the whole international endeavour in Afghanistan was not overseen by a civilian agency, be it a High Representative or coordinating council, meaning that there was little in the way of strategic direction. An attempt in 2007–8 to appoint the former High Representative to Bosnia, Paddy Ashdown, as a robust special representative to Afghanistan was rejected by the Afghan government on the grounds that it would mean ceding too much authority to an unelected foreigner.

An ineffective approach to reconstruction　While the PRT model might be a useful way of conducting civil affairs operations in order to improve the peacekeepers' image, it is not a suitable vanguard for state-building. The twenty-five different PRTs run by twelve different countries were highly fragmented and left the process of reconstruction without any overarching direction. Moreover, as is well understood by the relevant British and US military doctrine, while military peacekeepers realize that they may be required to fulfil reconstruction duties on a temporary basis while civilian capacity is built, ultimately, only civilian agencies have the capabilities needed to reconstruct states and societies. Despite this, the PRT model gives the military a significant direct role to play in reconstruction. Finally, in line with peace support operations doctrine, the PRTs focused on delivering assistance rather than building Afghan capacity.

There is no doubt that Afghanistan presents the most difficult environment of all the peace support operations discussed in this chapter and that, irrespective of ISAF's composition and performance, international actors would be facing immense challenges there. However, there are clear lessons to be learned from peace support operations doctrine, particularly the importance of large and robust forces, clear mandates, the role of consent management, and civilian leadership.

12.3 Challenges for peace support operations

Although conceptually sound, peace support operations have run into difficulty in practice. First, the IFOR and ISAF experiences suggest that one way of closing the mandate–means gap may be to interpret the mandate very narrowly, for example by limiting operations to a small geographic area or restricting the military engagement to explicitly military matters in a manner akin to traditional peacekeeping. The first strategy is reminiscent of Mary Kaldor's suggestion that international society should be in the business of creating 'safety zones' (1999: 125). The logic is that security can be established within a small territorial space and that over time, as that area develops economically, this security will be transmitted throughout the entire state. The problem, of course, is that the 'safe areas' idea was tried, tested and failed spectacularly in Bosnia. Moreover, although life may be cosy within the zone of peace, a geographically limited operation may inadvertently encourage (usually much larger) 'zones of violence' elsewhere. This was a particularly worrying potential problem in Afghanistan but was also a concern during IFOR's first few months, when the international assistance was focused almost exclusively on Croat–Muslim Federation territory. As the US army found in Iraq and subsequently wrote into its peace operations doctrine, however, there is a small window of opportunity immediately upon deployment when significant progress can be made (Joint Publication 2007). Ideally, a peace support operation should be at its largest, most robust and most proactive immediately upon deployment – as KFOR and INTERFET were – in order to restructure the military and political environment rapidly, provide public security, and support the rebuilding of infrastructure, the provision of utilities and the delivery of humanitarian aid until civilian agencies have the capacity to take over. In practice, however, that may not always be either possible, because of capacity constraints, or politically popular, on account of concerns about casualties and 'mission creep'.

Second, although it is desirable, a clear objective is not always politically possible, as KFOR and ISAF reveal. Fuzzy political goals (as in Kosovo) make it difficult to develop coherent strategies and measure progress, and may be wrongly interpreted as mission creep. A misplaced concern about mission creep prompted ISAF's mandate writers to instil political clarity by creating an artificial timetable that bore little correlation to the mission's goals. Later on, though, an absence of clarity contributed to the mission's fragmentation, made most apparent by the different PRTs and the lack of an overarching reconstruction strategy.

Third, the trend towards single pivotal states or established international organizations taking the lead in assembling a force and devising its mandate in conjunction with the Security Council is a useful practical way of closing the mandate–means gap and fosters greater vertical and horizontal cooperation (see figure 12.2). However, this approach to constructing and managing peace operations takes it further away from the original notion of collective action pursued by the Security Council. It raises important issues about the accountability of troop contributors and pivotal states and about the relationship between the UN and regional organizations. The Indian government and its supporters have been particularly vocal on this. Satish Nambiar, for instance, argued that the UN runs the risk of 'becoming a toothless and impotent organisation' held 'hostage to the machinations of a few powerful countries of the Western world' (2000: 261, 268).

This leads to two further concerns about peace support operations that impact upon the role of peace operations in global politics more broadly. The first issue is that the peace support operations concept is not universally applied or endorsed. As discussed in chapter 8, some current peacekeeping operations still bear all the negative hallmarks of wider peacekeeping. What, therefore, is to be done when no powerful actor or state wants to take the lead? Or when there are no means available to secure even the narrowest mandate in the world's most hazardous places? The danger is that, by selectively applying the peace support operations concept, the West in particular risks creating a two-tier system of peace operations. On the one hand there are well-equipped, well-funded operations led by one of the world's richer states trying to secure an achievable mandate. On the other hand there are peacekeepers, particularly in Africa, whose primary function remains 'burying the dead' (Chan 1997).

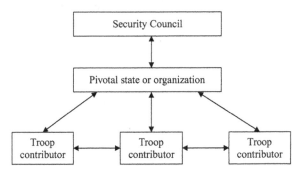

Figure 12.2 *Horizontal and vertical cooperation in peace support operations*

The other problem is closely related to the first. IFOR/SFOR in Bosnia, KFOR in Kosovo and INTERFET in East Timor (though conspicuously not ISAF on account of UNAMA's 'light footprint' approach) were in the business of creating a secure environment for the establishment of liberal democratic institutions. Peace support operations aim to promote liberal democracy and enforce a post-Westphalian conceptualization of the liberal peace. This assumes that there is agreement within international society that this should be peacekeeping's primary role in global politics. However, as we discussed in chapter 1, consensus on this point is fragile at best. The pursuit of liberal democracy therefore only adds to the sense of bifurcation between two competing visions of the role of peace operations. One vision is relatively well funded and supported by the West. The other is not. Given the disparities of funding and capability granted to each type of mission, it is unsurprising that peace support operations are heralded as successful while more traditional approaches are lambasted for being ineffective.

The final challenge concerns the relationship between military peacekeepers and civilian agencies. While both British and American doctrine have made important strides in clarifying the most appropriate relationship, in practice it remains complex and fraught with difficulties. Three major pitfalls identified in the preceding case studies are:

1 military peacekeepers become involved in executing the political demands of civilian agents such as the High Representative in Bosnia. Although this can provide vital support to the civilian effort it comes at the cost of a loss of perceived impartiality and local consent.

2 expectations are generated that military peacekeepers will be able to perform public order functions (pursue and arrest criminals, riot control) for which they are neither trained nor equipped to perform. The dangers here are that military peacekeepers either overreact and act disproportionately or take too long to respond to emergencies because they are unsure about how to act.

3 military peacekeepers are expected to play a leading role in reconstruction because they have more resources than civilian agencies. In the long run, however, only civilian agencies have the necessary skills and resources to build the local capacities needed for self-sustaining peace.

PART IV

Contemporary Challenges

CHAPTER THIRTEEN

Regionalization

In debates about peace operations, regionalization is commonly understood in both empirical and explicitly normative terms. Empirically, it is often used as a label to denote the increased level of activities that regional organizations have undertaken in regard to conflict management in general and peace operations in particular. In normative terms, it refers to the idea that each region of the world 'should be responsible for its own peacemaking and peacekeeping, with some financial and technical support from the West but few, if any, military or police contingents from outside the region' (Goulding 2002: 217). With global demand for peacekeepers increasing and the UN's capacity to deliver straining, many analysts look to regionalization as a potential solution.

As a short-hand descriptor for what is happening across the contemporary peacekeeping landscape, 'regionalization' is rather misleading in several respects. First, as this book has pointed out, regional organizations are not the only important non-UN actors in relation to peace operations; coalitions and individual states (see chapter 2), as well as private contractors (see chapter 14), all play significant roles. Second, regionalization is occurring unevenly across the planet. Thus while some parts of the world have regional organizations that are willing and able to conduct peace operations, others have the will but lack the relevant capabilities, some dislike the idea of conducting military operations but are keen to undertake political and observer missions, still others have no desire to engage in collective peace operations of any sort, and some parts of the world have no significant regional arrangements that deal with conflict management issues at all. Third, not all regional organizations have confined their activities to their own region. Some in the West, for instance, have operated well beyond their own neighbourhood. Nevertheless, although we must be aware of the limitations of regionalization as a description of contemporary realities, the debate about the place of regional organizations in peace operations and their relationship to the UN is a very important issue. As former UN Secretary-General Kofi Annan put it, 'multilateral institutions and regional security organizations have never been more important than today' (2002b). The major regional associations explicitly involved in peace and security activities are listed in table 13.1.

TABLE 13.1 Major regional arrangements with security provisions, 1945–2007

Region	Regional arrangement

Africa	• Organization of African Unity/African Union
	• Intergovernmental Authority on Drought and Development/
	  Intergovernmental Authority on Development
	• Economic Community of West African States
	• Southern African Development Coordination Conference/Southern
	  African Development Community
	• Economic and Monetary Community of Central African States

Europe	• European Community/European Union • Western European Union • North Atlantic Treaty Organization • (Warsaw Pact) • Organization for Security and Cooperation in Europe • Commonwealth of Independent States • Collective Security Treaty Organization
Asia	• (Southeast Asia Treaty Organization) • Association of Southeast Asian Nations • South Asian Association for Regional Cooperation • ASEAN Regional Forum • Shanghai Cooperation Organization • Central Asian Cooperation Organization • Islamic Conference Organization
Middle East	• League of Arab States • (Central Treaty Organization) • Gulf Cooperation Council • Arab Maghreb Union • (Arab Cooperation Council) • Economic Cooperation Organization • Islamic Conference Organization
Americas	• Organization of American States • Caribbean Community • Organization of Eastern Caribbean States • The Southern Common Market
Australasia	• The Australia, New Zealand, United States Security Treaty • South Pacific Forum/Pacific Island Forum

Notes: Parentheses indicate that an institution is now defunct. A slash indicates a change of name.

Two fundamental characteristics of the UN system form the starting point for understanding the challenge of regionalization. The first is to recall that Chapter VIII of the UN Charter encourages 'regional arrangements' to be proactive in peacefully resolving conflicts that occur within their neighbourhood. In this sense, the UN Charter created a system flexible enough not to grant the Security Council a monopoly of authority on issues of international peace and security (see Roberts, Adam 2003). The second fundamental characteristic is the UN's lack of standing armed forces (see box 6.4, pp. 168–9). This has meant that the UN often needs to delegate other actors to undertake its operations, especially those involving large-scale enforcement activities. The growing number of regional organizations that have taken an explicit interest in conflict management has thus provided the UN with an expanding set of options.

Within this international context, the challenge for the UN is to find an appropriate relationship with those regional organizations that are in the business of conducting peace operations. In order to analyse these issues, the chapter proceeds in three parts. The first section summarizes the debate about regionalization that has taken place within the UN. Although this is an old debate, it has become more prominent since NATO's intervention in Kosovo/Yugoslavia in 1999. We end this section with a brief summary of the main regional peace operations conducted in the twenty-first century. The second section then provides a more detailed overview of the major strengths and limitations of regional organizations as peacekeepers. In the final section we analyse three important cases of regional operations: the ECOWAS operation in Liberia (1990–7), NATO's intervention in Kosovo (1999), and the Pacific Islands Forum operation in the Solomon Islands (2003–present).

13.1 The United Nations debate on regionalization

During the debates that led to the UN's creation, several of its architects favoured a regionalist, as opposed to a globalist, approach whereby the great powers would assume responsibility for maintaining international peace and security in their respective spheres of influence (Morris and McCoubrey 1999: 133). The British prime minister Winston Churchill, for instance, proposed that the UN system should be based upon the pillars of 'several regional councils'. Other state leaders, especially those in South America, expressed reservations about the potential for regional hegemony implicit within such an approach. Ultimately, the globalist vision carried the day and the Security Council was given primary responsibility for the maintenance of international peace and security.

Under the UN Charter system, the majority of regional activity relating to international peace and security is governed under Article 33 (Chapter VI) and Articles 52–4 (Chapter VIII). Article 51, however, acknowledges the right of states to act in collective self-defence, which permits regional organizations to defend member states without prior authorization from the UN Security Council. Article 33(1) specifies that parties to a dispute should first of all seek to resolve their difficulties through negotiation and/or by 'resort to regional agencies or arrangements'. According to Article 52, regional organizations may engage in matters of international peace and security, provided their activities uphold the principles and purposes of the UN Charter. Article 53, however, emphasizes that regional organizations may not conduct enforcement actions without authorization from the UN Security Council. Article 54 stipulates that regional organizations must keep the Security Council fully informed of their activities. Despite this relatively clear framework, in practice the legal bases both for cooperation between the UN and regional organizations and for peacekeeping and enforcement action by regional organizations have not been made clear within the resolutions of either the Security Council or the organizations concerned (see Gray 2004: esp. ch. 9).

The practice of regional conflict management began in 1948 when the UN entered into formal cooperation with the OAS, the first body to be recognized as a regional organization under Chapter VIII of the UN Charter. Despite this early partnership, the geopolitical context of the Cold War often stifled the effective use of Chapter VIII. In addition, Boutros-Ghali noted that 'regional arrangements worked on occasion against resolving disputes in the manner foreseen in the Charter' (1992: § 60). It was also commonplace for both the United States and the Soviet Union to manage disputes through regional organizations that they effectively controlled. Crises in the Western hemisphere were thus often dealt with through the OAS, while crises in Eastern Europe were dealt with through the 'socialist community' of the Warsaw Pact (Weiss et al. 1994: 34).

Because the UN Security Council does not possess a monopoly of authority on issues relating to international peace and security, it is hardly surprising that the question of where authority resides in relation to peace operations has frequently proved controversial (see Padelford 1954; Wilcox 1965). For example, the issue arose over Palestine in 1948 (in relation to the Arab League), Hungary in 1956 (in relation to the Warsaw Pact), and the Dominican Republic in 1965 (in relation to the OAS) (see Bellamy and Williams 2005b: 161–4). These cases raised two main questions. First, was it legitimate for non-UN actors to uphold the UN's principles and purposes without the organization's prior authorization? Second, when the crisis in question lay within a regional organization's borders, did it or the UN have the principal authority to act?

The case of Palestine provides an example of the first question. In 1948 the League of Arab States claimed that it was acting to uphold the principles and purposes of the UN Charter when its forces entered Palestine in response to Israel's declaration of independence. This plea was rejected by the United States and not discussed further within the Security Council. A ceasefire agreement was arranged the following year, and one of the UN's first peace operations, UNTSO, was deployed to monitor it. The case of Hungary illustrates the second question. In 1956 the Soviet Union justified its intervention there to suppress a pro-democracy movement not by insisting that it was upholding the principles and purposes of the UN but by arguing that, within its zone, the Warsaw Pact took precedence over the UN Charter. Once again, though, the Security Council did not discuss the question at length.

The OAS operation in the Dominican Republic in 1965 is more instructive precisely because the Security Council discussed it at some length. As violence spread through the republic following a coup, US soldiers were deployed, ostensibly to protect US citizens. Following criticism from both OAS members and wider international society, the United States pushed for the mission to be brought under OAS auspices. It succeeded despite the deep misgivings of some of the organization's members, notably Brazil. In the Security Council, the Soviet Union, France, and the Asian and African representatives were highly critical of the United States, insisting that only the Security Council had the authority to mandate military actions. The US argued that Chapter VIII of the Charter gave the OAS a legitimate role to play, but it failed to persuade the Council of its case. Nevertheless, it continued to argue that it was legitimate for regional organizations to take action within their sphere of influence without UN authorization (Eide 1966: 129).

After these early debates, regionalization did not emerge as a significant issue at the UN until the early 1990s. Indeed, between 1945 and 1990, Security Council resolutions contained only three references to regional organizations (Gray 2000: 202). This situation changed dramatically after 1991, with references to regional organizations appearing in numerous Security Council resolutions, including those relating to Angola, Haiti, Mozambique, the former Soviet Union, the former Yugoslavia and Western Sahara. This was largely to do with the increased level of regional conflict management activities. As Diehl and Cho have shown, before 1975 regional organizations conducted an average of only approximately two mediations each year. Between 1989 and 1995, however, regional organizations conducted 116 attempts at mediation, representing almost twenty attempts per year (2006: 193).

By 1992, the prospect of increased cooperation with regional organizations prompted Boutros-Ghali to urge the UN to make better use of their potential in matters of international peace and security. However, he did not outline a blueprint for a formal relationship with them. Instead, the UN and regional organizations were to engage in informal consultations and joint undertakings, in the hope that such cooperation would imbue regional efforts with a greater degree of legitimacy and simultaneously generate the impression of greater participation in international decision-making (see box 13.1). As we discuss below, Boutros-Ghali did not remain as optimistic about the prospects for regional peacekeeping as this document suggested, but at the time it played an important role in heralding a new era of UN cooperation with regional arrangements.

After the end of the Cold War, the UN entered into a variety of relationships with regional organizations in matters of international peace and security. In some conflicts the Security Council took a back seat to the relevant regional organization, such as the OSCE in Nagorno-Karabakh, Moldova, South Ossetia and Chechnya, and the OAU in Burundi. In others, such as Liberia (UNOMIL), Georgia (UNMOGIP), Tajikistan (UNMOT) and Sierra Leone (UNOMSIL), the UN

> ### Box 13.1 Boutros-Ghali on the UN and regional arrangements (1992)
>
> ...in this new era of opportunity, regional arrangements or agencies can render great service if their activities are undertaken in a manner consistent with the purposes and principles of the Charter, and if their relationship with the United Nations, and particularly the Security Council, is governed by Chapter VIII....Under the Charter, the Security Council has and will continue to have primary responsibility for maintaining international peace and security, but regional action as a matter of decentralization, delegation and cooperation with the United Nations efforts could not only lighten the burden of the Council but also contribute to a deeper sense of participation, consensus and democratization in international affairs....and should the Security Council choose specifically to authorize a regional arrangement or organization to take the lead in addressing a crisis within its region, it could serve to lend the weight of the United Nations to the validity of the regional effort. (Boutros-Ghali 1992: §§ 63–5)

and regional peacekeeping forces engaged in joint or parallel activities. In others still, the Security Council delegated the use of force to particular regional organizations under Chapter VII, as in the former Yugoslavia (1992), Haiti (1993) and Sierra Leone (1997). With this increase in practical cooperation, Boutros-Ghali's *Supplement to An Agenda for Peace* (1995a) described the forms that such cooperation was taking – namely, consultation, diplomatic support, operational support, co-deployment and joint operations. He also instigated a series of high-level meetings between the UN and regional organizations. By 2007, seven such meetings had been convened.

Once again, however, controversy began to re-emerge in earnest at the end of the 1990s. This time it was sparked by NATO's intervention in Kosovo during 1999 (see companion website). Although ECOWAS (three times), SADC (twice) and NATO (once) had engaged in enforcement actions earlier in the decade, the relationship between these regional arrangements and the UN had received relatively little attention. NATO's 1995 Operation Deliberate Force and subsequent IFOR and SFOR missions were authorized by the UN and thus did not generate much controversy with regard to their legitimacy. Similarly, despite significant rifts within ECOWAS, the Security Council initially ignored and then retroactively endorsed its operations in Liberia in 1990, Sierra Leone in 1997, and Guinea-Bissau in 1999.

SADC's operations, however, were more problematic. In 1998 two different groups of states claimed to be operating under its authority when they conducted military operations in Lesotho (South Africa and Botswana) and in the DRC (Angola, Namibia and Zimbabwe) (see Coleman 2007: chs 4–5). Both cases were examples of 'intervention by invitation' and hence, although they involved enforcement activities without an explicit Security Council resolution, were legally justifiable under Article 51's concept of collective defence.

Whereas the Security Council did not publicly discuss the South African-led Operation Boleas in Lesotho, it did comment on the operations in the DRC but neither explicitly endorsed nor explicitly condemned them. Initially, it emphasized 'the need for all States to refrain from any interference in each other's internal affairs' (UN 1998: 2). Later, however, it distinguished between invited and uninvited (primarily Rwandan and Ugandan) forces within the DRC (in Security Council Resolution 1234). When Zimbabwe argued that its intervention was in accordance with UN principles and purposes to uphold the territorial integrity of a member state and to prevent its government from being toppled by invading forces, the Council did not explicitly reject its line of reasoning. In contrast, it explicitly rejected the argument put forward by Rwanda and Uganda that their military intervention in the DRC was justified in terms of national self-defence (in Resolution 1304 of 16 June 2000).

During much of the 1990s, therefore, peace operations conducted (and sometimes authorized) by regional organizations tended either to be uncontroversial in terms of their legitimacy and their wider impact on the international rules governing the use of force or were ignored by the Security Council. This was not the case in relation to NATO's Operation Allied Force in Kosovo (see also companion website).

On the eve of NATO's bombardment of Kosovo/Yugoslavia, the DPKO's Lessons Learned Unit generated eighteen principles it hoped would shape the relationship between the UN and regional organizations in relation to peacekeeping. These principles were designed to ensure that:

- primary responsibility for maintaining international peace and security remains within the Security Council;
- cooperation is viewed as a dynamic process which is enhanced by clear and concise mandates based on realistic timetables;
- cooperation is based on consultation that involves effective information-sharing;
- all cooperating parties share a common understanding of basic doctrine and operational rules of engagement;
- personnel are sufficiently trained and equipped;
- attempts to maintain peace and security do not end with the departure of a UN or regional operation but entail long-term efforts to strengthen civic associations committed to democracy, human rights and the rule of law. (UN 1999)

The report also suggested a variety of mechanisms for implementing these principles. These mechanisms can be summarized as ensuring multiple channels for regular communication; establishing a strategic planning group and relevant planning cells that would involve regular, senior-level meetings; intensifying joint training; and engaging in international conferences or meetings of a 'Group of Friends' in order to foster communication and develop a common code of conduct.

Clearly, NATO's actions went well beyond traditional peacekeeping and into the realm of enforcement. As we discuss in more detail below, this stimulated several reactions. On the one hand, a group of states led by Russia denounced NATO's actions as illegal. In contrast, the perceived success of the bombing campaign encouraged some Western leaders openly to advocate regionalization. For example, US President Bill Clinton's Presidential Decision Directive 71, released on 24 February 2000, identified the strengthening of the capacity of regional organizations as a major objective. This was because Washington thought NATO could conduct more effective operations than the UN and possessed the political authority to mandate such actions (see companon website).

As it turned out, NATO's actions did not stop the increase in regional peacekeeping around the world. As table 13.2 illustrates, a variety of regional associations undertook peace operations in the post-Cold War period, although these were concentrated in Europe and sub-Saharan Africa. Table 13.3 shows the extent to which this activity represents a huge increase in the number of peacekeeping operations conducted by regional organizations since the Cold War.

TABLE 13.2 Examples of peace operations conducted by regional organizations since 1990

Organization	Peace operations
African Union	Burundi (2003–4), Sudan (2004–present), the Comoros (2006, 2008), Somalia (2007–present)
Commonwealth of Independent States	Abkhazia, Georgia (1994–present), Tajikistan (1993–2003)
Economic and Monetary Community of Central African States	Central African Republic (2002–present)
Economic Community of West African States	Liberia (1990–9, 2003), Côte d'Ivoire (2002–3), Guinea-Bissau (1998–9), Sierra Leone (1997–2000)
European Community/Union	Macedonia (2003–5), Bosnia (2004–present), DRC (2003, 2006), Kosovo (2008)
Intergovernmental Authority on Development	Somalia (2005) [authorized but never deployed]
North Atlantic Treaty Organization	Bosnia and Hercegovina (1995–2003), Kosovo (1999–present), Macedonia (1999–2003), Afghanistan (2003–present)
Pacific Islands Forum	Solomon Islands (2003–present)
Southern African Development Community	Lesotho (1998–9), DRC (1998–2002)

TABLE 13.3 Peacekeeping initiated by the UN and regional organizations, 1947–2005

Period	Regional organizations	United Nations
Pre-1954	1	2
1955–1971	3	8
1972–1988	5	6
1989–2005	31	44

Source: Diehl and Cho (2006: 195).

In the twenty-first century, regional associations in Africa have continued to conduct more peace operations than those on any other continent. For some analysts, this represents the continuation of the post-Cold War trend whereby the great powers 'dumped' conflict management onto international organizations, especially in areas which they considered to be of little strategic value (Diehl and Cho 2006: 198). In recent years, African organizations have conducted several peace operations of short duration before handing over to UN forces. This occurred in the ECOWAS operations in Côte d'Ivoire (2002–3) and Liberia (2003) and the AU operation in Burundi (2003–4). The AU's mission in Somalia (2007–present) is also scheduled to be subsumed within a new UN peacekeeping operation. At the end of 2007 the AU mission in the Darfur region of Sudan was merged into a unique hybrid AU–UN operation known as UNAMID (see chapter 8). Only in its operations in the Comoros (2006 and 2008) did the AU not seek to hand over the mission (Williams 2009). The other ongoing regional operation, the CEMAC force in the Central African Republic, also continued to stand alone. The plethora of regional activity in Africa led the UN to focus particularly hard upon its relationship with the continent's regional associations. In November 2006, this produced a ten-year UN–AU plan to enhance Africa's peacekeeping capacity.

The EU conducted a variety of military peace operations in the Balkans and the DRC and a variety of rule of law and security sector reform operations elsewhere, most controversially in Kosovo after its unilateral declaration of independence in February 2008. In the DRC case, the EU temporarily helped to stabilize the situation for UN peacekeepers already present in the country before withdrawing, while in Bosnia and Macedonia it gradually took the place of NATO forces. In the former Soviet Union, the Russian-dominated CIS operation in Abkhazia has stoked considerable controversy. This was related primarily to persistent criticisms that this force was neither neutral nor impartial but was instead part of Moscow's efforts to bolster the independence claims of the breakaway region (see MacFarlane 2001). The suspicions were somewhat vindicated by Russia's August 2008 intervention in Georgia and Moscow's unilateral recognition of the two regions of Abkhazia and

South Ossetia. The Asian exception is the Australian-led peace operation conducted in the Solomon Islands, which has been under the aegis of the Pacific Islands Forum since 2003. Elsewhere in Asia and the Americas, regional organizations have maintained their reluctance to undertake collective peace operations.

13.2 The strengths and weaknesses of regionalization

The potentially double-edged nature of UN cooperation with regional organizations was recognized by Kofi Annan in a 1998 report on conflict issues in Africa. Here, Annan noted that support from regional organizations was vital because the UN lacked 'the capacity, resources and expertise' to tackle the continent's problems. On the other hand, he acknowledged that they could 'face political, structural, financial, or planning limitations' as well as charges of adopting a partisan approach (Annan 1998b). He concluded that the UN must exercise 'judgment and caution' when dealing with regional organizations, but should not lose sight of 'the potential for positive cooperation' (UN 1999: § 20). In light of this warning, this section identifies some broad generalizations which provide clues as to the challenges and opportunities raised by the UN's cooperation with regional organizations.

Potential advantages

Given the significant limitations of the UN's peacekeeping capabilities, it would be foolish to assume that regional organizations cannot play some useful roles in conflict management. First, in some conflicts, they can provide greater legitimacy and sensitivity borne of a greater working knowledge of the relevant circumstances. As the Uruguayan representative to the UN Security Council recently put it, 'the States of a region have a better grasp of a conflict situation and its cultural backdrop than other nations do' (UN 2007a: 3). This local knowledge has helped regional organizations enjoy some success in providing diplomatic windows of opportunity to respective warring parties through the use of their 'good offices'.

Second, their geographical proximity allows regional actors to deploy and supply troops relatively quickly. In the extreme case of the former Soviet Union, the Russian troops that became part of the CIS peace operation in Abkhazia, Georgia, for example, were already present in the country because they had not withdrawn from the Soviet garrisons.

A third potential benefit is that in some instances parties to a conflict may prefer the involvement of regional actors rather than the UN or other external bodies; hence the frequent calls for 'Arab', 'African' or 'Asian' solutions to regional problems. This argument 'relies on the notion that the people and governments in a region have a natural affinity with those in that geographic area and an inherent suspicion of what they perceive as outside intervention'

(Diehl 2007: 541). This has certainly been the case in a variety of conflicts – for example, in Chechnya, where the OSCE was granted access when the UN was not; in Zimbabwe, where Mugabe's government preferred regional and continental bodies as election observers to personnel from non-African organizations; between Ethiopia and Eritrea, when the Eritrean government called for UNMEE to expel peacekeepers from the EU; and in Darfur, where for four years Sudan would permit only African, and not UN, peacekeepers.

A fourth argument suggests that the region's proximity to the crisis in question means that its members have to live with the consequences of unresolved conflicts. As a result, regional associations are unable to disentangle themselves from an issue and hence may be more likely to sustain engagement over the long term. The EU's experiences in Bosnia, for example, would appear to support this argument.

Finally, regional operations may be the only realistic option in conflicts where the UN has declined to intervene. In this sense, regional arrangements can help fill some of the gaps in international conflict management left by the UN Security Council's selective approach. For example, after the debacle in Mogadishu in October 1993, the Security Council turned down requests for peacekeeping missions to be deployed to Burundi, Congo-Brazzaville and Liberia. This left the OAU and the relevant subregional arrangements to deal with these conflicts; in Liberia's case at least, ECOWAS deployed a peace operation (see section 13.3). More recently, in 2003, the African Union deployed a peacekeeping operation to Burundi at a time when the UN declined on the basis that a permanent ceasefire did not exist.

Potential disadvantages

A variety of senior figures connected with UN peacekeeping have voiced concerns about the problems of regionalization. For example, although the former UN Secretary-General Boutros Boutros-Ghali began his period in office by calling for greater involvement of regional arrangements in peacekeeping, most notably in *An Agenda for Peace* (discussed above), he later changed his mind and condemned regionalization as a 'dangerous' idea that threatened to weaken the internationalist basis of the UN (Boutros-Ghali 1999: 306). A former head of the UN's Department of Political Affairs, Marrack Goulding, also cautioned that most regional arrangements lacked the experience, bureaucratic structures, and resources necessary to conduct peace operations effectively (2002: 217). Similarly, a former head of the DPKO, Jean-Marie Guéhenno (2003), warned that regionalization encouraged an 'only in my backyard' approach that spelt trouble for regions that lack the necessary capacities.

In more specific terms, regional organizations not only suffer from the same constraints and problems faced by the UN, but also encounter other distinct disadvantages. First, geographic proximity to a conflict does not automatically generate a regional consensus on how to respond. As Paul Diehl has pointed out, although 'one might expect regional organizations to have an advantage over the United Nations because their membership is more homogenous', in fact, the 'most common threats to regional peace – internal threats – are exactly those least likely to generate consensus' (2007: 540–1).

A second, related point is that regional organizations are particularly susceptible to the pull of partisan interests, especially those associated with a regional hegemon such as Nigeria in ECOWAS, South Africa in SADC, Russia in the CIS, Australia in the PIF, and arguably the US in NATO. Because of the inability of regional organizations to act against their most powerful members, regional peace operations 'are unlikely to be authorized in conflicts that directly involve the global powers or regional powers' (Diehl 2007: 543). Think, for instance, how unlikely it would have been to see a CIS operation in Chechnya or an ECOWAS operation deployed to the Niger Delta. Instead, local hegemons have used regional arrangements to legitimize their activities in conflicts that are of direct relevance to them rather than those going on inside their borders. This kind of manipulation was clearly evident in the Nigerian-led ECOWAS operations in Liberia (1990) and Sierra Leone (1997), the South African-led SADC operation in Lesotho, the Russian-led CIS operation in Abkhazia/Georgia (1994), and the Australian-led PIF operation in the Solomon Islands (2003).

Third, compared to the UN, regional organizations lack the experience of conducting peace operations. Even the busiest regional organizations (the EU, AU and ECOWAS) have undertaken only a small fraction of the operations conducted by the UN. In this sense, some of these organizations have had to learn the techniques of peacekeeping as they go. In some cases, the organizations also lack provisions to undertake peace operations in their respective charters (e.g. NATO and the PIF).

As Goulding observed, a fourth weakness is that, with the possible exceptions of NATO and the EU, regional organizations tend to operate with relatively small bureaucracies and budgets and lack the administrative, logistical and command structures necessary to manage large-scale military operations. The problem is, as Diehl has noted, '[m]erely having the authority to carry out a conflict management activity is not enough if the organization lacks the requisite resources [financial, political and military] to take effective action' (2007: 546). This can be particularly problematic given that deploying a poorly equipped and funded peace operation can generate various problems in the area concerned, notably force protection and civilian protection issues, as occurred in the AU's mission in Sudan (see chapter 8).

A fifth problem stems from the uneven levels and types of regionalization evident around the globe. In particular, some parts of the world, including areas of intense confrontation between India and Pakistan or in the Middle East, have no regional organizations capable of conducting peacekeeping operations (Morris and McCoubrey 1999: 137). Here, attempting to subcontract the UN's responsibilities to the regional level could have disastrous effects. Finally, it has been pointed out that, although the Security Council suffers from a number of significant problems, no other organization can consistently generate as much international legitimacy as the UN (see Coleman 2007).

Overall, therefore, the general case for an increased reliance upon regional organizations as peacekeepers is rather weak. Interestingly, this has not stopped a discernible increase in their use as mechanisms of conflict management. The next section therefore analyses some regional peace operations in more detail. (An additional case study, on NATO's 1999 intervention in the Federal Republic of Yugoslavia, is provided on the companion website.)

13.3 Regional peace operations in practice

ECOWAS and the UN in Liberia (1990–1997)

In December 1989 Charles Taylor's National Patriotic Front of Liberia (NPFL) instigated a rebellion against Samuel Doe, Liberia's president since 1980. Despite a number of internal splits within the rebel groups, by the summer of 1990 Taylor's forces controlled approximately 90 per cent of Liberian territory and were approaching the capital, Monrovia. Increasingly worried about Taylor's advance, the Liberian government sought a UN intervention in June 1990, but the Security Council refused to become involved until January 1991. Despite its long-standing historic ties to Liberia, the US chose not to intervene in order to resolve the conflict, although it did send 2,000 marines, then stationed off the West African coast, to evacuate US and other foreign citizens (Ellis 1999: 4). The fighting continued sporadically until August 1996, resulting in approximately 200,000, mainly civilian, deaths, 1.2 million displaced persons and spillover conflicts in Sierra Leone, Côte d'Ivoire and Guinea. Taylor assumed Liberia's presidency.

In August 1990, in response to the rebellion, the ECOWAS Standing Mediation Committee met in Banjul, Gambia. Of the sixteen ECOWAS members, only five (Gambia, Nigeria, Ghana, Guinea and Sierra Leone) were present at this meeting (Adebajo and Landsberg 2000). The committee called for a ceasefire and established ECOMOG, the ECOWAS Monitoring Group, which initially comprised some 3,000 troops from Nigeria, Ghana, Guinea and Sierra Leone (Mali joined the operation in 1991). The ECOMOG troops arrived in Monrovia with a mandate to supervise a ceasefire and establish an interim government, which was to organize elections after a year. In December 1990, after considerable negotiations between the parties, an interim government was duly established under President Amos Sawyer. This was treated as the legitimate representative of Liberia at the UN. However, the ceasefire broke down in August 1992, after which the NPFL attacked Monrovia and the

Map 13.1 *Liberia*

ECOMOG forces defending it. ECOMOG retaliated by driving the NPFL back, pursuing its forces and recapturing some of the territory they had gained. In engaging directly in combat against the NPFL, ECOMOG forces lost even the flimsy façade of impartiality they may have enjoyed beforehand.

The ECOWAS Standing Committee justified its actions on three main grounds: limiting the effects of Liberia's war on regional stability; protecting ECOWAS nationals (including 3,000 Nigerian, Ghanaian and Sierra Leonean citizens held hostage by Taylor at the start of the war); and relieving the humanitarian crisis in Liberia. However, despite these laudable objectives, several observers questioned the legal basis of ECOMOG's actions (Adebajo and Landsberg 2000; Gray 2000: 212–13). First, the intervention did not conform to either the ECOWAS 1978 Protocol on Non-Aggression or the 1981 Protocol relating to Mutual Assistance and Defence. Second, the ECOWAS Standing Mediation Committee was mandated only to establish 'mediation procedures' (under Article 4), not to impose solutions on conflicts. Third, while President Doe and Prince Johnson (leader of a breakaway faction of the NPFL) did consent to ECOMOG's presence, Taylor's NPFL, which effectively controlled most of the country, did not. Although Taylor's consent was not legally required, his hostility destroyed any hope of ECOMOG playing an impartial role in the conflict. Finally, several francophone ECOWAS states, notably Burkina Faso, Côte d'Ivoire and Senegal, opposed ECOMOG's activities on the grounds that they represented a usurpation of ECOWAS powers in order to promote Nigeria's hegemonic aspirations in the region. These fears were diluted when Senegal eventually contributed 3,000 troops to ECOMOG, paid for by the US (Weller 1994: 174). Even then Burkina Faso and Côte d'Ivoire provided military assistance to the NPFL.

In spite of these criticisms, ECOMOG gained a significant and widespread degree of legitimacy, not least from powerful Western states, the OAU Secretary-General, Salim Ahmed Salim, and later the UN. However, other groups accused the forces of brutality, partisanship and engaging in corruption on a massive scale (Tuck 2000; Howe 2001: ch. 4). In its communications with the UN, ECOWAS did not refer explicitly to Chapter VIII of the UN Charter, although Nigeria did describe ECOMOG's actions as being in accordance with Chapter VIII. Similarly, ECOWAS did not seek Security Council authorization for ECOMOG, but it did inform the UN of its actions, albeit several months after the deployment. Consequently, at its first debate on Liberia, in January 1991, the Security Council supported ECOMOG only cautiously. However, the Council became gradually more supportive and in Resolution 788 (19 November 1992) it imposed an arms embargo, recalled Chapter VIII and commended ECOWAS for its efforts, although it did not mention ECOMOG by name. After the Cotonou Peace Accord of July 1993, in which the UN was heavily involved, the Security Council passed Resolution 866 (22 September 1993). This did refer to ECOMOG by name and also established a mission of 368 military observers, UNOMIL, the first UN peacekeeping operation to cooperate with a force set up by another organization.

From the outset, a clear division of labour existed between ECOMOG and UNOMIL. The former was the lynchpin of the operations and was tasked to look after all enforcement aspects, while the latter was to monitor compliance with the ceasefire. However, renewed fighting prevented UNOMIL from carrying out its responsibilities. It was reduced in size in October 1994, after over forty of its personnel were detained by the NPFL, and terminated in September 1997, after Taylor assumed the presidency. UNOMIL's operations also suffered from several disagreements with ECOMOG commanders (Adebajo 2002: 57). First, ECOMOG soldiers complained that UNOMIL withheld its vehicles and helicopters from their use. Second, ECOMOG officials were annoyed by what they saw as unilateral disarmament negotiations with the local parties by UN Special Representative Trevor Gordon-Somers. Third, ECOMOG argued for a far tougher approach to disarming the NPFL than did

UNOMIL. Finally, ECOMOG commanders were angered by UNOMIL's failure to consult with them before deploying troops. For their part, UNOMIL personnel complained that ECOMOG troops were incapable of protecting them.

While ECOMOG did succeed in restoring a degree of order to Liberia, this case highlights several important issues about the relationship between the UN and regional organizations. First, because it was deployed without the Security Council's authorization, ECOMOG represented a challenge to the UN's primacy in this field. Second, it was deployed without the consent of one of the major belligerents, Charles Taylor's NPFL. While the existing government did offer its consent, Taylor's hostility made it virtually impossible for ECOMOG to act as a neutral and impartial force. And, despite its best efforts, ECOMOG succeeded only in postponing Taylor's acquisition of the presidential mansion. This led directly to the third problematic issue – namely, that ECOMOG was often perceived as a vehicle for Nigeria's hegemonic aspirations in the region. In particular, its inevitable clashes with the NPFL fuelled suspicions that it was a Nigerian-dominated attempt to prevent Taylor becoming Liberia's president. Moreover, many observers noted with concern the irony that Nigeria, at the time ruled by a military junta, was purportedly fighting for democracy in Liberia. Fourth, quarrels developed between UNOMIL and ECOMOG personnel over a variety of operational issues. Finally, ECOMOG suffered from a severe lack of funding and resources, even with the support of a trust fund set up by the UN Secretary-General to which the US, Britain and Denmark contributed. ECOMOG's activities in Liberia therefore suggest that, while regional organizations can deploy troops quickly to trouble spots that do not grab the attention of the great powers, not only are they afflicted by similar resource constraints and dilemmas as the UN, but the participation of the regional hegemon (in this case Nigeria) can also fuel suspicions as to the motives for intervention and thus reduce the level of local support for the operation.

The Pacific Islands Forum and the Solomon Islands (2003–)

The Solomon Islands achieved independence from Britain in 1978. Through the 1980s and 1990s, however, the local economy gradually deteriorated, thanks largely to a combination of corruption and mismanagement. Within this context of growing economic hardship, Malaitan migration to the island of Guadalcanal helped fuel ethnic resentment. In late 1998 the Guadalcanal Revolutionary Army/Isatabu Freedom Movement (IFM) embarked on a campaign of violence and intimidation against Malaitans, forcing some 20,000 to flee. Malaitans responded by forming the Malaita Eagle Force (MEF), which countered IFM attacks and demanded – and sometimes violently claimed – compensation for the destruction of property. In 2001 Australia brokered the Townsville Agreement, which provided for elections overseen by an International Peace Monitoring Team (IPMT), comprising forty-nine people.

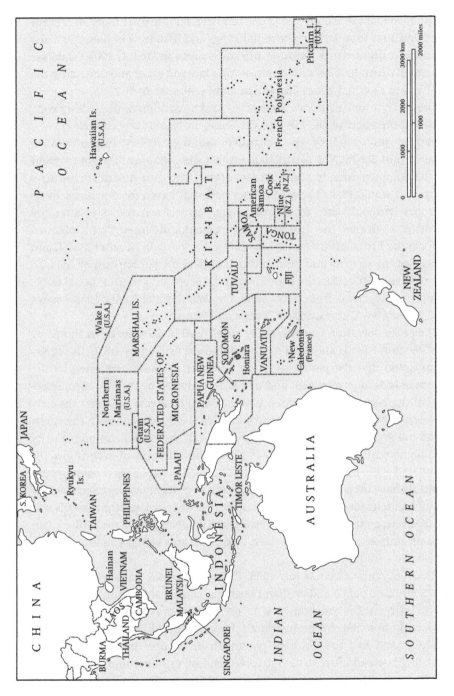

Map 13.2 *Economic and Social Commission for Asia and the Pacific (showing the Solomon Islands)*

Sir Allan Kemakaze was elected prime minister, but the IPMT failed to prevent the ex-militias from forming criminal gangs and withdrew in June 2002. The situation continued to deteriorate into lawlessness, and in July 2003 Kemakaze requested Australian assistance in restoring law and order and disarming the militia and criminal gangs (McMullan and Peebles 2006: 5).

The catalyst for Australia's decision to lead a coalition of the willing comprised of members of the PIF into the Solomon Islands was the release of a report in July 2003 by the Australian Strategic Policy Institute (ASPI) (Wainwright 2003a). The report claimed that the collapse of the government in the Solomon Islands posed an important threat to Australian security because it would make the Solomons a potential haven for organized international criminals and, more worryingly, terrorists. A few days after the report was released, the Australian government announced that it planned to form the Regional Assistance Mission to the Solomon Islands (RAMSI) and reiterated the security and humanitarian arguments put forward by ASPI. To help win support within the region, Australia proposed a multinational force, comprising elements from New Zealand as well as other Pacific Island states (Fiji, Papua New Guinea, Samoa, Tonga and Vanuatu).

The peace operation was effectively authorized by an agreement signed by the Solomon Islands and each of the interveners on 24 July 2003. The agreement noted that the peace operation had been formally requested by the Solomon Islands government and had been endorsed by the PIF, encompassing all the region's island states. It went on to delineate precisely the new force's mandate, chain of command and rules of engagement. Both the agreement and RAMSI itself had the strong support of the overwhelming majority of Solomon Islanders. Interestingly, when the question of securing a UN mandate for the mission was raised (which, given the 2003 agreement, would probably have been a formality), the Australian government rejected the idea out of hand. Its foreign minister, Alexander Downer, argued that the UN was an ineffective instrument and that a regional coalition of the willing had greater authority to authorize such a mission and would conduct it more effectively without the UN.

RAMSI began work on 24 July 2003. The initial RAMSI operation comprised 2,225 military, police and civilian personnel (among their number were 325 police officers). The political head of the mission was Nick Warner, a well-respected diplomat from Australia's Department of Foreign Affairs and Trade. RAMSI had two primary phases. In phase one, it was tasked with restoring law and order, which involved ending criminal impunity and disarming the militia and criminal gangs. Although the whole mission was characterized as 'police led' (Wainwright 2003b: 493), the reality is that, during this first phase, different parts of the mission were led by different agencies. The military contingent led efforts to disarm the militia and criminal groups, and by November 2003 they had removed from circulation 3,700 weapons, including 660 high-powered weapons. In August 2003 one of the most notorious criminal leaders, Harold Keke, surrendered to RAMSI. Meanwhile, the police contingent focused on investigating crimes committed by militias and criminals with the aim of ending impunity and cleaning up the Royal Solomon Islands Police (RSIP) as a precursor to enhancing its capacity to maintain law and order. By the end of 2003, 733 people had been arrested on 1,168 charges (McMullan and Peebles 2006). Over time, around one-third of RSIP personnel were removed and prosecuted on corruption charges. The first phase of the operation was therefore relatively successful.

Phase two was more complex and protracted. This aimed to build the capacity of the Solomon Islands government to maintain law and order and to facilitate the resolution of the conflict. During this phase, the military component was withdrawn almost entirely and the focus of the mission came to rest on the 200 or so Australian police officers. Their mission was further broken down into eight distinct phases, which included the detailed specification of institutional problems in the Solomon's law and justice system, community relationship-building measures, the identification, mentoring and coaching of key RSIP personnel, identifying gaps between what the authorities ought to be able to accomplish in an effective and legitimate manner and what they could actually accomplish, the establishment of a transparent institutional processes, and devising a meaningful exit strategy (AFP 2006: 58). Throughout 2005, steady progress was made. High-profile cases were successfully brought to trial and the Australian police handed over primary responsibility for policing almost entirely to the RSIP. The wider nation-building and conflict resolution parts of the mission proved less successful, as the April 2006 riots demonstrated.

The riots that broke out in the capital city of Honiara were fuelled by a mixture of political intrigue and racism which sent the country into lawlessness. The unrest, which went largely unchecked for days by the RSIP, exposed the limits of capacity-building, and it was left to the international police contingent to protect parliamentarians and gradually restore order. The RSIP was able to prevent the spread of violence but the international contingent sustained thirty-one casualties, including five serious injuries and the destruction of eleven vehicles (AFP 2006: 59). In the aftermath of the riots, capacity-building efforts resumed and several prominent Solomon Islanders were prosecuted for their part in the violence. This alone suggests that progress was made in relation to capacity-building in the justice sector but that the system remained fragile and required external assistance to respond to crises such as rioting and widespread disorder.

The RAMSI experience illustrates some of the benefits and shortcomings of regional operations. On the one hand, the mission proved relatively successful largely on account of its rapid deployment and overwhelming capability (McMullan and Peebles 2006: 6). Both the military and police contingents fared relatively well in the Solomon Islands because they were able to remove potential troublemakers rapidly and bring prominent criminals to trial.

Similarly, the 2006 riots did not escalate or spread because RAMSI was able to provide timely support to the RSIP. On the downside, however, some critics suggest that RAMSI failed to build stable peace in the Solomon Islands precisely because it lacks the peacebuilding capacity of the UN. Other critics argued that, as an Australian-led mission, it carried neocolonial connotations that impeded efforts to promote local ownership and build sustainable peace (Fickling 2003).

13.4 Conclusion

In some parts of the world, notably Europe and sub-Saharan Africa, regional arrangements are clearly an increasingly important feature of the contemporary landscape of peace operations. In other areas, however, notably Asia and the Americas, regional organizations have chosen not to get involved in conducting military peace operations. Regionalization thus remains a very uneven process. Moreover, those regions that have been involved in peace operations have not been able to escape from the same sets of challenges that have long confronted the UN's peacekeepers.

The challenge for the UN has been to develop constructive relationships with those regional organizations that are in the peace operations business and ensure that they do not undermine its attempts to build stable peace. This is especially important in circumstances where enforcement activities are likely to occur. Although the UN Charter clearly stipulates that regional arrangements must receive Security Council authorization before force is used, in practice the Council's selective and inconsistent response to organizations that have violated the letter of the law has encouraged challenges to this legal framework, particularly in Africa. Of all the world's regional associations, it is only those in the West, namely the EU and NATO, that have conducted operations beyond their own borders. In addition, these are the only regional institutions that have the resources necessary to sustain relatively large operations in the field for a considerable period of time. Other regional organizations, especially those in Africa, lack the resources to sustain the deployment of even a relatively small number of peacekeepers. In this sense, regional organizations are, at best, a useful complement to the UN in certain circumstances. It would be unwise, therefore, to suggest that regionalization in its normative sense provides a sound basis on which to maintain international peace and security across the entire globe.

CHAPTER FOURTEEN

Privatization

In the last two decades especially, private security companies (PSCs) have played increasingly significant roles in peace operations, raising questions about their potential to help satisfy the increasing global demand for peacekeeping. For their critics, today's PSCs represent little more than the contemporary face of mercenary activity. The former UN Special Rapporteur on the mercenary question, Enrique Ballesteros, for instance, suggested that the activities of PSCs represented a kind of 'formally tolerated mercenary intervention' and that there was 'a clear association' between their activities and 'mercenary acts' (Ballesteros 1997: §§ 58–9). From this perspective, it would be unwise for the UN and other peacekeepers to rely too heavily upon private military firms. For their supporters, on the other hand, these contractors work in legitimate corporations that undertake important and lawful work related to peace and security and should not be described as mercenaries. Indeed, they argue that, given the parlous state of the UN's resources and the increasing demand for peacekeepers worldwide, contingency contractors should be permitted to play an even larger role in peace operations than they already do. The challenge facing the UN and other international organizations is thus to find an appropriate balance between the public and private provision of peacekeeping.

This chapter proceeds in three parts. In the first section, we provide an overview of the private security industry and its relationship with peace operations. The second section then analyses the advantages and disadvantages commonly associated with the privatization of peace operations. In the final section, we address the most controversial issue of all – namely, whether the UN should hire private contractors in enforcement roles.

14.1 The private security industry and peace operations

Reading the UN's official documents on peace operations will not reveal much information about the roles that private contractors play within them. For example, the Brahimi Report makes only two brief and vague references to supporting private contractors; the Best Practices Unit's *Handbook on UN Multidimensional Peacekeeping Operations* (2003) alludes to the 'private sector' a couple of times, but not to PSCs specifically; while the UN *Principles and*

Guidelines (2008) document does not mention them at all. This is surprising because private contractors have played important roles in the conduct of peace operations and have done so for a considerable period.

As Jeffrey Herbst (1999: 108) has noted, before the twentieth century the privatization of violence 'was a routine aspect of international relations'. The private security industry is thus not a new phenomenon, but it has experienced a huge boom since the 1980s and has developed in some novel ways. Its expansion and its rise to greater prominence within the area of peace operations came about as a result of four interrelated developments (see Shearer 1998b; Singer 2003a; Avant 2005: 26–38).

First, the ideological justification for privatizing security services was given a major boost with the election to power of Ronald Reagan's administration in the US and Margaret Thatcher's Conservative government in the UK. The neoliberal economic policies espoused by both these leaders supported the further privatization of many domestic enterprises, including the provision of security. As more and more domestic companies began providing security services to everything from nightclubs to prisons, as well as the armed forces, some of them developed transnational dimensions and became the core of today's contractors involved in peace operations.

The second major factor was the end of the Cold War. This produced a vacuum in the market for security and a concomitant reduction in the levels of Western and Soviet armed forces. The subsequent downsizing of the armed forces on both sides left thousands of former soldiers without an obvious source of income. And, particularly on the Soviet side, it also produced a massive surplus of cheap and accessible weaponry, ranging from small arms and light weapons to helicopter gunships.

The third factor involved the transformations taking place in the nature of contemporary warfare, especially the increasingly important requirements of high-technology weapons systems in the Western world that dramatically increased the need for specialized, and often civilian, IT and communications expertise. In the world's weaker states, on the other hand, the erosion of the sovereign state's ability to enforce its legal monopoly on the use of organized violence and the continued prevalence of civil wars during the 1990s provided the private security industry with a significant demand for its services. In its most extreme form this involved embattled regimes in weak states such as Angola and Sierra Leone looking to hire armies to tackle insurgencies.

Finally, as discussed in chapter 4, the early 1990s witnessed a large increase in the number and size of peace operations. At this time, the private security industry was well placed to help fill the capacity gaps faced by the UN and other international organizations.

The privatized security industry was generating approximately $20 billion a year by the beginning of the twenty-first century, and was expected to be worth many times that figure by 2010 (Singer 2001: 199; 2003a: 78–9). It currently supports an unspecified but significant – well over 300 – number of firms, but a consolidation into larger transnational companies is under way. Mirroring trends which globalization has encouraged across the arms industry more generally (see Hayward 2000), many of the most active PSCs (such as MPRI and ArmorGroup) are subsidiaries of larger corporations listed on public stock exchanges, including Dyncorp and TRW (Singer 2001: 192). In 2002, for instance, all but two of the Fortune 500 firms in the US were involved in some form of armament production (Nordstrom 2002: 257). It is thus not surprising that most PSCs hail from advanced industrialized states, most notably, the US, the UK, France and Israel (although the personnel hired by these firms come from a much wider pool of countries). An important exception was South Africa, which after the end of apartheid and the subsequent downsizing of its defence force provided the personnel for the now defunct company Executive Outcomes (see box 14.3).

As in other areas of commercial activity, PSCs have become members of trade groups and associations. These include the American Society for Industrial Security, the International Federation of Risk & Insurance Management Associations, and the International Peace Operations Association (IPOA). A profile of the last of these groups is provided in box 14.1.

Not surprisingly, the private security industry is far from monolithic. As a result, analysts have devised various methods to categorize different aspects of it. Of most relevance here are those elements that deal with military and policing issues. Indeed, some groups are now referring to themselves as the 'peace and stability industry', 'contingency contractors' or 'battlespace contractors' in order to emphasize their specific focus (see box 14.1). The key to understanding these different types of firms and activities lies in developing a good grasp of the services the companies provide and the contracts they are hired to undertake. With this in mind, Deborah Avant (2005) has provided a useful overview of the industry as it relates to military and policing activities. Figure 14.1 illustrates some of the different types of military and policing activities undertaken by PSCs and their relationship with the front line of combat operations. Table 14.1 uses the distinction between the financing and delivery of security services to map the industry. The shaded boxes in this table (the two outermost rows and columns) represent Avant's definition of the term *privatization* – i.e. referring to decisions to devolve delivery or financing of services to private entities.

Private firms have long been involved in the conduct of peace operations, and many of them are listed on the supply database for UN and UN-related organizations. In broad terms, they have played advisory roles (e.g. MPRI in Croatia) and provided logistical, intelligence and other forms of support (e.g. DSL in the DRC). To give just a few examples, a wide variety of operations, including UNAMSIL, ECOMOG and AMIS, received logistical support from PAE; DSL provided security for UN infrastructure and personnel in Kinshasa; and a private security firm, Brown and Root (now KBR), provided all the support services at the US military base in Kosovo, Camp Bondsteel.

Box 14.1 The International Peace Operations Association

Founded in 2001 and based in Washington, DC, the International Peace Operations Association (IPOA) is a non-profit trade association whose mission is to promote high operational and ethical standards of firms active in the peace and stability industry; to engage in a constructive dialogue with policy-makers about the growing and positive contribution of these firms to the enhancement of international peace, development and human security; and to inform the concerned public about the activities and role of the industry.

IPOA's stated aims are better supervision of private companies operating under the umbrella of UN or government-led operations and better coordination between private organizations, government, NGOs and international organizations. IPOA members provide a wide range of services, including aviation, base support, communications, consultancy, de-mining and unexploded ordinance removal, insurance, intelligence, logistics, medical, risk management, satellite tracking, supply, surveillance and training. The association strives for greater awareness of private sector contributions in peace and stability affairs and raising the standards of companies in the peace and stability industry, while recognizing the leadership of government and international organizations in peacekeeping operations.

As of August 2008, IPOA had fifty-one full corporate members. Applicant companies must complete a formal application process, which does not automatically guarantee acceptance. If accepted into membership, companies must continue to uphold the ethical standards of the association as set out in the IPOA Code of Conduct. This is intended to promote accountability and high operational and ethical standards. To this end, the IPOA has conducted governmental advocacy; engaged all relevant stakeholders; hosted roundtables and forums; published research; provided information to media; shared information with NGOs; provided training courses; and fielded complaints about the industry.

Source: paraphrased from http://ipoaworld.org/eng/faqipoa.html
(accessed 25 August 2008).

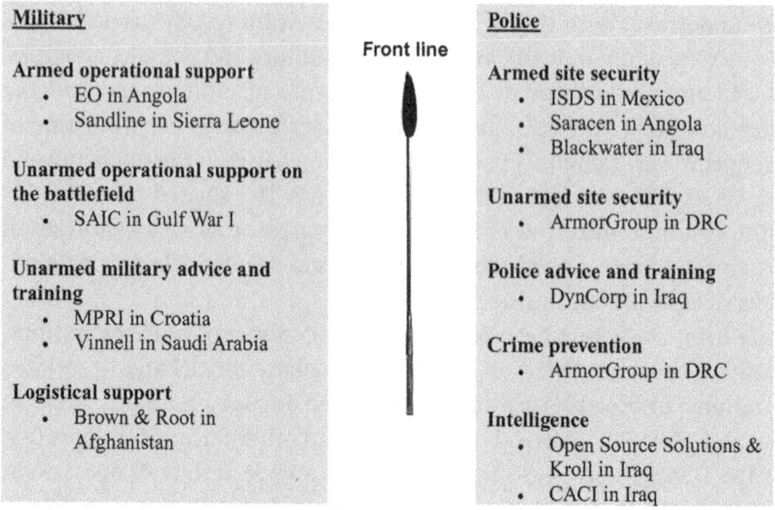

Military

Front line

Armed operational support
- EO in Angola
- Sandline in Sierra Leone

Unarmed operational support on the battlefield
- SAIC in Gulf War I

Unarmed military advice and training
- MPRI in Croatia
- Vinnell in Saudi Arabia

Logistical support
- Brown & Root in Afghanistan

Police

Armed site security
- ISDS in Mexico
- Saracen in Angola
- Blackwater in Iraq

Unarmed site security
- ArmorGroup in DRC

Police advice and training
- DynCorp in Iraq

Crime prevention
- ArmorGroup in DRC

Intelligence
- Open Source Solutions & Kroll in Iraq
- CACI in Iraq

Source: Avant (2005: 17).

Figure 14.1 *Contracts in battlespace*

TABLE 14.1 The variety of arrangements for allocating violence

Financing for security services

Delivery of security services	National financing	Foreign national financing	Multi-national financing	Private (for-profit) financing	Private (not-for-profit) financing
National delivery	• US in WWII	• German troops in the American Revolution	• The first Gulf War	• Shell financing Nigerian forces	• WWF financing park guards in the DRC
Foreign national delivery	• German troops in the American Revolution	• Korean troops fighting for the US in Vietnam	• The first Gulf War	• Branch group contributing to Nigerian forces in Sierra Leone	
Multi-national delivery	• NATO in Kosovo	• Muslim states' contribution to Western military aid in Bosnia	• UN peace-keeping		
Private (for-profit) delivery	• MPRI's provision of ROTC trainers to the US	• MPRI's work in Croatia	• MPRI's work in Bosnia	• DSL working for Lonhro in Mozambique	• DSL working for ICRC around the world
Private (not-for-profit) delivery			• 'Green Cross'	• BP financing Colombian paramilitaries	• Wildaid in Asia

Source: Avant (2005: 25).

Box 14.2 provides a profile of one of these multidimensional firms and the roles it played during the wars of Yugoslav succession in the 1990s. As discussed in more detail in section 14.3, to date, the UN has shied away from using contractors in front-line enforcement activities. In other areas, however, it has made increasing use of private capabilities.

Two good examples are intelligence and de-mining. Within the UN system, many states have consistently balked at the creation of a centralized intelligence-gathering capability. This is in spite of the fact that complex peace operations are very difficult to undertake effectively without good intelligence. The existence of PSCs offering intelligence-related services means that these capabilities can be purchased through the global marketplace and the concerns of UN members about centralized intelligence structures can be

---

Box 14.2 Military Professional Resources Incorporated (MPRI) in the Balkans

Founded in 1990, MPRI is a US company based near Washington, DC, and subject to US law. It is headed by retired senior military personnel and has a core staff of roughly 400 and a database comprising between 7,000 and 12,000 ex-security personnel, including over 200 former generals and flag officers. The company emerged as a direct result of American military downsizing and privatization and by 1998 had a turnover of $48 million. It undertakes work for the US government in a number of areas such as training and evaluation. Most of its work is for the US government but it has undertaken contracts elsewhere, including, for example, a small training operation in Nigeria. Again, in 1998, MPRI was managing twenty contracts worth more than $90 million. Of these, only three were international, but together they accounted for roughly half of the total income.

In 1994 MPRI was contracted by the Croatian government to design a programme to improve the capabilities of the Croatian armed forces and 'to enhance the possibility of Croatia becoming a suitable candidate' for NATO's Partnership for Peace Programme. It received a licence from the State Department for this contract, which it began in January 1995.

Many people argued that later in 1995 Croatian forces performed unexpectedly well in Operation Storm, an offensive against Serb forces in the Krajina region. The fact that the Croatian attack was better planned and coordinated than on any previous occasion has left many analysts with the view that the Croatian armed forces had profited from their relationship with MPRI, though no one has suggested that it was directly involved. MPRI deny any connection and maintain that their involvement was limited to classroom instruction.

MPRI also won a contract to 'assist the Army of the Federation [in Bosnia] in becoming a self-sufficient and fully operable force'. Unlike its contract in Croatia, this involved MPRI with teaching combat skills to the Bosnian/Croat armed forces. This contract was paid for by a trust fund to which a number of Muslim countries contributed and was licensed by the US State Department as a part of their 'Train and Equip' policy in Bosnia. It involved some 200 former US military personnel and is thought to have had a major impact on the effectiveness of the federation armed forces.

Sources: House of Commons (2002: 13); Duffield (2001: 67); Singer (2001: 201).

bypassed. One example saw the UN hire a private firm to provide intelligence on the 'guns for gems' trade being run by UNITA rebels in Angola (Singer 2003a: 182). De-mining and the removal of unexploded ordinance is another area where companies such as ArmorGroup, RONCO Consulting and DynCorp International have played a prominent role. Although it is clearly a very important part of any peacebuilding operation, removing landmines is also a lucrative business, with one estimate suggesting that the cost of undertaking this worldwide could exceed $33 billion (cited in Spearin 2008: 368). This has been described as a 'pot of gold' for private contractors with the relevant skills (Singer 2003a: 82).

14.2 The costs and benefits of privatizing peace operations

In late 1994 international society was debating how to deal with the large numbers of Rwandan refugees who had fled into Zaire in the wake of the genocide. The problem was that remnants of the genocidal regime and its armed forces had embedded themselves in the refugee camps near Rwanda's border. The subsequent turmoil led UNHCR to conclude that the situation was beyond its scope and mandate. As a result, the UN Secretary-General told UNHCR that the DPKO would consider the option of sending a force to keep the peace in the camps. In November, the DPKO laid out three options: Option A involved deployment of a large-scale force (c.7,000) under Chapter VII of the UN Charter; Option B was to assemble a smaller UN peacekeeping force of around 3,000 to 5,000 personnel under Chapter VI; Option C was to hire a private company to provide protection in the camps (Jones 2001: 140–3). The particulars of Option C involved an offer from a British firm to provide training and logistical support for Zairian soldiers. Although the proposal received some support, including from one permanent member of the Security Council, other states rejected it because of the high costs and on principle: they considered hiring a private contractor to take the lead 'was tantamount to shirking…an international public responsibility' (ibid.: 142).

In the end, the private proposal was rejected and no peacekeeping force was ever deployed, with the result that the Rwandan armed forces took matters into their own hands and hostilities resumed on the Rwanda–Zaire border. Nevertheless, these debates revealed the general reluctance of the UN's member states to countenance a privatized peace operation. Four years later, UN Secretary-General Kofi Annan still concluded that 'the world may not be ready to privatise peace' (Annan 1998a). As noted above, however, the general reluctance of its members to establish a peace operation led by private actors did not stop the UN hiring private contractors to conduct a wide variety of tasks within its own peace operations. It has also not prevented organized contractors from becoming significant 'expert' voices in contemporary debates about peace operations. In relation to the crisis in

Darfur, for instance, private contractors were involved from the start, 'providing logistics, base construction, management and operations, medical services, and helicopters and vehicles for the AU troops' (Doug Brooks, cited in Leander and van Munster 2007: 202). In this sense it is undisputed that the private security industry adds to the list of options available to the UN and other actors for the conduct of their peace operations. But which options should be utilized further and which should be rejected?

Potential benefits

Most advocates for the further privatization of peace operations begin by pointing to the current inadequacies of the UN and other international organizations, as well as to the fact that most victims of war crimes do not really care who stops their tormentors as long as they are stopped. Put bluntly, the argument is that private firms can help fill the existing capacity gaps left by the UN and other organizations. Whereas the UN is slow, expensive and militarily inefficient, private firms claim they will be able to deploy better equipped personnel quickly and cheaply (Brooks and Laroia 2005).

A related argument is that the better paid and equipped contractors will have a greater incentive to perform well than some UN peacekeepers – think, for example, of the disastrous conduct of the Bangladeshi contingent in UNAMIR, which regularly disobeyed orders and refused to undertake risky missions. Private firms are more likely to have better personnel, it is argued, because they are not only able to target their recruiting for capable personnel far more flexibly than the UN, but are also less threatened by internal national tensions that plague multinational forces (Singer 2003a: 183).

Another argument in favour of privatization suggests that, because contractors are less concerned than governments about the 'body-bag syndrome' – the idea that domestic opinion will turn against participation in a peace operation if its troops suffer casualties – they are willing (as long as the price is right) to go where governments fear to tread (see Shearer 1998a). In this sense, PSCs might be particularly well suited to forming a type of rapid reaction capability able to add military muscle to a peace operation. Although Executive Outcomes suffered the loss of around fifty personnel during its operations in Angola (1993–5), it did not pull out. This compares favourably alongside some state militaries. For example, the US withdrew from Somalia in the wake of the October 1993 'Black Hawk Down' incident and shortly afterwards refused to deploy peacekeepers to Haiti when its troops were confronted by a group of local thugs. Similarly, the Belgian government withdrew its peacekeepers from UNAMIR in April 1994 after ten of them were killed in the first days of the Rwandan genocide.

When attempting to counter likely criticisms, advocates of privatizing peace operations argue that any firms which prove inefficient, unreliable, corrupt or abusive will ultimately be forced out of business by market forces.

In sum, bad companies will soon get a bad reputation and will go out of business. This line of argument was regularly used by Executive Outcomes personnel, one of whom suggested that the 'fastest thing that would get us out of business is human-rights violations' (cited in Spearin 2002: 247). More generally, the author of a recent report by the Peace Operations Institute – an off-shoot of the IPOA – argued that '[a] company's failure to respect the association code of conduct would result in a tarnished image and the loss of a competitive edge within the industry' (Rochester 2007: 47).

Part of the problem with these arguments is the way in which individual companies have been closed down but the people behind them simply set up a new firm and continue their career within the industry. The track record of the former British army colonel Tim Spicer is a good example. As chief executive officer of Sandline International from 1996, Spicer presided over two highly controversial episodes before landing one of the biggest private security contracts ever recorded. The first episode, in 1997, was the debacle of Operation Contravene in Papua New Guinea. This involved Sandline entering into a contract of 'questionable legality' to defeat a group of rebels on the island of Bougainville. It also saw Spicer arrested and the activities of his company provoke violent riots and almost a full-blown civil war (Singer 2003a: 191–6). The second, in 1998, was the so-called Arms to Africa scandal, in which the British Foreign Office was found to have colluded with Sandline International to bring 30 tonnes of arms and ammunition into Sierra Leone in apparent contravention of a UN arms embargo (see Foreign Affairs Committee 1999). Despite such controversy, in 2004 Spicer's new company, Aegis Defence Services, landed a $293 million Pentagon contract to coordinate security for reconstruction projects, as well as support for other private military companies, in Iraq (Baer 2007).

Potential costs

In terms of potential costs, critics of the privatization of peace operations raise several issues. First, they point out that, within the UN system, responsibility for maintaining international peace and security lies with the member states in general and the permanent five members of the Security Council in particular. Resorting to private contractors represents an abdication of this public responsibility. As a former head of the DPKO, Jean-Marie Guéhenno, has argued, by deploying 'private troops, the first signal you send is: this is important, but not important enough to risk our own people' (cited in Spearin 2002: 243). As our earlier discussion of the attempts to establish a peace operation amid the refugee camps in Zaire in 1994 demonstrates, this principle of state-led action still retains significant appeal at the UN.

Second, private contractors have a distinctly mixed track record when it comes to issues of accountability and transparency. Before the recent scandals concerning Blackwater's operations in Iraq, one of the more publicized negative episodes occurred in 2002 when DynCorp employees contracted by the US government to train the Bosnian police were accused of raping and trafficking local women and girls (although it should be noted that they were apparently part of a larger network involving other UN personnel). DynCorp's Bosnia site supervisor even videotaped himself raping two women. While the offenders were moved out of Bosnia without facing prosecution, some of Dyncorp's employees who attempted to blow the whistle on these crimes were fired by the company (Singer 2003a: 222). To help overcome these problems, it will be necessary to establish mechanisms and structures that can maintain competition to ensure quality and replacement; make certain the company in question is not linked to a business network with stakes in the conflict zone concerned; secure outside vetting of personnel and the attachment of independent observer teams; and make sure that contractors place themselves under the jurisdiction of international tribunals for any violations of the laws of war (ibid.: 187). Of course, similar problems of conduct have been evident in peace operations undertaken by states and international organizations (see chapter 16), but until considerable advances are made in regulating the private sector there can be no guarantees that contractors will act in a transparent manner or be held accountable for any abuses (on the debate over regulation, see House of Commons 2002; Spear 2006).

A third common complaint centres on the profit motive driving private firms. From this perspective, critics are concerned about several factors. Not only might contractors have an incentive to maintain a state of conflict and attempt to make their clients dependent upon their services, but the personnel they attract are likely to include those that find significant gratification in warfare. One attempt to get around the profit motive problem but still tap into the expertise within the private sector is the Global Peace and Security Partnership (GPSP). This aims to 'provide a professional and experienced rapid response capability, with a strong service ethos, to complement the traditional peacekeeping forces deployed by the United Nations.' It would consist of a multinational contingent of between 5,000 and 10,000 personnel drawn primarily from the ranks of retired security sector or humanitarian relief workers and listed on a GPSP-managed database. This would not be an intervention force designed to fight 'its way into environments under its own authority'; rather, it would act as a private source of support for UN operations (Spearin 2002: 244).

As discussed earlier, proponents of privatization point to the staying power of firms relative to states. There are, however, also examples of private contractors fleeing the theatre when things go wrong. To take the example of Sierra Leone's civil war, it is often forgotten that the reason why Executive Outcomes received its contract in the first place was to take over from Gurkha Security Guards, which had left the country shortly after being hired when rebels killed several of its employees in an ambush. It is also not clear that private firms could assemble the numbers of personnel (i.e. approximately 20,000) needed to maintain a large peace support operation on their own. In this sense, private firms might at best be able to perform a spearhead or vanguard function for a larger UN force. The problem is that, in such a scenario, UN peacekeepers are likely to resent the presence of better paid and better equipped private contractors, as happens with better paid and equipped Blue Helmets. Nor is there much evidence that contractors are trained in the skills that make a good peacebuilder as opposed to a good warrior. Until that is the case, they will be able to deal only with the symptoms of armed conflicts; it will require other actors to treat the underlying causes.

Finally, contractors both contribute to and reflect the growing erosion of the state's monopoly on the legitimate instruments of military force. Securing the state's control over other sources of military power is something that international society has worked hard to achieve over several centuries. Indeed, the privatization of military force is a major part of the problem confronting much of the developing world, where wealthy actors now find it relatively easy to acquire military means with which to pursue their agendas. By encouraging the dispersal of military capacity and expertise, private firms are likely to make already complex emergencies more complicated, increase the prevalence and legitimacy of using military means to address political problems, and thus make it harder to bring the instruments of violence under democratic control. A further concern is that deploying contractors into conflict zones raises important moral questions about placing 'civilians' (albeit security guards, etc.) in harm's way. At the very least, it risks further eroding the distinction between combatants and non-combatants that is crucial to the limitation of war.

14.3 Privatized peace enforcement?

Although the vast majority of private companies have not been hired to take part in direct combat and enforcement operations, some of them have done so. The most famous case is that of Executive Outcomes (EO), the now defunct South African firm hired to defeat local resistance in several armed conflicts during the 1990s. A summary of EO's enforcement operations in Angola (1993–5) is provided in box 14.3. Its most thoroughly documented operations, however, are those it conducted in Sierra Leone.

Between May 1995 and January 1997, EO was hired by Captain Valentine Strasser's military junta to break the Revolutionary United Front's (RUF) control of the Sierra Leone's lucrative diamond mines (see Harding 1997; Musah 2000; Howe 2001: ch. 5). Strasser had apparently heard of EO's achievements in Angola and was keen to hire them to solve his own rebel problem. EO's fee for the twenty-one months was approximately $35 million (when it could not pay the monthly fee, Strasser's regime reportedly gave significant mining concessions to the EO–Branch Group). As instructed, EO's operatives

Box 14.3 Executive Outcomes in Angola, 1993–5

Mercenaries have played a negative part in the Angolan conflict on several occasions. British and American mercenaries fought for the FNLA in 1975–6, the MPLA was supported by exiled Katangese gendarmes and later by Cuban troops (for whom it paid the Cuban government), and a variety of mercenaries have been associated with UNITA. In 1992 UN-supervised elections were held in Angola, with the MPLA emerging victorious. UNITA subsequently withdrew its troops from the army and one month later attempted a coup. This failed and the war resumed.

In 1993, Executive Outcomes (EO) was hired by Sonangol, an Angolan parastatal company, to secure the Soyo oilfield and the computerized pumping station owned by Chevron, Petrangol, Texaco and Elf–Fina–Gulf. This had been under attack since a 1992 UN-brokered peace agreement collapsed. A small force from EO backed by two Angolan battalions regained the oilfield early in 1993. EO then withdrew, leaving the Angolan battalions in place, but Soyo was subsequently recaptured by UNITA. In September that same year the Angolan government agreed a more far-reaching contract with EO to conquer and defend diamond-mining areas in Cafunfo province and elsewhere, to train their troops and to direct operations against UNITA. The contract, reportedly worth significantly more than $60 million per annum, included a supply of arms as well as training. With the assistance and sometimes participation of EO personnel, Angolan government forces won a series of victories during 1994. The recapture of the diamond fields in Lunda Note in June 1994 is commonly seen as a turning point in the war, partly because it reduced UNITA's capacity to pay for its operations. In November 1994 UNITA signed a peace agreement in Lusaka, which included a provision for the withdrawal of foreign forces. Nevertheless, EO remained in Angola until December 1995, when it was withdrawn, reportedly at US insistence.

Although EO never had more than 500 men in Angola (indeed it often had far fewer), it is generally regarded as having tilted the military balance in Angola at a far lower cost, politically and fiscally, than could have been accomplished through direct aid to Angola's military. This, in turn, facilitated the ceasefire and the Lusaka Peace Agreement. EO's fee for its operations in Angola was $40 million per annum plus an undisclosed number of mineral concessions, one of which, the Yetwene mine, was worth at least $25 million per year. Even these figures, however, are still around half of UNAVEM III's budget, which between 1996 and 1997 was $135 million. EO lost eleven personnel (with seven missing).

Sources: House of Commons (2002: 11); Spearin (2001: 28); Reno (1998: 61–7); Howe (2001: 205); Shearer (1998b: 79).

were able successfully to train some of the government's soldiers and the self-defence militias known as the *kamajors* and work with them to break the RUF's resistance. They were so successful that the RUF sued for peace and demanded that the terms of the agreement include a clause stating that EO could not continue to work in the country. Only four months after the termination of its contract, and probably as a direct result of EO's withdrawal, the newly elected government of Ahmed Tejan Kabbah was overthrown in a military coup and the capital, Freetown, was sacked by the RUF.

EO's activities in Sierra Leone generated heated debate about the most appropriate relationship between the UN and private firms in relation to peace enforcement. EO's ability to tilt local balances of power is particularly significant, given that the concept of peace support operations (discussed in chapter 12) also attempts to alter local politics in favour of those actors that support the construction of liberal states and societies as a long-term solution to conflict. This coincidence of interests led some commentators to propose that the UN should seriously consider making more explicit use of contractors as part of its own enforcement operations. David Shearer, for instance, suggested that, had there been a structured relationship between EO and the UN in Sierra Leone, the military coup that ousted President Kabbah could have been avoided. EO personnel, Shearer argued, could have maintained a threat of enforcement against the RUF, giving the UN the breathing space it needed to implement its post-conflict programmes fully and to provide adequate reassurances for the RUF to demobilize (Shearer 1998b: 78–9). As it turned out, Sierra Leone's war ended only after British and UN forces helped ensure the military defeat of the RUF in late 2000. Would it therefore have been illegitimate for international society to support private means of achieving the same end four years earlier?

Despite EO's track record in Angola and Sierra Leone, and in spite of the problems UN and other peacekeepers encountered when dealing with spoiler groups, the consensus at the UN remained that contractors should not be hired to conduct enforcement actions. This position was recently confirmed in May 2007, when the governments of the US, the UK, the Netherlands and Norway, as well as companies in the extractive and energy sectors and various NGOs, developed a set of Voluntary Principles on Security and Human Rights (see Voluntary Principles 2007) to guide companies 'in maintaining the safety and security of their operations within an operating framework that ensures respect for human rights and fundamental freedoms'. Although this was directed at firms in the extractive and energy sectors, one of the principles was that private contractors should use force only for defensive purposes: 'Consistent with their function, private security should provide only preventative and defensive services and should not engage in activities exclusively the responsibility of state military or law enforcement authorities. Companies should designate services, technology and equipment capable of offensive and defensive purposes as being for defensive use only.'

As a general rule, this approach retains the backing of the world's governments, which remain deeply sceptical of endorsing the proactive use of force by private actors. However, some advocates of the industry have posed the question of what should happen on those occasions when the UN is either unwilling or unable to respond effectively to stop cases of genocide and mass killing, or when the UN and other organizations are unable to provide defensive humanitarian security for populations trapped in displacement camps and other areas. Would it be acceptable for contractors to deploy to the area in question, defeat any local opposition or protect certain 'safe areas', set up infrastructures, and then hand over to UN or other peacekeepers (Singer

> **Box 14.4 Stopping the next genocide?**
>
> Violence breaks out in a small African state. The local government collapses and reports emerge that civilians are being massacred by the tens of thousands. Refugees stream out in pitiable columns. As scenes reminiscent of the Rwanda genocide are played out on the world's television screens once again, pressure mounts to do something. The U.N.'s calls for action fall on deaf ears. In the U.S., the leadership remains busy with the war on terrorism and Iraq and decides that the political risks of doing nothing are far lower than the risks of losing any American soldiers' lives in what is essentially a mission of charity. Other nations follow its lead, and none are willing to risk their own troops. As the international community dithers, innocent men, women, and children die by the hour. It is at this point that a private company steps forward with a novel offer. Using its own employees, the firm will establish protected safe havens where civilians can take refuge and receive assistance from international aid agencies. Thousands of lives might be saved. All the company asks is a check for $150 million. (Singer 2003b)

2003a: 185)? Box 14.4 describes a potential scenario in which this might be considered legitimate, especially viewed from the perspective of the victims of the atrocities.

As we now know, EO did explore whether it would have had the capacity to intervene in the Rwandan genocide of 1994 (see Singer 2003b). Internal plans claim that the company could have had armed troops on the ground within fourteen days of its hire and been fully deployed with over 1,500 of its own soldiers, along with air and fire support (roughly the equivalent of the US Marine force that first deployed into Afghanistan), within six weeks. The cost for a six-month operation to provide protected safe havens from the genocide was estimated at $150 million (around $600,000 a day). Of course, these soldiers would not have been able to save the many thousands of people killed in the first two weeks of the genocide, nor will we ever know if they could have brought it to an end. But the evidence from UNAMIR's ability to save some locals with only very meagre resources suggests their presence could have made a big difference in their areas of deployment.

It is thus in circumstances where a robust response from the UN or relevant regional organizations to mass killing is unlikely that the 'EO option' deserves most serious consideration. In particular, there are at least four scenarios in which it might be contemplated. First, should the UN Security Council consider hiring a private army in situations of genocide where member states are unwilling to send their own soldiers (e.g. Rwanda, 1994)? Second, should it be considered in cases where the Security Council is divided on how to respond to a clear case of mass killing (e.g. Kosovo, 1999, or Darfur, 2004)? Third, should there be a role for contractors in conflicts such as those in Liberia or Burundi in the early 1990s when the Security Council explicitly agrees that a peace operation is inappropriate but where huge levels of civilian suffering are evident? Finally, would it be legitimate for contractors to be hired to supplement the firepower of an already existing peacekeeping operation, specifically to provide defensive security for designated 'safe areas'? It is only in the first of these scenarios that the Security Council might even contemplate the EO option. In the second and third cases it would be either unable to agree on a particular response (and it is highly doubtful that an EO option would be agreeable where others were not) or united in agreement that external intervention is unwise. Given the inability of peacekeepers to protect civilians in places as disparate as Srebrenica, Darfur and Bunia, arguably it is the fourth scenario which should receive most attention.

Although the victims of genocide would almost certainly support the deployment of any actors (public or private) with a mandate to stop it, there are good reasons why the Security Council is unlikely seriously to entertain the EO option. First, resorting to private contractors would highlight the Council's abdication of its responsibility to maintain international peace and security. It is hard to envisage the circumstances when this would not irreparably damage the Council's reputation and credibility. Second, it would undermine a cardinal principle of modern international society that limiting the number of actors entitled to use force is pivotal in reducing the incidence of warfare. The norm that states, and states alone, should have the monopoly on the legitimate use of military force would be severely dented if private firms were allowed to use violence for anything other than defensive purposes. A third problem is that the UN's member states appear to hold a strong collective conviction that contractors are not sufficiently transparent in their operations, and that there are no mechanisms in place that are robust enough to ensure that they will be held accountable for their actions. Although the last problem could be addressed by creating new international laws and the fact that some contractors have developed a good track record of service, others have engaged in ill-disciplined and criminal behaviour and displayed a worrying lack of restraint in relation to the use of force.

14.4 Conclusion

Private contractors have played important roles in the provision of peace operations for a long time and, especially since the end of the Cold War, their role has increased rather than diminished. This has had several consequences. First, it has generated a serious debate about the most appropriate forms of regulation for the private security industry (see House of Commons 2002). Second, it has prompted attempts to think about the legal status of civilian contractors in the world's conflict zones (Singer 2004). Third, private firms and the trade associations which represent them have gained greater acceptance as legitimate experts within debates about peace operations. To date, the UN and other international organizations have hired contractors to undertake a wide range of (often behind-the-scenes) activities, without which peace operations would simply not be able to function. In this sense, there is no reason to think that the privatization of peace operations will diminish any time soon. Nevertheless, the UN and other international organizations have so far refused to hire private firms to conduct enforcement operations, and this remains the most controversial area of the debate over privatization. Although the operations conducted by Executive Outcomes in Angola and Sierra Leone intensified calls for contractors to be given a leading role in stopping instances of genocide and the mass killing of civilians, this has not happened in practice. At present, the international climate is one in which the Security Council is unlikely to hire a private army, even in cases where it is loath to send a UN or UN-authorized force. Whether it should hire contractors to act as force multipliers for UN operations already on the ground and facing difficulties is perhaps a more urgent question. To date, therefore, it remains unclear whether the UN has found the correct balance between the public and private peacekeeping.

CHAPTER FIFTEEN

Protection of Civilians

In chapter 5 we argued that one of the most significant ideas put forward by the Brahimi Report in 2000 was that UN peacekeepers should be in the business of protecting civilians in their areas of deployment. Specifically, peacekeepers should be able to 'silence a deadly source of force that is directed at United Nations troops or the people they are charged to protect' (UN 2000: § 49). It maintained that UN peacekeepers should be granted the means to defend both themselves and those they are charged with protecting and that the protection of civilians should be a 'presumed' mandate for all UN missions. Before 2000, peace operations were largely guided by a 'culture of impartiality' that resisted the temptation to take proactive and forceful measures to protect civilians (Barnett and Finnemore 2004: 133). In the 1990s there were fleeting and uncertain attempts to give peacekeepers a limited role in the protection of civilians. From 1992 onwards the UNPROFOR mission in Bosnia had a mandate to use force to protect the delivery of humanitarian relief, and from 1993 it was mandated to deter armed attacks on Bosnia's 'safe areas' (Resolution 770, 13 August 1992, and Resolution 836, 4 June 1993). Indeed, Resolution 836 authorized UNPROFOR to 'take necessary measures, including the use of force' in protecting the safe areas (see Gow 1997: 111–14; Honig and Both 1996: 111–17).

In the short term, the well-publicized failure to protect civilians from genocide in Rwanda and Srebrenica, and from warlord violence in Somalia, only confirmed the belief that the UN should not be in the business of civilian protection. For example, Boutros-Ghali told African leaders that the 'UN mentality' was to 'maintain peace' not 'impose' it (Barnett and Finnemore 2004: 134). As we noted in chapter 4, however, the UN's own reports on these failures made this type of thinking increasingly untenable. According to the report on Srebrenica, 'the cardinal lesson of Srebrenica is that a deliberate and systematic attempt to terrorize, expel or murder an entire people must be met decisively with all necessary means', and the use of force was sometimes required 'to bring a halt to the planned and systematic killing and expulsion of civilians' (Annan 1999e: § 499).

This chapter explores the challenges raised by defining the protection of civilians as a core function of contemporary peace operations. Although there is now broad agreement that peace operations should be in the business of protecting civilians, there is much less agreement about what protection implies, which types of agencies are best placed to provide protection, and how protection is most effectively enabled (see Jones and Cater 2001). This chapter evaluates each of these questions in turn.

15.1 The emergence of the protection of civilians

Four major, interconnected factors explain the increasing importance given to civilian protection: greater interest in the subject from the Security Council; the gradual incorporation of protection into peace operations mandates; the adoption of protection agendas by humanitarian agencies; and the political commitment to the 'responsibility to protect' principle at the 2005 World Summit.

Increasing Security Council attention

Although the Security Council had passed resolutions addressing civilian protection in the early 1990s, the issue did not gain sustained prominence until the end of the decade, when Canada persuaded it to adopt a presidential statement (12 February 1999) requesting that the Secretary-General submit a report on how the UN might improve the physical and legal protection of civilians and committing to periodic Council reviews of the issue. Since then, the Council has informally agreed to hold two open debates annually (in June and December) on the protection of civilians. Soon after NATO's intervention in Kosovo, the Council adopted Resolution 1265 (17 September 1999), expressing its 'willingness' to 'respond to situations of armed conflict where civilians are being targeted or where humanitarian assistance to civilians is being deliberately obstructed' (§ 10) and committing it to consider adopting 'appropriate measures'. The resolution also called on states to ratify key human rights treaties and work towards ending the 'culture of impunity' by prosecuting those responsible for genocide, crimes against humanity and 'serious violations of international humanitarian law', endorsing the Security Council's ad hoc criminal tribunals for Yugoslavia and Rwanda (ICTY, ICTR). Finally, and most importantly for our purposes, Resolution 1265 expressed the Council's willingness to explore how peacekeeping mandates might be reframed to afford better protection to endangered civilians. The resolution enjoyed broad support from the Council and the wider membership, which was invited to participate in the dialogue (S/PV.4046, 16 September 1999).

There were, however, some notable criticisms from governments who believed that the UN should not move beyond its 'culture of impartiality' to embrace the protection of civilians. These criticisms prompted the Council to focus its energy on the ongoing work of its peace operations rather than the broad principles associated with the protection of civilians. A subsequent report by the Secretary-General was greeted with a further resolution (Resolution 1296, 19 April 2000) focusing on operational matters to improve the capacity of UN peace operations in protecting civilians. Two years later, at the urging of Norway, the Council issued an *Aide-Memoire* on civilian protection, which identified a range of specific measures necessary for the UN's peacekeeping and other operations (table 15.1). The *Aide-Memoire* was intended

TABLE 15.1 Excerpts from *Aide-Memoire* on the protection of civilians issued by the Security Council (2002)

Primary objectives	Issues for consideration
Facilitate safe and unimpeded access to vulnerable populations as the fundamental prerequisite for humanitarian assistance and protection	• Appropriate security arrangements (e.g. role of multinational force; safe corridors; protected areas; armed escorts) • Engagement in sustained dialogue with all parties to the armed conflict • Facilitate the delivery of humanitarian assistance • Safety and security of humanitarian and associated personnel • Compliance with obligations under relevant international humanitarian, human rights law and refugee law
Maintain the humanitarian and civilian character of camps for refugees and internally displaced persons	• Ensure cooperation with host state in provision of security measures, including through technical assistance and training • Provision of external and internal security for camps, including screening procedures to identify armed elements, disarmament measures, assistance from international civilian police and/or military observers • Regional approach to massive population displacement, including appropriate security arrangements • Location of camps at a significant distance from international borders and risk zones • Deployment of multidisciplinary assessment and security evaluation teams
Address the specific needs of women for assistance and protection	• Special measures to protect women and girls from gender-based discrimination, violence, rape and other forms of sexual abuse (access to legal redress, crisis centres, shelters, counselling and other assistance programmes; monitoring and reporting mechanisms) • Effective measures to disarm, demobilize, reintegrate and rehabilitate women and girl soldiers • Mainstreaming of gender perspective, including by integration of gender advisers in peace operations • Expand the role and contribution of women in UN field-based operations (among military observers, civilian police, humanitarian and human rights personnel) • Increased participation of women at all decision-making levels (organization and management of refugee and IDP camps; design and distribution of assistance; rehabilitation policies)
Ensure the safety and security of humanitarian, UN and associated personnel	• Urge all parties to the conflict to respect the impartiality and neutrality of humanitarian operations • Ensure a safe and secure environment for humanitarian personnel

Source: UN Security Council Presidential Statement (15 March 2002), Annex: *Aide-Memore*.

to help guide the Council's future deliberations, but it also served as a 'check-list' for reports to the Council on the protection of civilian measures under-taken by individual peace operations. It was adopted and developed by OCHA to guide its work and inform humanitarian agencies (OCHA 2004). Unfortunately, the *Aide-Memoire* approach proved too cumbersome, as the list of potential recommendations grew. In late 2003, therefore, the Under-Secretary-General for Humanitarian Affairs put forward a 'Ten Point Platform' which identified priority areas, specific tasks and obstacles to be overcome (Bowden 2006: 61). Many of those tasks and obstacles related directly to the work of peace operations (table 15.2).

Since then, the Council has passed several important resolutions on the issue of civilian protection. Among the most important was Resolution 1674 (28 April 2006), which reiterated the Council's demand for access to be granted to humanitarian agencies, stated its willingness to take action in cases where civilians are deliberately targeted and the host state is unwilling or unable to protect them, and endorsed the 'responsibility to protect' idea (R2P) that had previously been agreed in the UN World Summit outcome document of September 2005.

Mandates for UN peace operations

The second key source of concerns about civilian protection was the man-dates for peace operations handed down by the Security Council. Although during the early 1990s many force commanders had debated the extent to which their mandates involved civilian protection, it was not until the end of the decade that the Council began to make this an explicit feature of many mandates. While the Brahimi Report insisted that peacekeepers who witness violence against civilians should 'be presumed to be authorized to stop it, within their means', it also cautioned against the granting of 'blanket mandates' which might be unachievable given the scale of the threat and limited resources of the peacekeepers. The report therefore recommended that:

> The potentially large mismatch between desired objective and resources available to meet it raises the prospect of continuing disappointment with United Nations follow-through in this area. If an operation is given a mandate to protect civilians...it must be given the specific resources needed to carry out that mandate. (UN 2000: 111)

The Security Council took heed of this advice in two ways. First, it has tended to authorize larger missions. The peace operations in Sierra Leone, Liberia, the DRC and Sudan, for example, all – at one stage or another – had more than 10,000 soldiers. Second, it has applied a variety of caveats to the wording of its civilian protection mandates. These have usually been geographic (restricting protection duties to areas of deployment), temporal (limiting the duration of protection missions), or based on the actual capabilities of

TABLE 15.2 Platform on the protection of civilians (summary)

Priority	Tasks	Constraints
Sexual violence against women	– Prevent abuse occurring through peacekeeping deployments – Mitigate effects by changing cultural attitudes – Better treatment of HIV/AIDS	– Peace operations deployed after abuse has occurred – Needs of survivors and communities not well understood
Violence against children	– Prevent abuse occurring through peacekeeping deployments – Mitigate effects by changing cultural attitudes – Re-educate and provide livelihood opportunities for survivors	– Peacekeepers deployed after abuse has occurred – Needs of survivors not well understood – Long-term reintegration programmes typically underfunded
Violence against IDPs and refugees	– Prevent infiltration of IDP and refugee groups by armed groups through deployment of peacekeepers – Design and negotiate minimum standards for camps and areas hosting displaced people	– Slow deployment of peacekeepers, monitors and humanitarian staff – Poor camp management skills
Limited access	– Establish closer relations with local communities to press for better access – Make improved access key part of negotiations with belligerents	– Negotiations require different type of analysis – Needs assessment requires objective analysis
Targeting of humanitarian staff	– Better understanding of risks – Early warning of risks – Increase political costs to would-be targeters	– Poor understanding of local environment – Association with peacekeepers can detract from perceptions of impartiality – Distinction between military and humanitarians not made sufficiently clear
Impunity	– Build local capacities for rule of law – Participation in political negotiations – Should make political support contingent on protection of civilians – Protection of civilians should be a feature of military aid and training programmes – Greater use of targeted sanctions – Prosecute individuals for attacks on civilians	– Preventive local capacity-building poorly funded – Member states traditionally reluctant to link protection and inclusion – Difficulty in targeting sanctions – Little movement on persuading states of links between peace and protection – Ineffective use of media – Monitoring and reporting needed to support prosecutions

Source: Adapted from Bowden (2006: 63–6).

the peacekeepers (i.e. leaving the decision whether or not to use force in the hands of the commanders on the ground).

Humanitarian agencies

The third avenue through which the protection of civilians has risen to prominence is the agenda's adoption by a number of leading humanitarian agencies. Traditionally, 'protection' was understood by humanitarian agencies such as the ICRC, UNICEF and UNHCR as relating to the legal protection of individual human rights and hence with the verification of governmental compliance with international humanitarian law (see Forsythe 2005: 168; Quéguiner 2006). This began to change in the 1990s with the emergence of what Duffield (1997; 2001: 16) described as the 'new aid paradigm', which recognized that security and stability are closely related to traditional humanitarian concerns with social and economic development, good governance and human rights (Cooper and Pugh 2002: 14). As the conflicts in Rwanda, Bosnia, eastern DRC and elsewhere demonstrated, assistance without protection could create the 'well fed dead' syndrome – civilians given food, housing and medical support by humanitarian agencies only to be killed by armed groups. This recognition significantly increased the number of humanitarian actors engaged in protection and broadened the meaning of protection well beyond the relatively narrow legalistic view taken by the mandated actors (box 15.1; O'Callaghan and Pantuliano 2007: 13).

Box 15.1 Humanitarian agencies and their approach to protection

ICRC: protection encompasses those activities aimed at preventing and/or ending violations of international humanitarian law and ensuring that authorities and belligerents meet their legal obligations.

UNHCR: measures ensure that people of concern to the UNHCR have equal access to and enjoyment of their rights under international (refugee) law.

UNICEF: protection means freedom from violence, injury or abuse, neglect, maltreatment or exploitation.

OCHA: activities aim at ensuring respect for the rights of individuals in accordance with international human rights law, international humanitarian law, and refugee law.

IRC: activities aim at ensuring full respect for the rights of the individual in accordance with international law.

WFP: programming designed to promote safety and dignity.

Oxfam: protection is understood as safety from violence, coercion and deliberate deprivation.

Save the Children: protection is described as freedom from violence, injury or abuse, neglect, maltreatment or exploitation.

Source: Paraphrased from O'Callaghan and Pantuliano (2007: 13).

Recognition of the relationship between the protection of civilians and wider social development goals can be seen in the work programmes of a range of different civilian agencies. Since the mid-1990s, the World Bank and IMF have identified the protection of civilians as an important prerequisite to economic development, a view explicitly set out by one of the bank's leading researchers, Paul Collier (2007). Likewise, Oxfam International (2003) mainstreamed protection into all its programmes, became a key advocate of R2P, and outlined its own strategy for protecting civilians in war and combining protection with the delivery of emergency and development assistance (see also Oxfam 2008). Other initiatives included the ODI handbook to guide humanitarian agencies in the development, management and assessment of protection programmes (Slim and Bonwick 2005) and the Centre for Humanitarian Dialogue's manual on field strategies for civilian protection (Mahoney 2006).

The adoption of protection by humanitarian agencies has not been without its dissenters, however. Critics argue that protection places uncertain and contested principles of justice and human rights ahead of humanitarian principles of neutrality and universality, making humanitarian action subject to political whims (Fox 2001; Rieff 2002; Terry 2002). Others argue that protection makes for nice rhetoric but in practice makes very little difference to humanitarian activities (see Macrae 2002). Another line of criticism, commonly associated with Médecins Sans Frontières (MSF), rejects the idea that humanitarian agencies should be directly engaged in protection. The argument here is not only that protection contradicts the basic principles of humanitarianism but also that, in practice, agencies can do little to protect civilians and that, by trying to do so, they risk transferring the responsibility to protect away from the national authorities which are charged with protecting their citizens (O'Callaghan and Pantuliano 2007: 8). As MSF's legal counsel, Françoise Bouchet-Saulnier, put it, 'physical protection is a matter of power – of police, armies or whatever – and no NGO or humanitarian organization will be able to provide physical protection to people that are going to be bombed' (in OCHA 2003: 3). Finally, as humanitarian agencies become more heavily involved in local politics as a result of the adoption of protection programmes, so the risks faced by their staff increase (see Stoddard et al. 2006).

The responsibility to protect

The fourth source of support for the protection of civilians in peace operations is the international commitment to the 'responsibility to protect' (R2P). After the General Assembly's endorsement of the principle at the 2005 World Summit, the UN Secretary-General appointed a Special Adviser on matters relating to R2P (who would work in cooperation with the Special Representative for the Prevention of Genocide). Using peace operations to protect civilians under threat has already been identified as one of the main ways of operationalizing R2P (e.g. Holt and Berkman 2006; Johansen 2006; Breau 2007). In addition, R2P has also begun to influence the way that some regional organizations approach issues of peace and security (see Williams 2007; Von Schloriemer 2007). Article 4(h) of the AU's Constitutive Act, for example, enshrines the Union's right to intervene in the affairs of its member states in issues relating to genocide and mass atrocities, and the AU's mission in Sudan has included civilian protection as part of its mandate (see chapter 8).

Taken together, these four factors have elevated the protection of civilians into a core role for peace operations. Nowadays, outside observers and policy-makers alike expect peace operations to protect civilians under their care, using force to do so if necessary. However, precisely because the civilian protection agenda draws from these different sources, there are many different ideas about what it actually means and entails.

15.2 What is civilian protection?

What is civilian protection and what role can peacekeepers play in providing it? This section discusses three different ways of thinking about civilian protection (see table 15.3), while the following section focuses on the different types of actors that are involved in providing it. Overall, we suggest that (1) protection needs to be understood holistically; (2) the objective should be to empower victims and strengthen the measures that local communities can take to protect themselves; (3) that different agencies are best placed to fulfil different aspects of the protection agenda; but (4) the endeavour needs to be coordinated and given a political presence.

TABLE 15.3 Three approaches to protection

Label	Description	Advocates
Protection of rights	Protection is concerned primarily with the fulfilment of human rights and the maintenance of an environment that permits individuals to claim the rights owed to them by international human rights and humanitarian law.	ICRC
Humanitarian protection	Protection is concerned primarily with satisfying the basic needs for human survival.	Oxfam
Military protection	Protection is primarily about preventing and limiting physical attacks on the civilian population and securing humanitarian access.	DPKO, NATO

Protection as rights

According to the ICRC, protection encompasses 'all activities aimed at ensuring full respect for the rights of the individual in accordance with the letter and the spirit of the relevant bodies of law, i.e. human rights law, international humanitarian law, and refugee law' (Giossi Caverzasio 2001: 19). This definition has also been adopted by the UN's Inter-Agency Standing Committee (IASC), which comprises all the UN's major agencies and offices (IASC 2000: 4). The IASC argued that the focus on already existing rights helped to clarify the extent and focus of protection, set minimum standards for the treatment of civilians in war and was comprehensive in scope, covering not just physical security but also the civil, political, economic, social and cultural rights enshrined in international human rights law.

The main problems with this approach are fourfold. First, it defines protection in incredibly broad terms, making it almost synonymous with human rights (see Bonwick 2006: 271). Second, not all relevant legal conventions – among them the 1951 Refugee Convention and the Rome Statute of the International Criminal Court – are universally accepted. Third, while the rights-based approach helps clarify what the civilian victims of conflict are due – for example, women have a right not to be raped and to expect that they be protected from sexual assault – it does not provide a definition of protection that can act as a catalyst for strategies to provide protection in practice (ibid.). Fourth, the rights-based approach overlooks the fact that in reality civilians can claim respect for their rights only if their basic needs (food, shelter, medicine, physical security) are met first.

Humanitarian protection

A second approach accepts that international law sets useful benchmarks but begins by asking what it takes to keep people safe (Bonwick 2006: 271). As set out by Oxfam, humanitarian protection is concerned with preventing and mitigating the most damaging effects (direct and indirect) that armed conflicts have on civilians. Thus protection involves all measures necessary to enable civilians to live free from:

- *violence*, including murder, rape, torture, abuse and abduction;
- *coercion*, such as forced displacement or prevented return, forced prostitution, forced recruitment into armed groups, etc.;
- *deprivation* – a lack of the necessities of life (food, shelter, medicine, means of earning a living) and freedom from impediments on those necessities. (Oxfam 2003: 6)

Accomplishing these three goals requires that humanitarian agencies adopt a multifaceted approach that goes well beyond the delivery of material assistance – though it certainly includes such deliveries. Where civilians are under imminent threat, humanitarian protection implies two types of activity for these organizations: *political engagement* and *proactive presence*.

The first of these suggests that humanitarian protection involves engagement in local and global politics – something which traditional approaches to humanitarianism typically tried to avoid. This might involve negotiating with local authorities; raising awareness in foreign capitals of potential problems so that these states can apply the necessary diplomatic pressure; and calling for the deployment of peacekeepers (Oxfam 2003: 16–17). *Proactive presence* refers to a doctrine of humanitarian protection developed in 2006 which involves 'actions and strategies that deter or dissuade against abuses, persuade abusers to behave differently, strengthen or expand civilian capacity for self-protection, and foster institutional reform' (Mahoney 2006: 13). In practice, this works in three ways: raising the costs of committing abuses by publicizing and delegitimizing such activities; encouraging and enabling local civil society to protect itself by increasing the number of choices that are available to them; and using influence to identify and support individuals and groups within government institutions that can promote respect for civilians (ibid.: 14–27). While innovative in several respects, proactive presence is no substitute for protection either by national authorities or by international peacekeepers, particularly in areas considered by the belligerent parties to be strategically important. What is more, proactive presence provides protection only in a very limited geographic space. Indeed, one major humanitarian organization reportedly concluded that the protective shield it could provide extended only 500 metres from the agency's offices and lasted only until 5 pm (Bonwick 2006: 276).

This humanitarian or needs-based approach to protection is therefore first and foremost about keeping people safe. It is in some ways more limited than the rights-based approach in asking only what it takes to keep people from immediate harm rather than about the full panoply of their rights, though it draws on the idea of human rights. But its narrowness has the effect of making protection a clear and coherent policy agenda. What this approach exposes, however, is the limited ability of civilian agencies to protect endangered people. This brings us to the question of how the world's militaries understand protection.

Military protection

Although civilian protection has become a core task for many peacekeepers, there are few detailed discussions of what it involves in military terms. Arguably the closest the UN came was in its 2003 *Handbook on United Nations Multidimensional Peacekeeping Operations*. This suggested that protection was largely synonymous with providing a secure environment (DPKO 2003: 56–7). 'As part of the task of providing a secure environment', the *Handbook* continued, 'the military component may be asked to provide a visible deterrent presence, control movement and access through checkpoints, provide armed escort for safety and to facilitate access, conduct cordon and search operations, control crowds or confiscate weapons' (ibid.: 60). Since then, little clarification has been made, despite calls by Kofi Annan (2005c) to do precisely this and the recent attempts by the DPKO to develop its 'principles and guidelines' (DPKO 2006, 2007, 2008a). Nor have national militaries fared much better. Key states such as Canada, the UK, the US, the Netherlands, France and India, as well as organizations such as NATO, have also been slow to include specific guidelines on civilian protection in their own military doctrines (Holt and Berkman 2006: 114–28).

In their landmark work on the topic, Victoria Holt and Tobias Berkman (2006: 37–46) identified six ways of conceptualizing the military approach to civilian protection, some of which were identified by military actors themselves and some of which were developed by humanitarian agencies. These are set out in table 15.4 and provide a useful starting point.

Table 15.4 helps demonstrate that military protection is concerned primarily with protecting civilians from imminent physical danger, though it can also play a crucial role in supporting efforts to deal with deprivation. As such, it sets out a narrower agenda than rights-based or humanitarian protection. It also highlights an important distinction between *direct* and *indirect* protection. *Direct* protection implies that the peacekeepers are undertaking measures designed to protect civilians under immediate threat (e.g. guarding and demilitarizing refugee and IDP camps, patrolling villages and establishing checkpoints, protecting safe corridors, etc.). *Indirect* measures might contribute to the creation of an environment conducive to civilian protection but do not provide immediate protection (e.g. enforcement operations against armed groups, disarmament and demobilization, etc.). This brings us to the question of who should protect civilians, the subject of the following section.

15.3 Who can protect civilians?

Clearly, the protection of civilians requires a wide variety of activities and will involve a broad range of military and civilian actors. In general, the most effective forms of protection are provided by local communities themselves through what are often referred to as 'coping strategies'. For analytical purposes, modes of self-protection can be divided into three broad types: *in situ* self-protection (including 'coping economies'), flight from danger, and armed resistance (see Bonwick 2006: 274; Pantuliano and O'Callaghan 2006; O'Callaghan and Pantuliano 2007: 4; Dolan and Hovil 2006: 5; Pugh and Cooper 2004: 9). As a consequence, the aim of external assistance should be to enable and support these self-protection activities, in part by helping to improve local decision-making about risk management (see Slim and Eguren 2004; Bonwick 2006). In this context, both peacekeepers and engaged humanitarian agencies can have important roles to play in efforts to protect local civilians.

TABLE 15.4 Six conceptions of military protection

Concept	Description	Typical tasks
Obligation of military law	Militaries are obliged to protect civilians by obeying the laws of war	• No targeting of civilians • Measures to minimize collateral damage • Grant access to humanitarian agencies where possible • Provide assistance to sick, wounded and prisoners
Indirect protection through use of force	Protection is a result of successful war waged on those who attack civilians	• Use of force with humanitarian aim • Defeat enemy as quickly as possible
Provision of humanitarian space	Military force should create safe humanitarian space for agencies to work in	• Create geographical areas that are free from armed attack • Secure freedom of movement and access for humanitarian agencies • Maintain distinction between military and civilian actors
Aid in the operational design of assistance	Peacekeepers should aid in designing assistance plans (e.g. where to locate camps, how to organize them, etc.)	• Joint planning with humanitarian agencies • Planning of relief activities
Protection as part of peace operation	Peacekeepers should implement specific civilian protection mandates set out by the Security Council	• Supporting law and order • Escorting convoys • Protecting camps and safe havens • Breaking up militias • Organizing disarmament and demobilization • Intervening to protect threatened communities
Intervention to prevent mass killing	The use of force to stop or prevent mass killing	• Identify perpetrators • Use force to compel them to cease their attacks on civilians

Source: Based on Holt and Berkman (2006: 37–42).

Peace operations

For peacekeepers, the protection of civilians is largely about providing 'coercive protection' – the positioning of military forces between the civilian population and those that threaten them (see Weiss 2004b: 48). This can involve military measures to defeat and eliminate armed groups that threaten civilians. Since 2002, the UN's Standing Rules of Engagement for peace operations (which are not a matter of public record but are handed out to peacekeepers) have authorized the use of force 'to defend any civilian person who is in need of protection' (in Blocq 2006: 205). Sometimes, coercive protection may simply involve measures short of force, such as erecting military barriers around civilian populations and the gradual removal of threats through negotiated (and sometimes coerced) disarmament (Holt and Berkman 2006: 52). In the absence of relevant military doctrine, however, we have a much less clear understanding of how these tasks should be accomplished. This raises difficult questions about the relative importance of civilian protection and the holy trinity of consent, impartiality and minimum force (see chapter 7). Draft UN training modules reportedly insist that the holy trinity does not justify inactivity in the face of atrocities but do not provide guidance on how these concerns should be reconciled (ibid.: 190). For more detailed guidance, therefore, we have to make do with learning lessons from current and past missions.

The UN's official answers to these questions can be found in the series of reports provided to the Security Council by the UN Secretary-General. Kofi Annan's 1999 report, for instance, identified a series of tasks, including discouraging the abuse of civilians; providing stability; supporting institution building in areas such as human rights and law enforcement; protecting humanitarian workers; delivering humanitarian assistance; maintaining the security and stability of refugee camps; separating combatants from non-combatants in refugee camps; maintaining 'safe zones' for civilians; arresting war criminals; and using force to protect civilians when mandated by the Security Council (Annan 1999c: § 57). The 2002 *Aide-Memoire* described earlier returned to the tasks that peacekeepers ought to undertake but, as we saw (table 15.1), limited its recommendations to maintaining that peacekeepers should assist humanitarian agencies by providing security in camps. This represents a significant reduction compared to the protection role set out by Annan in 1999 (Holt and Berkman 2006: 46). In his 2004 report, Annan suggested the priorities should be protecting people in transit and upon return to their homes, and protecting women and girls from sexual and gender-based violence (Annan 2004a: §§ 25–9). His next report reiterated this message and returned to his earlier advocacy of a role for peacekeepers in maintaining the civilian character of camps and securing humanitarian access routes (Annan 2005c). In his first report on the matter, Ban Ki-moon (2007) noted the extent to which the UN's peace operations were already engaged in the protection of civilians and called for further study.

Beyond the UN, researchers at the the Henry L. Stimson Center in Washington, DC, have provided a useful starting point for thinking about these issues (box 15.2). When it comes to implementation, the first thing to note is that, in practice, the context of the operation is crucial. Specifically, there are three broad types of operations that are relevant: those where protection is the primary goal; those where it is one component of a multidimensional mission; and those where the military's role is limited to providing 'humanitarian space...for activities that result in civilian protection' (Holt 2005: 17–18).

A good example of the dilemmas and challenges involved in civilian protection is provided by the efforts by MONUC to protect civilians in eastern DRC between 2003 and 2004. Although civilian protection had been written into MONUC's mandate since early 2000, it was not until much later that it started to carry this role out. One of the most widely debated aspects of this was Operation Artemis, a French-led operation comprising approximately 1,800

Box 15.2 Protection tasks for peacekeepers
- Securing safe corridors and the passage of convoys
- Establishing safe havens
- Separating armed elements (especially in relation to border control, IDP camps and roads)
- Military observation and surveillance
- Preventing mob violence and crowd control
- Disarmament, demobilization and reintegration (DDR)
- Coercive disarmament
- Seizing arms caches
- De-mining
- Facilitating humanitarian access to conflict areas
- Securing key facilities and cultural properties
- Enforcing curfews
- Ensuring freedom of movement
- Supporting police presence and patrols
- Protecting VIPs
- Providing back-up for high-risk arrests
- Eliminating special threats
- Handling detainees
- Preventing looting and pilfering
- Supporting the prosecution of human rights abuses
- Transmitting information about human rights abuses to monitoring groups
- Training local security forces
- Providing intelligence support focused on civilian protection
- Stopping hate media
- Direct use of force against killers

Source: Holt and Berkman (2006: 43).

troops drawn from nine states (France, Germany, Greece, Belgium, Sweden, the UK, South Africa, Brazil and Canada). It was deployed to the town of Bunia in eastern DRC between early June and 1 September 2003 to help the existing MONUC peacekeepers put an end to the periodic killing of civilians there and to protect the 5,000 to 8,000 civilians who sought refuge near to the UN's compound. The deployment of well-armed troops with air support had a rapid impact on the security situation in Bunia, granting international NGOs greater freedom of movement and 'severely weakening' the key spoiler in the region, the so-called Union of Congolese Patriots. However, because the mission was limited temporally (Artemis was only a three-month deployment) and geographically (its mandate extended only to the town of Bunia and its environs), its contribution to saving lives in the wider Ituri province was 'minimal' (Grignon 2003: 3). Armed groups simply withdrew to the countryside around Bunia and continued their abusive behaviour after Artemis troops withdrew.

In the aftermath of Artemis and a similar episode of civilian slaughter in the town of Bukavu in mid-2004, MONUC adopted a much more robust posture in eastern DRC. In 2005 it began a process of compulsory disarmament in Ituri province around Bunia, removing weapons from around 15,000 combatants by June. Some groups opposed forcible disarmament, and in February 2005 fighters from the Nationalist and Integrationist Front (FNI) attacked and killed nine Bangladeshi peacekeepers. In response, Nepalese, Pakistani and South African peacekeepers, supported by Indian attack helicopters, pursued the FNI, killed between fifty and sixty belligerents and neutralized their threat to civilians (Holt and Berkman 2006: 165). For its part, the Security Council further strengthened MONUC's mandate and explicitly authorized the conducting of 'cordon-and-search' operations against 'illegal armed groups' thought to be threatening the civilian population (Resolution 1592, March 2005).

MONUC's Pakistani contingent also adopted a robust civilian protection posture in South Kivu. Acting alongside Guatemalan special forces, the Pakistanis rooted out Hutu Forces Démocratiques de Libération du Rwanda (FDLR) militia who were associated with the 1994 Rwandan genocide and subsequent abuse of civilians in the DRC. In October 2005 MONUC issued a disarmament ultimatum to FDLR and, when it refused to cooperate, used helicopter gunships to destroy over thirteen camps. Although the mission succeeded in weakening the FDLR and restricting its freedom of movement, it neither destroyed the militia nor forced them to disarm (Holt and Berkman 2006: 166–7). As well as coercing the perpetrators of attacks on the civilian population, the Pakistanis used innovative methods to protect civilians. For example, they organized a community watch in villages in Walungu territory and taught them to bang pots and blow whistles when danger was imminent. Pakistani peacekeepers were kept on high alert in the vicinity to respond to such warnings (ibid.: 166).

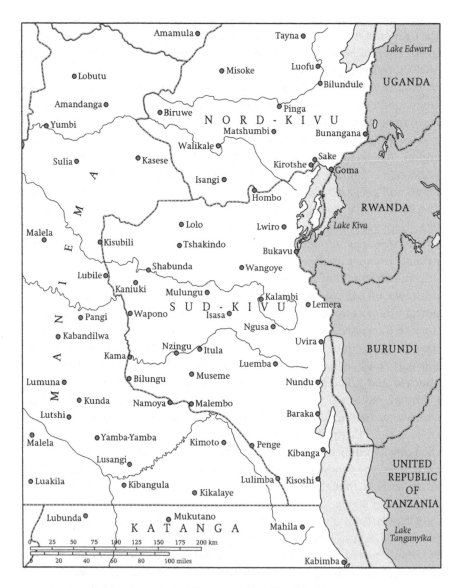

Map 15.1 *Eastern-Central Democratic Republic of the Congo*

In addition to illuminating the way in which the use of force can physically protect civilians who are in immediate danger, the MONUC/Artemis example raises important questions about the geographic scope of civilian protection. Despite MONUC's best efforts in 2005–6, comprehensive country-wide protection was simply impossible to achieve. This gave rise to calls for focusing protection efforts on specific geographical areas, be they 'safe havens/areas/zones' or 'safe corridors' for transit. (It is worth noting that, even where safe areas are not consciously designated, civilians under imminent threat often gravitate towards UN compounds in search of security.)

This model was first tried in northern Iraq, where American, British, French and Dutch troops and airpower were deployed to protect camps housing some 60,000 Kurds who had fled a post-Gulf War onslaught unleashed by Saddam Hussein. Operation Provide Comfort succeeded in reducing the number of Kurds killed by Iraqi forces and disease by providing immediate physical security and facilitating the delivery of humanitarian relief. It also created conditions that enabled the Kurds to return safely to their homes (see Wheeler 2000: 151; Seybolt 2007: 51). Nevertheless, the safe haven covered only one-quarter of the Iraqi territory inhabited by Kurds and, while it succeeded in (probably) reducing the number of Iraqi incursions, it did nothing to prevent Turkish incursions, which even by the Turkish government's estimates killed some 20,000 Kurds by 1995 (see Keen 1993). A similar approach was repeated in Bosnia with the creation of safe areas. But, as discussed in chapter 8, UNPROFOR peacekeepers were given neither the capability nor the mandate to protect the safe areas, with devastating consequences, most notably in Srebrenica but also in Gorazde and Sarajevo (see McQueen 2005).

The experiences in northern Iraq and Bosnia point towards some intrinsic problems with the safe areas approach, identified recently by Ian Johnstone. First, when local expectations that peacekeepers will protect civilians go unfulfilled, this is likely to generate anger against the peace operation, reducing levels of consent and cooperation. Second, limiting protection geographically encourages population displacement as civilians move to find shelter under the protection of peacekeepers (and not only are displaced civilians incapable of protecting their assets and property, they are also more vulnerable than those able to cope *in situ*). Finally, protecting civilians in one area leaves them vulnerable to violence elsewhere. The corollaries to havens of peace are zones of instability, where civilians are left to fend for themselves (Johnstone 2006: 7).

In practice, the military component of peace operations has to date limited their embrace of civilian protection to one of three scenarios. First, peacekeepers sometimes use force to defeat armed groups that kill and threaten the civilian population. Examples of this type of action include the British-led action against the 'West Side Boys' militia in Sierra Leone; the use of force by MINUSTAH against criminal gangs in Port-au-Prince; and MONUC's use of force against militia loyal to the renegade General Laurent Nkunda. Second, as described earlier, peacekeepers use force and the threat of force to establish safe areas/havens/zones, as in northern Iraq and Bosnia. Moreover, even when such areas are not self-consciously proclaimed, locals may treat the areas in and around peacekeeping bases as de facto safe havens. For example, when a Uruguayan MONUC battalion entered Bunia in eastern DRC in 2003, thousands of civilians sought shelter near its bases, despite the fact that the battalion was neither configured nor mandated for civilian protection duties (DPKO 2004c: 7). Third, and most commonly, peace operations take on some of the tasks associated with civilian protection, such as protecting convoys and humanitarian corridors, but without making protection their core business. In all three scenarios, it is important that the work of military peace-keepers be carefully calibrated with activities undertaken by humanitarian agencies.

Humanitarian agencies

While humanitarian agencies are rarely able physically to protect civilians in imminent danger, they do have significant roles to play in the protection agenda. According to a recent landmark report, at least six tasks are particularly important (O'Callaghan and Pantuliano 2007: 34–8).

1 *Use assistance to reduce vulnerability.* There are two ways in which humanitarian agencies can help reduce vulnerability: target assistance either at vulnerable groups or at the groups that endanger others in order to reduce tensions and the perceived benefits of abusing civilians. In Darfur, for example, the WFP distributed food to nomadic groups engaged in conflict in order to reduce attacks on vulnerable populations (O'Callaghan and Pantuliano 2007: 34). Both approaches have the potential to backfire, however. Targeting resources at vulnerable populations without the armed protection of peacekeepers might make them more attractive targets to predatory armed groups. The WFP strategy thus risks encouraging and rewarding the abuse of civilians. Groups not receiving aid might be encouraged to attack civilians in order to win access to WFP assistance.

2 *Prevent displacement as much as possible.* Although flight can be an effective means of protection against imminent attack, it is a risky endeavour that heightens the likelihood of malnutrition, disease and impoverishment and exposes individuals to future attack. It is preferable therefore to provide protection to people where they live, if at all possible. In Darfur, while most agencies focused their attention on camps, the ICRC provided assistance to people who had secure access to land, helping them to sustain themselves and reducing their dependency on camps (see ICRC 2005: 116–17). Although it is clearly preferential for individuals to remain in their homes, it is important to recognize that in many instances this is simply not possible and that the ICRC strategy is only viable in regions not directly affected by armed conflict.

3 *Use conditionalities to encourage the national authorities to fulfil their responsibility to protect.* Humanitarian agencies can place conditions on the delivery of assistance, for example by requiring national authorities to guarantee access and provide a safe and secure environment in return for assistance. This approach depends on governments wanting to reduce suffering and limit potential international criticism and places humanitarian

agencies in the difficult position of potentially having to limit assistance for political reasons. Critics argue that, in crises, governments seldom have such concerns for those considered enemies and that this approach exaggerates the influence wielded by humanitarian agencies (see Leader 2000: 47).

4 *Provide the information that people need to avoid threats.* When individuals make decisions about how best to protect themselves, they calculate the relative risks of different courses of action. For example, they repeatedly review whether to stay or flee. If they flee, they assess where should they go – a camp (where is the nearest and safest?), a neighbouring country, rebel or government held territory, a safe town? If they stay, should they plant crops, conceal assets, etc.? And should the whole family stay together or should they separate to manage their individual vulnerabilities (Slim and Bonwick 2005: 95)? Often, however, the information they use is 'inaccurate, incomplete or biased', thus increasing the risks and reducing the effectiveness of self-protection (O'Callaghan and Pantuliano 2007: 35). Humanitarian agencies can assist by improving both the quality of and access to information. They can provide simple technical information about health or livelihood issues, information about the whereabouts of family members and information about human rights, and inform IDPs and refugees about the security situation in areas to which they may be considering returning (Slim and Bonwick 2005: 96). During the Kosovo crisis, for example, the ICRC created mobile communication units that enabled people to contact family members by satellite phones and share information about their situation, safety issues and needs (IASC 2002: 109). A further way of using information is to support local early warning efforts by providing bells, whistles or mobile phones for use by 'neighbourhood watch' type initiatives.

5 *Assist in keeping people safe.* There are a range of activities that can contribute to the safety of individuals by reducing exposure to threat. Among these are supplying stoves that require less firewood, thus lowering the need to leave the safety of camps and villages to secure fuel; providing paid work within camps and other settings to reduce the need to acquire firewood for sale, lessen potential competition for resources and reduce perceived incentives associated with joining armed groups; and designing camps to maximize safety by erecting fences and reducing exposure to vulnerable areas.

6 *Decrease threats through monitoring and reporting.* Information gathered by humanitarian agencies can fulfil a number of indirect protection functions. Such information can contribute to the evidence base on the perpetration of war crimes and crimes against humanity; illuminate trends to improve policy-making; and inform the Security Council and individual governments about protection issues. According to MSF's legal counsel, while they cannot protect civilians from immediate danger,

humanitarian agencies can 'trigger other mechanisms of responsibility that are not humanitarian but, rather, political or military' (in OCHA 2003: 3). In order to facilitate the collection and dissemination of information, OCHA has created a database for collating incident reports from humanitarian agencies (O'Callaghan and Pantuliano 2007: 36). Although it is increasingly popular, there are a number of problems with this approach, not least that host governments tend to resist and obstruct accurate reporting, especially when government agencies are implicated in wrongdoing. Governments might react by withdrawing cooperation, expelling agencies or harassing its personnel. In addition, there are fears that reporting incidents breaches principles of confidentiality and attracts reprisals against those known to have cooperated with international agencies (Slim and Bonwick 2005: 63).

While each of these strategies has potential side-effects, they can make a positive contribution to the protection of civilians when used appropriately. At the same time, they are no substitute for robust peacekeepers or responsible national authorities and they can do little to remove people from imminent danger. This brings us, finally, to the question of cooperation between military and civilian agencies.

The problem of coordination: towards 'one UN'?

With so many actors engaged in providing protection, strategic coordination between them is crucial. Yet this is usually very difficult to achieve, not least because these actors have their own agendas, mandates, donors, standard operating procedures and interests. Of all the obstacles involved, it is often the relationship between civilian agencies and the military that poses most problems, but is also arguably the most important to get right. One fundamental problem is resource allocation, whereby the civilian components of peace operations typically have much less capacity than the military, yet the military do not have the skills to implement the civilian (diplomatic, legal, institutional, human rights, educational) elements of the mandate properly (Golberg 2006: 75). Another problem is that, from the perspective of many civilian agencies, even the appearance of cooperating in military agendas impairs their impartiality and neutrality and makes civilian agencies more vulnerable to attack. These concerns were not helped when US Secretary of State Colin Powell (2001) described humanitarian agencies in the war against terrorism in Afghanistan as 'force multipliers' (see Lischer 2007).

Even within the UN there are 'sharp divisions' between humanitarian and political agencies (Bagshaw and Paul 2004: 4). Many senior humanitarian officials believe that their job should not involve political engagement on protection issues. Several officials told the authors of a major study on the issue that it was not their job to raise protection issues with host governments either publicly or privately (ibid.: 40). In the rare cases where the UN's senior in-country humanitarian coordinator puts political pressure on host governments to live up to their protection obligations, they often find a lack of political support from UN headquarters. This creates a powerful disincentive which only reinforces the view that the UN's humanitarian officers should not be in the business of protection if it involves (as it does) political activism. In the most notorious case, the UN's senior humanitarian official in Sudan, Jan Pronk, was expelled by the government for his criticism of the killing and forced displacement of civilians in Darfur. Rather than support Pronk, the UN headquarters accepted the expulsion, appointed a new official and chose not to reassign him.

Similar divisions run through peace operations as well, ensuring that coordination of UN activities is somewhat haphazard. The UN's solution to this problem was the so-called collaborative approach, set out by the Secretary-General in 1997. Rather than designating lead agencies, the collaborative approach seeks to make protection incumbent on all UN agencies (Annan 1997; IASC 2000: 2). The problem with the collaborative approach, however, is that, by making everybody a leader on civilian protection, the effect was often to produce a situation where nobody was leading (Holbrooke 2000). For example, the delivery of humanitarian relief and protection to IDPs at the outset of the crisis in Darfur was delayed and hampered by UNHCR's initial decision not to take the lead there, forcing less well-placed agencies to lead in the crucial first year of the crisis.

One of the proposals under consideration for addressing these problems is the 'one UN' concept – the idea that all the UN's activities in a given country should fall under a common umbrella, giving them coherence and credibility. Although in its infancy, 'one UN' has already run into difficulties because large agencies and programmes, such as UNDP, UNHCR and the WHO, are reluctant to cede their independence. In addition, several of these agencies – especially the UNDP – insist that their work ought to be non-political and reject the encroachment of politics implied by 'one UN'. As such, the concept is evolving into the idea that UN agencies will share common office facilities and attend meetings but will not coordinate much beyond that.

These considerations are made even more complex by the presence of peacekeepers in a given country. Military peacekeepers have the capacity to render assistance to humanitarian agencies (VENRO 2003: 18), but, when large peace operations are deployed, the UN's civilian agencies sometimes worry that their work will be marginalized or associated with the work of the military peacekeepers. The question of how to coordinate civilian and military activities without obscuring the distinctions that civilian agencies believe to be necessary is crucial, and there are several broad models, set out in box 15.3.

Box 15.3 Models for civil–military cooperation in the protection of civilians

OCHA: 1994 Oslo Guidelines
- *Complementarity*: the military acts only in areas where civilian capacity is lacking.
- *Civil control*: military capacities must be under civilian control.
- *Costs*: the military should provide capacities to civilian agencies free of charge.

ICRC: 2001 Guidelines for Civil–Military Cooperation
1 The ICRC is not involved in conflict resolution.
2 Humanitarian activities must not be subordinated to military objectives.
3 The task of armed forces is limited to security and conflict resolution.
4 The ICRC must maintain its independence while coordinating at all levels with armed forces.

Overseas Development Institute: 2002 Criteria for Civil–Military Relations
- Cooperation must be led from a humanitarian perspective – all actors should commit to humanitarian principles.
- Military activities should be evaluated separately from civilian activities.
- Actors should avoid labelling political or military objectives as humanitarian.

Source: VENRO (2003: 16–17).

15.4 Conclusion

It is now widely expected that peace operations should be in the business of protecting civilians, but there is no consensus about what protection entails, how civilians are best protected, or who is primarily responsible for protection. Taking a holistic view, the protection of civilians involves measures to protect them physically from immediate harm and enable them to sustain a decent standard of living. Although there are many different ways of approaching protection, the starting point must be to understand how the local population tries to protect itself and to develop strategies that empower them by ensuring that threats are mitigated, the quality and quantity of information is enhanced, and material assistance is provided where it is most needed. Beyond this general approach, however, huge gaps remain in both the theory and practice of civilian protection and the role peacekeepers and humanitarian agencies should play in conflict zones. Moreover, the Security Council, the UN Secretariat and troop contributors have displayed marked hesitancy about applying the protection of civilians in practice. As such, civilian protection remains a hugely important ongoing challenge for peacekeepers.

CHAPTER SIXTEEN

Gender

A central challenge for today's peacekeepers lies in improving their gender sensitivity and ensuring that members of peace operations do not engage in the sexual exploitation and abuse (SEA) of local populations. In recent years both the gendered dynamics of peace operations and the behaviour of individual peacekeepers have come under intense international scrutiny. In particular, reports documenting the SEA of local populations by peacekeepers in a variety of missions badly damaged the UN's reputation. The biggest scandals were generated by reports – notably from Save the Children (2008), the UNHCR and then the UN Office of Internal Oversight Services – focusing on UN operations in the DRC and Liberia, but peacekeepers have a longer history of engaging in such activities. In this regard, UNTAC (1992–3) should have been 'the wake-up call for UN member states' after some of its personnel were caught engaging in various forms of SEA and fuelling the local commercial sex industry (Bazergan 2003: 38). Unfortunately, it was not. Instead, it highlighted the UN's disregard for such issues. This was exemplified by the comment made by the UN Secretary-General's Special Representative Yasushi Akashi that UNTAC's misdemeanours were just 'boys being boys' (cited in Whitworth 2004: 13). Surprisingly, it was not until October 2003 that the UN established official rules prohibiting its personnel from engaging in SEA. The challenge for the UN is thus to ensure that the behaviour of its peacekeepers in the field does not bring the organization into disrepute and, more importantly, does not further threaten the victims of armed conflict.

The basis for the UN's recent reflection on these issues is the obvious but often neglected point that armed conflicts affect people in different ways. Specifically, as the UN officially recognized in Security Council Resolution 1325 (2000), warfare affects men and women and girls and boys differently. In a similar fashion, peace operations also affect different segments of the local population in different ways. While peace operations are clearly intended to help make local populations more secure, sometimes they have had the opposite effect. In particular, they have been accused of having a damaging influence on local economies, of stimulating increased levels of prostitution, human trafficking and SEA, and even of being a significant vector of HIV/AIDS.

These issues raise important questions not only about the unintended consequences of peace operations but also about the type of person that makes a good peacekeeper. While traditional peacekeeping and enforcement operations clearly required a military presence, the world's militaries are not well suited to conducting the broader tasks of peacebuilding. This has led to calls for greater numbers of civilians and women to participate in peace operations and for the mainstreaming of what the UN calls a gender perspective in all of its operations, as well as in its approach to peace and security issues more generally (e.g. Weiss 2008: 115–19). This will help ensure that peace operations can make all local civilians more secure and that the operations themselves can be designed in such a way as to understand and positively influence gender dynamics within the society in question.

This chapter addresses these issues in three parts. It begins by providing an overview of the complicated inter-relationships between gender dynamics, armed conflict and contemporary peace operations while paying particular attention to the process that produced Security Council Resolution 1325. The second section then examines some of the negative unintended consequences of peace operations, focusing specifically on SEA, the spread of HIV/AIDS, and the problems generated by not taking local women seriously as agents of peace. The final section analyses the UN's stated solution to these problems – namely, gender mainstreaming.

16.1 Gender, armed conflict and peace operations

As we use the term here, gender refers to the social construction of ideas about masculinity and femininity. It is not the same as sex, which refers to differences in human biology between males and females. Our gender identities are therefore more malleable than our sexual identities, but they also shape how we think about what counts as masculine and feminine forms of behaviour within society.

How we think about gender is significant in all walks of life, but it has played a particularly important role in shaping our understandings of warfare and how it is conducted (see Elshtain 1987; Goldstein 2001). In addition, women have always been integral to armed conflict, both as participants and as victims. In general, however, warfare has affected the sexes differently; specifically, and of most relevance here, women and girls have always borne the brunt of sexual violence – though there is also evidence in recent wars of sexual violence against men and boys (see Carpenter 2006; Del Zotto and Jones 2002). There are many reasons why acts of sexual violence are committed during armed conflicts, but they have commonly been used to torture, terrorize, demoralize, injure, degrade, intimidate and punish affected populations. Such acts can occur in at least three types of generalized environments: those where sexual violence is widespread and systematic (i.e. it is undertaken as part of a war strategy); those where it is widespread and opportunistic (i.e. it is conducted en masse by those taking advantage of the breakdown of rule of law); and those where such acts are isolated and random (i.e. primarily as a criminal by-product of warfare) (Wilton Park 2008).

In recent decades sexual violence has been very widespread in areas where contemporary peace operations have been deployed. For example, in the conflicts in Sierra Leone (1991–2002) and Liberia (1989–2003), evidence suggests that at least 50 per cent of women suffered some form of sexual violence, rising to over 80 per cent in IDP and refugee camps (Wilton Park 2008: 2). Similarly, the war in eastern DRC (1998–present) generated huge levels of sexual violence and slavery (see Human Rights Watch 2002). By the time UN peacekeepers were deployed to the region, the problems brought on by displacement, extreme poverty and widespread corruption meant that many women, girls and boys were already regularly engaging in various forms of 'survival sex' – that is, 'trading sex for food, shelter, or money in order to provide for themselves and their families' (ibid.: 21). It was in this context that some UN peacekeepers engaged in various acts of SEA.

Statistics such as these generated calls for international society to do more to protect women and girls from sexual violence. But it was also noted that women should not be viewed solely as victims. International actors should also recognize and support the positive roles that women's organizations play in peace processes by helping to empower these traditionally disempowered groups. Efforts to do both these things were given a significant boost when the UN Security Council passed Resolution 1325 on 31 October 2000.

As noted above, the starting point for the UN's recent approach to gender and armed conflict as codified in Resolution 1325 stemmed from its recognition that warfare has different effects upon women and men and boys and girls. The resolution was the product of intensive involvement of activist and lobbying NGOs from outside the UN. It called upon member states and all parties to take action in four areas: (1) to promote the participation of women in decision-making and peace processes; (2) to integrate gender perspectives and training in peacekeeping; (3) to protect women in armed conflict; and (4) to mainstream gender issues in UN reporting systems and programmes related to conflict and peacebuilding. Resolution 1325 was an important breakthrough not least because, as one DPKO publication put it, '[an] understanding of how conflict has affected the lives of women as compared to men, and girls compared to boys, helps peacekeeping personnel to better understand the context in which they are working' (DPKO 2004a: x).

Although it was an important milestone, Resolution 1325 built upon earlier attempts to highlight the challenges facing women in the world's war zones (see Binder et al. 2008: 23). In 1969, for example, the report of the Commission on the Status of Women addressed the issue of whether special protection should be accorded to women and children during armed conflict and in emergency situations. During the 1970s the General Assembly made several relevant declarations. In 1974, for instance, it adopted the Declaration on the Protection of Women and Children in Emergency and Armed Conflict and proclaimed 1975 International Women's Year. The latter was intended, at least in part, to increase women's contribution to strengthening world peace. This was followed by the UN's declaration that the period from 1976 to 1985 should be known as the UN Decade for Women: Equality, Development and Peace. Finally, in 1979, the General Assembly adopted the Convention on the Elimination of all Forms of Discrimination against Women (CEDAW), which entered into force in 1981. This convention was intended to serve as an instrument to promote equality of women and men in crucial areas, including social economic rights (Articles 10–14), family rights (Article 16), and women's right to political participation (Articles 7 and 8). It did not, however, specifically address the situation of women in conflict situations. Since then, the various World Conferences on Women have played an important role in highlighting the plight of women and girls, as well as the positive contribution that they could make to building stable peace. They are also at least partly responsible for introducing a gender-sensitive perspective into the UN approach to maintaining international peace and security. Specifically, the Office of the Special Adviser to the Secretary-General on Gender Issues and Advancement of Women was established in March 1997, initially with the explicit aim of implementing the 1995 Beijing Declaration, itself the outcome of the Fourth World Conference on Women.

Since the passing of Resolution 1325, the UN Secretary-General has issued four reports and the Security Council has held seven open debates on women, peace and security that resulted in the adoption of statements by the president of the Security Council. At the national level, a number of states, among them the UK, Denmark, Sweden, Norway and Fiji, have adopted national action plans to implement Resolution 1325. Other countries, such as Canada and Austria, are currently in the process of adopting such plans. One of the important aims of these statements and plans is the commitment to increase the level of women's participation in UN peace operations. Just a few months before Resolution 1325, the Brahimi Report also recognized the need for equitable gender representation in UN peace operations (UN 2000: § 101). As discussed in more detail in section 16.3, this is something the UN has now endorsed. And yet peace operations continued to remain heavily male-dominated and military-dominated (in terms of numbers of personnel and financial support), and with very few women serving in senior positions. Box 16.1 provides a snapshot of the level of women's participation in peace operations seven and a half years after Resolution 1325. It demonstrates that there is significant room for improvement. Similarly, as box 16.2 shows, out of more than sixty UN peacekeeping operations, only seven women have held the post of Special Representative of the Secretary-General.

Advocates for more women in peace operations argue that this will help reduce some of the negative effects that peace operations have had upon host societies. The next section provides an overview of some of those negative effects, while the final section analyses the UN's response to them.

Box 16.1 Snapshot of women in UN peace operations (as of April 2008)

- There was one female head of mission (Liberia) and four women deputies (Burundi, Chad, Liberia and Sudan).
- Only 1.9 per cent of UN military personnel were women (1,408 of a total of 73,348 troops, military observers and staff officers), and no forces were led by a woman.
- Only 7.3 per cent of UN police were women (865 of a total of 11,182), including two female senior police advisers. In professional posts, six women were in the standing police capacity, five women were in the police division, and five women were in field missions.
- Approximately 29.8 per cent of international civilian staff was composed of women (of a total of 4,857) – a number that decreases to 10 per cent in management positions at the D-1 level or above.
- Women made up 19.6 per cent of nationally recruited civilian staff (of a total of 11,501), of whom many are relegated to service and clerical posts at the lowest grades.

Source: WIIS (2008: 23).

Box 16.2 Women Special Representatives of the Secretary-General in peace operations

Ellen Margrethe Løj (Denmark): Liberia (UNMIL) 2008–present
Carolyn McAskie (Canada): Burundi (ONUB) 2004–6
Heidi Tagliavini (Switzerland): Georgia (UNOMIG) 2002–6
Ann Hercus (New Zealand): Cyprus (UNFICYP) 1998–9
Elisabeth Rehn (Finland): Bosnia (UNMIBH) 1995–2001
Angela King (Jamaica): South Africa (UNOMSA) 1992–4
Margaret Joan Anstee (United Kingdom): Angola (UNAVEM II) 1992–3

Source: WIIS (2008: 29).

16.2 Some unintended consequences of peace operations

It is often forgotten that the arrival of a peace operation does not always make local lives more peaceful and secure. For some analysts, a major part of the problem is the contradiction at the heart of most peace operations: they are conducted by soldiers trained in the art of war. Unlike war-fighting, peace-building often requires impartiality, sensitivity and empathy, attributes that may have been discouraged by military training (Higate and Henry 2004: 484). In this sense, the traits that make good warriors do not necessarily make good peacekeepers (Whitworth 2004). In the heated atmosphere of real missions, asking warriors to 'keep a lid on' these attributes can contribute to what Sandra Whitworth calls explosions of hyper- or militarized masculinity, such as the sexual abuse of women and children or overt racism towards the local society. For Whitworth, such 'explosions' challenge 'the easy and often auto-matic association of peacekeeping with actual and substantive alternatives to military violence'. Indeed, on occasions the arrival of peacekeepers 'served to increase some local people's insecurity rather than alleviate it' (ibid.: 12).

Instances of SEA are one of the ways in which peacekeepers can make the lives of local women more insecure. Such exploitation and abuse can be understood as an unintended consequence of peace operations. Unintended consequences refer to any developments directly generated by the operation that were not intended by those who planned it (see Aoi et al. 2007). Some unintended consequences can be foreseen and anticipated; others might be impossible to predict. Moreover, such side-effects are not necessarily negative; they can also generate politically neutral or positive outcomes. While the negative consequences – such as SEA or alleged rises in HIV infection rates – have captured the media headlines, other activities conducted outside of the formal mandate – such as peacekeepers donating blood to local hospitals or helping to build schools and children's play areas – have generally been considered less newsworthy. One thing that can be said for certain is that, when large peace operations deploy into the complex social systems that characterize war-torn societies, some unintended consequences are inevitable (ibid.: 7). Negative unintended consequences can be damaging in several respects. First, they can cause suffering for individuals and communities where peace operations are deployed. Second, they can weaken the ability of the peacekeepers to achieve their intended objectives. At a more general level, they can also undermine the idea that peace operations are positive phenom-ena that should be encouraged and supported. And, finally, they can erode the legitimacy of the organizations that authorize and supposedly supervise them (ibid.: 8).

Clearly not all negative unintended consequences are about gender issues. Racism, for example, also seems to have been at the heart of the events of 1993 when members of Canada's airborne regiment, deployed to Somalia as part of the UN operations, ended up shooting two Somali civilians and tortur-ing and murdering another – sixteen-year-old Shidane Abukar Arone (see Whitworth 2004: 85–117). There have also been cases where peacekeepers have facilitated and even encouraged the growth of organized crime. Sometimes this has been directly related to gender issues, sometimes it has not. In the Balkans, for instance, numerous examples demonstrate both how peace operations can fuel and facilitate organized crime and how individual peacekeepers may participate directly in it (see Andreas 2008). In the spring of 1996, for instance, an open-air black market bazaar developed near Brcko in northern Bosnia. Commonly known as 'Arizona Market', it was established close to approximately 4,000 peacekeepers and the large brothels that catered for the sexual desires of those peacekeepers. According to Cockayne and Pfister, '[b]ilateral donors funded those involved in the market, hoping it might foster inter-ethnic interaction and even reconciliation. But the Arizona

Market quickly became a major black market and smuggling hub for guns, drugs, cars, and other consumer goods smuggled into Bosnia, many from far afield in Western Europe' (2008: 24). In another similar example, UN peace-keepers reportedly helped to ensure that goods purchased on the black market found their way to the beleaguered residents of Bihac, who were struggling to survive on humanitarian assistance alone (ibid.: 29).

Peace operations 'may also create a demand for goods supplied through organised crime such as pirated DVDs or smuggled cigarettes, and, notably, commercial sex' (Cockayne and Pfister 2008: 26). The Balkans, for instance, witnessed a major rise in the sex trafficking industry in the region which persisted well after the wars. It also 'provided a basis for criminal organiza-tions that had flourished during the war to move into more legitimate hotel and nightclub operations' (ibid.). In addition, peacekeepers may engage in criminal activities, whether as 'bribe-takers, transporters, informants, money couriers, and brokers/intermediaries facilitating commerce (often between warring parties)' (ibid.: 27).

While issues of race and criminality are important, the rest of this chapter focuses on three negative unintended consequences where gender issues play the central role: SEA, the alleged spread of HIV/AIDS, and the extent to which peacekeepers have ignored the ability of local women to act as agents of peace.

SEA and peace operations

In 2003, the UN Secretary-General defined 'sexual exploitation' as 'any actual or attempted abuse of a position of vulnerability, differential power, or trust, for sexual purposes, including, but not limited to, profiting monetarily, socially or politically from the sexual exploitation of another' (UN Secretary-General 2003). The term 'sexual abuse' was said to refer to 'actual or threat-ened physical intrusion of a sexual nature, whether by force or under unequal or coercive conditions'.

Analysts disagree over the extent to which peacekeepers have engaged in the SEA of local populations. This is not surprising given the delicate, often taboo nature of the topic and the concomitant difficulty of gathering accurate statistics. One of the early official estimates suggested that, within the UN system, the number of reported allegations from all forty-seven entities totalled 121 in 2004 (up from fifty-three allegations in 2003). The DPKO was responsible for 105 of these, eighty-nine against uniformed personnel and sixteen against civilian personnel (UN 2005a: 8). The nature of these allega-tions varied, with 45 per cent involving sex with minors, 31 per cent concern-ing prostitution with adult women, and 15 per cent involving rape or sexual assault. Well under half of the allegations (fifty-three) were subsequently substantiated by the Board of Inquiry (UN Secretary-General 2005: 2–4). More recent reports by the UN Secretary-General suggest that, between 2004 and

2006, of the 856 allegations of sexual misconduct towards adults and children made against the DPKO, United Nations Volunteers, the WFP, and the Office of the UNHCR, only 324 had been resolved within the year in which they had been reported. This left 532 allegations of abuse – 62 per cent of the total – that had not been resolved within that same year (in Csáky 2008: 15).

A brief look at the case of Timor-Leste provides an insight into both the positive and the negative consequences for gender issues that the arrival of UN peace operations can herald. The UN's peace operations there – particularly UNTAET and UNMISET – clearly intended to mainstream gender and promote women's advancement in Timorese society. Specifically, UN documents in 2002 set out the mission's objectives in this area as being to ensure gender mainstreaming within the mission, establish a Gender Affairs Unit, encourage the inclusion of East Timorese women in decision-making processes, incorporate gender issues into the constitution, and support campaigns against domestic violence (Koyama and Myrttinen 2007: 28). At the outset, it is important to recognize that UNMISET did go some way towards achieving these objectives, perhaps most notably in terms of getting gender issues incorporated into the constitution, but also by creating an unprecedented range of job opportunities for women who had previously been marginalized in the local labour markets. As Koyama and Myrttinen observed, the UN's arrival brought 'an influx of new concepts, new attitudes and new behavioural patterns with regard to gender roles being displayed by the expatriates'. Overall, this amounted to 'a gender revolution' (ibid.: 39).

On the other hand, UN personnel also contributed to some negative developments in relation to gender issues. While prostitution was not illegal in Timor-Leste and did not begin with the arrival of peacekeepers, the UN presence does appear to have increased the size of the industry, particularly in the capital, Dili. Part of the problem was that the UN did not initially adopt a unified policy on what to do when its personnel bought sexual services. In addition, different contingents within UNMISET took on different approaches to the issue: while some contingents imposed an early curfew on their peacekeepers, others, such as the Portuguese, had a more laissez-faire attitude to the nocturnal activities of its soldiers 'and hence gained a certain notoriety in Dili' (Koyama and Myrttinen 2007: 36). In 2003 the Special Representative of the Secretary-General barred UN staff from visiting places where prostitution took place. However, this directive did not include a 'blacklist' of bars or nightclubs for the mission and hence proved less than watertight. In practice such establishments did continue to be frequented by UN personnel, including some Singaporean police who were repatriated as a result. Overall, Koyama and Myrttinen's study showed that clients of sex workers were both locals and internationals, and the majority of them were male and civilian. They concluded that 'Quantifying the correlation between the existence of UNMISET and the scale of prostitution is difficult.

However, according to our interviews with both sex workers and clients, 'business' had reduced dramatically with the drawing down of the UNMISET staff' (ibid.: 35).

In addition to the question of prostitution, there were accusations of sexual assault, including rape, made against UN personnel. These apparently led to the court-martialling of several members of the Jordanian contingent. Upon their departure, UN personnel were also reported to have left behind local 'widows' and 'orphans'. Koyama and Myrttinen (2007: 36–8) draw attention to the case of a Portuguese peacekeeper who fathered a child with a mute and deaf Timorese woman and then refused them support.

HIV/AIDS and peace operations

One major issue related to SEA in peace operations is the spread of HIV/AIDS. It is often suggested that peace operations and infection rates in the area of deployment are related. Indeed, some analysts have gone as far as to suggest that '[p]eacekeeping forces are in fact among the primary mechanisms of spreading the disease at a mass level to new areas' (Singer 2002: 152; see also Elbe 2003: 39–44). Once again, however, accurate information about this issue is difficult if not impossible to obtain, and the evidence does not seem to sustain this case. While it seems clear that some peacekeepers have helped spread the disease, it is less clear whether the presence of a peace operation necessarily encourages a significant rise in infection rates. In 2001, for example, the US General Accounting Office suggested that 32 per cent of peacekeepers in Sierra Leone, 17 per cent of those in Ethiopia/Eritrea, 8 per cent of those in Croatia and the DRC, 6 per cent of those in Western Sahara and 5 per cent of those in Kosovo had HIV/AIDS (cited in Bazergan 2003: 30). But without accurate information of prevalence rates in national militaries before and after peace operations – information most governments are reluctant to make public – it is impossible to specify the effect of peace operations on host states or vice versa.

To date, some of the most detailed research on this issue relates to the UNTAC operation in Cambodia between February 1992 and September 1993 (see chapter 10). Here, the Cambodian Women's Development Association estimated that the number of prostitutes in Cambodia rose from about 6,000 in 1992 to 25,000 at the height of the mission. Unsurprisingly, they claim that this led to a rise in HIV/AIDS, with the result that locals began describing UNTAC as 'the United Nations Transmission of AIDS to Cambodia'. The official solution in this case was asking UNTAC personnel to be more discrete when visiting brothels and to ship 800,000 condoms to Cambodia (see Whitworth 2004: 67–9). The problem with these perceptions is that estimates from the World Health Organization (WHO) suggest that the numbers of people in Cambodia living with HIV began to climb steeply well before UNTAC arrived and that the rise in infection rates remained fairly constant during and after its deployment. In particular, WHO figures suggest that the major rise in infection rates occurred between 1990 and 1991, and that the rise in levels remained fairly constant until 1997, when they started to decline (see figure 16.1). If these estimates are accurate, it would be fair to conclude that there was little, if any, causal connection between the deployment of UNTAC and prevalence of HIV in Cambodia.

Since the Cambodian case, international blame games over responsibility for HIV rates have become common. For example, the Sierra Leone government blamed Nigerian military personnel in ECOMOG and UNAMSIL for the rise in HIV/AIDS, whereas the Nigerian military said its troops were not highly infected before their deployment to Sierra Leone. Once again, WHO estimates suggest that Sierra Leone experienced a fairly steady rise in infections from 1990 until 2006. Indeed, from 1997 to 1999, the period which saw the greatest numbers of ECOMOG troops deployed in the country, the rate of infection appears to have increased at a slower rate than previously (WHO 2008). Although imprecise, in the absence of sound evidence to the contrary, such figures cast serious doubt on the alleged link between ECOMOG and HIV/AIDS infections. Nevertheless, similar perceptions about the relationship between infection rates and peace operations led the Croatian government to try and keep African peacekeepers out of its country in the 1990s, on the grounds that they were a vector of HIV (Bazergan 2003: 37–8). More recently, in 2005 the government of Sudan announced a new 'behavioural code' which called for compulsory HIV testing of all employees of foreign organizations and peacekeepers, ostensibly to ensure that they did not increase infection rates in the country.

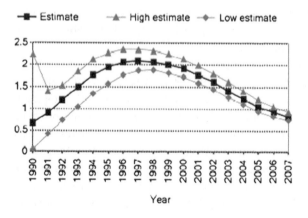

Source: WHO 2008.

Figure 16.1 World Health Organization estimates of HIV among adults aged 15 to 49 in Cambodia, 1990–2007 (%)

Part of the difficulty is that troop-contributing countries (TCCs) do not always ensure that their soldiers are free of the disease. For example, despite the high levels of HIV/AIDS recorded within UNAMSIL, the TCCs of the operation's eleven contingents all said they had a policy of testing prospective peacekeepers before deployment (Bazergan 2003: 41). This was in line with the second edition of the DPKO's *Medical Support Manual for United Nations Peacekeeping Operations* (1999), which recommended that HIV-positive personnel not be used. However, mandatory testing before, during or after deployment would run counter to the UN's preference not to discriminate against HIV-positive individuals and may constitute a violation of human rights (Davies 2009: ch. 2). In addition, denying HIV-positive individuals the right to be part of a mission makes presumptions about how they would behave. As a result, the default position is that the responsibility to assess the 'fitness to work' of personnel lies with the TCCs, not the UN. Unfortunately, it remains the case that 'Member states are often quicker to protect their reputation through denial than to protect the troops they deploy in the field' (Bazergan 2003: 48).

Women as peacemakers

Even after the passing of Resolution 1325, too few women have been included in formal peace processes. As the UN Secretary-General noted in 2004, the contribution of women to informal peace processes is well known, but gender perspectives have not been systematically incorporated into formal peace processes (UN Secretary-General 2004: 6). This raises the question of why this is the case.

At a general level, four main arguments have been used to excuse the lack of female participation in peace processes (see Anderlini 2007: 61–3). First, policy-makers have claimed that the negotiation table is not an appropriate venue for discussing gender equality or women's issues, which, although clearly important, should be reserved for a later stage. Not only does this assume that women are concerned solely with 'women's issues', it also fails to appreciate the extent to which gender issues are a crucial part of crafting a legitimate and hence stable peace. Second, international mediators have suggested that the key local parties with whom they are engaged have often failed to include women among their senior representatives. In such circumstances, external forces should not try and impose quotas of female representatives on these parties. While this is certainly true at one level, given all the other conditionalities imposed by external peacebuilders and international organizations, it is not unreasonable to expect serious efforts to encourage greater levels of participation among women. Indeed, this is already happening, even in societies that have displayed very conservative attitudes towards women. For example, the 2002 *loya jirga* in Afghanistan had a much larger proportion of women participating than those of 1964 and 1977, in which only four and twelve women respectively took part (UN Secretary-General 2004: 12). The greater number of women in the 2002 *loya jirga* came about, in part, because of the insistence of external actors, and yet the process has been widely supported as a good model for building legitimate institutions of government (e.g. Barnett 2006).

Third, there is a widespread belief that peace accords are gender neutral because they deal with such universal issues as human rights and justice. However, the way these concepts get interpreted and implemented in practice often delays or even damages the cause of gender equality, women's rights, or addressing issues of sexual violence. Finally, because women's groups do not tend to act as spoilers (i.e. those who take up arms to disrupt a peace process), they are often perceived as less important than the militant groups and hence get ignored. This stance is short-sighted and rests on the dubious assumption that those actors which gain most from wielding the instruments of violence will have a serious commitment to ending the armed conflict in question.

Rebutting these arguments is important because the historical record provides ample evidence of women playing critical roles in building stable and legitimate political orders. As we discuss further below, peacekeepers would be helping themselves by engineering as many openings as possible for women to participate in peace processes. As Sanam Anderlini has aptly put it,

> Whether by choice or necessity, conflict brings women to the fore. It changes social and gender relations. Devastating as war and conflict are for women, they are also a time when women step into the fray and empower themselves. They get a glimpse of how their roles in the family and society at large can be different. They are also a time when men's reliance on women increases. They learn to respect women for their abilities to cope, survive, protect, and recover....[People] must not box women as victims only. (2007: 228)

In summary, therefore, issues related to SEA, HIV/AIDS and the marginalization of women as agents of peace are clearly complicated, but it would be unwise to try and engineer solutions without first trying to understand why they occur in the first place.

At a general level, four types of explanations have been advanced for why these problems occur. One approach locates the problem in hyper-masculine values and the culture that forms the basis of most military training programmes from which most peacekeepers are drawn. This culture is said to encourage SEA and other forms of sexual adventurism that is common among soldiers, and hence also common among peacekeepers (e.g. Whitworth 2004; Martin 2005). The problem with this view is that, relatively speaking, complaints against UN military personnel occur with approximately the same frequency as those against civilian personnel. Using the 2004 figures noted earlier, there was approximately one complaint for every 628 military peacekeepers and every 625 civilian members of a peace operation. The culture of hyper-masculinity, however, is also believed to encourage a tradition of silence and of denouncing and shunning whistle-blowers. If hyper-masculinity is the problem, then the solution would appear to lie in ensuring that peacekeepers undergo different forms of training. The problem with this view is that it does not explain why civilian members of peace operations who have not been trained in this hyper-masculine culture also engage with similar frequency in acts of SEA.

A second explanation points to the political economy of the war-shattered societies into which peacekeepers are deployed. As noted above, not only does the nexus of war, displacement, poverty and corruption force many women into 'survival sex', but the massively unequal pay levels evident between foreign peacekeepers and their local hosts exacerbates the problem. Observers in the DRC, for example, received between 500 and 1,000 times the average per capita income of the local population (Higate and Henry 2004: 485). When large peace operations are deployed into impoverished conflict zones a unique peacekeeping economy is established where the informal sphere becomes particularly important. In such an environment peacekeepers are likely to be offered sexual favours in return for money, jobs and/or food. From this perspective, a reduction in exploitative and abusive practices by peacekeepers would be more likely if substantial changes were made in the local economy. In particular, a solution would involve providing income generation for women to improve their status and micro-credit to start businesses (Martin 2005: 24, 26). An alternative approach would be to impose a ban on peacekeepers leaving their base when they are off duty, thus preventing them from interacting with the local population or frequenting particular establishments.

A third factor identified in the literature is the so-called culture of protection that developed among UN agencies and NGOs, whereby there was a strong tendency to protect their staff rather than to hold them accountable for their actions (Kent 2007: 58). Peacekeeping is often a very difficult job carried out under extremely demanding circumstances. In such circumstances, peacekeepers are likely to form strong bonds of camaraderie with their colleagues which may make them less inclined to report any abuses they witness.

A related perspective points to those on the receiving end of the exploitation and abuse by suggesting that there are a variety of factors which discourage them from speaking out about such practices. First, they might fear losing much-needed material assistance if they report abuse. In particular, children who trade sex for food or other forms of support are unwilling to jeopardize this survival tactic (Csáky 2008: 12). Additional factors include a fear of stigmatization, threats of retribution or retaliation made by their abusers, and a lack of faith in the ability of the authorities to ensure an effective and timely response, as well as the basic issue that many of the victims may not know how to report abuse (ibid.: 12–14).

In sum, there are several different factors at play, and organizations engaged in keeping the peace need to design their responses accordingly. It is to a discussion of those responses that we now turn.

16.3 The UN's response: gender mainstreaming

In spite of the long history of problems related to SEA and peace operations, it was not until late 2003 that the UN established official rules prohibiting its personnel from engaging in such practices. At this point the Secretary-General's bulletin focused on 'special measures for protection from sexual exploitation and abuse'. Among other things, this strongly discouraged 'sexual relationships between UN staff and beneficiaries of assistance, since they are based on unequal power dynamics [and] undermine the integrity and credibility of the UN'. The UN also forbade any of its personnel to have sex with anyone under the age of eighteen.

The following year, 2004, three particularly important developments took place that aimed to address the gender-related problems associated with peace operations. First of all, the DPKO published its *Gender Resource Package for Peacekeeping Operations*. According to department head Jean-Marie Guéhenno, this 208-page document offered 'concrete guidance on how to identify the various gender issues in peacekeeping and how to integrate, or mainstream, gender into all aspects of peacekeeping' (DPKO 2004a: v). He also stated that doing this would considerably 'improve the effectiveness' of peacekeeping operations. The resource package was anchored to the concept of gender mainstreaming, which it defined as:

> the process of assessing the implications for women and men of any planned action including legislation, policies, or programmes in all areas and at all levels. It is a strategy for making the concerns and experiences of women and men an integral dimension of design, implementation, monitoring and evaluation of policies and programmes in all political, economic and societal spheres so that women and men benefit equally and inequality is not perpetuated. The ultimate goal is to achieve gender equality. (Ibid.: 3)

In line with the UN's overall goal of achieving a 50:50 ratio of men and women in all categories of posts within the UN system, the DPKO stated its intention to achieve a 50:50 balance of the sexes at all levels at headquarters as well as in peacekeeping operations for all national and international civilian staff (ibid.: 69). It also explored ways to encourage a greater number of women to serve as uniformed members of its peace operations (i.e. as troops, military observers and police).

The second important development in 2004 was Kofi Annan's decision to invite Prince Zeid Ra'ad Zeid Al-Hussein, the Permanent Representative of Jordan, to act as his adviser on sexual exploitation and abuse by UN peacekeeping personnel. The third development was the DPKO's decision, late that year, to create a multidisciplinary task force on SEA led by the Assistant

Secretary-General Jane Holl Lute. It also began to introduce some mission-specific measures to eliminate abuses. In MONUC, for example, the UN established a Personnel Conduct Unit, introduced a strict non-fraternization policy and curfew for military contingents, designated off-limits areas and premises, and required the wearing of military uniforms at all times outside the military camp. In similar fashion, MINUSTAH forbade its members to engage in sex with locals (Martin 2005: 16). Finally, the DPKO pushed for the incorporation of gender concerns in mission mandates, and by 2004 they were part of all new peacekeeping mandates. This included specific mandates for the protection of women and children in the operations in Burundi (ONUB SCR1545), Côte d'Ivoire (UNOCI SCR1528), Haiti (MINUSTAH SCR1542) and Liberia (UNMIL SCR1509) (UN Secretary-General 2004: 7).

In March 2005, Prince Zeid's report was released to the public. It concentrated on four main areas of concern: the current rules on standards of conduct; the investigative process; organizational, managerial and command responsibility; and individual disciplinary, financial and criminal accountability (UN 2005a; see Weiss 2008: 197). As Zeid's report noted, the factors encouraging SEA were varied. Peacekeepers were sometimes offered sex by locals in exchange for money, jobs and/or food. This chimed with evidence from a 2003 study of the production of masculine subject positions of MONUC and UNAMSIL personnel, which revealed that peacekeepers constructed their sexual behaviour in one of three ways (Higate and Henry 2004: 489ff.):

- as 'natural' men who were legitimately involved with local women (giving money for sex could even be seen as a benevolent act);
- as victims of the predatory advances of local women (women may have chosen to go into prostitution and to target rich foreigners);
- as disciplined men who were attempting to avoid a multitude of sexual 'temptations'.

Zeid's report drew attention additionally to the phenomena of local 'wives' and 'peacekeeper babies', which were often abandoned after the mission (or the person involved) withdrew. These issues generated calls for the introduction of DNA testing to establish parenthood and for peacekeepers to pay their 'wives' and children a portion of their wages. They also produced angry reactions from locals, such as instances of blackmail and violent retaliation against peacekeepers accused of engaging in these activities.

As for the way forward, Zeid made numerous recommendations. First, because they are responsible for the conduct and discipline of their soldiers, states should agree to prosecute their own troops as part of agreeing to become a TCC. In theory, this should not be a problem because most TCCs have accepted the rules set out in the publications *Ten Rules: Code of Personal Conduct for Blue Helmets* and *We Are United Nations Peacekeepers*. When things go wrong, however, the disciplinary process raises a vexing set of issues related to the legal status of peacekeepers and other UN personnel (see Kent 2007:

49–52). As far as military members of national contingents are concerned, they remain under the exclusive criminal jurisdiction of their own national authorities and therefore have immunity from local prosecution. If the TCCs do not prosecute their soldiers in the manner Zeid suggested then the UN is left with few disciplinary options other than repatriation. Given that UN staff generally have a difficult job recruiting enough troops to fill their operations, 'naming and shaming' the countries of offending soldiers in SEA cases is likely to make that task even harder. This is a delicate matter given that numerous allegations of SEA have been made against personnel from key UN TCCs, such as Pakistan, Uruguay, Morocco, Tunisia, South Africa, Jordan and Nepal. Civilian personnel, on the other hand, are obliged to respect local laws and customs. Consequently, if they commit illegal acts they can be subject to local civil and criminal jurisdiction. The problem is that, in practice, many peace operations are deployed in areas where the local rule of law has broken down, and hence initiating any form of prosecution is very difficult. This means it may sometimes be easier to discipline military personnel than civilians (Martin 2005: 17).

Zeid also made several other recommendations, notably that the UN should do more to train its personnel, increase its outreach with local communities, and improve data-tracking of all allegations and investigations. It was also crucial to change the environment of de facto impunity within operations and the perception that whistle-blowers would not be protected (UN 2005a: 10). In sum, Zeid's report concluded that the UN must be able 'to ensure that those unjustly accused are able to clear their names and that those justly accused would be found culpable' (ibid.: 16). This, he suggested, would require a professional investigative capacity and more female personnel.

Despite these efforts, critics have pointed to various problems in the UN's gender mainstreaming approach. In his 2004 report, for instance, Kofi Annan concluded that '[i]n no area of peace and security work are gender perspectives systematically incorporated in planning, implementation, monitoring and reporting' (UN Secretary-General 2004: 24). Moreover, external critics such as Sandra Whitworth (2004: 17, 130–1) have argued that the way in which gender mainstreaming occurred 'largely emptied gender concerns of their critical content'. 'Gender critiques', she suggested, were 'forced to fit into the UN's "way of doing business" without transforming how that business is done.' In addition, she highlighted the lack of funding given to gender units; the minimal direct access they were given to UN headquarters in New York; the way in which the creation of separate offices had tended to marginalize those women's organizations; and the challenges that several of the units faced once they were in place.

By September 2007, the position of the Secretary-General, Ban Ki-moon, had become more up-beat in tone; he spoke of 'significant advances' and 'progress, though uneven', in 'many substantive areas' (UN Secretary-General 2007: 17). In relation to peacekeeping, he pointed out that eleven of the eighteen ongoing missions had a full-time gender adviser and, in February 2007, the first all-female police contingent from India was deployed to Liberia (ibid.: 6). In relation to SEA by UN peacekeepers, the report suggested that progress on the UN's 'zero tolerance' approach would be facilitated by the establishment of specific procedures within the DPKO for investigation and monitoring in all peace operations. It also made reference to the creation in December 2006 of the Gender Community of Practice, which is intended to facilitate the sharing of good practices and lessons learned in relation to peacekeeping operations. While it is fair to say that progress is being made, the Secretary-General's point that it is uneven is important. Moreover, there is clearly a long way to go before the UN meets its own standards in this area.

16.4 Conclusion

If the UN is to live up to its goal of genuinely mainstreaming gender issues within its policy objectives and processes, and if its peace operations are really going to eliminate SEA, several things need to happen. First, troop- and police-contributing countries need to increase the number of female peacekeepers they deploy. More women would enhance the operational effectiveness of peace operations, not least because women are recognized to have a comparative advantage both in intelligence-gathering as military observers and in community liaison/cordon and search operations (see Wilton Park 2008: 8; WIIS 2008: 39–42). In addition, their presence is important because, as a 1995 study undertaken by the UN Division for the Advancement of Women found, 'incidents of rape and prostitution fall significantly with just a token female presence, signifying that "men behave when in the presence of women from their own culture…as it more closely resembles civilian society"' (cited in Kent 2007: 56).

Second, more women need to be hired and retained in senior positions related to peace operations. To date, however, several factors have made this difficult to achieve. One problem is that the (often highly politicized) hiring process for senior UN posts disadvantages women in several respects (see WIIS 2008). Another is that the 'vast majority of DPKO missions are designated as non-family duty posts even in locations where the staff of other UN agencies and funds are permitted to bring spouses and children. The non-family duty issue was repeatedly cited [by female UN personnel] as a disincentive to accepting peacekeeping positions' (ibid.: 47). As one UN Development Programme employee wryly noted, 'To be successful in the UN, one must be single, widowed, or divorced' (ibid.: 9).

A third necessary change must occur in relation to the bureaucratic and management culture within the UN system. Specifically, incentive structures need to be devised that make it absolutely clear to senior managers that their jobs depend on the effective implementation of the UN's stated goals on gender issues. Until senior managers take these issues seriously the goals will not be achieved. Furthermore, the UN should make it clear that it will protect whistle-blowers.

A fourth set of improvements needs to come in relation to empowering local women in the areas where peace operations are deployed. This is important in at least two senses. As noted above, local economies need to be reconfigured so that women there are given alternatives to selling their bodies as a survival tactic, and peace operations need to find ways to increase the level of women's participation with formal peace processes.

A fifth issue is related to the sort of training and education that peacekeepers receive, both before they arrive in the field and once they deploy. In particular, would-be peacekeepers need to be educated in the arts of peace-building and war-fighting. As Whitworth has observed, '[i]t is often the non-warrior qualities of soldiering that leave an impact on local people's security: building a park, reopening a hospital, or repairing a local school. Soldiers do not always make the best peacekeepers; sometimes it is carpenters, doctors, or lawyers who do, and sometimes it is soldiers who bring to bear a variety of skills that are not unique to soldiering' (2004: 18–19). This will require more specialized centres devoted to training peacekeepers rather than simply warriors. It would also involve making sure that peacekeepers are familiar with relevant resources found outside the UN system, such as the Keeping Children Safe Toolkit, developed in 2006 by a coalition of NGOs. However, we should not fall into the trap of thinking that the civilianization of peace operations would automatically make their personnel less likely to commit acts of SEA. This is because civilian members of peace operations appear just as likely as soldiers to commit these crimes.

Ultimately, all these issues require the UN and other actors to reflect upon how militarized they want their peace operations to be. While robust forces are clearly important in certain settings, in other circumstances it might make more sense for the UN to focus greater resources on the civilian dimensions of the operations. In a provocative critique of UN peacekeeping, Whitworth suggested that this might involve deploying 'contingents of doctors, feminists, linguists, and engineers; regiments of construction workers and carpenters; armies of midwives, cultural critics, anthropologists, and social workers; battalions of artists, musicians, poets, writers, and social critics' (2004: 186). This is not simply wishful thinking. In April 2003, for example, the Secretary-General of the OAS proposed that post-conflict operations should follow his organization's example in Nicaragua and involve only civilian personnel. If this approach worked in Nicaragua, perhaps it could work elsewhere.

CHAPTER SEVENTEEN

Policing

One of the defining characteristics of contemporary peace operations is that they play a greater part than earlier operations in the provision of public security and the rule of law. This raises the thorny question of whether soldiers or police should take the lead in providing public security and, if the latter, whether the capacity exists for police forces to fulfil this role. Although police contingents have been deployed as part of UN missions since the early 1960s (in ONUC) and under the umbrella of 'UN Civpol' since 1964 (in UNFICYP), the role of civilian policing in peace operations has increased dramatically in the past decade (Broer and Emery 1998: 367; Hansen 2002). In mid-2008, more than 10,000 police officers from eighty countries were participating in sixteen different operations around the globe. Indeed, policing is now recognized as a core part of UN peace operations. For example, when the UN Security Council authorized the deployment of UNAMID to Darfur in 2007, it insisted that up to 5,000 police accompany the 17,000 or so soldiers. Traditionally, the UN's police contingents were managed by the military command structure but, in recognition of their growing importance, the DPKO created a separate office in 2007 to manage its 'rule of law' operations, covering policing, the judicial system and corrections.

This chapter analyses the challenges faced by peacekeepers when they are asked to provide public security. It does so in three parts. After providing a brief historical overview of policing in peace operations, it considers some of the challenges that confront police, focusing in particular on the problem of staffing. In the final part of the chapter we assess four different types of policing mission.

17.1 The evolution of policing in peace operations

Traditionally, the policing component of a peace operation was unarmed and small, numbering not more than a few hundred officers. Even during the 1990s, for instance, the UN consistently deployed only a combined total of approximately 2,000 police across all of its operations. The UN's earliest traditional peacekeeping operations were not mandated to conduct policing activities, and, although UNEF forces occasionally assisted with law enforcement in the Gaza strip, these activities were more akin to military support for civilian authorities than policing as such (Schmidl 1998: 19). The early assisting transition operation, UNTEA, relied exclusively on the local police force for public order.

ONUC was the first mission to have a police component attached to it – a small Ghanaian police unit deployed in Kinshasa. Military peacekeepers were also involved in dealing with riots, though they lacked both the training and the equipment to do so effectively. The police unit was tasked with assisting the local police in the maintenance of public order. Within the space of a few months, however, the unit became embroiled in Congolese politics and had to be withdrawn (Schmidl 1998: 20). It was replaced by a 400-strong Nigerian police contingent, which assisted the military in the provision of public security and established small outposts in regional centres such as Bukavu and Kisangani. When the mission was withdrawn in 1964, several UN officials complained that the police component had proven very costly for its contribution to the overall mission (ibid.: 22).

The term 'Civpol' itself originated with the UNFICYP mission in Cyprus (see chapter 7). When it was first deployed, in 1964, UNFICYP was mandated to prevent civil unrest between the Greek and Turkish communities throughout the island. The SRSG, José Rolz-Bennett, proposed the deployment of military police to support this effort, but U Thant's military adviser, Indar Jit Rikhye, counselled that military police would be inappropriate for this role. UNFICYP's force commander, Lieutenant-General P. S. Gyani, then proposed the deployment of a civilian police attachment, with small detachments of thirty officers in every district with a mandate to support and supervise the Cypriot police (Schmidl 1998: 23). As with later policing operations, UNFICYP had trouble recruiting the necessary officers, primarily because the constant domestic demands placed on national police services meant that there was little spare capacity for international deployments. In the end, 173 officers from Australia, New Zealand, Scandinavia and Austria were employed. Unlike later operations, these officers operated in national contingents (ibid.: 23–4).

For much of this time, Civpol focused on fulfilling five interrelated tasks, which involved mainly monitoring compliance with peace agreements and the provision of advice to host governments. A training booklet produced in 1995 for Civpol officers by the DPKO and the Centre for Human Rights defined those tasks as 'SMART':

- Supporting human rights;
- Monitoring local policing;
- Advising the local police on best practice;
- Reporting on incidents to the UN;
- Training local police on best practice and human rights. (Hartz 2000: 30–1)

Such tasks fitted comfortably with the prevailing view of peace operations as concerned primarily with the maintenance of peace between states or (as in Congo) the consolidation of a state's territorial integrity. Even in large missions, the policing component deferred to the sovereignty of the host country by remaining small in size, foregoing the authority to conduct investigations or apprehend suspects, and being unarmed as a matter of principle (McFarlane and Maley 2001: 198). For example, UNFICYP's police component was mandated to occupy police stations/observation posts in sensitive regions, investigate and report on incidents that involved the Turkish and Greek communities (but not bring them to prosecution), and cooperate with the local police forces. Some commentators credit the contingent with defusing several local-level disputes that might have escalated if left unchecked. The Turkish invasion of Cyprus in 1974 transformed UNFICYP into a more traditional peacekeeping operation charged with monitoring a ceasefire line. This reduced the need for Civpol and the police contingent was downsized (Schmidl 1998: 24).

The place of policing in peace operations began to change in the mid-1990s, as UN peacekeepers were charged with facilitating the implementation of complex peace agreements and maintaining a basic degree of public security in the immediate aftermath of war. Typically, though, the police component remained limited to supervising and assisting the indigenous police force (O'Neill 2008: 94). For instance, ONUSAL in El Salvador oversaw the transformation of the former government police into a new national force that also comprised some former rebels, though their relatively small number was a source of concern and criticism (Costa 1995: 368; see companion website). Likewise, the policing component of the civilian mission to Haiti (MICIVIH) was mandated only to obtain information on human rights and make that information available to the Haitian government (O'Neill 2008: 94).

The limits of SMART policing in complex operations were most clearly exposed, however, by the UNTAC mission in Cambodia (1992–3). Despite being staffed with 3,600 international police observers (at the time, a larger number than all the other police units combined), UNTAC's Civpol component was 'widely perceived as disastrous', primarily because in its early phases it lacked the authority to arrest and detain criminal suspects (see chapter 11; Findlay 1995: 144). It also proved extremely difficult to acquire the kind of local knowledge that good policing requires. Although it was granted the power of arrest in January 1993 – the first example of such powers being authorized to UN police forces – no major human rights cases were brought to prosecution, largely because of the restrictive interpretation of UNTAC's mandate (Berdal and Leifer 1996: 45).

The key turning points came with the International Police Task Force (IPTF) deployed to Bosnia after the end of the war there in 1995 and the place of policing in the subsequent transitional administrations in Kosovo and East Timor from 1999. According to William O'Neill (2008: 95), 'Since 1999, the centrality of the rule of law has become accepted in all peace operations.' Under the Dayton Peace Agreement for Bosnia, the IPTF was charged with two overarching goals. First, it was required to conduct 'executive policing'.

In other words, it was expected physically to police Bosnia, investigate crimes, apprehend suspects, assist with prosecutions, manage the roads, and conduct the full range of activities associated with policing until such a time as the Bosnian police force was able to take over these tasks. Over the course of the following decade the IPTF (which was taken over by the European Union in 2002) gradually handed over responsibility for executive policing to the Bosnian authorities, though the international force retained its legal authority. Second, the IPTF was charged with training the new Bosnian police and assisting with the construction of a new justice system. To achieve all this, it had a maximum mandated size of 2,015 (Dziedzic 1998b: 6). This was less than one-twentieth the mandated size of the international military effort in post-war Bosnia. Similarly, the missions in Kosovo and East Timor gave policing a central role in both the immediate provision of security and the longer-term establishment of stable peace as part of the UN's nation-building effort. Yet in both of those missions, too, the police component was much smaller than the military one.

More recently, this type of policing expanded beyond transitional administrations into a wider range of peace operations. Since 2001, all UN peace operations have been explicitly authorized to engage in rule of law or policing activities (O'Neill 2008: 95). For example, the maintenance of law and order was commonly identified as the principal purpose of the UN Mission to Haiti (MINUSTAH) deployed in 2004, and the international police contingent there has been involved in a number of operations against organized criminals (see companion website). Similarly, UNAMA was mandated to establish a fair and transparent judicial system in Afghanistan, as was ONUB in Burundi. For its part, MONUC was given the broad task of providing public security and establishing the rule of law (ibid.: 96). The 2004 Australian-led mission in the Solomon Islands was unique in that the police formed the lead agency (see Peake and Studdard Brown 2005), and the more recent multinational operation in East Timor, deployed in 2006, is widely understood as a policing-focused mission.

The principal reason for the expansion of policing in peace operations is the growing recognition from the mid-1990s onwards that establishing the rule of law is a crucial element in the transition from war to stable peace. As Thomas Carothers (1998: 77) caustically remarked, 'one cannot get through a foreign policy debate nowadays without someone proposing the rule of law as a solution to the world's troubles'. When crises erupt, as in Kosovo in 2004 and East Timor in 2006, it is often the local police service that is best placed to deal with the problem. Where local services lack the capacity to handle sporadic outbursts of violence, relatively low-level crises can escalate rapidly into problems that threaten to unseat governments or unravel peace processes. Contemporary analysts are in broad agreement that the rule of law is a key foundation of stable peace and that peace operations ought to be in the business of helping to establish it (e.g. Bull 2008; Call 2006; Stromseth et al.

2006). Moreover, in the long term, military peacekeepers are ill-suited to performing the policing tasks and capacity-building measures necessary to support the establishment of the rule of law.

This idea sits comfortably with the post-Westphalian view that stable peace requires the transformation of states and societies along liberal democratic lines. It has also been widely taken up by governments and the UN. Like so much else in relation to peace operations, the connection between stable peace and the rule of law was first recognized by Boutros-Ghali's *An Agenda for Peace* (1992: § 59), which highlighted their 'obvious connection'. The Brahimi Report also emphasized the importance of the rule of law to peace operations and made a series of recommendations to improve the UN's capacity in this area, focusing in particular on increasing member states' contribution to UN policing (see box 17.1).

In 2002 the UN created a two-person Law and Judicial Affairs unit and in 2003 established a network of state representatives on the rule of law. In 2004 Kofi Annan released a high-profile report on the rule of law and transitional justice in conflict and post-conflict societies, in which he identified the rule of law as a crucial component of stable peace and placed the matter firmly

---

Box 17.1 Improving the UN's rule of law capacity: the Brahimi Report

2(b) The Panel recommends a doctrinal shift in the use of civilian police, other rule of law elements and human rights experts in complex peace operations to reflect an increased focus on strengthening rule of law institutions and improving respect for human rights in post-conflict environments;

...

10(a) Member States are encouraged to each establish a national pool of civilian police officers that would be ready for deployment to United Nations peace operations on short notice, within the context of the United Nations standby arrangements system [UNSAS];

10(b) Member States are encouraged to enter into regional training partnerships for civilian police in the respective national pools, to promote a common level of preparedness in accordance with guidelines, standard operating procedures and performance standards to be promulgated by the United Nations;

10(c) Member States are encouraged to designate a single point of contact within their governmental structures for the provision of police to United Nations peace operations;

10(d) The Panel recommends that a revolving list of about 100 police officers and related experts be created in UNSAS to be available on seven days notice with teams trained to create the civilian police component of a new peacekeeping operation, train incoming personnel and give the component greater coherence at an earlier date;

10(e) The Panel recommends that parallel arrangements to recommendations (a), (b) and (c) above be established for judicial, penal, human rights and other relevant specialists, who with specialist police will make up collegial 'rule of law' teams.

Source: Brahimi Report, cited in Smith et al. (2007a: 8).

Box 17.2 The rule of law and transitional justice

The 'rule of law' is a concept at the very heart of the Organization's mission. It refers to a principle of governance in which all persons, institutions and entities, public and private, including the State itself, are accountable to laws that are publicly promulgated, equally enforced and independently adjudicated, and which are consistent with international human rights norms and standards. It requires, as well, measures to ensure adherence to the principles of supremacy of law, equality before the law, accountability to the law, fairness in the application of the law, separation of powers, participation in decision-making, legal certainty, avoidance of arbitrariness and procedural and legal transparency. (Annan 2004b: § 6)

on the Security Council's agenda (see box 17.2). A year later, the Secretary-General called for the establishment of a rule of law assistance unit, which was endorsed by the 2005 World Summit and established in 2006 as the Rule of Law Coordination and Resource Group (Hurwitz 2008: 2). In the same year the UN also set up a small standing police capacity to improve mission planning and quicken deployment times, which gave policing operations the same status as military operations within the DPKO. This was much less than the early advocates for a UN standing police capacity had called for, however (see Hills 1998). Numbering around twenty-five people, the standing police capacity focused mainly on pre-planning and training. Its first mission, completed in 2008, involved training a specialized police unit in Chad to support the MINURCAT mission there (UN News 2008). One of the most noticeable effects of these reforms was a change in the terminology used to describe police contingents. After 2007 it was no longer appropriate to refer to them as 'Civpol' because the 'Civ' was traditionally used to distinguish civilian police from their military colleagues. Given its own institutional status within the DPKO, Civpol became UNPOL (UN police).

The impetus created by the growing recognition of the connection between the rule of law and stable peace was supported by two other factors. First, many governments and analysts believed that, in an interdependent and globalized world, security threats tended to cross borders. This gave (particularly Western) governments a vested interest in ensuring that their neighbours and other states were well governed and orderly (see Bayley 2006). As Krasner and Pascual (2005: 153) put it, 'in today's increasingly interconnected world, weak and failed states pose an acute risk to US and global security'. Thanks to globalization, these analysts argue, it is no longer possible to protect a country by simply policing its borders. It is much better to address the sources of such problems at their root by assisting with the establishment of the rule of law. Although this widely held view is empirically problematic (see Patrick 2006; Williams 2008), it has been very influential and helps explain why states such as the US have embraced the promotion of the rule of law through peace operations.

Second, it is widely acknowledged nowadays that economic development can succeed only if it is accompanied by measures to improve security. According to an increasing number of analysts, over the past few decades governments have poured significant resources into development aid without having a noticeable impact on economic growth. This was largely because much of it was siphoned off by corrupt officials or went into projects that failed to deliver economic growth because of criminal behaviour and sporadic outbreaks of disorder. In response, by 2003, 60 per cent of UNDP funds were being used for democratic governance programmes, including the rule of law (Call 2006: 4). In sum, economic development is widely thought to require a basic degree of law and order which can only be achieved with external assistance (Hurwitz 2008: 6–7).

The broadening of the place of policing within peace operations therefore reflects a profound shift in thinking about the purpose of such operations. Whereas they were once understood in Westphalian terms as providing a degree of confidence in the aftermath of armed conflict that would create a safe space for conflict resolution, today the prevailing view is post-Westphalian: that their purpose extends to building stable peace and providing security to vulnerable individuals. As the UN's former senior police adviser put it, whereas 'old' UN police officers were 'watchers' – monitoring and reporting on local policing efforts – 'new' officers are 'coaches' – preparing the way for stable peace (Kroeker 2007). The heightened profile of policing also points to a growing recognition that soldiers alone are ill-suited to providing security across the wide range of threats confronted by war-torn societies (see chapter 12).

To summarize, the role of policing in peace operations has been radically transformed in recent years. Until the twenty-first century, policing was seen as a peripheral part of peace operations and was normally limited to monitoring local police. However, with the recognition that military peacekeepers are often confronted with situations (such as riots and organized crime) which they are neither trained nor equipped to deal with, as well as the growing influence of the post-Westphalian idea that there is a positive connection between the rule of law and stable peace, there has been a massive expansion of policing in peace operations. This has created new challenges in relation to the sourcing and organization of police contingents.

17.2 The challenges of policing

While there has been a quantum leap in the role and responsibilities given to UN police, this has not been matched by supporting infrastructure and resources (Day and Freeman 2005: 140). Because most donor countries confront a shortage of police themselves, they remain reluctant to send their most qualified officers on overseas deployments. This has created an almost permanent shortfall of available officers which has in turn encouraged states occasionally to send unqualified, inexperienced and/or underperforming officers on international missions (Serafino 2004: 14). The UN has attempted to alleviate these problems by drawing up best practice guidelines and establishing minimum skill sets for police officers, with the implication that those officers who do not pass muster ought not to be deployed. However, while it certainly has the legal right to determine which individuals are sent on its missions, political considerations and a general shortage of personnel can prevent the UN from rejecting contributions that do not adhere to the guidelines or possess the required skill sets – though this has, on occasion, occurred. For example, a majority of candidates for the UNMIL mission in Liberia 'failed to meet basic UN standards'. Many were unable to drive and could not speak the mission's language (Durch et al. 2003: 80). Although some offers were rejected, many who did not meet the minimum standards were deployed nonetheless. Likewise, a review of UNPOL in Sierra Leone found that most officers 'had little knowledge of international norms and standards for democratic policing and some had less professional experience and competence than the local police they were supposed to be advising' (in Smith et al. 2007b: 6).

In addition, problems have been identified in relation to the failure of multinational operations to offer a common interpretation of the law, leading to different applications of the law within the same mission. Such problems are exacerbated by an absence of joint training and common standard operating procedures. Reflecting on arguably the best resourced policing mission, UNMIK in Kosovo, two scholars suggested that it 'demonstrates that international Civpol missions are always likely to suffer...insufficient training and harmonisation of rules of engagement, deficient conceptual planning and faulty operative co-ordination at command levels' (Heinemann-Gruder and Grebenschikov 2006: 49). Given that policing involves a much deeper relationship with the host population than that required in military operations, these problems significantly impede an operation's ability to fulfil its mandate. In Kosovo, for example, it took ten months for those contributing police to agree to a common legal code. In the meantime, individual policing contingents resorted to their own legal codes, some of which were highly authoritarian and involved practices commonly labelled in Europe as human rights abuses. What is more, the absence of common procedures relating to criminal investigations resulted in the contamination of evidence and collapse of high-profile cases against the leaders of organized crime (Rausch 2002: 18–19).

Around the world, governments have experimented with different ways of sourcing personnel for international policing missions. As we noted earlier, this is more difficult than sourcing military peacekeepers because of the competing domestic demands on police services. The entire American international policing endeavour, for example, is subcontracted through companies such as DynCorp (see chapter 14). In 2008, the US had some 2,000 people working on international policing missions, all of whom were private contractors. This model, however, comes with its own problems. Personnel tend to be retirees rather than the best officers America has to offer, and there are problems of accountability and consistency. In the late 1990s, for example, it was discovered that DynCorp personnel working with the international policing mission in Bosnia were involved in various illegal activities, including sex trafficking (Lynch 2001). The officers involved went unpunished, however, because they were not government employees.

An alternative model emerged in 2004 when the Australian Federal Police (AFP) established an International Deployment Group (IDG) comprised of 1,200 officers. The IDG was tasked with providing the Australian government with a standing capability to deploy police officers overseas in order to contribute to international and regional security through law enforcement interventions, peacekeeping and capacity-building programmes (AFP 2006: 55). The IDG assumed primary responsibility for RAMSI in the Solomon Islands, deployed police to East Timor to restore order during the 2006 crisis, contributes police to UNFICYP, and provides training and capacity-building programmes in Iraq, Afghanistan, Tonga, Vanuatu and Papua New Guinea. Other countries, including Canada and China, also began to develop their own standing international police capacity.

The other aspect of the staffing problem relates to the way in which states contribute police officers to peace operations. After UNFICYP, where police contingents were organized along national lines, the UN typically recruited individual police personnel. This was labour intensive and led to the deployment of fragmented police missions (Smith et al. 2007b: 2). More recently, governments have been encouraged to provide 'formed police units' (FPUs) – groups of police capable of performing a particular specialism (e.g. riot control, forensics, investigation) – though in practice most FPUs (initially labelled specialized police units) have taken the form of paramilitary police. This approach was first adopted in Kosovo (UNMIK) in 1999, and FPUs became a regular part of UN operations after they were used in Liberia (UNMIL). By 2007 there were approximately thirty-five units deployed on UN operations, accounting for 4,000 officers – approximately half the entire UNPOL effort (ibid.). FPUs have at least four key advantages over the recruitment of individuals and create the potential for the deployment of large-scale police-led operations.

1 They are better able to deal with riots and organized criminal elements.
2 They are more cost effective than individually recruited officers (ibid.: 3–4).
3 They improve a mission's coherence because they have trained and operated together before deployment.
4 They can deploy more quickly than individually recruited officers.

However, by themselves FPUs do not resolve the myriad staffing issues mentioned earlier.

Because the police sector is structurally different to the military sector, in that a state's police service has a permanent domestic role to play, the expansion of international policing has created some acute staffing problems that go beyond those usually associated with an absence of political will. Different ways of addressing this situation include subcontracting police activities to private companies, creating police divisions that are reserved for international deployment and building FPUs. While none of these approaches is perfect, the latter two have enabled international society to provide a substantially increased number of police officers to peace operations. In the following section we consider in more detail what these officers do.

17.3 Types of policing operations

With the rapid expansion of policing operations, it is useful to distinguish between different types of mission. One way of doing this is to think of a continuum of authority as set out in figure 17.1. At one end of the spectrum, international police officers provide advice and support to the local authorities but do not monitor them, let alone perform policing functions. At the other end, in transitional administrations, the international police contingent assumes executive authority and conducts the full range of policing activities with the authority to arrest and detain suspects. In practice, most operations fit somewhere between the two poles. Another way of distinguishing between different types of mission is according to the activities they undertake, as set out in figure 17.2. Doing this helps illuminate the fact that

Capacity-building   Traditional monitoring   Multidimensional   Executive

Figure 17.1 *The spectrum of international policing operations*

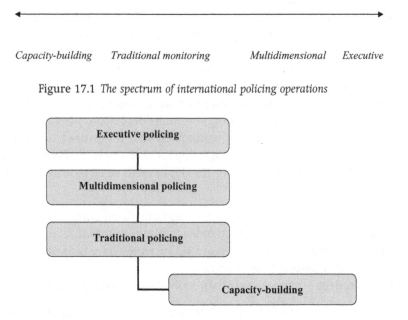

Figure 17.2 *Policing operations organized by activities*

larger, more intrusive operations are also engaged in monitoring and capac-ity-building – both of which are necessary for establishing a sustainable rule of law (see Hansen 2003: 186).

In the rest of this section we briefly examine these four basic types of opera-tion, drawing on a typology developed by researchers at the University of Queensland in Australia (Lin and Law 2008).

Capacity-building

Almost all policing missions (with the exception of those engaged in tradi-tional policing) have a capacity-building element in that they aim to support the establishment of effective, legitimate and sustainable indigenous police services. For example, the European Union Policing Mission (EUPM) in Bosnia-Hercegovina, which succeeded the IPTF in 2003, was mandated to reform the Bosnian police into a 'professional, political and ethnically neutral institu-tion for judicial enforcement' (Osland 2004: 552). According to Frank Harris (2005: 50), capacity-building operations typically aim to 'develop or modify the knowledge, skills, and character traits of police officers and support staff through a planned and systematic learning experience, thereby achieving effectiveness in a wide range of activities'. These missions are intended to 'allow police staff to acquire abilities in order to perform given tasks to an adequate level or degree'. Typically, they attempt not only to improve the police service's functional capacity but also to use the police service as a vanguard for wider societal transformation by using the reform process as a 'transmission mechanism' (Paris 2002). The basic idea here is that, in divided societies, reforms to create a multi-ethnic, gender-sensitive, democratic police service can have positive effects beyond their immediate impact on the police service itself, helping to embed these values – generally considered funda-mental for stable peace – within the wider society (Celador 2005: 372–3).

Capacity-building activities can cover a wide spectrum, embracing activi-ties designed to increase the effectiveness of criminal investigations, the police service's capacity to prevent and deal with civil unrest, and measures to improve the local police force's accountability and compliance with inter-national human rights norms. In practice, capacity-building includes mea-sures such as training programmes covering both practical policing issues (e.g. how to practise effective crowd control or how to issue parking fines) and normative issues, for example democratic policing, human rights and gender mainstreaming, the provision of equipment, planning support for senior management, and the creation of systems of accountability such as transparent budgeting and accounting (Lin and Law 2008).

According to Lin and Law (2008), there are two broad types of capacity-building operations. The first they label 'advising and supporting operations'. These are the least intrusive of all police operations and aim to provide 'tech-nical assistance and strategic support to increase the capacity and widen the capabilities of the local police service' and/or 'support the local police service by contributing to ongoing investigations, providing intelligence and threat assessments, and advising in planning processes' (ibid.: 15). Typically, these missions are small in size – numbering fewer than a hundred officers – and are deployed with the consent (and often specific invitation) of the host government. Significantly, Lin and Law argue that personnel deployed on advising and supporting missions do not take direct responsibility for delivering training programmes or crafting reform initiatives. Instead, their role is limited to making recommendations to the local authorities, which are then entitled to do whatever they like with the advice provided (see box 17.3).

The second type of capacity-building operation is labelled 'training and mentoring' (Lin and Law 2008). In these operations, which are somewhat more intrusive, the international police are 'directly engaged in the delivery of capacity-building measures that aim to reform the behaviour of domestic police and increase the skills standards and capacity of the service through the provision of training and mentoring' (ibid.: 17). Typically, these missions focus on the creation of competent specialized units, enhancing a police service's capacity to train its own future officers, and providing mentoring in the field in order to improve the indigenous police service's competency, professionalism and compliance with international human rights standards. Typically, mentoring is undertaken through the conducting of joint patrols and assigning officers to oversee the administration of the indigenous police service – both of which are common activities undertaken by UNPOL (DPKO 2008b).

A good example of this sort of operation is MIPONUH, a force of 300 civilian police personnel which was deployed in Haiti between December 1997 and

---

Box 17.3 Advising and supporting: Vanuatu Police Force Capacity-Building Project (VPFCBP)

The bilateral assistance programme between Australia and the Vanuatu Police Force (VPF) was carried out in two parts. The first part, which began in 2003, is considered the interim phase. It extended until September 2005 and involved the provision of 'training, policy and organisational reform'. This was followed by the five-year VPFCBP. The stated aim of VPFCBP was to support the government of Vanuatu in the creation of a 'professional, accountable and community-oriented police force while enhancing existing crime prevention and victim support services'. The focus on advising and supporting, rather than the provision of direct and/or large-scale training and intrusive intervention, can be inferred from the stated main components of the project. Furthermore, the intervening police were not endowed with decision-making powers with regards to the VPF. Further highlighting the light footprint of the operation is its physical size and the labelling of those deployed as advisers rather than trainers. The deployment consists of only eight full-time police advisers, with the prospect of a further eight part-time technical advisers to be deployed over the life of the project.

Source: Lin and Law (2008: 16).

March 2000 (Lin and Law 2008: 18). MIPONUH's primary aim was to support the professionalization of the Haitian police by training specialized units and their future trainers, monitoring police performance, guiding the day-to-day activities of the Haitian National Police, providing strategic advice, and improving the central police directorate's capacity to disburse aid provided on a bilateral or multilateral basis (Annan 1999a, 1999b; Lin and Law 2008: 18). Training was provided in community policing, crowd control, border monitoring, judiciary–police relations, record-keeping and report-writing (Annan 1999b: 4).

Capacity-building operations have had some success. For example, analysts observed that the Haitian police 'gradually improved' as a result of the assistance provided by MIPONUH and 'began to operate in a reasonably professional manner' (Stromseth et al. 2006: 215). However, they also confront some major problems. First, as stand-alone operations, they are entirely dependent on the consent of the host government and must cooperate closely with it. This can create problems in contexts where the host government does not enjoy a high degree of local legitimacy or where the police service is dominated by a particular ethnic group. Second, it has proved very difficult to sustain reforms and behavioural change in the long term, as Haiti's post-2000 history shows only too well. On the one hand, this points to a wider problem with using the police as a 'transmission mechanism'. If the values inculcated by police reforms (e.g. respect for human rights norms, gender mainstreaming, etc.) are not shared by the political elite and wider society, they are unlikely to be sustained. On the other hand, as we discuss later, the specific problems with MIPONUH point to the problem of treating the police in isolation from other aspects of the criminal justice system. Third, by purging corrupt and abusive officers and disrupting key systems, police reform can actually reduce a police service's capacity in the short term to respond to emergencies and deal effectively with violent crime (Cawthra and Luckham 2003: 314–15). According to Charles Call (2003: 843), police reform in El Salvador disrupted the internal security network by – for instance – requiring the re-creation of a system of informants from scratch and dramatically reducing the number of police personnel (in this case from 60,000 to 6,000), thus creating a 'public security gap'. Similarly, in Guatemala the disruption created by police reform meant that the military had to be called onto the streets to deal with civil unrest (Höglund 2008: 90). Finally, the provision of training can be quite haphazard in multinational operations where different contingents lead different aspects of the mission. Not only does the quality of training delivered vary across the mission, but the different national styles imparted leaves the local police service with myriad and not always complementary systems and techniques. For example, US officers complained that MIPONUH trainers did not provide sufficient mentoring, preferring to deliver training classes in the post where they were stationed and routine checks on remote posts (Call and Barnett 2000: 57).

Traditional operations

Traditional policing operations involve the deployment of unarmed police officers to 'monitor and oversee implementation of police reform and/or relevant aspects of a peace agreement' (Lin and Law 2008: 13; Smith et al. 2007a: 17). They have tended to accompany traditional, wider peacekeeping or assisting transition operations such as UNTAG, MINURSO, UNAVEM II and ONUMOZ, and their principal purpose is to serve as a confidence-building measure by helping to reassure the host population that abuses by the indigenous police service will become less frequent (Smith et al. 2007a: 17). Traditional police missions focus on monitoring compliance with peace agreements. Typically, this involves a combination of three core roles: first, verifying that indigenous police activities are consistent with the terms of the peace agreement, second, monitoring the extent to which local police activities are consistent with international human rights norms (ibid.: 19). Finally, traditional operations may be called upon to assist the verification of critical processes such as disarmament and demobilization or elections (Lin and Law 2008: 13).

Traditional operations are not necessarily larger than capacity-building operations and can consist of a small deployment of personnel, such as the six police officers that were deployed as part of MINURSO, who were tasked with overseeing the 'safe passage of flights facilitating family visits between refugees and their families' (Lin and Law 2008: 14). On the other hand, they may also involve relatively large deployments. For example, the ONUMOZ police component was given a traditional mandate but was enlarged from 128 officers to 1,144 on account of concerns about human rights abuse committed by the local police and rising crime rates (Smith et al. 2007a: 17; see below).

According to Lin and Law (2008), traditional operations observe and report on a wide range of actors, processes and activities but do not play a direct role in training and reforming the host's police service. They typically lack the authority to enforce the law and can only record and report infringements to indigenous law enforcement services or to the operation's political leadership (ibid.: 14). This limits the impact that traditional police operations can have on human rights abuse and crime rates. For instance, despite its expansion, ONUMOZ police were only able to report abuses to the National Police Affairs Commission, which would then pass the information to the Ministry of Interior. Reports were frequently not followed up and human rights abuse by the police persisted (see below; Woods 1998: 162–3). In practice, police engaged in traditional operations have sometimes acted outside their mandate to plug some of these gaps. For instance, UN police in El Salvador assumed limited law enforcement duties in remote areas that had no local police coverage, despite a mandate only to monitor local police (Smith et al. 2007a: 19).

As we suggested earlier, the policing experience in ONUMOZ provides good insights into traditional policing operations. Independently of the Mozambique peace agreement between the government and RENAMO rebels, the UN created a policing mission to monitor the conduct of the local police (Woods 1998: 150). This was loudly endorsed by RENAMO, but the government was opposed, with the result that the police mission was very small (128 officers) at the outset. In February 1994 the UN Secretary-General set out its seven tasks (box 17.4), while insisting that responsibility for maintaining law and order lay exclusively with the Mozambique authorities.

As we mentioned earlier, the mission's mandated size was increased to 1,144 owing to concerns about human rights abuse by the Mozambique police and the persistently high crime rate. At its peak, the mission comprised 1,028 police officers drawn from twenty-nine countries – a figure somewhat lower than the mandated number on account of financial shortfalls in the mission (Woods 1998: 155). Overall, the police mission established offices in the capital (Maputo) and the provincial capitals, set up eighty-three field posts, investigated 511 complaints, sixty-one of which were related to human rights violations, and helped monitor national elections. Typically, human rights monitoring had most impact on behaviour in remote areas where the local police was unaware of the UN police's lack of authority and feared that adverse reports would be submitted to their superiors (ibid.: 156).

Perhaps the most difficult element of the police mission's work was its oversight of the extension of Mozambican authority over areas previously

---

Box 17.4 Traditional policing: ONUMOZ policing tasks

- To monitor all police activities in the country, including those of PRM [Mozambican police] and any other police and security agencies and verify that their actions are fully consistent with the General Peace Agreement.
- To monitor the respect of rights and civil liberties of Mozambican citizens throughout the country.
- To provide technical support to the National Police Commission.
- To verify that the activities of private protection and security agencies do not violate the General Peace Agreement.
- To verify the strength and location of the government police forces, their materiel, as well as any other information that might be needed in support of the peace process.
- To monitor and verify the process of the reorganization and retraining of the quick reaction police and their activities, as well as to verify their weapons and equipment.
- To monitor, together with ONUMOZ components, the proper conduct of the electoral campaign and verify that political rights of individuals, groups and political organizations are respected, in accordance with the General Peace Agreement and relevant electoral documents.

Woods (1998: 153)

held by RENAMO. Under the peace agreement the two armies were to unite into a single national army, but this was not possible in the police sector because RENAMO did not have a police entity. Thus, national integration in police amounted to the extension of government police into rebel-held areas. RENAMO was understandably worried about this, especially as it became clear that weapons and personnel were being transferred from the army to the police, particularly the paramilitary presidential guard (Woods 1998: 157). The UN police personnel were given the role of overseeing the extension of the Mozambican police's authority but were often unable to influence the process. For example, they were denied the authority to verify claims about the transfer of weapons from the army to the police and denied access to police training camps.

The ONUMOZ experience demonstrates some of the strengths and weaknesses of traditional policing operations. Overall, the mission is usually described as a 'qualified success' (Woods 1998: 162). On the positive side, it made a contribution to the holding of peaceful elections and helped allay fears of police brutality. It also had a positive impact on the human rights situation in remote areas (ibid.: 161). On the downside, the mission had only a minor effect on the Mozambican police, and this effect dissipated quickly after its withdrawal. This was partly a result of the limitations placed on the mission by its status as a traditional operation. It had no authority to train, authoritatively verify or enforce. But its weaknesses were also partly caused by inadequacies with the UN police personnel themselves. Many of them were not trained to perform the tasks assigned to them and could not speak the mission language, and some could not even drive vehicles (ibid.: 162–3).

Multidimensional operations

Multidimensional policing operations are deployed to help establish and maintain public security and to reform, restructure and/or rebuild indigenous law enforcement capacity (Smith et al. 2007a: 19). Since the 1990s, the UN and other actors have conducted several multidimensional policing operations, among them UNMIH/MINUSTAH, UNMIL, MONUC and UNMIS. The first goal of multidimensional police operations is to assist the host government in all policing functions necessary to establish and maintain public security (Lin and Law 2008: 19). Among other things, this may involve conducting patrols in support of military peacekeepers, managing criminal investigations, and performing crowd control functions. Multidimensional operations often include armed police units and FPUs and usually have the power of arrest and detention, though they do so under the authority of the host government not in their own right. Because multidimensional operations derive their local authority from the host government, the local authorities reserve the right to withdraw and modify the authority to arrest, detain and carry arms (ibid.: 21). The second goal is to help create a sustainable and legitimate indigenous police service capable of sustaining the rule of law. As indicated in figure 17.2, this involves undertaking tasks associated with capacity-building and monitoring, such as providing training, equipment, doctrine and bureaucratic processes, monitoring practice, and instilling values such as democratic policing, international human rights and gender mainstreaming.

The policing components of the UNMIH and MINUSTAH missions in Haiti provide good insights into the challenges confronted by multidimensional policing operations. UNMIH's police component was mandated to assist in establishing public security and creating a new national police force. It was succeeded by MIPONUH (see Bailey et al. 1998). Good progress was made, and towards the end of the 1990s the Haitian police began prosecuting many of its own officers that had engaged in corrupt or abusive behaviour (Stromseth et al. 2006: 215). However, police reform was not supported by wider political reform, and many of those trained by MIPONUH were forced out of the service as it became politicized once again (ibid.: 216). When MINUSTAH was deployed in 2004, it was mandated to assist in the maintenance of public security in cooperation with the police, to protect civilians under threat of imminent violence and to support the establishment of the rule of law (Resolution 1542, 30 April 2004; see box 17.5 and chapter 9). Security Council Resolution 1542 was commended as an 'immense improvement' on previous policing mandates because of its clarity and its integration of policing within a broader rule of law framework, including the judiciary and corrections system (Smith et al. 2007a: 33).

The first part of MINUSTAH's mandate produced a robust and proactive approach to policing. For example, as part of their contribution to law

---

Box 17.5 MINUSTAH'S rule of law mandate

[MINUSTAH shall] assist the Transitional Government in monitoring, restructuring, and reforming the Haitian National Police, consistent with democratic policing standards, including the vetting and certification of its personnel, advising on its reorganization and retraining, including gender training, as well as monitoring/mentoring members of the Haitian National Police...

...assist with the restoration and maintenance of the rule of law, public safety and public order through the provision *inter alia* of operational support to the Haitian National Police...as well as with their institutional strengthening, including the re-establishment of the corrections system.

MINUSTAH in collaboration with other partners shall provide advice and assistance within its capacity to the Transitional Government: (a) in the investigation of human rights violations and violations of international future law, in collaboration with the Office of the High Commissioner for Human Rights, to put an end to impunity; (b) in the development of a strategy for reform and institutional strengthening of the judiciary.

Security Council Resolution 1542, as paraphrased in Smith et al. (2007a: 33)

enforcement, FPUs forcibly engaged and inflicted casualties on armed gangs and conducted aggressive operations to free hostages (see Holt and Berkman 2006: 95–8). Learning from UNMIH and MIPONUH, where police reform was conducted in isolation from other aspects of the rule of law, MINUSTAH embarked on a broader process of reform and restructuring that included the judicial and corrections systems. Moreover, it also provided advice on legislation and offered guidance to civil society organizations on how to monitor the courts' activities (Smith et al. 2007a: 21). In doing so, it made a significant difference to public security in Haiti, though considerable challenges remained.

Executive policing

Executive policing operations are similar to multidimensional operations in terms of their activities (Perito 2002: 85). Their principal role is to assume responsibility for public security while building local capacity and managing the transition to local ownership. For example, UNMIK's policing component was organized into four phases: (1) executive policing; (2) capacity-building; (3) transitioning the conduct of policing from UNMIK to the Kosovo Police Service (KPS); and (4) monitoring the KPS (Decker 2006: 502). The key difference between this type and multidimensional policing is that full sovereign authority is conferred upon an executive police mission. Thus, it enjoys the right to arrest, detain and carry arms in its own right and is not subject to the host government. Typically, these operations are deployed alongside a transitional administration and in the absence of any viable local law enforcement institutions. As such, the executive police mission is often required to take on full responsibility for law enforcement (Lin and Law 2008: 22). These operations are accountable to the international administration or the mandating authority – usually the UN Security Council (see chapter 11).

Like transitional administrations, executive policing operations are rare – the only examples being UNTAES, UNMIK and UNTAET. Compared to other police contingents, they are usually deployed in relatively large numbers because they are expected to assume all policing responsibilities. UNMIK, for instance, was authorized to contain up to 4,700 police. Of course, this is still much smaller than the military component, leaving transitional administrations with the unique (and unhelpful) status of having more soldiers than police officers (see Dziedzic 2002: 36; box 17.6). The result is that executive police operations are sometimes unable to maintain order in the face of major disturbances. For instance, UNMIK police lacked the capacity to respond effectively to the outbreak of violence in Kosovo in 2004.

There are therefore many different types of policing contributions to peace operations, ranging from small missions designed to provide advice to the indigenous police service to executive operations that assume full responsibility for law enforcement and the creation of new police services. Besides

Box 17.6 UNMIK: policing in Kosovo

UNMIK, being the sole governing authority, was the source of command for all policing agencies in Kosovo and by definition, therefore, was an executive policing operation. It had the power of arrest and detention and the authority to carry arms. UNMIK Police took over the civil policing from the multinational military force that stabilized Kosovo in June 1999, its objectives being to maintain 'civil law and order, including establishing local police forces and meanwhile through the deployment of international police personnel to serve in Kosovo; protecting and promoting human rights; assuring the safe and unimpeded return of all refugees and displaced persons to their homes in Kosovo'. Specialized units such as the Special Police Units and the Border Police, which were distinctive parts of the force, were responsible for providing protection to vulnerable witnesses, targeting trafficking in human beings, and fighting other forms of organized crime. While UNMIK Police provided interim law enforcement services, the Kosovo Police Service (KPS) was being established under centralized UN administration. However, while it supervised KPS operations and undertook its executive policing duties, UNMIK Police was not responsible for creating and developing the KPS, whose training and professional development was the responsibility of the OSCE. Upon graduation from the Kosovo Police Service School, the new police officers undergo an additional nineteen weeks of structured field training provided by UNMIK Police field training officers. Despite the formal separation of roles between UNMIK Police and the OSCE police mission, the two have to be conceived as distinct parts of one single police mission, and the executive authority applies to both.

Source: Paraphrased from Lin and Law (2008).

the rapid expansion of policing itself, there has been an important transformation of the way in which policing is conceptualized. Once seen as a more or less stand-alone activity, it is now embedded within a broader rule of law approach that incorporates reform of the judicial and corrections systems. This transformation is clearly seen in the context of the three missions to Haiti discussed earlier (UNMIH, MIPONUH, MINUSTAH). Whereas UNMIH and MIPONUH focused exclusively on policing and failed to produce sustainable reform, MINUSTAH was granted a broader mandate to support the maintenance of public security and establish the rule of law, including through reform of the judicial and corrections systems. Indeed, every UN operation with a rule of law component mandated between 2003 and 2007 (UNMIL, MINUSTAH, ONUB, UNMIS, UNMIT) was specifically mandated to cover policing, the judicial system and corrections (Smith et al. 2007a: 35).

17.4 Conclusion

There has been a quantum leap in the role of policing in peace operations. This reflects a shift from a Westphalian conception of the purpose of peace operations to a post-Westphalian view, which holds that there is a link between stable peace and the rule of law within domestic societies, and that peacekeepers ought to be in the business of establishing the rule of law and then building a sustainable capacity to maintain it in the long term. Today, it is common for peace operations to contain a significant multidimensional policing contingent tasked with assisting in the provision of public security and building the capacity of the indigenous police service. Moreover, since 2003 policing has been embedded within a broader concern for the rule of law, including the judicial and corrections systems.

The principal challenge that confronts the policing components of peace operations is ensuring a sufficient number of adequately trained officers. Unlike in the military sphere, international police missions have to contend with high domestic demand for experienced police officers. As a result, governments are often reluctant to provide highly capable police for international missions, creating shortfalls in numbers and expertise. A number of different solutions have been developed, among them the use of private contractors, the establishment of national police groups specifically earmarked for international deployment, and the creation of a standing police capacity at the UN. The other aspect of this problem is the way in which police officers are recruited and deployed. While recruiting police officers on an individual basis was feasible when police contingents were rare and small, it is simply not a viable way of enlisting the 10,000 plus officers needed for UN missions in 2008. In response to this problem, many governments are switching to contributing FPUs. Finally, with the widening of policing to cover other aspects of the rule of law, the UN is likely to need a large pool of civilian experts capable of being deployed at short notice and in large numbers.

Conclusion

This book has outlined the key theories, concepts and practical developments in relation to peace operations and analysed the central debates, dilemmas and challenges that surround them. Although the concept of 'peacekeeping' did not acquire general usage until the 1950s, peace operations of one sort or another have a much longer history. In recent decades, however, they have become international society's most concerted attempt to manage armed conflict and assist in the transition from war to peace.

When we completed the manuscript for the first edition of *Understanding Peacekeeping* (in early 2003), we noted the early signs of a rebirth in peace operations but also issued a word of caution about the nature and scope of that rebirth. Since that time, the trends have become clearer. Relatively successful operations in Kosovo and East Timor and the bailing out of the UN missions in Sierra Leone and the DRC, which faced severe crises at the turn of the century, helped reaffirm belief in the utility of peace operations. With this renewed confidence came a greater demand for peacekeepers and a growing consensus around the post-Westphalian idea that they should be in the business of enabling stable peace by facilitating social, political and economic transformation of a particular kind. This agenda has raised difficult questions as to how such complicated tasks might be achieved as well as which actors are best placed to achieve them.

In order to understand the roles that peace operations play in contemporary world politics, we first need to understand the relevant theories and the context in which they operate. For us, contemporary globalization provides the crucial backdrop that has influenced peace operations in important ways and on several different levels. We noted in chapter 1 that recent years have witnessed a steady and welcome proliferation of theories and conceptually informed approaches to peace operations. By utilizing different methods and being reflective about the units and levels on which we choose to focus, these theories help us to understand peace operations better. In chapter 2, we outlined how the world's principal peacekeepers have authorized, assembled, managed and financed peace operations, while in part II of the book (chapters 3–5) we provided a historical narrative of how peace operations developed from the nineteenth to the twenty-first century.

In part III (chapters 6–12) we identified and evaluated seven broad types of peace operations, ranging from those designed to prevent the outbreak of armed conflict to missions created to impose the will of the UN Security Council, as well as those intended to transform war-torn societies by temporarily assuming the reins of sovereign authority. These seven types were distinguished by the primary role that the peacekeepers were meant to play, not by the size of the mission or its individual tasks.

In preventive operations peacekeepers are deployed with the consent of the host state in order to prevent armed conflict by building confidence, encouraging disarmament, deterring violence, acting as a trip-wire, and assisting in the building of state capacity. Also based on the consent of the belligerents, traditional peacekeeping typically takes place in the space between a ceasefire and a political settlement. Here, peacekeepers monitor the ceasefire in the hope of creating conditions that will encourage the belligerents to reach a lasting political settlement. In contrast, wider peacekeeping takes place within a 'new wars' context of persistent violence and unreliable ceasefires. These peacekeepers are given 'wider' tasks such as assisting humanitarian agencies, but continue to be guided by the traditional concepts of consent, impartiality and the minimum use of force. The fourth type of operation we identified was peace enforcement. This involves the forcible imposition of the will of the Security Council, either on states that commit acts of aggression against their neighbours ('Westphalian' enforcement) or on non-state actors in support of other peace operations activities ('post-Westphalian' enforcement).

Next we identified two types of 'transitional' operations. These multidimensional operations involve military, police and/or civilian personnel to assist the parties to a conflict in the implementation of a political agreement or in the transition from a peace heavily supported by international agencies to a self-sustaining peace. There are many different subcategories of transitional operations, but the most pronounced difference is between missions that aim to *assist transitions* and *transitional administrations*: the former work in cooperation with the host state and under its authority, whereas the latter assume the full reins of government and sovereign authority. Finally, we examined peace support operations, a type developed by several Western countries. These operations combine the idea that peacekeepers should fulfil wider tasks and support the broader civilian mission with the insistence on robust military forces capable of defending themselves, their mandate and civilians under their protection.

In part IV of the book (chapters 13–17) we identified a number of contemporary challenges facing the world's peacekeepers. These fall into one of two broad categories that are related to the recent rebirth of peace operations in the twenty-first century. The first challenge revolves around the heightened demand for peacekeepers and two potential solutions to this problem: regional arrangements and private contractors. In exploring these options, we expressed doubt about the capacity of either to become a viable alternative to the UN and argued that regional organizations and private companies should be thought of as useful partners for the UN but not as alternatives to it. The second challenge relates to the increasing functional complexity of peace operations. Here, we focused on three of the most important challenges – the protection of civilians, gender issues and policing.

Themes and issues

In the first edition of *Understanding Peacekeeping* we identified three themes and reflected on those themes in the conclusion. In this section, we briefly reprise those themes and set out some emerging new ones. The first theme that we identified in 2003 was the ongoing debate between proponents of Westphalian and post-Westphalian approaches to peace operations. We argued that, although the terms 'Westphalian' and 'post-Westphalian' were useful analytical devices, most actors fell somewhere between the two poles and might adopt different positions in relation to different operations. For instance, most advocates of the post-Westphalian approach do not argue that peacekeepers should always be in the business of constructing liberal polities, economies and societies. There was no suggestion, for example, that UNMEE should enforce democratization and human rights standards on Ethiopia and Eritrea. Likewise, those governments that are most sceptical of the post-Westphalian agenda do not argue that it is *never* appropriate for international society to impose its will on belligerents or assist in the creation of liberal and democratic states. While India and Pakistan are among the most sceptical members of international society when it comes to the post-Westphalian approach, their personnel have provided the backbone of UN operations all over the world, including those implementing post-Westphalian agendas.

Although this debate is ongoing, there is evidence that the post-Westphalian approach has gained the upper hand. At the global level this is perhaps best evidenced by the 2005 World Summit declaration, in which international society recognized that states have a 'responsibility to protect' their populations from genocide, war crimes, crimes against humanity and ethnic cleansing, and that the society of states as a whole has a duty to take timely and decisive action when the state manifestly fails in its responsibility (see Evans 2008; Bellamy 2009). In relation to peace operations, this is reflected in the Security Council's increasing willingness to grant peacekeepers a role in the protection of civilians, as well as in the rapid expansion of the rule of law component of peace operations, which involves deep and protracted engagement with host states and their societies.

The second theme we noted in 2003 was a gap between the theory and practice of peace operations. We argued that this gap was largely a product of the ad hoc nature of peace operations and their inherently political nature. As we noted in chapter 1, in recent years there have been significant developments in theories of peace operations, and these have gone a long way towards closing this gap. First, they have given us a much better idea of the overall contribution of peace operations to international peace and security and the conditions for success and failure. Second, the application of constructivist and 'world culture' theories, as well as more detailed empirical analysis, has helped shed light on why countries engage in peace operations and how shared expectations develop about the ultimate purpose of peace operations. Third, the development of normative theories of peace operations is helping both to evaluate the contribution of peace operations to broader goals such as conflict resolution and the promotion of human rights and to suggest pathways for future development. Fourth, the application of critical and feminist theories has helped to uncover the deep structures that underpin violent conflict and shape international society's response and to identify possibilities for immanent critique and potential; it has also given voice to some of those whose perspectives on peace operations were too often overlooked. Finally, there is now a more sophisticated discussion about the relationship between different levels and units of analysis, particularly the regional dimensions of many armed conflicts. Although more work is still needed, significant inroads have been made into closing the gap between theory and practice.

Our third theme from the first edition – the proliferation of actors associated with peace operations – remains just as salient. Today, peacekeepers have to deal with state leaders and their militaries, warlords and their militias, community-based armed self-defence units, private security companies, and refugees, the displaced and other civilian victims of war. At the same time, the number and variety of actors essential to building peace has also expanded. Contemporary peace operations involve UN soldiers and police, non-UN soldiers and police, civilian staff from the UN, and civilians in humanitarian agencies both governmental and non-governmental, as well as members of the local population. Each of these groups may come with their own agenda, timetable, operating procedures, sources of funding and methods for evaluating both the mission and the factors contributing to success. All of this makes coordination, let alone command and control, exceedingly difficult.

The additional themes we would like to highlight stem from developments in the past six years that we have charted in the preceding chapters. The first relates to the fundamental issue of means and ends: as peace operations have come to be seen as an effective tool for managing conflicts, demand for peacekeepers is starting to outstrip international society's willingness and capacity to provide them. In particular, those countries most able to deploy well-trained and equipped peacekeepers have become noticeably less willing to do so, at least under a UN banner. Evidence of this can be seen across various contemporary operations, as can the effects. In Timor-Leste, the UN withdrew precipitately, leaving Asia's newest state incapable of dealing with a political emergency in 2006. Likewise, in Darfur, international society first failed to deliver promised support to AMIS, then failed to provide UNAMID with the resources it required to protect civilians in need, and at the time of writing (early 2009) it seems likely that a similar fate awaits the missions in Chad and the CAR. A similar situation continues to fester in the DRC. Although MONUC has undergone several phases of enhancement, it remains woefully under-equipped for addressing the huge problems facing the DRC. These and other examples suggest that the UN will struggle to satisfy the demand for large and complex operations, often in areas of the world that lack even basic levels of infrastructure. Consequently, different forms of hybridity or 'partnership peacekeeping' are likely to emerge and develop. As they do, we can only hope that the development of policy in this area is based on evidence of what works rather than ideological preferences.

The second additional theme to emerge from this edition of the book is the increasing professionalization of peace operations. Whether it be criminal activity in the form of SEA or incapacity and incompetence, it is clear that unprofessional behaviour by both civilian and military staff can have signifi-cant and negative consequences for the immediate victims, the mission and the legitimacy of the UN or non-UN actors themselves. Moreover, as the scope of peace operations widens, so the need for specially trained units of soldiers, police and civilians with expertise in and skills relevant for peacebuilding becomes more apparent. Unfortunately, while the scope of peace operations has expanded dramatically, international society has failed to develop rele-vant doctrine or training programmes, and the organization of missions remains painfully ad hoc.

Whither peace operations?

To use a well-known phrase, contemporary peace operations once again stand at a fork in the road. In some respects, their theory and practice has come a long way in recent years, but with increasing demand comes new strains and the potential for catastrophic failure. By way of a conclusion, we offer four thoughts about the potential future direction of peace operations. First, the debate between advocates of Westphalian and post-Westphalian approaches is likely to continue, especially if international society develops in a more multipolar direction. We should not, however, let this obscure the fact that traditional peacekeeping and assisting transition operations remain the most effective types of missions. It is not unreasonable to argue, there-fore, that consent-based operations such as these should be used wherever it is practically feasible.

Second, although regional organizations will continue to conduct their own operations, the trend towards hybrid forms of peacekeeping is likely to continue, especially if the reluctance of Western powers to contribute soldiers to UN operations persists. If current trends continue, Western contributions to UN operations are likely to involve either small niche components or limited interventions in support – but not under the command – of UN peacekeepers. This will only add to the complexity of command and coordination and, as we mentioned earlier, is an area that requires much more study and high-level deliberation focusing especially on the relationship between the UN and regional associations and the role of private contractors.

Third, the legitimacy of peace operations will be tied to their capacity to protect civilians in the areas of their deployment. As we noted in chapter 4, few things do more damage to the legitimacy of peace operations and the UN as a global institution than the failure to protect populations from genocide and mass atrocities. One of the most significant changes over the past two decades is that civil societies and an increasing number of governments expect the UN and other actors to stand between vulnerable populations and their tormentors. For civilian protection to be effective, however, significant changes need to occur, not least in relation to the level of resources given to peacekeepers and the development of relevant military doctrine, as well as more serious thinking about the use of special forces and intelligence-gathering in peace operations.

Finally, great power politics will continue to shape the geopolitical context within which peace operations take place. Although US influence waned somewhat under the George W. Bush administration, Washington remains the single largest source of funds and the single most influential member of the UN Security Council. But it remains to be seen where peace operations will fit into its list of priorities and whether the Obama administration will play a more constructive role than its predecessor. Elsewhere, China's growing contribution to peace operations seems likely to continue, although it is unknown how this commitment will play out in areas where energy resources are Beijing's number one priority. As far as Russia is concerned, there are few signs that it will seek to deploy significant numbers of troops beyond its 'near abroad'.

Since the first edition of this book, there is much more conclusive evidence that peace operations can help manage conflicts and lay the foundations for stable peace. We have a better idea of the conditions that breed success and the factors that lead to failure. We also have a more comprehensive understanding of how peace operations should be organized. Yet, as we write, civilians in the eastern DRC, many parts of Sudan, Chad, Afghanistan, Somalia, Haiti, Côte d'Ivoire and elsewhere remain at risk and several peace operations teeter on the brink of collapse. As we argued at the outset, understanding peacekeeping is important because the stakes are so high.

References

Abbott, K. W., and D. Snidal (1998) 'Why States Act through Formal International Organizations', *Journal of Conflict Resolution*, 42(1): 3–32.

Abi-Saab, G. (1978) *The United Nations Operation in the Congo 1960–1964* (Oxford: Oxford University Press).

Adebajo, A. (2002) *Building Peace in West Africa* (Boulder, CO: Lynne Rienner).

Adebjao, A. (2004) 'Ethiopia/Eritrea', in D. Malone (ed.), *The UN Security Council* (Boulder, CO: Lynne Rienner), pp. 575–88.

Adebajo, A., and D. Keen (2007) 'Sierra Leone', in M. Berdal and S. Economides (eds), *United Nations Interventionism, 1991–2004* (Cambridge: Cambridge University Press), pp. 246–73.

Adebajo, A., and C. Landsberg (2000) 'Back to the Future: UN Peacekeeping in Africa', *International Peacekeeping*, 7(4): 161–88.

Adelman, H., and A. Suhrke (1996) *Early Warning and Conflict Management*, Study II of *The International Response to Conflict and Genocide: Lessons from the Rwanda Experience* (Copenhagen: DANIDA).

Adibe, C. E. (1998) 'The Liberian Conflict and the ECOWAS–UN Partnership', in T. G. Weiss (ed.), *Beyond UN Subcontracting* (Basingstoke: Macmillan), pp. 67–90.

AFP (Australian Federal Police) (2006) *Annual Report 2005–06* (Canberra: Commonwealth of Australia).

Akashi, Y. (1994) 'The Challenge of Peacekeeping in Cambodia', *International Peacekeeping*, 1(2): 204–15.

Akashi, Y. (1995) 'Report to the Secretary-General', in *The United Nations and Cambodia 1991–1995* (New York: United Nations), pp. 205–6.

Akashi, Y. (1998) 'Managing United Nations Peacekeeping', in W. Biermann and M. Vadset (eds), *UN Peacekeeping in Trouble* (Aldershot: Ashgate), pp. 125–36.

Akashi, Y. (2001) 'The Politics of UN Peacekeeping from Cambodia to Yugoslavia', in R. Thakur and A. Schnabel (eds), *United Nations Peacekeeping Operations* (Tokyo: UN University Press), pp. 149–54.

Alagappa, M. (1998) 'Regional Arrangements, the UN, and International Security: A Framework for Analysis', in T. G Weiss (ed.), *Beyond UN Subcontracting* (Basingstoke: Macmillan), pp. 3–29.

Albert, S. (2000) 'International Law and National Reconciliation in Peacebuilding: Transcaucasia', in M. Pugh (ed.), *Regeneration of War-Torn Societies* (London: Macmillan), pp. 177–94.

Alden, C. (1997) 'The Issue of the Military: UN Demobilisation, Disarmament and Reintegration in Southern Africa', in J. Ginifer (ed.), *Beyond the Emergency* (London: Frank Cass), pp. 51–69.

Anderlini, S. N. (2007) *Women Building Peace* (Boulder, CO: Lynne Rienner).

Andreas, P. (2008) *Blue Helmets and Black Markets* (Ithaca, NY: Cornell University Press).

Annan, K. (1996) 'Press Release', GA/9212, 18 December.

Annan, K. (1997) *Report of the Secretary-General on the Reform of the UN System* (UN doc. A/51/950).

Annan, K. (1998a) Speech at Ditchley Park, UK. UN press release SG/SM/6613, 26 June.

Annan, K. (1998b) *The Causes of Conflict and the Promotion of Durable Peace and Sustainable Development in Africa* (New York: Report of the UN Secretary-General, April).

Annan, K. (1999a) *Report of the Secretary-General on the United Nations Civilian Police Mission in Haiti* (UN doc. S/1999/181, 19 February).

Annan, K. (1999b) *Report of the Secretary-General on the United Nations Civilian Police Mission in Haiti* (UN doc. S/1999/579, 18 May).

Annan, K. (1999c) *Report of the Secretary-General on the Protection of Civilians in Armed Conflict* (UN doc. S/1999/957, 8 September).

Annan, K. (1999d) 'Address of the Secretary-General to the UN General Assembly', 20 September (GA/9596).

Annan, K. (1999e) *Report of the Secretary-General Pursuant to General Assembly Resolution 53/55: The Fall of Srebrenica* (UN doc. A/54/549, 15 November).

Annan, K. (1999f) 'Statement on Receiving the Report of the Independent Inquiry into the Actions of the United Nations during the 1994 Genocide in Rwanda', 16 December, www.un.org/News/ossg/sgsm_rwanda.htm.

Annan, K. (2000a) *Report of the Secretary-General on the United Nations Transitional Administration in East Timor* (UN doc. S/2000/53, 26 January).

Annan, K. (2000b) *Report of the Secretary-General on the Implementation of the Report of the Panel on United Nations Peace Operations* (UN doc. A/55/502, 20 October).

Annan, K. (2000c) *Resource Requirements for Implementation of the Report of the Panel on United Nations Peace Operations* (UN doc. A/55/507, 27 October).

Annan, K. (2001a) *Prevention of Armed Conflict* (UN doc. A/55/985-S/2001/574).

Annan, K. (2001b) *No Exit without Strategy: Security Council Decision-Making and the Closure or Transition of United Nations Peacekeeping Operations* (UN doc. S/2001/394, 20 April).

Annan, K. (2001c) *Implementation of the Recommendations of the Special Committee on Peacekeeping Operations and the Panel on United Nations Peace Operations* (UN doc. A/55/977, 1 June).

Annan, K. (2001d) *Implementation of the Report of the Panel on United Nations Peace Operations: Report of the Secretary-General* (UN doc. A/56/732, 21 December).

Annan, K. (2002a) *Report of the Secretary-General on the Situation in Afghanistan and its Implications for International Peace and Security* (UN doc. A/56/875 S/2002/278, 18 March).

Annan, K. (2002b) 'Regional Security Organizations Never More Important than Today' (UN doc. SG/SM/8543, 9 December).

Annan, K. (2004a) *Report of the Secretary-General on the Protection of Civilians in Armed Conflict* (UN doc. S/2004/431, 28 May).

Annan, K. (2004b) *The Rule of Law and Transitional Justice in Conflict and Post-Conflict Societies* (UN doc. S/2004/616, 23 August).

Annan, K. (2005a) *In Larger Freedom: Towards Development, Security and Human Rights for All* (UN doc. A/59/2005, 21 March).

Annan, K. (2005b) *Monthly Report of the UN Secretary-General on Darfur* (UN doc. S/2005/467, 18 July).

Annan, K. (2005c) *Report of the Secretary-General on the Protection of Civilians in Armed Conflict* (UN doc. S/2005/740, 28 November).

Annan, K. (2005d) *Implementation of the Recommendations of the Special Committee on Peacekeeping* (UN doc. A/60/640, 29 December).

Annan, K. (2006) *Report of the Secretary-General on Darfur* (UN doc. S/2006/591, 28 July).

Anstee, M. (1996) *Orphan of the Cold War: The Inside Story of the Collapse of the Angolan Peace Process, 1992–1993* (New York: St Martin's Press).

Aoi, C., C. de Coning and R. Thakur (2007) 'Unintended Consequences, Complex Peace Operations and Peacebuilding Systems', in C. Aoi, C. de Coning and R. Thakur (eds), *Unintended Consequences of Peacekeeping Operations* (Tokyo: UN University Press), pp. 3–19.

Armstrong, D. (1982) *The Rise of International Organisation* (London: Macmillan).

AU (2004a) AU Communiqué, PSC/PR/Comm. (XIII), 27 July.

AU (2004b) AU Communiqué, PSC/PR/Comm. (XVII), 20 October.

AU (2005a) AU Communiqué, PSC/PR/Comm. (XXVIII), 28 April.

AU (2005b) *Report of the Chairperson of the Commission on the Situation in the Darfur Region of the Sudan* (AU doc. PSC/PR/2 (XXVIII), 28 April).

AU (2006) AU doc. PSC/PR/2(XLV), 12 January.

Avant, D. (2005) *The Market for Force* (Cambridge: Cambridge University Press).

Baehr, P. R., and L. Gordenker (1994) *The United Nations in the 1990s*, 2nd edn (Basingstoke: Macmillan).

Baer, R. (2007) 'Iraq's Mercenary King', *Vanity Fair*, April, pp. 146–56.

Bagshaw, S., and D. Paul (2004) *Protect or Neglect? Toward a More Effective United Nations Approach to the Protection of Internally Displaced Persons* (Washington, DC: Brookings Institution and UN OCHA).

Bailey, M., R. Maguire and J. G. Pouliot (1998) 'Haiti: Military–Police Partnership for Public Security', in R. Oakley, M. Dziedzic and E. Goldberg (eds), *Policing the New World Disorder* (Washington, DC: National Defense University Press), pp. 135–48.

Bailey, S. D., and S. Daws (1995) *The United Nations: A Concise Political Guide*, 3rd edn (Basingstoke: Macmillan).

Bailey, S. D., and S. Daws (1998) *The Procedure of the UN Security Council*, 3rd edn (Oxford: Clarendon Press).

Ballesteros, E. (1997) *Report on the Question of the Use of Mercenaries as a Means of Violating Human Rights and Impeding the Exercise of the Right of Peoples to Self-Determination* (UN doc. A/52/495, 16 October).

Ban, K.-m. (2007) *Report of the Secretary-General on the Protection of Civilians in Armed Conflict* (UN doc. S/2007/643, 28 October).

Barcena, A. (2007) 'Introductory Remarks by the Under-Secretary-General for the Department of Management to the UN General Assembly Fifth Committee', 5 June, www.centerforunreform.org/node/29.

Barkawi, T. (2006) *Globalization and War* (Lanham, MD: Rowman & Littlefield).

Barkawi, T., and M. Laffey (1999) 'The Imperial Peace: Democracy, Force and Globalization', *European Journal of International Relations*, 5(4): 403–34.

Barnett, M. N. (2002) *Eyewitness to a Genocide: The United Nations and Rwanda* (Ithaca, NY: Cornell University Press).

Barnett, M. N. (2006) 'Building a Republican Peace: Stabilizing States after War', *International Security*, 30(4): 87–112.

Barnett, M. N., and M. Finnemore (2004) *Rules for the World: International Organizations in Global Politics* (Ithaca, NY: Cornell University Press).

Barnett, M. N., H. Kim, M. O'Donnell and L. Sitea (2007) 'Peacebuilding: What Is in a Name?', *Global Governance*, 13(1): 35–58.

Bartlett, C. J. (1992) *The Global Conflict: 1880–1970* (Harlow: Longman).

Baskin, M. (2006) 'Local Governance in Kosovo: A Link to Democratic Development?', in T. B. Knudsen and C. B. Laustsen (eds), *Kosovo between War and Peace* (London: Routledge), pp. 76–95.

Bass, G. J. (2008) *Freedom's Battle: The Origins of Humanitarian Intervention* (New York: Alfred Knopf).

Bayley, D. H. (2006) *Changing the Guard: Developing Democratic Police Abroad* (Oxford: Oxford University Press).

Baylis, J. (2001) 'International and Global Security in the Post-Cold War Era', in J. Baylis and S. Smith (eds), *The Globalization of World Politics*, 2nd edn (Oxford: Oxford University Press), pp. 254–76.

Bazergan, R. (2003) 'Intervention and Intercourse: HIV/AIDS and Peacekeepers', *Conflict, Security & Development*, 3(1): 27–51.

Bell, P. D., and G. Tousignant (2001) 'Getting Beyond New York: Reforming Peacekeeping in the Field', *World Policy Journal*, 28(3): 41–6.

Bellamy, A. J. (2002a) *Kosovo and International Society* (Basingstoke: Palgrave).

Bellamy, A. J. (2002b) 'The New Wolves at the Door: Conflict in Macedonia', *Civil Wars*, 5(1): 117–44.

Bellamy, A. J. (2009) *Responsibility to Protect: The Global Effort to End Mass Atrocities* (Cambridge: Polity).

Bellamy, A. J., and P. Williams (eds) (2005a) *Peace Operations and Global Order* (London: Frank Cass).

Bellamy, A. J., and P. D. Williams (2005b) 'Who's Keeping the Peace? Regionalization and Contemporary Peace Operations', *International Security*, 29(4): 157–95.

Bellamy, A. J., and P. D. Williams (2009) 'The West and Contemporary Peace Operations', *Journal of Peace Research*, 46(1): 39–57.

Bennis, P. (2000) *Calling the Shots: How Washington Dominates Today's UN* (New York: Olive Branch Press).

Berdal, M. (1993) *Whither UN Peacekeeping?* (Adelphi Paper no. 281, London: Oxford University Press for the IISS).

Berdal, M. (2001) 'United Nations Peace Operations: The *Brahimi Report* in Context', *Studies in Contemporary History and Security Policy*, 9: 35–53.

Berdal, M., and S. Economides (eds) (2007) *United Nations Interventionism, 1991–2004* (Cambridge: Cambridge University Press).

Berdal, M., and M. Leifer (1996) 'Cambodia', in J. Mayall (ed.), *The New Interventionism 1991–1994* (Cambridge: Cambridge University Press), pp. 25–58.

Berman, E., and K. Sams (2000) *Peacekeeping in Africa: Capabilities and Culpabilities* (Geneva: UNIDIR and ISS).

Bert, W. (1997) *The Reluctant Superpower: The United States' Policy in Bosnia 1991–1995* (Basingstoke: Macmillan).

Biermann, W., and M. Vadset (1998) 'Setting the Scene: The Challenge to the United Nations: Peacekeeping in a Civil War', in W. Biermann and M. Vadset (eds), *UN Peacekeeping in Trouble* (Aldershot: Ashgate), pp. 17–26.

Bildt, C. (1998) *Peace Journey: The Struggle for Peace in Bosnia* (London: Weidenfeld & Nicolson).

Binder, C., K. Lukas and R. Schweiger (2008) 'Empty Words or Real Achievement? The Impact of Security Council Resolution 1325 on Women in Armed Conflicts', *Radical History Review*, 101: 22–41.

Birgisson, K. T. (1993) 'UN Good Offices Mission in Afghanistan and Pakistan', in W. J. Durch (ed.), *The Evolution of UN Peacekeeping* (New York: St Martin's Press), pp. 273–84.

Birgisson, K. T. (1994a) 'United Nations Special Committee on the Balkans', in W. J. Durch (ed.), *The Evolution of UN Peacekeeping* (Basingstoke: Macmillan), pp. 77–83.

Birgisson, K. T. (1994b) 'United Nations Peacekeeping Force in Cyprus', in W. J. Durch (ed.), *The Evolution of UN Peacekeeping* (Basingstoke: Macmillan), pp. 219–36.

Blair, T. (1999) 'Doctrine of the International Community', speech to the Economic Club of Chicago, Hilton Hotel, Chicago, 22 April.

Blocq, D. S. (2006) 'The Fog of UN Peacekeeping: Ethical Issues Regarding the Use of Force to Protect Civilians in UN Operations', *Journal of Military Ethics*, 5(3): 201–13.

Blum, A. (2000) 'Blue Helmets from the South', *Journal of Conflict Studies*, 20(1): 53–73.

Bonwick, A. (2006) 'Who Really Protects Civilians?', *Development in Practice*, 16(3/4): 270–7.

Booth, K. (2007) *Theory of World Security* (Cambridge: Cambridge University Press).

Booth, K., and N. J. Wheeler (2008) *The Security Dilemma* (Basingstoke: Palgrave-Macmillan).

Bose, S. (2002) *Bosnia after Dayton* (London: Hurst).

Boulding, K. (1978) *Stable Peace* (Austin: University of Texas Press).

Boutros-Ghali, B. (1992) *An Agenda for Peace* (New York: UN Department of Public Information).

Boutros-Ghali, B. (1993) 'Further Report of the Secretary-General on the United Nations Angola Verification Mission' (UN doc. S/26434, 13 September).

Boutros-Ghali, B. (1994) 'Report of the Secretary-General Pursuant to Resolution 871' (UN doc. S/1994/300).

Boutros-Ghali, B. (1995a) *Supplement to An Agenda for Peace* (UN doc. A/47/277 – S/24111, 3 January).

Boutros-Ghali, B. (1995b) 'Introduction', in *The United Nations and Cambodia, 1991–1995* (New York: United Nations), pp. 3–66.

Boutros-Ghali, B. (1995c) *Confronting New Challenges: Annual Report on the Work of the Organization* (New York: United Nations).

Boutros-Ghali, B. (1996) *An Agenda for Democratization* (New York: United Nations).

Boutros-Ghali, B. (1999) *Unvanquished: A US–UN Saga* (London: I. B. Tauris).

Bowden, M. (2006) 'The Protection of Civilians', *International Studies in Human Rights*, 87: 59–68 [special issue].

Breau, S. C. (2007) 'The Impact of Responsibility to Protect on Peacekeeping', *Journal of Conflict and Security Law*, 11(3): 429–64.

Briscoe, N. (2004) *Britain and UN Peacekeeping, 1948–1967* (Basingstoke: Palgrave).

Britt, T. W., and A. B. Adler (2003) 'The Psychology of the Peacekeeper: An Introductory Framework', in T. W. Britt and A. B. Adler (eds), *The Psychology of the Peacekeepers* (Westport, CT: Praeger), pp. 3–10.

Broer, H., and M. Emery (1998) 'Civilian Police in UN Peacekeeping Operations', in R. Oakley, M. Dziedzic and E. Goldberg (eds), *Policing the New World Disorder* (Washington, DC: National Defense University Press), pp. 365–98.

Brooks, D., and G. Laroia (2005) 'Privatized Peacekeeping', *National Interest*, 80 (summer): 121–5.

Brownlie, I. (1963) *International Law and the Use of Force by States* (Oxford: Clarendon Press).

Bull, C. (2008) *No Entry without Strategy: Building the Rule of Law under UN Transitional Administration* (Tokyo: UN University Press).

Bull, H. (1977) *The Anarchical Society* (Basingstoke: Macmillan).

Bull, H., and A. Watson (eds) (1984), *The Expansion of International Society* (Oxford: Clarendon Press).

Bures, O. (2007) 'Wanted: A Mid-Range Theory of International Peacekeeping', *International Studies Review*, 9(3): 407–36.

Burg, S. L., and P. L. Shoup (1999) *The War in Bosnia-Herzegovina* (London: M. E. Sharpe).

Bush, G. H. W. (1991) 'A New World Order', speech to the House of Representatives, Washington, DC, 6 March.

Buzan, B., and R. Little (2000) *International Systems in World History* (Oxford: Oxford University Press).

Byers, M., and S. Chesterman (2000) ' "You the People": Pro-Democratic Intervention in Internal Law', in G. H. Fox and B. R. Roth (eds), *Democratic Governance and International Law* (Cambridge: Cambridge University Press), pp. 259–92.

Call, C. T. (2003) 'Democratisation, War and State-Building: Constructing the Rule of Law in El Salvador', *Journal of Latin American Studies*, 35(4): 827–62.

Call, C. T. (2006) *Constructing Justice and Security after War* (Washington, DC: US Institute of Peace).

Call, C. T., and M. Barnett (2000) 'Looking for a Few Good Cops: Peacekeeping, Peacebuilding and CIVPOL', in T. T. Holm and E. B. Eide (eds), *Peacebuilding and Police Reform* (London: Frank Cass), pp. 43–68.

Caney, S. (2005) *Justice beyond Borders* (Oxford: Oxford University Press).

Caplan, R. (2002) *A New Trusteeship? The International Administration of War-Torn Territories* (Adelphi Paper no. 341, Oxford: Oxford University Press).

Caplan, R. (2005) *International Governance of War-Torn Territories* (Oxford: Oxford University Press).

Cardenas, E. J. (2000) 'UN Financing: Some Reflections', *European Journal of International Law*, 11(1): 67–75.

Carnegie Commission on Preventing Deadly Conflict (1997) *Preventing Deadly Conflict: Final Report* (New York: Carnegie Corporation).

Carothers, T. (1998) 'The Rule of Law Revival', *Foreign Affairs*, 77(2): 95–106.

Carpenter, C. (2006) 'Recognising Gender-Based Violence against Men and Boys in Conflict Situations', *Security Dialogue*, 37(1): 83–103.

Carr, E. H. ([1939] 1995) *The Twenty Years' Crisis: An Introduction to the Study of International Relations* (London: Macmillan).

Cawthra, G., and R. Luckham (2003) *Governing Insecurity: Democratic Control of Military and Security Establishments in Transitional Democracies* (London: Zed Books).

Celador, G. C. (2005) 'Police Reform: Peacebuilding through "Democratic Policing"?', *International Peacekeeping*, 12(3): 364–76.

Chalk, P. (2001) *Australian Foreign and Defense Policy in the Wake of the 1999/2000 East Timor Intervention* (Washington, DC: RAND).

Chan, S. (1997) 'And What Do Peacekeeping Troops Do apart from Bury the Dead Then?', *International Relations*, 13(5): 27–36.

Chandler, D. (1997) 'Three Visions of Politics in Cambodia', in M. W. Doyle, I. Johnstone and R. C. Orr (eds), *Keeping the Peace* (Cambridge: Cambridge University Press), pp. 25–52.

Chandler, D. (2000) *Faking Democracy: Bosnia after Dayton* (London: Pluto Press).

Chandler, D. (2001) 'Universal Ethics and Elite Politics: The Limits of Normative Human Rights Theory', *International Journal of Human Rights*, 5(4): 72–89.

Chandler, D. (2006) *Empire in Denial: The Politics of State-Building* (London: Pluto Press).

Charters, D. A. (2000) 'Canada–US Defense Cooperation', presentation given at Defense Forum, Fredericton, New Brunswick, 12 April.

Chesterman, S. (2001) *Just War or Just Peace? Humanitarian Intervention and International Law* (Oxford: Oxford University Press).

Chesterman, S. (2002) 'East Timor in Transition: Self-Determination, State-Building and the United Nations', *International Peacekeeping*, 9(1): 45–76.

Chesterman, S. (2004) *You, the People: The United Nations, Transitional Administration, and State-Building* (Oxford: Oxford University Press).

Chesterman, S. (2006) *Shared Secrets: Intelligence and National Security* (Sydney: Lowy Institute Paper no. 10).

Chesterman, S., M. Ignatieff and R. Thakur (eds) (2005) *Making States Work* (Tokyo: UN University Press).

Chopra, J. (2000a) 'The UN's Kingdom of East Timor', *Survival*, 42(3): 27–40.

Chopra, J. (2000b) 'Introductory Note to UNTAET Regulation 13', *International Legal Materials*, 36.

Chopra, J. (2002) 'Building State Failure in East Timor', *Development and Change*, 33(5): 979–1000.

Chopra, J., and T. Hohe (2004a) 'Participatory Intervention', *Global Governance*, 10(2): 289–305.

Chopra, J., and T. Hohe (2004b) 'Participatory Peacebuilding', in T. Keating and W. A. Knight (eds), *Building Sustainable Peace* (Tokyo: UN University Press), pp. 241–62.

CIC (Center on International Cooperation) (2006) *Annual Review of Global Peace Operations 2006* (Boulder, CO: Lynne Rienner).

CIC (Center on International Cooperation) (2007) *Annual Review of Global Peace Operations 2007* (Boulder, CO: Lynne Rienner).

CIC (Center on International Cooperation) (2008) *Annual Review of Global Peace Operations 2008* (Boulder, CO: Lynne Rienner).

Cilliers, J. (2008) *The African Standby Force: An Update on Progress* (Pretoria: ISS Paper 160).

Clapham, C. (1998) 'Rwanda: The Perils of Peacemaking', *Journal of Peace Research*, 35(2): 193–210.

Clapham, C. (2002) 'Problems of Peace Enforcement', in T. Zack-Williams et al. (eds), *Africa in Crisis* (London: Pluto Press), pp. 196–215.

Clark, H. (2000) *Civil Resistance in Kosovo* (London: Pluto Press).

Clark, I. (1997) *Globalization and Fragmentation* (Oxford: Oxford University Press).

Clark, I. (2005) *Legitimacy in International Society* (Oxford: Oxford University Press).

Clark, J. (1993) 'Debacle in Somalia: Failure of the Collective Response', in L. F. Damrosch (ed.), *Enforcing Restraint* (New York: Council on Foreign Relations Press), pp. 205–39.

Clark, W. (2001) *Waging Modern War: Bosnia, Kosovo and the Future of Combat* (New York: Public Affairs).

Clarke, W., and J. Herbst (eds) (1997), *Learning from Somalia* (Boulder, CO: Westview Press).

Claude, I. L. (1963) *Swords into Ploughshares: The Problems and Progress of International Organization*, 4th edn (London: McGraw Hill).

Claude, I. L. (1966) 'Collective Legitimization as a Political Function of the United Nations', *International Organization*, 20(3): 367–79.

Cockayne, J., and D. M. Malone (2007) 'Relations with the Security Council', in S. Chesterman (ed.), *Secretary or General? The UN Secretary-General in World Politics* (Cambridge: Cambridge University Press), pp. 69–85.

Cockayne, J., and D. Pfister (2008) *Peace Operations and Organized Crime* (Geneva Papers no.2, Geneva: Geneva Centre for Security Policy)

Coleman, K. P. (2007) *International Organizations and Peace Enforcement* (Cambridge: Cambridge University Press).

Collelo, T. (1989) 'Historical Setting, Lebanon, the Civil War 1975–6', in T. Collelo (ed.), *Lebanon: A Country Study* (Washington, DC: Federal Research Division, Library of Congress), pp. 1–29.

Collier, P. (2007) *The Bottom Billion* (Oxford: Oxford University Press).

Collier, P., V. Elliott, H. Håvard, A. Hoeffler, A. Reynal-Querol and N. Sambanis (2003) *Breaking the Conflict Trap* (Oxford: Oxford University Press for the World Bank).

Commission of Inquiry (1994) *Report of the Commission of Inquiry Established Pursuant to Security Council Resolution 885 (1993) to Investigate Armed Attacks on UNOSOM II Personnel which Led to Casualties among Them*, New York, 24 February.

Conforti, B. (2000) *The Law and Practice of the United Nations* (The Hague: Kluwer International Law).

Conklin, A. L. (1997) *A Mission to Civilize: The Republican Idea of Empire in France and West Africa, 1895–1930* (Stanford, CA: Stanford University Press).

Connaughton, R. (1995) 'Wider Peacekeeping – How Wide of the Mark', *British Army Review*', 11: 62–5.

Cooper, N., and M. Pugh (2002) 'Security Sector Transformation in Post-Conflict Societies', *CDS Working Papers*, no. 5.

Cortright, D., and G. A. Lopez (2000) *The Sanctions Decade* (Boulder, CO: Lynne Rienner).

Cortright, D., and G. A. Lopez (2002) *Sanctions and the Search for Security* (Boulder, CO: Lynne Rienner).

Cortright, D., G. A. Lopez and L. Gerber-Stellingwerf (2008) 'The Sanctions Era', in V. Lowe et al. (eds), *The United Nations Security Council and War* (Oxford: Oxford University Press), pp. 205–25.

Costa, G. (1995) 'The United Nations and Reform of the Police in El Salvador', *International Peacekeeping*, 2(3): 365–90.

Cottey, A., T. Edmunds, and A. Forster (eds) (2002) *The Democratic Control of Armed Forces in Postcommunist Europe* (London: Palgrave Macmillan).

Cousens, E. M. (2001) 'Building Peace in Bosnia', in E. M. Cousens and C. Kumar (eds), *Peacebuilding as Politics* (Boulder, CO: Lynne Rienner), pp. 113–52.

Cousens, E. M., and D. Harland (2006) 'Post-Dayton Bosnia and Herzegovina', in W. J. Durch (ed.), *Twenty-First Century Peace Operations* (Washington, DC: US Institute of Peace), pp. 49–140.

Cox, R. W. (1981) 'Social Forces, States and World Orders', *Millennium*, 10(2): 126–55.

Cox, R. W. with T. Sinclair (1996) *Approaches to World Order* (Cambridge: Cambridge University Press).

Csáky, C. (2008) *No One to Turn to: the Under-Reporting of Child Sexual Exploitation and Abuse by Aid Workers and Peacekeepers* (London: Save the Children, UK).

Curran, D., and T. Woodhouse (2007) 'Cosmopolitan Peacekeeping and Peacebuilding in Sierra Leone', *International Affairs*, 83(6): 1055–70.

Daianu, D., and T. Veremis (2001) 'Introduction', in T. Veremis and D. Daianu (eds), *Balkan Reconstruction* (London: Frank Cass), pp. 1–11.

Dallaire, R., with B. Beardsley (2003) *Shake Hands with the Devil: The Failure of Humanity in Rwanda* (Toronto: Da Capo Press).

Davies, S. E. (2007) *Legitimising Rejection? International Refugee Law in Southeast Asia* (The Hague: Martinus Nijhoff).

Davies, S. E. (2009) *The Global Politics of Health* (Cambridge: Polity).

Day, G., and C. Freeman (2005) 'Operationalizing the Responsibility to Protect – the Policekeeping Approach', *Global Governance*, 11(1): 139–47.

Dayal, R. (1976) *Mission for Hammarskjöld: The Congo Crisis* (Oxford: Oxford University Press).

Decker, D. C. (2006) 'Enforcing Human Rights: The Role of the UN Civilian Police in Kosovo', *International Peacekeeping*, 13(4): 502–16.

Dee, M. (2001) '"Coalitions of the Willing" and Humanitarian Intervention', *International Peacekeeping*, 8(3): 1–20.

Del Zotto, A., and A. Jones (2002) 'Male-on-Male Sexual Violence in Wartime: Human Rights' Last Taboo?', paper presented to the International Studies Association, New Orleans, 23–7 March.

Demurenko, A., and A. Nikitin (1997) 'Basic Terminology and Concepts in International Peacekeeping Operations', *Low Intensity Conflict and Law Enforcement*, 6(1): 111–26.

Deng, F. M. (2004) 'The Impact of State Failure on Migration', *Mediterranean Quarterly*, 15(4): 16–36.

Deng, F. M., S. Kimaro, T. Lyons, D. Rothchild and I. W. Zartman (1996) *Sovereignty as Responsibility: Conflict Management in Africa* (Washington, DC: Brookings Institution).

Department of the Army (US) (2003) *Stability Operations and Support Operations*, FM 3-07 (FM 100-20) (Washington, DC: Department of the Army).

Des Forges, A. (1999) *Leave None to Tell the Story* (New York: Human Rights Watch).

Destexhe, A. (1995) *Rwanda and Genocide in the Twentieth Century* (London: Pluto Press).

Diehl, P. F. (1994) *International Peacekeeping* (Baltimore: Johns Hopkins University Press).

Diehl, P. F. (2000) 'Forks in the Road: Theoretical and Policy Concerns for 21st Century Peacekeeping', *Global Society*, 14(3): 337–60.

Diehl, P. F. (2007) 'New Roles for Regional Organizations', in C. A. Crocker, F. O. Hampson and P. Aall (eds), *Leashing the Dogs of War* (Washington, DC: US Institute of Peace), pp. 535–51.

Diehl, P. F. (2008) *Peace Operations* (Cambridge: Polity).

Diehl, P. F., and Y.-I. Cho (2006) 'Passing the Buck in Conflict Management: The Role of Regional Organizations in the Post-Cold War Era', *Brown Journal of World Affairs*, 12(2): 191–202.

Diehl, P. F., and S. R. Jurado (1993) 'United Nations Election Supervision in South Africa: Lessons from the Namibian Peacekeeping Experience', *Terrorism*, 16(1): 61–74.

Diehl, P. F., D. Druckman and J. Wall (1998) 'International Peacekeeping and Conflict Resolution: A Taxonomic Analysis with Implications', *Journal of Conflict Resolution*, 42(1): 35–55.

Dobbins, J., J. G. McGinn, K. Crane, S. G. Jones, R. Lal, A. Rathmell, R. M. Swanger and A. Timilsina (2003) *America's Role in Nation-Building* (Santa Monica, CA: RAND).

Dolan, C., and L. Hovil (2006) *Humanitarian Protection in Uganda: A Trojan Horse?* (London: HPG Background Paper for the Overseas Development Institute).

Donald, D. (2002) 'Neutrality, Impartiality and UN Peacekeeping at the Beginning of the 21st Century', *International Peacekeeping*, 9(4): 21–8.

Doyle, M. W. (1994) 'UNTAC – Sources of Success and Failure', in H. Smith (ed.), *International Peacekeeping* (Canberra: Australian Defence Studies Centre), pp. 79–98.

Doyle, M. W. (1995) *UN Peacekeeping in Cambodia: UNTAC's Civil Mandate* (Boulder, CO: Lynne Rienner).

Doyle, M. W., and N. Sambanis (2000) 'International Peacebuilding: A Theoretical and Quantitative Analysis', *American Political Science Review*, 94(4): 779–801.

Doyle, M. W., and N. Sambanis (2006) *Making War and Building Peace: United Nations Peace Operations* (Princeton, NJ: Princeton University Press).

Doyle, M. W., and N. Suntharalingam (1994) 'The UN in Cambodia: Lessons from Complex Peacekeeping', *International Peacekeeping*, 1(2): 117–47.

Doyle, M. W., I. Johnstone and R. C. Orr (eds) (1997) *Keeping the Peace* (Cambridge: Cambridge University Press).

DPKO (1996) *Comprehensive Report on Lessons Learned from United Nations Assistance Mission for Rwanda (UNAMIR) October 1993 – April 1996*, Lessons Learned Unit, December.

DPKO (2003) *Handbook on United Nations Multidimensional Peacekeeping Operations* (New York: DPKO Best Practices Unit).

DPKO (2004a) *Gender Resource Package for Peacekeeping Operations* (UN DPKO Best Practices Unit).

DPKO (2004b) *UNOCI Evaluation: After Action Report* (Peacekeeping Best Practices Unit, December).

DPKO (2004c), *Operation Artemis: The Lessons of the Interim Emergency Multinational Force* (Peacekeeping Best Practices Unit, Military Division, October).

DPKO (2006) Draft Capstone Doctrine for United Nations Peacekeeping Operations – Draft 2.

DPKO (2007) United Nations Peacekeeping Operations Principles and Guidelines (Capstone Doctrine Draft 3) (29 June).

DPKO (2008a) *United Nations Peacekeeping Operations: Principles and Guidelines* (Department of Field Support, 18 January).

DPKO (2008b) *United Nations Police* (New York: United Nations).

Druckman, D., and P. C. Stern (1999) 'Perspectives on Evaluating Peacekeeping Missions', *International Journal of Peace Studies*, 4(1): 181–92.

Duffield, M. (1997) 'NGO Relief in War Zones: Towards an Analysis of the New Aid Paradigm', *Third World Quarterly*, 18(3): 527–42.

Duffield, M. (2001) *Global Governance and the New Wars* (London: Zed Books).

Duffield, M. (2007) *Development, Security and Unending War* (Cambridge: Polity).

Dunbabin, J. P. D. (2008) 'The Security Council in the Wings: Exploring the Security Council's Non-Involvement in Wars', in V. Lowe et al. (eds), *The United Nations Security Council and War* (Oxford: Oxford University Press), pp. 494–517.

Durch, W. J. (1993a) 'Getting Involved: Political–Military Context', in W. J. Durch (ed.), *The Evolution of UN Peacekeeping* (New York: St Martin's Press), pp. 16–38.

Durch, W. J. (ed.) (1993b) *The Evolution of UN Peacekeeping* (London: Macmillan).

Durch, W. J. (1994a) 'Introduction', in W. J. Durch (ed.), *The Evolution of UN Peacekeeping* (Basingstoke: Macmillan), pp. 1–15.

Durch, W. J. (1994b) 'Paying the Tab: Financial Crises', in W J. Durch (ed.), *The Evolution of UN Peacekeeping* (Basingstoke: Macmillan), pp. 39–58.

Durch, W. J. (1994c) 'Running the Show: Planning and Implementation', in W. J. Durch (ed.), *The Evolution of UN Peacekeeping* (Basingstoke: Macmillan), pp. 59–75.

Durch, W. J. (1996a) 'Keeping the Peace: Policy and Lessons of the 1990s' in W. J. Durch (ed.), *UN Peacekeeping, American Policy and the Uncivil Wars of the 1990s* (London: Macmillan), pp. 1–34.

Durch, W. J. (ed.) (1996b) *UN Peacekeeping, American Policy and the Uncivil Wars of the 1990s* (London: Macmillan).

Durch, W. J. (2001) *UN Peace Operations and the 'Brahimi Report'* (Washington, DC: Henry L. Stimson Center).

Durch, W. J. (2003) *The UN System and Post-Conflict Iraq* (Washington, DC: Henry Stimson Center).

Durch, W. J. (2006a) 'Preface', in W. J. Durch (ed.), *Twenty-First-Century Peace Operations* (Washington, DC: US Institute of Peace), pp. xvii–xviii.

Durch, W. J. (ed.) (2006b) *Twenty-First-Century Peace Operations* (Washington, DC: US Institute of Peace).

Durch. W. J., and T. C. Berkman (2006) 'Restoring and Maintaining Peace: What we Know So Far', in W. J. Durch (ed.), *Twenty-First Century Peace Operations* (Washington, DC: US Institute of Peace), pp. 1–48.

Durch, W. J., V. K. Holt, C. R. Earle and M. K. Shanahan (2003) *The Brahimi Report and the Future of UN Peace Operations* (Washington, DC: Henry L. Stimson Center).

Dziedzic, M. (1998b) 'Introduction', in R. Oakley, M. Dziedzic and E. Goldberg (eds), *Policing the New World Disorder* (Washington, DC: National Defense University Press), pp. 3–18.

Dziedzic, M. (2002) 'Policing from Above: Executive Policing and Peace Implementation in Kosovo', in R. Dwan (ed.), *Executive Policing* (Oxford: Oxford University Press for SIPRI), pp. 33–52.

Eide, A. (1966) 'Peace-Keeping and Enforcement by Regional Organizations: Its Place in the United Nations System', *Journal of Peace Research*, 3(2): 125–44.

Elabray, N. (1987) 'The Office of the Secretary-General and the Maintenance of International Peace and Security', in J. P. Renniger (ed.), *The United Nations and the Maintenance of International Peace and Security* (Boston: Martinus Nijhoff), pp. 161–75.

Elbe, S. (2003) *Strategic Implications of HIV/AIDS* (Adelphi Paper no.357, Oxford: Oxford University Press).

Ellis, S. (1999) *The Mask of Anarchy* (London: Hurst).

Elshtain, J. B. (1987) *Women and War* (New York: Basic Books).

Esman, M. J. (1995) 'Survey of Interventions', in M. J. Esman and S. Telhami (eds), *International Organisations and Ethnic Conflict* (Ithaca, NY: Cornell University Press), pp. 21–47.

Evans, G. (1993) *Cooperating for Peace: The Global Agenda for the 1990s and Beyond* (St Leonards, NSW: Allen & Unwin).

Evans, G. (2004) 'When is it Right to Fight?', *Survival* 46(3): 59–82.

Evans, G. (2006a) 'A World in Crisis: Prevention and the International Crisis Group', speech to Norwegian Red Cross Humanitarian Forum, Oslo, 26 September, www.crisisgroup.org/home/index.cfm?id=4396&l=1.

Evans, G. (2006b) 'What Difference Would the Peacebuilding Commission Make?: The Case of Burundi', presentation to EPC/IRRI Workshop on the Peacebuilding Commission and Human Rights Council, Brussels, 20 January.

Evans, G. (2008) *The Responsibility to Protect: Ending Mass Atrocity Crimes Once and for All* (Washington, DC: Brookings Institution).

Evans, G., and K. Rowley (1990) *Red Brotherhood at War: Vietnam, Cambodia and Laos since 1975*, 2nd edn (London: Verso).

Fetherston, A. B. (1995) *Towards a Theory of United Nations Peacekeeping* (New York: St Martin's Press).

Fickling, D. (2003) 'The Bad Old Days of Colonialism', *The Guardian*, 21 July.

Findlay, T. (1995) *Cambodia: The Legacy and Lessons of UNTAC*, SIPRI Research Report no. 9 (Oxford: Oxford University Press).

Findlay, T. (ed.) (1996) *Challenges for the New Peacekeepers* (Oxford: Oxford University Press for SIPRI).

Findlay, T. (2002) *The Use of Force in UN Peace Operations* (Oxford: Oxford University Press for SIPRI).

Finnemore, M. (1996) 'Norms, Culture, and World Politics: Insights from Sociology's Institutionalism', *International Organization*, 50(2): 325–47.

Finnemore, M. (2003) *The Purpose of Intervention* (Ithaca, NY: Cornell University Press).

Fleitz, F. (2002) *Peacekeeping Fiascos of the 1990s* (Westport, CT: Praeger).

Flint, E. (2001) 'Civil Affairs: Soldiers Building Bridges', in D. S. Gordon and F. H. Toase (eds), *Aspects of Peacekeeping* (London: Frank Cass), pp. 230–52.

Flint, J., and A. de Waal (2005) *Darfur: A Short History of a Long War* (London: Zed Books).

Foreign Affairs Committee (UK) (1999) *Second Report: Sierra Leone* (London: House of Commons, 9 February).

Forsythe, D. P. (2005) *The Humanitarians: The International Committee of the Red Cross* (Cambridge: Cambridge University Press).

Fortna, V. P. (1993a) 'United Nations Angola Verification Mission I', in W. J. Durch (ed.), *The Evolution of UN Peacekeeping* (New York: St Martin's Press), pp. 376–87.

Fortna, V. P. (1993b) 'United Nations Angola Verification Mission II', in W. J. Durch (ed.), *The Evolution of UN Peacekeeping* (New York: St Martin's Press), pp. 388–405.

Fortna, V. P. (1994) 'The United Nations Transition Assistance Group in Namibia', in W. J. Durch (ed.), *The Evolution of UN Peacekeeping* (Basingstoke: Macmillan), pp. 353–75.

Fortna, V. P. (2003) 'Inside and Out: Peacekeeping and the Duration of Peace after Civil and Interstate Wars', *International Studies Review*, 5(4): 97–114.

Fortna, V. P. (2004) 'Does Peacekeeping Keep Peace? International Intervention and the Duration of Peace after Civil War', *International Studies Quarterly*, 48(2): 269–92.

Fortna, V. P. (2008a) 'Peacekeeping and Democratization', in A. K. Jarstad and T. D. Sisk (eds), *From War to Democracy* (Cambridge: Cambridge University Press), pp. 39–79.

Fortna, V. P. (2008b) *Does Peacekeeping Work? Shaping Belligerents' Choices after Civil War* (Princeton, NJ: Princeton University Press).

Fox, F. (2001) 'New Humanitarianism: Does it Provide a Moral Banner for the 21st Century?', *Disasters*, 25(4): 275–89.

Fox, G. H. (2008) *Humanitarian Occupation* (Cambridge: Cambridge University Press).

Fravel, M. T. (1996) 'China's Attitude towards UN Peacekeeping Operations since 1989', *Asian Survey*, 36(11): 1102–22.

Freedman, L. (1994) 'The Balkan Tragedy: Why the West Failed', *Foreign Policy*, 97 (winter): 52–7.

Freedman, L. (1998) *The Revolution in Military Affairs* (Adelphi Paper no. 318, Oxford: Oxford University Press).

Fukuyama, F. (1989) 'The End of History?', *National Interest*, 16: 3–18.

Fukuyama, F. (ed.) (2005) *Nation-Building: Beyond Afghanistan and Iraq* (Baltimore: Johns Hopkins University Press).

Galtung, J. (1975) *War, Peace and Defence – Essays in Peace Research*, vol. 2 (Copenhagen: Christian Ejlers).

German Government (2002) 'The Stability Pact and German Policy on South-Eastern Europe', German Foreign Ministry, www.auswaertiges-amt.de.

Ghali, M. (1994a) 'United Nations Truce Supervision Organisation', in W. J. Durch (ed.), *The Evolution of UN Peacekeeping* (Basingstoke: Macmillan), pp. 84–103.

Ghali, M. (1994b) 'United Nations Emergency Force I', in W. J. Durch (ed.), *The Evolution of UN Peacekeeping* (Basingstoke: Macmillan), pp. 104–130.

Giossi Caverzasio, S. (ed.) (2001) *Strengthening Protection in War* (Geneva: ICRC).

Gligorov, V. (2000) 'The Stability Pact for South-East Europe', unpublished paper.

Golberg, E. (2006) 'Operationalising the Protection of Civilians', *International Studies in Human Rights*, 87: 71–8 [special issue].

Goldstein, J. S. (2001) *War and Gender* (Cambridge: Cambridge University Press).

Goldstone, J. (2008) *Using Quantitative and Qualitative Models to Forecast Instability* (Washington, DC: USIP Special Report 204).

Goodrich, L. M., and M. J. Carroll (eds) (1947) *Documents on American Foreign Relations*, vol. VII (Princeton, NJ: Princeton University Press).

Goulding, M. (1993) 'The Evolution of United Nations Peacekeeping', *International Affairs*, 69(3): 451–64.

Goulding, M. (1996) 'The Use of Force by the United Nations', *International Peacekeeping*, 3(1): 1–18.

Goulding, M. (2002) *Peacemonger* (London: John Murray).

Gow, J. (1997) *The Triumph of the Lack of Will: International Diplomacy and the Yugoslav War of Succession* (London: Hurst).

Gow, J., and J. D. D. Smith (1992) *Peace-Making, Peace-Keeping: European Security and the Yugoslav Wars* (London: Brassey's).

Gray, C. (2000) *International Law and the Use of Force* (Oxford: Oxford University Press).

Gray, C. (2001) 'Peacekeeping after the Brahimi Report: Is there a Crisis of Credibility for the UN?', *Journal of Conflict and Security Law*, 6(2): 267–88.

Gray, C. (2004) *International Law and the Use of Force*, 2nd edn (Oxford: Oxford University Press).

Greig, J. M., and P. F. Diehl (2005) 'The Peacekeeping–Peacemaking Dilemma', *International Studies Quarterly*, 49(4): 621–45.

Grignon, F. (2003) 'The Artemis Operation in the Democratic Republic of Congo: Lessons for the Future of EU Peacekeeping in Africa', paper presented at 'The Challenges of Europe-Africa Relations: An Agenda of Priorities', conference, Lisbon, 23–4 October.

Grindle, M. S. (1997) 'The Good Government Imperative', in M. S. Grindle (ed.), *Getting Good Government* (Cambridge, MA: Harvard University Press), pp. 3–31.

Guéhenno, J.-M. (2002) 'On the Challenges and Achievements of Reforming UN Peace Operations', *International Peacekeeping*, 9(2): 69–80.

Guéhenno, J.-M. (2003) 'Everybody's Doing It', *World Today*, 59(8/9): 35–6.

Gutiérrez, I. C. (2006) *European Union Operations in the Democratic Republic of the Congo (DRC)*, doc. A/1954, 20 December (Brussels: Assembly of the Western European Union).

Hampson, F. O. (1996), *Nurturing Peace: Why Peace Settlements Succeed or Fail* (Washington, DC: US Institute of Peace).

Hampson, F. O., and D. Malone (2002) 'Improving the UN's Capacity for Conflict Prevention', *International Peacekeeping*, 9(1): 77–98.

Hansen, A. S. (2002) *From Congo to Kosovo: Civilian Police in Peace Operations* (Adelphi Paper no. 343, Oxford: Oxford University Press).

Hansen, A. S. (2003) 'Strengthening Indigenous Police Capacity and the Rule of Law in the Balkans', in M. Pugh and W. P. S. Sidhu (eds), *The United Nations and Regional Security* (Boulder, CO: Lynne Rienner), pp. 175–91.

Harbom, L., S. Högbladh and P. Wallensteen (2006) 'Armed Conflict and Peace Agreements', *Journal of Peace Research*, 43(5): 617–31.

Harding, J. (1997) 'The Mercenary Business: "Executive Outcomes"', *Review of African Political Economy*, 71: 87–97.

Harland, D. (2003) 'The Brahimi Report: Challenges to Implementation', remarks at International Peace Academy Seminar, Vienna, 4 July.

Harris, F. (2005) *The Role of Capacity-Building in Police Reform* (Pristina: OSCE).

Hartz, H. (2000) 'CIVPOL: The UN Instrument for Police Reform', in T. T. Holm and E. B. Eide (eds), *Peacebuilding and Police Reform* (London: Frank Cass), pp. 27–42.

Hay, C. (2000) 'Contemporary Capitalism, Globalization, Regionalization and the Persistence of National Variation', *Review of International Studies*, 26(4): 509–31.

Hayward, K. (2000) 'The Globalisation of Defence Industries', *Survival*, 42(2): 115–32.

Hegre, H. (2000) 'Development and the Democratic Peace: What Does it Take to be a Trading State?', *Journal of Peace Research*, 37(1): 5–30.

Heinemann-Gruder, A., and I. Grebenschikov (2006) 'Security Governance by Internationals: The Case of Kosovo', *International Peacekeeping*, 13(1): 43–59.

Held, D. (1995) *Democracy and the Global Order* (Cambridge: Polity).

Held, D. (1998) 'Democracy and Globalization', in D. Archibugi, D. Held and M. Köhler (eds), *Re-Imagining Political Community* (Stanford, CA: Stanford University Press), pp. 11–27.

Held, D., A. McGrew, D. Goldblatt and J. Perraton (1999) *Global Transformations* (Cambridge: Polity).

Heldt, B. (2008) 'Trends from 1945 to 2005', in D. C. F. Daniel, P. Taft and S. Wiharta (eds), *Peace Operations* (Washington, DC: Georgetown University Press), pp. 9–26.

Herbst, J. (1999) 'The Regulation of Private Security Forces', in G. Mills and J. Stremlau (eds), *The Privatisation of Security in Africa* (Braamfontein: South African Institute of International Affairs), pp. 107–27.

Higate, P., and M. Henry (2004) 'Engendering (In)security in Peace Support Operations', *Security Dialogue*, 35(4): 481–98.

Higgins, R. (1969) *United Nations Peacekeeping 1946–1967: Documents and Commentary*, Vol. I: *The Middle East* (London: Oxford University Press).

Higgins, R. (1981) *United Nations Peacekeeping: Documents and Commentary*, Vol. IV: *Europe 1946–1979* (London: Oxford University Press).

Hillen, J. (1998) *Blue Helmets: The Strategy of UN Military Operations* (Washington, DC: Brassey's).

Hills, A. (1998) 'International Peace Support Operations and CIVPOL', *International Peacekeeping*, 5(3): 26–41.

Hirsch, J. L. (2001) *Sierra Leone: Diamonds and the Struggle for Democracy* (Boulder, CO: Lynne Rienner).

Hirsch, J. L. (2004) 'Sierra Leone', in D. M. Malone (ed.), *The United Nations Security Council* (Boulder, CO: Lynne Rienner), pp. 521–35.

Hirsch, J. L., and R. B. Oakley (1995) *Somalia and Operation Restore Hope* (Washington, DC: US Institute of Peace).

Hirst, P. (2001) *War and Power in the Twenty-First Century* (Cambridge: Polity).

HMSO (1995) *Wider Peacekeeping* (London: Ministry of Defence).

HMSO (1999) *Joint Warfare Publication 3–50: Peace Support Operations* (London: HMSO).

Hobsbawm, E. (1962) *The Age of Revolution 1989–1848* (London: Weidenfeld & Nicolson).

Höglund, K. (2008) 'Violence in War-to-Democracy Transitions', in A. K. Jarstad and T. D. Sisk (eds), *From War to Democracy* (Cambridge: Cambridge University Press), pp. 80–102.

Holbrooke, R. C. (1998) *To End a War* (New York: Random House).

Holbrooke, R. C. (2000) 'Statement by Ambassador Richard C. Holbrooke, United States Permanent Representative to the United Nations', Cardozo Law School, New York, 28 March.

Hollis, M., and S. Smith (1991) *Explaining and Understanding International Relations* (Oxford: Clarendon Press).

Holsti, K. J. (1991) *Peace and War: Armed Conflicts and International Order 1648–1989* (Cambridge: Cambridge University Press).

Holt, V. K. (2005) *The Responsibility to Protect: Considering the Operational Capacity for Civilian Protection* (Washington, DC: Henry L. Stimson Center).

Holt, V. K., and T. C. Berkman (2006) *The Impossible Mandate? Military Preparedness, the Responsibility to Protect and Modern Peace Operations* (Washington, DC: Henry L. Stimson Center).

Honig, J. W., and N. Both (1996) *Srebrenica: Record of a War Crime* (London: Penguin).

Hoon, G. (2001) 'The International Security Assistance Force for Kabul', speech to the House of Commons, London, 19 December.

Horkheimer, M. (1972) *Critical Theory: Selected Essays*, trans. M. J. O'Connell et al. (New York: Seabury Press).

Horta, R. (2008) 'Interview with Andrew Denton', ABC Australia, screened 4 August.

House of Commons (UK) (1993) *The Expanding Role of the United Nations and its Implications for United Kingdom Policy*, vol. 1, Foreign Affairs Select Committee (London: HMSO).

House of Commons, UK (2002) *Private Military Companies: Options for Regulation* (Green Paper HC 577, London: HMSO).

Howard, L. M. (2008) *UN Peacekeeping in Civil Wars* (Cambridge: Cambridge University Press).

Howe, H. (2001) *Ambiguous Order: Military Forces in African States* (Boulder, CO: Lynne Rienner).

Hulton, S. C. (2004) 'Council Working Methods and Procedure', in D. M. Malone (ed.), *The United Nations Security Council* (Boulder, CO: Lynne Rienner), pp. 237–51.

Human Rights Watch (2002) *The War Within: Sexual Violence against Women and Girls in Eastern Congo* (New York: Human Rights Watch).

Human Security Centre (2005) *Human Security Report 2005* (Oxford: Oxford University Press).

Human Security Centre (2008) *Human Security Brief 2007*, www.humansecuritybrief. info/.

Hurwitz, A. (2008) 'Civil War and the Rule of Law: Toward Security, Development and Human Rights', in A. Hurwitz (ed.), *Civil War and the Rule of Law* (Boulder, CO: Lynne Rienner), pp. 1–20.

IASC (Inter-Agency Standing Committee) (2000) *Protection of Internally Displaced Persons*, Inter-Agency Standing Committee Policy Paper Series, no. 2 (New York: United Nations).

IASC (Inter-Agency Standing Committee) (2002) *Growing the Sheltering Tree: Protecting Human Rights through Humanitarian Action, Programmes and Practices Gathered from the Field* (Geneva: IASC).

ICG (International Crisis Group) (2000) *Elections in Kosovo: Moving Toward Democracy?* (Balkans Report no. 87).

ICG (International Crisis Group) (2001) *No Early Exit: NATO's Continuing Challenge in Bosnia* (Balkans Report no. 110).

ICG (International Crisis Group) (2002) *Securing Afghanistan: The Need for More International Action* (Afghanistan Briefing).

ICG (International Crisis Group) (2006) *Resolving Timor-Leste's Crisis* (Asia Report no. 120).

ICG (International Crisis Group) (2008a) *Afghanistan: The Need for International Resolve* (Asia Report no. 145, 6 February).

ICG (International Crisis Group) (2008b) *Timor-Leste's Displacement Crisis* (Asia Report no. 148).

ICRC (2005) *Annual Report: Sudan* (Geneva: ICRC).

IICK (Independent International Commission on Kosovo) (2000) *Kosovo Report* (Oxford: Oxford University Press).

IISS (2001) *The Military Balance 2001/2002* (London: Oxford University Press).

Ikenberry, G. J. (2001) *After Victory: Institutions, Strategic Restraint and the Rebuilding of Order after Major Wars* (Princeton, NJ: Princeton University Press).

Independent Inquiry (1999) *Report of the Independent Inquiry into the Actions of the United Nations during the 1994 Genocide in Rwanda* (UN doc. S/1999/1257, 12 December).

International Commission of Inquiry on Darfur (2005) *Report to the Secretary-General, Pursuant to Security Council Resolution 1564 (2004) of 18 September 2004* (UN doc. S/2005/60, annex).

International Peace Academy (1984) *Peacekeeper's Handbook* (New York: International Peace Academy).

International Peace Academy (2006) 'The UN Peacebuilding Commission: Benefits and Challenges', background paper prepared for the regional seminars organized by the Friedrich-Ebert-Stiftung, 6 June.

Jackson, K. D. (1989) 'The Khmer Rouge in Context', in K. D. Jackson (ed.), *Cambodia 1975–1978* (Princeton, NJ: Princeton University Press), pp. 3–11.

Jackson, R. (2000) *The Global Covenant* (Oxford: Oxford University Press).

Jackson, R. (2001) 'The Evolution of International Society', in J. Baylis and S. Smith (eds), *The Globalization of World Politics*, 2nd edn (Oxford: Oxford University Press), pp. 35–50.

Jackson, R. (2005) *Classical and Modern Thought on International Relations* (London: Palgrave Macmillan).

Jakobsen, P. V. (2002) 'The Transformation of United Nations Peace Operations in the 1990s', *Cooperation and Conflict*, 37(3): 267–82.

James, A. (1969) *The Politics of Peacekeeping* (London: Chatto & Windus).

James, A. (1989) 'The UN Force in Cyprus', *International Affairs*, 65(3): 481–500.

James, A. (1990) *Peacekeeping in International Politics* (Basingstoke: Macmillan with the IISS).

James, A. (1994a) 'International Peacekeeping', in D. A. Charters (ed.), *Peacekeeping and the Challenge of Civil Conflict Resolution* (New Brunswick: New Brunswick University Press), pp. 17–31.

James, A. (1994b) 'Is there a Second Generation of Peacekeeping?', *International Peacekeeping*, 1(4): 110–13.

James, A. (1994c) 'The Congo Controversies', *International Peacekeeping*, 1(1): 44–58.

Jardine, M. (2000) 'East Timor, the United Nations, and the International Community', *Pacifica Review*, 12(1): 47–62.

Jarstad, A. K. (2008) 'Power Sharing: Former Enemies in Joint Government', in A. K. Jarstad and T. D. Sisk (eds), *From War to Democracy* (Cambridge: Cambridge University Press), pp. 105–33.

Jarstad, A. K., and T. D. Sisk (eds) (2008), *From War to Democracy* (Cambridge: Cambridge University Press).

Jaster, R. (1990) *The 1988 Peace Accords and the Future of South-Western Africa* (Adelphi Paper no. 253, London: Oxford University Press for the IISS).

Jett, D. (1999) *Why Peacekeeping Fails* (New York: St Martin's Press).

Johansen, R. C. (ed.) (2006) *A United Nations Emergency Peace Service* (New York: World Federalist Movement).

Johnstone, I. (2006) 'Dilemmas of Robust Peace Operations', in *Annual Review of Global Peace Operations 2006* (Boulder, CO: Lynne Rienner), pp. 1–17.

Joint Publication (2007) *Peace Operations 3.07-03* (Washington, DC: Joint Chiefs of Staff).

Jones, B. D. (2001) *Peacemaking in Rwanda* (Boulder, CO: Lynne Rienner).

Jones, B. D., and C. K. Cater (2001) 'From Chaos to Coherence? Toward a Regime for Protecting Civilians in War', in S. Chesterman (ed.), *Civilians in War* (Boulder, CO: Lynne Rienner), pp. 247–62.

Jones, B. D., with F. Cherif (2004) *Evolving Models of Peacekeeping: Policy Implications and Responses* (UN: Peacekeeping Best Practices Unit External Study), http://pbpu.unlb.org/pbpu/library/Bruce%20Jones%20paper%20with%20logo.pdf.

Judah, T. (2000) *Kosovo: War and Revenge* (London: Yale University Press).

Kaldor, M. (1997) 'Introduction', in M. Kaldor and B. Vashee (eds), *Restructuring the Global Military Sector*, vol. 1: *New Wars* (London: Pinter), pp. 3–33.

Kaldor, M. (1999) *New and Old Wars* (Cambridge: Polity).

Kaldor, M. (2006) *New and Old Wars*, 2nd edn (Cambridge: Polity).

Kaplan, R. (1994) *Balkan Ghosts* (New York: Vintage Books).

Keating, C. (2004) 'Rwanda: An Insider's Account', in D. M. Malone (ed.), *The United Nations Security Council* (Boulder, CO: Lynne Rienner), pp. 500–11.

Keen, D. (1993) *The Kurds in Iraq: How Safe is their Haven Now?* (London: Save the Children).

Keen, D. (1998) *The Economic Functions of Violence in Civil Wars* (Adelphi Paper no. 320, Oxford: Oxford University Press for the IISS).

Keen, D. (2001) 'War and Peace: What's the Difference?', in A. Adebajo and C. L. Sriram (eds), *Managing Armed Conflict in the 21st Century* (London: Frank Cass), pp. 1–22.

Keen, D. (2008) *Complex Emergencies* (Cambridge: Polity).

Keene, E. (2002) *Beyond the Anarchical Society* (Cambridge: Cambridge University Press).

Keith, A. B. (1919) *The Belgian Congo and the Berlin Act* (Oxford: Clarendon Press).

Kekic, L. (2001) 'Aid to the Balkans: Addicts and Pushers', in T. Veremis and D. Daianu (eds), *Balkan Reconstruction* (London: Frank Cass), pp. 20–40.

Kennedy, D. (2004) *The Dark Sides of Virtue* (Princeton, NJ: Princeton University Press).

Kent, V. (2007) 'Protecting Civilians from UN Peacekeepers and Humanitarian Workers', in C. Aoi, C. de Coning and R. Thakur (eds), *Unintended Consequences of Peacekeeping Operations* (Tokyo: UN University Press), pp. 44–66.

Kieh, G. K. (1998) 'International Organizations and Peacekeeping in Africa', in K. P. Magyar and E. Conteh-Morgan (eds), *Peacekeeping in Africa* (Basingstoke: Macmillan), pp. 12–31.

Kim, J. (2005) 'Bosnia and the European Union Military Force (EUFOR): Post-NATO Transition', CRS Report for Congress, 14 March.

Kissinger, H. (1994) *Diplomacy* (London: Simon & Schuster).

Knaus, G., and F. Martin (2003) 'The Travails of a European Raj', *Journal of Democracy*, 14(3): 60–74.

Knudsen, T. B. (2006) 'From UNMIK to Self-Determination? The Puzzle of Kosovo's Future Status', in T. B. Knudsen and C. B. Laustsen (eds), *Kosovo between War and Peace* (London: Routledge), pp. 156–67.

Kolsto, P. (2000) *Political Construction Sites: Nation-Building in Russia and the Post-Soviet States* (Boulder, CO: Westview Press).

Koyama, S., and H. Myrttinen (2007) 'Unintended Consequences of Peace Operations on Timor Leste from a Gender Perspective', in C. Aoi, C. de Coning and R. Thakur (eds), *Unintended Consequences of Peacekeeping Operations* (Tokyo: UN University Press), pp. 23–43.

Krain, M. (2005) 'International Intervention and the Severity of Genocides and Politicides', *International Studies Quarterly*, 49(2): 363–87.

Krasner, S. D., and C. Pascual (2005) 'Addressing State Failure', *Foreign Affairs*, 84(4): 153–63.

Kroeker, M. (2007) 'Role of UN Police from Observing to "Coaching", Top Adviser Says', *UN News Service*, 27 January.

Kroslak, D. (2007) *The Role of France in the Rwandan Genocide* (London: Hurst).

Kupchan, C., and C. Kupchan (1991) 'Concerts, Collective Security and the Future of Europe', *International Security*, 16(1): 23–51.

Lake, A. (1990) *After the Wars: Reconstruction in Afghanistan, Indochina, Central America, South Africa and the Horn of Africa* (New Brunswick, NJ: Transaction Books).

Langille, H. P. (2000) 'Conflict Prevention: Options for Rapid Deployment and UN Standing Forces', *International Peacekeeping*, 7(1): 219–53.

Lauterpacht, H. (1933) *The Function of Law in the International Community* (Oxford: Clarendon Press).

Le Billon, P. (2008) 'Corrupting Peace? Peacebuilding and Post-Conflict Corruption', *International Peacekeeping*, 15(3): 344–61.

Le Billon, P., and K. Bakker (2000) 'Cambodia: Genocide, Autocracy and the Overpoliticized State', in E. W. Nafziger, F. Stewart and R. Vayrynen (eds), *War, Hunger and Displacement*, Vol. 2: *Case Studies* (Oxford: Oxford University Press), pp. 53–88.

Leader, N. (2000) *The Politics of Principle* (London: HPG Report 2 for the ODI).

Leander, A., and R. van Munster (2007) 'Private Security Contractors in the Debate about Darfur', *International Relations*, 21(2): 201–16.

Lederach, J. P. (1995) *Preparing for Peace* (Syracuse, NY: Syracuse University Press).

Lee Kim, C. M., and M. Metrikas (1997) 'Holding a Fragile Peace: The Military and Civilian Components of UNTAC', in M. W. Doyle, I. Johnstone and R. C. Orr (eds), *Keeping the Peace* (Cambridge: Cambridge University Press), pp. 107–33.

Lehmann, I. A. (ed.) (1999) *Peacekeeping and Public Information* (London: Frank Cass).

Licklider, R. (1995) 'The Consequences of Negotiated Settlements in Civil Wars, 1945–1993,' *American Political Science Review*, 89(3): 681–90.

Lin, T., and P. Law (2008) 'Objectives-Based Policing Typology', paper presented to the Oceanic Conference on International Studies, 2–4 July.

Linklater, A. (1992) 'What is a Good International Citizen?', in P. Keal (ed.), *Ethics and Foreign Policy* (Sydney: Allen & Unwin), pp. 42–63.

Linklater, A. (1998) *The Transformation of Political Community* (Cambridge: Polity).

Lischer, S. K. (2007) 'Military Intervention and the Humanitarian "Force Multiplier"', *Global Governance*, 13(1): 99–118.

Lizee, P. (1993) 'The Challenge of Conflict Resolution in Cambodia', *Cambodia Defence Quarterly*, 23(1): 35–44.

Lodico, Y. C. (1996) 'A Peace that Fell Apart: The United Nations and the War in Angola', in W. J. Durch (ed.), *UN Peacekeeping, American Policy, and the Uncivil Wars of the 1990s* (London: Macmillan), pp. 103–34.

Lorenz, J. P. (1999) *Peace, Power and the United Nations* (Boulder, CO: Westview Press).

Lowe, V., A. Roberts, J. Welsh and D. Zaum (2008) 'Introduction', in V. Lowe et al. (eds), *The United Nations Security Council and War* (Oxford: Oxford University Press), pp. 1–58.

Luck, E. (2006) *UN Security Council: Practice and Promise* (London: Routledge).

Lynch, C. (2001) 'Misconduct, Corruption by US Police Mar Bosnia Mission', *Washington Post*, 14 July.

Lynch, M. (2008) 'Lie to Me: Sanctions on Iraq, Moral Argument and the International Politics of Hypocrisy', in R. Price (ed.), *Moral Limit and Possibility in World Politics* (Cambridge: Cambridge University Press), pp. 165–96.

Lyons, T. (2006) *Avoiding Conflict in the Horn of Africa* (Washington, DC: Council on Foreign Relations).

Lyons, T., and A. I. Samatar (1995) *Somalia: State Collapse, Multilateral Intervention and Strategies for Political Reconstruction* (Washington, DC: Brookings Institution).

McCoubrey, H., and J. Morris (2000) *Regional Peacekeeping in the Post Cold War Era* (The Hague: Kluwer Law International).

McDermott, A. (1994) 'Peacekeeping Operations: Funding Problems and Solutions', in D. A. Charters (ed.), *Peacekeeping and the Challenge of Civil Conflict Resolution* (Fredericton: Centre for Conflict Studies, University of New Brunswick), pp. 143–60.

McDermott, A., and K. Skjelsbaek (eds) (1991) *The Multinational Force in Beirut, 1982–1984* (Miami: Florida International University Press).

McFarlane, J., and W. Maley (2001) 'Civilian Police in UN Peace Operations: Some Lessons from Recent Australian Experience', in R. Thakur and A. Schnabel (eds), *United Nations Peacekeeping Operations* (Tokyo: UN University Press), pp. 182–212.

MacFarlane, S. N. (2001) 'Regional Peacekeeping in the CIS', in R. Thakur and A. Schnabel (eds), *United Nations Peacekeeping Operations* (Tokyo: UN University Press), pp. 77–99.

MacGinty, R., and G. Robinson (2001) 'Peacekeeping and the Violence in Ethnic Conflict', in R. Thakur and A. Schnabel (eds), *United Nations Peacekeeping Operations* (Tokyo: UN University Press), pp. 26–45.

Mack, A. (2007) *Global Political Violence: Explaining the Post Cold War Decline* (Coping with Crisis Working Paper, New York: International Peace Academy).

Mackinlay, J. (1989) *The Peacekeepers* (London: Unwin Hyman).

Mackinlay, J. (ed.) (1996) *A Guide to Peace Support Operations* (Providence, RI: Thomas J. Watson Institute for International Studies).

Mackinlay, J. (1998) 'Beyond the Logjam: A Doctrine for Complex Emergencies', *Small Wars and Insurgencies*, 9(1): 114–31.

Mackinlay, J., and J. Chopra (1992) 'Second Generation Multinational Operations', *Washington Quarterly*, 15(3): 113–31.

MacKinnon, M. G. (2000) *The Evolution of US Peacekeeping under Clinton* (London: Frank Cass).

McMahon, P. C. (2002) 'What Have We Wrought? Assessing the International Involvement in Bosnia', *Problems of Post-Communism*, 49(1): 18–29.

McMullan, B., and D. Peebles (2006) 'The Responsibility to Protect: Lessons from RAMSI', unpublished paper.

McNeill, T. (1997) 'Humanitarian Intervention and Peacekeeping in the Former Soviet Union and Eastern Europe', *International Political Science Review*, 18(1): 95–113.

McQueen, C. (2005) *Humanitarian Intervention and Safety Zones* (Basingstoke: Palgrave Macmillan).

MacQueen, N. (2002) *United Nations Peacekeeping in Africa since 1960* (London: Longman).

MacQueen, N. (2006) *Peacekeeping and the International System* (London: Routledge).

Macrae, J. (ed.) (2002) *The New Humanitarianisms* (London: HPG Report 11 for the ODI).

Magnarella, P. J. (2000) *Justice in Africa* (Aldershot: Ashgate).

Mahoney, L. (2006) *Proactive Presence: Field Strategies for Civilian Protection* (Geneva: Centre for Humanitarian Dialogue).

Malcolm, N. (1994) *Bosnia: A Short History* (London: Macmillan).

Maley, W. (2000) 'The UN and East Timor', *Pacifica Review*, 12(1): 63–76.

Malone, D. M., and K. Wermester (2001) 'Boom and Bust? The Changing Nature of UN Peacekeeping', in A. Adebajo and C. L. Sriram (eds), *Managing Armed Conflicts in the 21st Century* (London: Frank Cass), pp. 37–54.

Malone, D. M., and R. Thakur (2001) 'UN Peacekeeping: Lessons Learned?', *Global Governance*, 7(1): 11–17.

Mandelbaum, M. (2002) *The Ideas that Conquered the World* (New York: Public Affairs).

Mann, M. (1986) *The Sources of Social Power*, vol. I: *A History of Power from the Beginning to AD 1760* (Cambridge: Cambridge University Press).

Mann, M. (1993) *The Sources of Social Power*, vol. II: *The Rise of Classes and Nation-States, 1760–1914* (Cambridge: Cambridge University Press).

Månsson, K. (2005) 'The Forgotten Agenda: Human Rights Protection and Promotion in Cold War Peacekeeping', *Journal of Conflict and Security Law*, 10(3): 379–403.

Marten, K. Z. (2004) *Enforcing the Peace: Learning from the Imperial Past* (New York: Columbia University Press).

Martin, I. (2004) 'Keeping the Peace: The UN Mission in Ethiopia and Eritrea', in J.-B. Berdal and M. Plaut (eds), *Unfinished Business: Ethiopia and Eritrea at War* (Trenton, NJ: Red Sea Press), pp. 135–49.

Martin, S. (2005) *Must Boys Be Boys: Ending Sexual Exploitation and Abuse in UN Peacekeeping Missions* (Washington, DC: Refugees International).

Mearsheimer, J. J. (1994) 'The False Promise of International Institutions', *International Security*, 19(3): 5–49.

Medlicott, W. N. (1956) *Bismarck, Gladstone and the Concert of Europe* (London: Athlone Press).

Meisler, S. (1995) 'Dateline UN: A New Hammarskjöld?', *Foreign Policy*, 98(spring): 180–97.

Meisler, S. (2007) *Kofi Annan: A Man of Peace in a World of War* (London: John Wiley).

Melvern, L. (1995) *The Ultimate Crime: Who Betrayed the UN and Why* (London: Allison & Busby).

Melvern, L. (1997) 'Genocide behind the Thin Blue Line', *Security Dialogue*, 28(3): 333–46.

Melvern, L. (2000) *A People Betrayed: The Role of the West in Rwanda's Genocide* (London: Zed Books).

Melvern, L. (2006) *Conspiracy to Murder: The Rwanda Genocide*, 2nd edn (London: Verso).

Menkhaus, K. (2004) 'Conflict Prevention and Human Security: Issues and Challenges', *Conflict, Security & Development*, 4(3): 419–63.

Mersiades, M. (2005) 'Peacekeeping and Legitimacy: Lessons from Cambodia and Somalia', *International Peacekeeping*, 12(2): 205–21.

Miall, H., O. Ramsbotham and T. Woodhouse (1999) *Contemporary Conflict Resolution* (Cambridge: Polity); 2nd edn, 2005.

Mill, J. S. (1991) *Considerations on Representative Government* (Amherst, MA: Prometheus Books).

Mitzen, J. (2005) 'Reading Habermas in Anarchy: Multilateral Diplomacy and Global Public Spheres', *American Political Science Review*, 99(3): 401–17.

Morphet, S. (2000) 'China as a Permanent Member of the Security Council, October 1971–December 1999', *Security Dialogue*, 31(2): 151–66.

Morris, J., and H. McCoubrey (1999) 'Regional Peacekeeping in the Post-Cold War Era', *International Peacekeeping*, 6(2): 129–51.

Münkler, H. (2005) *The New Wars*, trans. P. Camiller (Cambridge: Polity).

Murray, R. W., and S. Gordon (1998) *The Road to Peace: NATO and the International Community in Bosnia* (London: Casemate).

Musah, A.-F. (2000) 'A Country under Siege: State Decay and Corporate Military Intervention in Sierra Leone', in A.-F. Musah and J. K. Feyemi (eds), *Mercenaries* (London: Pluto Press), pp. 76–116.

Nambiar, S. (2000) 'India: An Uneasy Precedent', in A. Schnabel and R. Thakur (eds), *Kosovo and the Challenge of Humanitarian Intervention* (Tokyo: UN University Press), pp. 260–70.

NATO (2002) *NATO Handbook* (Brussels: NATO).

Newman, E. (2004) 'The "New Wars" Debate: A Historical Perspective is Needed', *Security Dialogue*, 35(2): 173–89.

Nordstrom, C. (2002) *Shadows of War* (Berkeley: University of California Press).

O'Ballance, E. (1966) *The Greek Civil War, 1944–1949* (London: Faber).

O'Callaghan, S., and S. Pantuliano (2007) *Protective Action: Incorporating Civilian Protection in Humanitarian Response* (Report 26, London: Overseas Development Institute, Humanitarian Policy Group); www.odi.org.uk/resources/download/1020.pdf.

OCHA (2003) *Special Report: Civilian Protection in Armed Conflict* (New York, OCHA Integrated Regional Information Network).

OCHA (2004) *Aide-Memoire for the Consideration of Issues Pertaining to the Protection of Civilians* (New York, OCHA Policy Development and Studies Branch).

Ohmae, K. (1995) *The End of the Nation State* (New York: Free Press).

Olonisakin, F. (2000) *Reinventing Peacekeeping in Africa* (The Hague: Kluwer International Law).

Olonisakin, F. (2008) *Peacekeeping in Sierra Leone* (Boulder, CO: Lynne Rienner).

O'Neill, W. G. (2008), 'UN Peacekeeping Operations and Rule of Law Programs', in A. Hurwitz (ed.), *Civil War and the Rule of Law* (Boulder, CO: Lynne Rienner), pp. 91–113.

O'Shea, B. (2002) 'The Future of UN Peacekeeping', *Conflict and Terrorism*, 25(2): 145–8.

Osland, K. M. (2004) 'The EU Police Mission in Bosnia and Herzegovina', *International Peacekeeping*, 11(3): 544–60.

Ottaway, M., and B. Lacina (2003) 'International Interventions and Imperialism: Lessons from the 1990s', *SAIS Review*, 23(2): 71–92.

Owen, J. M. (1994) 'How Liberalism Produces Democratic Peace', *International Security*, 19(2): 87–125.

Owen, J. M. (2000) 'International Law and the "Liberal Peace"', in G. H. Fox and B. R. Roth (eds), *Democratic Governance and International Law* (Cambridge: Cambridge University Press), pp. 251–73.

Oxfam International (2003) *Beyond the Headlines: An Agenda for Action to Protect Civilians in Neglected Conflicts* (Oxford: Oxfam GB for Oxfam International).

Oxfam International (2008) *For a Safer Tomorrow: Protecting Civilians in a Multipolar World* (Oxfam Research Paper, September).

Padelford, N. J. (1954) 'Regional Organizations and the United Nations', *International Organization*, 8(2): 203–16.

Pantuliano, S., and S. O'Callaghan (2006) *The 'Protection Crisis': A Review of Field-Based Strategies for Humanist Protection in Darfur* (London: Humanitarian Policy Group Discussion Paper for the Overseas Development Institute).

Paris, R. (1997) 'Peacebuilding and the Limits of Liberal Internationalism', *International Security*, 22(2): 54–89.

Paris, R. (2000) 'Broadening the Study of Peace Operations', *International Studies Review*, 2(3): 27–44.

Paris, R. (2002) 'International Peacebuilding and the *Mission Civilisatrice*', *Review of International Studies*, 28(4): 637–56.

Paris, R. (2003) 'Peacekeeping and the Constraints of Global Culture', *European Journal of International Relations*, 9(3): 441–73.

Paris, R. (2004) *At War's End: Building Peace after Civil Conflict* (Cambridge: Cambridge University Press).

Paris, R. (2007a) 'Understanding the "Coordination Problem" in Postwar State Building', working paper, Ottawa: Research Partnership on Postwar State-Building.

Paris, R. (2007b) 'NATO's Choice in Afghanistan: Go Big or Go Home', *Policy Options*, December–January, pp. 35–43.

Paris, R., and T. Sisk (eds) (2008) *The Dilemmas of Statebuilding* (London: Routledge).

Parsons, A. (1995) *From Cold War to Hot Peace* (London: Michael Joseph).

Patrick, S. (2006) 'Weak States and Global Threats: Fact or Fiction?', *Washington Quarterly*, 29(2): 27–53.

PBSO (2007) 'The UN Peacebuilding Fund (PBF)', presentation by the Peacebuilding Support Office, 3 July.

Peake, G., and K. Studdard Brown (2005) 'Policebuilding: The International Deployment Group in the Solomon Islands', *International Peacekeeping*, 12(4): 520–32.

Pelcovits, N. A. (1993) *The Long Armistice: UN Peacekeeping and the Arab–Israeli Conflict* (Boulder, CO: Westview Press).

Peou, S. (ed.) (1997) *Conflict Neutralization in the Cambodia War* (New York: Oxford University Press).

Pérez de Cuéllar, J. (1990) *Report of the Secretary-General on the Work of the Organization* (UN doc. A/45/1, 12 January).

Perito, R. (2002) 'National Police Training within an Executive Policing Operation', in R. Dwan (ed.), *Executive Policing: Enforcing the Law in Peace Operations* (Oxford: Oxford University Press for SIPRI), pp. 85–101.

Pilger, J. (1994) *Distant Voices* (London: Vintage).

Polman, L. (2003) *We Did Nothing: Why the Truth Doesn't Always Come Out When the UN Goes in* (London: Viking).

Ponzio, R. (2007) 'The United Nations Peacebuilding Commission: Origins and Initial Practice', *Disarmament Forum* (UNIDIR), 2: 5–16.

Pouligny, B. (2006) *Peace Operations Seen from Below: UN Missions and Local People* (London: Hurst).

Powell, C. L. (2001) 'Remarks to the National Foreign Policy Conference for Leaders of NGOs', US Department of State, 26 October.

Power, S. (2002a) 'Raising the Cost of Genocide', *Dissent*, 49(2): 69–77.

Power, S. (2002b) *A Problem from Hell* (New York: Basic Books).

Prunier, G. (1995) *The Rwanda Crisis* (London: Hurst).

Prunier, G. (1999) 'Operation Turquoise', in H. Adelman and A. Suhrke (eds), *The Path of a Genocide* (New York: Transaction Books), pp. 238–62.

Prunier, G. (2005) *Darfur: The Ambiguous Genocide* (London: Hurst).

Prunier, G. (2009) *Africa's World War* (Oxford: Oxford University Press).

Pugh, M. (1995) 'Peacebuilding as Developmentalism: Concepts from Disaster Research', *Contemporary Security Policy*, 16(3): 320–46.

Pugh, M. (2003) 'The World Order Politics of Regionalization', in M. Pugh and W. P. S. Sidhu (eds), *The United Nations and Regional Security* (Boulder, CO: Lynne Rienner), pp. 31–46.

Pugh, M. (2004) 'Peacekeeping and Critical Theory', *International Peacekeeping*, 11(1): 39–58.

Pugh, M. (2006) 'Crime and Capitalism in Kosovo's Transformation', in T. B. Knudsen and C. B. Laustsen (eds), *Kosovo between War and Peace* (London: Routledge), pp. 116–34.

Pugh, M. (2008) 'Peace Operations', in P. D. Williams (ed.), *Security Studies: An Introduction* (London: Routledge), pp. 407–21.

Pugh, M., and N. Cooper (2004) *War Economies in a Regional Context* (Boulder, CO: Lynne Rienner).

Quéguiner, J.-F. (2006) 'Precautions under the Law Governing the Conduct of Hostilities', *International Review of the Red Cross*, 88(864): 793–821.

Ramsbotham, O., and T. Woodhouse (1999) *Encyclopedia of International Peacekeeping Operations* (Santa Barbara, CA: ABC-Clio).

Ratner, S. R. (1996) *The New UN Peacekeeping* (New York: St Martin's Press).

Rausch, C. (2002) 'The Assumption of Authority in Kosovo and East Timor', in R. Dwan (ed.), *Executive Policing* (Oxford: Oxford University Press SIPRI Research Report no. 16).

Razack, S. H. (2004) *The Somalia Affair, Peacekeeping and the New Imperialism* (Toronto: University of Toronto Press).

Reno, W. (1998) *Warlord Politics and African States* (Boulder, CO: Lynne Rienner).

Richmond, O. (2003) 'Introduction: NGOs, Peace and Human Security', in O. Richmond (ed.), *Mitigating Conflict: The Role of NGOs* (London: Frank Cass), pp. 1–11.

Rieff, D. (2002) *A Bed for the Night: Humanitarianism in Crisis* (New York: Vintage).

Rifkind, M. (1993) 'Peacekeeping or Peacemaking? Implications and Prospects', *RUSI Journal*, 138(2): 1–6.

Rikhye, I. J. (1978) *The Sinai Blunder* (New Delhi: IBH).

Rikhye, I. J. (1984) *The Theory and Practice of Peacekeeping* (London: Hurst).

Rikhye, I. J., M. Harbottle and B. Egge (1974) *The Thin Blue Line* (New Haven, CT: Yale University Press).

Roberts, A. (1993) 'The UN and International Security', *Survival*, 35(2): 3–30.

Roberts, A. (1995) 'From San Francisco to Sarajevo: The UN and the Use of Force', *Survival*, 37(4): 7–28.

Roberts, A. (1996) 'The United Nations: Variants of Collective Security', in N. Woods (ed.), *Explaining International Relations Since 1945* (Oxford: Oxford University Press), pp. 309–36.

Roberts, A. (2003) 'Law and the Use of Force after Iraq', *Survival*, 45(2): 31–56.

Roberts, A. (2008) 'Proposals for UN Standing Forces: History, Tasks and Obstacles', in V. Lowe et al. (eds), *The United Nations Security Council and War* (Oxford: Oxford University Press), pp. 99–130.

Roberts, A., and B. Kingsbury (2000) 'Introduction: The UN's Role in International Society', in A. Roberts and B. Kingsbury (eds), *United Nations, Divided World*, 2nd edn (Oxford: Oxford University Press), pp. 1–62.

Roberts, Anna (2003) ' "Soldiering on in Hope": United Nations Peacekeeping in Civil Wars', *New York Journal of International Law and Politics*, 35: 839–91.

Roberts, D. (2001) *Political Transition in Cambodia 1991–1999* (Richmond: Curzon).

Robinson, P. (2002) *The CNN Effect* (London: Routledge).

Rochester, C. (2007) *A Private Alternative to a Standing United Nations Peacekeeping Force* (White Paper, Washington, DC: Peace Operations Institute).

Roe, P. (2005) *Ethnic Violence and the Societal Security Dilemma* (London: Routledge).

Roessler, P., and J. Prendergast (2006) 'Democratic Republic of the Congo', in W. J. Durch (ed.), *Twenty-First-Century Peace Operations* (Washington, DC: US Institute of Peace), pp. 229–318.

Rose, M. (1998) *Fighting for Peace: Bosnia 1994* (London: Harvill Press).

Ross, W. (2003) 'Bedlam in Bunia', *BBC Focus on Africa*, 14(3): 20–3.

Roth, B. R. (1999) *Governmental Illegitimacy in International Law* (Oxford: Clarendon Press).

Roth, K. (2004) *The War in Iraq: Justified as Humanitarian Intervention?* Kroc Institute Occasional Paper no. 25 (Notre Dame, IN: Joan B. Kroc Institute).

Rupesinghe, K. (1989) 'Sri Lanka: Peacekeeping and Peacebuilding', *Security Dialogue*, 20(1): 335–50.

Ryan, S. (1990) *Ethnic Conflict and International Relations* (Brookfield, VT: Dartmouth).

Ryan, S. (2000) 'United Nations Peacekeeping: A Matter of Principles?', in O. Ramsbotham and T. Woodhouse (eds), *Peacekeeping and Conflict Resolution* (Portland, OR: Frank Cass), pp. 27–47.

Sahnoun, M. (1994) *Somalia: The Missed Opportunities* (Washington, DC: US Institute of Peace).

Said, E. (1994) *Representations of the Intellectual* (London: Vintage).

Sambanis, N. (1999) 'The United Nations Operation in Cyprus', *International Peacekeeping*, 6(1): 79–108.

Sanderson, J. (2001) 'The Cambodian Experience: A Success Story Still?', in R. Thakur and A. Schnabel (eds), *United Nations Peacekeeping Operations* (Tokyo: UN University Press), pp. 155–66.

Sarooshi, D. (2000) *The United Nations and the Development of Collective Security* (Oxford: Oxford University Press).

Save the Children (2008) *No One to Turn To: The Under-Reporting of Child Sexual Exploitation and Abuse by Aid Workers and Peacekeepers* (London: Save the Children).

Schear, J. A. (1997) 'Riding the Tiger: The United Nations and Cambodia's Struggle for Peace', in W. J. Durch (ed.), *UN Peacekeeping, American Policy and the Uncivil Wars of the 1990s* (Basingstoke: Macmillan), pp. 135–92.

Schechter, M. G. (2005) 'Possibilities for Preventive Diplomacy, Early Warning and Global Monitoring in the Post-Cold War Era; or, The Limits to Global Structural Change', in W. A. Knight (ed.), *Adapting the United Nations to a Postmodern Era*, 2nd edn (London: Palgrave), pp. 52–64.

Scheffer, D. J. (1992) 'Challenges Confronting Collective Security: Humanitarian Intervention', in D. J. Scheffer, R. N. Gardner and G. B. Helman, *Post-Gulf War Challenges to the UN Collective Security System* (Washington, DC: US Institute of Peace), pp. 1–13.

Schierup, C.-U. (ed.) (1999), *Scramble for the Balkans* (Basingstoke, Macmillan).

Schmidl, E. (1998) 'Police Functions in Peace Operations: An Historical Overview', in R. Oakley, M. Dziedzic and E. Goldberg (eds), *Policing the New World Disorder* (Washington, DC: National Defense University Press), pp. 19–40.

Schmidl, E. A. (2000) 'The Evolution of Peace Operations from the Nineteenth Century', in E. A. Schmidl (ed.), *Peace Operations Between War and Peace* (London: Frank Cass), pp. 4–20.

Scobell, A. (1994) 'Politics, Professionalism and Peacekeeping: An Analysis of the 1987 Coup in Fiji', *Comparative Politics*, 26(2): 176–97.

Scott, C. (2007) *Assessing ISAF: A Baseline Study of NATO's Role in Afghanistan* (London: British American Security Information Council).

Security Council Report (2008a) *Ethiopia/Eritrea* (Update Report no. 5, 31 July).

Security Council Report (2008b) *Security Council Action under Chapter VII: Myths and Realities* (SCR: Special Research Report, 23 June).

Senlis (2008) *Afghanistan – Decision Point 2008* (London: MF Publishing); www. icosgroup.net/documents/decision_point_08.pdf.

Serafino, N. (2004) 'Policing in Peacekeeping and Related Stability Operations: Problems and Proposed Solutions', Washington, DC: Library of Congress, 30 March.

Seybolt, T. (2007) *Humanitarian Military Intervention* (Oxford: Oxford University Press for SIPRI).

Shaw, M. N. (2003) *International Law*, 5th edn (Cambridge: Cambridge University Press).

Shearer, D. (1998a) *Private Armies and Military Intervention* (Adelphi Paper no. 316, London: Oxford University Press).

Shearer, D. (1998b) 'Outsourcing War', *Foreign Policy*, 112(fall): 68–81.

Simpson, G. (2004) *Great Powers and Outlaw States* (Cambridge: Cambridge University Press).

Singer, P. W. (2001) 'Corporate Warriors', *International Security*, 26(3): 186–220.

Singer, P. W. (2002) 'Aids and International Security', *Survival*, 44(1): 145–58.

Singer, P. W. (2003a) *Corporate Warriors: The Rise of the Privatized Military Industry* (Ithaca, NY: Cornell University Press).

Singer, P. W. (2003b) 'Peacekeepers, Inc.', *Policy Review*, 119; www.hoover.org/ publications/policyreview/3448831.html.

Singer, P. W. (2004) 'War, Profits and the Vacuum of Law: Privatized Military Firms and International Law', *Columbia Journal of Transnational Law*, 42: 521–49.

SIPRI (2007a) *SIPRI Military Expenditure Database*, www.sipri.org/contents/milap/ milex/mex_database1.html.

SIPRI (2007b) *United Nations Arms Embargoes: Their Impact on Arms Flows and Target Behaviour* (Stockholm: SIPRI).

Sisk, T. (1996) *Power Sharing and International Mediation in Ethnic Conflict* (Washington, DC: Carnegie Corporation of New York).

Slim, H. (1997) 'The Stretcher and the Drum: Civil–Military Relations in Peace Support Operations', in J. Ginifer (ed.), *Beyond the Emergency* (London: Frank Cass), pp. 123–40.

Slim, H. (2001a) 'Positioning Humanitarianism in War', in D. S. Gordon and F. H. Toase (eds), *Aspects of Peacekeeping* (London: Frank Cass), pp. 125–40.

Slim, H. (2001b), 'Violence and Humanitarianism: Moral Paradox and the Protection of Civilians', *Security Dialogue*, 32(3): 325–339.

Slim, H. (2008) *Killing Civilians: Method, Madness and Morality in War* (New York: Columbia University Press).

Slim, H., and A. Bonwick (2005) *Protection: An ALNAP Guide for Humanitarian Agencies* (London: ALNAP/Overseas Development Institute).

Slim, H., and L. E. Eguren (2004) *Humanitarian Protection: A Guidance Booklet* (London: ALNAP/Overseas Development Institute).

Smith, B. D., and W. J. Durch (1993) 'United Nations Central America Observer Group', in W. J. Durch (ed.), *The Evolution of UN Peacekeeping* (New York: St Martin's Press), pp. 436–62.

Smith, J. G., V. K. Holt and W. J. Durch (2007a) *Enhancing United Nations Capacity to Support Post-Conflict Policing and Rule of Law* (Washington, DC: Henry L. Stimson Center).

Smith, J. G., V. K. Holt and W. J. Durch (2007b) *From Timor-Leste to Darfur: New Initiatives for Enhancing UN Civilian Policing Capacity* (Washington, DC: Henry L. Stimson Center, Issue Brief, August).

Smith, M. G., and M. Dee (2003) *Peacekeeping in East Timor* (Boulder, CO: Lynne Rienner).

Snyder, J., and R. Jervis (1999) 'Civil War and the Security Dilemma', in B. F. Walter and J. Snyder (eds), *Civil Wars, Insecurity and Intervention* (New York: Columbia University Press), pp. 53–81.

Søbjerg, L. M. (2006) 'The Kosovo Experiment: Peacebuilding through an International Trusteeship', in T. B. Knudsen and C. B. Laustsen (eds), *Kosovo between War and Peace* (London: Routledge), pp. 57–75.

Solana, J. (2007) Presentation by EU High Representative for the CFSP, on the Democratic Republic of Congo/EUFOR New York, 9 January, www.consilium.europa.eu/ueDocs/cms_Data/docs/pressdata/en/discours/92360.pdf.

Spear, J. (2006) *Market Forces: The Political Economy of Private Military Companies* (Oslo: FAFO, Report 531).

Spearin, C. (2001) 'Private Security Companies and Humanitarians', *International Peacekeeping*, 8(1): 20–43.

Spearin, C. (2002) 'Between Public Peacekeepers and Private Forces', *International Peacekeeping*, 12(2): 240–52.

Spearin, C. (2008) 'Private, Armed and Humanitarian? States, NGOs, International Private Security Companies and Shifting Humanitarianism', *Security Dialogue*, 39(4): 363–82.

Stamnes, E. (2004) 'Critical Security Studies and the United Nations Preventive Deployment in Macedonia', *International Peacekeeping*, 11(1): 161–81.

Stamnes, E. (ed.) (2007) *Peace Support Operations: Nordic Perspectives*, special issue of *International Peacekeeping*, 14(4).

Stanley, W., and D. Holiday (1997) 'Peace Mission Strategy and Domestic Actors: UN Mediation, Verification and Institution-Building in El Salvador', *International Peacekeeping*, 4(2): 22–49.

Stedman, S. (1997) 'Spoiler Problems in Peace Processes', *International Security*, 22(2): 5–53.

Stedman, S. J. (2001) 'The New Interventionists', *Foreign Affairs*, 72(1): 1–16.

Stefanova, R. (1997) 'Conflict Prevention in Europe: The Case of Macedonia', *International Spectator*, 32 (3/4): 97–113.

Stephenson, J. (2007) *Losing the Golden Hour* (Washington, DC: Potomac Books).

Stern, G. (1999) *The Structure of International Society* (London: Pinter).

Stewart, B. (1993) *Broken Lives: A Personal View of the Bosnian Conflict* (London: Harper Collins).

Stimson Center (2006) *The Darfur Peace Agreement: A Tough Job for Peacekeepers?* (Washington, DC: Henry L. Stimson Center); www.stimson.org/fopo/pdf/StimsonCenter_DarfurPeaceAgreement.pdf.

Stimson Center (2007) 'UN Peacebuilding Commission' (Washington, DC: Henry L. Stimson Center, Peace Operations Fact Sheet Series).

Stoddard, A., A. Harmer and K. Haver (2006) *Providing Aid in Insecure Environments* (London: Overseas Development Institute, Humanitarian Policy Group, Report 23).

Strange, S. (1996) *The Retreat of the State* (Cambridge: Cambridge University Press).

Stromseth, J., D. Wippman and R. Brooks (2006), *Can Might Make Rights? Building the Rule of Law after Military Interventions* (Cambridge: Cambridge University Press).

Stueck, W. (2008) 'The United Nations, the Security Council, and the Korean War', in V. Lowe et al. (eds), *The United Nations Security Council and War* (Oxford: Oxford University Press), pp. 265–79.

Sudan Tribune (2006) 'AU reacts to ICG report on Darfur peace deal', 25 June.

Suhrke, A. (1998) 'Facing Genocide: The Record of the Belgian Battalion in Rwanda', *Security Dialogue*, 29(1): 37–48.

Suhrke, A., and I. Samset (2007) 'What's in a Figure? Estimating the Recurrence of Civil War', *International Peacekeeping*, 14(2): 195–203.

Terry, F. (2002) *Condemned to Repeat? The Paradox of Humanitarian Action* (Ithaca, NY: Cornell University Press).

Thakur, R. (1984) *Peacekeeping in Vietnam* (Edmonton: University of Alberta Press).

Thakur, R. (2001) 'Cambodia, East Timor and the Brahimi Report', *International Peacekeeping*, 8(3): 115–24.

Thakur, R. (2006) *The United Nations, Peace and Security* (Cambridge: Cambridge University Press).

Thakur, R., and A. Schnabel (2001) 'Cascading Generations of Peacekeeping: Across the Mogadishu Line to Kosovo and Timor', in R. Thakur and A. Schnabel (eds), *United Nations Peacekeeping Operations* (Tokyo: UN University Press), pp. 3–25.

Thakur, R. C., and C. A. Thayer (eds) (1995) *A Crisis of Expectations: UN Peacekeeping in the 1990s* (Boulder, CO: Westview Press).

Tharoor, S. (1995) 'Should UN Peacekeeping Go Back to Basics?', *Survival*, 37(4): 52–64.

Tharoor, S. (1996) 'The Changing Face of Peacekeeping', in B. Benton (ed.), *Soldiers for Peace* (New York: Facts on File), pp. 208–23.

Thatcher, M. (1993) *The Downing Street Years* (New York: Harper Collins).

Thayer, C. A. (1998) 'The United Nations Transitional Authority in Cambodia: The Restoration of Sovereignty', in T. Woodhouse, R. Bruce and M. Dando (eds), *Peacekeeping and Peacemaking* (New York: St Martin's Press), pp. 145–65.

Thier, J. A. (2006) 'Afghanistan', in W. J. Durch (ed.), *Twenty-First Century Peace Operations* (Washington, DC: US Institute of Peace), pp. 467–572.

Tierney, D. (2005) 'Irrelevant or Malevolent? UN Arms Embargoes in Civil Wars', *Review of International Studies*, 31(4): 645–64.

Tilly, C. (1992) *Coercion, Capital and European States AD 990–1990* (Oxford: Blackwell).

Traub, J. (2006) *The Best Intentions: Kofi Annan and the UN in an Era of American Power* (London: Bloomsbury).

Treacher, A. (2003) *French Interventionism: Europe's Last Global Player?* (Aldershot: Ashgate).

Tuck, C. (2000) '"Every Car or Moving Object Gone": The ECOMOG Intervention in Liberia', *African Studies Quarterly*, 4(1); www.web.africa.ufl.edu/asq.

UN (1959) Transcript of press conference no. 1961, 2 April.

UN (1960) *Annual Report of the Secretary-General* (UN doc. A/4390, 31 August).

UN (1990) *The Blue Helmets: A Review of United Nations Peacekeeping*, 2nd edn (New York: UN Department of Public Information).

UN (1994) *Report of the Secretary-General Pursuant to Resolution 844 (1993)* (UN doc. S/1994/555).

UN (1998) UN doc. S/PV.3922, 31 August.

UN (1999) *Cooperation between the United Nations and Regional Organizations/Arrangements in a Peacekeeping Environment: Suggested Principles and Mechanisms* (UN, Lessons Learned Unit).

UN (2000) *Report of the Panel on United Nations Peace Operations* (New York: General Assembly, UN doc. A/55/305 S/2000/809) [Brahimi Report].

UN (2005a) *A Comprehensive Strategy to Eliminate Future Sexual Exploitation and Abuse in United Nations Peacekeeping Operations* (UN doc. A/59/710, 24 March).

UN (2005b) *Outcome Document of the 2005 World Summit* (UN doc. A/60/1, 24 October).

UN (2007a) UN doc. S/PV.5649 (Resumption 1), 28 March.

UN (2007b) 'Darfur: New Donations Keep Aid Workers Airborne', UN News, 11 June.

UNDP (1997) *Governance for Sustainable Human Development: A UNDP Policy Document* (New York: UNDP).

UN General Assembly (2002) *Report of the Special Committee on Peacekeeping Operations: Comprehensive Review of the Whole Question of Peacekeeping Operations in All their Aspects* (UN doc. A/56/863, 11 March).

UN General Assembly (2006) *Report of the Special Committee on Peacekeeping Operations and its Working Group at the 2006 Substantive Session* (UN doc. A/60/19, 22 March).

UN News (2008) 'UN Standing Police Capacity Completes its First Field Mission' (UN News Centre, 18 August).

UN Secretary-General (2003) *UN Secretary-General's Bulletin: Special Measures for Protection from Sexual Exploitation and Sexual Abuse* (ST/SGB/2003/13, 9 October).

UN Secretary-General (2004) Report of the Secretary-General, *Women and Peace and Security* (UN doc. S/2004/814, 13 October).

UN Secretary-General (2005) *Special Measures for Protection from Sexual Exploitation and Sexual Abuse* (UN doc. A/59/782, 15 April).

UN Secretary-General (2007) *Women and Peace and Security* (UN doc. S/2007/567, 12 September).

UN Secretary-General (2008a) *Ethiopia and Eritrea* (UN doc. S/2008/40, 23 January).

UN Secretary-General (2008b) *Ethiopia and Eritrea* (UN doc. S/2008/226, 7 April).

UNSG High-Level Panel on Threats, Challenges and Change (2004), *A More Secure World: Our Shared Responsibility* (UN doc.A/59/565, 2 December).

Urquhart, B. E. (1993) *Ralph Bunche: An American Life* (New York: Norton).

Urquhart, B. E. (1994) *Hammarskjöld* (New York: Norton).

Urquhart, B. E. (1995) 'Prospects for a UN Rapid Response Capability', address to the 25th Vienna Seminar on Peace-Making and Peace-Keeping for the Next Century, Government of Austria and International Peace academy, Vienna, 3 March.

Urquhart, B. E. (2000) 'The UN and International Security after the Cold War', in A. Roberts and B. Kingsbury (eds), *United Nations, Divided World*, 2nd edn (Oxford: Oxford University Press), pp. 81–103.

Urquhart, B. E. (2007) 'The Evolution of the Secretary-General', in S. Chesterman (ed.), *Secretary or General? The UN Secretary-General in World Politics* (Cambridge: Cambridge University Press), pp. 15–32.

Urquhart, B., and G. Sick (eds) (1987) *The United Nations and the Iran–Iraq War* (New York: Ford Foundation, Conference Report).

Uvin, P. (1998) *Aiding Violence: The Development Enterprise in Rwanda* (West Hartford, CT: Kumarian Press).

Vallieres-Roland, P. (2002) *Prosecuting War Criminals* (Brussels: Centre for European Security and Disarmament, Briefing Paper).

VENRO (Verband Entwicklungspolitik Deutscher Nichtregierungs-Organisationen) (2003) *Armed Forces as Humanitarian Aid Workers* (Berlin: VENRO Position Paper, May).

Vickers, M. (1998) *Between Serb and Albanian: A History of Kosovo* (London: Hurst).

Voluntary Principles on Security and Human Rights (2007) www.voluntaryprinciples.org/files/voluntary_principles.pdf.

Von Schloriemer, S. (2007) *The Responsibility to Protect as an Element of Peace: Recommendations for its Operationalisation* (Bonn: Stiftung Entwicklung und Frieden, Policy Paper 28).

Wainwright, E. (2003a) *The Solomon Islands: Our Failing Neighbour* (Canberra: Australian Strategic Policy Institute).

Wainwright, E. (2003b) 'Responding to State Failure: The Case of Australia and the Solomon Islands', *Australian Journal of International Affairs*, 57(3): 485–98.

Walters, F. P. (1969) *The League of Nations* (Oxford: Oxford University Press).

Waltz, K. (1959) *Man, the State and War* (New York: Columbia University Press).

Weiss, T. G. (ed.) (1995) *The United Nations and Civil Wars* (Boulder, CO: Lynne Rienner).

Weiss, T. G. (1997) 'Rekindling Hope in UN Humanitarian Intervention', in W. Clarke and J. Herbst (eds), *Learning from Somalia* (Boulder, CO: Westview Press), pp. 207–28.

Weiss, T. G. (1999) *Military–Civilian Interactions* (Oxford: Rowman & Littlefield).

Weiss, T. G. (2004a) 'The Sunset of Humanitarian Intervention? The Responsibility to Protect in a Unipolar Era', *Security Dialogue*, 35(2): 135–53.

Weiss, T. G. (2004b) 'The Humanitarian Impulse', in D. M. Malone (ed.), *The United Nations Security Council* (Boulder, CO: Lynne Rienner), pp. 37–54.

Weiss, T. G. (2007) *Humanitarian Intervention* (Cambridge: Polity).

Weiss, T. G. (2008) *What's Wrong with the United Nations and How to Fix It* (Cambridge: Polity).

Weiss, T. G., and S. Daws (eds) (2007) *The Oxford Handbook on the United Nations* (Oxford: Oxford University Press).

Weiss, T. G., D. P. Forsythe and R. A. Coate (1994) *The United Nations and Changing World Politics* (Boulder, CO: Westview Press).

Weller, M. (ed.) (1994) *Regional Peacekeeping and International Enforcement: The Liberian Crisis* (Cambridge: Grotius).

Weller, M. (2008) 'Kosovo's Final Status', *International Affairs*, 84(6): 1223–43.

Westlake, J. (1910) *International Law*, 2nd edn (Cambridge: Cambridge University Press).

Wheeler, N. J. (2000) *Saving Strangers: Humanitarian Intervention in International Society* (Oxford: Oxford University Press).

Wheeler, N. J. (2001) 'Reflections on the Legality and Legitimacy of NATO's Intervention in Kosovo', in K. Booth (ed.), *The Kosovo Tragedy* (London: Frank Cass), pp. 145–63.

Wheeler, N. J., and A. J. Bellamy (2005) 'Humanitarian Intervention in World Politics', in J. Baylis and S. Smith (eds), *The Globalization of World Politics*, 3rd edn (Oxford: Oxford University Press), pp. 555–78.

White, N. D. (2001) 'Commentary on the Report of the Panel on United Nations Peace Operations (Brahimi Report)', *Journal of Conflict and Security Law*, 6(1): 127–46.

Whitworth, S. (2004) *Men, Militarism and UN Peacekeeping* (Boulder, CO: Lynne Rienner).

WHO (World Health Organization) (2008) *Global Health Atlas: Epidemiological Fact Sheets*, www.who.int/globalatlas/predefinedReports/default.asp.

Wight, C. (2006) *Agents, Structures and International Relations* (Cambridge: Cambridge University Press).

WIIS (Women in International Security) (2008) *Women in United Nations Peace Operations: Increasing the Leadership Opportunities* (Washington, DC: WIIS).

Wilcox, F. O. (1965) 'Regionalism and the United Nations', *International Organization*, 19(3): 789–811.

Wilkinson, P. (2000) 'Sharpening the Weapons of Peace: Peace Support Operations and Complex Emergencies', *International Peacekeeping*, 7(1): 61–79.

Willetts, P. (2008) 'Transnational Actors and International Organizations in Global Politics', in J. Baylis, S. Smith and P. Owens (eds), *The Globalization of World Politics*, 4th edn (Oxford: Oxford University Press), pp. 330–47.

Williams, A. (2000) *Preventing War: The UN and Macedonia* (Lanham, MD: Rowman & Littlefield).

Williams, P. D. (2001) 'Fighting for Freetown: British Military Intervention in Sierra Leone', *Contemporary Security Policy*, 22(3): 140–68.

Williams, P. D. (2004) 'Peace Operations and the International Financial Institutions: Insights from Rwanda and Sierra Leone', *International Peacekeeping*, 11(1): 103–23.

Williams, P. D. (2006) 'Military Responses to Mass Killing: The African Union Mission in Sudan', *International Peacekeeping*, 13(2): 168–83.

Williams, P. D. (2007) 'From Non-Intervention to Non-Indifference: The Origins and Development of the African Union's Security Culture', *African Affairs*, 106(423): 253–79.

Williams, P. D. (2008) 'State Failure in Africa', in *Africa South of the Sahara 2009* (London: Routledge), pp. 20–8.

Williams, P. D. (2009) 'The African Union's Peace Operations: A Comparative Analysis', *African Security*, 2(2–3): 97–118.

Williams, P. D. (2010) 'Peace Operations', in R. Denemark et al. (eds), *The International Studies Compendium Project* (Oxford: Blackwell).

Wilton Park (2008), *Report on Wilton Park Conference 914: Women Targeted or Affected by Armed Conflict: What Role for Military Peacekeepers?* (Wilton Park, Steyning, West Sussex, 27–9 May).

Woodhouse, T. (1999) 'The Gentle Hand of Peace? British Peacekeeping and Conflict Resolution in Complex Political Emergencies', *International Peacekeeping*, 6(2): 24–37.

Woodhouse, T., and O. Ramsbotham (1998) 'Peacekeeping and Humanitarian Intervention in Post-Cold War Conflict', in T. Woodhouse, R. Bruce and M. Dando (eds), *Peacekeeping and Peacemaking* (Basingstoke: Macmillan), pp. 39–73.

Woodhouse, T., and O. Ramsbotham (2005) 'Cosmopolitan Peacekeeping and the Globalization of Security', *International Peacekeeping*, 12(2): 139–56.

Woods, J. L. (1998) 'Mozambique: The CIVPOL Operation', in R. Oakley, M. Dziedzic and E. Goldberg (eds), *Policing the New World Disorder* (Washington, DC: National Defense University Press), pp. 143–74.

Woodward, S. (2008) 'The Security Council and the Wars in the Former Yugoslavia', in V. Lowe et al. (eds), *The United Nations Security Council and War* (Oxford: Oxford University Press), pp. 406–41.

Wyn Jones, R. (1999) *Security, Strategy and Critical Theory* (Boulder, CO: Lynne Rienner).

Yannis, A. (2004) 'The UN as Government in Kosovo', *Global Governance*, 10(1): 67–81.

Zacher, M. W. (1970) *Dag Hammarskjöld's United Nations* (New York: Columbia University Press).

Zanotti, L. (2006) 'Taming Chaos: A Foucauldian View of UN Peacekeeping, Democracy and Normalization', *International Peacekeeping*, 13(2): 150–67.

Zartman, I. W. (1985) *Ripe for Resolution: Conflict and Intervention in Africa* (Oxford: Oxford University Press).

Zaum, D. (2008) 'The Security Council, the General Assembly, and War', in V. Lowe et al. (eds), *The United Nations Security Council and War* (Oxford: Oxford University Press), pp. 154–74.

Index